ADVENTURES IN CRIMINOLOGY

Sir Leon Radzinowicz is one of the leading figures in the development of criminology in the twentieth century, working as an academic criminologist, an adviser to governments and as the founding Director of the Institute of Criminology at the University of Cambridge.

This account intertwines Sir Leon's personal narrative as a criminologist with the development of criminology itself. Drawing on his long career spanning seventy years, from the 1920s to the present day, he writes about fundamental changes which have affected our understanding of crime and criminals, of criminal justice and penal systems, and of the tensions and dilemmas these pose for democratic societies.

He offers a unique perspective on the intellectual and institutional history of criminology within a wide comparative perspective.

ADVENTURES IN CRIMINOLOGY

Sir Leon Radzinowicz LL D FBA

Fellow of Trinity College
Emeritus Wolfson Professor of Criminology
and
former Director of the Institute of Criminology
University of Cambridge

FOREWORD
by
The Rt. Hon. The Lord Woolf
Master of the Rolls

London and New York

First published 1999
by Routledge
11 New Fetter Lane, London EC4P 4EE

Simultaneously published in the USA and Canada
by Routledge
29 West 35th Street, New York, NY 10001

© 1999 Sir Leon Radzinowicz

Typeset in Garamond by RefineCatch Limited, Bungay, Suffolk
Printed and bound in Great Britain by
TJ International Ltd, Padstow, Cornwall

All rights reserved. No part of this book may be reprinted or
reproduced or utilized in any form or by any electronic,
mechanical, or other means, now known or hereafter
invented, including photocopying and recording, or in any
information storage or retrieval system, without permission in
writing from the publishers.

British Library Cataloguing in Publication Data
A catalogue record for this book is available from the British Library

Library of Congress Cataloging in Publication Data
Radzinowicz, Leon, Sir.
Adventures in criminology / Sir Leon Radzinowicz.
p.   cm.
Includes bibliographical references and index.
1. Radzinowicz, Leon, Sir. 2. Criminologists – Great Britain –
Biography. 3. Criminology – Great Britain – History. I. Title.
HV6023.R33A3   1999
364′.092 – dc21
[B]   98–35440
CIP

ISBN 0–415–19875–5

CONTENTS

List of plates   x
Foreword by The Rt. Hon. The Lord Woolf, Master of the Rolls   xi
Acknowledgements   xiv

1 **At the creation**   1
   The maestro 1
   The status quo 4
   New horizons 9
   The design of a Code of Social Defence 14
   The demise of criminological positivism 19

2 **From an active volcano to a well-ordered scenery**   26
   Return to Geneva 26
   Swiss old and new ways 30
   Carl Stooss 32
   Searching for a via-media 33
   Going beyond traditional punishment 36
   Social defence slides into social aggression 38
   The pioneer left behind his œuvre 41
   Some preconditions for penal progress 43

3 **Towards a medical model of criminal justice**   48
   Pressures for change in Belgium 48
   Criminal anthropology at work 54
       Dr Louis Vervaeck
       Anthropological penitentiary services
       Psychiatric annexes
   Devising a penal network 62
   Psychiatrists at the penal helm 66

CONTENTS

4 **A penological cul-de-sac**   71
   An uninspiring academic cast 71
   A reactionary Ministry of Justice 72
   Moving towards authoritarianism 73
   Involvement and frustration 74
   A put-up job to discredit me 77
   My departure 77
   Jumping ahead in time: tempting me to return to Poland (1945) and a disappointing visit (1978) 78

5 **Trying to break down traditional barriers**   80
   My mission to England 80
   Paradoxical and unique institutions 81
   New directions in sentencing policy 86
   Grappling with persistent offenders 91
      The young-adult recidivist
      The habitual and professional criminal
      The mentally defective
   A landmark in penal legislation 104

6 **The socio-liberal approach to criminal policy**   111
   Idealism versus realism 111
   An environment conducive to continued penal reform 114
   The threat of reversal 119
   Retribution–deterrence–reformation: could a balance be struck? 122
   Two Home Secretaries: two contrasting profiles 125
   Epilogue 130

7 **Reaching the harbour**   132
   My debt to the Howard League for Penal Reform 132
   My first English friend 133
   The Cambridge legacy in criminal science 135
      Sir James Fitzjames Stephen: a rigid Victorian
      Courtney Stanhope Kenny: a more subtle Edwardian
   The first step 141
   Six thrusts to indicate the relevance of criminology to criminal law 143
   Time for some personal work 153

CONTENTS

8 Putting criminology on the national map 164
Mr Butler takes charge of the Home Office 164
He resolves to become a reforming Home Secretary 168
Criminological research built into the Home Office 172
The grounding of independent criminological research and teaching 175
   The initial step
   The first hurdle
   The second hurdle
   The course still bumpy

9 Making it work: infusing reality into an idea 192
Some false assumptions 192
The Cambridge Institute of Criminology 200
   Inter-disciplinary foundation
   The postgraduate course
   Doctorates in criminology
   Undergraduate teaching
   Building bridges with the practical world: the Advanced Course in Criminology
   Another bridge: the Cropwood Fellowships
   Yet another bridge: Cropwood Round-Table Conferences
   Visiting Fellows to the Institute
   Programme of research
   Miscellaneous but connected activities
   National Conferences of Research and Teaching in Criminology
   Cambridge Studies in Criminology
   Building an international library of criminology
   Concluding remarks
Welcomed recognitions 237
Essential acknowledgements 239
Lord Butler: a few scattered reminiscences 242

10 The awkward question of capital punishment 245
The six inconclusive but revealing stages 245
   A deep-rooted schism disclosed
   A glimmer of hope
   A painful rebuff
   A resurgence of abolitionist pressures
   Followed by a humiliating rejection
   The government in the dock

CONTENTS

The Royal Commission on Capital Punishment 1949–53: a new departure or a move 'to delay' and 'to postpone'? 252
   The Chairman and the Secretary
   Some of its members
The search for solutions 260
Reaching the end of the road 263
Yet a further period of equivocation 268
My further unexpected involvement in the subject 274
A very high potential for ferocity 278

11 **An issue which refuses to go away**   280
   A bolt of lightning 280
   Inspirations for change: humanity, religion, politics 282
   Totalitarian distortions 286
   The deadly weight of the United States 288
   Forces of resistance 291

12 **A prison system in crisis**   294
   A great escape 294
   The perplexing concept of security 297
   Lord Mountbatten takes command 299
   Challenging Mountbatten's solution 303
   Moving towards a British Alcatraz? 307
   Mountbatten's report in abeyance 310
   The zigzags of Mr Roy Jenkins 313
   Rules of fairness to be observed when passing judgment on an inquiry 318

13 **A fruitful approach to penal reform**   322
   Setting up an Advisory Council 322
   An influential and dedicated group 324
   A twenty-year involvement 327
   No need for apology 331

14 **The death of a Royal Commission**   333
   My early misgivings 333
   Trying to avoid a catastrophe 337
   On a collision course with the Home Office 341
   Moving towards disintegration 344
   The need to 'revise' Lord Windlesham's account of how the end came about 346
   The final lesson 351

CONTENTS

15 Seeking international solutions   353
The big issue out of the way 354
First steps towards penal co-operation 357
Governmental sponsorship of an international commission 359
Cracks and collapse 364
A plethora of voluntary initiatives 369
Penal standards and the League of Nations 376
Lending a hand at the United Nations 380
New congresses – old problems 387
Lending a hand at the Council of Europe 394
Summing-up 402

16 Some forays abroad and at home   405
Consultative work 405
   Australia
   South Africa
   New York
   Washington
Preaching the criminological gospel 416
Helping to transplant a foreign institution into English soil 421
A surprised co-midwife 424

17 A grim penal outlook   426
The authoritarian model 426
Tensions and dilemmas in democratic societies 429

18 A brief for criminology   440
This 'barbarous neologism' 440
The sterile search for the causes of crime 441
Limitations and prospects 448

Index of Names   470

PLATES

1 Enrico Ferri (1856–1929)
2 Paul Logoz (1888–1973)
3 Louis Vervaeck (1872–1943)
4 Paul-Émile Janson (1872–1944)
5 Comte Henri Carton de Wiart (1869–1951)
6 Henri Donnedieu de Vabres (1886–1968)
7 Cecil Turner (1886–1968)
8 H.A. Hollond (1884–1974)
9 Lord Butler (1902–82)
10 Herbert Wechsler (photographed in 1975)
11 Roger Hood (photographed in 1992)
12 Marc Ancel (1902–90)
13 Cambridge Institute of Criminology (photographed in 1968)
14 G.M. Trevelyan (1876–1962)
15 Sir Leon Radzinowicz (photographed in 1953)
16 Sir Leon Radzinowicz (photographed in 1965)

FOREWORD

By The Rt. Hon. The Lord Woolf
Master of the Rolls

How marvellous that Sir Leon has been spared to write this great book. He approaches his ninety-second birthday and his century is in sight. His admirers and disciples all over the world will celebrate its publication and will want to congratulate him on yet another marvellous achievement. After all, it is a quarter of a century since he retired in 1972 and a more impressive seventy years since he graduated at the age of twenty-two, *magna cum laude*, from the Institute of Criminology in Rome. Professor Roger Hood, in the introduction to Sir Leon's Festschrift – *Crime, Criminology and Public Policy* (1973) – accurately forecast it was impossible to imagine him in a state of leisurely retirement.

There could not be a better time for the *Adventures* to be published. Criminology, thanks to Sir Leon's influence, may be flourishing in Britain but the penal system of the country has lost its way. We have forsaken Sir Leon's message and instead of tackling the fundamental causes of crime we are sending more and more people to prison for longer and longer periods, ignoring the expense and ignoring the effect of overcrowding on the ability of the Prison Service to promote training and education for the inmates which are its responsibility. In the early 1990s, the prison population was 40,000 and falling. The Prison Service was focusing on developing regimes, preparing prisoners for release and maintaining family links. The service was seeking to make the criticism, that prisons are an expensive way of making people worse, unjustified. Now the population is over 60,000 and rising and we are back to crisis management. Once again the cancer of overcrowding is eating at the heart of constructive initiatives promoted by the service. The lessons learnt as a result of the Strangeways epidemic of riots are being forgotten. Recent events underline the relevance of Sir Leon's comment that 'international experience shows that as public concern about crime and its control increases, pressures to roll back the liberal procedures for bringing offenders to justice become more acute' (see p. 118).

The present Labour government is having to pay for its failure to vigorously oppose the populist penal policies of the previous Conservative government. The sad spectacle of the previous government and the Opposition competing for the title of being the toughest on crime is now haunting the present government. As I write, a prison for child offenders is being established.[1] The tabloids which bayed for the sentences which led to its creation are now expressing outrage at the cost of looking after the young criminals, said to be at least £125,000 per child per year. The only justification for this cost that the present government can give is that, by the time it took office, to cancel this folly would not have resulted in any saving. The clear implication being that the new prison does not have anything of real worth to offer, notwithstanding the huge costs involved.

I wholeheartedly endorse Sir Leon's statement that 'no meaningful advance in penal matters can be achieved in contemporary democratic societies so long as it remains a topic of party political controversy instead of a matter of national concern' (see p. 49). Sir Leon was a member of the Royal Commission on Capital Punishment. The non-party political approach which resulted in its abolition demonstrates what can be achieved in the way of enlightened reform when politicians are able to discard their party labels. The state of our penal policy has caused Lord Bingham, the Lord Chief Justice, to call for the establishment of a Royal Commission to report on the situation. This is a remedy about which Sir Leon expresses reservations in Chapter 14. These reservations need to be borne in mind if, as I hope, Lord Bingham's call is answered.

I accept Sir Leon's advice that 'much good can be achieved in promoting progress and readjustments in the penal system not so much by putting on the agenda of reform huge, ambitious schemes of "reconstruction", but by coming to grips with a series of much more limited and much more precisely defined topics in response to certain obvious, yet not adequately satisfied, needs' (see p. 331). Yet, surely, the time is fast approaching when an overwhelming consensus will develop that, in order to protect the public against crime, some radical alternative response is required to those tattered remedies which are being currently deployed. When this happens, this work, which with eloquence and style surveys the timeless contribution of Sir Leon to criminal justice over his magnificently long lifetime, will be available to direct a new way forward. If we learn from his unique personal involvement, his unrivalled international experience and great wisdom, we should be able to avoid repeating the majority of the mistakes and the lost opportunities of the past. To quote Sir Leon again, we 'are too often inclined to forget that there was always a time when the past was the present and that it is therefore prudent and fair to ascertain whether some of the solutions of the past do not contain a worthy message or a wise indication with respect to matters which

---

1 The Medway Secure Training Centre; Group 4 has a fifteen-year contract to run the Centre.

FOREWORD

still preserve their significance and utility in spite of the inexorable passage of time' (see p. 43).

It is an immense honour to be associated with this book by being asked to contribute this foreword. I suspect that this invitation is Sir Leon's way of endorsing the reforms I recommended in my report on Prison Disturbances. If my suspicions are correct, I regard it as a huge compliment which I wish I could have repaid by the quality of this short foreword. Alas, as will be self-evident, I lack the abilities required to achieve this. I have found it impossible to convey as this book does the international and comparative scale of Sir Leon's work, the dimensions of his personal experience, the breadth of his interests and the universality and timelessness of his criminology. It requires the erudition and elegance of a Sir Leon Radzinowicz to do justice to Sir Leon and that is exactly what this book does. It confirms that what Sir Leon has to say remains essential reading for anyone remotely interested in the subject which he has made his own: criminology.

ACKNOWLEDGEMENTS

It is a very great honour and an enduring pleasure to have my last book introduced in such a generous way by Lord Woolf, Master of the Rolls, and the author of the memorable report on our prison conditions. Penal reform demands not only a firm dose of realism but also a genuine social conscience and a deep concern for justice.

Roger Hood, the first Professor of Criminology in the University of Oxford, was an exceptionally able student of mine. This relationship rapidly grew into solid friendship and close collaboration which, in the course of over thirty years, has assumed many forms. An unrepentant scribbler who easily might slip into overwriting – amongst other sins – I badly needed an exceptional editor. Roger Hood, not surprisingly, discharged this function to perfection. The fact that he knows the dark corners of our discipline so well made his task so much less strenuous. I am delighted to acknowledge that I am greatly indebted to him.

I am grateful to Lloyd Cutler, the eminent Washington lawyer (he was legal counsel to two presidents) for introducing me to Judge Patrick Cudahy, the Chairman of the Patrick and Ann M. Cudahy Foundation. The trustees graciously voted to make a grant towards my research expenses. And so did the Wakefield Trust, established by Mrs Priscilla Mitchell, a dear friend of mine and a benefactor of the Cambridge Institute of Criminology. I may perhaps mention that I also made a contribution.

It is very pleasing to have this book published by the widely respected publishing house of Routledge and to be taken care of by David Hill, the managing director. Our friendship goes back to the time when he, following his father, Alan Hill of Heinemann, became the publisher of the *Cambridge Studies in Criminology* series.

I would like to renew my warm thanks to the following for providing me with much useful information – either through correspondence or by allowing me to visit them: Giuliano Vassalli, the former Professor of Criminal Law in Rome, Minister of Justice and now a member of the Constitutional Court of Italy; Professors Hans-Heinrich Jescheck, Günther Kaiser and Dr Barbara Huber of the Max Planck Institute for Foreign and International Criminal

ACKNOWLEDGEMENTS

Law in Freiburg i. Br; M. Eugène Frencken, then the Secrétaire général of the Belgian Ministry of Justice and Professors Françoise Tulkens and Dan Kaminski of the Department of Criminology and Criminal Law in the Catholic University of Louvain-la-Neuve; Professor Hans Schultz of the University of Berne and the Federal Department of Justice in Switzerland; Eduardo Vetere and Irène Melup of the United Nations; Aglaia Tsitsoura of the Council of Europe; and last but not least the Home Office for enabling me to lose myself in the mass of papers relating to the period of my involvement.

I have found the following three libraries indispensable in my work and I wish to express my appreciation to: Mrs Elizabeth Kelly, Director of the Biddle Law Library of the University of Pennsylvania Law School, and to Mrs Marta Tarnawsky; to Professor Joseph Kürzinger of the Max Planck Institute; and to Mrs Helen Krarup of the Radzinowicz Library, Cambridge Institute of Criminology. Miss Frances Hoenigswald, on the staff of the Biddle Law Library, has always found time to help me in the search for, and classification of, the material I needed. Her devoted assistance has been most effective. I am happy to say that our collaboration continues.

My secretary, Mrs Margaret Thompson, has again typed all my drafts with her usual exemplary reliability. As the drafts progressed through the word processor towards publication Humaira Erfan Ahmed and Hannah Bichard were asked to give a hand. I would like to thank them very much for their help.

[* * *]

When a man as old as I am decides to write a book he requires all the good will he can muster. I have been very fortunate in this respect, receiving support and encouragement from many quarters. As a further insurance I have taken to heart the following message conveyed by the great English actor Sir Ralph Richardson when interviewed by Russell Harty for the *New Yorker* magazine in 1977:

HARTY: Are you viewing the prospect of old age with regret or happiness?

SIR RALPH: I'm amazed that I'm so old as I am. I always had the idea that when I was old I'd get frightfully clever. I'd get awfully learned. I'd get jolly sage. People would come to me for advice. But nobody ever comes to me for anything, and I don't know a thing.

L.R.
June 1998

1

AT THE CREATION

The maestro

'What are you reading, young friend?'
'Cesare Lombroso's *L'Uomo Delinquente.*'
'Very good. But always remember that Lombroso was a genius who lacked talent.'

This was one of my first conversations with Enrico Ferri. It took place over seventy years ago, more precisely in September 1927 at his Institute of Criminology in Rome. He must have attached importance to his comment for a few months later, while talking to me in his splendid villa about the work of Lombroso, he pointed to Lombroso's bust on his desk and said: 'My young friend, do not make the mistake common to so many of Lombroso's detractors and always remember that he was a man of genius though he was without talent.'

I followed up my legal studies in Paris and Geneva and went to Rome at the age of twenty-two. I had gone to Rome because it was there that criminology in an undiluted and expansive form was being shaped. So began what was to be a lifetime's adventure in criminology. It was Cesare Lombroso, a medical man, who had launched the idea and followed it up in several vital, though often flawed, confused and contradictory directions. Enrico Ferri, the jurist, had taken it up with unusual imagination and zeal, and had deepened, widened and made more coherent its scope and contents, moulding the corpus of evolving knowledge and radical penal proposals under the aegis of a new school, the Scuola Positiva di Diritto Criminale. He had joined Lombroso in earnest in 1878 when, at the age of twenty-two, he had reviewed the second edition of *L'Uomo Delinquente* in the *Rivista Europea*, and he toiled in undisturbed cordial and fruitful collaboration with Lombroso for thirty-one years, until the latter passed away in 1909. By then Ferri was acknowledged throughout the world as the authoritative exponent and leader of the new creed.

Like everyone else I was fascinated by his appearance and presence. Tall, lean, bent slightly backward, with sensitive hands, elongated neck, superb head, piercing and oscillating eyes, engaging smile and a beautiful pliable voice which could express a whole range of moods: he embodied an altogether exceptional human being. 'A man of really unusual physical beauty', remarked Helen Zimmern in her book *The Italy of the Italians* (1906, p. 189), 'is Enrico Ferri, as well as of charm of manner and of eloquence, which, when stirred to a theme dear to his heart, carries all before it.' This was in harmony with the intellectual quality he radiated, for he was a man of many exciting parts and many considerable talents. No wonder one would come across him in all sorts of out of the way publications, and certainly not the kinds of places where the species of law professor would be expected to appear. This combination would have been unusual in anyone under any circumstances but it was particularly so in his case because the background from which he stemmed stood in the starkest possible contrast with his achievements. He, the fervent believer in the decisive influences of hereditary transmission and environmental constellation, must have been puzzled more than once when relating them to his own past (see Plate 1).

He was born on 25 February 1856 in the small town of San Benedett-Po in the province of Mantua. His father, though he tried hard, proved to be a total failure. A purveyor of goods to a military unit, he became bankrupt and by a narrow margin escaped imprisonment for debt. The family continued to live, or rather to vegetate, in miserable conditions. All nine of his siblings died at an early age and in 1875 his father also passed away. His mother, by then fifty-three years old, became a cook and a laundress, and afterwards opened and ran a small tobacconist shop to support herself and her son through the lycée and the University of Bologna. They had no one in the world except each other and she became an integral part of his life, even after Ferri had married and had his own family. Their household became her home in the most intimate meaning of the term. At the age of fifty-seven she embarked upon learning the alphabet in order to read what was written about her son. And a tremendous lot was pouring in from all over the world; it warmed her heart and made her feel the happiest woman on earth, after so many dark and hard years of emotional and material deprivations. She lived to be ninety and Ferri saluted her memory in an article – 'In memoria di mia madre' – published in the *Scuola Positiva*, the journal of the new school, in January 1896. 'Era forte e buona' was the motto of his moving tribute, written without inhibition and affectation.

His was a truly meteoric career. It was forged within the brief span of fifteen years, but its worth, diversity and scale would easily have required the full lifespan of any but an exceptionally endowed individual. It started in 1878 when, as a young man of twenty-two, he submitted his dissertation to the Faculty of Law of Bologna – instantaneously provoking acclaim and criticism, both of which continued to resound for many decades to come. He began to accumulate a criminological luggage of published work which, well before he was forty-five, had placed him definitely at the very forefront of the scholars in his chosen field. As a professor in several universities and finally in Rome his reputation was enthusiastically upheld by generations of grateful and admiring students. As a lecturer on a variety of subjects, frequently well outside the confines of criminal science proper, he was in steady demand far beyond Italy. His lectures were invariably regarded as brilliant, and so were his frequent interventions in international penal congresses. He was also an editor of *Avanti*, the mouthpiece of the left, and of *Scuola Positiva*, the authoritative organ of the new criminological school. Effective involvement and remarkable success in a series of sensational civil, criminal and political cases established him, again when he was not yet forty-five, as the pre-eminent advocate of Italy. Finally, as an orator, in a country renowned for its talent in flowery and passionate eloquence, he remained an undimmed star. The lionization was eagerly shared by the genteel ladies of literary circles whether in Naples or Florence, by not so easily satisfied academic audiences, by members of a stormy Parliament, in exacting courts of justice, and, most dramatically, by the masses – peasants in Sicily and workers in Milan – often hungry and in revolt. His socialist allegiance had faded away before I appeared on the scene and more will be said about it later (pp. 21–24).

He was vain, very vain, but after all he was Italian and human and furthermore there was a tremendous amount to be justifiably proud of. He was self-centred, extrovert, yet subtle in human relations and public situations, persistent but not overbearing. There was nothing mean in him, indeed he was capable of generous gestures. His concentration and energy came close to being terrifying. His entire existence was geared to the objectives he had assigned to himself at an early stage. And all the 'mechanics' of life were at hand to sustain him. The family life was perfect. Sheer physical strength, unquenchable drive and well-balanced emotions were perfectly attuned to each other. Except for his early youth, his style of life could hardly have been made more agreeable and comfortable. Yet its enjoyment was strictly controlled, in many ways even spartan.

He shared with us, his students, in the regular course on criminal law, as part of the curriculum of the faculty and in the smaller group at the institute – then known as La Scuola d'Applicazione Giuridico-Criminale – his scientific findings and postulates. With his superb gifts of exposition it came so easily to him, free of technicalities and hesitations. Always alert and indefatigable in pouncing on the weaknesses or inconsistencies in the work of his numerous adversaries, he hardly ever bothered to draw our attention to flaws or ambiguities inherent in his positivist version of criminology. Apparently Clemenceau used to say that he could always identify an article written by Jean Jaurès (the famous socialist leader), even when unsigned, simply because 'it never ended with a question mark but always with a point of exclamation'. This characteristic admirably fitted the maestro and I suppose it would also have fitted Karl Marx or Sigmund Freud, indeed anyone with a mission to convey and a crusade to conduct. It was imperative for Ferri that we should digest, absorb and retain unchanged the doctrine as laid down by him and destined to last forever. Raising the slightest doubt made him visibly impatient, not to say bored. I was then too inexperienced to ponder upon the intense, intolerant, one-sided and often dangerous streaks of an innovator. This was to come much later. I was very young (twenty-two years old) and could hardly resist the invigorating criminological indoctrination, especially as it occurred at a time in my life when I needed to believe: much more to believe than to discern, to sift or to weigh up.

The status quo

> Concentrate on the study of criminal procedure, rather than on the substantive criminal law, because in the latter field there remains little to be added to what has already been done by your fathers.
>
> (Francesco Carrara)

The second half of the nineteenth century witnessed the emergence and radiation of powerful currents of thought which affected so many aspects of individual *and* society and of the individual *in* society. Auguste Comte – the visionary and inspiring projector of human destiny; Herbert Spencer – the pedantic and yet reassuring promoter of social engineering grounded on the developing industrial society; Karl Marx – the relentless and dramatic inquisitor of the capitalist economy, leaving no alternatives to his doctrinal precepts; Charles Darwin – the unassuming and yet supremely authoritative explorer of evolutionary processes in plants and animals, as well as in human beings. Their vitality and productivity were stupendous and their refutation of criticisms matched the fierceness of their opponents' attacks.

I plunged into them in the last year of my schooling in Poland with the easily predictable adverse effect on my final diploma (*matura*). With unabated enthusiasm I continued to peruse them in Paris and Geneva in addition to my appointed legal studies. Naturally I was very often left hazy, indeed confused, though the total impact was exciting and durable. I felt that humanity was at a cross-roads and continued to be so because many of the messages and their implications remained largely unfulfilled.

Ferri was in the midst of this seemingly inexhaustible ferment at the very time he was seeking to form his outlook on life and to sharpen his scientific convictions. With his superb intelligence, sensibility and ambitions, he could not have remained a passive onlooker and was bound to become an active participant. He was captivated by the many-sided onslaught and the process of his intellectual and emotional identification with it was accelerated by the early and continuing influence exercised on him by Roberto

Ardigò – his teacher in his lycée who soon was to become a noted philosopher in Italy. Ferri urged me to make his acquaintance. I ploughed through a portion of his *œuvre* – twelve volumes *in toto* – but I felt that Ferri had exaggerated the significance of the man. However, Ardigò was a trumpeter of change and this appealed to Ferri enormously. By 1890, when he was not yet thirty-three, Ferri had made up his mind where he stood and remained faithful to this scientific posture for nearly four decades.

It led him to make two assumptions: one flawed and ephemeral, the other correct and enduring. By ingenuous and tempting twists he convinced himself, and tried to convince others, that, putting aside some differences in interpretation and method, the four major currents of thought which so mightily agitated the contemporary mind, in effect, supplemented each other. Indeed, in the final analysis, they formed a harmonious and perfectly integrated symbiosis – with Karl Marx leading them all to the altar. How Comte, Marx, Darwin and Spencer would have responded to this offer of fusion is not difficult to anticipate, although rather difficult to prove for the simple reason that the first passed away in 1857, the second in 1883, and the third in 1882. Spencer was still alive, indeed very much so (he died in 1903), and his response was tart and succinct. In a letter to an Italian newspaper Spencer expressed 'his astonishment at the audacity of him who has made use of [my] *name* to defend socialism'. Ferri, undeterred, remarked, in a spirited reply, there was no one in Italy who would

> misuse so grotesquely the name of Herbert Spencer, whose extreme individualism is known to all the world. But the personal opinion of Herbert Spencer is a quite different thing from the logical consequence of the scientific theories concerning universal evolution which he has developed more fully and better than anyone else but of which he has not the official monopoly nor the power to prohibit their free expansion by the labour of other thinkers.

Ferri also met with violent opposition from within his own camp. Baron Raffaele Garofalo, the other eminent figure of the positivist school of criminal law and criminology, opened his attack through his pamphlet *The Socialist Superstition* (*La Superstizione Socialista*, 1895). From Marxist circles came the castigating voice of Antonio Labriola, who warned both the leadership of the Italian socialist party (through Filippo Turati) and the German party (through Friedrich Engels) of the dangerous consequences likely to emanate from Ferri's interpretation, which diluted, indeed emasculated, Marxism through an opportunistic ideological accommodation. He conferred upon Ferri the insulting epithet of 'signal charlatan'.

Nevertheless, it is difficult to deny that Ferri's book *Socialism and Positive Science* (*Darwin–Spencer–Marx*) had a long and vigorous life. Its first appearance in Italy in 1894 was followed by two editions. Soon afterwards it was translated into French, Spanish and German. It went though three editions in the United States, the first in 1901, the last in 1909; and it landed in Britain as a volume in *The Socialist Library* in 1909, passing through five editions. Ramsay MacDonald, the editor of the series, wrote an interesting and eulogistic foreword. And some twenty years later, as Prime Minister, he attempted to erect a bridge in a government of national unity between the Tories and Labour, not unlike Ferri's hope of reconciling Spencer with Marx.

When I arrived in Rome in 1928 no one seemed to be discussing or even to be aware of these polemics. However, the maestro must have been still troubled by the problem of how to reconcile his faded socialism with the triumphant ascendancy of fascism and with the role that a positivist criminology could play within the orbit of an authoritative state without negating its very essence, scientific and moral. The way in which he thought he had solved this dilemma will emerge later.

In the mean time, it is important to delineate the second of his assumptions because of its intrinsic and permanent value. It had imposed itself on Ferri's mind from his early days and he shared it with us, eager to listen to him. Powerful thrusts of thought which affected the roots of individual and societal existence must inevitably have an impact on the major institutions regulating life. The impact may not always be acknowledged, it may vary in intensity, it may or may not be beneficial, but it is always there. The institution of criminal law and the system of criminal justice could not avoid such reverberations. And yet to the reformers of the day it appeared undeniable that these currents had been bypassing the structure of criminal law and its functioning. Isolated, unbent, static, supremely confident, the existing penal system was drawing its solutions from ideological and scientific resources primarily belonging to a phase of development which was losing much of its significance. To discover the theoretical model of criminal law embodying this outlook of the status quo one has to turn to Italy and direct one's searchlights on Francesco Carrara. To find the practical model of its enforcement the road leads to the Criminal Codes of France and their numerous imitators.

Born in Lucca in 1805, Carrara spent the first fifty-four years of his life there, teaching in a lycée and practising as a highly respected provincial lawyer in his beloved Tuscany. He was apparently also scribbling in his free time, but nothing seems to have come out of it. Not surprisingly he was little known. In 1859, he was called to occupy the Chair of Criminal Law at the University of Pisa, and almost immediately he became famous in Italy and indeed throughout Europe. Within a few years ten hefty volumes of his *Programma del Corso di Diritto Criminale* made their appearance and a further eight volumes of *Opuscoli*, containing his speeches, articles and shorter treatises, followed. He lived to be ninety-three and, although blind for the last few years of his life, he continued to teach. Ferri told us one day how, anxious to meet Carrara in the flesh, he had gone to visit him in his house at Pisa and how, on that very occasion, a man accused of adultery (which was then a criminal offence) also called on Carrara to consult him about his predicament. The leading criminal jurist of the world had still felt that he needed further advice and the young Enrico was ordered to bring down from the upper shelves of Carrara's library the treatise of Benedict Carpzow (1635) which, for a century, had a deep influence on criminal law and its interpretation in Saxony and beyond. Modest and unassuming, he was loaded with all imaginable honours and died as a venerable Senator of the Realm. The lovely and quaint Lucca has not forgotten him. In visiting the city, as I sometimes do when indulging in my *picola cura* in Montecatini, I cannot fail to come across the handsome monument erected in his memory, nor can I fail to make a note of the magnificent library he gave to the University of Pisa and the personal papers locked in the archives of the Courts of Justice of Lucca.

There can be no proper discipline of criminal law and no satisfactory system of criminal justice, stated Carrara in the opening paragraphs of the introduction to his *magnum opus*, unless we discover the very basic principle which should inspire and guide them and see how this principle is adhered to when theoretical concepts are developed and practical solutions are set on foot.[1] This is how he postulated the 'fundamental principle and its formula'. First, 'crime is not a factual entity but a juridical entity' ('il delitto non è un ente di fatto, ma un ente juridico'). Second, 'criminal science has for its mission to curb abuses of authority' ('la scienza criminale ha per sua missione di moderare gli abusi dell'autorità'). The two, he confidently asserted, contain in themselves 'the germ of everything that is true in criminal science' ('il germe di tutte le verità della scienza criminale'). The first signals that moral, psychological or sociological investigations and findings are not, and should not be, the concern of the criminal law. The business of criminal law is to deal with crime as a juridical fact, or still better, as a juridical artefact: to identify and to define it in objective legal terms by means of strict logical dissection and synthesis and place it appropriately within the catalogue of all the other acts of commission or omission brought within the orbit of the criminal law in force. The second element implies that the system of criminal justice should be grounded on a rule of law which disowns arbitrariness, excesses and all the devious pressures in prosecution, trial and conviction which had been sanctioned and freely practised under the *ancien régime*.

The very institution of punishment has to be subordinated to this principle and conform to its two limbs. Its purpose is not to relate to the criminal perpetrator, to potential criminals or to society at large. When adroitly applied, punishment may well have an effect on these elements but they should be regarded as secondary, derivative and even accidental, because the basic justification of punishment is to ensure as far as possible 'juridical

---

1 F. Carrara, *Opuscoli di Diritto Criminale*, 2 vols (Lucca, 1859–67), vol. 1.

protection' ('tutela juridica'). Although expiation, retribution and deterrence may flow from punishment they are but by-products of it and not its essence.

Karl Roeder of Heidelberg University, a noted professor and penal reformer and a contemporary of Carrara, advocated reformation as the major purpose of punishment.[2] The latter lost no time in raising his voice against it, maintaining that, at best, this cannot be but an 'accessory of punishment' ('chè un accessario della pena'); that 'the rehabilitation of a criminal can be ascertained only through a most difficult experimentation absolutely unobtainable in social life' ('la correzione del colpevole è verificabile solo attraverso un difficilissimo sperimentalismo assolutamente irrealizzabile nella vita sociale'); and that by pushing this objective to the forefront one endangers the individual's rights and assigns to the state — but an agent of criminal law enforcement — functions and prerogatives which do not belong to it. To the extent that punishment departs from its formal purpose and aims at securing this, or any other external objectives, criminal justice inevitably becomes less legal, more administratively oriented, more ideological and consequently more relativistic and unpredictable. The surest way to avoid these evils, states Carrara, echoing almost verbatim Beccaria, and to ensure that punishment does not become an act of violence, is to make it absolutely certain that it is public, prompt, necessary, the least severe in given circumstances, proportionate to the offence and fixed by law.

In reviving these fiery polemics of the 1870s, one comes so very close to the controversies initiated by the Nordic criminologists and their counterparts in the United States and Britain in the 1970s, and cannot fail to react to them as something *déjà vu*. They are mostly radicals, whereas Carrara was a fervent Catholic and a liberal. It is one of the most attractive and puzzling features of criminology that when its evolution is retraced historically it reveals an almost incurable tendency to give birth to strange bedfellows. Enrico Ferri was an agnostic and a socialist.

This entire classical vision, in an embryonic form, was first portrayed by Cesare Beccaria, whose *Crimes and Punishments* appeared for the first time in 1765. Beccaria had a genius for composing a stirring manifesto, but neither by intellectual temperament nor professional preparation was he capable of writing (or willing to write) a systematic treatise. It is here that Carrara stepped in. He constructed a system that encompassed the entire field of criminal science; its General Part, conferring rules such as those regulating criminal responsibility, attempts, complicity, provocation and premeditation; its Special Part including all the major offences; and its penal economy devised to secure an effective enforcement under legitimate public authority. And, because of its exceptional all-round quality, the treatise continued to be acknowledged up to the beginning of the twentieth century as the authorita-

---

2 K. Roeder, *Rivista Penale* (1875), vol. 2.

tive and authentic text of the classical school of criminal law (I had in my library at Cambridge its tenth edition of 1924).

Looking at the leading penal laws of the period and the professional literature supporting them. Carrara could not fail to feel exhilarated. He – the sophisticated scrutineer of the past – had become the unashamed troubadour of the present. In his inaugural lecture in 1873 he went so far as to exhort the undergraduates of the University of Pisa to concentrate on the study of criminal procedure rather than on the substantive criminal law, because in the latter field 'there remains little to be added to what has already been done by your fathers'.

New horizons

Criminal law urgently needs radically new horizons.
(Enrico Ferri)

Carrara never failed to emphasize his indebtedness to Beccaria, nor did Ferri fail to express his admiration for both. But he was left unconvinced. To him the entire system needed urgently to be reshaped, root and branch. Partial reforms might appear to be useful but, in the long run, would prove to be pernicious because they would simply hide the basic structural failings and postpone the inevitable necessity for radical solutions. And, no question, the programme of penal reconstruction he taught me was the most radical of its kind ever presented anywhere in the course of the entire twentieth century and still remains so even today. In many ways it went much further than the reforms advocated by Beccaria and by Carrara following the French Revolution. What follows is an attempt to provide the gist of the new doctrine as faithfully and succinctly as I can. To amplify it by the findings and counter-findings of the very many studies generated by it would gravely unbalance my memoir.

To take the point of departure: the fundamental principle formulated by Carrara and implied by Beccaria – which the French would be inclined to accept as their *l'idée-force* – was one-sided and incomplete. In consequence, it was not valid as the exclusive basis of the penal system. Yes, it was true that crime is a 'juridical entity' defined by strict normative legal rules and should continue to be so regarded, otherwise the frontiers of criminal law would be expanded far beyond what is necessary and justifiable. Other forms of behaviour labelled as anti-social, immoral, amoral, deviant, dissident, or even marginal, would fatally be brought within the scope of criminal behaviour. The very stability and coherence of the criminal law would be endangered beyond repair with far-reaching negative socio-political repercussions. Nevertheless, the formula as it stands had to be converted, or, more precisely, turned round: crime is an entity of fact (*ente di fatto*) before it becomes a juridical entity. The perception of crime as a *natural* phenomenon, i.e. the expression of a particular individual personality acting within the context of a specific social environment, must take precedence over the perception of crime as a *formal* phenomenon, i.e. the violation of a prohibition laid down under the penal law. The *empirical* approach is more basic and one which should be given priority over the dogmatic approach. Surely, the legal syllogism by itself produced a meticulously symmetrical construction grounded solely on aprioristic and deductive premises, an abstraction which would distort both the substance of criminal science and the purposes of a criminal code.

And now to pass to the second limb of the classical position. Yes, it is true that criminal science and penal law should 'have for their mission to curb abuses of authority' and Ferri was profuse in his eulogy of this aspect of the classical school's contribution. It represented through its basic ideological core, as well as through its specific provisions, a most generous reaction against the laws and traditions of the medieval ages: a reaction against the barbarisms inflicted upon individuals by a punitive and non-accountable state which exceeded by far its proper limits, thus uprooting in the penal sphere the zealous respect for individual rights, the solemn affirmation of which would forever remain the glory of the French Revolution. Yet Ferri believed that the time had come for a fundamental demarcation to be recognized. Whereas Beccaria had made his appeal to the old Europe at the dawn of a new social and political epoch, Carrara developed the doctrine in a period of social and political stability, when the view that criminal law should guarantee legality to all citizens, including criminals, had gained wide theoretical and practical acceptance. Though vigilance to preserve this most precious conquest should never subside, the battle had been won and firm conclusions flowed from it. From now on, the ingredient of liberal individualism, which by its very nature is static, should recede into the background in comparison with a vigorous social component, which by its very nature is dynamic. There should be no cleavage between crime and criminal, between criminal and society. Criminal policy should link up with social policy and the Magna Carta Criminal Code should merge into a Social Defence Code.

If these two reformulations were to be thrown into the whirlpool of unfettered academic criminological explorations, nothing monolithic and radical was likely to emerge, simply because of the very many complex and dissonant questions inherent in them. But the situation would dramatically change if they were laid down in a categorical manner to serve as directives in the construction of a positivist criminal code. This is, in effect, what the maestro had in mind. With undiluted boldness, and in utter disregard of centuries-long moral and legal heritage, he drew from the reformulations two such directives.

First, the total elimination from penal codes of the concept of criminal responsibility; second, a similar rejection of the concept of punishment. There is, of course, a natural connection between the two: both evoke a deep echo in the philosophy of individual and social life as felt, perceived and taught by virtually all religious creeds across the world. Furthermore, the classicists assumed the existence of criminal responsibility as an essential part of the liberal creed of individual choice – the grounding for their retributive system. The positivists rejected it as being incompatible with social and personal determinism: an obstacle to their scheme for protective measures of crime control.

The limitations of human free will were being revealed more and more clearly by the solid advances in medical and social sciences and they told against the rule of making offenders accountable for their offences whenever they could be held 'responsible' for their actions (or omissions). In practice, however, even the most sophisticated and subtle legal formulae proved to be unsatisfactory when they came to be applied to complex individual cases, except when in one way or another extreme insanity was beyond dispute. Not knowing what one was doing and not being able to control one's actions are the two kernels of all such definitions. The very inclusion in penal legislation of the mental condition called 'diminished responsibility' was a recognition of the growing scepticism. And so were the so-often undignified and sterile confrontations between lawyers and medico-psychiatric experts acting on behalf of the prosecution and defence. The effectiveness and credibility of the system of criminal justice as a whole were affected by it.

'Every active perpetrator of a crime', stated Ferri, who was never tired of repeating it,

> is always legally responsible, provided that the act is his own, i.e., that it is an expression of his own personality, no matter what was his physical and psychological condition when he considered it and carried it out. Man is always responsible for every one of his acts, for the sole reason that he lives in society, and for as long as he does so.

Legal responsibility is all that is needed.

Similarly, punishment, as it was perceived and regulated in contemporary legislation, drew its *raison d'être* from roots identical to those which maintained the traditional concept of responsibility: namely, free will and moral guilt with their deeply embedded attributes of expiation, retribution and deterrence. Punishment was the restorative and responsibility was the declarative aspect of the same component. And to make it operative and visible – the classicists insisted – it was essential to ensure, as closely as possible, proportionality between the nature of the crime committed and the quality of the punishment inflicted. This – the positivists insisted – was again a largely abstract, dogmatic process of thinking which contained neither guarantee nor hope that it would produce socially useful results in curtailing crime. There was no room for the institution of punishment within a Code of Social Defence. It should be erased and replaced by 'Sanctions' or 'Measures of Social Defence'.

This was not a mere reshuffling of terminology. The possibility, the probability, or the certainty of reversion to crime constituted the offender's 'state of danger' (*pericolosità*). It was this which should be regarded as the decisive criterion in selecting an appropriate response to crime in each particular instance. The nature of the crime would still be taken into consideration, but it would be only one of the many factors indicative of the delinquent's future course of life. The concept was not altogether new: it can be retraced in the nineteenth-century legislation introduced in many countries to try to cope with vagrancy and mendacity; in the very many reflexes of preventive police laws; in attempts to deal with recidivists and in deciding what to do with people suffering from insanity in its various shades. But never before had this concept been pushed into a central position in criminology, penal legislation and administration.

It was Garofalo, the other major figure of positivism, who took up the idea in his memorable essay *Di un Criterio Positivo della Penalità* (1880), gave it a new look and, more importantly, a new dimension. Ferri, drawing upon this as well as upon his rich criminological knowledge and court experiences, elaborated the formula in several directions. He specified it with a detailed precision, making it readily available to be used as a spearhead in the imposition, enforcement and revocation of sanctions. It led to the following terse and novel syllogism to govern the process of sentencing and its aftermath: within the limits laid down by law a sanction is to be applicable to a delinquent in accordance with his state of danger – the degree of dangerousness to be determined by the gravity and kind of the criminal act, his dominant motives and his personality.

The state of danger could be of two kinds, major or minor, the first to be assessed by seventeen criteria and circumstances, the second by eight. There was hardly any indicative aspect of the delinquent's personality which was not to be explored in depth and recorded: such as the delinquent's psycho-biological make-up; social, family and professional background; criminal or any anti-social past; motivation and *modus operandi*; connection with or attitude towards the victim, before and after the commission of the offence. The cumulative effect of these indicators (my enumeration is not exhaustive but illustrative), providing that they were thoroughly and correctly registered and collated, could hardly fail to reconstruct a minutely individualized profile of a transgressor which, in the final analysis, would lay a foundation for the choice of an appropriate individualized sanction. The expectation was that, as a general rule, offenders declared to exhibit a maximum state of danger would, in their conduct, reveal a minimum of social adaptability, whereas the conduct of those evidencing a minor state of danger would demonstrate a maximum of social adaptability.

The positivists also held that the customary differentiation of offences, into those directed against property, person, sex and state, was hardly of any use in the processes of assessing the state of danger and choosing a sanction. This was simply because, in reality, the same type of delinquent might commit offences belonging to either or several of these classes and, inversely, because offences in any of these classes might be committed by different types of offenders. One needed to look at crime as a whole and then single out and describe the basic categories of criminals who produced it. Ferri regarded this as a pivotal task for criminological research as well as an essential adjunct to the sentencing and enforcement processes of criminal justice. At an early stage of his work he built up such a classification, enriching and refining it greatly as he went along in his explorations. It was made up of five primary categories: the born criminal, by instinct or congenital tendency; the insane criminal; the habitual criminal; the occasional criminal; and the criminal from passion. To these five he further added: the criminal couple; the criminal crowd; non-intentional transgressors; and, cutting across the entire spectrum, the group of young offenders. Each of these broad categories was supported by a many-sided characterization which revealed them not as skeletons derived from abstract schematizations, but as living human beings whom we may fear, despise, hate or sympathize with, but also whom we should not fail to acknowledge as the product of their individual personalities influenced by the socio-cultural environment from which they came and continued to be part of.

I must refrain from describing in greater detail this aspect of criminological positivism because of the nature of this book, but there is a point which I feel should not pass unnoticed. In arriving at this classification Ferri had relied heavily on material harnessed by many researchers, starting with Lombroso, but he had also made an original and major contribution himself. At an early age and single-handed he embarked upon an inquiry into the crime of murder – concentrating on 1,550 (in round figures) individuals, made up of 700 soldiers (his control group), 300 of the insane and 550 convicted murderers – with the object of throwing empirical light on this, the gravest of crimes, and of checking the relevance of his group classification. The volume embodying the results appeared in 1895 but it is the fifth edition of 1925, thoroughly revised in substance and presentation, which should be remembered.[3]

In his lectures at the school and at the institute Ferri frequently shared with us his major findings, proving how vitally important it is to go beyond the crime of murder defined in legal terms and to concentrate on murderers within the context of their environment. The many important differences

---

3 E. Ferri, *L'Omicida nella Psicologia e nella Psicopatologia Criminale*, including *L'Omicidio-Suicidio* (5th edn, 1925).

between the five classes emerged distinctly: to take the extreme examples, the first category of murderers (the murderer by instinct or congenital tendency) revealed sixty characteristics and the last (occasional murderer) only fifteen. Some time ago I made a rather extensive summary of all his findings and showed it to Dr Donald West (Emeritus Professor of Clinical Criminology at the Cambridge Institute) whom I esteem greatly, not least for his cautious and critical mind. Although he naturally regarded the theoretical basis developed by Ferri as rather archaic he nevertheless agreed that 'the factual observations on many points have since been observed and rediscovered by others'. This was the first major piece of criminological research I had come into contact with and I was fascinated by its modernity and exceptional insight. I continue to regret that this opus, today virtually unknown, has not been made available in English (or French for that matter).

It was no less fascinating and instructive, though on an altogether different plane, to watch the maestro try to test his classification against the gallery of heroes and villains painted by the gripping literary imagination and magnetic language of Shakespeare, Dante, Dostoyevsky, Balzac or Zola: deranged or immoral; bent by a degenerative heritage or corrupted by a vicious environment; spurred by the lowest or by the noblest of instincts and motives – greedy and mean, ruthless and violent, calculating or emotional, weak or cowardly. He usually had no difficulty in rediscovering his criminal types in their *œuvres* and, carried away by his Italian emotionality, he would come near to conferring upon them (posthumously of course) the accolade he usually reserved only for a few most loyal criminological positivists. He published these bold interpretations in a book which met with instant success. It was translated into several languages (not into English as far as I know) and though somewhat erratic and strained it still makes for delightful reading.[4]

The design of a Code of Social Defence

Young people are, as a general rule, much more interested in ideas than in their practicality. I was no exception. I am therefore particularly grateful to Ferri for having directed my attention to this at an early stage of my life. He was good at it. One of his favourite sayings was to the effect that however beautiful the branches and leaves of a tree may happen to be, that tree could not prove viable unless it also had firm and healthy roots. Thus, the mapping out of concrete and detailed plans of crime control, by which he meant both prevention and repression, figured prominently in his general approach and found a conspicuous place in his teaching. Furthermore, for those of us desirous to get a more thorough insight, there was always the possibility of

---

4 E. Ferri, *Delinquenti nell' Arte* (1st edn, 1896; 2nd revised edn, 1926).

consulting his books, articles and legislative proposals, knowing that he would always find time to respond to our queries.

The classification of criminals into certain empirically proved categories and according to their state of danger, also empirically assessed, were the two basic elements which formed the core of the positivist criminal policy. Ferri formulated it very early, somewhere towards the end of the nineteenth century, and there was nothing in the literature of the period, or in practice, to compare with it for coherence, comprehensiveness, specificity and, last but not least, boldness. It would be unfair to pretend that everything originated from his design and he would have been the first to acknowledge it. Neither the International Association of Criminal Law nor the International Penitentiary Commission, both of which began to spread their beneficial effects on penal developments in Europe from 1900 onwards, contained a single proposal, major or minor, which had not already become part and parcel of Ferri's scheme. In effect, he kept his eyes wide open for legislative innovations and practical reforms emanating from several European centres as well as from a few of the South American states. But he followed his own path.

He honoured in full the penological legacy of the Enlightenment and of the French Revolution; indeed he went far beyond it, by expunging from his system any solution which belonged to, or displayed, the slightest affinity with the past. There was to be no transportation; no detention on public works, in chains or otherwise; no flogging, or any other devices inflicting immediate physical pain; no forceful exposure to the public; no police supervision as a penal sanction; no grounding of the prison system on solitary confinement; no capital punishment for any kind of crime. Even as late as 1900 the International Association of Criminal Law had ascertained a truly daunting list of aggravations to the enforcement of deprivation of liberty, pliable enough to be used as instruments of arbitrariness and torture, in the regulations governing at least forty-five European prisons. Yet the general assembly of the association, having taken note of this deplorable evidence, nevertheless concluded that these aggravations 'could not be avoided'. Twelve years later, Franz von Liszt, the guiding spirit of the association, felt that it was still essential to do something about it and he moved a recommendation that aggravation in the enforcement of imprisonment should be unconditionally rejected. Stringent solitary confinement, baptized by Ferri as 'one of the aberrations of the twentieth century', still continued to play a prominent part in penitentiary organization everywhere.

In the 1920s, when I was staying in Rome, evidence started to come in pointing to the emergence of ominous regressive trends affecting the entire penal sphere. Ferri's deeply felt concern that criminal policy, because of its subject-matter, could not avoid at times making painful, tough decisions, but that it could and should nevertheless strive to be effective without being inhuman, began to be looked upon in certain influential quarters as just another faded socio-liberal shibboleth. Seemingly indifferent to the gathering storm, Ferri kept a firm grip on his vision of criminal policy. Untrammelled by the so-often tortuous process of harmonizing the legal definition of responsibility with the mental state of the particular offender; disregarding the traditional concepts of moral guilt, expiation or retribution; rejecting the insistence upon proportionality between crime and punishment and determining the latter, on the basis of predominantly utilitarian concerns of social defence, Ferri was enabled to give full rein to his resourcefulness and imagination in redesigning a system of unorthodox, variegated and elastic sanctions.

There was to be a group of ten sanctions to deal with first and occasional delinquents, removed as far as possible from the imposition of short terms of imprisonment. Another rather unusual nucleus of sanctions was directed towards political offenders and those held responsible for crimes of passion. A welcomed expansion of fines was projected, making them more stringent and at the same time more effectively readjusted to the economic situation of individual delinquents. The idea of giving much fuller scope to compensation for damages inflicted upon the victims (physical, moral, social or material), first expounded by Garofalo, was taken up by Ferri and developed on a large scale throughout the whole penal spectrum, both as an independent measure and jointly with other types of sanctions. Elaborate separate institutions for those mentally affected, and a highly diversified system with special rules of criminal procedure and specialized courts inspired by a predominant reformative bent, were to be made available for young and young-adult transgressors.

Brushing aside any objections or hesitations, both of which could justifiably be entertained with respect to indeterminate sentences, Ferri proposed two types: relatively indeterminate and absolutely indeterminate – that is to say, with a minimum and a maximum, or with a minimum but no maximum. Their use was to depend on whether offenders were early recidivists, habitual or dangerous or born criminals, on the degree of their state of danger and the probability of their social readaptation. The minimum could be as high as five or ten years and the maximum as drastic as twenty years or even for life. However, the possibility of a conditional discharge remained, although its use was to be regulated by a strict procedure. An imaginative and widespread system of after-care endowed with ample resources should become an integral part of the whole penal structure and not just left to sporadic, blatantly ineffectual, half-measures. Possibly inspired by Bentham's scheme for criminal prophylaxy before crime is committed (*ante delictum*), Ferri recommended a combination of precautionary and preventive measures to be pursued on a systematic and regular basis. He called them 'penal substitutes'.

Finally one has to add to it all, or more precisely 'superadd', the exceptionally prominent part that Ferri expected the judge to play. The judge, to put it tersely and succinctly, was the centre of the system. His task was to ascertain the criminal category and the state of danger, minor or major, with respect to each individual offender; they were to select out of the rich well of sanctions the one that they regarded as the most appropriate in furthering the objectives of social defence, whether to secure readaptation or to activate prolonged, even permanent, segregation through the imposition of an indeterminate sentence. Judges were also expected to be involved with penal administration in many crucial matters such as conditional discharge from, or revocation of, an indeterminate sentence. It is true that some directives were laid down to guide them in their sentencing capacity but these were minimal when contrasted with the reality of judges' enormous discretionary power. I do not know of any code in force, or any projected penal code, during the entire period of Ferri's scientific and legislative activity (which extended over fifty years), nor in the course of the sixty-nine years since his death, which can bear any significant comparison with this aspect of the positivist design.

But Ferri did not conceal his conviction that, as a general rule, the judiciary of his day was not up to the satisfactory discharge of so formidable a task. He proposed two changes to raise their standards, not only for the benefit of the exigencies of the sentencing process but for the benefit of the system of criminal justice as a whole. First, that the judiciary should be split into two branches: one dealing with civil and the other with criminal matters. This division should be stringently observed throughout all levels of the court organization. There should be an established career as a criminal judge. They would be carefully selected, well rewarded and held in high esteem. It was a foregone conclusion that there was no room under his design for the jury system. It was too amateurish, too emotional and too unpredictable. By its very nature and constantly changing composition it was inimical to a scientific, rational approach. Its total removal, even with respect to those charged with political offences, was essential, maintained Ferri, the professor who as an advocate had been their hero and darling for so many decades.

Second, the curriculum of law school, which in Italy (as in Europe generally) was of three years' duration, should be split into two phases. The first phase, occupying the first two years, should be concerned with the predominantly juridical study of the various branches of the law, including criminal law and criminal procedure. Ferri never denied the importance of the discipline – after all he had, at one time, been a successor of Carrara in Pisa. But here too he had definite views as to how it should be taught. He fulminated against the excesses of dogmatic, logistic and deductive study and interpretation. This so often led to sterile, splitting-of-the-hair disquisitions which lost sight of the fact that crime is foremost a natural and social fact. Almost as if it were provocation to the traditional scholars of criminal law, Ferri's major opus on *Murder* contained hardly any reference to the crime of murder in its legal perception nor the hotly debated issues of 'malice aforethought' or 'constructive malice'. Instead the volume opened with two substantial chapters tracing the crime of murder amongst animals and amongst so-called primitive people, fascinating chapters which, according to the expert opinions I have consulted, have survived remarkably well the test of time. His *bête noire* in this respect was the German tradition. On this he was in full agreement with his contemporary Franz von Liszt, the head of the innovative criminal science school of Germany. No doubt in the eyes of the formidable Karl Binding, the unsurpassed master of dogmatic exposition, Ferri would share with Von Liszt the epitaph of *Di Dilettanten*. And Von Liszt would have to suffer the epitaph conferred by the classicist Luccini on Ferri: *Gli Simplicisti*.

The second stage of law school, comprising the last year, should be devoted to criminology in its widest possible sense, comprising all the basic auxiliary disciplines concerned with the study of the phenomenon of crime and its control. In addition, there should be institutes of criminology attached to faculties of law ready to receive all those who desired to specialize in criminal science and practice. And at this juncture came the crucial requirement: no one should be appointed to be a criminal judge who had failed to follow this pattern of academic study.

Thus, when a total view was taken, it was a vision of a system of criminal policy and criminal justice, dynamic and experimental, under which every single offence was regarded as a signal for launching a remedial and protective action with respect to its perpetrator. It was a system which, far removed from the early versions of Lombroso's hypothesis of the origin of criminal behaviour, recognized the impact of social environment, yet regarded individual disposition as an independent and major factor in the etiology of crime, though of varying degree of intensity. It was a system which was not afraid of losing its juridical physiognomy by borrowing from the social and medical sciences any scheme or design which could be of help. It was a system which pleaded for closer integration between the various sectors of criminal justice in order to make better use of available resources. It was a system which was bent upon raising the status of criminal policy and the role of criminal justice in the governance of a country and one which would combine effectiveness with humanity. It was a system which acknowledged the value of criminology and expected it to monitor failings and achievements and new initiatives in a systematic and critical way. It was a system inspired by vigorous optimism, an optimism which was grounded in the dominant belief of the inevitability of expanding progress in all the major spheres of national life. In its wake, crime, as a mass phenomenon, was bound to disappear, except for that committed by a residue of predisposed criminals. The rest would be achieved by shaking off a criminal policy shaped by the classical school. It was a system incompatible, from the very start to the very end, with the under-developed and often distorted prevailing penal structures run routinely by a narrow-minded, self-satisfied bureaucracy closed to outside independent and thorough evaluation.

Ferri usually kept cool when criticisms, however severe, were directed against him and his school. Indeed, in some ways, he was too indifferent or even condescending, but he was certainly justified in feeling scornful when the eminent philosopher Giovanni Gentile castigated the positivists with the gibe that 'the delinquent of Lombroso is not a delinquent, but the body of a delinquent'. In contrast, it warmed the heart of the positivists struggling hard for recognition when a Dutch professor of international reputation who was not a positivist stated: 'L'école classique exhorte les Hommes à connâitre la justice; l'école positiviste exhorts la justice à connâitre les Hommes.' Gerard Anton van Hamel put it as a heading to his paper written in honour of Lombroso and the aphorism made a *tour du monde*.

The demise of criminological positivism

To dislodge a philosophy and a doctrine as meaningful and so masterly communicated as the classical doctrine, to challenge the credibility of the major criminal codes of the period which were so firmly entrenched in the political culture, was a truly formidable undertaking. Yet Ferri never faltered in believing that, however long and bumpy the road towards recognition would prove to be, the essence of criminological positivism, clothed in obligatory legislative language, would ultimately win the day. He and his associates would then share in the glory of Beccaria and Carrara as having initiated a new phase of criminal jurisprudence and practice in that major European country which, for centuries, had enjoyed the reputation of being *la patria del diritto penale*.

In the years 1919–21 they seemed to have come close, very close, to achieving this truly extraordinary triumph. Italy was to be endowed with a Positivist Criminal Code and positivism was to become a potent sociopolitical factor in the life of the country. Ludovico Mortara, the Minister of Justice and a former First President of the Supreme Court, felt that the time had come to replace the classical Code of Zanardelli, in force since 1885. By Royal Decree a Commission for the Reform of the Criminal Laws of the country was set up under the chairmanship of Enrico Ferri, packed with positivists or their close sympathizers. This was in 1919. In 1921 Ferri presented a Project of a Penal Code, containing its general part, together with an introduction which expounded its basic principles and signalled its main solutions. It was a remarkable document: of great clarity, precision, conciseness and force, but at the same time highly controversial. At once translated into several languages, it evoked intense interest all over the world. By 1927 it was dead and dead for good. Its burial was not, to paraphrase the title of a famous film, in 'Italian Style'. There were no rites, no condolences, no recriminations, no memorial services, and seemingly no sadness and no joy. It was accepted as yet another event in the inevitable chain of events leading to a new chapter in Italy's history. A fresh commission was appointed, this time under the direction of Arturo Rocco, the powerful Minister of Justice in Mussolini's government, and its project of 1927 became the *Codice Rocco*. It remained in force until the downfall of the fascist regime, chasing away for ever the dream of a *Codice Ferri*.

The stage was set for a dramatic denouement in conformity with Ferri's personality and life, but nothing of this sort happened. What his thoughts were in this supreme crisis I did not know and, of course, I could not expect to know: I was too young, too insignificant and too foreign. I am pretty certain he did not share them with many, for, in spite of being so eminently sociable and clubbable, he firmly kept issues of grave importance to himself. As a matter of fact, I was rather glad to be ignored and so was everybody else. I had not come to Rome to be a public prosecutor, defender, judge or jury of Ferri's conclusions. I came to see whether I could be inspired by him to believe that criminology had a substance and a message which made it worth pursuing.

With the perspective now of more than six decades, I can perceive more clearly the four alternatives open to him at that time. He could, like Giacomo Matteotti, have engaged in an active fight against the fascist onslaught and, most likely, he would have shared the fate of Matteotti, who was brutally murdered by the fascist Falangists under Mussolini's direct orders, his murderers remaining undiscovered. He could have left the country and continued in exile, say from Paris, his uncompromising opposition to all things fascist – the road followed by Filippo Turati, the central figure of the Italian socialist party with whom Ferri often crossed swords but whom he held in high esteem. He could have remained in the country, abandoning his previous political allegiance, abstaining from any direct or indirect action hostile towards the regime, yet not supporting it – to be a kind of silent outsider, but one who was not cut off from his natural environment. And, finally, he could have tried to arrange an accommodation, genuine or opportunistic, or both (in high politics it is often a mixture), with the new political reality and so in appearance or substance become part of it. The maestro must have been aware that his past could never be rekindled, and he therefore concentrated upon building a bridge between bygone positivism and the ruling fascist legal establishment.

Ferri left the socialist party following the end of the First World War, obviously disillusioned like so many others. The party was in a dire state, bitterly divided between its left and right wing, incapable on its own of assuming power and opposed to sharing it with some other democratic non-socialist party. It was thus reduced to impotence and, in the mean time, the country was plunging into chaos. This is acknowledged both by reputable historians of socialism as well as by historians generally, though of course this was not the only element of the national drama. 'People, such as Croce, the liberal high priest,' writes Denis Mack Smith, the leading English historian of modern Italy, 'advocated Mussolini's assumption of power as better than the existing anarchy, and believed that fascism might be gently directed into good constitutional usage.' Nevertheless he judges harshly Ferri's political activity, seemingly supporting the view of a number of Ferri's socialist colleagues who regarded him as 'a notorious opportunist who never adhered to one policy for very long . . . a clever and dangerous man'.[5]

His attempt to secure criminological readjustments expressed itself in several ways. Some could not fail to appear rather theatrical and others consisted primarily in repainting the labels to the detriment of the substance. In 1926 he undertook the defence of Violet Gibson, an Englishwoman, obviously deranged, who attacked Benito Mussolini in circumstances most unpropitious for a successful assassination.[6] She was held to be not responsible, discharged and sent back to England.

This episode warmed the hearts of loyal fascists. As a general rule only an abnormal person could contemplate the killing of *Il Duce* and that person should therefore be declared insane and sent to a mental institution. But a person who happened to be clearly politically motivated should be sentenced to death and put to death. All his life Ferri had been in favour of the total abolition of capital punishment but in 1926 he postulated a differentiation. There should still be no capital punishment for any common offence, including murder, but it could be justified in certain cases as an extreme and exceptional remedy in response to abnormal conditions prevailing in a society at a particular stage. And thus he gave his support to the Law of the Defence of the State of 25 November 1926, reintroducing capital punishment following four attempts on the life of Mussolini within twelve months, also with the object of 'giving satisfaction to the deep feelings of public opinion'.[7] And shortly afterwards, as might have been expected, the fascist legislators, forgetting the legacy of Beccaria and Carrara, reintroduced capital punishment within the wider context of their new Criminal Code.

A much commented upon piece entitled *Fascismo e Criminologia Una Lettera di Enrico Ferri* published in the *Popolo d'Italia* (19 December 1923) had already revealed the imminent ideological shift, but of decisive significance was the forty-page article published initially in the *Scuola Positiva* (July 1926) and reissued in his *Studi sulla Criminalità*.[8] This clinched the issue. It was a piece which so vividly brought to life the Ferri of the past. Pugnacious, dialectical, eloquent, theatrical and at the same time often moving, well equipped with factual information, rich in comparative thrusts relating to several countries and long periods of penal history – trying to justify the

---

5 Denis Mack Smith, *Italy: A Modern History* (1969 edn), pp. 228 and 369–70.
6 Enrico Ferri, 'A Character Study and Life History of Violet Gibson, Who Attempted the Life of Benito Mussolini on the 7th of April 1926', *Journal of the American Institute of Criminal Law and Criminology*, vol. 19 (1928–9), pp. 211–19.
7 *Sociologia Criminale*, vol. 2 (5th edn, 1930), p. 488.
8 2nd edn, 1926, p. 696.

present not only by its intrinsic merits but also by the missed opportunities of the past. It was a veritable *tour de force*. There he stood trying to preserve the legacy he had built up over half a century – the vibrant essence of his entire life. But it was also a thoroughly sad piece. What he intended to prove could not be proved in good faith. The very title of his essay, 'Fascism and the Positive School in Social Defence against Criminality', contained contradictions which could not be satisfactorily sorted out and the more he tried to do it the more strained and disingenuous his attempt appeared to be.

According to Ferri the divergence between positivism and Fascism would only exist if by positivism one understood a 'philosophical system' such as that of Comte, Spencer or Ardigò. The revival of the spiritualist trend in philosophy, also embraced by the fascist ideology, was easily to be explained as a justified reaction against the fatalism, determinism and materialism associated with philosophical positivism. However, a confusion had arisen only because of terminological misunderstanding. What he and his school meant by positivism was not the philosophical system of positivism but the positivist method of study and perception, and more precisely its empirical approach, an approach which was also common to fascism. This was obviously more of a dialectical twist than a serious argument.

His second attempt at clarification was no less fallacious and possibly even more perilous. It was concerned with the central issue of the position of the individual in relation to society and the state. Here, Ferri asserted, there was no room for any misunderstanding. Long before fascism came to power he and his close followers had emphasized on more than one occasion that, in general, but more particularly in the penal sphere, the preservation of individual rights had gone too far at the expense of the legitimate concerns of the collective authority. Their draft Penal Code project of 1921, with its wide range of indeterminate sentences and other types of sanctions, had given ample proof of their concern. What positivism urged in the penal sphere, fascism 'proclaimed in the sociological and political sphere, more specifically the reaffirmation of the pre-eminently sovereign rights of the state in the face of the excesses of the democratic individualism which is fast becoming demagogical and substantially anarchic . . . a state to which Benito Mussolini has affixed with good reasons a dynamic obituary'. In 1927 a second edition of his pamphlet *Mussolini, Uomo di Stato* appeared. A similar tribute is contained in two more of Ferri's pamphlets which appeared at about the same time. This assertion, translated into plain language, meant that criminological positivism fits perfectly the purposes of fascism and could be adopted with good results as its criminal policy. Coming from the head of the positivist school such an assertion could perhaps, in the short run, yield a few dividends. But in the long run this self-inflicted deep wound placed him in a morally impossible position.

Pushing his analysis further, Ferri singled out sixteen initiatives taken by the fascist regime which showed the strong imprint of positivism. It was a very mixed bag. A few of these reforms, projected or implemented, were innocuous or even progressive, belonging to that early stage of fascism when it was still warmly praised in many influential international circles as the first movement of national renovation in the history of Italy which could make its trains run on time. Some others on this shopping list unmistakably revealed the iron fist of the regime aimed at reducing the margin of freedom and building up a machinery of justice which would secure a more insidious control. The few which could be shown to have a direct linkage with positivism are primarily those which were pliable enough to be part of an authoritarian criminal policy. The jury system was abolished but for reasons different from those adduced by Ferri. It was not because juries were not qualified to return sound and purposeful verdicts, it was because the verdicts could contain unwanted surprises prejudicial to the authorities, whereas the judges who owed allegiance to the regime could be relied upon. The discretionary power of the judges on criminal matters had been extended along the lines of Ferri's project, not in order to ensure enlightened individualization but to make it easier to hit hard both actual and potential offenders. For the same reason, the state of danger was accepted as one of the criteria to determine the quality and degree of punishment to be imposed. Indeterminate sentences which replaced punishment were rejected. Instead a constellation of security measures of very long duration were introduced for certain categories of 'dangerous' offenders. These would be served after they had undergone punishments proportionate to the gravity of their offences and their culpability. In certain cases the police were given the power of administrative interference before the commission of an offence through the exercise of regular supervision or, still worse, through the exile to one of the less known isolated islands off the coast of Italy, well protected from innocent tourist intrusion or pointed impartial inspection. The Lombroso-Ferrian type of born criminal had at last found a niche in the famous Article 18 of the Criminal Code of Rocco, which reaffirmed an hereditary or otherwise determined individual disposition towards criminal behaviour as contrasted with the view which proclaimed the predominance of environmental factors, a view which had never found favour with fascist ideology.

The maestro's embrace was not spurned. He was still too important and still too widely remembered to be ignored. He was asked to join the commission set up by Rocco to formulate a new Criminal Code. The Institute of Criminology of Rome, the first of its kind in the world, which he had established in 1911 and which continued to be so close to his heart, received substantial support from the Ministry of Justice. He was appointed leader of the Italian delegation to the International Penal Congress held in London in 1925 and on his return presented a report to the government entitled 'The Triumph of Italian Science'. And he was made, like Francesco Carrara before him, a Senator of the Realm. One point should not be lost sight of in retracing these sad events because it makes them less painful and, in some ways, more redeeming. Throughout this period, perhaps in order to erase the bitter taste of the accommodation with fascism, or, more importantly, because he wished to leave his scientific legacy unblemished and untarnished, and perhaps also because of a feeling that he would not live much longer, he embarked at the age of seventy upon scholarly work no less demanding than that he had undertaken as a young man when he had decided to break the status quo of his beloved discipline and make the world a better place. This entailed a new edition of his *Studies in Criminality*; a drastic revision of his major research on *Murder*; a *Treatise on the Principles of Criminal Law*; an intense preparation of the fifth edition of his *magnum opus, Criminal Sociology*.[9] Here no apology was needed, no embarrassment was caused. Full praise was due.

It seems to me that there are two ways of assessing the role and worth of the Scuola Positiva. First, in relation to what existed in the field of the study of crime at the time of its emergence. Second, what its qualities and limitations proved to be in the longer perspective of the subsequent evolution of criminology as a whole. Both approaches are required for a proper assessment and I shall attempt to say something about them when I have progressed further in retracing this evolution.

In the mean time I have to close my Roman chapter. It was a wonderful experience. I was already fully aware at the time that it would remain for ever a permanent part of my being – and it proved to be so. I had been fortunate to have, as my Professors of Criminal Law, Henri Donnedieu de Vabres at the Sorbonne and Paul Logoz at Geneva. I owe them a lot. But Enrico Ferri was my first maestro and the only one I had. As it happened I was his last foreign pupil and follower. My work was rewarded by a doctorate of law *cum laude* and by a diploma of the Criminological Institute. Encouraged by Ferri I translated my doctoral dissertation from Italian into French and, no doubt largely because he volunteered to write a preface, I had no difficulty in finding a well-known Parisian publisher to launch it in 1929. On the eve of my departure from Rome Ferri invited me to come to see him again. He asked me whether I had made up my mind to follow the academic path and on receiving an affirmative answer he said:

---

9 Thorsten Sellin noted in his significant article on Ferri that when the fourth edition had been published in 1900, Ferri had claimed that 'he had examined all the literature of the previous decade to complete his document'. The fifth edition was published (in two volumes in 1929 and 1930) posthumously. Arturo Santoro, who had been assisting Ferri, completed the footnotes and saw the manuscript through to publication. Sellin commented: 'It seems clear that in the nearly three decades between the two editions, Ferri had found less and less time to keep up with the literature, except in his own country. Of the *circa* 4,700 footnote references in the fifth edition less than 1,100 date from this century and 75 per cent of these are to Italian sources . . . Ferri used to say during his later years that he found nothing written of such importance that it had caused him to change his views.' See Thorsten Sellin, 'Enrico Ferri 1856–1929', in Hermann Mannheim (ed.) *Pioneers in Criminology* (1960), pp. 277–300, at p. 287, fn. 19.

One alternative would be the eternally exciting Paris; the other Geneva – a place of serene and civilized stability. You may feel somewhat isolated there, but you are not likely to lose yourself. I recommend Geneva. And I would like, if you will allow me, to send to Paul Logoz your 'criminological profile' as I see it. I shall be writing to him tomorrow.

Only once more did I see Ferri; it was on 10 January 1929, when I had the honour to convey the homage of the University of Geneva at the sumptuous festivities mounted by the University of Rome to celebrate half a century of teaching in the context of his entire scientific activity. This was followed by the publication of a splendid volume *In Onore di Enrico Ferri*, containing articles from fifty authors and a list of over five hundred personalities from all over the world who wished to pay a tribute to him. Soon afterwards, on 2 April 1929, Ferri died at the age of seventy-three. I understand that, unlike his turbulent life, his passing away was peaceful.

2
FROM AN ACTIVE VOLCANO TO A WELL-ORDERED SCENERY

Return to Geneva

The title I have chosen for this chapter reflects a personal feeling that got hold of me almost immediately on my return to Geneva. I remember that feeling vividly, but I am far from certain whether I can adequately recapture it. And yet, I should try, because the contrast which my title expresses not only relates to matters which may well be regarded as trivial, but also is a metaphor for a radically different attitude towards crime and punishment which prompts reflections of a more general character.

Instead of being admitted to a sumptuous villa *à la Ferri* by a formally dressed servant, it was Professor Paul Logoz himself who opened the door of his charming chalet in the mountains near Geneva and ushered me into his small sitting-room, modestly furnished, with a few books on the shelves and a few handsome vases engraved with rustic designs. Criminology hardly figured in our conversation. Instead, the professor asked me whether I was attracted by mountains and whether I indulged in ski-ing – 'it is important to start as early as possible if you wish to be good at it', he announced authoritatively. He was certain that I had enjoyed my stay in Rome – and left it at that. He had no reasons to doubt that his recommendation that I should be appointed *Privat-Dozent* would be approved by the faculty. I should be prepared to start giving a course in the coming semester (in October) and I would be well advised to give some thought forthwith to the topic of my inaugural lecture, the choice of which he left entirely to me, refraining from making any suggestions. Nor did he enquire whether I already had a theme in mind which I was anxious to develop. He did, however, go out of his way to assure me that everything would turn out to be pleasing and worthwhile simply because, as far as he was aware, the faculty had never had so young a *Privat-Dozent*. Indeed, he said he was pretty certain that I would be the youngest in Europe. 'To use the local language,' he said, 'it would be an exciting mountaineering expedition.' He would try to come on the appointed day to listen to me. The meeting was brief, exceedingly amiable, but at such a low key that it could hardly have been lower (see Plate 2).

In vain would one look for hundreds and hundreds of students flocking to the faculty's premises for instruction like at the Sorbonne or in Rome. The Law School in Geneva consisted of, perhaps, two hundred students *in toto* and a regular class contained a mere fifty to sixty-five. I was one of only two foreign students, the other being a dear Polish friend of mine. Later, as a heroic and brilliant journalist, he was executed by the Nazis in Warsaw. Everyone else was Swiss and, with hardly any exceptions, they were from the leading legal and social circles of Geneva. All of them were visibly very comfortably off, well groomed, tastefully dressed, impeccably polite, confident and at ease. They could expect, in the natural course of events, to find their place in the legal establishment, in banks and important corporations, in public administration and in politics. Nor was there any difference in these respects between the pupils and their teachers. I do not remember a single professor who was not a *Genevois*. They too were part of *la crème de la crème* of this small but perfectly attuned world. They were neither anxious nor desirous to establish contacts with the eminent foreign lawyers who, at the time, were working in the League of Nations or the International Labour Office. They valued their self-sufficiency above all. They were a highly competent and thoroughly conscientious body of instructors.

The Law Faculty building was somewhat sombre but, in a surprisingly transparent manner, it conveyed a relaxed, even-handed atmosphere which, without any disparaging intent, could be described as a faculty *en famille*. It could not have been better situated: in a charming, intimate park adjoining the most imposing part of the city, the Parc des Bastions. The stark monument of John Calvin, the most famous inhabitant of Geneva (next to Jean-Jacques Rousseau), stood close at hand to remind one that law and morals should always be intimate and faithful allies.

Privat-Dozent is a term unknown in the English-speaking academic world and, as such, it calls for a brief explanation. The appointment did not entitle admission to the inner circle of the faculty. But, if conferred by a university of good repute, it signified a professorial potential and it marked the essential first step in an academic career. As a general rule no one could become a professor unless, at some stage, that person had been a *Privat-Dozent* and one could not become a *Privat-Dozent* unless one had obtained a doctorate and had written a special dissertation, the substance of which would be made use of in the inaugural lecture. A *Privat-Dozent* was expected to give a course of lectures which had to be approved by the faculty, but was hardly ever assigned teaching which was part of the required legal curriculum of the school. Students attended these lectures on a voluntary basis, they were not marked and there were no examinations. Indeed, their value was precisely that they related to topics and problems which could not be integrated into the formal programme – either because of lack of time or space or because it was thought that the time was not yet ripe to tackle them in a less informal and more systematic manner. The post had a long and respectable tradition behind it and was firmly established in the universities of Germany, Switzerland and Italy, where it was known as *Libere-Docente*. Many people, including students, guided by an engaging politeness often bordering upon meaningless flattery, were in the habit of addressing one as 'Monsieur le Professeur'. I must confess that as a *Privat-Dozent*, twenty-three years old and in an unusual foreign environment, I found it rather pleasing, but whether it was really good for me is another matter.

I was informed by the Department of Public Education that I was dispensed from submitting a dissertation but that on 16 October 1928 at 3:15 p.m. in auditorium 50 I was to present 'devant le corps de professeurs de la faculté une leçon sur "La crise et l'avenir du droit pénal"' ('The crisis and the future of the criminal law'). The lecture, forty pages long, was almost immediately published in Paris by Marcel Rivière. Its theme was one which a seasoned professor close to the end of his career might have considered desirable to reflect upon. But for a young 'Monsieur le Professeur' to tackle such a truly formidable assignment required a mixture of boldness and temerity. Looking at it again when composing this section of my memoir, it is easy to see its strengths and weaknesses. I had tried to make a good choice of historical and legal sources and to use apt quotations to bring to life important points. I had attempted to express my conclusions in concise yet forcible language. But, in spite of all this, the whole exercise now conveys a strong impression of being more of a polemical manifesto than a scholarly disquisition. It erred by making too many obvious simplifications of complex historical situations and problems, and frequently confused causes and effects in relation to certain vital stages in the evolution of criminal law and the working of criminal justice. To this extent my *tour de force* was open to justified criticism.

Taking a very broad view of the subject I distinguished three phases in the evolution of penal ideas. First, the primitive phase, which extended to the Middle Ages and exhibited extreme cruelty and capriciousness in dealing with suspected or convicted criminals. Second, the classical phase engendered by the impact of the Enlightenment and the French Revolution. And third, the positivist phase with its three layers: anthropological, socio-psychological and juridical. Without being conscious of it, I made use of this categorization thirty-eight years later in my *Ideology and Crime: A Study of Crime in its Social and Historical Context* (1966). But, in my inaugural, any acknowledgement of the contribution of the classical school was submerged by a remorseless attempt totally to demolish it. Everything that appeared lacking or unsatisfactory in the system of criminal justice – including its impact on the level of crime – I hurled mercilessly at the door of the classicists.

Drawing upon comparative criminal statistics I concluded that the proportion of recidivists ('which with good reason is looked upon as the touchstone of criminality') amongst those convicted of crime varied between 40 and 45 per cent. I regarded even this as an understatement and believed that the proportion was steadily rising. Again, perhaps even more disturbing, was the level of juvenile criminality – juveniles accounting for a quarter of all convictions. Solitary confinement, the basis of penitentiary organization, was more and more disputed or rejected, while the sentencing infrastructure was becoming rapidly discredited for being neither reforming nor deterring. One-third of all prison sentences were one month and less and as many as nine out of ten did not extend beyond six months. Virtually all trends of crime were showing no decline, not even a halt, but instead a sharp turn for the worse.

I welcomed the emerging penal code for Switzerland as offering, at last, tangible hope that this crisis of criminal law enforcement could be overcome. But I nevertheless held fast and firmly to my conviction that the projected code was but a transitional project which, in due course, would lead to the formulation and adoption of a code of social defence conceived in undiluted positivist terms. Moreover, I declared, to confine oneself to the task of formulating a penal code, however urgent and necessary it undoubtedly was, would be following a gravely faulted road. To reach the evil of crime at its roots it was imperative to attack its economic and social causes and to implement a social policy boldly directed towards the fulfilment of collective equality and justice. I continued:

> The sociologists and the economists expect, from the centuries to come, a definitive solution of the social question. It was for us, jurists and criminologists, to harbour and foster a firm belief that this future will also bring with it a solution to the formidable problem of criminality which like a dismal shadow seems to follow humanity for ever. Happy are those who will live in this golden age.

There were many at that time, besides me, who were infected by such an exhilarating and touchingly naïve optimism. But there were also those who had begun to witness at closer quarters a frightening regression. And not so much later a mass of humanity was to be annihilated by evil forces in their seemingly insuperable ascendancy.

The basic tenor and bent of my lecture stood in striking contrast to the political and penal climate then prevailing not only in the Canton of Geneva but in Switzerland as a whole. Professor Logoz was not an exception, and yet this did not hinder him in the slightest from promoting my academic career. To pay a modest tribute to the largesse of his outlook I dedicated to him another book of mine which appeared at that time, a product of my interest in social sciences and demography.[1] Paul Logoz continued to lead a serene and eminently useful life, first as the Professor of Criminal Law and Criminal

---

1   *Le Problème de la population en France* (Marcel Rivière, Paris, 1929).

Procedure at the Faculty of Law in Geneva and then as a judge at the highest court of Switzerland, the Federal Tribunal in Lausanne. He also continued to discharge public duties of the first order, such as the Vice-Presidency of the International Red Cross. He left behind a *Commentaire du Code Pénal Suisse* in three volumes which by its clarity and precision is still held in high esteem. He died on 30 June 1973 at the age of eighty-five. The admiring tributes paid to him by Professor François Clerc (to mark his eightieth birthday) and the posthumous tribute by Jean Graven were just right.[2] And he remained friendly and well disposed towards me.

The audience, which filled one of the largest auditoriums of the university, were extremely generous in their response to my lecture. As I cast my eyes at the benches I saw sitting next to the professor my father, who had come from Poland to be with me on this occasion. I could hardly have wished for more.

Swiss old and new ways

Fortunately, my fervent beliefs in positivism did not induce me to turn a blind eye to the exciting way in which the Swiss were, at that time, pioneering penal reform. The knowledge I thus acquired stood me in good stead in the years to come when I gained greater maturity and better balance of judgement.

Switzerland, small in size and population, was made up of twenty-five cantons, all of them proud of their substantial autonomous status within an equally proud Confederation which, in its turn, united all the Swiss as a nation irrespective of their cantonal provenance. This closely integrated structure prompted admiration in many parts of the world but hardly ever a true and workable reproduction, largely because it was a unique historical product of interwoven interests, circumstances, events and expectations. But Switzerland was also a country positioned at the heart of Europe, trilingual and surrounded by three major states. Hence it could hardly escape (even if it had wished to do so) their potent, persistent and diversified influences. The effect of all this in the penal sphere was an extraordinary mosaic.

Swiss delinquents committing a crime in Switzerland could, in practice, face any one of twenty-three criminal codes plus two common-law uncodified legal systems and as many codes of criminal procedure, largely depending on the canton in which they happened to break the law. There were, of course, several drawbacks in dispersing the authority of the criminal law. One of them was the disparity in the punishments imposed in different cantons with respect to offences closely akin: disparities so flagrant and so unjustifiable that they presented a threat to the very notion of equality and legality in

---

2 In *Revue Pénale Suisse*, vol. 84 (1968), p. 7 and vol. 89 (1973), p. 255.

a sphere which, in historical perspective, has proved to be especially vulnerable to arbitrary decisions and even abuses. Professor J. Hurtado Pozo reminds us that in 1896 the Federal Council pointed out that the same illegal act was punishable in one canton by penal servitude, in another by imprisonment and in a third one by a fine. In one it was prosecuted ex officio, in another by complaint, and in yet others it was never prosecuted or not even punishable.

A country with two dozen or so criminal codes, amidst European states endowed with formal, stable, codified and uniform penal structures, could hardly avoid criticism. The elaboration of a uniform Civil Code and Code of Obligations, accomplished with flying flags by Eugene Huber and put into binding effect for the entire Swiss Confederation, also could not fail to intensify the embarrassment and the frustration felt by many criminal lawyers, academics and practitioners. The fact that throughout Europe powerful currents of thought pressed for a vast reform of penal laws and penal systems could not fail to foster the suspicion that the reluctance in certain legal and political circles of Switzerland to forge a uniform code was caused not so much by the concern to protect the traditional autonomy of the cantons but rather by the fear that it might bring with it a drastic revision of the classical penal heritage which was so strongly embedded in so many of them.

Yet the conviction that a thoroughly modern state should have a modern uniform criminal code was too deeply felt for it to be kept off the national agenda. As early as 1860, and again in 1872 and 1887, the Society of Swiss Jurists – a highly respected and influential group – urged the Federal Council to set on foot preparatory work with a view of bringing about the full implementation of this emerging vision. Largely in response to this initiative, Carl Stooss was appointed to tackle this complex and delicate task at the age of forty-one.

Committed to the principle that a good codification calls for a good stock-taking of the status quo, his three massive volumes (1890–3) contain a comparative digest of the entire cantonal penal diversity, revealing in an accessible form the most important similarities and differences in content and formulation. In 1893 appeared his *Avant-Projet de Code Pénal Suisse: Partie Générale*, followed a year later by the Special Part which was accompanied by an *Exposé des Motifs*. The original German text prepared by Stooss was masterly translated into French by Professor Alfred Gautier, Logoz's predecessor at Geneva. A little later Stooss also produced a *Unified Code of Criminal Procedure*, which still remains in the form of a project. The attractiveness of his *œuvre* was greatly enhanced by his remarkable linguistic capacity, for he was a superb draftsman as well as a very gifted writer.

Carl Stooss

In this context, the contrast between Enrico Ferri and Carl Stooss in personality, lifestyle, ambitions, reforming vision and strategy of approach could hardly be more stark and unbridgeable. Carl Stooss, strange as it may seem, became a lawyer almost *malgré lui*. In his delightful autobiographical sketch, which reveals his engaging personality, he informs us that 'As I had no scientific, artistic or technical gifts, I became early in 1868 a jurist, in fact without following a disposition or a vocation'. Once he decided to follow this path he followed it at the exclusion of any other pursuit. He was not attracted by extensive travels abroad, not keen to agitate for the adoption of his penal views in endless conferences and congresses, not interested in political discourse or campaigns. He was nowhere more perfectly content as in his native Berne, in the simplicity, intimacy and warmth of his family life. Guided by his impeccable sense of duty, he gave up at an early stage of his preparatory codifying labour both his professorship at the University of Berne and his judicial position in order to devote all his time and energy to the task which, in his endearing modesty, he had never expected to be entrusted with.

From the outset Stooss was anxious to avoid ideological, or personally loaded, confrontations. There was a lot he did not like in the cantonal criminal legislations across Switzerland and he did not hesitate to say so, but his criticisms were hardly ever fierce or hurting. Firmly believing in the value of having a diversity of penal views, he was ready to compromise and anxious to avoid controversial issues unless their resolution was absolutely vital for an effective control of crime. And he had no illusions that a successful construction of a revised and unified code commanding general approbation would prove to be a painful and exhausting exercise requiring much endurance as well as patience. What Sir Cecil Carr said about Lord Brougham was also largely true of Enrico Ferri: 'a better beginner than finisher. His fire was over full of irons, they could not all stay hot.' This remark could not be affixed to Carl Stooss.

To assess fully the significance of Stooss's *œuvre* it would obviously be essential to study his legislative text and the motives behind it. But I have also found it particularly revealing, and in some ways more direct and personal, to ponder over nine of his many articles which appeared between the years 1891 and 1925 in the *Revue Pénale Suisse* (founded by him in 1888 and still going strong). Their very titles convey what I mean: 'What does Criminal Policy Expect from a Federal Penal Code?' (1891), 'What is Criminal Policy?' (1894), 'The Ethical and Social Foundations of the Criminal Law' (1896), 'The Spirit of a Modern Criminal Legislation' (1896), 'Crime and Punishment viewed from a Criminal Policy Angle' (1901), 'Punishment and Security Measures' (1905), 'Treatment of Youth in the new Swiss Project of Criminal Code' (1915), 'Montesquieu and Criminal Policy' (1919) and 'Security Measures in Earlier Times' (1925).

Behind these pieces you can easily discover a man who lived at a time when criminal law and criminal policy were at odds with each other, a man who studied carefully their conflicting trends, who had no axe to grind but who was nevertheless anxious and determined to produce a construct that would satisfy the needs of the period by more effectively controlling crime and saving human waste whenever it was possible and realistic to do so. But he was also a man who firmly believed in the necessity of maintaining public order and the authority of the state.

Stooss also firmly believed that free will and moral responsibility were much too deeply embedded in the human psyche and the fabric of society to be expunged from a criminal code. 'I acknowledge', he stated, 'the retributive character of punishment historically proven', and, on another occasion, he declared that he who has committed a criminal deed 'should suffer pain in proportionate relationship to his culpability'. And still on another occasion he emphasized that punishments have to be retained both in substance and terminology, because they reflect the need for retribution which, not unlike free will and moral responsibility, are basic to individual life and social existence. But when a traditional punishment proved to be ineffective or inappropriate it should be supplemented, or even replaced, by a type of sanction which was likely to be more useful in controlling crime. Indeed he was convinced that several of these traditional concepts could not remain intact in the face of scientific progress and new social ideals. The time had come to readjust them.

Stooss was, of course, well aware of the positivists and of the programme of the International Association of Criminal Law. Yet, like so many others, he was discouraged by the extreme position taken up by the positivists, as the following remark illustrates: 'The foundation of Lombroso's theory proved to be untenable. There is no born criminal and crime cannot be explained by the scalp and body of the criminal.' He gravitated towards the Association. In the final analysis, however, his work was, to a decisive extent, intrinsically the expression of his personality and of what he felt were, at the time, the urgent and attainable objectives of penal renovation.

Searching for a via-media

A formula was constructed to redefine responsibility under criminal law which some of the contemporary Swiss students (such as Michèle Rusca or Hurtado Pozo) characterized as 'penal capacity'. This meant that psychiatric, psychological and social considerations would come into play in each individual case so as to ensure that no one would be punished who, at the time of committing the offence, was in a state of 'insanity, idiocy or grave disturbance of mental competency'. These conditions were not defined but were to be left to the determination of the judge. The project rightly abandoned the classical requirement of 'not knowing what one did or not being able to control it', but regrettably it was reintroduced in subsequent drafts and in the Code.

The assumption that people can be naturally and categorically split into the normal and the abnormal was regarded as being too simplistic and unreal and a new category of diminished responsibility was introduced, again described in very broad terms: 'mentally disturbed, or his mental competency diminished, or if he was mentally retarded to the extent that his capacity to recognize the illegality of his act or his capacity to act in accordance with insight was diminished'. If judges encountered difficulties in determining the condition of irresponsibility or diminished responsibility, they were to be allowed to call on experts to help them.

The redoubtable positivist concept of the state of danger as the regulator of the quality and amount of penal response in each individual case of the violation of the law was not adopted by the Code. But nor was the classical criterion that the basis of sentencing should be the objective gravity of the offence. It was overshadowed by a cluster of subjective criteria, and prominence was given to the principle of individualization. The project declared: 'The judge will fix the punishment according to culpability taking into account the motives, the antecedents and the personal situation of the offender.' This principle was to be applied however serious or minor the offence might be, whenever the judge had to consider mitigating or aggravating factors, and also in those cases where consecutive sentences might be imposed.

Especially noteworthy was the emphasis on assessing and weighing up the motives for the commission of the crime. A subtle and diversified range of considerations appeared in numerous provisions of the Special Part of the Code as well as in its General Part. Thus, a provision relating to the circumstances when punishment could be aggravated, so as to exceed the normal level, reads like an assessment by a highly trained Jungian or Freudian exponent of human motivation: 'bassesse de caractère, en particulier par méchanceté, brutalité, ruse, vengeance, cupidité, joie de nuire ou simple plaisir criminel'. No one would envy the judge who had to try to disentangle this formidable labyrinth of conscious or subconscious drives and turns of human nature.

There were many other features of the projected Code which marked a new stage in penological thinking. In general it had a moderate sentencing structure compared to that in France, Germany, Italy and Britain. It provided for the elimination of capital punishment; a very limited use of sentences for life; a flexible system of aggravating and attenuating circumstances centred round the personality of the offender; an attempt to prevent as far as possible the substitution of short-term imprisonment for a fine; conditional suspension of a prison sentence; the conditional discharge of those undergoing detention; supervision and after-care. In the prison system there was to be a drastic curtailment of solitary confinement, requiring it only for the first three months of penal servitude or imprisonment, except when the court decided otherwise or the offender asked for it; insistence on the introduction of the progressive system throughout the whole range of penal institutions; separate cellular detention by night; and prison work which, as far as possible, could be adjusted to the aptitudes of the prisoners to make it easier for them to earn their livelihood after discharge. Surprisingly, the statutory minimum deprivation of liberty was still very low: one day for detention and eight days for imprisonment. No less surprising was the retention of the traditional classical distinction between two types of deprivation of liberty: imprisonment and penal servitude.

Nor should one overlook the bold and elastic network of measures to deal with juvenile criminality. There were to be no criminal proceedings against children who at the time of the commission of the offence were under fourteen years old. For those between fourteen and eighteen years of age the classical criterion — whether they had acted with or without discernment — was abolished. Stooss repeatedly emphasized that, at this age, maturity and will should be the guiding indicators. It was the judge's job to examine 'their moral and mental development'. Many facilities would be put at the judge's disposal for making this preliminary, but essential, diagnosis. A range of educative and ameliorative measures was to be applied. Nevertheless, if offenders were in need of a disciplinary regime it should be 'vigorous and prolonged'. The court could order their detention in a house of correction for young delinquents for a period of between one and six years, but they could not be detained beyond the age of twenty-one. And again, if an adolescent aged more than sixteen but less than eighteen was 'showing criminal disposition', but did not yet merit detention in a house of correction, ordinary punishment would be applied but substantially reduced. Hopes were running high that these developments would lead to a notable diminution of criminality and especially to a decrease of recidivism among young offenders. As a distinguished contemporary Swiss commentator noted:

> Among the many problems of penal policy, two stand out because of their urgency and gravity: first the treatment of young delinquents and second the treatment of dangerous recidivists who have become professional delinquents. Rescue the former and subdue the latter; a legislator who would succeed in achieving this double objective would count among the benefactors of society.

All along there was a tendency not to go too fast or too far. Thus, for instance, the already noted adoption of the suspended sentence was undoubtedly a bold move for the time. But it was made dependent on certain preconditions characteristic of the tenor of the Code as a whole. It could be ordered by the court only if the offender was convicted for the first time;

there were no vile motives behind the offence; if the imposed punishment did not exceed six months' imprisonment; if one could anticipate that the conditional suspension was likely to prevent the delinquent becoming a recidivist. Should the offender commit a new offence within a period of five years the penalty first imposed should be undergone, leaving the possibility of imposing further measures because of this recidivism.

Going beyond traditional punishment

Viewing the project as a whole, it is undeniable that what attracted most attention everywhere was its system of 'measures of security'. 'Sichernde Maßnahmen', 'misure di sicurezza' and 'mesures de sûreté' were the nomenclatures given to it in German, Italian and French professional literature and practice. In English the term 'security measures' seems to be a faithful translation but is rather unfortunate, for it carries the connotation of being some sort of police measure, or some kind of emergency measure facing an imminent danger. Professor Franz Exner, who dedicated an entire book *Theorie der Sicherungsmittel* (1914) to these measures, maintained that the Swiss Project was the first legislation in Europe to introduce a system which would operate alongside the traditional system of punishments: indeed it was this very project which used the term 'security measures' to describe the idea. My own subsequent studies confirm this view. And Paul Logoz was perfectly right when, in the 1920s, he stated in his report to the National Council for the Unification of Swiss Penal Law:

> To Professor Carl Stooss belongs, one can say, almost the glory to have been the first in his Project of 1894, to perceive and legislatively to implement this idea which to-day has almost become banal: a security measure must figure in the penal code alongside punishment, as the second and powerful measure of social reaction against crime, and more exactly against certain criminals.

To Exner, Logoz and many others, this innovation was not to be regarded as a smart, shifty compromise which would bring to rest the fierce struggle between the classical, the positivist and the eclectic schools of criminal law, but as a true solution which would at last vitalize and invigorate the criminal codes while, at the same time, helping to preserve the traditional nature of punishment. But not everyone was so hopeful. Karl von Birkmeyer of Munich, for instance, declared categorically that 'the Criminal Law Legislator must declare himself either in favour of the old or the new School'. And even Professor Ernest Hafter of Zürich, a collaborator and friend of Stooss, prophesied as early as 1904 that this was nothing but a tactical arrangement and one which would not prove to be workable. The separation of punishment and security measures was too artificial, too strained, leading in practice to confusion and injustice. A further more definitive clarification of this fundamental issue had to wait another four decades. And I shall have many critical things to say about it.

The security measure had, in common with the punishment to imprisonment, a combination of features which have to be kept clearly in mind. It had to be explicitly stipulated in the criminal code or statute in force. It had to relate directly to a commission (or omission) of an act declared to be an offence under existing law. It could be imposed only if the established rules of criminal procedure had been followed. It could be suspended, revoked or reinstituted in individual cases. When suspended or terminated it could be followed by supervision and after-care.

On the other hand, it differed from imprisonment in several fundamental respects. It could not be applied to all kinds of offenders, as it were across the board, but only to those who were singled out under the law as being liable to be dealt with by a defined security measure. That did not mean that all such offenders had to be mandatorily subjected to it: judges were to exercise their discretion on the basis of certain laid-down criteria and according to each particular case. It was not to be imposed for a fixed term for it was essentially an indeterminate sentence – either absolute (i.e. without a minimum and maximum) or relative (i.e. with a minimum and maximum covering a rather wide range). In contrast to punishment, which was primarily inspired by considerations of retribution, deterrence or expiation, the purpose of the sanction was treatment, reformation or incapacitation. It was not to be enforced alongside deprivation of liberty imposed as a punishment but, as a general rule, in a separate network of diversified establishments, with their own regimes and personnel.

The project distinguished six categories of offenders to whom security measures might or should be applied: the insane, the partially insane, those convicted of disorderly conduct or idleness, habitual drunkards, recidivists and juveniles. Sometimes the enforcement of a security measure was to precede the enforcement of the punishment of imprisonment; sometimes it was expected to follow imprisonment; sometimes it was left to the court to decide whether both should be imposed in a particular case and, if so, in which order they should be enforced. More often than not, these alternatives and combinations were fixed by law. The Swiss experts were inclined to define this development in legislation and sentencing not as a 'dual system' but as a 'monistic system'.

Particularly instructive was Stooss's attempt to deal with criminal recidivists. The persistency and extent of recidivism were being increasingly revealed by the progress made in the organization and interpretation of criminal statistics in the leading countries of Europe. It was rapidly becoming recognized as the 'number one problem' of criminal policy. In particular, a crisis in penal ideology emerged as the limitations of fixed short terms of imprisonment were revealed. Any radical departure from the traditional mode of punishment would undermine the principle of proportionality between crime and punishment and, in its turn, the very legality of the criminal process. Certainly, Stooss made no attempt to avoid this issue or to cover it up. Indeed, he constructed a system which was unique at the time and, thereafter, highly revealing of the new thinking about crime problems which was then emerging.

When a criminal who had undergone several sentences committed a new offence within the period of five years following the expiration of the last punishment, and when the court was 'convinced of the ineffectiveness of the ordinary penalty to prevent further crimes', it could, after having passed sentence, but before ordering the enforcement of the penalty, hand the criminal over to a Federal Commission which would be responsible for determining whether, in this case, a special measure of internment should be imposed. In order to reach this conclusion, the commission was to collect all the relevant information about 'the antecedents of the convicted recidivist, his education, family, his means of existence, his physical and mental health, the crimes he has committed and the punishments he has undergone'. If, in the light of this thorough inquiry, it appeared beyond doubt that criminals would continue to commit offences for a considerable time, even after having undergone their newly imposed sentence, the commission could determine that, instead of imposing a fixed punishment, the criminals should be interned in a special establishment for a period of not less than ten and not more than twenty years. If, after having served five years, it appeared that they would no longer commit further offences, they could be conditionally set free, but only if this was the first time that they had been ordered to be interned. If they abused the conditions under which they had been given their liberty they would be ordered to undergo the entire period of internment. If, however, the commission formed the view that they should not be interned, their case would go back to the court which would then order that they should serve the sentence to imprisonment initially imposed by the court which had tried them.

Social defence slides into social aggression

It was correctly observed by Michèle Rusca that this model (especially the idea of a mixed commission with the ultimate power of decision) was, in all probability, inspired by Lombroso. At some stage Stooss had strongly recommended that the sentencing process as a whole should be split into two, with the judge determining the guilt of the accused and a mixed commission deciding both the type of the sanction to be chosen and the mode of its enforcement. Stooss was particularly keen on this solution because, as he put it, 'the jurists have a tendency simply and swiftly to decide cases'. But a motivation behind this gripping solution and the expectations of what it would lead to in practice, if accepted, went far beyond the attempt to improve the sentencing process. They were revealed by Alfred Gautier at the very time when the draft project was passing through the initial very important stages of consolidation by the official commission of experts. Gautier was a highly respected Professor of Criminal Law and Criminal Procedure at the University of Geneva, the official translator into French of Stooss's Code and his very close friend and associate. The revealing statement is to be found in his report presented to the International Congress of Comparative Law held in Paris in 1900.[3] What follows is a faithful summary of Gautier's text, almost invariably in direct quotations.

> The term 'recidivist' is not used in the formalistic meaning adopted by criminal codes, but in order to designate those hardened delinquents who, even if their deeds in themselves do not present a high degree of seriousness, have nevertheless shown that they have become insensitive to ordinary punishment. Undoubtedly this sorting out ('ce tirage') is a delicate exercise. However, although it is virtually impossible to describe *a priori* the general characteristics of the class of incorrigible offenders, it is, in general, possible to appraise in a particular case whether the offender in question belongs to this species. 'This is not a question of law but of social policy.'
>
> Strange is the obstinacy of those who refuse to recognize that even a light offence following a long series of offences already punished, often suffices to characterize their perpetrators so as to include them among professional delinquents. While recognizing the futility of such an exercise, the courts nevertheless continue everywhere to feed the judicial records of such offenders with a heap of small penalties which simply make them laugh. This situation calls for the introduction and rigorous application of measures of 'special treatment'.
>
> The dominant part of the Federal Commission which should decide about the outcome of all such cases should not be made up by 'theoretical jurists', but by those who by their avocation or profession are in constant touch with the criminal world, such as prison chaplains, prison governors, prison doctors and magistrates. A permanent secretary should be attached to the commission whose business it should be to centralize and to keep up to date the information relating to that 'dangerous class', its composition and ways of life, 'with the ultimate objective of drawing up and maintaining a list of the criminal inventory of the army of crime'.
>
> The internment should be conceived as a 'measure of social defence' and its regimen should reduce the interned offenders to the

---

3 'La lutte contre le crime dans le projet de Code Pénal Suisse', *Procès-Verbaux des Séances et Documents* (1st edn, Paris, 1905), pp. 580–96, at pp. 585–8.

pure and simple condition of being unable to do any more harm, to isolate them from society against which they had decided to be in a 'state of war', and also to isolate them from less hardened prisoners, whom they would exhort to be in a 'state of revolt'. Incarceration should not be in solitary confinement but in a special establishment along with severe and sustained work for a period of between five and twenty years. However, in order not to discourage 'repentance however improbable', conditional discharge, but never earlier than after five years, should be allowed.

Why try to do more? Why dissipate the heavy expenses involved in the establishment and running of solitary confinement, or of the various attempts at rehabilitation with respect to those from whom no good can be expected? The unanimous testimony of our prison directors confirms the existence of a class of delinquents with respect to whom punishment does not bite anymore. For them, crime is a chosen career and they live by it. By the damage which they cause, by the teaching and example which they propagate, by the imitators who are procured by an unintelligent repression, those professionals put the country in danger. It is high time to ward it off. 'Judicious provisions'; 'energetic measures of purification', are, 'a far too long delayed action against this breed'.

But, at the very time when Gautier was making the case for this radical penal philosophy, the solution was quietly expunged from the project by the governmental commission. In eloquent terms he grieved and mourned over its precocious demise. He also raised the pertinent question: how could this have happened? It is difficult to conjecture, but perhaps it was found that the solution if effectively implemented would lead to a multiplication of detention establishments? Perhaps the increased expenditure which this 'rational justice' would inevitably call for would frighten the electorate and indeed put in danger the very idea of penal unification through a national code? This, Gautier confidently asserted, was bad politics because the decrease in the number of crimes which this solution would have brought about would lead to substantial savings, amply sufficient to cover the initial expenditure. Perhaps the authorities allowed themselves to be frightened by the clamours of classical jurists, hostile towards any kind of innovation. Are you going to intern people for ten or twenty years, they were likely to ask, without taking into account the gravity of the last committed offence? Are you not aware that, by acting in this way, you would ruin the sacrosanct principle of the proportion between punishment and crime?

The Swiss Project was alone among the several other projected European new criminal codes at the end of the nineteenth and the beginning of the twentieth century to attempt to bring the criminal class within the orbit of the dangerous classes, to tame it and, in the final analysis, to eliminate it through the operation of suitably adapted penal legislation. A vital aspect of the penal question was identified as an aspect of the social question. A penal solution was advocated on grounds of social expediency and the law was reduced to a crude tool. Ultimately the solution adopted was much less extreme, but it was still controversial.

According to Article 42 of the Code, the detention of an habitual criminal could be ordered by the court for an indeterminate period, 'if he shows a tendency to commit crimes or medium offences, or towards disorderly conduct or idleness, and if he again commits such offences'. The security measure would then be ordered instead of the sentence to imprisonment pronounced by the court. It would be for a period of no less than three years, but, if the initial sentence was for a longer period of imprisonment, it would have to be for the duration of such term. When detainees had served a period corresponding to the term of imprisonment originally pronounced, they could be considered for conditional release, combined with supervision for a period of three years. If during this period, they committed a new offence, they could be detained for a second time for a period of no less than five years.

The pioneer left behind his *œuvre*

> But a few days of life are left to the texts [of cantonal penal legislations]... The work for the adoption of a Criminal Code applicable to the whole of Switzerland is almost completed.

Thus wrote Professor Alfred Gautier in his report presented to the International Congress of Comparative Law which took place in Paris in 1900, and there was hardly anyone in Switzerland who could presume to speak on this subject with an authority comparable to his. And yet it needed a further forty years to pass by before this cheerful prophecy was fulfilled. There were hardly any positivists in Switzerland who would obstruct the adoption of the Code because it did not go far enough, but there were very many classicists and conservatives who rallied against it because it seemed to them to have gone much too far in the direction of leniency.

The opposition, especially in the early stages, was, therefore, resolute and persistent. A warning of things to come was given by a respected colleague of Stooss, Professor Heinrich Pfenninger of Zürich, when instructed (about the same time as Stooss) to prepare a new penal code for the Canton of Uri. In Article 3 he laid down that in the enforcement of penal servitude prisoners should be kept in darkness and sustained by water and bread alone; that their chains could be removed at the beginning of the third month, but solitary confinement should last a minimum of one year. No wonder the first Commission of Experts, composed of twenty members, made little progress in their examination of Stooss's project. Although the second commission, reduced to seven members, made substantial advances, the lack of support was so discouraging that, in 1896, Carl Stooss decided not to continue as the rapporteur, a decision which, in view of his patience and perseverance which had seemed inexhaustible, was characteristic of the prevailing tensions.

He was then at the height of his international reputation and was forthwith invited to occupy the Chair of Criminal Law and Criminal Procedure at the University of Vienna. Yet, deeply chagrined, he became an exile *malgré lui*. After several unhappy years he left Vienna (and a *Treatise of Austrian Criminal Law* in two volumes, 1910) for Switzerland. He was not allowed to take with him his legitimately earned pension and settled in Graz in rather restricted financial conditions. His project continued to be considered by several commissions and experts, by the Department of Justice and by the Federal Government and underwent several revisions. Stooss was consulted from time to time but hardly ever very closely. Isolated, lonely and sad (I do not believe he was a man who could feel bitter) not to see his life's work becoming the law of the land – a work which continued to evoke growing adulation in many parts of the world – he died on 24 February 1934 at the age of eighty-five. The Code at last came into force on 1 January 1942, nearly half a century after its formulation. We are assured by modern Swiss authorities, such as the late Professor O.A. German (of Basle) and Emeritus Professor Hans Schultz (of Berne) that the Code, in spite of its many revisions, remained faithful to its initial creation in shape, bent and ideology.

Carl Stooss's project not only became the Criminal Code of Switzerland, but its reputation continued to grow even in the face of doctrinal disagreements. It served as a model in no fewer than eleven countries and a Swiss professor was not exaggerating when he referred to its *rayonnement*. It became the avant-garde Penal Code of the twentieth century. Enrico Ferri's project by contrast was buried in the country of its birth and remained a disappointed outsider. The only two countries which adopted the essence of its doctrine were Cuba and the Soviet Union. They did so in their Criminal Codes of 1923 and 1926 respectively. It required but a brief span of time for the worst possible testimonies to emerge. No pride could be derived from them.

A very competent translation into English of *The Swiss Federal Criminal Code of 21 December 1937* by Walter Friedlander and W. Abraham Goldberg appeared in 1939 as a supplement to the *Journal of Criminal Law and Criminology*.[4] But the Code has hardly ever been referred to in the United States in works on criminal law, penal policy or codification. Even Jerome Michael and Herbert Wechsler's pioneering treatise *Criminal Law and its Administration* (1940), which made good use of comparative material, was not an exception.

---

4 Vol. 30, no. 1 (1939).

To revive interest amongst English-speaking scholars and teachers I suggested that the Cambridge Department of Criminal Science, of which I was then a member, should provide a survey of the central provisions of the Swiss Criminal Code in the form of replies to our questionnaire by a recognized Swiss expert. Cecil Turner, my close friend and collaborator, required no persuasion and played an important part in framing the questions. Dr Helen Pfander, a senior member of the Permanent Secretariat of the International Penal and Penitentiary Commission, supplied the answers under the direction of Professor E. Delaquis. Dr (later Professor) Kurt Lipstein ably translated them into English and Dr Gutteridge, the first holder of the Chair of Comparative Law in the University of Cambridge, wrote a stimulating preface. The piece appeared as the tenth pamphlet in our *English Studies in Criminal Science* and also in the *Canadian Bar Review* for 1944. But at the end of the day our initiative could hardly be judged a success. Comparative studies in criminal law and criminal policy, as well as in criminology, did not at that time – to put it mildly – find many enthusiasts.

Some preconditions for penal progress

A few reflections, some of them tentative, can be drawn from my criminological experience in Switzerland.

First, comparativists and reformers are too often inclined to forget that there was always a time when the past was the present and that it is therefore prudent and fair to ascertain whether some of the solutions of the past do not contain a worthy message or a wise indication with respect to matters which still preserve their significance and utility in spite of the inexorable passage of time. The elimination of so many codes operating within one country and their replacement by one Code gave an impetus to those aspects of comparative studies which Professor Hurtado Pozo defined as the 'circulation of juridical models'. It helped to clarify such concepts in criminal codification as 'influence', 'penetration', 'infiltration', 'imposition', 'reception', 'transplantation' or 'loan'.[5] It certainly had a beneficial effect on the production of comparative penal studies.

Second, although it may be true – as the famous English White Paper *Penal Practice in a Changing Society* (1959) put it – that 'delinquency cannot be dealt with effectively without more knowledge of its causes', the connection between criminological research and penal reform should not be too dogmatically insisted upon. Many path-breaking innovations were not devised on the strength of fresh and precise criminological knowledge. On the whole, they can be shown to have evolved under the influence of growing

---

5 In his report to the Thirteenth International Congress of Comparative Law, Montreal, 19–24 August 1990.

social consciousness; of religious movements and philanthropic stimulus; from some temporary measure; or just from straightforward common sense, supported by experience. This point of view, to which I shall refer again in due course, also impressed itself on my mind.

Third, I would respectfully but decidedly qualify the late Professor German's view that Stooss's projects were 'grounded on criminological insights, although these were not yet scientifically fully established'.[6] Stooss, to my mind, acted not as a criminologist but as a *Kriminalpolitiker, par excellence*. This is clearly evident in the articles which he published in the *Revue Pénale Suisse* as he proceeded to try to find a solution to specific problems of criminal policy. It is not an accident that the political philosopher whom Stooss held in especially high regard, and to whom he devoted an unreservedly admiring article, was Montesquieu. It may well be that the architect of a good Criminal Code should be a *Kriminalpolitiker*, but one who has at his elbow a good criminologist as one of his leading advisers.

Fourth, criminological sophistication and techniques were badly needed but not available, or not made available, when it was necessary to assess empirically several of his basic assumptions or bold expectations. One of the very few studies of its kind was the *enquête* launched in 1893 under the direction of Dr Guillaume (Head of the Statistical Office of Berne, a noted penologist and a close friend of Stooss) on the subject of recidivists and incorrigible offenders.[7] This, however, left many vital questions unanswered. Indeed, the same can be said about the official explanation provided by the Federal Government in 1918.[8] And it is only fair to observe that criminology proper made a rather late entry into Switzerland. This impression, which I had at the time, has now been confirmed by two learned essays, one by Professor Günther Kaiser and the other by Stefan von Banhofer.[9] I am also inclined to think that the excesses of positivism must have played an important part in hindering criminological studies in Switzerland.[10]

Fifth, it is truly fascinating to note how this cautious, observant and reliable Swiss lawyer, without being aware of it (or so it appears), found himself

---

6 In *Revue Pénale Suisse*, vol. 67 (1952), p. 8.
7 In *Revue Pénale Suisse*, vol. 6 (1893), pp. 292–312.
8 *Message du Conseil Fédéral ... à l'appui d'un projet de Code Pénal Suisse of 23 July 1918*, pp. 18–19.
9 G. Kaiser, 'Kriminologie in Zürich', *Revue Pénale Suisse*, vol. 101 (1984), pp. 367–90, and S. Banhofer, 'Kriminologie in der Schweiz', *Revue Pénale Suisse*, vol. 97 (1980), pp. 145–74.
10 It would, however, be grossly misleading if this statement were construed to suggest that there has been no proper recognition of criminology in Switzerland. The report presented by Professor Hans Schultz of Berne to the Council of Europe's Criminological Conference in 1968 on 'L'identification des problèmes-clés de la recherche criminologique: du point de vue de justice', in *Études relative à la recherche criminologique*, vol. vi, pp. 137–55, serves as a most persuasive rebuttal of such a contention.

to be in total agreement with the impetuous Enrico Ferri on two important issues. Like Enrico Ferri, Stooss had no doubts that a very large proportion of those offenders who suffered from diminished responsibility or chronic alcoholism, or were inveterate social parasites recoiling from regular honest work, or were criminally advanced young offenders, or habitual criminals, could be effectively treated, reformed and readjusted to the stormy, tempting outside world and not return to their anti-social past. Nor did he seem fully to appreciate the danger of arbitrary administrative interference by prison authorities or over-zealous sentencing commissions or courts, indeed of the wider political and social implications of what he was proposing.

Sixth, no doubt Foucault would have seized upon Stooss's system of security measures, especially the mode of dealing with recidivists, as an unmistakable indicator of the way in which the ruling class which emerged out of the industrial revolution aimed to keep down and contain its other product, the dangerous classes. No doubt Switzerland also had its industrial revolution and some of the social tensions engendered by it which William Rappard, my Professor of Political Economy, meritoriously retraced in his book *La Révolution Industrielle . . . en Suisse* (1914). (He was the only professor I ever met who wore two watches: one very opulent with a golden chain across his vest and a second, no less opulent, on his wrist.) But this was not the type of industrial revolution which would have attracted Engels's or Marx's attention: it did not produce a serious potential for revolt. Nevertheless, an industrial society requires for its functioning good order and social subordination and its impatience and irritation when faced with crime, especially in its chronic manifestations, cannot be ignored. There was, at the time, a rather widely felt disappointment that since the abolition of capital punishment in 1874 there seemed to have been an increase in crime and premeditated murder. But its cause was attributed to an influx of migrant workers and drunkenness rather than to abolition itself. Several cantons, however, did bring capital punishment back, but no executions were carried out.[11] Stooss himself acknowledged his hopes that under his system persistent criminals would in the long run become extinct. If discharged they would have lost their prowess to re-embark upon criminal activities. Indeed, they would become the 'lost generation of criminals', a kind of senior citizens of crime, innocuous and ignored. But it appears that, under the system initially conceived, there was a tendency to confuse the concept of social defence with that of social aggression with hardly any attempt to pay attention to the liberal and classical requirement that, as far as possible, punishment should be proportionate to the gravity of the offence.

---

11 The pamphlet by Dr Guillaume, *État actuel de la question de la peine de mort en Suisse* (1866) and its thorough discussion in the London *Times*, including the leading article, *The Times* (28 July 1886), pp. 3 and 9, are so very reminiscent of today's debates on the subject.

Seventh, the Swiss Code also contained a vast array of measures and recommendations which were definitely and genuinely attuned to progressive, humanitarian goals. This was largely to be accounted for by the atmosphere of optimism and the belief in the inevitability of progress then prevailing in Europe, and which affected so many areas of social life. Even Stooss's deeply ingrained realism could not escape this invigorating incubation. Not to recognize this aspect of the criminal policy of the period and to regard it merely as hypocrisy is to add flagrant partiality to inexcusable ignorance.

Eighth, the Swiss experience seems also to provide strong evidence that in a truly democratic and richly diversified society there can be no monolithic Criminal Code emanating solely from one school of thought. This can be effectively secured only in countries run by an emperor or a dictator or under an authoritarian regime.

Ninth, it provided evidence of how important it is to strike the right kind of balance between moderation and strictness which was one of the leading characteristics of the project. A resolve to make it clear that anxious as the penal law was to show understanding and humanity it was no less anxious to avoid the appearance of sentimentality and weakness.

Tenth, nor can it be denied that steadiness, moderation and legality, displayed throughout the entire spectrum of criminal law and the system of criminal justice, can be practised and preserved over long historical periods only in a country which is happily endowed with ethnic and social cohesion, political maturity, economic well-being and a jealously preserved national independence. It will still have crime but hardly ever a chronic or massive crime problem. Professor Marshall Clinard brought this out in his illuminating comparative study *Countries with Little Crime: The Case of Switzerland* (1978). Professor Freda Adler, writing five years later, reached a similar conclusion in her assessment of Switzerland, *Nations Not Obsessed with Crime* (1983, pp. 15–23). And although Flemming Balvig, in his study *The Snow White Image: The Hidden Reality of Crime in Switzerland* (1988), has effectively shown that Clinard (and Adler) substantially underestimated the incidence of crime in Switzerland, nevertheless the fundamental thesis still holds good. We do not have, alas, many such countries.

Eleventh, when a country reaches and preserves these attributes for a long time, it is likely to be unsympathetic to radical criminological solutions, for that matter any radical solutions. It will be anxious to maintain what it has achieved and what seems to work satisfactorily, if not perfectly; it will gravitate towards the maintenance of the status quo, which is the first but very essential step towards conservatism.

Twelfth, no doctrines, however enlightened and comprehensive, are destined to be permanent. Like other ideological tides they were the product of changing historical situations. None of them are perfect, even if they might appear to be so at the time of their birth and challenge. In fact, all had some inherent weaknesses and could, in circumstances not always foreseeable, lead to perilous consequences.

Following my inaugural lecture, I embarked upon teaching and gave a course of lectures on 'The typology of criminals in the light of criminology and criminal policy'. However, after three terms of residence, I started to look around to see whether I could find a place where I could witness and study not so much new departures in criminal legislation, but rather some clearly articulated practical attempts to reshape the traditional penal infrastructure. I wanted to find a country with a penal system in the process of radical change conceived in practical terms. My preliminary enquiries seemed to indicate that Belgium at that time was such a country and so I went there.

3

TOWARDS A MEDICAL MODEL OF CRIMINAL JUSTICE

Pressures for change in Belgium

I went to Belgium knowing no one there, neither in the academic world nor in the field of criminal administration. No one asked me, or suggested that I should come, nor did I receive any grant or encouragement to undertake any task. This is how I wanted it to be. I was keen to settle down in Brussels for a while in unfettered freedom and with no commitments, just to study and to look around to see whether there was something going on in the penal sphere that was worthwhile to explore and eventually write about.

In order to do this I needed some official support and it seemed to me that my best bet would be to go to the very top, to the Chef de Cabinet of the Ministry of Justice. This title and post are unknown in the governmental structure of the English-speaking world, but common to virtually all ministries in Europe and certainly to those in the French-speaking countries. Chefs de Cabinet are neither Permanent Under-Secretaries of State in the English style nor, for that matter, are they directors of departments inside the ministry, although they could be. They are the *portes-paroles*, the spokesmen of ministers, expected to organize Ministers' official lives and implement their initiatives and desires across the whole spectrum of the ministry. The Chef de Cabinet is frequently, but not always, a political appointment that changes with the change of minister. Monsieur Paul-Émile Janson (a liberal) was then the Minister of Justice and Monsieur Maurice Poll was his Chef de Cabinet and Directeur Général in the ministry.

Monsieur Poll received me graciously and we had a lengthy conversation. He confirmed that the Belgium penal system was at a stage when far-reaching changes were taking place and that he welcomed my intention to make it an object of extensive study on the spot, as well as through library work. Accordingly, he said he would inform a wide range of penal administrators about my projected study and also take steps to facilitate my use of published material, internal documents, ministerial orders and directives, parliamentary debates and exchanges of views in important conferences. He also most generously volunteered to put me in touch with a few judges, public prosecutors and academics. He wished me well in my enterprise and expressed the hope to see me again when I felt that I had made some tangible progress with my inquiry. It was an encouraging start.

I concentrated all my efforts in the initial stage of my ambitious undertaking on acquiring some knowledge of the criminological and penal history of the country. And I drew from it five conclusions which seemed to me to be particularly relevant, not only to the movement for penal reform in Belgium, but also to the better understanding of the processes which prompt penal renovation in general.

Belgium was the first country in Europe — indeed I dare say in the world — where a penal reform was initiated and supported by a political consensus between its three major parties. This did not, of course, mean that there was complete agreement on all the issues involved, but the differences which cropped up from time to time were mainly matters of emphasis or related to the allocation of priorities. They were hardly ever issues of substance.

The support of the Catholic Party can be traced back to Jules Le Jeune, a powerful Minister of Justice (1887–94), Minister of State and Senator, and to the highly respected Comte Henri Carton de Wiart (Minister of Justice 1911–18), who had similar qualifications. The commitment of the Socialist Party originated with its acknowledged leader, Émile Vandervelde, who had also been Minister of Justice (1919–22). And it was fully shared by the influential Liberal Party beginning with Henri Jaspar, and continued by Paul-Émile Janson, who was Minister of Justice at the time of my arrival in Belgium. I do not know of any other country which has provided so fervent and consistent a 'national union' in favour of remodelling its system of criminal justice. As recently as 1991, I stressed that no meaningful advance in penal matters can be achieved in contemporary democratic societies so long as it remains a topic of party political controversy instead of a matter of national concern, cutting across the conventional political alignments.[1]

Another feature which added novelty to my inquiry was the course which the projected reform was taking. Italy was characteristic, indeed typical, of how reforms were handled elsewhere in the world: a change in criminal legislation, if endorsed, would hopefully be followed in due course by changes and readjustments in the penal infrastructure. Enrico Ferri, when introducing his Criminal Code Project, recognized that his legislative proposals would necessitate a radical and costly reconstruction of the entire penal system. But his statement that 'this was not the business of his Criminal Law Reform Commission and should be tackled by others' was, to put it mildly, cavalier. Moreover, it was (and largely still is) typical of very many reformers who, although no doubt well intentioned, are dangerously detached from penal reality. No such criticism could have been levelled in

---

1 'Penal Regressions', *Cambridge Law Journal*, vol. 50 (1991), pp. 422–44, at p. 444.

good faith at the Belgian crusaders. Some of the very early signals of how they intended to proceed had been laid down in legislation, such as the law of 31 May 1888 (known as Loi Le Jeune); of 31 May 1888 on conviction and conditional discharge; the law of 21 November 1891 on the repression of vagrancy and mendacity; or the law of 15 May 1911 (known as Loi Carton de Wiart) relating to delinquent children and very young offenders.

When the work of renovation in Belgium was taken up in earnest, it started at the very bottom of the penal system, more precisely amongst the prison population itself. And it continued at this primary level for a very long time before it extended its tentacles, sharpened its thrusts, and directed its objectives towards a bold and specific revision of the legislation in conformity with the conclusions reached by its initial experimentation in the prisons. It was a fascinating trajectory from the very bottom to the very top.

Yet another feature was the high degree to which this reforming movement was in effect nourished, and even moulded, in negative as well as positive terms, by a resurgence of ideas belonging to the past. After all, this was the country where the social study of crime had emerged from the statistical illuminations of Adolphe Quetelet, the Royal Astronomer of genius. No man of this rank followed him (it would be truly extraordinary if one had come along) but a number of scholars of high calibre did succeed in developing a distinct discipline – criminal sociology.

The influence of economic conditions, especially of crisis and depression, was effectively grasped and communicated by Hector Denis (Professor of the Free University of Brussels, a leading member of the Solvay Institute of Sociology and a socialist Member of Parliament). H. Joly and C. Jacquart, a decade or two later, endeavoured to retrace the evolution and trends of criminality as a 'total social fact' and not just an amalgamation of individual anti-legal episodes. Raymond de Ryckere's thorough, hefty and ponderous book on larceny by domestic servants pioneered the study of crime committed by those in intrinsically honest professions. A dozen students of penal matters concentrated on recidivism, which they viewed as the hard core of the crime problem. Even stalwarts of the neo-classical Criminal Code in force (of 1867), such as J. Haus or Fernand Thiry, were not inhibited from presenting unusual proposals to curb so called 'incorrigible' offenders. A slow but steady improvement in the official criminal statistics, both in their content and presentation, was proving beneficial to the criminal justice system as well as providing a tool for criminological investigation. Nor should one forget the scholarly volumes published at the end of the nineteenth century by Professor J.J. Thonissen of the University of Louvain, a firm opponent of the death penalty. His analysis of the growth of the criminal law and its system of punishment in the ancient world (contained in several learned volumes) provided many perspectives relevant to the modern period.

The other side of this ongoing quest was possibly more compelling and more intriguing. It went down to the very bones and the very instincts of human beings in order to extricate out of their total make-up those characteristics and dispositions which could be identified as making them vulnerable to becoming delinquents. Innumerable hypotheses were juggled and tossed about frequently with little regard for methodological considerations and the concept of degeneracy was widely used and hardly ever convincingly defined. Individual etiology of criminal conduct was contrasted with the environmental etiology of crime, or as the current terminology so frequently expressed it: endogenous factors as against the exogenous ones. But, as a general rule, the former were not expected to rule out the latter. More frequently than not, they were assumed to act in close conjunction.

One could easily discover in this ferment of ideas and hypotheses an unmistakable echo of Lombroso and of the positivists, as well as the criticism they received, not only in Italy, but also in France, Germany and the Netherlands. And thus, in the academic world of Belgium, hitherto assiduously pursuing the study of criminal law and criminal policy primarily from a traditional legal perspective, in the universities of Brussels, Liège, Ghent and Louvain, a strange term emerged on the scene and floated in scientific discourses, in reports to learned societies, in national and international conferences, in articles and books by established professors. 'Criminal anthropology' was the term used to label these currents of thought.

I refer to the books of Xavier Francotte (*L'Anthropologie criminelle*, 1891), L'Abbé Maurice de Baets (*L'École d'anthropologie criminelle*, 1893) and Jules Dallemagne (*Théories de la criminalité*, 1896, and *Stigmates anatomiques de la criminalité*, 1896). There were also the articles by Paul Héger, Jean De Moor, F. Semal and several others in the *Bulletin de la Société d'Anthropologie de Bruxelles* and the communications of Émile Houzé and D. Warnotte presented at the International Congresses of Criminal Anthropology, Biology and Sociology, especially the one which took place in Brussels in 1893. Three of the International Congresses of the Association of Criminal Law also took place in Belgium – in 1889, 1894 and 1910. Not surprisingly Enrico Ferri was to be found in Brussels in those exciting days. Between 1895 and 1905 he was a visiting professor at the newly established L'Université Nouvelle (rather than the more traditional Université de Bruxelles), where he preached his criminological positivism and published a book in French which summarized his lectures. It was only quite recently that I learned from a lively and informative essay by Françoise Digneffe, that Ferri found in the highly influential Guillaume de Greef – one of the founding fathers of Belgian sociology – a staunch supporter of his conception and programme of 'criminal sociology'.[2]

Many others, whose contributions were of varying quality and importance, also contributed to the debate. Their total output produced a feeling of moral

---

2 F. Digneffe, 'La sociologie en Belgique de 1880–1914', in F. Tulkens (ed.) *Généalogie de la défense sociale en Belgique* (1988), pp. 245–97, at pp. 262–3.

and intellectual insecurity and added to the doubts expressed about the very basis of the system. The traditional institution of punishment, as conceived by the classical school, began to appear largely irrelevant and rather external to the reality of crime and its effective control.

What, however, was urgently needed in order to turn this ferment into the reality of change was the support of a persuasive personality with firm roots in the Belgian soil. This person would need to be of high calibre and standing in the scientific world as well as in public life, able to embrace and absorb all these approaches, both foreign and domestic, and expound with clarity, persistence and conviction, a doctrinal programme in the crucial sectors of criminal policy. Adolphe Prins (1845–1919) was the man. And he did it in his capacity as university professor, Inspector General of Prisons and co-founder and, at times, President of the International Association of Criminal Law. He was the author of numerous articles and of three highly readable and influential books which even today fully deserve study and reflection: *Criminalité et répression* (1886), *Science pénale et droit positif* (1899) and *La défense sociale et les transformations du droit pénal* (1910; reprinted 1986). The bulk of the views therein expressed were those which had been laid down and developed on very many occasions by Enrico Ferri. They were also repeated in the writings and pronouncements of Von Liszt and Van Hamel. And, if by any chance they had been clothed in legislative language, I doubt whether I would be far off the mark by saying that a 'Prins Criminal Code' would have been somewhere in between a 'Ferri Code' and a 'Stooss Code'.

Within the Belgian criminological context, the label 'criminal anthropology' had added to it the label of 'social defence'. As the work of reform expanded, the latter term became very influential. It will be evident later that this was not just a simple shift in terminology. In the mean time, I should mention that in 1907 a periodical was founded by Raymond de Ryckere and Henri Jaspar under the patronage of Jules Le Jeune in collaboration with twenty-four personalities from the medical, legal, academic and ministerial world – all of them Belgian – *Criminologie* was added to *Droit Pénal* and it was further stated on the title page that the *Revue de Droit Pénal et Criminologie* would also act as the organ of the Belgian section of the International Association of Criminal Law. These facts fit neatly into my preceding account and have a special significance.

As a general rule, the chances that a projected reform will be successful are likely to be increased considerably if it manages to concentrate its attention from the very start on a simple, clearly discernible, object of basic importance and current public concern. This was so in Belgium, for there the reform centred round the issue of what should be the core of the penal system. The Auburnian System – separation by night and association by day – had been introduced by Vilain XIII in the prison of Ghent. For several decades it attracted admiring penologists from many countries (including four visits from John Howard). But by the end of the eighteenth century it collapsed ignominiously, leaving a vacuum which could not be ignored for long. A new era of penitentiary history opened in Belgium when Edouard Ducpétiaux, the head of its penal system in the 1830s, adopted the Pennsylvania System, which involved separation by day as well as by night. A truly remarkable and colourful man, Ducpétiaux left a mark on several sectors of social and philanthropic life. Two volumes, closely packed, were needed to review his initiatives and achievements as well as his failures.[3] And, quite recently, there was room for another spirited study of his contributions.[4] Ducpétiaux was followed by J. Stevens who continued in his path, with less panache, it is true, but with similar thoroughness and consistency. Between 1850 and 1895 the country was covered by a network of prisons organized on the basis of extreme solitary confinement. The central prison of Louvain, the jewel of the entire system, gained an international reputation equal if not superior to that of Pentonville in London. Indeed, in the battle of penitentiary ideas and models which raged across Europe and North America, what became known as the Belgian System acquired special significance. It was acclaimed by the International Penal and Penitentiary Commission at its Congress at Washington in 1910, and it even became the subject of a doctoral dissertation in the University of Paris when a young candidate, Henri Martin, wrote his thesis on 'La cellule belge' (1900).

Ducpétiaux, the Commander-in-Chief of the new prison system, was also a gifted and effective writer, as may be seen from the statements which I have extracted from the policy pronouncement contained in his *Rapport sur l'état actuel des prisons en Belgiques etc.* (1833). The first extract expresses his vision of the essence of punishment and the other, one sentence long, of the essence of the prison regime. The two, taken jointly, were the epitome of the Pennsylvania System and can also be regarded as reflecting the doctrine of the classical school in the penitentiary sphere:

> To be effective the penalty of imprisonment must satisfy the following conditions:
> It must render the offender incapable of doing harm during his sentence
> It must punish him and must let him expiate his offence
> It must be exemplary, it must strike with solitary fear those who might be tempted to break the law
> It must put the convicted man in sufficient fear to make him give up his criminal career
> It must, if possible, bring about his reformation.

---

3   E. Rubens, *Edouard Ducpétiaux*, 2 vols (Brussels, 1922–3).
4   M.-S. Dupont-Bouchat, 'Ducpétiaux ou la rêve cellulaire', *Deviance et Société*, vol. 12 (1988), pp. 1–27.

As a consequence,

> a criminal when he becomes a prisoner should be placed in a position as if he were the only one in the penal institution in question.

Starting with the First International Penitentiary Congress in Frankfurt, held in September 1846, the classical penitentiary school of solitary confinement, of which Ducpétiaux became one of the most respected leaders, emerged victorious, even with respect to criminals undergoing sentences of life imprisonment (although not for political offenders).

This does not mean, of course, that it escaped criticism in Belgium. Adolphe Prins forcefully and eloquently condemned the system as 'un bloc énorme, massif, rigide, ne laissant passer nulle part un peu d'air, de lumière ou de vie'. But the system and its ideology were so firmly entrenched that, as Professor Françoise Tulkens – an admirer of Prins – notes, the building of prisons grounded on solitary confinement continued undisturbed during the entire period during which Prins occupied the post of Inspector General of Prisons. Indeed, it lasted longer: the last such prison was opened in 1919.

A year later, Émile Vandervelde, in his capacity as Minister of Justice, told the Senate in the course of his speech of 8 July 1920:

> I was struck, at the outset, by the absurdity of the logical consequences of the solitary imprisonment ... the concern with isolation has been carried so far that on Sunday when the prisoners go to Mass, they are put in a separate box which allows them to see the officiating priest, but prevents them from seeing one another. At the school not only are they shut up in a sort of cupboard but they cannot reply to the question of the instructor except by gestures. Another fact struck me with equal force, one which no doubt strikes you: it is that in Belgian prisons, the cowl was still worn as it was in the Middle Ages.

I was most anxious to see, ten years after this simple but immensely moving statement was made, how far Belgium had left this heritage behind, in what direction things were moving, and at what speed.

Criminal anthropology at work

Dr Louis Vervaeck

These strands of ferment and pressure were exciting and indicative of the growing acknowledgement that a radical change in penal practice and criminological thinking were becoming imperative. But they were often too disparate, too generalized, too hypothetical and too contradictory to provide a firm and coherent basis for a policy of renovation. For this a model was needed which would inspire a course of action — gradual though it might well have to be — with a well-defined objective and a practical appeal, for this was a national characteristic of Belgians. And it needed someone with proper qualifications and a resolve to take up this task as his exclusive lifelong commitment. Dr Louis Vervaeck was this kind of man (see Plate 3).

When I arrived in Belgium, Dr Vervaeck was at the top of his career and reputation, deeply respected and carefully listened to by Ministers of Justice of all political affiliations. Highly decorated, he was not only the Head of the entire Service of Criminal Anthropology (SAP), but was also given the rank of Directeur Général of the Ministry of Justice. A long and strenuous road had led to this ultimate recognition. He obtained his medical degree with high distinction from the University of Brussels in 1895 and was awarded the Prix Alvarang by the Royal Academy of Medicine. In 1902 he joined the prison service and started work at the age of thirty as a prison doctor in the prison of Nîmes. In 1910, he published an important article 'La théorie Lombrosienne et l'évolution de l'anthropologie criminelle' in the *Archives d'Anthropologie Criminelle*, which shows that already at an early stage he had formed a clear idea of the direction that he would like his life to take.[5] He was greatly helped by two medical friends, both sophisticated and influential professors at the University of Brussels (Fernand Héger-Gilbert and A. Ley), but it is to him alone that full credit is due for leading the criminal-anthropological school of Belgium and being the driving force of penal reform inspired by this medical outlook.

When Vervaeck started on his career he subscribed to Von Liszt's dictum, which he defined as follows:

> Criminal Anthropology should be the scientific study of the physical and mental aspects of the individual who becomes a delinquent, taking into account that his individuality is in part innate and in part acquired.

Three decades later, when providing a final account of his views concerning the whole subject-matter, he still retained the essence of his early definition, but expressed it in a somewhat different way:

> Criminal Anthropology is the science the object of which is the study of delinquents, or more precisely the study of the human being who becomes a delinquent taking into account that his personality is in

---

5   Vol. 25, no. 12 (1910), p. 561.

part innate and in part acquired in the different environments in which it developed.[6]

But, as he went along, the social component receded into the background compared with the anthropological side. Vervaeck was neither a socialist nor a liberal, but an enlightened Catholic: this in itself was a great advantage. He was a very reserved man, not particularly sophisticated in manner or speech and with little sense of humour. Nevertheless, he was very impressive, largely because he was totally and unflinchingly dedicated to his work and his vision of reform. Vervaeck was often referred to as the 'Homme des Prisons' and sometimes as the 'Belgian Lombroso'. This latter ascription was, in spite of his very considerable worth, an untenable exaggeration. He was the author of very many articles, most of which were concerned with criminals and their characteristics, based on his exceptional experience gathered in the *laboratoires* and the *annexes*, yet he was also interested in a variety of topics falling within the province of social and medical prophylaxis. He was not a gifted and engaging writer, but he was solid and anxious to inform. Vandervelde's hope that one day Vervaeck would publish his *beau livre* on criminals never materialized. He simply did not have it in him, and the book he published, *Cours d'anthropologie criminelle* (1939), shows it. A tempting comparison with Charles Goring suggests itself. Much younger, less experienced, with rather restricted empirical material at his disposal and hardly any assistance, Goring nevertheless produced a book (*The English Convict*, 1913) which marks a stage in the development of English criminology.[7] But he left no impact on the evolution of the penal system as such, whereas Vervaeck succeeded in redirecting it. He died in 1943 at the age of 71.

I frequently visited him in the prison of Forest in Brussels and made it a particular point in my inquiry to be present on occasions when he was carrying out his laborious examinations. He most generously gave me much of his besieged time to answer my questions and engage in discussions on some major matters. On one such occasion I overheard Dr Vervaeck, who was not expecting me to join him, murmuring to himself while seeing my silhouette in the mirror facing his desk: 'Le visage n'est pas mal, mais les oreilles sont un peu anormales' ('The face is not bad, but the ears are somewhat abnormal'). I wonder what his diagnosis would be today, after sixty-eight years have passed by, both in relation to my ears and to my face.

---

6 See Vervaeck's *Cours d'anthropologie criminelle* (1939), p. 81.
7 L. Radzinowicz and R. Hood, *A History of English Criminal Law*, vol. 5, *The Emergence of Penal Policy* (1986), pp. 20–7.

Anthropological penitentiary services

The first step to be taken in embarking on the reform was the establishment of what was sometimes known as the Laboratory of Penitentiary Anthropology, but more often went under the name of the Laboratory of Criminal Anthropology. It passed through three stages: in the first, still experimental stage, it was set up in 1907 in the old prison of Nîmes; in the second it was moved in 1911 to the newly erected prison of Forest in Brussels, and by Royal Decree was accorded permanent existence; in the third stage, beginning in 1920, it was extended so as to cover the main penal institutions of the kingdom.

It is important to note that at each of these stages the laboratory increased in importance and in the expectations it aroused. The aim in the first stage was described by Monsieur Renkin (the Minister of Justice) as an attempt to identify the anthropological characteristics of those convicted, their abnormalities and their deformities, their disorders of speech and sensibility, their mental and psychological condition. The results of these manifold studies and observations would be 'brought together, classified, compared, and the publication of these investigations would no doubt contribute to the progress of penitentiary science'. Thus, in the first stage, the purpose assigned to the new organization was primarily scientific. In the second stage the Minister of Justice (Léon de Lantsheere) looked upon the Laboratory from a more practical angle. It would be an essential ingredient of penal organization, which by the very weight of 'its precise and numerous data with respect to the personality of the offenders' would help to identify those who were likely to be reformed in addition to being punished. This would contribute 'to a more exact determination of their treatment while in prison'. It was in the third stage, initiated in 1920 by Émile Vandervelde (the Minister of Justice), that a radical transition took place. 'Until now,' he declared in his speech in the Senate (on 8 July 1920), 'the work of Dr Vervaeck was mainly scientific work, a kind of preliminary study to the *beau livre* which one day he will write about the criminals he has studied. Our thought directs us that one should invest the organization of anthropological services with a practical character.'

As a consequence, a Service Anthropologique Pénitentiaire (SAP) was established, with a network of ten such laboratories in the main prisons throughout the country. The laboratory in the Forest Prison in Brussels acted as a co-ordinating centre, a centre which I described at the time, in my book, as 'le coeur battant et palpitant des tendances modernes dans les realisations pénitentiares'. Considering the number of prisoners in the Belgian system, this service was of considerable size. The average population of the twenty-nine prisons as of 31 December 1928 consisted (in round figures) of 1,100 men in central prisons and 2,900 men and 350 women in secondary ones. Special regulations were issued for the organization and the functioning of the laboratories. The set-up was rather simple, consisting of a doctor well versed in the disciplines concerned with the study of human personality, of crime and prison life, an assistant charged with taking all kinds of measurements and a clerk.

Its commanding instrument was the *Dossier Criminologique du Laboratoire d'Anthropologie Pénitentiare*. And a truly formidable instrument it was. All delinquents sentenced to imprisonment exceeding three months were subjected to it, except those convicted of political offences or fiscal transgressions. The *Dossier* comprised two dozen large-scale closely packed pages with innumerable divisions and subdivisions. It was so bulky that a special directive was issued, under the signature of the Director General of the Ministry of Justice, to the medical heads of the provincial centres instructing them to take special care that 'dossiers soient éxpédiés roulés et pourvu d'un emballage résistant'. Just to give an idea: the document contained some 300 anthropometric measurements and 600 items relating to neuro-psychological examinations. All told there were about 1,300 items which probed from all imaginable angles and perspectives into the personality of an imprisoned delinquent. It ended with: 'Conclusions – Criminological Diagnosis – Penitentiary Treatment – Improvement – Reclassification – Suggested Measures'. The *Dossier* of every prisoner examined was made available to the governor of the prison, his close collaborators, and the chaplain. They were all expected to confer regularly to review the prisoner's condition in the light of his *Dossier*.

The purpose of the SAP was not only to make the principle of individualization a reality in the prison setting but also to help to establish a valid classification of prisoners, which was regarded as an indispensable preliminary to a rational differentiation of penal institutions. The leaders called it 'sériation' and did not object in the least to the way in which I attempted to express the essence of their criminal-anthropological programme: 'Le cadre anthropologique doit nécessairement être complété par la sériation psychiatrique'. They claimed to have identified five basic groups, each of them containing several sub-groups. And although my purpose was to retrace, as faithfully as I could, the work of the Belgian reform movement I could not refrain from commenting upon the so-often illusory nature of all such classifications, a comment which perhaps I may be permitted to reproduce here:

> Every criminologist, even one of second order, tends to have his own classification; he severely criticizes those belonging to others, emphasizing their imperfections and gaps. He then proceeds to forge one of his own, which naturally he considers to be perfect, but which soon afterwards is ousted by the classifications of others. And the series of classification continues. To have one has become a question of prestige, almost self-respect. Only a criminologist who does not respect himself would be content with a classification made by

somebody else; and even if he happens to agree 'in principle' with somebody else's classification he cannot bring himself to accept it unless he makes certain ameliorations to it and thus feels happy to present it in its new form.

No doubt this comment of mine was somewhat exaggerated, but I venture to say it contained a large measure of truth. It certainly also applies to the contemporary trend of presenting 'criminological theories', a trend which calls for some further comments (see Chapter 18).

The broad conclusion was that 47 per cent of prisoners examined could be regarded as 'normal' and 53 per cent as 'abnormal'. Among the latter were included the 'constitutionally amoral' and the psychopaths who accounted for 36 and 14 per cent respectively. As regards recidivists, the incidence of 'abnormality' was declared to be higher. Yet it was rather difficult to find an authoritative and precise definition of these categories. Nor was a thorough comparative investigation carried out with corresponding strata of the non-criminal population. I devoted sixty pages of my book to the examination of the *Dossier*, on the basis of the material provided by Dr Vervaeck and the main literature which served as the background to it. These were largely sources published in French. There were hardly any references to books on psychiatry and psychology of English, American and German origin which, it is only fair to say, at that time were superior in depth and precision to their French counterparts. As the years passed by, the background was considerably widened but the main conclusion remained unaltered.

Every working day of the year in the many prisons dotted around the country, yet more of these individual compendia were created, all of them ultimately reaching their home at the criminal-anthropological headquarters at the Forest Prison in Brussels. In the area of the capital alone about 2,000 *Dossiers* found their way there every year, neatly placed and effectively secured under the vigilant eye of Louis Vervaeck. When I appeared on the scene no fewer than 18,000 *Dossiers* were already in existence, each remaining in the prison where the convicted delinquents were serving their sentence and each deposited in the archives at Forest after the prisoners were discharged. In 1937 (seven years after I left Belgium), the SAP comprised 33,605 'Dossiers d'observation méthodique de délinquants'.[8]

Psychiatric annexes

The second arm of the penitentiary reform were the Annexes Psychiatriques. They sprang from the same belief as the SAP and directly challenged the classical belief that criminals, by and large, were a homogeneous mass from

8   Vervaeck, *Cours d'anthropologie criminelle* (1939), p. 17.

the point of view of their physical and mental make up, a belief obstinately reaffirmed by the penitentiary doctrine of the uniform system of total solitary confinement. In many ways the annex was auxiliary to the laboratory and in practice they supported and reinforced each other. They also differed, and differed essentially, in their total significance. The laboratories were the spearhead of the whole movement of reform, with consequences affecting many sections of the criminal justice system. The annexes dealt with certain obvious flaws in controlling the prison population in closely defined circumstances. Only much later were they also expected to play an important role in the determination of the disposal of all kinds of delinquents.

The first two annexes were established in 1921 and several others followed, primarily in those central prisons of the country already endowed with laboratories. An annex was, in effect, a kind of small mental home within a prison. It was composed of a ward with ten beds, a further room with three beds, a few cells, and auxiliary quarters of one kind or another. At the head of the annex was the doctor in charge of the anthropological service (with its laboratory). The doctor was assisted by two or three hospital attendants who had previously acquired a good knowledge of the object and functioning of an annex. They were expected to exercise supervision by day and night and keep a register recording all the events which occurred within twenty-four hours. In this they were helped by two trustworthy prisoners. The doctor was expected to visit daily all those placed in the annex; all the detainees were to undergo a thorough medical examination on admittance, even if they already had their *Dossier*. The regimen to which detainees in the annex were submitted depended on the penal category to which they belonged. In general, the detainees enjoyed all the privileges accorded to ordinary prisoners; though in exceptional cases the doctor could prescribe a special regime concerning visits and correspondence. The cells of the annex were bigger than those in the ordinary prison; they had more light, but the bars on the windows were always there to remind inmates of the penal nature of their stay. Smoking and alcoholic beverages were absolutely prohibited. But punishments were seldom administered: the most serious was the removal from the common quarters into one of the cells, known as the *cellule nude* because they had no furniture of any kind in them. To disturbed and agitated detainees a long bath was administered to calm them.

The annex was set up to deal with three groups of convicted prisoners. First, those who presented acute and persistent difficulties when under the ordinary prison routine and to whom, therefore, hard and largely unproductive disciplinary measures were being applied, often in an automatic and indiscriminate manner. They were, in effect, 'problem prisoners' whose problems were often accentuated by the very fact of being confined within the four walls of a cell. The role of the annex in such cases was not only the negative one of securing 'prison épuration', but also the positive one of trying to recondition them, in one way or another, in the light of diagnosis and observation. The second group were those who were suspected of simulating problems. It was virtually impossible for prisoners to simulate anything substantial over a longer period in the different environment of the annex where they were under the constant supervision of experienced observers. The third group were those who, on admission to prison and in the process of being examined by the head of the laboratory with a view to drawing up their criminological *Dossier*, had revealed certain features, the elucidation of which required their being removed to an annex for a period of time.

On average between 350 and 450 were admitted every year for observation and a total of 1,850 had been subjected to this experience within the seven-year period between 1921 and 1927. By 1939, noted Dr Vervaeck, the annexes had been able to assemble 14,200 'clinical observations of abnormal and mentally ill delinquents displaying anti-social reactions'. A sombre statement indeed. The period of observations and detention was intense but brief. Roughly speaking, 25 per cent of all cases were detained for a period of between eleven and twenty days; 20 per cent between twenty-one and thirty days; 15 per cent were there between thirty-one and forty days; and only 16 per cent between fifty-one and sixty days; less than three dozen remained there for more than sixty days. The bulk of the cases sent to the annexes originated with the prison authorities, but there was also a contingent sent by public prosecutors and committing magistrates.

A few other broad figures are needed, first with respect to the diagnosis and second with respect to the measures taken. The most numerous group was that diagnosed as 'Psychopathes, déséquilibrés, debiles mentaux', amounting to 31 per cent of the total of all cases. It was followed by 'Neuropathes à crises' with 21 per cent. Those declared to suffer from 'Psychoses et démences' added another 16 per cent, and those utterly unspecified but marked as 'Divers' made up 17 per cent. The fact is that nearly seven out of every ten removed to the annexes were declared to be mentally abnormal. The measures adopted therefore reflected this psychiatric diagnosis, though not completely. A total of 42 per cent were sent to mental asylums, psychiatric colonies, prisons for epileptics and mentally deficients, or to special quarters set aside in prisons for the abnormal. Nevertheless, as many as 46 per cent were sent back to the prison cells from which they came ('réintégrés en cellules' was the quaint terminology). I myself also analysed 1,056 completed *Dossiers* belonging to the Forest Laboratory and the Louvain Prison. But a few years later I came to realize that my methodology had slipped up rather seriously and that I fully deserved the severe castigation by Jerome Michael and Mortimer Adler in their vigilant report on *Crime, Law and Social Sciences* (1933).

Devising a penal network

The experience gained by these two engines of reform led to a blue-print for a differentiated penitentiary organization, a veritable network of specialized institutions or wings with varying regimes and often with different cadres of personnel. And yet there was always the possibility of shifting prisoners from one type of institution into another for periods of varying duration should their condition change or needed to be changed.

The implementation of this ambitious programme was particularly facilitated by the fact that a vast complex of buildings and much land – used in the beginning of the twentieth century for colonies to deal with the very many vagrants and mendicants – was made vacant because vagrancy and mendicancy ceased to be a problem in statistical terms. Appropriate structural changes were also carried out wherever possible in a number of prisons up and down the country so as to fit some of the new requirements, especially those applying to work and education which had been turned into sterile exercises in misery under the solitary confinement system. Steps were also taken to abandon philanthropic after-care and replace it by an 'Office of Social Readaptation', supported by steady governmental and local grants and based on principles and techniques inspired by social work. Indeed social workers were being appointed in increasing numbers to the staff of the laboratories to provide them with information of a social nature relating to an offender's environmental background as well as to act as a link between the laboratories and those delinquents who had been absolutely or conditionally discharged from prison. No impression should be conveyed that the scheme had been put into effect in its totality at the time I made my inquiry, far from it. It was still largely a blue-print, but advances had been made and there was an unequivocal commitment to securing the entire objective.

The organizational vision

1 Schools of care for young offenders between the ages of sixteen and twenty-one
2 Schools of correction for those of similar age but vicious or undisciplined
3 Ordinary prisons for normal prisoners and corrigible recidivists
4 Quarters or prisons in cells for those vicious or undisciplined
5 Industrial workshops under severe regimen
6 Agricultural colonies under mild regimen
7 Deportation colonies
8 Institutions for incurable recidivists
9 Penitentiary hospitals and hostels for infirm prisoners or those afflicted by chronic illness
10 A sanatorium and hospital for those afflicted by tuberculosis
11 An establishment for prisoners afflicted by neuroses and by illnesses of the nervous system

12 A sanatorium for alcoholics and drug addicts
13 Prison asylums for the degenerated, abnormal, mentally deficient
14 Criminal asylums for the criminal insane and those suspected of being irresponsible
15 A special section for kleptomaniacs, the moral insane and sexual maniacs

The organizational scheme had nothing definitive and rigid about it: it would be constantly kept under review and changed in the light of new circumstances and new experiences. But its seven objectives would remain constant because they responded to the basic needs and characteristics of the offenders, as well as to the exigencies of social defence against crime in an enlightened society. This meant a concentration on young delinquents, corrigible offenders, habitual recidivists, abnormal offenders, sex offenders, insane offenders, and alcohol-abusing and drug-taking delinquents. There was an apprehension in certain quarters that, because the medical profession had had so much to say in giving birth and direction to this penal reform, that its reformative purposes would recede into the background as compared with curative and eventually incapacitating concerns. Clearly this was by no means a foregone conclusion, but it was a conclusion which could not be ignored.

At the very beginning of the reform, for example, a 'Prison École' was established to deal with offenders between the ages of sixteen to twenty-one with the sole objective of reformation and re-education. And also, from the very start, the principle of *seriation* was rigorously applied. Only offenders sentenced to imprisonment for six months or more could be admitted; those declared mentally deficient could not be admitted; nor those afflicted by venereal diseases; nor those convicted of sexual offences; nor those suspected of homosexuality; nor those who had previously already served at least three sentences of three months or more; and finally not those who displayed persistent lack of discipline. This left an 'elitist' group of between sixty and eighty. A young and ardent partisan of the new ideas, Monsieur Adolphe Delierneux, was put in charge of the institution and he kept an account of his doings there.[9] However, no account could replace a thorough personal visit to the Prison École at Merxplas; I went twice, once on purpose when the director was absent, and spent many hours there. This was for all practical purposes an institution which would have warmed the hearts of Zebulon Brockway of Elmira Prison and of Sir Alexander Paterson of the English Borstal system. I devoted twelve pages of my book to the analysis of its methods and achievement. And even now this captive society of young delinquents at Merxplas, which engendered so much vitality, benevolence and hope, still captivates my memory. But it should not be ignored that

9 See *Revue de Droit Pénal et Criminologie* (December 1923), p. 1080.

this was a very elitist establishment catering for a carefully selected group and, even so, no attempt was made to gather the data which would have made it possible to assess the inmates' after-conduct and incidence of relapse into recidivism.

As the anthropological reform was forging ahead, the hold of the solitary confinement ideology was weakening. Its retreat, however, was by no means smooth and amiable, for at every stage of this process the defenders of the status quo fought a fierce rearguard action. In 1922 the Société Générale des Prisons of Paris – an influential and elitist body if ever there was one – put on its agenda the subject of the *Mouvement Anticellulaire*. Two lengthy debates were devoted to it, debates which frequently came close to embarrassing personal confrontations.[10] Professor Paul Cuche, the highly regarded author of the first modern penitentiary treatise in French, was the rapporteur.[11] Émile Garçon, the leading *pénaliste* of France, and Henri Joly, Membre de l'Institut, were at hand. A delegation from Belgium was invited, consisting amongst others of Dr Louis Vervaeck and the formidable Monsieur Ernest Bertrand, the Governor of the Central Prison at Louvain – the symbol and the embodiment of the classical penal system. Cuche made one of the most effective speeches in favour of the cell, remarkably well expressed and argued. Bertrand launched a full-scale attack on the entire Belgian programme of reform and Vervaeck responded in a dignified but firm manner. Unquestionably the tenor of the debates was in favour of the solitary confinement system: obligatory and absolute for all offenders undergoing short terms of imprisonment and the first stage for all those sentenced to a long term or for life. Moreover there was a tendency to avoid any precision concerning the duration of solitary confinement in either instances.

In 1930, when the English Select Committee on Capital Punishment was exploring a system of alternative punishment to the death penalty, they looked towards Louvain. The evidence which they received on the conditions prevailing there was simply frightful. When I went there, Monsieur Bertrand was still in command. By his very presence and appearance he looked like a penological Savonarola. This fervent apostle of the *cellule redemptrice* (redemptive cell) thundered against any proposal for change with a fierceness, even more blatant than usual: perhaps because of the growing realization that the tide was moving against everything that he stood for. Even in the 1950s the regime was still very strict, stricter than that of other prisons for long-term prisoners which were visited elsewhere by the Royal Commission on Capital Punishment of 1949–53.[12] Nevertheless, the commissioners

---

10 See *Revue Pénitentiaire et de Droit Pénal* (18 July 1922) and (27 May 1922), vol. 46, pp. 39–76 and 346–92, and 'Enquête', *ibid.*, pp. 515–37.
11 *Traité de la science et de législation pénitentiaires* (1905).
12 *Report*, Cmd 8932 (1953), pp. 484–5.

'emphatically stated that solitary confinement in the sense in which that term is ordinarily understood no longer exists'.

The prison reform owed a lot to criminology. It was, to a large extent, because criminology created this *esprit d'inquiétude* about the penal status quo that a reform was set in motion. As the reform gained in recognition, in turn it contributed considerably to raising the status of criminology. It became a mutually fertilizing interaction. As usual, the beginnings are fascinating. They can be traced back to the year 1890, when Henri Jaspar (subsequently a distinguished public figure), at that time a student of law at the Free University of Brussels and a fervent pupil of Adolphe Prins, established a 'Cercle de Criminologie'; to the initiative of Comte Henri Carton de Wiart, who in 1913 sent Raymond de Ryckere, a well-known magistrate, to learn more about some of the new Schools of Criminal Science in France, Switzerland and Italy; and to Émile Vandervelde, who in 1921 established the École de Criminologie et Police Scientifique in Brussels under the aegis of the Ministry of Justice. And then, in the period between 1921 and 1938, centres were set up at each of the major universities of the country, known as the 'School of Criminal Sciences', 'School of Criminology' or 'School of Criminology and Criminal Sciences'. At a much more modest but hardly less important level, 'criminal anthropology', 'penitentiary science' or 'criminology' appeared in one form or another as part of the curriculum adopted for the professional training of prison personnel of various grades. For a period, the innovative zeal of the anthropological services went much too far: somewhere around the 1920s, forty-two hours of a course lasting forty-eight hours were devoted to 'medical sciences' and only six to elements of criminal law, penitentiary science and prison regulations. This invasion was, however, effectively pushed back.

I noted some of these developments but I did not examine them at that time, for my object was to concentrate on the prison reform as such and its criminological and penal implications. However, some thirty years later, when I was called upon in Cambridge to help to establish a Criminological Institute, all these centres naturally attracted my renewed attention and I shall refer to them again at the stage of this memoir when I try to evaluate criminological thought and study across the world.

In order to ensure that the reform should not – like so many other reforms in so many sectors of public life and in so many countries – lose its impetus, its vision and its aptitude for keeping under constant, independent and critical review all kind of matters affecting directly the prison system and indirectly the criminal justice system as a whole, a Superior Council of Prisons was established in June 1929 under a Royal Decree and in pursuance of a recommendation made by the Minister of Justice. It was composed of fourteen personalities of high standing and acknowledged competence who were to be 'formed into a permanent consultative commission'. They were not to meddle with the work carried out routinely by the penitentiary administration, but to be a promoter, a supporter and a guardian of changes which – to quote again the Minister of Justice – 'would bring into harmony the teaching of criminology with the exigencies of humanity and the concerns of social defence against crime'.

Psychiatrists at the penal helm

The spiral which made itself felt on so many aspects of penal thought and practice, directly or indirectly and over so long a period of time, was reaching the decisive stage of legal implementation. The changes from below were producing changes at the top. The new modalities of enforcing sanctions demanded new types of sanctions. Criminal anthropology was expected to inspire social defence. Administration and legislation were expected to come closer to each other and act jointly. The traditional juridical basis was to be preserved as long as *La Lutte contre le crime* was not hampered and encumbered by it. In a discreet, low-keyed but determined manner the foundation was laid for this final denouement of the old classical system. Monsieur Maurice Dulaerts, the Director General in the Ministry of Justice, kindly put at my disposal the government's dossier on the projected *Loi de Défense Sociale*, a term intended for the first time to be used in statutory language. It was fascinating to be able to retrace step by step this multitude of efforts, initiatives, confrontations and compromises, the ups and downs of the preparatory work, leading to the day of triumph when the project adopted by Parliament received the Royal Assent and became part of the statute book of the realm.

First, the abnormal offender. Here the dispositions of the Code relating to responsibility, irresponsibility and diminished responsibility were largely brushed aside and a radically different formula was adopted to serve the concerns and needs of social defence. Intervention was justified when 'there were reasons to believe that the accused was in a state of insanity, or in a grave state of mental imbalance or mental debility which made him incapable of controlling his actions' ('l'inculpé est en état de démence, ou dans un état grave de déséquilibre mental ou de débilité mentale, le rendant incapable de contrôle de ses actions'). The power of intervention was given not only to courts sitting in judgment but also to prosecutorial and investigative authorities. It allowed them to order that the accused be placed in one of the psychiatric annexes. If the suspicion of the abnormality was confirmed, these authorities – unless it was a case of political crime or crimes concerned with the liberty of the press – had the authority to order the accused to be 'put at the disposal of the government' for a period of five, ten or fifteen years.

In each local jurisdiction across the country a special commission was set up which selected the establishment in which the accused should be interned. The commission also had the power to change the establishment in the course of the detention as well as the vital authority to order a conditional or definitive discharge in all cases of internment. No wonder that Monsieur Jean Servais, the *Procureur Général* of the Realm, an Honorary Professor of Criminal Law at the Free University of Brussels and a supporter of the entire social defence package, nevertheless warned the Consultative Council to proceed cautiously and not to give too much power to the doctors. Otherwise the new law would be identified in the public mind with the *Lettres de Cachet* of the *ancien régime*. The commission deliberated in private and could ask for additional advice from the doctor, the head of the laboratory, or from the penitentiary administration. A representative of the Readaptation Office could ask to be allowed to attend the deliberations. The public prosecutor, the interned criminal and the lawyer were expected to make a statement. The discharge would take place 'when the mental state is sufficiently amended to make believe that the offender does not constitute a social danger any more'.

Nothing communicates better the spirit which animated the whole approach to this agonizing problem than the following cheerful passage from the *Exposé des Motifs*:

> Throughout the entire economy of the project, the abnormals are dealt with not as delinquents but as ill ('en malades'); this is what the Law of 1912 does with respect to children. Internment is not a punishment, but it is at the same time a measure of social defence and a measure of humanity; an abnormal put in a condition where he can do no damage any more is subjected to a curative regime scientifically organized.

The enormous potential of this segment of the law may be easily gauged from the fact that the Minister of Justice – in his report to the Chamber of Representatives – fell back on the authority of Dr Vervaeck, according to whom

> approximately two-thirds of the penitentiary population should be considered in different degrees as abnormal, constitutional or acquired, mentally deficient, ill or intoxicated, and that in consequence it would be childish to try to define abnormality through a simplified formula.

The social defence system directed towards habitual offenders (the term more frequently used was recidivists) was not so complex, but no less incisive. The provisions of the Penal Code, which gave the judge the power to apply aggravating circumstances and order police supervision after the expiration of the increased punishment, were brushed aside. They were regarded as utterly ineffective and irrational with respect to the mass of recidivists graphically described by Adolphe Prins as the 'vieux chevaux de retour'. The three new alternatives were as follows. In the case of a repetition of crime following a previous conviction for a crime (but not if it was a political crime) the judge *must* put recidivists 'at the disposition of the government' for twenty years, after they had undergone the imposed punishment. Second, in the case of crime following a *délit* (a transgression inferior to crime in gravity and defined as such in the Code) or *délit* after *délit* the judge *may* put recidivists, after the expiration of their punishment, at the disposition of the government for a period of between five or ten years if the undergone punishment was less than one year. Third, an identical measure *may* be imposed on delinquents if they were found guilty of crime following a *délit*, or when within the last fifteen years they had committed at least three offences each punishable by imprisonment of not less than six months, and on condition that these recidivists 'present a persistent tendency towards criminality'. The establishment provided for these additional measures of social defence were usually to be workhouses or agricultural colonies.

In all three instances the recidivists could ask for their discharge, but only after having undergone the initial punishments. They had then to make an appeal to the general prosecutor attached to the Court of Appeal of the district in which they were tried. The prosecutor had to collect all the information and communicate it to the Correctional Chamber of the court which would give reasons for its decision, after having heard the offender assisted by counsel. Offenders could appeal after three years if their internment was for ten years and only after five years if their internment went beyond the ten-year period. Here again, the powers provided by the social defence doctrine and intended practice were truly formidable. First of all, a dual system was imposed in contrast to that used for the abnormal offender. Second, hardly any description or definition of recidivism was given except the objective, mechanical criterion of the number of their legally defined transgressions. The potential scope of this arm of the law was exceptionally wide. It was generally agreed that every second offender was a recidivist, that half of the recidivists were found guilty of three or more offences and that the incidence of abnormality amongst recidivists was declared to be much higher than amongst first offenders.

Throughout these lengthy and elaborate deliberations, the old, seasoned heavy guns – Vandervelde, Jaspar, Carton de Wiart and Janson – gave unfailing and subtle support, while behind the scene, one could easily discern the firm hand of Dr Vervaeck. In the early stages, when the projected provisions were even wider than those ultimately accepted, there was some opposition towards them on the part of the magistrature, the Bar and a few Members of Parliament. But when the moment for the final decision came, there was a virtually unanimous endorsement of the provisions. Thus Belgium became the first country in Europe, indeed in the world, where a radical penitentiary reform led to a radical reform in penal legislation, both being propelled and directed by the medical profession initially acting under the flag of criminal anthropology and – as some would say four or five decades later – inevitably sliding into the murky area of social defence. Belgium, in penal terms, had become a kind of criminological laboratory to be watched and evaluated by all those who, in many parts of the world, were involved or interested in criminological advances and in social progress. Optimism ran high. The role of anthropological laboratories as the engine of penal reform was put on the agenda of the International Penitentiary Congress in London (1925) and all the reports presented on this subject came out strongly in favour of it, a belief which was reaffirmed in a recommendation approved by the Congress as a whole. At the very time that I published my book two very laudatory accounts of the Belgian developments appeared – both unknown to me – one in Germany and the other in France.[13] Even more importantly an observer as cautious and vigilant as my dear and respected friend, Professor Thorsten Sellin, wrote in 1926:

> No student of criminology can do else but hope for the successful realization of this program, not solely because it embodies his dreams and materialises his visions, but also because it would be carried out under conditions which would permit the measurement and the evaluation of the results, a most desirable thing in these days of 'crime waves' and other humbug.

I tried to do a little more than hope and attempted to give a full and fervent account of this experiment in my book *La Lutte moderne contre le crime*, which was published at the end of my stay in Belgium by Ferdinand Larcier of Brussels in 1930, with an important seven-page preface by Comte Henri Carton de Wiart and an exquisite letter from Paul-Émile Janson (see Plates 4 and 5). The book was presented to the Royal Academy of Belgium and went out of print within a year. I was invited to give a series of lectures on aspects of it in many parts of the country: in the Free University of Brussels, at the headquarters of the Bar in Anvers, and in the Palais de Justice in Brussels under the auspices of the Belgian section of the International Association of Criminal Law.

On my return to Geneva, or more precisely, on 1 September 1930, I was informed by the Minister of Foreign Affairs that the King of Belgium had conferred upon me the decoration of the Chevalier de l'Ordre de Léopold, an utterly unexpected honour which I cherish greatly. Carton de Wiart, I understand, unmolested by the Nazis, died at the age of eighty-two. Paul-Émile Janson, alas, was arrested by Germans in France and sent to Buchenwald where he died in 1944. I continue to remember them vividly with respect and affection, not only because of their personal qualities and opinions but

---

13 Dr Werner Petrzilka, *Persönlichkeitsforschung und Differenzeirung im Strafvollzug* (Munich, 1930) and Jean Buffelain, *Reforme pénitentiaire en Belgique* (Toulouse, 1930).

also because they were so kind and so encouraging to a rather disputatious young man who arrived in their country out of the blue, anxious to understand the foundations and capture the spirit of a new edifice of criminal justice which both of them for so many years had struggled so hard to make a reality.

In June 1988 when I was planning this memoir I returned to the old battlefield for a rapid visit to look at some of the most sensitive threads of the Belgium reform and to assess how relevant they still were to the contemporary development of thought and practice in criminology. I shall not fail to do so within the wider context of this book.

When one is young, absorbed and excited by one's work, time seems to become unreal. But not for ever, and a moment comes when a cooler approach prompts a closer look at the calendar. This happened to me on my return to Geneva later in 1930. On 1 June 1924 I had received my school certificate of maturity and a month later at the age of eighteen I registered as a law student at the Sorbonne. Six years had gone by in learning, researching and lecturing in Paris, Rome, Geneva and Brussels. I felt that I had reached the stage when I should go back from whence I came, not necessarily for ever, but for long enough to test my roots and to look at Poland against the much wider West European background which by then had become so much part of me. Some time in 1931, at the age of twenty-five, I found myself in Warsaw.

4

A PENOLOGICAL CUL-DE-SAC

An uninspiring academic cast

It took me some time before I reached the conclusion that the criminological prospects in Poland were dim. In the country's five universities, chairs of criminal law and criminal procedure were firmly established. The six professors (in one university there were two) were, as usual, in the Faculties of Law and all had tenure. Naturally they differed in personality, style and scholarly weight. But, with one or two exceptions, they shared in common the classical or neo-classical attitude towards the discipline of criminal science. Their focus was on the juridical, dogmatic study of the criminal law and, in particular, on the interpretation of the Criminal Code in force. In hardly any of the Law Faculties (and this also applied to the Faculties of Social and Political Sciences) was there a professor of criminology, or criminal policy; not even *Dozents* were encouraged to initiate a wider approach. A small criminological window, but a very small one, had been opened at the University of Warsaw: a thoughtful assistant (who held both a medical and a law degree) had been charged with conducting a seminar on criminological topics, was editing the 'criminological archives', and was pursuing his own researches. But he was virtually isolated from the professor, whose attitude was blatantly non-committal. In another place, there was a gifted *Dozent* of criminal policy who had to await many long years before he became a professor. And yet somewhere else, a promising student was sent to the United States to study under Edwin Sutherland just before the war, but hélas was murdered by the Nazis soon after his return. There were a number of able young men keen to work in this field but no support came from above to launch them properly and in reasonable time. There were no foundations which could be persuaded to help set on foot an empirical inquiry which might focus public attention on the potentialities of criminology. The only place where criminology was recognized as a distinct academic subject was at the Free University of Warsaw. But this institution, meritorious as it was in many ways, was not equal in either its formal or its legal status to the state universities, and moreover it had no Faculty of Law, the subject being adopted by the Faculty of Political and Social Studies. Paradoxically, this innovation was stultified by the fact that the professor in charge was an orthodox, monolithic, Marxist to whom criminology and criminal policy pursued within the context of a capitalistic class-ridden society was a farce, an illusion, an escapade. The other professor there, a judge of the Supreme Court, had in his younger years studied in Paris under Émile Garçon and had written at that time an interesting book on the *Lutte des écoles*; he, however, had discontinued scholarly work a long time ago and now merely diligently followed the official criminal policy.

A reactionary Ministry of Justice

In the circumstances, the only place from which a rescue could have been mounted was the Ministry of Justice. But there too the situation was pretty hopeless. The two ministers who were in office during my presence in Poland were political figures closely connected with the Pilsudski regime. They considered that their main function was to use the coercive machinery of the ministry for the preservation of the new order. At least the first was a cultured man whereas the second was a young public prosecutor of no distinction whatsoever. His appointment had evoked widespread surprise even amongst those who sympathized with the group in power. The Vice-Minister was a man of an altogether different outlook and sensibility, but he had no influence over important appointments or decisions: he was kept simply because the ministry needed somebody who had the knowledge and experience necessary for dealing with professional and technical matters. It goes without saying that no research of any kind was carried on in the ministry. The regular publication of separate criminal statistics was discontinued, and instead some very rudimentary information was included in the general *Statistical Account* of the country. No provision was made, and no intention was expressed, to promote an independent examination of the working of some of the more controversial solutions of the new Criminal Code of 1932. The two most senior occupants of the post of Counsellors in the Prison Department, who were expected to plan new initiatives and throw out new ideas, were two worn-out bureaucrats. For years they had been in the habit of offering their subservient allegiance to the directors of the department who, as a general rule, were former senior public prosecutors. *Parliamentary Discussions of the Budget of the Ministry* were empty of significant facts or constructive critical commentaries. The police fell within the province of the Ministry of the Interior which, as might be expected, was enveloped by a thick and impenetrable blanket of secrecy and, in practical terms, of far-reaching public non-accountability.

The academic and ministerial world was closed to criminology but could these fortresses ever be persuaded to abandon, or at least to attenuate, their hostile or indifferent attitude?

A PENOLOGICAL CUL-DE-SAC

Moving towards authoritarianism

The Polish Republic was born in November 1918. 'Rarely, if ever,' writes Norman Davies in his major work on the history of Poland, 'was a newly independent country subjected to such eloquent and gratuitous abuse.'[1] As a matter of fact, considerable progress was achieved in many sectors of national life by the New Republic and it was grossly unfair not to recognize it. But it was also true that the schism between promise and reality was becoming painfully deep. The Constitution of 17 March 1921 reads like an exotic extravaganza in political poetry. And, as the years passed by, the image of a coherent, stable and prosperous liberal democracy was fading away. 'Inter-war Warsaw', to quote Norman Davies again,

> possessed an unmistakable, bitter-sweet quality. It was characterized on the one hand by the pride and optimism generated by national independence, and on the other hand by the sad realisation that the appalling problems of poverty, politics, and prejudice could not be alleviated by existing resources.

Pilsudski's *coup d'état* of 12–14 May 1926 largely destroyed what was left of a state presumed to be based on the rule of law. Although the new regime had not acquired the character of a military dictatorship as practised intermittently by several South American states, the regime of the Colonels (which followed Pilsudski's death) – political adventurers *par excellence*, deprived of legitimacy, of public support and respect, continuously assaulted by formidable national problems and the worsening of the international situation – was moving towards a similar formula of government. Davies was right in concluding that 'the Second Republic was indeed destined for destruction' and if 'it had not been foully murdered in 1939 by external agents, there is little doubt that it would soon have sickened from internal causes'.

The study of criminal law, if primarily conceived as the study of the juridical, legal and formal contents of acts or omissions labelled as offences, can be comfortably pursued within the context of conservative states, and even (though to a much lesser degree) within the authoritarian ones. There will always be room there for a Binding or Luccini, but a Ferri or a Von Liszt, in search of 'New Horizons in Criminal Law', would soon be left with hardly any elbow room. Criminology needs for its birth, growth and recognition, a political, social and, indeed, a moral environment of an altogether different nature. It is this perception, arising out of my reacquaintance with the Polish

---

[1] For the motley epitaphs bestowed on Poland, varying from Stalin, Molotov and Hitler, to David Lloyd George, Louis Namier, E.H. Carr and J.M. Keynes, see Norman Davies's *God's Playground: A History of Poland*, vol. 2 (1986 edn), p. 392.

reality of that time, that left an indelible impression on me and remained with me for ever in my comparative studies of criminology and criminal justice systems across the world.

Involvement and frustration

Soon after my return to Poland (more precisely in 1931) the Professor of Criminal Law at Cracow graciously suggested that I should add to my foreign degrees the degree of *Doctoris Juris* of the University of Cracow. The faculty accepted my Roman dissertation and asked me to pass examinations on only a few distinctly Polish legal topics. I was also invited to give, as an open lecture to the university, my inaugural lecture at Geneva, but this time in Polish. In due course it was published by the highly respected *Contemporary Review* of Cracow. All this gave me much pleasure. In 1933, after having been assigned to a committing judge acting within the province of the Court of Appeal of Warsaw for the stipulated period of a year, I passed the required examinations and received a diploma of 'juridical practice'. This was regarded as an essential step (following university studies) in the career of a public prosecutor, judge or advocate. None of these openings appealed to me, but I was anxious to acquire some knowledge at first hand of the functioning of the machinery of justice at its essential stages from the time a crime came to the cognizance of the police through to investigation, prosecution, indictment, trial and sentencing.

A year earlier (in 1932) I had received an invitation from the Rector of the Free University of Warsaw to become a member of the Faculty of Political and Social Studies in the capacity of a *Dozent* 'in the field of criminal policy'. It was intimated to me by Professor Wladyslaw Maliniak, the Dean of the Faculty – a noble and learned personage who, together with all the other professors, was massacred by the Nazis during their occupation of Warsaw – that, if I decided to settle down and pursue an academic career, a professorship would follow in due course. I had no inclination at that time to enter into such commitment but I greatly valued my academic *pied-à-terre*.

At about the same time I was asked by the Director of Penal Institutions in the Ministry of Justice whether I had any suggestions to make with respect to the activities of his department, very much to the obvious displeasure of the two Counsellors to whom I have already referred. I ventured to throw out three ideas. First, the establishment of a regular *Review of the Penitentiary System*, broad in scope and conducted in a liberal spirit. Second, a drastic reorganization of the school for the professional training of prison personnel of both the higher and lower grades. And third, a vigorous impetus to launch an ambitious programme of domestic penal colonies, which would be primarily agricultural, so as to escape the legacy of the jails inherited from the Russian, German and Austrian occupying powers in the odious past. Soon afterwards I was informed that all three of my suggestions had met with approval and I was asked to give a hand in planning their development, indeed more than that – to become a regular contributor to the *Revue*, a professor at the Penitentiary School (at both levels) and an adviser on the establishment and subsequent assessment of the colonies. I accepted all three assignments and was looking forward with great anticipation to their implementation.

These commitments were not intended in any way to replace or to diminish my scholarly efforts in the area of criminal science, where so much remained to be done.

I intended to assemble and analyse statistical material relating to the structure, incidence of and trends in criminality in Poland over a lengthy period of time. In this field silence, generalities, or vague hypotheses had held sway, often simply to give 'substance' to a priori views or, worse still, to feed perilous prejudices. I received permission from the Director of the Statistical Office to work on the accumulated but unused material deposited there. I could study it in my own home or in the office. From time to time, I was allowed to enlist one of the employees to help me with the necessary laborious calculations. For this, I remunerated him personally. The first instalment of my labours was published in the *Criminological Archives* under the title of 'Structure of criminality' and it was followed soon afterwards by a substantial monograph on *The State of Crime in Poland*. The second task which I assigned myself was to write a treatise on penitentiary discipline in its historical and contemporary setting and to do so on a comparative scale. This was an ambitious undertaking but there was a crying need for it. An understanding of criminal policy, both as a system of thought and practical deployment, needs a rich and enlightened perspective on the modes of enforcing sanctions in general and deprivation of liberty in particular.

Out of these explorations grew a volume of 455 pages entitled *The Fundamentals of Penitentiary Science*. The third publication, *Contemporary Evolution of Criminal Anthropology*, aimed to show that despite the flaws and distortions of its Lombrosian phase, it was evolving in a more subtle, pliable and balanced fashion and that it could still be of value in the enforcement of criminal justice. The first two books evoked much interest and gained much approval. The penitentiary treatise was the first of its kind and continued to be so for several decades. The book on the state of crime was followed in time by more sophisticated publications. Its appearance stimulated pressure for the setting up in the Ministry of Justice of a well-equipped centre of criminal statistics – but nothing came out of it. The third book met with a rather mixed reception because it was viewed in some quarters as a reaffirmation of Lombrosian doctrine – a perception which was utterly incorrect but could not be ignored. A dozen articles on a variety of subjects, including developments abroad, also found their way into the leading periodicals of the period.

I had by this time acquired a certain knowledge of systems of criminal justice and criminological interpretations in Western Europe and I took advantage of my presence in Poland to extend my inquiries to Germany. I improved my knowledge of German, built a substantial library of German criminal science literature, and paid several visits to the famous centre built up by Von Liszt in the Law Faculty of the University of Berlin, which was directed with distinction by Professor Kohlrausch. I loved this feverish period of activity and regarded myself fortunate to have the strength, the zeal and the financial resources to make it all possible.

Absorbed as I had been by this work, I could hardly have failed to note the darkening of the penal horizon and my comments upon it and my more elaborate disquisitions became increasingly unpopular. For instance, I evolved a method which enabled me to relate the economic situation of certain strata of society to the trends in crime among them in the period 1928–34 – which covered the peak of prosperity and then through depression. I was able to demonstrate that the massive increase in crime was not to be explained by a spread of wickedness and greed, justifying a more rigorous penal repression, but by the direct and powerful impact of economic plight. Another example was the way in which sentencing practices had become distorted by the unscrupulous acquiescence of the ministerial authorities. The Code of 1932, praised for its 'liberal spirit', had established a special security measure of long duration to follow the enforcement of imprisonment for 'incorrigible offenders'. An 'Establishment for Incorrigible Offenders' was dutifully set up by the authorities. I made a thorough study of the files of the criminals so labelled, visited the establishment on several occasions and concluded that a large proportion of the inmates were about twenty-five years of age and had been found guilty of only a few offences against property unattended by violence or any other aggravating circumstances. This was the first time that I became acutely conscious that the lofty principles of 'social defence' could be effortlessly distorted into cruel patterns of 'social aggression'. The three articles which followed had titles which are self-explanatory: 'Crisis of the Prison System', 'The Crisis of Criminal Policy in Poland' and 'Factors Shaping the Evolution of Criminal Policy', with an emphasis on the influence of the Nazi ideology.

As the *Proceedings* of the International Penitentiary Congress held in Berlin in 1935 had shown, the Nazis were no longer content with planting their penal concepts at home but were anxious to export them and to have them acknowledged internationally as the penal solution of the future. I pointed out that, in this respect, Poland was at a turning point and that extreme vigilance was needed to prevent it succumbing to these distortions. I was also rather free with my remarks when teaching at the Penitentiary School (my regular course dealt with 'Potentialities and limitations of reformative processes within a traditional prison system') as well as on my visits to penal institutions around the country. These comments were reported to the Director of the Department (often distorted by the informants or by him) and led to several rather unpleasant exchanges of views. I was obviously becoming a nuisance, indeed a kind of criminological dissident.

A put-up job to discredit me

In 1936 a person unknown to me, but who from time to time contributed articles in the *Penitentiary Review* (issued by the department) on the historical origins of the Polish prison system, published privately a twelve-page tract entitled *The Fundamentals of Penitentiary Science* – the very title of my book. It was a virulent attack on everything in it, including an accusation of two instances of plagiarism. It was so distorted that it was clear to me that I should not bother to reply, but simply ignore it. Yet I also felt that I should ask for an outside, totally detached, opinion. The Professor of Criminal Law at the University of Poznan – a man of impeccable integrity and common sense – categorically advised me to take no account of it. My book appeared in 1933 and the tract in 1936. Why did the author take three years to react in this way? The author himself was uneasy about this strange incongruity, raised it, but was incapable of providing an explanation. It was obviously a put-up job. I am pretty certain who was behind this villainy, but I refrain from mentioning their names because it would be unfair to accuse persons who are no longer able to respond. (I have made arrangements for the tract to be deposited in the Radzinowicz Library at the Cambridge Institute of Criminology.)

My departure

Poland has often been referred to as a country of contradictions and indeed I have been made aware of it on several occasions. Although penal conditions had reached a very low level, the interest in what was going on abroad was still very much alive, even in relation to countries as different as Britain. Articles, of varying quality, appeared on the Borstal system, on probation, on juvenile courts. They made me keen to know more. Consequently, when the Vice-Minister suggested that I should go to Britain to inquire into certain salient features of its penal system and present a report on the subject, I did not hesitate. I set off under my own steam and at my own expense. I had not the slightest premonition that this would mark my final departure from Poland. In consequence, and in contrast to the chronological order which I have followed up to now in my account, I will jump ahead and relate two episodes which confirmed my decision not to return to my country of birth.

Jumping ahead in time: tempting me to return to Poland (1945) and a disappointing visit (1978)

One day when I was sitting in my home in Cranmer Road in Cambridge (I do not remember the exact day, but it was at the time when Stalin imposed the communist government on Poland) the doorbell rang and two men, with broad shoulders and wearing heavy coats, obviously from Eastern Europe, asked me whether they could take a few moments of my time. They brought me the greetings of the Minister of Justice, who would like to make me aware of the records they kept of scholars originally from Poland. They distinguished two categories: those with fascist leanings and those lost to Polish science. I was classified as belonging to the second category. And they would like to welcome me back as a professor of criminology, a director of a criminological institute and, should I wish, as a high functionary in the ministry. I asked them to convey to the Minister my appreciation of his invitation to which, however, I did not intend to respond. The conversation was brief and without any recrimination on either side. They graciously left me, leaving behind two bottles of *Wódka Wyborowa* ('Perfect Vodka'), the best Polish product.

Some thirty-three years passed by until, if I remember correctly, sometime in 1978 the private secretary to the Home Secretary wrote to me that the Polish Minister of Justice was on an official visit to Britain. He, as well as the Home Secretary, had expressed the hope that I would be able to attend a lunch which was to be given in his honour. After the lunch the Minister suggested that we should go to see the Ambassador and have a glass of port with him. At the embassy they both said how very much they would like me to visit Poland. They were fully aware that I would not like to go there in any official or formal capacity, but they had in mind a private visit: by a happy coincidence, they said, a group of American and English naturalized citizens originally from Poland were about to make a tour of the country.

I accepted the invitation but stipulated that I could stay no longer than a few days and preferably in Warsaw; that I wished to come with my two children who, although born and educated in England and permanently settled there, would nevertheless like to see the country of my birth. It was also agreed that I would give one lecture in Warsaw under appropriate auspices; that I should be unfettered in what I could say; and that the text of my address in Polish would be made available by the organizing authorities to all present. The promise was not honoured and there were in the audience not many people who could fully and correctly follow my delivery in English. A partial simultaneous translation by a member of our visiting group was useful but inevitably could not do full justice to the text. Again a subsequent promise that my piece would be published in a leading Polish periodical was also not honoured. On my return to England I was invited by the late Melvin Lasky to publish it in *Encounter* where it appeared in 1979 under the original title 'Illusions about crimes and justice'.[2] The ten points (on pp. 38–9) which I formulated as being 'the essentials of a decent and law abiding system of criminal justice' ran against the very existence of an authoritarian regime, whether fascist or communist. I was not surprised that my address failed to evoke a warm applause from an audience obviously picked for the occasion. The chairman of the meeting made it clear that questions and exchange of views would not be welcomed. I was pleased to see my piece translated into German and published by *Der Monat*.[3]

I am not well informed about what is now going on in Poland in the sphere of criminal justice and the development of criminology. I was told by Professor Wasik of the University of Lublin and his colleagues, when I had the pleasure of meeting them at the Max Planck Institute of Comparative Criminal Law in Freiburg a few years ago, that things were changing and moving in the right direction.[4] They would have to change radically to reach an acceptable civilized level. And the process of penal reconstruction will be painful and obdurate because a set of genuine values, and not just smooth rhetoric or clever texts, will have to be forged and cultivated to give inspiration and veracity to the new order of things. Even when everything is said and done, in applying criminological techniques or in thrashing out criminal policy concepts, a system of criminal justice should ultimately still be judged by its intrinsic morality.

---

2 No. 180 (February–March 1979), pp. 31–9.
3 No. 284 (July–September 1982), pp. 83–90.
4 See, for instance, 'Erstes deutsch-polnisches Kolloquium über Strafrecht und Kriminologie', held in Warsaw, 1–4 December 1981, the *Proceedings* of which were subsequently published by H.-H. Jescheck and Günther Kaiser (1983). Also several articles by A. Wasik (of Lublin University) and S. Frankowski (of St Louis University), the most recent being 'Polish Criminal Law and Procedure', in *Legal Reform in Post-Communist Europe* (1995), pp. 275–308. For a valuable informative account of Polish criminology in the very difficult post-war period, see Professor J. Jasinsky, 'Poland', in Elmer H. Johnson (ed.) *Handbook of Contemporary Developments in Criminology* (1983), pp. 511–25.

5

TRYING TO BREAK DOWN TRADITIONAL BARRIERS

My mission to England

My first visit to Britain was in 1925 when I was still a second-year law student in Geneva, and it had been prompted by different considerations. Largely influenced by my reading of Benjamin Disraeli and Jack London, I had felt the urge to go to England to see for myself how the 'other nation' lived. From London's Victoria Station, I went straight to the Docklands area, knocked at the door of one of the most miserable looking houses and announced, in my very broken English, to the surprised (not to say bewildered) owner that I would like to rent a room for a month or two. He asked me a few pertinent questions and said with firmness that, before we reached an agreement, I had better have a look at the premises and the room which could be made available to me. Undeterred by what I saw, I insisted and was accepted. It was a simple and loving family. The wife ran the household. Her husband and their two children, a daughter and a son both close to my age, worked during the day not far from their home, joining together for the evening meal. They were all very patriotic, very proud to be English, with no class hatred or envy. Nevertheless, conscious of the prevailing inequalities, they lived in hope that in the days to come their lot would substantially improve. I was very happy staying with them and learned a great deal about aspects of the country which, in normal circumstances, would not have been accessible to me.

On the eve of my departure, they, and a few of their friends, whom I had met before, gave me a dinner in the leading pub of the neighbourhood. I was urged to come back to settle in England for good. My continental background, indeed the continent of Europe as a whole, hardly figured in their mental horizon. At that time an episode occurred which still keeps a firm hold on my memory. It was late evening and London was enveloped by a fog which reduced visibility almost to nil. As I was struggling to find my way towards Piccadilly Circus I was confronted by the headline in big black letters of the *Evening Standard*, exhibited on a newspaper stand, announcing: 'Continent of Europe cut off from England'.

The Master of Trinity, George Trevelyan, with his romantic disposition, liked my first English experience and sometimes referred to it at High Table, invariably rounding off with his loudly proclaimed conviction that 'many Fellows of this College should have had Radzi's experience'. I was flattered but I doubt very much whether I produced many imitators amongst them.

When I came in 1936 it was in an altogether different capacity. Armed with an official letter from the Polish Ministry of Justice addressed 'To whom it may concern', I arrived in London and settled in a small hotel in one of the lovely Bloomsbury squares which have since been swept away by the University of London. The head of the Polish Consulate in London politely drew my attention to the fact that England was much more formal and low keyed than the continent. Consequently, I would be well advised not to go personally to the Home Office, but send my letter to the secretary to the Permanent Under-Secretary of State at the Home Office (a title which at the time baffled me very much), with a note expressing the hope that, in spite of his heavy duties, he might be able to help me. I acted accordingly and almost by return of post he rang me up to say that Sir Alexander Maxwell would like to see me, suggesting a very early date for the meeting. Thus, with hardly any delay I was ready to move.

Paradoxical and unique institutions

I remember precisely how perplexed, confused and uncertain I became as I began to try to sort out, weigh up and draw some kind of coherent picture from the scanty and diverse preliminary information I had assembled. 'In England,' stated Ernst Schuster, a leading German expert who had been invited by Von Liszt to review the English legal system, 'there is a criminal literature, but there is no criminal science.'[1] Although he had written this at the end of the nineteenth century, a similar view continued to prevail in authoritative continental circles for many years to come. Sir James Fitzjames Stephen was the only criminal lawyer who was occasionally referred to. More often than not, and rather paradoxically, one had to turn to the historian Lord Macaulay's Penal Code of India to find elegantly expressed principled formulations.

'Do they have a criminal code?' asked a French jurist. On being told 'they do not have one and they seem not to like to have one', he could hardly hide his astonishment. For after all, France (or more precisely Napoleon) was the country which had given to itself, as well as to many countries across the world, an imposing and enduring model of what could be achieved.

---

1   Ernst Schuster, in *Die Strafgesetzgebung der Gegenwart in Rechtsvergleichender Darstellung*, vol. 1 (1894), pp. 609–90, at p. 616.

How influential could the judiciary be in such circumstances? According to Sir James Fitzjames Stephen, the criminal laws of England were 'the product of the most powerful legislature and judiciary that the world has ever known'. But of course he became one of them. To dispose of the suspicion of partiality we have at hand the view of Professor Henri Lévy-Ullmann of the University of Paris, an authority in the field of comparative law in general and of the English system in particular. According to him, the only two juridical systems to have influenced the modern world are the Roman and the English systems. Referring to the latter, this sober and restrained comparatiste became quite poetical:

> un système planétaire dont le droit d'Angleterre serait le soleil. Autour de lui, tout le système gravite. Il en est la source vitale, l'entretien de sa lumière. Il est le centre et le foyer.[2]

The Law Lords, the High Court judges, the recorders, the chairmen of Quarter Sessions, the mass of justices of the peace (unpaid and, as a general rule, not lawyers though discharging wide responsibilities) and last but not least the venerable jury system, completed this extraordinarily rich juridical framework. The discretionary power of the courts was tremendous. The common law was widely revered and it continued to excite the intellectual curiosity of eminent foreign legal minds, as can be gathered from Raoul van Caenegan's book, *The Birth of the English Common Law* (1973).[3]

The lack of a prosecutorial system and of committing magistrates as known on the continent of Europe and elsewhere, as well as the absence of a national centralized police force, added naturally to my bewilderment. And so did the principle of the presumption of innocence which cut across many sectors of criminal justice, reaffirming its fundamental directive in matters large and small, prosaic or spectacular. It expressed itself in the maxim that it is better that ten guilty persons escape than one innocent man should suffer. The formulation of this ancient maxim varied in time. William Paley proposed ten guilty men to one innocent man, whereas Jeremy Bentham spoke of a hundred to one. Sir John Fortescue a few hundred years earlier proposed twenty to one, Sir Matthew Hale spoke of five to one. According to Sir Carleton Allen the ten to one relation had been adopted only at the beginning of the nineteenth century.[4] But with a few reservations (foremost by

---

2 H. Lévy-Ullmann, *Le Système juridique de l'Angleterre* (1935), p. 10. Translated into English as *The English Legal Tradition*, with a preface by Sir William Holdsworth (1935).
3 Especially Chapter 4, 'English Law and the Continent', at pp. 85–110.
4 See Allen's article – still worth remembering – 'The Presumption of Innocence', in *Legal Duties and Other Essays in Jurisprudence* (1931), p. 257.

Paley and Bentham) it was accepted pervasively. The belief that it was strictly adhered to throughout the entire system was a source of national pride.

Even so resolute (not to say ruthless) a judge as Sir James Fitzjames Stephen did not wish to depart from it to any extent. Comparing the legal tradition and the administration of criminal justice of France and England, he questioned whether under the French system the chances of impunity were in fact less than in England. And he contended that even if they were, it was a pernicious political arrangement to increase the odds against crime by endangering the essential liberties of the citizen. Indeed, he who castigated any kind of weakness in criminal law, went so far as to maintain that a certain margin of impunity was but a modest price to pay for safeguarding the higher constitutional objectives protected by criminal procedure. On this, the conservative James Fitzjames Stephen and the liberal Courtney Kenny saw eye to eye. Both regarded the continental system as inferior. 'The restrictions imposed by the English rules of evidence', wrote Courtney Kenny,

> are in startling contrast to the laxity of proof allowed in Continental tribunals. But the constitutional value of our stringency is great, for it has done much towards producing that general confidence in our criminal courts which has kept popular feeling in full sympathy with the administration of the criminal law, and has thereby facilitated the task of government to an extent surprising to Continental observers.

English criminal procedure (also not codified), with its unmistakably liberal bent, continued to evoke admiration, respect and even the envy of political philosophers, practising jurists and professors, visitors and observers of the English national scene and its institutions.

In comparison with leading European countries, the incidence of crime in Britain had not been disturbingly high. Indeed, judging from statistics, but remembering that international comparisons can be grossly misleading, criminality in Britain at the end of the nineteenth and at the beginning of the twentieth centuries was on the decrease, whereas abroad it was definitely going up.[5] Particularly important from the point of view of criminal policy was the incidence and quality of violent crime. In this respect Britain stood out most favourably. In effect, violent crime was so low that, from the eighteenth century onwards, foreign experts and visitors repeatedly commented upon it. But trends in crime are not immutable. How would public opinion react to bold changes and innovations in the field of criminal policy if the condition of crime were to become threatening? This was another topical

---

5 See L. Radzinowicz and R. Hood, *A History of English Criminal Law*, vol. 5, *The Emergence of Penal Policy* (1986), pp. 113–29.

question. Connected with it, but also grounded in the early constitutional position of police (as envisaged by Sir Robert Peel, its founder), was the fact that, alone amongst the major countries of the world, the British police were not armed (not even in the big cities) and did not wish to be armed, but they were in favour of capital punishment.

With respect to the central direction of the system of criminal justice, Britain again differed radically from the 'cut-off continent'. In every country of Europe, small or large, there was a Ministry of the Interior and a Ministry of Justice. Police and all kinds of auxiliary services having a direct bearing on the maintenance of public order fell within the competence of the Ministry of the Interior. Everything relating to the preparation of criminal legislation, the enforcement of criminal law and the administration of penal institutions, the appointment of judges, magistrates and public prosecutors, was decided by the Ministry of Justice. There was, of course, no Ministry of the Interior nor Ministry of Justice in Britain. Most of these matters were dealt with by the Home Office, though by no means all of them. Some, such as the selection of judges, the functioning of the courts and the appointment of justices of the peace, belonged to the Lord Chancellor's Department.

Between 1845 and 1875 and again in 1918 the question was debated whether Britain should not be endowed with a full-blooded Ministry of Justice, but it was ultimately decided 'in favour of leaving things alone'. It may not be left alone now that the Labour Party is in power. Whatever the future might bring with respect to this or any other subject in the criminal sphere, one thing appeared to me to be certain: the future of the Blue Books in British public life was assured (see pp. 154–8). This included the many kinds of inquiries set up as the result of governmental or parliamentary initiatives, such as Royal Commissions, departmental committees or select committees. It has been said that the first thing four Englishmen stranded on a desert island would do is to frame terms of reference, select a chairman and members and set up a committee, start by investigating and taking evidence and conclude with recommendations. Even Karl Marx, not particularly inclined to say nice things about England, was full of praise of the Blue Books and used them extensively in his *Das Capital*. In the field of criminal policy, they are simply indispensable. I do not know of any major topic which, in the course of time, had not been selected for examination under their aegis before any legislative or administrative action had been taken.

I would go so far as to say that one cannot claim any expertise in British criminal policy unless one has in the background a thorough knowledge derived from this source of information, expository and critical. The reports, minutes of evidence, memoranda, recommendations and, of course, minority reports and notes of reservation, are indispensable sources. No country in the world has such vast and variegated material stretching over nearly three hundred years.

It was at this stage that I came across this source for the first time and found it so fertile that I entertained the hope that perhaps one day I might be able to devote sufficient time to retrace its evolution and to absorb its major contents. This was to come, but in the mean time there were quite a number of such reports (some fifteen) which I had to study because they had an impact on the period I was investigating.

In contrast, there was hardly any English criminology in the continental meaning of the word. 'England', remarked Sir Evelyn Ruggles-Brise (the former Chairman of the Prison Commission and President of the International Penal and Penitentiary Commission), who was well versed in this aspect of continental thought and traditions, 'has not participated to any great extent in the controversies of the criminological schools, which have been so active and have excited so much interest on the continent of Europe . . . It may almost be said that there is no school of criminology in England.' This lack of involvement had a long history. In 1885, the International Congresses of Criminal Anthropology, Biology and Sociology were founded and up to 1911 seven meetings took place. Only to the fourth congress in 1896 at Geneva did the Home Secretary send a delegate. In the subsequent years, the British were conspicuously absent. In 1889, the prestigious International Association of Criminal Law was set up. Here the number of British delegates, a mere six at the first meeting, dwindled to only one in 1913, a year in which the association's individual membership consisted of over twelve hundred, in addition to the collective membership of some Ministries of Justice and learned bodies. But this was not a true reflection of the attitude of the association. English penal developments were carefully watched and discussed within the national sections and at their international congresses. Important penal enactments were frequently translated (mostly into German) and appeared in the association's regular official publications.[6]

The International Penal and Penitentiary Commission was established in 1878 by a joint Anglo-American initiative. And yet Britain was not officially represented at the congresses of 1878, 1885 and 1890. Real collaboration started only when Sir Evelyn Ruggles-Brise became the head of the penal system of England and Wales. His observation on criminology which I quoted above was made in 1925. When I arrived in England, eleven years later, I found that it still held true, though with certain significant qualifications. But whatever may be said of the criminological interactions or contrasts between continental Europe and Britain, English criminal policy was a

---

6 In 1971 I had hoped to be able to make a modest dent in this traditional English attitude when I proposed the formation of a national group within the International Association of Criminal Law. But, apart from a few encouraging replies, my initiative was met either by a non-committed response or by a significant silence. I am glad to note that a definite change has taken place in this respect since the mid-1980s. Many fruitful bridges have been built between academic criminal lawyers and criminologists in the United Kingdom and those in continental Europe. But it is still only a beginning.

decisively original product, growing out of its own national experience and following its own evolutionary path to an extent that cannot be said of many other systems.

Its legal system and its criminal policy to my eyes clearly vindicated the well-known dictum of that eminent French historian of England, Professor Elie Halévy: 'Indeed, of all the nations of Europe, it is perhaps the English whose institutions must, in many respects, be regarded as being beyond the institutions of other people, paradoxical, "unique".'[7]

New directions in sentencing policy

I considered an understanding of this combination of features to be essential if one were to form an opinion about the English system, and I still do. But, of course, by their very nature they are in some way background factors. Although they have a deep influence on the structure of the system, they tell us little about how it functions in reality. I recognized that I needed to go further and ascertain, as precisely as possible, what use the courts were making of the measures put at their disposal by the legislature. Or, in other and simpler words, how offenders were being punished in Britain. Furthermore, in order to be able to draw meaningful conclusions, the exercise should cover a period of substantial length. In this instance, I chose the years from 1900 to 1936. I made no distinctions between the trends for adults and juveniles, which in the case of some punishments was quite substantial, because I was anxious to ascertain the overall picture.

The conclusions of my analysis were incorporated in an article entitled 'The Present Trend of English Penal Policy' which I submitted to the *Law Quarterly Review*. Its distinguished editor, Dr Arthur Goodhart (Professor of Jurisprudence in the University of Oxford), was so puzzled by its conclusions that he sent it for an opinion to Sir Alexander Paterson, the eminent Prison Commissioner and penal reformer. 'Dr Radzinowicz', stated Sir Alexander in his reply, which Goodhart graciously shared with me, 'is a scholar of international repute and you may accept the piece without any hesitation.' I must confess that I myself had been truly astonished by what the cold figures revealed and I had checked and rechecked my calculations, remembering that I am but a very rudimentary amateur statistician. The exposed trends were so crisp and so consistent over the entire period that only a few numerical indicators in round figures were needed to illustrate the sweep and depth of the accumulating changes and their ultimate effect on the evolution of the criminal justice system of the country.[8]

Capital punishment as related to the crime of murder had virtually lost

---

7 *A History of the English People*, vol. 1 (1924), preface, pp. x–xi.
8 *Law Quarterly Review*, vol. 55 (1939), pp. 273–88.

any statistical significance within the context of the total sentencing practice. The number convicted of murder remained much the same: twenty in 1900 and twenty-three in 1936, although the number executed fell from thirteen to eight. It is true that efforts to abolish the death penalty altogether had not succeeded, but nor was any weighty pressure exercised to expand its scope to other crimes besides murder, or to make its enforcement more strict, especially in relation to the operation of the system of the Royal Prerogative of Mercy. The abolitionists could not celebrate their final victory, but the retentionists were clearly on the defensive.

The punishment by whipping, so dear to Victorian mentality, presented an even more striking example. In 1900 it accounted for 7 per cent of all punishments. It dropped to 3 per cent in 1910, to a little more than 1 per cent in 1924 and it reached the level of 0.2 per cent in 1936. In 1900 every fourteenth penalty was a whipping, but in 1936 only every five-hundredth. The enormous drop was reflected more strikingly by absolute figures. The 3,200 cases ordered by the courts in 1900 dwindled in 1930 to a bare 157.

Perhaps less spectacular, but unquestionably more important, was the fate of penal servitude. The latter was devised when transportation was forced out of existence. This had been expected to provide a feeling of public security through its wholesale removal of English-born delinquents from their natural abodes to far away parts of the globe, a removal which more often than not proved to be permanent. It would have been unrealistic to expect penal servitude to do this, nevertheless it was hoped that it would still provide, by prolonged isolation and a rigorous regime, a stern bastion against serious and chronic criminality. But by 1895 it had proved to be a bastion in clay. Its minimum duration had been reduced from five to three years in 1893, and soon long sentences, as well as those of intermediate length, began to be less and less frequently imposed. In striking contrast, minimum sentences of three years went up from 42 per cent of all sentences of penal servitude imposed in 1900 to 69.0 per cent in 1936. Indeed, long terms of penal servitude had become so rare that they could without fear of exaggeration be considered as non-existent.

Trends in imprisonment (the normal maximum term of which was two years) were affected by this redirection of criminal policy. The courts began to use longer terms of imprisonment as an alternative to the declining rate of penal servitude. Out of every ten cases sentenced to imprisonment at Assizes and Quarter Sessions in 1900, six received up to six months and four had a longer period of custody imposed upon them. In 1936 the figures were just the opposite: six out of ten got longer than six months. The same trends occurred at Courts of Summary Jurisdiction: in 1900 only two out of every ten sentenced to imprisonment got over two months, while in 1936, five of every ten received such a sentence.

The major finding which emerged when penal servitude and imprisonment were lumped together was the declining use of deprivation of liberty with respect to both serious and minor offences. As a percentage of all sentences imposed in 1900, it was still as high as 49 per cent. By 1910, it had decreased, but only a little, to 45 per cent. But by 1924 it had shrunk to 28 per cent and in 1930 it had fallen still further, amounting to no more than 18 per cent. Thus, the proportion that involved total penal detention fell steadily and rapidly from nearly half of all sentences in 1900 to less than one-third in 1924 and less than one-fifth in 1936. It would be difficult to find a more expressive illustration of the process of depenalization of criminal policy anywhere.

A further, most eloquent reaffirmation of this process was to be found in the expansion of the three intrinsically non-penal measures, of dismissal, recognizance with a probation order and recognizance without a probation order. They were imposed on 17 per cent of all cases in 1900; in 32 per cent in 1910; in 47 per cent in 1924 and in 56 per cent in 1936. Thus, one-sixth of all sanctions imposed by courts of all kinds in 1900 involved unconditional or conditional release. Ten years later, in 1910, the proportion rose to one-third; after the First World War, it was nearly half and in 1936 more than half.

The practice followed by Assizes and Quarter Sessions was particularly instructive because they had no power to dismiss a case and also because they dealt with the more serious indictable offences. And yet, even there, the depenalization had firmly taken root. In 1936 nearly one-third of all persons sentenced by these courts were conditionally released in contrast to a little more than one-seventh in 1910.

The administration of criminal justice, or more precisely the very enforcement of criminal law in England and Wales, had been radically transformed. Thus, in 1900 out of every hundred offenders, forty-nine were deprived of their liberty by being sent to penal servitude or to prison, seventeen were conditionally discharged and seven were whipped, whereas in 1936 the figures were respectively 18, 56 and 0.2 per cent. And, looking at those figures beyond 1936, these trends had by no means reached the end of their cycle.

Inevitably, the penitentiary structure of the criminal population could not avoid being moulded by so vast and definite shifts in sentencing practice: first, through the reduction of the prison population in general, and second, through the shrinkage of the short-term contingent. The influence of the decline in convictions for many kinds of non-indictable offences, especially drunkenness, which took place during this thirty-five-year period was a very important factor indeed, but not the only one. Already, before the First World War the number of receptions into prison had declined from a high point of 197,000 in 1905 to 149,500 in 1913. After the war the number continued to fall rapidly. Since 1932 there had not been a single year in which the number of receptions had been higher or even remained the same as in the preceding year; indeed in every instance there had been a drop. The number in 1936 was only 17 per cent of the 1909 figure and 68 per cent of the 1924 figure: 188,000 receptions in 1909, 46,000 in 1924 and 31,000 in 1936.

The mass of imprisonment to very short terms – a phenomenon which haunted penologists and penal administrators everywhere in the world – had not been wiped out. But here also remarkable progress had been achieved. Thus, for instance, out of every hundred prisoners, thirty-seven had been sentenced to a week in 1924, but only fourteen in 1936. And again, every third prisoner in 1900, but only every seventh in 1936, served a term of up to seven days. If we take all sentences to imprisonment to less than four weeks, we see that out of every hundred prisoners, in 1900 as many as seventy-two served for terms of less than four weeks, while the corresponding figure for 1936 was only thirty-five. Or to put it more succinctly, whereas in 1900 nearly three-quarters of all prisoners were sent to prison for up to four weeks, in 1936 they numbered no more than one-third.

No wonder that under the impact of all these changes the daily average prison population of England and Wales hardly exceeded 11,000, the lowest number of prisoners in any of the major countries of the world. There are, alas, not many criminologists still alive who remember the stir that such figures produced amongst all those across the world who toiled and believed in penal progress. This unusual trend certainly did not escape the attention of the mentor of American criminologists, the late Edwin H. Sutherland, who devoted to it a substantial study on 'The Declining Prison Population of England'.[9]

Figures, as such, it is often remarked, are rather tedious. Indeed, frequently they make it difficult to reach broad but firm conclusions because they can be used and interpreted in so many different ways. Furthermore, the increasing complexity of social conditions and phenomena demand increasingly refined statistics, which are rather difficult to follow by those who are not statistically trained. This, in its turn, breeds new frustrations. But there comes a time when there is no substitute for them if one is anxious to gain a clear perception of a changing situation. Although statistics cannot by themselves provide causal explanations of changing realities they reveal, they may well suggest plausible hypotheses.

In spite of the already noted limitations inherent in statistical interpretations two sound conclusions can be derived. First, they challenge effectively the orthodox Marxist thesis that an increasingly intense penal repression is an inescapable concomitant of capitalistic society. Second, they provide a no less categorical rebuttal of Foucault's contention that there was an inevitable trend towards a widely spread use of mass imprisonment leading to a carceral archipelago.

---

9   *Journal of the American Institute of Criminal Law and Criminology*, vol. 54 (May–June 1933 to March–April 1934), pp. 880–900.

None of these changes had been brought about suddenly and from above. All were the end-product of a constant and gradual activity which steadily gained in strength and influence. And it would have been difficult to identify one single major change which had not been examined and recommended by one of the Blue Books, had not been carefully considered by the Home Office, thoroughly vetted by the standing committees of both Houses of Parliament, and ultimately closely scrutinized in the course of a parliamentary debate.

The point of departure when English criminal policy moved into the twentieth century was the Departmental Committee on Prisons of 1895, widely known as the Gladstone Committee.[10] Nevertheless, it would be historically and factually wrong to ignore continuity in English penal policy. As a distinguished philosopher has noted: 'there are, of course, differences between Victorian attitudes to penal institutions and those prevalent nowadays', but it is nevertheless true in broad but concrete terms to acknowledge that

> the criminal and penal system which we attempt to operate is, again in its essence, a product of the Victorian age: the use of imprisonment – rather than death, mutilation or exile – as the major means of enforcing the criminal law is something which became developed only during the reign of Queen Victoria.[11]

From the turn of the century onwards, advances were punctuated by statutes, each of them opening or facilitating new departures. Legislation and sentencing policy marched hand in hand with the result that a very old and traditional country acquired a very modern and experimental criminal policy. This convergence appeared to be exceptionally harmonious. There was no attempt on the part of the government, the legislature or the Home Office to go back on its statutory commitments, nor on the part of the courts to retrace their steps and fall back on the sentencing practices of the past. It was not the quality of crime that had changed. What had changed radically was the attitude towards crime and punishment, and the kind of equation between the two which was likely to serve better the interests of society.

---

10 In the second volume of his *History*, entitled *English Local Prisons, 1860–1900: Next Only to Death* (1995), Seán McConville throws fresh light on the Gladstone Committee. But despite his criticisms of the way in which it went about its task, he leaves intact the exceptional role played by the committee in the penal history of England.
11 See Sir Anthony Kenny, 'Victorian Values: Some Concluding Thoughts', in *Victorian Values* (*Proceedings of the British Academy*, 1992), pp. 78, 217–24, at p. 222.

Grappling with persistent offenders

In addition to the reshaping of the traditional system, an effort had also been made to build into it a nucleus of measures radically different from those associated with the traditional classical concept of punishment. Three such types of sanctions should be mentioned. The Prevention of Crime Act 1908, Part I, provided for certain classes of delinquents under twenty-one years of age a sanction known as Borstal Detention. The same Act under Part II introduced into penal legislation preventive detention, to be applied to certain categories of habitual criminals. And the Mental Deficiency Acts of 1913 and 1927 attempted for the first time to deal in a different way with offenders who were mentally affected, but not insane. Reformation, protection of the public and cure were the basic objectives which these three provisions aimed to secure. The fate of these three departures from the traditional system of punishment threw a further revealing light on the ideology behind the new criminal policy.

The young-adult recidivist

The Prevention of Crime Act 1908, Part I, gave power to sentence young people not less than sixteen or more than twenty-one convicted on indictment of an offence for which they were liable to be sentenced to penal servitude or to imprisonment, to detention under penal discipline in a Borstal Institution for a term of not less than one year nor more than three years. The age limit could be raised to twenty-three by an Order of Council and in 1936 it was raised. At any time, after six months (for male offenders) the Prison Commissioners could release the detainee on licence and under supervision 'if satisfied that there is a reasonable probability that he will abstain from crime and lead a useful and industrious life'. Conversely he was liable if he misbehaved to be recalled to serve out the remainder of his sentence. Furthermore, he was to continue under supervision for six months after his sentence expired and be liable to have his licence revoked for up to three months 'if necessary for his protection'. The power to pass a Borstal sentence belonged to higher courts. When, therefore, an offender was convicted by a Court of Summary Jurisdiction of an offence punishable by imprisonment but the court was of the opinion that he was qualified for Borstal 'by reason of his criminal habits or tendencies, or association with persons of bad character', it had to commit him in custody to Quarter Sessions for sentence. In all cases, before passing the Borstal sentence, the courts had to consider a report prepared by the Prison Commissioners on the offender's physical and mental condition and his suitability for this type of institution. And to conclude, the Secretary of State was given power not only to transfer 'incorrigibles' from Borstal to prison, but also to transfer hopeful cases from prison to Borstal.

The foundation was laid down by statute, but its continued evolution depended on administrative initiatives carried out by the Prison Commissioners under the authority of the Home Secretary. This development, it could be said without any fear of exaggeration, exhibited almost from its very start a luminous, meteoric projection. And it is a strange, though in many ways unusually attractive, reality to know how hesitant, how diffident its founder Sir Evelyn Ruggles-Brise was when, under the influence of the American reformatory at Elmira, he had put his idea into practice as a surprisingly modest experiment in 1902. Of course, one should not forget that he was English, indeed very English. The experiment began with eight selected young prisoners at Bedford Prison, one of the smaller local jails. Twelve months later part of Borstal convict prison in Kent was set aside for a class of young offenders selected from London prisons who had been sentenced to at least six months. The first party arrived there in chains. In 1903 the experiment was extended to Dartmoor for the worst young recidivists.

Within a few years the Borstal system had become – to use a German expression difficult to render into English – a *Wunderkind*, an 'infant prodigy' of criminology and penology. 'An epoch in the treatment of juvenile crime', declared *The Times* in its leading article of 29 January 1906, a view which was confirmed and continued to be held by foreign experts such as – to quote just a few – Professors Herman Kriegsmann, the author of an authoritative treatise on penitentiary science, Franz Exner of Leipzig, Leopold Quentin and Rudolf Sieverts of Hamburg, William Healy and B.S. Alper of Chicago, and W. Sokalski, Judge in the Supreme Court of Poland. The best account in English is still *Borstal Re-Assessed* (1965) by Roger Hood, which I had the pleasure to include as volume 20 in *Cambridge Studies in Criminology*.

From the 1920s onwards the Borstal system was acclaimed more and more. First, it was saluted as a definite solution to the problem of young adult offenders who were dangerously close, because of their previous records and personalities, to becoming determined recidivists. Second, as an economical and effective way of cutting off the future supply of habitual adult criminals. And last, but not least, because of the view – gaining in influence – that the Borstal system (with certain readaptations) might rejuvenate the traditional rigid prison system as a whole. There were many reformers eager to crusade for this and not afraid to experiment in order to prove that this could and should be done. It is characteristic that Sir Alexander Paterson did not hesitate to affirm in 1923, and to reaffirm in 1931, that 'the problem of Recidivism is small, diminishing, and not incapable of solution. Prison after prison would be closed down.' The conduct of released Borstal inmates (they used to be referred to even in official documents or pronouncements as 'lads') was closely monitored and great care was taken to gauge the complex realities of life at the stage of supervision and after-care that followed their discharge. But serious reservations existed which could not be lightly brushed aside.

There seems to be nothing more simple and more convincing than juggling with a few broad figures. But inescapably one entered a truly shaky minefield when one attempted to weigh up the results of after-conduct in a more realistic and differentiated manner. A particularly demonstrative illustration was provided much later by Roger Hood in a section of his already quoted book entitled 'Results'.[12] At the time of my inquiry, a general figure which was freely floated estimated that between 40 and 50 per cent of 'Borstalians' abstained from committing fresh crimes within three years of their discharge and that 70 per cent had no more than one further conviction.

Figures are important in penal matters, but very often it is the attitude of the public which settles the tone, and, in the case of Borstal, irrespective of the preciseness of available data, the tone was definitely optimistic. If a reliable opinion poll were taken in the 1920s I was (and still am) inclined to state that a good 70 per cent of the public would have been convinced that the system was an extremely fair and effective method for the remedial control of the young generation of the criminal population of the country.

In 1913, five years after the passing of the statute, the prison department received 571 offenders sentenced to Borstal and, by 1936, the number had risen to 868. With rates of success so encouraging and the substantial numbers involved, the contribution of the Borstal system to the prevention of crime in general was in practical terms undeniably significant. I have never come across an expert and detailed scrutiny of the expenditure required to run the system, and I myself have not felt qualified to attempt to ascertain it.

Borstal was not the product of admirable work done in one or two isolated institutions, but represented a system in the fullest meaning of the term and was planned, organized and directed as such. It started to operate immediately upon admission when offenders were placed for some two months in an observation centre. Here a diagnosis and prognosis was made before they were sent to an institution which had been set aside for offenders with their characteristics. A sophisticated network of twelve institutions was finally evolved to cater for different categories of offenders, with different locations, architecture, personnel and regime. An elaborate, after-care organization was built up as an integral part of the Borstal system and set in motion long before the offenders were released. The release was always on licence, conditional and revocable. The supervision was invariably of long duration. Freedom under control was considered as an essential stage leading towards uncontrolled freedom. Institutions were small and individual treatment was still further facilitated by the house system, in imitation of the great public schools of England. All of this called for a staff of high quality and genuine dedication much above the level prevailing in traditional prisons. The very high ideals set by the system, and the wealth and variety of arrangements put

---

12 *Borstal Re-Assessed* (1965), pp. 197–220.

at its disposal, acted as a magnet for drawing people of unusual calibre who were ready to work for its success, people to whom the ordinary prison system would not appeal.

There is also the elementary truth, yet so often ignored or underestimated, that if a system is to leave a mark it must exhale a mixture of atmosphere, tradition and involvement which is so difficult to put on paper and atomize in orderly sentences, still less in bureaucratic executive orders. The Borstal system was saved from sterile schematization because its mission was described by a man who, by his personal example and remarkable gifts of balanced and yet inspiring leadership, was its devoted artisan and inexhaustible leader. I refer to the little book entitled *Principles of Borstal System* (first edition in 1922 and second edition in 1932) written by Alexander (later Sir Alexander) Paterson who soon and most appropriately became the Prison Commissioner (there were four altogether) in charge of the Borstal system. In the course of my inquiry I visited several Borstals and returned to some of them for further information, on each occasion feeling more enlightened and more personally engaged. Dr Max Grünhut, the noble scholar-exile from Nazi Germany who had found a niche in Oxford and did a lot for developing criminological studies in England, concluded in his book, *Penal Reform* (1948, p. 382), 'that it is something to be proud of'. I entirely agree with him, but I wish to go further: when viewed in an international comparative perspective, the Borstal system stood out as the most impressive and the most successful achievement in applied penology the world had seen and is likely ever to see again.

The habitual and professional criminal

Whereas the Borstal sentence made penal history the indeterminate sentence of preventive detention, aimed at the habitual criminal, was virtually an instantaneous and unmitigated flop. The guiding formula for a new approach, expressed in arresting and succinct terms, had been laid down by the Gladstone Committee of 1895: 'to punish them for the particular offence is almost useless . . . the real offence was the wilful persistence in the deliberately acquired habit of crime' and consequently 'a new form of sentence should be placed at the disposal of the judges . . . consisting of a long period of detention under less onerous conditions'. In fact, the clamour about the evil of chronic and persistent criminality had rung loud and compellingly long before 1895. In the decade following the publication of the report the clamour grew even louder.

One of the first drafts of a Bill to provide a remedy was so radical, so positivist in tone and substance, that even Enrico Ferri, my Roman maestro, would not have hesitated to sponsor it. What finally emerged was a dual-track system: preventive detention of up to ten years was to follow the enforcement of a sentence to penal servitude. Continental Europe watched the

English developments with utmost attention, for there, also, enormous pressure was being exerted to change the law in a similar direction and for similar purposes. When the eminent criminologist Hans von Hentig of Heidelberg University visited Camp Hill soon after it was opened in 1911 he left an account vibrating with optimism that a solution to the problem of habitual criminality in legislative and penal terms had at last been found.[13] When I visited Camp Hill in 1937, I recorded a pitiful experience. I encountered a haphazardly collected small contingent of manifestly decrepit very senior citizens of crime, genuinely surprised to find themselves in these incoherent, aimless surroundings at the end of their anti-social careers. To my mind, the system which had given rise to so many expectations was beyond repair: it was and would remain a shambles.

Two official documents of the period provide a fascinating illustration of the mistrust (the word is not too strong) which this part of the Act evoked as well as of the liberal approach deployed to avoid, or at least to minimize, the dangers inherent in it. One was a memorandum by the Secretary of State for the Home Department, prefixed to draft rules prescribing the conditions which would have to be fulfilled before a sentence of preventive detention could be imposed (17 February 1911, under the signature of Winston Churchill) and the other a 'Copy of Circular Letter . . . issued by the Home Office to Police Authorities' (21 June 1911, under the signature of Sir Edward Troup, the powerful Permanent Under-Secretary of State). Despite the restrictions and exhortations for restraint emanating from the Home Office, the courts still displayed a dislike of the Act which they continued to demonstrate with increasing frequency. The total number of offenders sentenced to preventive detention for the entire period 1909–30 amounted to one hundred and thirteen; in only one of these years did the number reach thirty-eight, and the next highest annual figure was twenty-one. The average, which could hardly have been lower, was about five. And characteristically ninety-one out of the one hundred and thirteen were sentenced to the minimum of five years' and only three to the maximum of ten years' preventive detention. To put this in context: in 1908 Herbert Gladstone, the Home Secretary (afterwards Viscount Gladstone), stated in the Commons that there were in England and Wales about five thousand habitual, hardened criminals who were qualified to come within the scope of the new law.

The Prevention of Crime Act 1908, Part II, was dead soon after its enactment and yet for very many years nothing drastic was done about it, a strange omission especially as there was no division in public opinion as to the intrinsic importance of doing something effective to deal with recidivism. A

---

13 Hans von Hentig, 'Ein Besuch in Camp Hill, der Englischen Verwahrunganstalt für gewohnheitsmässige Verbrecher', *Revue Pénale Suisse*, vol. 26 (1913), pp. 403–12.

partial explanation may well be found in the well-known classical statement of Dicey, to be found in his *Law and Public Opinion*, that

> The opinion which changes the law is in one sense the opinion of the time when the law is actually altered; in another sense, it has often been in England the opinion prevalent some twenty or thirty years before that time; it has been as often as not in reality the opinion not of to-day but of yesterday.

But in this instance there was much more to it than that. The recognition of the complexity of the problem of habitual criminality in the 1930s was so much more sophisticated than at the turn of the century. Connected with it was the growing realization that this was a branch of criminal law and penology which should be approached with the utmost care because it could easily upset the always delicate balance between the rights of the individual and the interests of society. It could easily reverse the trend towards a more liberal approach to the problem of crime in general. The way in which reformers of the day held back on this particular topic, in striking contrast to so many of their other initiatives, seems to be indicative of some fundamental differences in penological opinions. Sir Samuel Hoare revealed that, while there was general agreement that the Prevention of Crime Act 1908 was in this respect ineffective, there was no clear-cut opinion as to any alternative. On the one hand, there was a widespread feeling against indeterminate sentences of the kind applied in other countries, and on the other there was a no less widespread conviction that short sentences did not protect the community from hardened criminals.[14] One could hardly ignore this. I hope that much more detailed evidence on this aspect of the penal law of the period will be explored by researchers, especially by those who consult the Home Office papers which I have not seen.

The first major step towards the reassessment of Part II of the 1908 Act took place in 1932 when a departmental committee was asked by the Home Secretary

> to enquire into the existing methods of dealing with Persistent Offenders, including Habitual Offenders who are liable to sentences of Preventive Detention and other classes of offenders who return to prison repeatedly, and to report what changes, if any, are desirable in the present law and administration.

The committee was a small, but highly respected, body with Sir John G. Dove-Wilson as Chairman, H. du Parcq (a future High Court judge), W.N.

---

14 Viscount Templewood, *Nine Troubled Years* (1954), p. 233.

East (later Sir Norwood East, a medical prison authority) and Alexander Maxwell (later Sir Alexander Maxwell, the outstanding Permanent Under-Secretary of State at the Home Office). Its report, *Persistent Offenders* (1932), should be regarded as an authoritative formulation of English penological thinking during this period. I remember vividly, when reading it a year later in Warsaw soon after it appeared, how deeply impressed I was by its substance and mode of presentation, in spite of my very poor English and exceedingly scanty knowledge of English penal conditions. Since then I have often quoted it in my university lectures and seminars in many parts of the world and in many consultative discussions relating to the problem of persistent criminality. I studied it again in England while working on my report and I took it off my library shelves yet again in Philadelphia to peruse it afresh in the perspective of more than six decades of penal history and criminological investigations. My admiration remained unaltered, but inevitably some serious reservations emerged.

At that time in Europe, taking a broad view, three systems for dealing with habitual criminality could be distinguished. The first, still firmly entrenched, was part of the classical doctrine of criminal law and criminal policy. You did not punish delinquents, however persistent they happened to be, for what they are, or, still more objectionable, for what they were likely to become. You punished them primarily in relation to the gravity of the specific offence of which they had been convicted at trial and in accordance with fixed provisions of the law in force at the time – thus, in utter conformity with the rule of law. Or, to put it differently but with the same meaning, they would be punished with little regard to their previous criminal record, the principle being to regard each specific kind of crime as carrying a precise punishment on a fixed standard. It was an honest guide drawn from the corpus of the classical doctrine of criminal law.

The second system, dramatically opposed to the first, was based on the positivist doctrine. The sanction imposed on habitual offenders should be grounded on their state of danger and probability of committing further offences, taking into account their whole social and criminal past (even if they already had undergone punishment for their past criminality). It should consist of an indeterminate sentence, preferably of absolute duration with very considerable powers vested in administrative authorities. This system hardly ever found favour in practice and largely remained a fierce theoretical challenge to the traditional classical and revisionist approaches to the subject.

The third formula, which may be labelled as neo-classical, eclectic or revisionist, was a kind of compromise between the classical and positivist approaches. It adopted the dual-track system: first, punishment proportionate to the offence, which was then followed by an indeterminate sentence, usually with a fixed maximum. But there was a fundamental difference between the motivation underlying the continental and the English 1908 approaches. On the European continent, the dual-track system was mainly to be explained by the doctrinal influence of the pure classical school of criminal law, according to which it was first essential to compel all offenders to pay a penalty proportionate to their moral responsibility and to the gravity of their offence, notwithstanding all other considerations of social utility. In England, it was primarily adopted to protect more effectively the rights of the individual and to restrict the scope of preventive detention by making its application contingent on the last offence committed being a serious crime warranting penal servitude.

The first system was becoming increasingly discredited because it provided no effective barrier against the intense recurrence of what on the continent of Europe was described as 'Les vieux chevaux de retour'. The second was regarded as much too controversial and prone to lead to arbitrariness and massive incarceration. The third was criticized as being too cumbersome, too artificial and indeed rather hypocritical. This last mentioned feature had thus been described by the well-known German Professor of Criminal Law, Graf zu Dohna:

> Imagine that an offender, after having served his sentence of ten or fifteen years of penal servitude, is ordered to come before the Governor of the prison. The following dialogue then takes place.
> The Governor:
>   'To-day the term of your punishment expires and considerations of justice require that you should regain your liberty.'
> When the prisoner, however, is about to depart, the Governor adds:
>   'Oh no, you cannot leave; now we must protect society and you have to go to an institution for preventive detention.'
> Upon this the offender asks:
>   'What change then is there to be in my life?'
> To which he will get the reply:
>   'Up to now you have been detained in the eastern wing of the prison; from now on you will be detained in the western wing.'[15]

An Italian prisoner's comment when asked if he had experienced any difference between the prison and the preventive detention was, as might have been expected, much more laconic, but no less trenchant: 'Ci, sono sempre 600 grammi di pane e sempre lo stesso minestrone' ('There are always the same 600 grammes of bread and always the same soup').[16]

---

15 See 20 *Tagung der deutschen Landesgruppe der I.K.V. in Innsbruck* (Mitteilungen, 1935), pp. 109 and 201.
16 Quoted by Gunnar Dybwad, *Theorie und Praxis des faschistischen Strafvollzugs* (1934), p. 59 – one of the best studies of its kind.

Behind these three approaches, although with significant differences in emphasis, there was a tendency to regard persistent, habitual criminality as something apart from the general, ordinary mass of criminality. In its extreme forms it was looked upon as part and parcel of the dangerous or parasitic strata of society, a cancerous growth on the striving industrial society upon which the economic progress of society as a whole so fundamentally depended. This had been the theme of penological debate in Britain during the period preceding the 1908 Act, and it was characteristic of much that had been written and reported upon in Europe at the end of the nineteenth and the beginning of the twentieth centuries. Indeed, it was sometimes brutally postulated by the leaders of the International Association of Criminal Law, such as Franz Von Liszt, Adolphe Prins and French criminal law authorities such as Paul Cuche, Emile Garçon and Pierre Garraud.[17]

And if this mosaic of alternative solutions were not sufficient there was still account to be taken of the cruel distortions which might follow when the direction of criminal policy of a country becomes part and parcel of an extreme authoritarian regime. Indeed, at the very time that new solutions were being sought for in Britain, the Nazis had adopted, by their law of 24 November 1933, a dual-track system and had lost no time in giving it a particular twist. A German penologist and an ardent expositor of the Nazi penal policy, Dr Wilke, frankly admitted that 'La loi met ainsi des armes terribles entre les mains du juge'. Dr Freisler, Secretary of State of the Ministry of Justice, went further and acknowledged that the indefinite character of preventive detention 'caused difficulties to arise in connection with the psychology of the judges' but, he added reassuringly, this 'we are trying to overcome'. And one is not surprised to learn that he succeeded. Within the three years 1934–7, fourteen thousand criminals were brought within its iron net.[18]

This was not the road that the English were prepared to take: certainly not in those days. The committee's point of departure was expressed in a simple, almost self-effacing, sentence which, however, was pregnant of far-reaching consequences:

> Every persistent offender has been at one time a 'first offender' and in a review of the methods of dealing with persistent offenders account must be taken of the methods of dealing with these persons before their persistence in crime has been developed or become manifest.

---

17 See Leon Radzinowicz, 'The Impact of Social Darwinism' and 'The Concern for Social Defense', in *The Roots of the International Association of Criminal Law and their Significance* (Freiburg, 1991), pp. 26–41.

18 This, to quote Professor Andrew Rutherford, falls neatly into his picture of 'Criminal Policy and the Eliminative Ideal': see *Social Policy and Administration*, vol. 31 (1997), pp. 116–35.

What followed was a rapid but highly persuasive review of the main stages in the handling of people found guilty for the first time within the existing system, which so often predetermines them 'soon to be among the prison "ins and outs"'. The committee reaffirmed as an unchallengeable fact that 'the first sentence of imprisonment is a turning point in an offender's career and his treatment in prison on this first occasion will often have a decisive influence on his future career'. It further expressed 'the hope that if the methods of dealing with offenders in the early stages of criminality are improved there will be fewer for whom prolonged terms of detention will be needed'.

Persistent offenders were not an homogeneous group. The committee divided them into three classes. First, there were the offenders of relatively strong character and mentality who deliberately chose a life of crime. Second, there were offenders of weaker mentality and weaker moral character who drifted into crime because they were unable to face the difficulties of ordinary social life. Third, there were the pathological and mental deficient cases. However, the committee was anxious to emphasize that

> there is of course no sharp distinction between those categories especially as between the first and second, and many cases belong to a broader region in which various causes of widely differing character appear to be at work.

From this classification and the more detailed characterizations it follows that not every persistent offender required prolonged detention: indeed, there were very many with respect to whom the imposition of such a sentence would be manifestly unfair and damaging. One factor which stood out and should have a great influence on the type of the sentence and the mode of its enforcement was the age of the offender. A young, a middle-aged and an old persistent offender were, as a general rule, three radically different entities and to ignore this would be to construct a legislative and penal system on faulty foundations.

The committee insisted that two types of sentences were needed for persistent offenders and the following three principles should form their core. They should be related not merely to the facts of the specific offence, but to the character of the offenders and to the necessity of subjecting them to such period of detention as was requisite either for their training or discipline or for the protection of the public. Such sentences should be served under conditions designed, as far as practicable, to fit the offender to take up life on release under normal conditions. And finally, the sentence should entail a prospect of release on licence as soon as there was a reasonable probability that detention had effected its object and that the offender would abstain from crime.

The first type of the new sentence, called 'detention', would be for any period of not less than two years and not more than four years. The second, called 'prolonged detention', would run for any period of not less than five and not more than ten years. The first would be imposed only if the offender had been convicted of an offence punishable by imprisonment for two years or by penal servitude and 'if it appears to the Court that by reason of the offender's criminal habits or tendencies his detention is expedient for the prevention of crime'.

The second type of sentence would be applicable only if the offender had been convicted since attaining the age of sixteen on at least three previous occasions of a crime (the term covers the more serious offence) and the court was of the opinion that 'his criminal habits and mode of life are such that his detention for a lengthened period of years is expedient for the protection of the public'.

Before either of these sentences was passed the prison authorities would be required to submit to the court a statement containing a report from the prison medical officer on the mental and physical condition of the offender, all information which could be collected as to his history and circumstances, as well as observations as to his suitability for a sentence to detention. And both sentences could be imposed only by Courts of Assize and Quarter Sessions. Power would be vested in the Secretary of State to release on licence any person who had completed one-third of the sentence if detention had effected its purpose and there was a reasonable probability of the offender abstaining from crime. There would also be power to license offenders after they had completed three-quarters of their sentence on the grounds of their good conduct and industry while under detention.

The committee was not content simply to lay down these principles but a substantial part of its report was devoted to defining and describing in many important details the regime of the various establishments for persons sentenced to both types of detention, with varying conditions to suit the different types of persistent offenders. For the younger offenders, those most likely to respond to reformative and educational influences, there should be training establishments similar to those tried at Wakefield and Chelmsford. Indeed, the principles which underlay the Borstal system should be adapted so far as possible to these older persistent offenders. Labour camps and minimum security units, as well as a parole system, should be launched. A case could be made for setting up clinics or specialized institutions to deal with mentally abnormal persistent offenders, including persistent sexual offenders, but, as the committee put it:

> we should be on guard lest words are substituted for facts until the efficacy of treatment is based on scientific data . . . whether the psychological treatment of delinquency is of sufficient value to justify statutory recognition as a means for the prevention and treatment of certain crimes.

In the mean time it recommended that a medical psychologist should be attached to one or more establishments to carry out psychological treatment of selected cases. The psychologist should be assisted by voluntary women workers. Arrangements for the after-care and reabsorption into industry of persons discharged from detention should be carefully reconsidered because the subject was an integral part of one and the same problem.

The scheme, and the ideology behind it, was a clear-cut rejection of the then prevailing dual-track system and marked a radical departure in comparative penology. It was a refreshing and, in many ways, an enlightened effort which breathed a large dose of optimism into a sector of criminal policy renowned everywhere for its gloom and resignation. Yet in spite of its careful wording and cautious use of penological concepts the report contained some very acute weaknesses. The dominant tenor of the committee was clearly influenced by the potentialities and achievements of the Borstal system. But hardly any evidence was provided to show that intrinsic similarities existed between the rank and file of Borstal inmates and the bulk of advanced recidivists, habitual and persistent offenders.

The report also seemed to me to underestimate what I am inclined to call the iron law of recidivism, which is largely determined by the social and penal pressures impinging on those who have advanced far in their criminal careers. There was no reference to the concept of incorrigibility and it was too hopeful, without providing any tangible evidence, that this time the courts would forgo their traditional hostility towards indeterminate detention even if it were better defined and regulated. It is true that the committee ignored the much more radical proposal to adopt an absolute indeterminate sentence put forward by Alexander Paterson in a memorandum submitted to it.[19] And it is safe to assume that it would not have accepted the other version of his solution for those included under number 5 of his projected classification: 'habitual criminals, who would be kept for indeterminate periods under conditions of comparative liberty. This class will include the petty recidivist as well as the man repeatedly guilty of more serious offences.'[20] But even so the committee's solution raised some apprehension in Parliament: 'we have gone too far in the way of fear of punishment', warned one Member, who expressed the hope that 'the heyday of Patersonian opinion in this matter has, at any rate for the time being, passed'. And last but not least, the committee failed to consider the very considerable expenditure involved in setting up and operating its sophisticated system and to weigh this against the likely diminution in the rates of reconvictions which in the best of circumstances would be very modest indeed.

---

19 'Recidivism and the Indeterminate Sentence', in S.K. Ruck, *Paterson on Prisons* (1950), pp. 55–67.
20 See Paterson's piece 'Classification', *ibid.*, pp. 45–55, at pp. 52–3.

The unanimously adopted recommendations of the committee were shelved. A solution to the problem of advanced recidivists, of habitual and persistent criminals in legislative and penal terms, had baffled (and still baffles) the imagination and experience of the most seasoned of eminent criminologists and penal administrators throughout the world. However, the inadequate protection of this vital flank of the criminal justice system was too glaring to be ignored. And yet, a further five years passed by before another attempt was made to resolve this complex and ideologically controversial issue.

The mentally defective

The first departure gave birth to a fully justified enthusiasm, the second marked an irremediable failure, and the third produced endless frustration. I refer to the Mental Deficiency Acts of 1913 and 1927 which provided relatively indeterminate detention to replace traditional types of punishment for certain categories of offenders who were declared to be mentally deficient. They were to be detained in a special institution for a period of one year in the first instance, but on medical certification it could be extended for a further year and after that for periods of five years at a time. The amount of thought which went into the attempts to find a more effective and humane way of treating mentally disordered offenders was tremendous. And so were the controversies which surrounded the topic. The history is exciting and instructive, even if very briefly told.

The Bill of 1913, largely inspired by the eugenics movement, was based on an unjustifiably wide definition of mental defect and gave drastic powers to the courts. The opposition at first had been rather insignificant due to the support that the Bill received from Winston Churchill and the Webbs, but it later became fierce and uncompromising. The opponents prevailed and rather unexpectedly the government withdrew the Bill. In its revised version the Bill of 1913 was passed into law. It was more moderate, although there was still stiff opposition to it from libertarians. The definition of mental deficiency was narrowed, its possible bearing upon criminal conduct made more precise, and the procedures to set the law in motion as well as the mechanism for discharge from an institution more protective of the rights of offenders declared to be mentally defective. And yet the criminal justice system was slow and hesitant (this applies both to the 1913 and to the 1927 Acts) to acclimatize to this new legislation.

By 1927, 168 offenders were reported to the courts to be certifiable under the Act (Section 8) and 67 were certified while undergoing their sentences (Section 9). A decade later, in 1937, the corresponding figures were just as inadequate to the needs of the situation: 152 and 131. Even ten years later, in 1947, they were as low as 287 and 40. The obstacles to modernizing the treatment of mentally abnormal offenders in general must have been formidable indeed. A highly qualified authority on the subject, Sir Norwood East (a former Commissioner of Prisons on the medical side), tried to derive comfort from such scanty data, observing plaintively: 'Although the figures are less impressive than the earlier forecasts they represent socio-medico-legal progress.' It is only fair to note that some meritorious administrative advances had been made in the prisons by identifying a number of prisoners suffering from very serious mental abnormalities, by separating them as far as possible from the ordinary mass of prisoners, and by readjusting their prison regime accordingly. Nevertheless, no one questioned that the legislation of 1913 had a negligible impact. Many of the formidable problems posed by mentally defective (now called 'learning disabled') offenders, and by others who are mentally affected, continue to haunt us.

A landmark in penal legislation

At the very time that I was reaching the final stages of my report, an important event took place at the Home Office which had an immediate bearing on my inquiry. On 28 May 1937 Sir Samuel Hoare succeeded Sir John Simon (afterwards Viscount Simon) as Home Secretary in Neville Chamberlain's administration. Just a week after he took office the Prison Vote had to be moved and he made a speech which he himself regarded as his 'most successful speech in the House of Commons'. He was right to be pleased. It was a fine speech: informative, well presented and full of promise for new achievements.[21]

Hardly a few months had passed before he was weighing up, in consultation with his senior advisers, the two alternatives with respect to a projected scheme of penal legislation. The first, to quote his own words,

> was to proceed with several small bills, each dealing with a limited aspect of penal reform, the second to collect all the proposals into a comprehensive Criminal Justice Bill. It was urged in favour of the first that as the small bills could be handed over to private members, there would be little or no demand on the Government's timetable. The objection against it was the loss of an impressive picture that would strike the imagination of the general public. I chose the second method.

'It would', he continued, 'give a valuable personal background to my forthcoming official agenda', and rekindle what he called his 'hereditary interest in prison questions' (Elizabeth Fry was his great-great-aunt and Samuel

---

21 'Supply Committee: Prisoners, England and Wales', *Parl. Debates*, HC, vol. 324 (1936–7), cols 1315–21, 4 June 1937.

Hoare his great-great-grandfather), and reinforce his resolve to innovate for he would try to 'gather together with a single Act the lessons of a generation of experience and experiment that were ready to hand, and were only awaiting to be used for bringing up to date our methods of penal treatment'.[22]

In November 1937 he circulated to the Cabinet an outline of his comprehensive Criminal Justice Bill and was given approval to introduce legislation. This was followed by detailed consultations with experts and interested professional bodies and organizations. 'I can imagine', he said, 'that few Ministers have ever had more interviews about a single measure than I had in connection with the Criminal Justice Bill.' It comprised eighty-three sections and ten schedules which in scope and complexity was sometimes compared to his Indian Bill. In embarking upon this expansive and bold undertaking he was fortunate in being able to draw upon the imagination, the experience and the skill of two senior civil servants in his department: the Permanent Under-Secretary of State, Sir Alexander Maxwell, the outstanding administrator, and Sir Alexander Paterson, the outstanding penal reformer. Hoare generously acknowledged their help:

> Alexander Maxwell in particular helped me with wise and stimulating advice. How lucky I was to have him! . . . Unruffled amidst the alarms and excursions that periodically shake a Ministry of Public Order, he possessed the imperturbable assurance essential to a department of historical traditions. He had also a sensitive sympathy with many new ideas that made itself felt in his attitude towards crime and punishment . . . Or . . . for instance, Alexander Paterson, nervous, assertive, transparently sincere, essentially the new man with the new ideas of prison treatment.

I was not expected, of course, to analyse the Bill in detail but to single out its most striking features: those which endorsed the achievements of the immediate past; improved their effectiveness; enhanced their more accurate understanding not only by those administering criminal justice but also by the general public; and promoted some further forward-looking developments along the lines hitherto pursued. I was to review all those provisions which, in spite of their memorable linkage to the Gladstone Committee of 1895, had been found clearly unworkable or straight counter-productive; and to mark those provisions which had been excised from the statute book, or Executive Orders and Prison Regulations which lingered on, unmistakably belonging to another epoch of social sensibility.

The Bill aimed to abolish corporal punishment (but not as a prison

---

22 See Viscount Templewood, *Nine Troubled Years* (1954), Chapter 18, 'Criminal Justice', pp. 225–35, *passim*.

disciplinary measure), a step which evoked much surprise abroad where it seemed that Britain, despite its civilized reputation, was determined to cling firmly to flogging forever. Hoare had met formidable opposition despite the unassailable evidence provided by a highly reputed departmental committee which unanimously recommended doing away with it (the Cadogan Report on Corporal Punishment of 1938). Many of his friends wondered why 'did he ask for trouble in putting it into the Bill at all?' and tried to persuade him: 'leave it out and you will get your Bill through with little or no opposition'. The party passed many resolutions in favour of flogging in the meetings of the National Union of Conservative Associations. At some stage Hoare was told by the chief whip that nine-tenths of the Conservative members were against him in the House of Commons. But he was determined to ignore this opposition.

On the subject of capital punishment Hoare was much more circumspect. In the light of his experiences as Home Secretary, he had formed the opinion that it should go. But he was also convinced that such a move, in addition to the abolition of flogging, would produce an opposition which could wreck the entire Bill. He therefore 'took the line that as capital punishment had always been given a unique place in the administration of justice, its abolition should be the subject of specific and not general legislation', a view which was adopted and legislation on the subject postponed.[23]

Highly significant was the intention to abolish the time-honoured distinction between penal servitude and imprisonment which, in its turn, led to the abolition of hard labour and of the ticket-of-leave system. This was heralded by reformers from abroad with admiration, but also with some degree of envy because for nearly five decades progressive penological authorities in Europe had tried to introduce the concept of the single unified sentence of imprisonment. But they had met with opposition on the grounds that the distinction in law was needed for purposes of retribution to mark out the punishment of certain especially heinous crimes.

The classification of sentences of imprisonment into three divisions, set up by the Prison Act 1898, was to be abolished. This again was a very characteristic change. It gave effect to the view that a rational classification of offenders sentenced to penal detention could not be left to the discretion of the judge. It should be the responsibility of prison administrators acting on the spot.

The Bill also contained a well-planned and bold legislative strategy to restrict and finally to abolish altogether imprisonment of young offenders up to twenty-one years of age. Even during the period 1937–46 some 25,000 young offenders between sixteen and twenty-three had been sentenced to

---

23 *Ibid.*, 'The Prerogative of Mercy', pp. 247–51. And see, in general, Templewood's highly readable and informative book, *The Shadow of the Gallows* (1951).

imprisonment. The Bill provided for the establishment of several types of new institutions such as state remand homes, compulsory attendance centres and Howard Houses (for 'residential control' of young-adult offenders) setting on foot radical and specific alternatives to imprisonment. Henceforth, Courts of Summary Jurisdiction were not to impose imprisonment on any person under seventeen years of age and Courts of Assize or Quarter Sessions on any person under fifteen years of age unless these courts had obtained and considered information about the young offender's condition and character; and should they then choose imprisonment they must set out their reasons for so doing in the warrant of commitment.

The Borstal system was to be further strengthened. The minimum period which had to be served before the Prison Commissioners could conditionally release a person from a Borstal institution was increased from six months to nine, but the maximum period (three years) remained unaltered. The Prison Commissioners, and not the court, would determine the length of detention within these limits. The expression of the 1908 statute 'Borstal Detention' was to be replaced by 'Borstal Training' – not a linguistic gimmick but a truthful and fully justifiable re-emphasis.

The process of readjusting the payment of fines to the economic condition of the offender, so as to ensure, in general, a more equitable assessment, but also to avoid the imposition of imprisonment in lieu of non-payment, was to be carried further with respect to Courts of Assize and Quarter Sessions.

Not even the provisions which provided for the dismissal after a charge had been proved – binding over with recognizances to keep the peace and suspension of the sentence under probation – all of which had been used so extensively, were left intact. The Bill recognized the fundamental difference between them and so they were more clearly separated and more precisely defined. Probation especially came out of this cleansing exercise a much improved sanction. To eradicate the feeling which could so easily be entertained in certain quarters, including some cynical delinquents, that being bound over on probation amounted, in effect, to a 'let off', it was enacted, after animated and long discussion at the committee stage, that, when making a probation order or discharging an offender unconditionally or conditionally, the courts were first to proceed to a conviction. It was characteristic of Hoare's view that controlled firmness should be balanced by mercy:

> Probation is not a form of acquittal. My personal view is that probation should follow a definite conviction, but that if the probationer makes good, the conviction should be erased.

Previously there had been no minimum duration of probation supervision, but under the Bill it was fixed at one year – another improvement. It also expanded the methods of treatment for those put on probation, one of the most important of which was the provision that the offender could, when on probation, be subjected to mental treatment. And to increase the effectiveness of the system as a whole, the Bill provided for a new distribution of probation areas.

To this necessarily abridged survey a note must be added on the subject of persistent offenders. The bankruptcy of the 1908 Act, Part I, was formally and definitely acknowledged by its repeal and a new system was to be adopted. With so many liberal provisions enacted, and in view of the widespread disappointment that so little was being done to secure a more stringent control of the army of recidivists, one would have been justified in expecting the adoption of a system of containment through prolonged and rather crudely conceived detention. So strong, however, was the dislike and the distrust of absolute and even of relative indeterminate sentences, so profound was the belief that in no sector of criminal law enforcement should the doors of possible reformation be closed for many years, often forever, that a formula was adopted which stood in very sharp contrast to continental thought and practice. Yet it fitted harmoniously into the evolving new English criminal policy.

It was in effect the formula laid down by the departmental committee's report of 1932, clothed in legislative language, and including one or two changes, such as new terminology: sentences of 'corrective training' and of 'preventive detention'. There was also to be a change in the duration of the second type of sentence: instead of no less than two and no more than ten years, it was to be for a term of no less than two and no more than four years if an offender had two previous serious convictions, and between four and ten years for offenders who had three or more or had previously served a sentence of corrective training or preventive detention. Corrective training could be imposed on offenders over twenty-one years of age who had been convicted of a serious offence, and had two or more previous convictions, if the court was satisfied that the reformation of him or her and the prevention of crime made it expedient to subject the offender to this type of sentence. Preventive detention could be imposed on offenders over the age of thirty who had been convicted on indictment of a serious offence and had previously been convicted on indictment of a serious offence, on at least three occasions, since they had attained the age of seventeen. In such cases the court had to be satisfied that 'it is expected for the protection of the public that such offenders should be detained in custody for a substantial time'. Rehabilitative training was to be the guiding principle of the first and protection of the public of the second. In both cases the court had to consider a report on the offender's physical and mental condition and suitability for such a sentence, a report which was to be presented by the Prison Commissioners.

In September 1939 the Bill of eighty-three sections and ten schedules which had been piloted with great skill by Sir Samuel Hoare was almost on the statute book. According to him, all that was then needed was a week or two for the report stage and its passage through the House of Lords. But then, as he put it, 'new developments that made the last lap take nine years instead of nine days' took place. The war broke out, Hoare joined the War Cabinet as Lord Privy Seal and for obvious reasons the Bill was 'left in cold storage'. It was taken up in 1948, however, this time by another Home Secretary, Chuter Ede, in the Labour administration led by Clement Attlee. By that time Hoare's active political career had come to an end. He left the Madrid Embassy in 1944 and soon afterwards went to the House of Lords and was made a viscount. From there he graciously gave a hand to Chuter Ede and was delighted to see the Criminal Justice Bill become at last the law of the land. I did notice, however, whenever I used to meet him, a regret that he the projector, through no fault of his, had failed to become its formal father – a fully understandable feeling.

The Criminal Justice Act 1948 was, in the main, a replica of the 1938 Bill, although as regards offenders under the age of twenty-one, Detention Centres ('the civilized alternative to the birch') replaced the milder Howard Houses proposed in 1938 and the sentence of preventive detention was made more severe, the maximum being raised from ten to fourteen years.[24] The problem of controlling habitual criminality was again revealing its ugly head. Once you reject the dual-track system or the absolute indeterminate sentence it is very hard indeed to come across a seemingly effective and workable solution. And yet without it, a vacuum is created and the penological, indeed the social and political balance of the whole corpus of the evolving criminal policy, calls for some kind of reassurance. This was noticed at the time, but not very often. One such voice, particularly impressive, was that of S.K. Ruck. It gave me great pleasure to see that his and my interpretation of the emerging sentencing trends moved along parallel lines.[25]

Soon after the passing of the 1948 Act, Sir Lionel Fox, Chairman of the Prison Commission, not unlike Sir Alexander Paterson some twenty years earlier, inhaled a large dose of optimism and was definitely convinced that at last an effective inroad would be made into the high and seemingly unalterable contingent of recruits to a life of recidivism. He seemed to agree that some 6,000 men then in prison would on further conviction of a serious indictable offence qualify for corrective training and some 4,000 men would qualify for the imposition of preventive detention. Whether this fresh effort would prove to be successful was a question which one would automatically expect to have arisen. At the time I would not have dared to answer it; nor could I have anticipated that fifteen years later I would become a member of

---

24 Also, the maximum age for a Borstal sentence, increased by Order in Council to twenty-three, was brought back to twenty-one because in the changed conditions following the war it was felt that men between twenty-two and twenty-five were too old for Borstal.
25 'The Increase of Crime in England', *Political Quarterly*, vol. 3 (1932), p. 206 – a periodical which would not be regularly noticed by criminologists or criminal lawyers.

a Home Office Committee called upon to assess the newly acquired experience and to recommend what else should be attempted, should the reassessment prove to be negative.

A note, however brief, is still needed to refer to the incessantly reappearing question of capital punishment, especially because the way it was dealt with in 1948 was very revealing of the changing attitude towards crime and punishment in general. By an exciting twist of penal history, this time it was not corporal punishment which threatened the fate of the Bill. That had been settled in 1938 and for good. Instead it was the question of capital punishment. Although, as already mentioned, Sir Samuel Hoare had been able to argue successfully in 1938 that it was too important an issue to be dealt within a general penal statute, now, because the abolitionist pressure had become much more pronounced, the Cabinet decided to allow a free vote on a new clause introduced by a Private Member proposing the elimination of capital punishment for an experimental period of five years. Chuter Ede, the new Home Secretary, opposed it on the grounds that public opinion was not ready for the change, that a substantial increase in violent crime was taking place, and that the careful final consideration of cases by the Home Secretary guaranteed that capital punishment would be put into effect only when it was absolutely justified. His advice was not followed and, as a result of one of the most dense and passionate parliamentary debates ever held on the subject, the amendment was adopted, but by a slender majority of 23 votes (245 to 222). However, when the Bill reached the House of Lords the clause was rejected by a large majority (181 votes to 28). Whereupon Chuter Ede tabled a compromise clause limiting the death penalty to a number of specific offences. This again was thrown out by the Lords. He then succeeded in convincing the Commons not to insist on the new clause, because the most likely outcome was that the Criminal Justice Bill would be postponed until the next session with the risks that the legislation as a whole might well be fatally endangered.[26]

Thus the Criminal Justice Act, purified by the elimination of juridical corporal punishment, was still tainted in the eyes of the reformers by the retention of the supreme penalty. However, by then it had become apparent that the question of abolition, although temporarily buried, was not dead.

---

26 On this important period in the history of capital punishment in Britain, see Chapter 10.

6

THE SOCIO-LIBERAL APPROACH TO CRIMINAL POLICY

Idealism versus realism

The Criminal Justice Act 1948 gave an official and definitive seal to the most progressive and coherent criminal policy, not simply conceived on paper, but pursued in practice of any major country in the world at that time. And perhaps I may be allowed to repeat a point already made but now somewhat amplified by personal experience. The parliamentary game to secure this objective continued to be played out to the unrestrained satisfaction of all concerned. I was given the opportunity to be present at some of the general debates and at the committee stage. For the first time (and it may well be the last) I witnessed the extraordinarily different connotation the promotion of penal progress assumes when it is tackled on non-partisan lines. The playing to the gallery, inciting feelings of prejudice, exaggerating fear, of promoting short-cuts and solutions which could not in the long run work but were accepted for extraneous opportunistic reasons, were all brushed aside or at least rendered innocuous.

The reformers were idealists but they were not sentimentalists. They did not wish to avoid confronting reality. They were, for example, without exception dead against the infliction of corporal punishment as a form of penal sanction and they made their point. But they agreed, though with some reluctance, to keep it in prison as a disciplinary measure for the offences of mutiny or incitement to mutiny, and for gross personal violence to a prison officer. The old argument that retaining it under these grave circumstances would have the effect of restraining prison officers from using violence under their own, emotionally strained authority without proper control, seemed to have retained its hold. This argument has always appeared to me rather fatuous, bringing home to me the easy-going Italian proverb: 'si non e vero e ben trovato' ('if it is not true it is well invented'). But even here a compromise was agreed upon: the maximum punishment of flogging was reduced to eighteen strokes of the cat or birch for men over twenty-one, and to twelve strokes of the birch for those under that age. When corporal punishment was inflicted no further punishment such as confinement in cells or restricted diet could be imposed; and, last but not least, it was abolished altogether in Borstal institutions.

Or to take another example: should the recording of conviction precede the imposition of a probation order? Or should probation be made use of without proceeding to a conviction? The traditionalists maintained that, although in practical terms probation is a form of treatment, it is nevertheless a species of punishment following the commission of an offence. In their view the abandonment of the prerequisite condition would go far to create the impression in the public mind that probation is equivalent to being 'let off'. The reformers, or at least a substantial number of them, contended that combining the two – conviction and treatment – would rob probation of its distinctive and basic character as an attempt to secure rehabilitation. The Departmental Committee on the Social Services in Courts of Summary Jurisdiction of 1936 had neatly and fairly set out the arguments for and against retaining the condition, but the division of opinion continued. In the end, a consensus emerged and the traditional view was accepted.

And still another illustration. Like all new regimes, the reformers often express their ideology and faith through aphorisms and slogans (some sceptics would describe them as signature-tunes) such as: 'It is impossible to train men for freedom in conditions of captivity' or 'Men come to prison as a punishment, not for punishment' or 'It is as hard to make men better by prison treatment as it is easy to make them worse'. They insisted that, in contrast to the general atmosphere and contaminated passivity of the old prison conditions, the regime which they advocated and set-up in practice was purposeful and invigorating, continuously requiring sustained efforts from the delinquents themselves. An extract from a report by the Governor of Portland Borstal Institution was frequently quoted as an example to dispose of the accusation that the new methods produced leniency and aimlessness: 'Many of them [Borstal detainees] prefer prison and apply to be transferred there when they find that the Borstal system demands something more positive and vital from them than mere attention to a list of prohibitions.'[1]

Sir Alexander Maxwell set the tone when he pointed out, in a lecture at Oxford in 1938, that not only 'more thought ought to be given to theories and principles', but also 'more information ought to be compiled about practices and results'.[2] A year earlier, the Under-Secretary of State in charge at the probation system at the Home Office frankly raised the question 'Is probation an effective cure or does it merely act as a temporary palliative?' He reported that in certain restricted areas where the subsequent

---

1 Annual Report of Prison Commissioners . . . for the year 1928, Cmd 3607 (1930), p. 39.
2 See *Treatment of Crime*, Barnett House Papers, 21 November 1938, p. 24.

behaviour of probationers could be clearly ascertained, experienced probation officers asserted, and their statement could be confidently accepted, that the number of failures was less than 5 or 10 per cent. On the other hand, some courts which had kept careful records of their results over a period of years had found that the failures were much more numerous. He acknowledged that the variation in the success of probation was as remarkable as the variation in its use and that there was clearly a strong case for further investigation. Indeed, he bluntly confirmed that, although 'there is no reason to fear the issue there can be no doubt that nothing could place the probation system on a stronger foundation than a scientific appraisal of its results'.[3]

And again, Britain was the first major country in Europe where the authorities initiated, conducted and published systematic after-conduct studies of many categories of offenders: by sex, age, previous records, kinds of sentences imposed, and whether unconditionally or conditionally discharged within a fixed period of time. They singled out reformatory schools, industrial schools, Borstal institutions, preventive detention and offenders found guilty of substantial offences for the first time in 1927. Moreover, they welcomed and supported similar undertakings by outside researchers. Soon much more sophisticated investigations of this kind would be set on foot, but in the mean time the material thus collected proved to be of great value, not only because of its intrinsic worth but also as a healthy insurance against excessive enthusiasm, and still worse, self-delusion. I derived much pleasure and gained a revealing insight when, in a piece ('The After-Conduct of Convicted Offenders in England') I tried to bring together all the available data and analyse them in a way which would show at least some limited comparative indicators.[4] Imperfect as they were, they showed that the road towards penal renovation was long and hard. But it was also one which did not seem to the reformers to be endless.

Most fittingly the Criminal Justice Act 1948 contained a provision which, for the first time, laid down the principle under statutory authority that the pursuance and financial support of criminological research should be a responsibility of the state. Clause 77(1)(b) referred to 'the conduct of research into the causes of delinquency and the treatment of offenders, and matters connected therewith'. I shall refer later, in a more appropriate context, to the far-reaching implications drawn from this clause.

I was sometimes asked in the course of my inquiry how I would describe the message conveyed by the period which I had been inquiring into and my

---

3 Sydney Harris (afterwards Sir Sydney Harris), 'Probation and other Social Work of the Courts' (Third Clarke Hall Lecture, 1937), pp. 18–20, 24–5, 35–6, *passim*.
4 Originally published in *Canadian Bar Review*, vol. 17, no. 8 (1939), pp. 558–78. A revised version appeared under the title 'The After-Conduct of Discharged Offenders', in L. Radzinowicz and J.W.C. Turner (eds) *The Modern Approach to Criminal Law* (vol. 4 of *English Studies in Criminal Science*) (1945), pp. 142–61.

reply was: 'treble confidence'. Confidence that the steps which were being taken would prove to be exceptionally effective. Confidence that the problem of crime which English society was then facing was in the long run well within the scope of durable control. And confidence that, irrespective of the circumstances, the view would not fail to prevail that the criminal policy pursued by England should be in harmony with a truly civilized state.

An environment conducive to continued penal reform

There was no single cause to which these vast and profound changes in criminal policy could have been safely attributed. They were the result of a number of factors and circumstances, each of which could not itself have been defined with precision, nor could their respective significances and possible interactions be adequately delineated and made convincingly clear.

The continuing commitment to humanitarian ideas and preoccupations; the predilection for social work, primarily voluntary, which had for so long been a marked element of the best in English life; the still strong religious feelings prompting wider communal sympathies and philanthropic initiatives; the relatively high degree of general prosperity compared with many other countries – despite the depression – making it possible, to a greater extent than in many other countries, to undertake expensive new schemes in social welfare and penal administration; a prolonged period of national security and a feeling of pride on having emerged victorious from the First World War; a relative absence of those exceptionally acute and lengthy social conflicts which tend to foster in the criminal sphere a policy of deterrence and intimidation in disregard of the rule of law; a system of social control rooted in social subordination; a coherent and ethnically homogeneous society; the widely shared public confidence in the ability of the police to prevent crimes through increased efficiency in the detection of crime and fairness in the handling of suspected offenders; the lack of anything exceptionally threatening in the total mass of criminality; the still low percentage of crimes of violence, the relatively modest volume of organized crime and the abeyance of serious political crime and serious outbreaks of terrorism; a more understanding and constructive attitude towards problems inherent in criminality within a modern, complex society; accompanied by a better knowledge of the flaws and limitations of the many traditional punishments tried again and again and always with disappointing results.

Several of these elements were gaining in emphasis through the expanding scope of the welfare state.[5] The conviction was growing that the orthodox

---

5   I owe this very interesting footnote to Dr José Harris, the Oxford historian, who replied to my question about the earliest uses of the term 'welfare state' as follows: 'the answer is not an entirely clear-cut one. The term was used by Alfred Zimmern in the 1930s (well before

liberal doctrine – which regarded the state primarily as an institution charged with the protection of individuals' rights – took too narrow a view of the purposes of man's social and political organization. This was followed by progressive and systematic interference by the state in many spheres of economic and social life and by the adoption of a weighty programme of legislation giving effect to these concerns. The continued advancement of social policy, in the widest sense of the term, was increasingly being recognized as one of the most vital and sensitive tasks of the state. This evolution inevitably exercised a profound influence on the evolution of criminal policy. A state which recognizes, as one of the basic aims of its domestic policy, improvement in the condition of the population, and especially of its poor and under-privileged strata of society, cannot maintain a merely formal, passive attitude towards penal repression. It is inclined to approach crime as a complex phenomenon which calls for a constructive remedial policy in which prevention and reformation play a prominent part. Under such a political climate social policy and criminal policy come closer to each other, indeed are impinging, one on the other, at certain sensitive crossings.

I hope I do not convey the impression that this interaction had reached the state of perfect symbiosis. The prison system, for example, was still not free of crude, or even cruel, edges. The magnificent survey carried out by S. Hobhouse and A.F. Brockway (*English Prisons Today*, 1922, recounting their experience and observations as conscientious objectors in the First World War) was still relevant to many aspects of prison life. The programme of new buildings was much too modest. In contrast to the splendid Borstal after-care organization, the after-care for adult prisoners was still under-developed. Unjustified disparities in sentencing appeared much too frequently, and a lot was needed to improve the professionalism and the training of the judiciary at its various levels. But important as these shortcomings were, no one could question that the forward trend was unmistakably and rapidly gaining in strength and scope.[6] Nor could one escape a comparison with the penal situation prevailing in major European countries and fail to notice their inferiority.

This was the dynamic, innovative aspect of the English administration of criminal justice, but it was not the only one. To the social substratum has to

---

William Temple) to distinguish the new functions of the State from its traditional defensive and police functions. But the term was used much earlier in its German form (in Weimar during the 1920s as a term of abuse, but earlier – e.g. by Ferdinand Tönnies – as a term of approval for Bismarckian social policies). I find it hard to believe that the German term was never noticed in England earlier – but I can't give you any concrete earlier references.'

6 'The improvements', Sir Louis Blom-Cooper observed correctly, 'were far from universal' and he quoted significant facts in support of this view. See his 'Penalty of Imprisonment' (Tanner Lecture, University of Cambridge, 1987), p. 17, *passim*.

be added the traditional liberal ingredient, though the latter requires an urgent but cautious clarification. The term 'liberal' has many connotations, some of which may appear to be contradictory. It often creates havoc of dissent among the most dedicated of liberals, while 'liberalism' never ceases to be a captivating topic in political science: but there also it often turns out to be an infuriating concept. Professor Alan Ryan, moving comfortably in this minefield, has produced a stylish and much needed essay.[7]

Within the province of criminal science and practice the meaning and impact of liberalism was much more easily identified and delineated, but the concept still requires careful handling. Perhaps the most classical of liberals in this field was Cesare Beccaria. But that was a very long time ago (his famous book, *Dei Delitti e delle Pene*, appeared in 1764) and even then the gentleness of the Enlightenment and the ruthlessness of the French Revolution were conveying conflicting signals to the humanitarian side of liberalism. In the unbent and undiluted sense of the term, liberalism in criminal justice postulates the following prescriptions: free will; criminal responsibility; proportionality between the gravity of the crime and the nature and degree of punishment; retribution and deterrence as the major, if not exclusive, functions of punishment; avoidance of indeterminate sentences and as much restriction as possible on administrative interferences in the enforcement of criminal law; discretionary power of the judges admitted to a certain degree but carefully regulated; only acts or omissions strictly defined as offences and declared to be such in laws duly enacted can be made subject to a penal response; no retroactivity and no filling the omissions or gaps in the law by *ad-hoc* elastic interpretations; judicial independence; openness of and accountability for decisions; a criminal procedure and evidence operating at each stage of the process in strict accordance with the rule of law and with respect for the presumption of innocence. These prescriptions constitute the core of the ideology of liberalism in the sphere of criminal law, but they are also the core of the classical school of criminal law, which, in its turn, was adhered to almost everywhere by genuine and devoted conservatives. Moreover, a distinction has to be made between two different usages of the term 'liberalism' in the criminal sphere. On the one hand it is frequently used as a term of abuse to castigate those who are regarded as caring too much for the welfare of criminals. Yet, on the other hand, the concept of 'liberalism' is rightly associated in the criminal law and criminal justice system with the fundamental concepts of fairness, legality and the rule of law, which have been embraced by Conservatives as well as by Liberals.

The constellation of many of these beliefs and principles was firmly rooted in the English political and legal soil and I saw no evidence that the reform-

---

7   See 'Liberalism', in Robert E. Goodin and Philip Pettit (eds) *A Companion to Contemporary Political Philosophy* (1993), pp. 291–311.

ers would wish to depart from them. But I strongly felt that one would obtain a distorted view of the English penal reality of the time if the social and the liberal facets were not clearly distinguished. I was inclined to define the evolving English penal legislation and penal practice of the period, for lack of a more elegant and unequivocal term, as social liberalism. It is in the nature of the 'social' to press for expansion of state intervention as it is in the nature of 'liberalism' to emphasize constraints on state power, and therefore a clash between the two approaches is sometimes unavoidable. But I also noticed that the new penal provisions and their mode of enforcement across the entire spectrum of criminal justice avoided extreme solutions. In a subtle, visible and honest way they managed to blend these two intrinsically different constructs within a harmonious and balanced system. Even so, schemes of criminal policy with a prominently socio-liberal bent are very fragile historical constructs indeed.[8]

The liberal ingredient on the continent of Europe was often conveyed through the famous dictum of Franz von Liszt that 'The Criminal Code is the Magna Carta of the Criminal'. I am fervently addicted to it, but I am inclined to extend this dictum and affirm that 'The Criminal Code is also the Magna Carta of the Citizen'. And the longer I live and cast my eyes on what is going on in the world at large I firmly endorse the saying of W.L. Birbeck that 'the jury and the law of evidence are Englishmen's two great safeguards against the worst of all oppressions – that oppression which hides itself under the mask of justice'.

I have not carried out a thorough inquiry to ascertain whether the liberalism of criminal procedure and rules of evidence at the time were fiercely challenged in responsible and influential quarters as having gone too far. But I have come across voices which expressed some concern. The judges, always very discreet, were at that time especially so. But, not surprisingly, Lord Goddard, CJ, in *R. v. Grondkowski and Malinowski* (1946),[9] said: 'The Judge must consider the interests of justice as well as the interests of the prisoners. It is too often nowadays thought, or seems to be thought, that the interests of justice means only the interests of the prisoners.' Among the academics, Sir Carleton Allen was the most outspoken on the subject. Reviewing one of our books (*The Modern Approach to Criminal Law*, in the *Oxford Magazine* for November 1945) he wrote:

> We shall hope, too, that some day this pioneer English School of Criminal Science will address its attention to what threatens to

---

8   For more extended comments on 'the liberal position' within the historical context of criminal policy see Leon Radzinowicz, *Ideology and Crime* (1966), pp. 1–28.
9   1 *All ER* 561. And, much earlier, a dictum of Parke B, in *R. v. Baldry* (1852) 2 Den. Cr.C. 430, at p. 445: 'I think there has been too much tenderness towards prisoners in this matter' (the law relating to confessions).

become a serious embarrassment to justice – namely, the constant complication of technicalities which make it difficult to obtain conviction even in the clearest cases.

Perhaps the most closely reasoned presentation of the most sensitive issues relating to criminal proceedings and trial, accompanied by specific proposals to redress the balance, came from A.C.L. Morrison, who wrote from his long experience as a former highly respected Senior Chief Clerk of the Metropolitan Magistrates' Court.[10] He wrote it at my instigation for I was anxious to obtain a reliable and informative rendition of this point of view.

It is true that, on the whole, the liberal ingredient in criminal justice in a country like Britain was much less susceptible than the social ingredient to radical change or insidious manipulations, for the simple reason that it is grounded in the constitutional fabric of the country. But, even so, its historical stability should not be taken for granted. The impact of a penal crisis, even upon this sector, should not be underestimated. International experience shows that, as public concern about crime and its control increases, pressures to roll back the liberal procedures for bringing offenders to justice become more acute. Then the precepts inherent in the concept of criminal law as an incarnation of 'Magna Carta' increasingly become regarded as a luxury in which the state cannot be expected to indulge. Today we have not yet reached this stage in Britain, but disturbing signals pointing in this direction are not difficult to identify.

It is also interesting to note that the point of departure of almost all of those who advocated anti-liberal procedural changes was to insist that the liberal measures dated from times when criminal justice was exceptionally crude and largely inaccessible to effective public accountability. They asserted that these conditions no longer applied:

> The question is whether under present conditions it is necessary for the rules to be observed with the same rigidity as in former days, when undoubtedly they served the cause of justice and humanity . . . Yet a rule that was once necessary may not be so for ever. Times change, and human relationships alter; the administration of the law becomes more humane. It may be asked whether some of the rules that have been valuable safeguards may not have become unnecessary obstacles in the way of justice . . . In these days, with impeccable judges, competent magistrates, wide publicity and a prevailing spirit of humanity, there would be no danger of a return to those evils, and

---

10 See 'The Protection of the Accused', *Journal of Criminal Science*, ed. by L. Radzinowicz and J.W.C. Turner, vol. 1 (1948), pp. 127–56.

that if any kind of impropriety occurred it would quickly be corrected in a higher court.[11]

This very comforting reasoning does not fit very easily into some of our more recent experiences and it raises the issue of the extent to which the very basic principles of liberalism should be viewed under the spectre of vague relativity.

The threat of reversal

There was little to suggest that public opinion was acutely concerned that the altered system of punishments and their enforcement were becoming too lenient compared with the not too remote past, although there was much in the system which could have been reinterpreted in this way. And there was a truly remarkable constructive relationship between the major political parties with respect to crime and the attitude to be adopted towards it. There were, of course, differences in emphasis and sometimes differences of principle. But there was no opportunistic desire to make political capital out of it: no desire to be awarded with the medals of 'law and order' and 'war against crime'. The role played throughout by the core of the Home Office department cannot be too highly emphasized. They provided the expertise and the balance: the red light when to stop and the green light when to start. 'There was a time', stated Herbert Samuel (afterwards Viscount Samuel and a former Home Secretary), in his introduction to Sir Sydney Harris's Third Clarke Hall Lecture in 1937, 'when it was believed in some quarters that the Home Office consisted of a body of heartless bureaucrats, who believed that prison sentences should be dealt out mechanically according to a fixed tariff', and whose only maxim was 'crush the criminals'. On the contrary, I am sure that every minister who has had the privilege of holding office in this department will bear witness to the fact that the fullest encouragement and the most cordial co-operation is forthcoming from the permanent staff for all measures of enlightened penal reform.[12]

Even at the time when innovative penal developments seemed to have taken firm roots there were weaknesses beneath the surface, not of the reformers' making, but from within society's structure. These could have affected adversely some of the favourable factors which I have listed in the

---

11 *Ibid.*, pp. 127, 138 and 146. See also Heber L. Hart, KC, *The Way to Justice: A Primer of Legal Reform* (Allen & Unwin, London, 1941), pp. 99, 100 and 103.
12 Introduction to Sir Sydney Harris's Third Clarke Hall Lecture, 'Probation and other Social Work of the Courts' (1937), p. 9. Harris was Under-Secretary of State at the Home Office.

preceding pages. For instance, in the 1920s and 1930s the volume of recorded indictable crime was already increasing regularly by about 5 per cent per year. And there was no guarantee that the rate of increase would not top 10 or 15 per cent. Nor was there any assurance that violent crime (and there are many modalities of it) would not become part of the rising curve. One did not have to be a particularly skilful projector to anticipate what the public response would be, should these two disturbing developments coincide with the establishment and expansion of the welfare state with which so many lofty hopes were so often linked. 'By far the most important means of securing diminution of crime', stated Herbert Samuel, the Home Secretary and keen penal reformer,

> is a general improvement in social conditions. The general level of prosperity, comfort, education, the whole standard of civilisation of the nation, is reflected in its criminal statistics.[13]

Or to take another sensitive element: what if the rate of relapse into crime by delinquents who had been subjected to the new experimental methods of treatment were to increase or, still worse, prove to be higher than for some of the traditional, primarily punitive, restraints? And to continue: what might happen if the effectiveness of deterrence were to appear problematic because of the rising chances of impunity stimulated by the poor and erratic incidence of detection?

Inevitably the other elements of punishment – retribution and even expiation – would raise their claims, loud and far across the land. Punishment in all probability would then acquire another dimension: it would become much more aggressive in the choice and enforcement of measures which might be expected to reverse the situation. Depending upon the political climate – the strength and commitment of the alignment of forces pressing for penal regression – the shift would be immediate or gradual. Punishment would become part and parcel of the package which goes under the name of 'law and order' which, in its turn, can so easily lead to the ideology and practice of a crude punitive and eliminatory action. And wide popular support would be forthcoming.

Delivering the Ninth Clarke Hall Lecture in 1949, Sir Alexander Maxwell, the highly respected permanent head of the Home Office and one of the architects of the new Act, frankly acknowledged that public opinion was still sometimes sharply divided on the desirability of some of the basic

---

13 'Supply: Committee – Home Office', *Parl. Debates*, HC, vol. 264, cols 1135–55, at col. 1146, 15 April 1932.

penal changes. Nevertheless, he seemed to imply that this was the product of prejudices, lack of proper information, or simply the weight of the past. He was confident that in time these divergences would disappear. But it is also only fair to acknowledge that he made no wild claims and, as the following quotation shows, he shifted the aims and possibilities of the penal system into more realistic channels:

> How far it is practicable to make men and women better by methods of prison treatment may be arguable. That it is possible to make them worse is incontestable, and the primary object of prison reforms is to mitigate the deformative effects of detention.[14]

A much less confident note was struck by Sir Norman Birkett, the great advocate of his day, a former Nuremberg judge, a High Court judge, and later a Law Lord and the first Chairman of the Home Office Advisory Council on the Treatment of Offenders. Speaking under the same distinguished auspices and only a year earlier he stated:

> The figures for the years 1939–45 are most disturbing. They show that in almost every form of what may be called serious crime there is a great increase not only in the number of offences committed, but in the number of persons convicted, an increase not confined to any particular age group or to either sex. In the year 1938, 78,000 persons were found guilty of indictable offences; in 1945, the comparable figure is 115,000 and the Home Secretary announced in the House of Commons that the prison population is higher now than at any time in the last twenty-six years. With this very considerable army of wrongdoers it would be idle to expect the community to be without the desire for retribution ... nor would it be in the true interests of the community if it were so.

And he added wisely:

> Problems of punishment during the last 200 years at least have always been controversial, which is indicative of their inherent difficulty.[15]

The well-known progressive views of Sir Norman Birkett could not be questioned nor his deep conviction doubted that 'one of the great tests of

---

14 'The Institutional Treatment of Delinquents' (1949), *passim*.
15 'Criminal Justice: Problems of Punishment' (Eighth Clarke Hall Lecture, 1948), pp. 24 and 29.

civilisation is the character of its criminal justice and the manner of its administration', and this is why the statement quoted above is so significant.

It was Chuter Ede, who as Home Secretary took so prominent a part in espousing the cause of penal reform, who said, when taking charge of the 1948 Criminal Justice Bill:

> I doubt very much whether, at the moment, public opinion is in favour of this change [suspension of capital punishment] but I doubt also, whether at any time during the past 100 years a plebiscite would have carried any of the great penal reforms which have been made.[16]

In 1936–8 when I was carrying out my inquiry I failed to discover any acute and substantial signs of frustration and urges for a counter-offensive: to paraphrase Eric Maria Remarque's famous dictum 'All's Quiet on the Penological Front'. But it became clear rather soon that the 'quiet' was not to last for long.

Retribution–deterrence–reformation: could a balance be struck?

In March 1934, by a happy coincidence (or maybe it was not a coincidence) the First Clarke Hall Lecture was given in the Hall of Gray's Inn by Dr William Temple, then the Archbishop of York. He was introduced by the Lord Chancellor, Lord Sankey, and Sir Herbert Samuel later provided a foreword when the lecture was published. It was an eagerly awaited occasion. The subject could not have been more topical. Dr Temple entitled it 'The Ethics of Penal Action'. It was a beautifully constructed disquisition, probing into the essence of a problem eternally situated at the centre of moral, social, political, philosophical and criminological thinking. This dissection of the essence of punishment under criminal law by a man of Dr William Temple's standing would command attention under any circumstances. But a special significance was added to it because the Archbishop was often referred to as the spiritual expositor and sympathizer of the emerging welfare state.[17]

The immediate objective should be 'of so working out the true principles

---

16 Statement attributed to him by the late Sir Arthur Peterson, former Chairman of the Prison Commission and Permanent Under-Secretary of State at the Home Office.

17 See F.A. Iremonger, *William Temple: His Life and Letters* (1948); Joseph Fletcher, *William Temple* (1963); John Kent, *William Temple* (1922) and, as a general guide, Iremonger's 'Temple, William (1881–1944)', in *Dictionary of National Biography 1941–50* (1959), cols 869–72. All pay homage to this remarkable spiritual leader and national figure.

of penal action that we may bring coherence and consistency into the chaos of our administration', and he continued, 'I believe that such a stage has been reached in the treatment of crime in this country'. One of the first premises, defined succinctly and categorically, stated: 'If we are to think clearly at all on this subject we must begin with a sharp distinction between revenge and punishment' and he quoted with obvious relish the widely known saying of Bacon: 'Revenge is a wild kind of justice.' Second, and very pointedly, was the total absence in his analysis of the traditional religious element of expiation. For even if it were to be taken into account it is obviously outside the competence of secular authorities and could not be assessed and acknowledged by them in individual cases.

Deterrence was admitted, but with certain important qualifications. Its essence 'is found rather in the threat of the penalty than in its execution' and it largely depended on the probability of detection. As such it 'belongs to the necessary mechanism of the state' and

> it is not without moral value, but that is not its primary quality ... deterrence, though the most obvious aspect of State-inflicted punishments, is peculiar in that it ignores the personal quality of the offender. The aim is to so treat any one who shall offend that none shall think it worth to offend; where deterrence is completely effective, the penalty is never inflicted ... In the infliction of a deterrent sentence, therefore, the State is treating the offender as a means to the good of others rather than as an end in himself: and if this is all that the State has in view it will be acting immorally, for it will be contravening the fundamental principle of morality as expressed in the Kantian maxim Treat humanity, whether in your own person or in others, always as an end withal and never only as a means.

These remarks should make it clear that 'the purely deterrent aspect of penal action ... is morally justifiable provided that it is subordinate'.

Does this, Dr Temple asked, lead us to assume, as it is so frequently contended, that the retributive element is the truly essential element in punishment? In this connection the role of the state under the authority of which punishments are inflicted cannot be overlooked.

> The first duty of the State is to dissociate itself from the act of its own member; to do this it must act, not only upon, but against that member. Just because he is a member his act implicates the community, unless the community repudiates it. The community must exhibit an antagonism in its will against the will of the offending member. This is necessary for the preservation of its own character, on what the character of its citizens largely depend.

And what follows may be regarded as the concluding assessment.

> But this action of the community must be painful, because its essential quality is antagonism to the criminal so far as he is criminal . . . The state does not represent only the injured party, not only all the other citizens; it acts for the whole of the community, including the offender himself.

In another passage he strongly warned: 'Though it is very easy to exaggerate the proportion of individual to corporate responsibility [in the commission of crime], yet to deny individual responsibility is to deny personality.' And indeed it should be recognized that 'Retributive punishment, even in brutally vindictive forms, does at least treat its victims as persons and moral agents, and has thus an ethical superiority to mere deterrence or to a merely medical treatment aiming at reformation.' A criminal 'never is only criminal and nothing else':

> Unless a man is wholly identified with evil, which only God could know him to be, it must be immoral and unjust to treat him as if he were . . . We are not what we appear, but what we are becoming: and if that is what we truly are, no penal system is fully just which treats us as anything else.

Thus the concluding formula is close at hand, a formula which is the product of deep spiritual and moral conviction but also of an acute social and political insight:

> though Retribution is the most fundamental element in penal action, and deterrence for practical reasons the most indispensable, yet the Reformative element is not only the most valuable in the sympathy which it exhibits and in the effects which it produces, but is also that which alone confers upon the other two the full quality of Justice.

The reformative aspect of penal action deserves all our thoughts and endeavours as long as 'this shall never take such forms as to destroy the Retributive and Deterrent elements'.

This inspiring and forcibly argued pronouncement contained many things that warmed the hearts of reformers and illuminated the long hard road which would be their destiny should they persevere in their endeavour. But it also signalled its heavy shadows. It contained an implicit, though not necessarily intended, ominous warning, a warning which may not necessarily cross the mind of a moralist or a philosopher, however perspicuous he may be, but which is conspicuously borne out by the penal history of the world at large.[18]

Two Home Secretaries: two contrasting profiles

Samuel Hoare and Chuter Ede: there could hardly be a greater contrast. Samuel Hoare was the son of Sir Samuel Hoare (afterwards the first baronet), a Conservative Member of Parliament for Norwich (1886–1908), settled in Sidestrand Hall, Norfolk, and a descendant of an old Norfolk banking family. James Chuter Ede, the son of James Ede a grocer, was born in Epsom, Surrey. Whereas young Samuel was educated at Harrow and New College, Oxford, and did very well there, James went to Epsom National Schools and, though he obtained a scholarship to go to Christ's College Cambridge, he left before taking a degree. He married Lilian Mary Stephens, a fellow member of the Surrey County Council. Hoare espoused Lady Maud Lygon, fifth daughter of the sixth Earl Beauchamp.

Chuter Ede started as an assistant master in Surrey elementary schools and continued in this capacity until 1914 when he enlisted in the armed forces, becoming a sergeant in the East Surreys and Royal Engineers. Hoare was appointed Assistant Private Secretary to Alfred Lyttleton, the Colonial Secretary. In 1910 he entered Parliament as Conservative Member for Chelsea and kept the seat until 1944. During the war, he served as a general staff officer with the rank of Lieutenant-Colonel in the military mission to Russia and then to Italy. Mentioned in dispatches, he was appointed Companion of the Order of St Michael and St George (CMG) and succeeded to the baronetcy in 1915.

Sir Samuel Hoare followed Sir John Simon (afterwards Viscount Simon) as Home Secretary in Neville Chamberlain's government. He was then fifty-eight years old and had behind him an exceptionally brilliant and varied political career. According to Charles Mott-Hadclyffe (the author of the note about Hoare in the *Dictionary of National Biography 1951–60*, 1971, cols 487–90, from which I borrow freely) 'he held more high offices of the state than any other contemporary minister, with the exception of Churchill'. He was Secretary of State for Air four times; Secretary of State for India; Foreign Secretary; First Lord of the Admiralty; Lord Privy Seal and a member of the War Cabinet; and Ambassador to Spain during the crucial years of the Second World War.

---

18 This was not the only piece Dr Temple wrote about the subject, but the other one, interesting as it also was, made no new points. 'Ethics of Punishment' (John Howard Anniversary Sermon, Howard League for Penal Reform, 1945). Also deserving attention is his paper on the 'Death Penalty', *Spectator*, vol. CLIV (25 January 1935), p. 112, and vol. CXCVI (29 June 1956), p. 880. He was a member of the National Council for Abolition of the Death Penalty.

Chuter Ede's career was a sharp contrast. He had joined the Labour Party in 1918 and held the seat for South Shields for many years (1929–31 and 1935–64). His only governmental experience was as Parliamentary Secretary to the Ministry of Education in the Coalition Government of 1940–5, when he worked in close association with Rab Butler, then the Minister of Education, piloting the major Education Act 1944. In 1945, at the age of sixty-three, Chuter Ede became Home Secretary in Clement Attlee's administration.

I heard it sometimes being said that Hoare was very anxious to make a big splash at the Home Office because he wanted to 'repaint' his public image which had been so catastrophically tainted by the 'Hoare–Laval pact', which proposed a deal with Mussolini over Abyssinia, in violent contrast to his 'sabre-rattling' speech made at the League of Nations Assembly on 11 September 1935. There was something in it, but only something. The following three factors were of incomparably greater importance. First, Hoare was a man deeply imbued in tradition: national and family tradition. The fact that, for nearly 200 years, two of his ancestors had been prominently involved in penal reform, acted as a stimulus to take up the cause in the changed conditions of the twentieth century and to carry it forward through a major step (his book *The Unbroken Thread*, 1950, makes this abundantly clear). But there was much more than that. Hoare genuinely cared for penal reform and continued to sponsor its cause practically to the end of his life. Second, he was by nature a builder. In none of his previously held ministerial offices did he content himself by being the senior routine administrator. He always strove hard to innovate, to bring about something which would prove to be durable and useful to national life. Third, he knew as well as anybody else that to promote a major progressive Bill of penal reform was a hazardous enterprise under any circumstances, and one which could be torpedoed by members of his own party. Nevertheless he was confident that he would succeed. This was not lack of modesty on his part but a sober awareness of his capacities. Thus, following the second round-table conference with respect to the new Constitution for India, Hoare was occupied in preparing the draft. When a select committee was set up which held 150 meetings and examined 120 witnesses, he was one of the principal witnesses and answered more than 10,000 questions in cross-examination. Lord Halifax noticed that this was done 'with a grasp of his subject that in comparable circumstances can never have been surpassed and seldom equalled by any previous minister of the Crown'.

Subsequently, when he piloted the India Bill of 478 sections and sixteen schedules through the Commons, he made a substantial proportion of the speeches which were over 1,900 in number. Lord Butler, who was known to be very judicious when paying compliments to his political associates, had this to say about some of Hoare's capacities: 'I have had a lifetime experience of politics and political offices and do not know any man in my long experience, including Churchill, who was more efficient at handling papers and dispatches.'[19]

Penal reform was not Chuter Ede's initial and dominant interest. In contrast, from the beginning and throughout the tenure of his office, he spent considerable efforts in building up the police force of the country as an efficient and fair institution, which would enjoy high status and respect in a democratic society. In matters concerning police, Labour was often accused of hostility, distrust or just lack of interest. Thus, from a broader electoral point of view, it was good to have a Labour Home Secretary proving the contrary. But this was not his motivation: he was genuinely and deeply interested in public order and respect for the law. However, once the Criminal Justice Bill became part of his agenda, he identified himself with it, though never forgetting to pay a handsome tribute to his Conservative predecessor.

Criminal policy issues were not the only major measures brought by him to their statutory conclusion: as a matter of fact he was extremely busy. In 1948 alone he sponsored six important and complex Bills. He was Home Secretary for six years (1945–51) and very few precedents of such longevity in this office can be quoted. That he was so eminently successful in carrying out his tasks was not surprising. He possessed many outstanding qualities. He had a quiet but determined will; he was fair and could be very persuasive; he disliked rhetoric and usually spoke only when he had something worthwhile to say; he was honest, sincere and warm-hearted; he stuck to his principles, yet acknowledged the role of compromise in a pluralistic society; he had not much conventional social polish, nor did he appear to be urbane. Indeed, he was somewhat provincial, perhaps suburban, yet dignified in demeanour and speech. He was not witty and did not aspire to be, but had a rather slow, sure sense of humour which sometimes could unexpectedly assume a rather raffish, although not malicious, flavour. I remember vividly when he came to deliver our Biennial Lecture in Criminal Science on 26 February 1954 and I took him to our most distinguished guest room in Trinity. There he saw the luxurious and majestic Victorian bed. He asked who had recently slept there and on being told that it was Lord Goddard, the Lord Chief Justice, who had come as a guest of the Law Society, he retorted with vivacity: 'Oh, I am not going to spend the night in Lord Goddard's bed.' And next morning, when delivering his address to a very large university audience, he referred in his introductory remarks to the little interest shown to him by the university in the past: 'It needed Dr Radzinowicz to come from Warsaw to bring me back to Cambridge.' I remember many things about him simply because he was not a man whom one was likely to forget.

---

19 See his foreword to J.H. Cross's solid and fair book, *Sir Samuel Hoare: A Political Biography* (1977), p. 1.

He became afterwards a deputy leader and then leader of the House of Commons, was appointed a Companion of Honour (CH) and in 1964 he went to the Lords as a life peer. To the very end, he kept his appearance largely intact and continued to look like an understanding, but watchful, schoolmaster. He was Labour all right but certainly not a socialist in the Marxist mould. He was too much of an old-fashioned liberal to be that. It seems to me that he belonged in the very first rank of Home Secretaries and one of the few who were utterly happy to get on with their job at the Home Office without continuously casting their desirous eyes at 10 Downing Street.

Comparisons continue to be tempting and tend to revive my early recollections. It is true that Hoare had no charisma; that he appeared to be cold and aloof; that he had no brilliant repartee or mordant wit; no gifts of lazy, engaging conversation or moving and exciting eloquence. These may be regarded as impediments in reaching the highest governmental office, but they did not seem to have been so in the case of Chamberlain, who held them all to a conspicuous degree, and certainly they should not prove to be fatal flaws in a Home Secretary. But Hoare had qualities which went very far to neutralize any of these possible shortcomings. He had a mind which, far from being static, was genuinely and solidly interested in things and issues round him; he was constantly ready to learn and he had the capacity to absorb rapidly new ideas and approaches and to adapt them speedily to existing circumstances. He had a very high sense of duty, was hard-working and always remarkably well prepared for any brief he intended to hold. His presentations were usually a model of conciseness and precision.

This logical and cerebral emphasis seemed on occasions to blind him to certain subtle and powerful reactions of public opinion. In this context, his address to the students of the University of Reading, 'The Balanced Life' (1938), which he delivered in his capacity as the Chancellor of the University, was very revealing. Those characteristics could, and did, lead to disasters in some of his foreign policy initiatives, but also to oversimplifications in the field of criminal policy. When urging the total and immediate abolition of capital punishment he tried to minimize unduly those deep and intricate roots of expiation and retribution in the individual and collective psyche.[20]

One could not fail to note and to be impressed by his skills, his professionalism and his capacity to cut across details and go for the central point. One could also not miss facing a political animal *par excellence* whose ambitions were not made of dreams but of realistically conceived moves. Though there was some truth in Hoare's statement that 'he was a Liberal amongst Conservatives and a Conservative amongst the Liberals' he was nevertheless a

---

20 See his weighty evidence to the *Royal Commission on Capital Punishment: Minutes of Evidence* (1949), paras 622–38.

faithful Tory and he looked like one. This was a precious bounty because penal reformers much too frequently were lumped together with leftist radicals, dreary intellectuals or insecure moralists. It continued to be a great encouragement to them when, after having relinquished virtually all of his public commitments, he kept the chairmanship of the Council of the Magistrates' Association (1947–52), but especially the presidency of the Howard League for Penal Reform from 1947 until his death. Most appropriately, his last speech in the Lords was on a subject of penal reform.[21] I may perhaps be allowed to add that, from the start, he evinced and continued to show his enthusiastic support for the development of criminological studies in Cambridge. It was a splendid occasion when he came to Cambridge wearing his LLD gown to inaugurate the series of Biennial Lectures in Criminal Science.[22] Nor can I forget his generous public acknowledgement of my efforts not only on this occasion but also when he gave evidence to the Royal Commission on Capital Punishment and in his book *The Shadow of the Gallows* (1951).

On retirement Hoare enjoyed living on his estate in Norfolk, and he 'was no mean naturalist' we are told. He continued to excel in skating (for which he had been awarded a silver medal) and tennis. He was President of the Lawn Tennis Association (1932–56), and all his life he had been a first-class shot. We are also told that 'he continued to shoot with astonishing accuracy until the year before his death', though J.H. Cross, his biographer, stated that he was 'of indifferent health almost amounting to hypochondria'. He also loved writing books. They make for interesting, lively reading and throw much light on many contemporary problems, domestic and international.

Chuter Ede's style of life and range of interests were narrower. Among his pleasures, we are informed by the late Sir Arthur Peterson,[23] were horse-racing (he always had a box at the Epsom Derby meeting), excursions on the Thames in a small motor-cruiser, and a yearly Christmas visit to the circus, to which he used to invite a party of children from a Surrey orphanage. Similarities started and terminated here: both were born the same year, though Chuter Ede lived eleven years longer (1882–1965 and 1882–1954). Both had no children. Both enjoyed long and exceptionally happy marriages. And they were both men of deep religious convictions.

As I witnessed at close quarters how much Samuel Hoare accomplished at the Home Office in so short a period of time, how effectively and gracefully he made use of the exceptionally high talent then available in the

---

21 *Parl. Debates*, HL, vol. 215, cols 415–20.
22 See the substance of his published address, *Crime and Punishment* (Stevens & Sons, London, 1947).
23 See his warm and informative note in *Dictionary of National Biography 1961–70* (1981), cols 216–17.

department, as I listened to some of his plans for the future, I had no doubt in my mind that a stay for a further three or four years in that office would have easily cemented his stature next to Sir Robert Peel, hitherto universally acknowledged to have been the most eminent of all Tory Home Secretaries of the past century.

Epilogue

My report found its place amongst the ashes of Warsaw and in the circumstances I left it at that. I had not felt it proper to forward it to Sir Alexander Maxwell for comment, but as a matter of courtesy I sent him the statistical part and received an amiable letter in response. I also thought it would have been rather pretentious to have tried to publish it in English. But I was very surprised and very pleased when several leading legal periodicals decided to publish a series of articles which grew out of my report.[24]

Looking at them again they seem to me still to make sense in the context of the penal situation prevailing more than half a century ago and they still contain some useful conclusions which are relevant to the present. When composing these papers, especially the one in which I attempted to characterize the leading features of the social and liberal components of English criminal policy, I was in communication with my old professor at the Sorbonne, Henri Donnedieu de Vabres who, at that time, was giving the final touches to his book *La Politique criminelle des pays autoritaires* (Paris, 1938) – a significant work which inevitably was overshadowed by the advent of the war (see Plate 6). Upon reading the substance of my conclusions, he invited me to Paris to give a fuller account. I gave a course of three lectures at the Faculty of Law and at the Institute of Criminology which led to a lively discussion. (In those days, my French was so much better than my English.) I was, however, greatly relieved to return to London by one of the last available civilian planes. I lost contact with the professor for a while but we remained good friends and I had the privilege to entertain him in Cambridge after the war had ended and on his return from Nuremberg where he had acted at the trial of the Nazi war criminals as the judge representing France.

Some twenty years later another distinguished Frenchman approached me, this time with a much more weighty proposal. Monsieur Marc Ancel (the head of the Comparative Law Centre in the University of Paris, Judge of the Supreme Court of France and a Membre de l'Institut) was planning a

---

24 Such as *Canadian Bar Review*, vol. 17, no. 8 (1939), pp. 538–78; *Modern Law Review*, vol. 3, no. 2 (1939), pp. 121–35; *Cambridge Law Journal*, vol. 7, no. 1 (1939), pp. 68–79; *Law Quarterly Review*, vol. 55, no. 218 (1939), pp. 273–88; *ibid.*, vol. 56, no. 224 (1940), pp. 483–503; also *Revue de Droit Pénal et Criminologie*, vol. 19 (1939), pp. 1114–48. These papers ultimately found their place in L. Radzinowicz and J.W.C. Turner (eds) *The Modern Approach to Criminal Law* (vol. 4 of *English Studies in Criminal Science*) (1945), *passim*.

series of 'Les Grands Systèmes de Droit Pénal Contemporain'. As a faithful anglophile he was anxious to start off with a volume on the English system, and he also wanted to know whether I still regarded my earlier interpretation of it as valid. He gave me a completely free hand in planning the volume. I was fortunate to meet with a very encouraging response from my English colleagues and *Introduction au droit criminel de l'Angleterre* appeared in 1959. A volume of 300 pages, admirably translated into French, it comprised nine chapters provided by distinguished collaborators such as Rupert (later Sir Rupert) Cross, Glanville Williams, G.H. (later Sir Guenter) Treitel, J.Ll.J. Edwards, D. Seabourne Davis, Sir Lionel Fox and T.S. Lodge. Marc Ancel wrote a foreword and I re-examined my early views in an 'Introduction' of thirty-five pages and found no reasons to question them.

The events and the ethos which inspired both Samuel Hoare and Chuter Ede, which I have tried to recall, amount to a 'period piece' unlikely ever to re-emerge again. But they took place at a time when a genuine and impressive effort was being made, largely cutting across party lines, to give the criminal justice system a more 'humane face'. Nearly half a century has gone by and perhaps I ought to indicate where I stand now. My initial depiction of the English scene fits more and more awkwardly with the present. The penal system has lost much of its vigour and fertility and the ideology which inspired it is rapidly fading away.[25]

---

25 Broadly speaking it was the system of criminal justice of the Nordic countries which bore the closest resemblance to the English experience. A remarkable account was provided by Marc Ancel and Ivan Strahl (eds) with the collaboration of Johs Andenaes and of Knut Waaben, *Le Droit Pénal des pays scandinaves* (Paris, 1969). See also the Swedish Criminal Code of 1962, designed by Karl Schlyter and translated into English by Thorsten Sellin with an introduction by Ivan Strahl (Ministry of Justice, Stockholm, 1965). The series, *Scandinavian Studies in Criminology*, was inaugurated in 1965 with Karl O. Christiansen as its first editor and continues to be valuable. In recent years, however, the systems of all Scandinavian countries have shifted a considerable distance away from the socio-liberal penal ideology. See the review of Anika Snare (ed.) *Beware of Punishment* (1995) by Andrew von Hirsch, *British Journal of Criminology*, vol. 37 (1997), pp. 686–9. This is also true to some extent of the Netherlands.

7

REACHING THE HARBOUR

My debt to the Howard League for Penal Reform

Like everybody else from abroad who wanted to learn about penal matters in England, I got in touch with the Howard League for Penal Reform. I valued this early contact greatly because its members made no attempt to 'indoctrinate' me in any way but simply helped me to see things from more than one particular point of view. This, because of the complexity of our subject-matter, is exceptionally important. I visited them occasionally and did some reading in their library. I could not fail to be impressed by how much valuable work had been done in these two crowded and modest rooms near London's Victoria Station by a small group of highly dedicated people. The pioneering effort of the late Gordon Rose, in retracing the early history of the Howard League and its predecessors (*The Struggle for Penal Reform*, 1961), now needs to be supplemented by a fresh up-to-date study.

This was the time when the League was at the height of its prestige and influence at home and abroad. Margery Fry (1874–1958) was its star. She was a remarkable woman from a remarkable family. Born a Quaker, she was the daughter of Sir Edward Fry, the distinguished High Court judge, and the sister of Roger Fry, the painter. She displayed her talents in several sectors of public life: as a governor of the British Broadcasting Corporation, a member of the BBC Brains Trust, a member of the University Grants Committee, and at some stage as the Principal of Somerville, her Oxford college. She was also a highly respected Chairman of London Juvenile Courts and one of the founders of the Magistrates' Association. But penal reform was closest to her heart. Since 1919, when she had become the Honorary Secretary of the Penal Reform League, and for the next four decades, she stood at the forefront of all such endeavours. Her book, *The Arms of the Law* (1951), proved to be very influential and her earlier lecture (the Fifth Clarke Hall Lecture, 1940), 'The Ancestral Child', revealed a woman of unusually refined mind and an outstanding writer. She referred to herself thus: 'I, on the other hand, am a life-long dilettante, jack of several trades, master of none.'[1]

Convinced that penal reform was a matter calling for international intervention, Margery Fry played a prominent part in putting it on the agenda of the League of Nations.[2] About this, and my collaboration with her in this endeavour, I shall say more a little later.

Miss Cicely Craven, also a graduate of Oxford and a Justice of the Peace, was the Honorary Secretary of the League. Although she was not of Margery Fry's calibre (few men or women are) she was equipped with a good critical mind and yielded a sharp, attractive pen. George (afterwards Sir George) Benson (1889–1973) was not a national figure, but was a respected parliamentarian and a member or chairman of several House of Commons committees. Inspired by his father, who was one of the founders of the Independent Labour Party and their long-time treasurer, he followed in his path as a faithful Labour Party member, belonging to its moderate wing. He also fell under the spell of Norman (afterwards Sir Norman) Angell and became a confirmed pacifist. His extended experiences in prison during the First World War as a conscientious objector deepened his involvement in penal reform. In 1938 he became the Chairman, and a very effective one, of the League.

They all gave me very many useful hints, but perhaps it is not immodest on my part to say that, to some extent, it was a 'two-way traffic' because they found my European experiences, negative or positive, of considerable interest.

One day Miss Craven said to me:

> We have hardly any Oxbridge members, but there is one, J.W.C. Turner of Trinity Hall, Cambridge, who could be helpful to you in your enquiry. He takes no part in any of our activities but he is a faithful supporter. I shall alert him of your desire to meet him.

I could not have surmised at the time that this utterly unpredictable encounter would prove to be such an important day in my life.

My first English friend

Graciously Cecil Turner was waiting for me at Cambridge railway station. He took me to his college, Trinity Hall, for lunch and then to his rooms for a talk. After an hour or so he told me that he would be happy to take me for a stroll in Cambridge. It was a beautiful afternoon and Cambridge responded to it. As I was walking, I remembered a remark made to me a few years earlier by an elegant French woman who urged me to visit Cambridge,

---

1 *The Arms of the Law* (1951), p. 7.
2 She was helped by Gertrude Eaton, who opened a small office in Geneva.

should one day I find myself in England: 'Monsieur,' she said, 'ce n'est pas une université mais c'est un paradis terrestre.' ('Monsieur, this is not a university but an earthly paradise.') Helped by a brisk walk I saw a lot and was truly enchanted. As the evening was setting in Cecil Turner said: 'Delay your return to London and let us have an early dinner at the Garden House Hotel.' In an uninhibited easy-going conversation we touched upon a wide range of topics as well as criminal law and criminology. At the end he said:

> I suggest that you come to Cambridge and help me to expand the study of crime and punishment, and hopefully, in good time, further beyond Cambridge. I shall try to help you as much as I can but I have many other concerns which I do not intend to relinquish or neglect. There is no opening within the University for the kind of things which are of interest to us, nor can I see one emerging in the foreseeable future. The road will most likely be long and tough, maybe with nothing or very little to show at the end of it, but it will be a rewarding experience.

I was attracted by this adventurous suggestion and startled by a strong impression that this was a friendship at first sight (see Plate 7). Three weeks later I was settled in Cambridge at the Garden House Hotel. Sixty years ago, it was a small and definitely unusual place, beautifully situated, with a good table, run with an iron fist by Mr Reynolds, its owner.

Cecil Turner, in spite of his noticeable simplicity, was a very complex being and in many ways a remarkable man. He was reserved, shy and often inexcusably modest. He was a kind of domesticated rebel with strong views. Greatly reluctant to compromise, perfectly content to go his own way, very sensitive and apt to take quick dislike. A happy family man (with six children), deeply attached to them and yet rather remote; a keen gardener; an inveterate teetotaller and a believer in simple healthy food who, however, looked with tolerant eyes on those displaying opposite tastes. He was a cricketer of some note, playing for his county, and a Greek and Latin scholar. William Buckland, the Regius Professor of Civil Law and one of the great Romanists of the period, thought of him at one time as his successor, but Turner shifted towards criminal law. He returned from the First World War with a Military Cross. He was devoted to his college, Trinity Hall, was its bursar for many years and one of the founders of the Department of Land Economy in the university. The first Cambridge don to visit Soviet Russia, and a determined anti-Communist, he became even more so after his visit. An agnostic, or perhaps even an atheist, but never failing in respect for those who believed, he finally became, with ultimate delight, the father-in-law of Dr Robert Runcie, the future Archbishop of Canterbury.

Turner was my first English friend and there was never a cloud in our long friendship extending over thirty-two years. He died in 1968 at the age of eighty-two. In the previous fifteen years our friendship had become much less intimate, partly because he was struck by severe rheumatism which considerably curtailed his mobility, and partly because these were the years when I was more busy than ever. Of course I was the loser.

The Cambridge legacy in criminal science

When one is trying to introduce something different into a settled environment it is intriguing to see whether there are aspects in the background, however remote or fragmentary, which can be seized upon with advantage as a point of departure. There were two men who stood out and cannot be forgotten when one touches upon the history of criminal law in its broader sense. They were both Cambridge men: James Fitzjames Stephen (1829–94) and Courtney Stanhope Kenny (1847–1930).

Sir James Fitzjames Stephen: a rigid Victorian

If one went by titles alone, there were in England in the latter part of the nineteenth century textbooks on criminal law. But intelligent students could not help but turn their backs upon the amorphous and disjointed structure of all these treatises. Case was heaped upon case and statute upon statute, all too often leaving the reader confused and bored. Stephen made a break with this lamentable situation through the publication in three volumes of his *magnum opus*, the *History of Criminal Law of England*, in 1883. He was the first to interpret the present state of the criminal law through an examination of its antecedents and to blend the historical and the expository mode of analysis. His statements were always lucid, succinct and almost invariably correct; many passages of the *History* are brilliant. He could vividly communicate the majesty and paths of a judicial process which wields the power to affix guilt when failings of human nature lead to crime, when tensions in society have jeopardized its peace, or when the vital interests of the state hang in the balance. It had been a formidable task. That he should have been able to find, from his crowded and exacting days as a High Court judge, enough leisure and strength to accomplish it, must evoke our unqualified admiration. Inevitably the work suffers from certain limitations and I had the audacity to draw attention to some of them in my Selden Society Lecture *Sir James Fitzjames Stephen* delivered in the Senate House of the University of London during the Eightieth Annual Meeting of the American Bar Association in 1957.[3] Yet I have always regarded Mr Justice Holmes's criticisms as excessive, and have contrasted them with the views of Sir Frederick Pollock and Professor John H. Wigmore.

---

3   Bernard Quaritch, London, 1957.

Stephen regarded the history of punishment as 'part of the history of the criminal law', and indeed perhaps 'the most curious' part of it (vol. 1, pp. ix and 457), but except for a brisk and trenchant formulation of what according to him should be the purpose of punishment under criminal law, he devoted scant space to the analysis of its penological aspects. For this, one has to turn to the galaxy of essays and articles he published in the leading periodicals of the period, such as *The Saturday Review, Cornhill Magazine, Fraser's Magazine for Town and Country, Quarterly Review of Jurisprudence, Law Magazine and Review, Fortnightly Review, The Nineteenth Century* and *Papers Read Before the Juridical Society.* On reading them I felt confident to state that I knew no one among the great criminal lawyers anywhere with a doctrine on punishment which was so consistent, so monolithic and so dogmatic. It bore the exact impression of his moral philosophy and indeed of his whole outlook on life. And it also happened to be the most rounded off and extreme formulation of what is known in continental Europe as the classical school of criminal law and criminal science. Actually, he went much further than many of the classical exponents of this criminal law doctrine because of his moral fervour which at times was truly frightening. In a statement worthy of Savonarola, he stated:

> It is highly desirable that criminals should be hated, that the punishments inflicted upon them should be so contrived as to give expression to that hatred, and to justify it so far as the public provision of means for expressing and gratifying a healthy natural sentiment can justify and encourage it.

In vain one would look for any sympathy with, or even a cursory notice of, the modern currents of thought in the field of criminology and criminal policy which were at that time battling for 'New Horizons' – to use Enrico Ferri's slogan – and agitating enlightened public opinion across the civilized world.

His contributions to the life of his college, Trinity (he was made an Honorary Fellow),[4] and his debates with William Harcourt (the future Home Secretary) at the Cambridge Union; his early remarkable essays on the growth of criminal law such as 'A General View of the Criminal Law of England';[5] his subsequent splendid career as a legal historian, political philosopher, publicist, jurisconsul in India, codifier of the criminal law of England, and ultimately a High Court judge – all contributed decisively to the profound respect in which he was held in Cambridge. Single-handedly he raised the status of

---

[4] His brother, Sir Leslie, was Honorary Fellow of Trinity Hall and Virginia Woolf was his niece.

[5] 1st edn, 1863, and 2nd edn completely written in 1890.

the criminal law and revealed its potentialities as an academic discipline of the first order. He put it on a par with the other branches of the law and showed it to be superior to many of them in its constitutional and political relevance.

But he did not – and could not have had – a direct impact on the new approaches to criminal law, and the changing public attitude towards traditional penal values and expectations. In fairness to him, it has to be said that he was too much of a realist and shrewd interpreter of trends of public opinion not to take cognizance of the widening schism between himself and the world around him. The penal legislation and the penal system then taking shape did not escape his concentrated and incisive eyes: he regarded them as the outcome of a 'misplaced and exaggerated' tenderness, but he also acknowledged that this

> springs from very deep roots, and that no considerable change in it can be expected unless the views current on several matters of deep importance should be greatly modified in what must at present be called an unpopular direction.[6]

Courtney Stanhope Kenny: a more subtle Edwardian

In contrast, Courtney Stanhope Kenny's impact on Cambridge was direct and penetrating. It proved to be so because Cambridge became the centre of his life and the academic study of criminal law his central academic preoccupation there. At first it did not seem it would be so. Born in Halifax, Yorkshire, he was the son of the town's solicitor who was descended from a family of French Huguenots named Du Quesne who had fled to Connaught in the seventeenth century. After an education at the local grammar school, Kenny was articled in 1868 to a Halifax firm of conveyancing solicitors and this was expected to be his career.

Four years later he decided to acquire a university education. He entered Downing College, Cambridge, in 1871, was elected to a foundation scholarship in 1872, and embarked upon an academic career which could not be described otherwise than as exceptionally brilliant. In the course of three successive years (1877–9), following his election to a fellowship of Downing College and appointment to lecture in law and moral science, he won three Yorke Prizes for outstanding essays which established him as a legal historian of the first order. In 1881, he was called to the Bar by Lincoln's Inn and joined the south-eastern circuit. The year 1885 could have heralded a radical reorientation of his life, but fortunately it did not. In that year he was elected

---

6 *History*, vol. 2, p. 93.

Member of Parliament as a follower of Mr Gladstone for the Barnsley division of Yorkshire and at the general election of June 1887 he was again returned. He proved to be a useful Member of the House and proposed a few legal reforms, but I do not believe he had it in him to develop into a distinguished parliamentarian or a leading political personality.

When in 1888 Frederick Maitland became the Downing Professor of the Laws of England, Kenny succeeded him as the University Reader in English Law and retired from Parliament. Henceforth, except for serving as Vice-Chairman of the Cambridgeshire County Council and as a Chairman of the Cambridgeshire Quarter Sessions, he toiled indefatigably to promote the academic study of criminal law. In 1907 he was elected to succeed Maitland as Downing Professor and he held the chair until 1918. He continued to live in Cambridge for another twelve years, not too busy but very happy and enjoying his deservedly earned high reputation.

His times were not like ours. It was not characteristic then to rush into print, but rather to take time, ample time, for one's ideas to mature and be clothed in appropriate language. But even on this account Kenny beat all the records. In view of his expertise and linguistic abilities one would be justified in expecting him to have published his projected book in three or four years. But he lectured on criminal law in Cambridge year by year throughout a quarter of a century before he handed over to his publisher the manuscript of his *Outlines of Criminal Law*. This occurred in 1902, and for the next twenty-seven years Kenny prepared with exemplary care, and saw through the press, its thirteen editions.[7] I can do no better than to quote three opinions amongst the very many which expressed eloquently and authoritatively the view which I formed when reading and reflecting upon the volume. 'It has become', stated A.L. Goodhart (in the *Dictionary of National Biography* from which I learned several facts),[8]

> a legal classic, being an indispensable textbook not only for students, but also by the bench and bar. It contains a clear and penetrating exposition of fundamental principles, illustrated by novel and vivid examples many of them borrowed from Continental legal literature, for Kenny had made a study of French, German, and Italian criminal law.

H.D. Haseltine (the author of the most complete sketch of C.S. Kenny's life) quotes many authorities confirming similar views and he maintains with some justification that Stephen's *History* cannot be regarded 'as equal to

---

7 The last revision by him was made in 1929; the French translation appeared in Paris in 1921. It was translated into Japanese (1949) and Hebrew (1954).
8 *Dictionary of National Biography 1922–30* (1937), pp. 466–7.

Kenny's treatise in analytical and constructive qualities'.[9] And the eminent A.V. Dicey praised its merits because the *Outlines*

> prove conclusively that the art of treating legal topics with literary skill makes a legal textbook a work, full not only of instruction, but of interest, may be displayed to-day quite as markedly as in the time of Blackstone.

Kenny was also one of the first to edit a collection of judicial decisions which was regarded as a model of its kind.[10]

His great talents as a legal scholar and writer were matched by his talent as a lecturer. He was, stated Goodhart, 'unquestionably the most successful of all the Cambridge Law teachers of his time'. And Percy Winfield (afterwards Sir Percy Winfield, Rouse Ball Professor of Law), a down-to-earth man, phlegmatic and rather dry, let himself go in describing his old teacher in these effusive terms: 'His lectures flame like a beacon in the memories of those who have attended them, and have been the altar at which excellent substance, lucid form, and resonant delivery mark in the highest degree the scholar, teacher, and orator.'[11]

Kenny took lengthy steps to emphasize that the dogmatic and juridical analysis of crime, essential as it is, does not exhaust the substance of the 'law of crime', because the latter 'is so closely linked with history, with ethics, with politics, with philanthropy' and because it is essential

> to trace out its connection with the past ... to explain the various historical anomalies with which it is still encumbered [and] to suggest the most important controversies, psychological, social, juridical – that it seems likely to arouse in the future.[12]

Two superb examples of this refreshing approach were 'The Nature of Crime' and 'The Purpose of Criminal Punishment', which formed the first two chapters of the *Outlines*.[13] And so was his article, 'The Death of Lombroso'.[14] I have continued unashamedly to make use of these three pieces, nearly a

---

9 *Proceedings of the British Academy*, vol. 18 (1932), pp. 345–406, at p. 375.
10 *A Selection of Cases Illustrative of English Criminal Law* (1st edn, 1901; 7th and last edn, 1928).
11 'Courtney Stanhope Kenny', in *Cambridge Legal Essays* (1926), pp. 17–20, at p. 19.
12 Extracts from the preface to the first edition of *Outlines of Criminal Law* (1st edn, 1902), which remained throughout all the successive editions.
13 See pp. 1–23 and 24–32 in *Outlines*.
14 It originally appeared in *Journal of the Society of Comparative Legislation*, and was reprinted as 'The Italian theory of crime: Cesare Lombroso', in L. Radzinowicz and J.W.C. Turner (eds) *The Modern Approach to Criminal Law* (1945), pp. 1–11.

century old, in my reflections, writings, and teaching and I would no less enthusiastically recommend the same to the present generation of scholars and students. Mind you, his interpretations and views would not always recommend themselves to some modern sensibilities. Fitzjames Stephen was a high Tory and Kenny a middle-of-the-road Liberal. He was much less extreme than Stephen, which was not very difficult to be, after all Stephen was *par excellence* Victorian and he an Edwardian, though still with noticeably strong Victorian roots which he was proud to emphasize.

'It is commonplace to say', stated Kenny, unhindered by the slightest of reservations,

> that every crime must contain two elements, both a physical and also a mental one. It is equally commonplace to say that criminal punishments are created for two purposes, that of Deterrence and that of Retribution.[15]

With unqualified endorsement, he quoted Lord Justice Fry that 'the object of punishment is to adjust the suffering to the sin'. Not unlike one of the leaders of the reformation of morals in the seventeenth century and joining hands with Bishop Wilberforce, he added:

> to elevate the moral standard of the less orderly classes of the country is undoubtedly one of the functions of the criminal law; but it is a function which must be discharged slowly and cautiously.[16]

And look at the ending to his chapter on punishment, with its attractive light touch and fertile after-thoughts:

> It cannot, however, be said that the theories of criminal punishment current among either our judges or our legislators have assumed, even at the present day, either a coherent or even a stable form. To this, in part, is due the fact that . . . our practical methods of applying punishment are themselves still in a stage which can only be regarded as one of experiment and transition.[17]

Would this not make a splendid examination question for criminal lawyers, criminologists and even Home Secretaries to discuss?

---

15 See his 'Some Recent Writers on Criminal Law', *Journal of Comparative Legislation and International Law*, third series, vol. 2 (1920), pp. 244–52, at p. 248.
16 *Outlines of Criminal Law* (1st edn, 1902), p. 27.
17 *Ibid.*, p. 36.

Fitzjames Stephen and Courtney Kenny served well and faithfully their chosen subject and they left a rich and enduring heritage.

The first step

The first step was the decision of the Cambridge Law Faculty to set up a standing committee 'to consider the promotion of research and teaching in Criminal Science'. It was a small body but one which had panache and influence. Professor Percy (afterwards Sir Percy) Winfield, a Doctor of Laws of Cambridge and an Honorary LLD of Harvard, Fellow of the British Academy and a Justice of the Peace, was its chairman. H.A. Hollond, Chairman of the Law Faculty and Vice-Master of Trinity College, and Cecil Turner, who was also asked to act as its Secretary, were its other members. Subsequently co-opted were H.C. Gutteridge, the first Professor of Comparative Law, C.C.W. Wade, the well-known constitutional authority, and R.M. Jackson, the future Downing Professor of the Laws of England and a pioneer writer on *The Machinery of Justice in England* (which is still going strong under the vigorous authorship of Professor John Spencer).[18] The important thing was that, to virtually all of them, the work of James Fitzjames Stephen was far from being foreign. Even more important was the fact that, with one exception, they had all attended the course on criminal law delivered by Courtney Kenny. They shared in common a lasting admiration for him and were thus psychologically predisposed to consider the wider aspects of criminal science. They never failed to give encouragement and advice. Characteristically, Cecil Turner went far beyond his initial promise of help and contributed heftily to the projected enterprise. He often joined me in preparing texts for publication which were to appear under our joint authorship; he was always ready to make comments both of substance and form on my own texts; as a general rule, we planned together the main initiatives which we hoped would give effect to the terms of reference assigned to the committee; and we collaborated closely in dealing with the rather considerable correspondence and personal contacts continuously required.

I was not a member of the committee but the brunt of the work fell on me. This is how it should have been. The committee was embarking upon an experimental, non-committal inquiry and it would have been wrong to convey the impression that their minds were made up. This was the time when, as I used to say, criminologists were looked upon with greater suspicion than criminals and this is how they continued to be regarded for a considerable time to come. I was in some ways 'on probation' and this also was largely

---

18 I was honoured when Meredith Jackson dedicated his book, *Enforcing the Law* (1967), to me. And I had also been honoured when Professor Hans von Hentig dedicated to me the third volume of his great work *Das Verbrechen* (1963).

understandable. It was a venerable Law School, going back to the Middle Ages, conscious of its tradition and the contribution it had made to learning. It was not boastful, but thoroughly satisfied with its *raison d'être* as part of one of the leading universities of the world. Such institutions do not need to embrace novelties to make a mark, indeed they are inclined to look upon them with suspicion and require exceptionally strong evidence of their intrinsic worth before even starting to consider their relevance and desirability within the context of their legal curriculum.

If asked whether, for example, criminology should be given a place within the Faculty of Social Sciences, they would most probably have said that they were not competent to express an opinion. Or they might have said that this would seem reasonable but that, even so, a special case would have to be made out. To adopt it as part of the study of law was an altogether different matter, prompting attitudes ranging from firm opposition to lingering hesitation. The basic approach of criminology and law, indeed, the very language, was fundamentally different. Criminology was born to be vague and was bound to remain so; the language of the law was precise and specific, with immediate practical implications. The promotion of criminology would give rise to an apprehension that the teaching of the subject and research into it would degenerate into the kind of sentimentality or pseudo-intellectual exchanges which have so often been associated with soft liberal or dreamy leftish beliefs. It was not the purpose of the Law Schools of Oxford or Cambridge to produce do-gooders. In their view, this mission could be safely left in the care of the Howard League for Penal Reform and other similar philanthropically minded groupings.

The fact that criminology was born in Italy and taken up in certain European quarters was not, to put it mildly, a tempting asset: this could well be seen as part of the 'Europe cut off from England' complex to which I shall refer later (see pp. 194–196). It was natural that it should attract the attention of the intellectually curious mind of a Kenny, but it still left the question widely open whether it should be thrust upon the rank and file of British jurists. These issues had not been frankly brought into the open, but they were undoubtedly prominent. It was clear that no progress could be made unless due account was taken of these undercurrents and unless we proceeded with caution and sensibility. But it was also no less clear that, if a breakthrough could be achieved, the benefit for the future of criminal science would be considerable. An advance of this kind, if accepted in Cambridge half a century ago, could not fail to have national, indeed, international, reverberations, precisely because of the standing of the university and its conservative reputation. And in effect it did, but not without hard and patient efforts.

Six thrusts to indicate the relevance of criminology to criminal law

To give a detailed account would be tedious, but a rapid review of the main thrusts directed towards the establishment of criminology is necessary. There were six of them. First, we wanted to indicate how important it is for the study of criminal science continuously to draw upon the practical working of the system of criminal justice, irrespective of whether it is reflected in penal reform or relapses into penal regression. We singled out eleven such segments, drew terms of reference for each of them, and approached eleven experienced collaborators. The theme was penal reform and the second and much larger edition of the book appeared in 1946.[19] The contributors are all dead by now but our debt to them is still vivid:

> I have read these Essays. I have learned a great deal of which I was unaware. The writers are all skilled in the subjects on which they have written. Whenever they offer an opinion or propose some approach to a problem their views deserve attention.

This is the opening paragraph of the preface to the volume written by the then Lord Chief Justice of England, Lord Caldecotte. No further encouragement was needed.

By a second thrust, we hoped to emphasize that there are big and complex problems of direct relevance to criminal law which criminal law can neither ignore nor solve by its own intellectual resources. It needed continual attributions of knowledge and experience emanating from a variety of disciplines. A classic example was the problem of mental abnormality, the implications of which were so much wider than that part of the law which dealt with the determination of criminal culpability, even wider than the relation between insanity and criminal responsibility as defined by the M'Naghten Rules, or, for that matter, any kind of rules. Within this context, we proceeded by three stages. First, we tried to take cognizance through intensive reading and selected interviews of what psychiatry and psychology had to offer. Second, we examined what ought to be regarded as the most urgent and reasonable readjustments of the rules of criminal procedure, provisions of the criminal law, and modes of treatment, that these disciplines suggested. And third, we followed the pattern set by our first successful venture. We selected thirteen topics which seemed to us to cover the main segments of the problem, drew up terms of reference for each of them, and invited thirteen of the leading medical authorities with major expertise of the criminal

---

19 L. Radzinowicz and J.W.C. Turner (eds) *Penal Reform in England* (vol. 1 of *English Studies in Criminal Science*) (2nd edn, 1946).

process to cover the ground thus delineated. In a lengthy introduction Cecil Turner and I attempted to bring into focus some of the central and topical issues emerging out of this exploratory and critical survey. No doubt this volume, *Mental Abnormality and Crime*, of some 316 pages written in attractive English, free of jargon, contained flaws and limitations, as did our introduction.[20] And no doubt the late Enoch Powell's comment when reviewing a book symposium also applied to our enterprise: 'The book suffers from the weakness of all symposia: the different voices seem to be saying their own thing without visibly taking account of one another.'[21] But no one in fairness could deny that this was the first publication of its kind in Britain or elsewhere, a publication which even today richly repays careful perusal and sustained reflection. Lord Birkett, who as Sir Norman Birkett commanded an unrivalled experience in criminal matters, a man with an outstanding critical mind, referred to our product in these terms:

> Any of your Lordships who have had the opportunity of looking at any of the publications which have come from [the Cambridge Department of Criminal Science] such as *Mental Abnormality and Crime*, will be convinced of the immense value not only of the Department of Criminal Science but of the Institute of Criminology of which that Department will in due course form a part.[22]

This again was good enough for us.

Our third thrust aimed at the criminal law proper. It was perfectly justified to maintain that some of the modern currents of thought, especially those of the early Lombrosian and positivist phases, had created the impression that the criminal law is (or should be) on the very periphery of criminal science. Indeed that its role was bound to shrink further and further as the biological, psychological and social approaches to criminal behaviour extended their influence, with the inevitable effect that the medical model of prophylaxis and treatment would reveal the irremediable limitations of the traditional juridical model. New descriptions and new claims were truly mushrooming. At one point I identified some twenty different terms in use. The list included criminology, criminal science, criminal anthropology, criminal biology, criminal psychology, criminal sociology, penal philosophy, penal policy, criminal policy, criminal jurisprudence, criminal statistics, penology, prison science, prison law, prison pedagogy, police science, crim-

---

20 L. Radzinowicz and J.W.C. Turner (eds) (vol. 2 of *English Studies in Criminal Science*) (1944).
21 Review of Andrew Adonis and Tim Hames (eds) *A Conservative Revolution? The Thatcher–Reagan Decade in Perspective*, in *Financial Times* (10 March 1994), p. 20.
22 See his speech in the debate on 'Crime and Penal Practice', *Parl. Debates*, HL, vol. 215, cols 436–44, at col. 437, 8 April 1959.

inalistics and criminal prophylaxis. In effect, these varied and bewildering titles simply represented several emerging lines of new types of inquiry. Nevertheless, it was difficult to justify such a plethora of expression, while the confusion was further accentuated by the fact that many of them had different meanings for different authors. Furthermore, their total impact seemed to provide strong support for the lingering suspicion that behind it all was the inclination to reduce the significance of the discipline of criminal law proper or even to ignore it altogether. If this were true, or likely to happen, there could have been no greater misfortune in political, social, moral and practical terms to a well-balanced system of criminal justice as a whole. Nor could one underestimate the strength of the opposition which such an attitude would provoke and a consequential resistance to adopt even the most moderate of changes in the criminal sphere if they happened to be promoted under the aegis of this brand of reform.

I strongly felt, particularly in relation to our aims and hopes, that a paper was needed which, in a succinct but authoritative manner, would clarify the situation and describe the scope and the basic ramifications of criminal science and the place of criminal law as an independent but integral part of it. Cecil Turner fell in with my suggestion and joined hands with me to produce such a paper. We were well aware that this was by no means an easy task, but the task was made easier because, although we strongly agreed that there was a need to consider the terminology and the contents of criminology, we deprecated no less strongly these elaborate subdivisions and the rather naïve belief that clear-cut definitions could be achieved and, more importantly, that they could serve a useful purpose in advancing criminological knowledge as well as rallying support for it.

There was something abstract, schematic and sterile about this whole cerebral exercise, especially if carried too far, as was so often the case. I am reminded of a remark made by Kenny in another context, yet also relevant to this one: 'Definitions', he said, 'belong, indeed, rather to the end of our knowledge than to the beginning of it.'[23] This is obviously not the place to go into the details of our analysis, but suffice it to say that we reached the conclusion that the whole subject-matter could conveniently be expressed under the neutral but characteristic generic term of 'criminal science', with three major constituents: 'criminology', 'criminal policy' and 'criminal law'. Our paper appeared in the *Cambridge Law Journal* under the title 'The Language of Criminal Science';[24] it was reproduced in a volume of our series under the title *The Meaning and Scope of Criminal Science*. It gave us great pleasure when Sir George Benson, Chairman of the Howard League for Penal

---

23 Preface to the third edition of his *Outlines of Criminal Law*, 1907, p. vii.
24 Vol. 7 (1940), pp. 224–37.

Reform, accepted it as a pamphlet under the League's auspices, and wrote a foreword.

Irrespective of any contribution likely to be made by criminology and criminal policy to the third branch of criminal science – criminal law proper – its study and exposition should always be fostered with unabated energy. Criminal law should include the complex of police powers and the complex of rules of criminal procedure – from the early stage when one is suspected of having transgressed through the stages of prosecution, trial and sentencing. Kenny had opened these new departures, but his contribution was condemned to fade away unless it were kept under constant review and propelled into ever-new directions to keep pace with the needs and the ethos of a modern society in evolution. With this purpose in mind, we mounted and prepared for publication another volume in our series, *The Modern Approach to Criminal Law* (1945), with the emphasis on the necessity for diversity. Of the twenty-one chapters of this 500-page volume, seven came from distinguished outside Cambridge experts who dealt with subjects as diverse as public mischief, police search, absolute prohibition in statutory offences, common law misdemeanours, child-killing, and the jury system.

Cecil Turner, for the first time, published the bulk of his novel insights into the structure of the general part of the criminal law and formulated his conclusions in four weighty chapters: the mental element in crimes of common law, attempts to commit crimes, common law assaults, and larceny. In two further chapters, we joined hands: one, already mentioned, dealt with the meaning and the scope of criminal science and the other was an outline of developments in punishment since the eighteenth century. We were the editors of the volume but as we happened also to be contributors, we felt that the preface should not come from us. We were delighted that Sir Percy Winfield, our chairman, was very willing to do it. And, as one might have expected, his preface was brief and wise. One of the points he made gave us special pleasure. He stressed that the volume illustrated the fulfilment of the hope we had entertained at the very inception of our committee: namely, that we might be able to stimulate the interest of experts from outside Cambridge and sometimes, if it were felt useful, might act as 'a centre of collaboration in criminal science'.

When a final account was made of this first phase of our work we estimated that some sixty leading authorities in the legal, medical and penal sphere had responded to our invitation and had given us the honour and the advantage of becoming our collaborators. It is a debt which we could never forget but also one which we could never adequately discharge.

At the head of the volume – the first chapter – we republished Kenny's essay 'The Italian Theory of Crime: Cesare Lombroso', in part to revive the memory of the Cambridge maestro and to pay him a tribute, but primarily to keep his *Outlines of Criminal Law* alive. For, after all, this was the first academic book on the subject which could be read with professional and intellectual profit and, I am inclined to add, with aesthetic pleasure. With criminal law changing so swiftly and in so many directions this could well have been no more than a chimerical hope. It was, therefore, a most welcome development when Cecil Turner accepted the invitation of the Cambridge University Press to become the editor of Kenny's tome on a regular basis. I do believe that no one could have discharged this duty more effectively and more expeditiously. He succeeded in prolonging its life for many years and through many editions.

But there was one difficulty that an editor could not overcome, indeed which to my mind no editor could have overcome: to preserve in its fullness the singular flavour of the book. I have always believed that legal textbooks which have gained the rare distinction of becoming a classic should not be kept alive in perpetuity, but, at some stage, not too far removed, should be allowed to die a dignified death, reminding us of their meaningful life. Turner was compelled, after laudable attempts to avoid it, to remove the first two memorable chapters of the *Outlines* into an appendix of some of his later editions and, soon afterwards, to dispense with them altogether. Ultimately in his forewords he acknowledged that he had had to rewrite large parts of the book with the result that inevitably it was neither the textbook of Kenny any more, nor Turner's. But in the critical time when we were trying to give effect to the terms of reference assigned to us by our standing committee, it was good that the book was still around to enjoy the glory of the past. Soon a new generation of criminal lawyers of outstanding calibre, such as Glanville Williams and Sir John Smith, stepped in to fill the gap by producing texts of undisputed refinement.

The fourth thrust aimed at indicating the values inherent in a comparative approach to criminal matters. If I did not have the courage to take risks I would certainly not have put this subject as prominently on the agenda of our endeavours. As early as the seventeenth century, no less an authority on the criminal law as Sir Matthew Hale sternly warned against taking it up. Referring to certain distinctions to be made in respect of homicide, as expounded by civilian and canon lawyers, he stated:

> But as the laws of several nations, in relation to crimes and punishments, differ, and yet may be excellently fitted to the exigencies and conveniences of every several state, so the laws of England are excellently fitted, in this and most other matters, to the conveniences of the English Government, and full of excellent reasons; and therefore I shall not trouble myself about other laws than those of England.

And if this did not indicate definitely enough where he stood, he added a comment which sounded like a verdict which could not be appealed against under any circumstances:

> Writers on English law have seldom compared the provisions of foreign systems of criminal jurisprudence with our own; and it has been a commonly received opinion that the laws of England are founded upon principles so peculiar and characteristic, that no advantage could be derived from their comparison.[25]

As time passed by, this solemn precept seemed to have enlisted an increasing number of adherents. Yet, not everybody. One of the most respectable and earliest opponents of this view were the commissioners appointed to revise (and if possible to codify) the criminal laws of England. In their fourth report, they took exactly the opposite view, and it was this view which particularly appealed to us. We adopted it (with some modifications) as our guide in this sector of our activities.

> In composing a mere treatise of English Law, intended for practical instruction, it would no doubt be impertinent and useless to allude to the laws of other countries and the opinion of foreign jurists, but where the existing laws of England are discussed, with a view to defining and improving them, their comparison with those of other nations will often be of material advantage. It is true, as Lord Hale observes, that the criminal laws of different nations vary; but at the same time, among many differences, many points of resemblance will always be found, because the object to which they are directed, being the prevention of crimes resulting from the common passions and tendencies of human nature, must be universally the same. The forms of procedure differ in different countries, but the characteristics of crimes are remarkably similar in all.

The commissioners had

> consulted most of the numerous codes which have appeared in Europe and America in modern times, as well as the writings of foreign jurists, and we are bound to acknowledge that in some instances they have furnished us with useful suggestions for the improvement of our law, while in others they have illustrated and confirmed our own previously conceived opinions.[26]

We first invited W.T.S. Stallybrass from Oxford to join us in our comparative plans and republished (with some changes from him) his substantial com-

---

25 Hale was Lord Chief Justice of England 1671–6 and the extracts are taken from his famous treatise, Hale, *Pleas of the Crown* (1678), p. 489.
26 *Parl. Papers*, 168, XIX (1839), p. xviii.

parative study of the general principles of criminal law of England as compared with the 'Progetto Definitivo di un Nuovo Codice Penale' of Arturo Rocco, the first fascist criminal code, which followed the abortive positivist project of Enrico Ferri.[27] We threw our net rather widely and prompted and secured papers on topics such as 'The Development of the German Penal System, 1920–1932', 'Modern Trends in the American Law of Arrest', 'Insanity in the Criminal Law in Australia', 'The Treatment of the Recidivist in the United States' and 'Swiss Criminal Code'. They were all produced by well-known foreign authors, were highly informative, and written in a way which made them easily accessible to English-speaking readers. But, as I mentioned previously, these were not yet very propitious times to plant genuine comparative interests. Even so, a beginning had to be made.

In this context, one experience proved to be particularly remarkable and as such deserves a more extended review. I refer to the initiative which we took in establishing a 'Commission of Penal Reconstruction and Development' in conjunction with our centre, not as a permanent institution, but as a temporary body to mark the importance which should be attached to criminal matters which would have to follow the victorious ending of the war. Systems of criminal justice, indeed, the very core of criminal jurisprudence as evolved by the Western world, had been ruthlessly deformed or simply wiped out by the axis powers and their satellites. Brutally interrupted developments needed to be revived and carried forward in circumstances which had been dramatically altered by this international cataclysm. And there was the more immediate and urgent problem of the extent to which principles of international criminal law and the laws regulating the conduct of the war had been violated. What kind of criminal justice should be made operative to ensure a fair trial and yet exact adequate punishment from those who had borne commanding responsibility for the commission of vast numbers of crimes which were covered not only by the conventional term of 'war crimes', but also by the horrible and unfortunately far too truthful term 'genocide'?

The first meeting of this unique enterprise took place on 14 November 1941. The countries represented were Belgium, Czechoslovakia, France, Greece, Luxembourg, the Netherlands, Norway, Poland and Yugoslavia. It included five ministers of justice, one minister of state, one ambassador, two presidents of superior courts and three senior officials. Dr J.A. Venn, the President of Queens' College and Vice-Chancellor of the University of Cambridge, struck the right note in the opening paragraph of his welcoming address when he said:

> This occasion must be unique in the annals of our University, for it
> can have fallen to the lot of none of my predecessors during the last

---

27 Chapter 20 of *The Modern Approach to Criminal Law* (1945), pp. 390–466.

500 years to be privileged to welcome at the same time representatives of no less than nine countries over-run by tyranny.

The occasion called for a lot of preparatory work and delicate discussions in order to classify some of the issues likely to arise. One to which we naturally attached the greatest importance was to make clear beyond doubt the academic independence of our centre both in appearance and in substance. To give tangible effect to our concern, as well as to project what the commission might properly undertake, Cecil Turner and I had drawn up a small memorandum which had been approved by our centre and agreed upon beforehand by the participants of the commission. It was read out at the opening of the meeting in the beautiful Syndicate Room in the Old Schools, following a speech by Professor Winfield. It was unanimously approved, as were the several detailed resolutions moved by Monsieur Victor Bodson (Minister of Justice of the Duchy of Luxembourg), Monsieur de Vleeschouwer (a minister in the Belgian Government in exile) and Monsieur Terge Wold (Minister of Justice of Norway), establishing the commission, appointing our centre to act as their adviser, and giving a broad outline of the immediately projected activities. It may be informative to mention the first three projects. 'The treatment of accused persons', 'Rules of penal law for recidivists' and 'Rules and procedure to govern the case of crimes against international public order'. Chairmen of the first two committees were elected by vote. On the third topic two incisive addresses were delivered, one by Monsieur René Cassin (General Commissioner of Justice and Public Education of France Libre) and by Dr A.L. Goodhart (Professor of Jurisprudence in Oxford), who acted as an observer to the commission. Soon afterwards Sir Arnold McNair (afterwards Lord McNair, President of the International Court of Justice at The Hague) and Professor Hersch Lauterpacht (afterwards Sir Hersch Lauterpacht and Judge of the International Court of Justice at The Hague) gave directions to the third committee and submitted major reports on the subject. Some of the initial material is to be found in the two pamphlets published by the Cambridge centre in collaboration with the *Canadian Bar Review* under the title 'Penal Reconstruction and Development' (March and June 1942). A lot of correspondence (and auxiliary papers) were deposited in the Radzinowicz Library at Cambridge, but several reports were destroyed at the time because of their confidential and exceptionally delicate political nature.

The commission was not expected to survive the war, but it played a modest role in the great turmoil of the times. As Professor Cecil A. Wright, KC, editor of the *Canadian Bar Review*, who extended the hospitality of its pages to the commission's publications, stated:

> It may seem surprising that in the midst of war such a meeting was even possible in England . . . but it is apparent that only secondary in

importance to the winning of the present war is the constitution of society prepared to benefit from the resulting peace.

Several members of the commission upon returning to their liberated countries played an important role in the juridical and penological sphere and, in spite of the pressure of time, we continued to be in touch with them to our mutual pleasure and profit. In the perspective of the half century which has since passed by, this initiative cannot fail to appear somewhat amateurish, seizing as it did upon a moment, and possibly not more than a moment. But, in fairness, there was a certain resolution and hope implied therein and certainly a profound conviction that an enlightened system of criminal justice constitutes an indispensable ingredient of a civilized and just society. Furthermore, that effort to secure this seemingly unreachable goal is an object worthy to figure high on the agenda of the community of nations, even in the darkest hours of their history.

Our fifth and sixth thrusts can be taken up jointly because they served a similar purpose. Looking at the very wide field of criminal science we concluded, in no time, that there were many problems of theory and practice in which an immediate interest could usefully be stimulated by concise treatment in pamphlet forms. By this method, the salient features of such problems could be brought out, and subsequent more thorough investigations encouraged. The setting up of a pamphlet series in parallel to the series of books was the consequence of this perception. On hearing of our scheme, Cecil Wright, on behalf of the Canadian Bar Association, most generously offered to publish in its *Review* these shorter studies and to reproduce them subsequently as pamphlets. Arrangements were made to make it possible to acquire them either from the *Canadian Bar Review* or direct from Cambridge. The first pamphlet in the series, *Conviction and Probation*, may be used as an example of our approach to this type of publication. The Probation Act 1907 comprised three rather unusual methods of treatment: dismissal, binding over without probation and binding over with probation. But a court of summary jurisdiction could not proceed to a conviction if it made an order under the Probation Act. On the other hand, Courts of Quarter Sessions and of Assizes had to convict before they could make an order under the Act. In practice, as the vast majority of indictable offences (nearly 90 per cent) were dealt with by courts of summary jurisdiction only an insignificant minority was convicted (7 per cent of the whole). The government, through the Criminal Justice Bill 1938, wanted to change this and make the ingredient of proceeding to a conviction an essential requirement for all courts. At one stroke of the pen the statistical map of crime would have been changed by the addition of many thousands of convicted offenders. This proposed change prompted an intense ideological confrontation. In the lengthy introductory note to the pamphlet, Cecil Turner and I retraced step-by-step the stages of the problem; one expert argued the case for amending the law in support of first proceeding to conviction and another argued against conviction. Sir George Benson, Chairman of the Howard League, provided 'An Account of the Proceedings in the House of Commons', and Professor Sutherland, responding to our invitation, examined 'The Position in the United States [the country where probation was born] with regard to Probation and Conviction'. A comment he made in his covering letter to us illustrated the exciting surprises that comparative studies contain: 'this is a question that has not been argued in the United States and I find that argument brings out many phases of a problem that do not at first occur to a person'. In England, it was the conservative current of thought that conviction should always precede putting a person on probation which ultimately prevailed in the Criminal Justice Act 1948, and this continues to be the law of the land.

It was this spirit of give and take, relativistic or categorical, reforming or preserving, that we attempted to bring to our series of *Criminal Science Pamphlets*. Sometimes we may have been trying to jump over too high a wall – in 'Psychoanalysis and Crime' (with a preface by Sir Cyril Burt) or 'The Social Problem Group' (by Caradog Jones with a preface by Lord Horder) or 'Punishment as Viewed by a Philosopher' (by A.C. Ewing) – but our thought behind them all was always to point out how diverse and how complex some of the problems involved in criminal behaviour can be in reality.

The sixth, and the last, of our thrusts fitted neatly into the whole, and its very title expressed its substance: 'Biennial Lectures in Criminal Science'. They were open to all members of the university, resident or not, and indeed to any member of the public interested in coming to listen. No tickets were issued and no fee was required. Any such restrictions would have adversely affected the intended purpose which, to put it as simply as possible, was to evoke interest in criminal science. Time was allowed for questions and discussion. The lectures were well advertised beforehand and were published in pamphlet form, mainly by Stevens & Sons of London, or in a leading periodical such as the *Law Quarterly Review*. The interest evoked was truly remarkable. As a general rule, the biggest of the rooms in the Old Schools was filled. In the audience students predominated as it should have been, but there was a respectable contingent of senior members of the university, justices of the peace, police, probation officers, members of the medical services and local citizens. The series was opened by Viscount Templewood (Sir Samuel Hoare) with 'Crime and punishment' as his subject. He was followed by Sir Alexander Maxwell (Permanent Under-Secretary of State) on 'The Home Office – its function relation to the treatment of offenders', Sir Harold Scott, the Commissioner of the Metropolitan Police, on 'Police problems of today' and Chuter Ede on 'Experiences as Home Secretary and as a Justice of the Peace'. At a later stage topics of a criminological nature began to appear and proved to be very popular, such as 'The significance of records of crime' by Professor Thorsten Sellin of Philadelphia, 'Le crime passionnel' by Monsieur Marc Ancel, Judge of the Supreme Court of France and leading comparative penologist, and Baroness Wootton on 'Diminished responsibility: a layman's view'.

These were wonderful occasions for us. We, the organizers, would come out of our little room in the attic of the Squire Law Library and witness how, in the skilful hands of the eminent lecturers, the chosen subject could touch the imagination of members of an *ad-hoc* assembled audience and make them talk the language of criminal science.

I suddenly remembered that Enrico Ferri was in the habit of inaugurating his regular course of criminal law in the University of Rome by selecting an important development which had taken place in Italy or abroad in the field of criminal science in the preceding year, making it into an opening self-contained address. It usually served admirably the purpose of acting as an 'hors d'œuvre' or an 'appetizer' to the course and was highly appreciated. I do not know of any Faculty of Law or Department of Criminology which has thought it worthwhile to imitate this.

Time for some personal work

All this was exceptionally fulfilling, but I still entertained the hope that I would have some energy and time left to pursue a little of my own work, as if it were on the side. I am so very glad that I managed to do it, for after all time is always a very precious and irreplaceable commodity.

I have already referred to the preparation for publication of my six articles which grew out of my report on English criminal legislation and policy. These had been well received and I still was making good use of them when in search of links of continuity, or more frequently of discontinuity, between the preceding and the contemporary phases of penal outlook and evolution in Britain.

A much more disconnected excursion was into the field of etiological statistics of criminal behaviour. This was more correctly defined as belonging to the province of criminal sociology. There were two such subjects which attracted my attention: the influence of economic conditions on crime and a comparison between the criminality of men and women. They were by no means new subjects: as a matter of fact they had been raised and explored ever since the social study of crime was launched early in the nineteenth century by Adolphe Quetelet, the Belgian astronomer of genius, who made some novel and far-reaching observations on the subject. The literature had become very considerable. Although I was acquainted with a lot of it, I continued not to be entirely satisfied. I felt that the findings could be sharper, more precise and significant if the methodological approaches could depart from the established rather rigid patterns, and other positions and angles of exploration were tried.

My studies were based on the criminal, economic and social statistics of Poland for the period from 1928 to 1934, a period which covered the peak of prosperity and the trough of depression. I made a reference to my methods of approach and some of the findings while still in Poland, but I had not published the relevant material. I brought the manuscripts with me when I left for England, so as to have a look at them again and to try to publish them in English. On consulting still further the literature I gained the impression, very much to my surprise, that my two studies covered new ground, that they had relevance far beyond Poland, and might well be of some interest to a wider international circle of criminologists and sociologists.

I was thrilled that Morris Ginsberg (Martin White Professor of Sociology at the London School of Economics and Political Science), a careful and sophisticated student of the problem of *Causality in the social sciences*, formed such a view, in spite of their rather colourless English, and welcomed their publication in the *Sociological Review* of which he was then the editor. There were four papers. A further, very pleasant recognition came my way soon afterwards when Professor Edwin Sutherland, the leading world authority in criminology, wrote to congratulate me on these studies because of their method of approach and the etiological significance of their findings.[28] He also kindly inquired whether I would consider visiting the United States in the near future. The two topics continued to be investigated by criminologists, particularly those with a sociological bent, especially in Britain and America, but I venture to suggest that my four pieces, old as they are, still deserve not to be forgotten.

But what had bitten me more than anything else at that time was the contribution made by the so-called Blue Books to the evolution of criminal policy of England. What intrigued me to start with was their rather odd designation. After much searching I concluded that I could not do better than to fall back on the explanation provided by H. Hale Bellot. He acknowledged that

> the bibliography of the printed versions of papers which came into the possession of both Houses [of Parliament] is confused in the first place by the popular use of the terms 'blue book' and 'white paper', which are merely descriptive of a physical difference in Parliamentary Papers and have no further bibliographical significance. They mean no more than a paper which is fat and one which is thin. When a book is so thick that you must sew instead of stitching, then you must glue the back, and therefore you must have something to

---

28 See 'Variability of the Sex-Ratio of Criminality', 'A Note on Methods of Establishing the Connexion between Economic Conditions and Crime', 'The Influence of Economic Conditions on Crime – I' and 'The Influence of Economic Conditions on Crime – II', *Sociological Review*, vol. 29 (1937), pp. 1–27, vol. 31 (1939), pp. 260–80, vol. 33 (1941), pp. 1–36 and 139–53.

cover the glue and the stuff that is there; and it so happened that the colour chosen for that cover was blue.[29]

The second, much more serious point which surprised me was that the leading authorities on criminal law had made very little use of, and hardly ever referred to, this source of information. For instance there are only three occasions on which Sir James Fitzjames Stephen refers to the Blue Books in his three volumes on the *History of the English Criminal Law*. One is when he describes the establishment of the Metropolitan Police Force, but his reference simply mentions in a footnote the series of Police Reports of 1816, 1817, 1818, 1822 and 1828, which dealt with the inadequate police organization before the passing of the 1829 Act. He then adds: 'The evidence given before them fills several blue books, and is curious and instructive.'[30] Again, there is nothing in the published works relating to criminal science of Professor Courtney Kenny to show that he made any extensive researches into the material contained in the Blue Books. Even in the chapter of his *Outlines of Criminal Law* which dealt with penal matters *par excellence* there were hardly any references, except for a few fragmentary figures taken from the annual volumes of *Criminal Statistics* or from the *Annual Reports of Prison Commissioners*. The only occasion when he took note of a report on criminal law is his reference to the Explanatory Memorandum prefixed to the Drafts of Criminal Code and Code of Criminal Procedure for the Island of Jamaica.[31] L.O. Pike in his pioneering work *History of Crime in England* also virtually ignored this source.

A rare and impressive exception was provided by Sidney and Beatrice Webb in their indispensable volume on *English Prisons under Local Government* (1920), despite the fact that in *Methods of Social Study* (1932) they drew attention to several limitations inherent in Blue Books.[32] And, of course, as might have been expected no criticism could be directed at German students of English public life and institutions for having neglected or underestimated the value of this source of knowledge. One of the most frequent characterizations used by them in this connection was 'ein ungeheuriges Urmaterial ... gewaltiges, unschätzbares Material zur Erforschung der ökonomischen, rechtlichen, und sozialen Entwicklung Englands' ('an enormous source material ... mighty and priceless material for the exploration of the economic, legal and social development of England').[33]

---

29 H. Hale Bellot, 'Parliamentary Printing, 1660–1837', *Bulletin of the Institute of Historical Research*, vol. 11, no. 32 (1933), p. 86.
30 Vol. 1, p. 196 and see also pp. 480 and 482 where there are two other brief references.
31 Kenny, *Outlines of Criminal Law* (1st edn, 1902), pp. 33 and 238.
32 Chapter VII, pp. 142–54.
33 Robert von Mohl and J. Redlich, among many others.

I needed no such encouragement. The series of Blue Books which I read when preparing my report for the Polish government had made it abundantly clear to me how vital and irreplaceable this source of information is for anyone who wishes to follow and to grasp the evolution of English penal thought, legislation and policy in historical perspective over a long period of time. The period which was of interest to me covered nearly two centuries, from 1750 to 1940. I plunged into this exploration with youthful enthusiasm and mobilized many of my limited resources in my desire to succeed. The formidable collection of state papers, like the awe-inspiring Matterhorn of Switzerland, was comfortably lodged on the top floor of the Cambridge University Library where I was given a corner to myself with an adequate chair and table nearby. I was given permission to remove from the shelves an unlimited number of reports and instructions were given that they were not to be removed from the table when I had finished my day's work. My secretary-typist was installed far away on the ground floor, so as not to distract visitors and readers by her fierce and continued typing of my summaries and selected extracts from the chosen volumes. On occasion I had to supplement the Cambridge collection by volumes at the library of the House of Lords, where the librarian could not have been more hospitable.

In broad terms I listed, extracted or summarized all the relevant material contained in the following three main groups of documents. First, the material originated by commission of inquiry, a generic term which covered the different kinds of commissions and committees, such as royal commissions, departmental committees, inter-departmental committees, select committees, joint committees of both Houses of Parliament and tribunals of inquiry. Second, the material embodied in what goes under the name of accounts and papers. These sometimes preceded the appointment of a particular commission of inquiry; sometimes followed the publication of a report emanating from a commission or committee, frequently owing their origin to a response to a question asked by a Member of Parliament; and sometimes were issued at the initiative of the government, in this case, the Home Office. They were rather brief, informative statements on specific issues. They had all been laid upon the table of the House and very often had given rise to a discussion. There was a very great mass of them. And third, I included the series of annual reports published by departments of state concerned with the administration or supervision of certain sectors of the machinery of justice of particular interest to Parliament and to the public in general. This group included such reports as those emanating from the Directors of Convict Prisons and the Prison Commissioners, of the Children's Branch of the Home Office, of the Public Prosecutors' Office, of the police, as well as the *Criminal Statistics*. As a general rule they were regular publications appearing annually.

It had not taken me much time to ascertain that all these groups (especially the first two) were largely a product of the English parliamentary system. It is in the Commons or in the Lords that is to be found the explanation of the circumstances which led to the setting up of a particular commission of inquiry, or the demand for an account or paper. It is there that the terms of reference usually defined by the government were debated, and again it is there that the recommendations of these bodies were taken note of and considered. It therefore appeared to me inescapable that in my catalogue and survey to the three groups of information parliamentary debates had to be added as the fourth interconnected tributary. Furthermore, for the whole story to be understood, elaborate cross-references between the four had to be constructed. I also formed the view that a purely chronological reproduction would be too mechanical, and too perfunctory to be of any deeper criminological and social significance. Instead I divided the whole area into 130 items and under each of them I grouped, as far as possible, the relevant primary references from the four categories of information I had brought into focus within the period of 1740–1940. Inevitably, cross-referencing made for an acute headache.

I may perhaps be allowed to cite a few figures to give an idea of the scope of the whole enterprise: my material consisted of about 1,250 reports of the different commissions of inquiry, about 3,000 accounts and papers, 800 annual reports and about 5,000 items abstracted from parliamentary debates. Under each of the 130 headings which referred to a given topic of criminal legislation and practice a student could find all the above noted sources relating to it over the entire 200-year period. Each document was recorded according to its full parliamentary description and a researcher would have had no difficulty in finding it in the bound set of Parliamentary Papers and the series of Parliamentary Debates, usually known as Hansard. My own summaries amounted to about 12,000 pages.

While engaged in this piece of research I was in touch with Winfield and Turner and when I finished it I sent them the end product with a memorandum. Shortly afterwards, they informed me that they had studied it, but before expressing an opinion they would like to send the whole to ten authorities eminently qualified to add their appraisal. A few weeks later I received from them this record. It was most encouraging and so was their own view. Winfield asked me to write an article on the subject, and expressed the desire to contribute a preface and to have the whole piece published in the *Cambridge Law Journal*. It appeared under the title 'Some sources of modern English criminal legislation. A preliminary report on the Blue Books and Parliamentary Debates for the period 1760–1940', with a note by Professor P.H. Winfield. He thus concluded his generous preface:

> Readers of his article will find that he has given historical research in Criminal Law a new starting point. He will remove from our

literature on the topic the reproach of having at hand a gold mine without having made any real effort to get and to use its riches.[34]

I could not have hoped for a better reward for my labours and a firmer encouragement to pursue the project beyond this stage.

A plan which had been floating in my mind for some time, largely as a result of my work on the *Parliamentary Papers*, had considerably gained in tightness and perspective. It prompted me to present an outline and to share it with some of my Cambridge friends. To the 'old' ones, Cecil Turner and Percy Winfield, I had been given the privilege of adding a new one: H.A. Hollond, the Vice-Master of Trinity College and Chairman of the Board of the Law Faculty. There could hardly have been a greater contrast than that between Turner and Hollond: contrast in background, physical constitution and appearance, education, indeed in their general outlook on life, society and human beings.

Harry Hollond was for all practical purposes a member of the traditional English establishment. He came from an old family connected with the Hoares of Norfolk, was educated at Rugby and Trinity, and was made an honorary bencher of Lincoln's Inn at the age of fifty-one. English legal history was his subject and it was widely thought at the time that he had it in him to develop into a worthy successor of the great Frederick Maitland. But this was not to be and, with his alert and sophisticated mind, he was painfully conscious of it. He held a few very strong prejudices mixed with a strong dose of snobbery. But he was also a man of very great kindness, loyalty and understanding. A persistent introspection and a melancholy disposition became a commanding part of his personality. In spite of a wide circle of friends, not only in Cambridge, but also in Oxford, London and America, and of much stylish entertainment, he was *au fond* a rather sad and lonely man (see Plate 8).

He had, however, found much compensation and earned a lot of gratitude for what he had done over nearly four decades to improve the structure and functioning of the university, to expand the collegial life of Trinity and, last but not least, to introduce legal studies into the colleges and to bring the Law School into the twentieth century. He had been elected a Fellow of Trinity College in 1909, a Reader in the University in 1919 and Rouse Ball Professor of English Law in 1943. These contributions were widely acknowledged and re-emphasized in a moving tribute to him at the gathering to mark his retirement as the professor on 18 November 1950.[35]

Turner was attracted to the study of criminal law and criminal science and his involvement deepened as our collaboration became more intense. Hollond

---

34 *Cambridge Law Journal*, vol. 8, no. 2 (1944), pp. 180–94.
35 'Speeches . . . in his honour . . .' and privately published in Cambridge in 1951.

disliked the subject both intellectually and emotionally. He felt that it needlessly added to his justified equivocation concerning social progress and individual destiny. He had already found it painful to watch the ways of the world and the very idea that this could be changed for the better in the sphere of crime and punishment made no sense to him. He emphasized this with his uninhibited frankness (some would say ignoring the canons of obvious average sensibility) at the luncheon he gave in honour of the representatives of the Allied governments when they assembled in the magnificent Hall of Trinity to set up the International Commission for Penal Reconstruction and Development. But it was also a speech of mellow wisdom with an incisive touch of realism.[36] He had a gift, inestimable in public-minded men of quality, of detaching his views or prejudices from himself so as not to make them into impediments to action urged by others, well meaning and competent. He thus acknowledged that the time had come to put criminal science on the map in research and teaching and that Cambridge should play a prominent part in it. He found my approach congenial and, as the result of our many conversations, a relationship developed within which we could discuss a variety of problems and events while looking critically in each other's eyes and yet remaining good friends. Next to Turner he was the man who welcomed me to Cambridge and who over the years generously continued to give me his disinterested and well-meaning support. He succeeded Winfield as the chairman of our centre and this in itself was good for our cause. The former gave us confidence in ourselves and stability — qualities which we then urgently needed. The latter harnessed prestige and influence for our undertaking and he was, with his wide circle of connections in Cambridge and in London, exceptionally good at it.

I had outlined a scheme for a multi-volume *History of English Criminal Law and its Administration from 1750* which would go beyond its static and isolated study primarily grounded on the dogmatic interpretation of acts and omissions declared to be criminal transgressions. It would, instead, pursue an approach, much more basic and incomparably wider, which would look upon criminal law as an instrument of criminal policy aimed at the control of crime. It would regard the criminal law as a historical category evolving within the social, political and moral context of society, which themselves by their very nature were far from being immutable. Hollond, after perusal of my outline and a talk about it with me, emphasized how important it was not to underestimate the magnitude and complexity of such an undertaking. Even so, he was firmly convinced that it should be undertaken, a view which both Winfield and Turner unreservedly endorsed. All three agreed that substantial support was needed to launch the attempt if it were to have a reasonable chance of success, support which it was vain to expect the

---

36 See Pamphlet Series (March 1942), pp. 26–9.

university or the Law Faculty to provide. Consequently, at least the initial involvement by an outside source of high standing and dependability was imperative.

Lord Macmillan, who at that time was the Chairman of the Pilgrim Trust, was approached. He asked for the outline of the first volume, *The Movement for Reform*, as well as for my article in the *Cambridge Law Journal* on the Blue Books, and the anticipated expenditure in relation to the first volume. Soon afterwards he informed us that he proposed to put the matter on the agenda of the forthcoming meeting of the trustees. Their decision was positive, but they also said that, in view of the novelty of the project, they would welcome the setting up of a standing committee. The chairman of that committee was Viscount Maugham (a former Lord Chancellor) and its members were Lord Wright, Lord Simonds (a former Lord Chancellor), Sir Arnold D. McNair (afterwards Lord McNair), Professor Sir Percy Winfield, Professor H.A. Hollond and J.W.C. Turner (also acting as secretary). This proved to be a very enjoyable experience. No formal meetings were convened by the committee but its members used to meet with me individually from time to time over tea or lunch, usually in London in the House of Lords. I hasten to add that I was left with a completely free hand in my research and writing: their purpose was simply to give me encouragement, to help me in any way I wished, and to take notice of the progress made. Lord Maugham (as befitted a brother of Somerset Maugham) was very keen on the way in which the formidable material I was handling was presented.

There was no single place where I could find all the necessary material but the libraries I needed were close at hand and very hospitable. The University of Cambridge Library allowed one to take books out (five at a time) and Lord Acton's collection was also valuable. There were plenty of old books in the Squire Law Library. But, even so, I had to go hunting in London and there the British Museum and the library of the London School of Economics never disappointed me. Like so many others, I was deeply grateful to Carlyle for having lost patience with the British Museum and so bringing into being that admirable institution, the London Library, of which I became an eternally grateful member. As I went along I built up a collection on many aspects of English history and soon found myself surrounded by 3,000 books of my own.

This was one of the most satisfying periods in my life, but also one of the most exacting for it demanded categorical concentration, sometimes accompanied by despair that the task would never end or end in chaos and defeat. When, in 1946, the moment came and the manuscript of 1,125 typed pages carefully packed went to my amiable London publisher, the late Hilary Stevens, I felt a terrifying emptiness taking hold of me: that ceaseless challenge which, for every single day of five years had made me curious and happy about what I might come across and try to write about, was no longer there. Although physically I felt much more comfortable, emotionally I felt nearly drained. I am referring to a stage which occurred half a century ago and I am aware that I should be restrained and economical in my references to it. And yet I cannot omit certain facts because they are an integral part of this account as a whole.

Lord Macmillan declared that the Pilgrim Trust would like the book to appear under its auspices – and it did – and that he would be happy to write a preface – which he did. It was a wonderful piece, four pages long, rich in mellow wisdom, and one which would warm the heart of any author. This first volume of the *History*, *The Movement for Reform*, appeared in 1948 and the eighty-odd reviews which my publisher showed me contained many review-articles contributed by distinguished scholars and public figures of the period. The tone was invariably laudatory and encouraging. Sometimes, as was inevitable in the case of a volume of this range and size and with such extensive supportive material, a few mistakes crept in here and there. But those who noticed them kindly went out of their way to praise the innovative features of the enterprise as a whole. One reason for the exceptional reception accorded to the volume was that the story it tried to retrace was so dramatic and so singular. Another reason was that, for the first time, an attempt had been made on a large scale to study the criminal law of England at a critical and controversial stage of its evolution as a social and political institution moulded by deeper forces. And yet another reason was, if I may be somewhat personal, that this dissection which went so sharply into the very core of the history of England, had been undertaken by somebody intrinsically and initially so alien to it. And my age was still in my favour: I was forty-two when the volume appeared.

George Trevelyan selected it as the book of the year, as important from a historical point of view as it was from the legal point of view, and praised its language. The Harvard Law School affixed to it its most coveted scientific award and I became the third recipient from Britain of the James Barr Ames Prize and Medal. When Thorsten Sellin retired as the General Secretary of the International Penal Commission, its leaders presented him with the volume, the second opening page of which bears their signatures. The Rockefeller Foundation most generously decided to provide the funds necessary for the next three volumes.

Harry Hollond, as the Chairman of the Law Faculty, had earlier asked me to give him a copy of my manuscript to put before the Appointments Committee of the Law Faculty and a copy which he, as Vice-Master of Trinity, would pass to Trevelyan. Soon afterwards two events took place which had a lasting and profound impact on my life. In 1946 I was appointed Assistant Director of Research in Criminal Science in the Faculty of Law and two years later (1948) I was elected into a fellowship of Trinity, also under a special category which allowed me, indeed which expected me, to concentrate on research with the same object in view. I was deeply proud and infinitely happy that the first volume of the *History* carried both posts on its title page.

Three years later, in 1951, the degree of Doctor of Laws was conferred upon me by the university. When, at the last fitting of my robe, I asked the well-known Cambridge cutter how I looked in it, the old man replied with some hesitation: 'Well Sir, with your dark complexion, black eyes and the rich red robe you look like Robespierre.' And when I told Trevelyan this episode, when he inquired how my doctorate was proceeding, his comment was: 'Rubbish, Robespierre had blue eyes.' More importantly, Cecil Turner, my dear comrade in arms, was also made a Doctor of Laws, a distinction which gave much pleasure to his family and to his friends (see Plate 7).

In 1949 the University of Cambridge established a Department of Criminal Science as part of the Law Faculty, with a more widely constituted committee of management. The department consisted of a director, assistant director of research, senior research officer and a secretary. All these posts had been accepted as a fixed academic responsibility of the university and the directorship had also been made, by special regulation, a teaching post.

On the recommendation of Dr Morris Ginsberg, and after I had interviewed him at length on two occasions, F.H. McClintock was invited to become the first Research Officer. His association with us, extending over twenty-five years, brought many fruitful benefits to criminology in Cambridge. From Assistant Director of Research, Fellow and Tutor of Churchill College, he moved in 1973 to Edinburgh as the first Professor of Criminology where he laid the foundations for a lively and active centre. He was not only my close collaborator but also a very dear friend and I know that I shall, as long as I live, continue to mourn his passing away in 1994. We were also fortunate that Derick McClintock gathered around him at the department research associates and consultants to help him with his various inquiries such as Miss N.G. Savill, J.H. Bagot, James (later Sir James) Nursaw and Mrs Monica Walker, the noted social statistician.

But research had to be supported by outside funds. Slowly empirical studies began to emerge: *The Results of Probation* (which in my view was too severely criticized), *Detention in Remand Homes*, and a major inquiry into *Sexual Offences*. Parallel to this, the series *English Studies in Criminal Science* was enriched by several notable volumes. The Squire Law Library offered hospitality in two of its rooms.

This was the culmination of never faltering efforts on the long road which had lasted a full decade. It had never ceased to be exhilarating, but it was not always free from stress and disappointments. This is how it should have been, for nothing durable and worthy should be achieved in life on the cheap. The added considerable satisfactions were the spirit and the loyalties which animated the small group who believed in the cause and acted accordingly.

The commitment of Cambridge evoked at the time considerable interest in Britain and abroad. The opening paragraph of a letter written to me by an old friend, Jean-André Roux (Professor of Criminal Law in Strasbourg and subsequently a judge of the Supreme Court of France) – an ardent Frenchman but also a staunch anglophile – was as follows: 'Cher ami, you have reached the harbour. Never fail to appreciate it and never try to abandon it.'

8

PUTTING CRIMINOLOGY ON THE NATIONAL MAP

Mr Butler takes charge of the Home Office

On Monday, 14 January 1957, Mr R.A. Butler was gazetted to the post of Home Secretary and Leader of the House of Commons, while retaining the office of Lord Privy Seal. This was not his preference. He wanted the Foreign Office and he told the Prime Minister so, but Harold Macmillan decided otherwise. This was possibly the lowest ebb in Butler's long political career, he was tired and looked tired, and in the circumstances it was natural that he should lean towards a stage in public office, further away from rivalries and tensions, stimulating and civilized.

The last thing he wanted was to be posted to a potential minefield. He knew the machinery of the government all too well and the turbulence of political life to have any illusions about it. Dining a few nights later at the Beefsteak Club, he records in his Memoirs:[1]

> I was reminded by a bright spark that Home Secretaries scarcely ever become Prime Ministers. But since the exceptions include Melbourne and Churchill, this 'rule' need depress no incumbent; nor was I ever Home Secretary *tout court*.

(I am rather puzzled why he should have omitted Sir Robert Peel.) And a few pages later he commented:[2]

> Of course, even for unadventurous spirits the Home Office can never provide a rest cure. It is a residuary legatee of every problem of internal government not specifically assigned to some other department, and many of these problems are politically sensitive, straddling the controversial borderline between liberty and order.

---

1 *The Art of the Possible* (1971), p. 196.
2 *Ibid.*, p. 198.

It is interesting to compare this with the views held by Lady Thatcher on the same subject, some two decades later:

> Home Secretaries never do have an easy time: it is sometimes said that they possess a unique combination of responsibility without power, taking the blame for matters ranging from breaches of royal security, to the misdemeanours of police officers, prison break-outs and the occasional riot, when their power to prevent them is indirect or non-existent.[3]

There seemed always to have been foul weather in the Home Office. Thus, in 1957 a distinguished departmental committee published a report (widely known as the Wolfenden Report) recommending a change in the law relating to prostitution and homosexuality. Butler asked his new Parliamentary Under-Secretary David Renton (afterwards Lord Renton and a Minister of State) to take charge of the Bill giving effect to the committee's recommendations, only to be told that he would gladly take charge of the prostitution part of the Bill but not the part relating to homosexuality 'because conscience would not allow him to do so with the first part on the homosexuals'.

Again the Home Secretary was greatly relieved when the Street Offences Act 1959 was passed, only to be tainted by a harsh attack launched against him by the Association for Moral and Social Hygiene, of which he was a Vice-President, on the ground that he had shamefully neglected the responsibility of men in prostitution, an attack particularly painful to Rab Butler because the Association was founded by Josephine Butler, the great Victorian social reformer and a relative of his. The discontent continued to be so strong that it left him no alternative but to resign his vice-presidency.

And to continue: 'Let him be a man and bring back corporal punishment for young offenders', exclaimed a 'mild-looking, motherly, Mrs Ruby Forth' at the Annual Conservative Women's Conference held in 1961 at the Central Hall, Westminster. The connection between a man's virility and his belief in flogging had hardly ever been so vociferously and crudely reiterated. And the unshaken credence that there is a positive causal relationship between lacerated posteriors of adult and young delinquents and a substantial and durable reduction of crime continued to be eagerly held, evoking highly pitched passions. Butler's stand on the matter led to severe criticisms, indeed to hardly veiled derision, in many influential Tory circles.

Capital punishment, always a tricky business, was incomparably much more so in those days. It had haunted Samuel Hoare mercilessly, but as I

---

3   Margaret Thatcher, *The Downing Street Years* (1993), p. 307.

have already mentioned, he found an ingenious escape route (see p. 106). In the case of Rab Butler it provided nothing but a chronic severe headache. Already in 1956, following the execution of John Christie and Timothy Evans, Butler was called upon to reply to Sydney Silverman's impressive attempt to get rid of the death penalty. In delivering a vigorous speech in favour of retaining it he had uttered the imprudent remark that no innocent man within living memory had been hanged and rounded it off by warning that life imprisonment – the only alternative – was incomparably more cruel.

Subsequently he gave his support to the messy attempt introduced by the Homicide Act 1957 to define degrees of murder in their ascendant villainy in order to distinguish capital murders from those which would not be punishable by death. Whether it was correct to point out, as the *Sunday Telegraph* did, that in effect he had been responsible for sending to the gallows more condemned-to-death offenders than any other post-war Home Secretary (quoted by Anthony Howard – the author of the thorough and attractively written biography of Butler on which I have drawn for several facts recorded here),[4] I am unable to confirm. Even if this were true, it would not mean much unless the comparative 'quality' of the cases had been convincingly analysed. But it would certainly appear that in the exercise of the Royal Prerogative of Mercy he showed no weakness: of the nineteen capital sentences he had to consider by the summer of 1959 he had commuted only eight. In his autobiography Butler throws no light on the cases in which execution followed, only on one or two for which he ordered that the law should not take its course. The ambiguous situation aggravated by the Homicide Act did not prevent Lord Parker, then the Lord Chief Justice, to criticize the Home Secretary on a public occasion at home and, what was much more unusual, in the course of his official visit to Canada, for his unsatisfactory attitude towards corporal and capital punishment. This, in its turn, encouraged many unpleasant criticisms of Butler in the Commons, particularly from members of his own party, or, more correctly, as his biographer stated, from 'his most natural supporters within the Tory Party'.

His hesitancy to come out one way or another was still there. At an important Conservative National Conference he resolutely and successfully opposed a strongly urged motion to extend capital punishment. But again, although he acknowledged that 'for the first time my own belief, now generally accepted, that a jury would not have convicted Evans in later days when they knew all the truth about Christie', he nevertheless refused to reopen the case of Timothy Evans.[5] Evans was posthumously granted a free pardon from the Queen on the advice of Roy Jenkins on 18 October 1966.

---

[4] Anthony Howard, *Rab: The Life of R.A. Butler* (1987), p. 273.
[5] R.A. Butler, *The Art of the Possible*, p. 202.

Another quotation cannot be ignored: 'By the end of my time at the Home Office', Butler writes, 'I began to see that the system could not go on, and present-day Secretaries of State are well relieved of the terrible power to decide between life and death.' It is somewhat surprising that a man of his superior intelligence and with full access to the massive evidence available in the Home Office needed so much time to reach this conclusion. Samuel Hoare, William Whitelaw and Douglas Hurd were much more forthright about it, and this in spite of the fact that their Prime Ministers were convinced retentionists. Alistair Horne informs us that 'while Rab constantly agonised over capital punishment, Macmillan admitted that he was against abolition', adding 'I don't remember Dorothy ever expressing views . . . it was not her kind of interest'.[6]

It may well be that Butler felt that the time was still not ripe for a total abolition of capital punishment; that an uncompromising insistence on this radical departure might endanger his new plans for a wider penal reform; that in the end a sagacious adherence to *The Art of the Possible* would yield better all-round results. Yet in the mean time his zigzags did not appear very alluring. In the end it would seem that to gauge where he stood one would have had to toss a coin for ever. At the same time the view was widely spread that *au fond* Mr Butler was a 'hidden' or 'secret' abolitionist. As a consequence, both camps were inclined to join hands in accusing him of equivocation and of lack of the essential governmental gift of decision at the very top when issues of deep import are involved.

The relationship with the Prime Minister could also not be ignored. Mr Macmillan was much more interested in the use of power and the influence which emanated from it than in matters of social policy. There was a time when he had been genuinely involved in a vital domestic policy issue with a component both social and electoral. I refer to his exceptionally successful Housing Crusade. However, this had been a long time ago, and anyhow, even under the most propitious of circumstances, no such dividend could be expected from embracing the cause of penal reform. But there was a more basic fact noted by his observant and sensitive biographer:

> Throughout the copious Macmillan diaries, with all their multifold interests, there is so conspicuously little reference to social reforms – urgently as many were needed – that one is entitled to reckon that they assumed a relatively low position in Macmillan's list of priorities.[7]

Butler could have had at the Home Office a quiet, comfortable life. With his

---

6   Alistair Horne, *Macmillan*, vol. 2 *(1957–86)* (1989), p. 81.
7   *Ibid.*, p. 81.

stately figure, deliberate manner of talking and impeccable traditional family background, he looked a part of it. He fitted the impressive old building in Whitehall and you could see him sitting in the huge room of the Secretary of State behind a cumbersome desk, near the Victorian fireplace, behaving like a lord of the manor. And even if he were not to do much, it would still be so much more than the exceptionally mediocre record of his predecessor, Gwilym Lloyd George (afterwards First Viscount Tenby). But, as a matter of fact, he wanted to do a lot and have it accomplished with invigorating speed. He wanted to revive the creative, forward-looking atmosphere generated by his great Education Act 1944.

He resolves to become a reforming Home Secretary

On 27 June 1958 Butler sent a rather attractive letter to Macmillan. He acknowledged that he had found the work in the Home Office 'most congenial and rewarding. In its quaint and graceful traditions, and the variety of its problems, the Home Office is unique among Government Departments.' But he continued:

> all is not steeped in history; and the longer I remain here, the more it is borne in upon me that the main part of my duty consists in taking what steps I can to carry out long overdue reforms in our penal system.

Indeed, what he had in mind was 'to press forward a comprehensive plan of penal reform'. The answer, as might have been expected, was positive but it lacked real understanding and warmth: 'and I take it,' stated Macmillan, 'it will mostly be the building of new prisons, but they will take some time, especially if the Ministry of Works have anything to do with the plans'.[8] In this context Butler referred in his Memoirs to Macmillan's 'indulgent scepticism'. Macmillan, himself, acknowledged that 'with regard to the Home Office there could be no doubt Butler was an excellent Minister and in addition led the House with conspicuous talent'. And he added, 'We had worked most successfully and loyally together during these troubled years'.[9] In effect, there was much more to it than that. There was an intense rivalry between the two men which even the tradition of well-known English good manners could not have hidden or diverted for long. Horne provides an incisive glimpse which goes far to illuminate the 'darker sides' of this very complex and increasingly painful relationship.[10] It is neither unfair nor unreasonable

---

8 This exchange of letters is reproduced in full by Howard, *Rab*, pp. 263–4.
9 Harold Macmillan, *Pointing the Way, 1959–1961* (1972), p. 17.
10 Horne, *Macmillan*, vol. 1, *1894–1956* (1988), pp. 296–8.

to guess that should something serious have gone wrong with Butler's 'comprehensive plan of penal reform' and he had turned to the Prime Minister for help, he would most likely have met with rather lukewarm support.

At that time any such anticipations or speculations were out of place simply because Mr Butler decided to become a truly reforming Home Secretary. This appeared unmistakably clear when, barely two months after he took office (on 11 March 1957), he made a weighty and eloquent statement during Supplementary Estimates for the Prison Commissioners,[11] and more incisively and comprehensively when, two years later (more exactly on 2 February 1959), a White Paper, *Penal Practice in a Changing Society*, was published under his authority.[12]

The programme consisted of two thrusts: penal reform and criminological research. Its significance consisted in the fact that, for the first time, their interdependence was laid bare. In substance this was a continuation of the socio-liberal model of criminal policy pursued with vigour and imagination some thirty years earlier. And this continuation, remarkable as it would have been under any circumstances, was so much more remarkable in the 1960s for, as it was so pointedly conveyed by the opening paragraph of the authoritative White Paper:

> It is a disquieting feature of our society that, in the years since the war, rising standards in material prosperity, education and social welfare have brought no decrease in the high rate of crime reached during the war: on the contrary, crime has increased and is still increasing. The purpose of this Paper is first to give the facts about this situation, then to set out proposals of the Government for dealing with some of its aspects. This Paper does not seek to deal with those deep-seated causes which, even were they fully understood, would be largely beyond the reach of Government action.

That in such unfavourable circumstances a reforming zeal should still be endorsed, and for that matter by a Conservative administration, was very unusual indeed. Nor should it be forgotten that it would not have happened but for Mr Butler. I do not like to indulge in gratuitous generalizations, yet I firmly believe that it would have been found virtually impossible to seek out another prominent political figure of the ruling party who at that time would have evinced the desire and the courage to be the captain of such a hazardous enterprise.

It is also fair to say that the Labour opposition had not tried to make political capital out of it and went out of their way to express admiration for

---

11 Mr Butler's speech in *Parl. Debates*, HC, vol. 566 (1956–7), cols 1140–206 and 1140–55.
12 Cmnd 645 (1959).

the Conservative Home Secretary. 'Certainly,' stated Anthony Greenwood, 'the tone of [the Home Secretary's] speech and the breadth of the canvas that he has painted has shown that we have great grounds for believing that he will live up to the high expectations that we have of him.' And he added significantly: 'I do not think that this is a subject which will create any very pronounced party differences.' 'After listening to the agreeable speech of Mr Anthony Greenwood,' stated another Member of the House, 'and especially after the very liberal speech made by the Home Secretary, I do not think that there will be any feeling of the party in the Committee.' There seemed to be no end to congratulations so effusive as to become politically embarrassing. 'We welcome with great warmth', stated another Member of the House,

> the statement made by the Home Secretary today. He brought new imagination to the subject, and new hope to those who have been advocating the cause of prison reform. If he will only implement the speech which he made to-day he will add another to crown his political career ... It is not a work which will gain any votes from anybody. It is a completely non-party matter.[13]

The penal reform aspect of Butler's programme formed a very important and substantial chapter in the penal history of this country but as such is outside the scope of this book, yet to ignore it would be a mistake. Suffice it to state that it encompassed both young and adult offenders, first offenders, occasional offenders, persistent offenders and those with psychiatric and psychological problems. Recognizing that sentencing should be the unfettered responsibility of the courts, it nevertheless promised to adopt measures which would cut the proportion of short sentences and deal with that part of the prison population which could be and should be avoided by adequate alternatives. It proposed the setting up of a series of new institutions or remodelling of some of the old ones. Remand and attendance centres, detention centres, Borstal, preventive detention, all were brought under a critical, but constructive review. Changes in the regime of all kinds of institution were envisaged to infuse a broader humanity and purposefulness into them, including work, earnings, education and medical services. The reorganization and the strengthening of the system and procedures regarding discharge and after-care were put on the agenda. An urgently needed building programme for new institutions was adopted as a long-term commitment and a start was

---

13 *Parl. Debates*, HC, vol. 566 (1957), cols 1153, 1165. At the time, a stir was produced by an open letter to the Home Secretary, filling several pages of the *New Statesman and Nation* (2 February 1957), pp. 135–41, on 'Prisons and Prisoners' written by C.H. Rolph, a former Chief Inspector of Police. A few years later I had the pleasure of asking him to give a seminar on the postgraduate course. He continued to be as refreshing and controversial as before. He died in 1994; see obituary notice in *The Times* (12 and 14 March 1994).

made. This combination of measures was aimed to raise the status of prison officers. There was to be an increase in the size of the prison staff so as to ensure three shifts of duty, a rise in their remuneration across all ranks, a more sophisticated process of selection of new members, and the setting up of a regular consultative committee between the prison staff and the governing centre. This was the time when the specific identity of the Prison Commissioners was still preserved, shortly before they became subsumed within the huge and inevitably largely depersonalized machinery of the Home Office.

The second and parallel thrust aimed at the promotion of proper, and properly used, criminological research. Mr Butler's speeches in Parliament, his other public pronouncements, and the recommendations of his commanding White Paper, provided unmistakable evidence that an important resolve had been made and speedy steps would be taken to implement it. Henceforth criminological research was to be regarded as an integral part of the criminal policy pursued by the Home Office. It was not to consist of disconnected inquiries, more or less casually launched and carried out, but it was, as a matter of routine, to underlie any significant penal moves whether of change, retrenchment or innovation. Nor was the research to be of exclusively official origin, but should be supplemented and encouraged in a systematic way by independent, non-official, preferably academic quarters.

Not unlike Samuel Hoare before him, Butler expressed his great appreciation of the senior Home Office staff and singled out Sir Charles Cunningham, the new Permanent Under-Secretary of State, Sir Lionel Fox (Chairman of the Prison Commission), Arthur Peterson (later Sir Arthur Peterson, Chairman of the Prison Commission and later Permanent Under-Secretary of State) and T.A. Critchley, the historian of the police. They provided the assistance, but Butler gave the indispensable direction. I was told that the White Paper passed through three or four drafts. I was of course very curious to know who was the main draftsman of a document which stands out so prominently because of its conciseness, precision, imagination and skilful presentation of several controversial aspects. The first three officials referred to by Butler were friends of long standing and well-proven trust. I used to meet them quite often but I would have never attempted to ask any one of them to provide the answer and they, in their turn, were too faithful to the proper Civil Service etiquette to satisfy my inquisitiveness.

Mr Butler did not rise to the Churchillian grandiloquence so avidly quoted by penal reformers or Home Secretaries – particularly when in distress – for he was neither a scintillating orator nor a disarming actor. But his modest, unadorned reflection has a moving, genuine and wise ring about it which will stand well the test of time:

> This is, of course, one of the most intensely and immensely varied problems which come within the sphere of my responsibility, that is

to say, the problem of the way in which society should treat offenders against its own laws. It is a problem as old as society itself, and I am aware that to-day I cannot give any final answer to it, because the problem changes as society changes. Each of us, in our own generation, must attempt to find a solution acceptable in terms of our own human understanding and our own store of knowledge and experience.[14]

It properly ends this section.

Criminological research built into the Home Office

'This is the biggest initial shock which has come to me in examining the problem', declared Mr Butler in the Commons when it transpired that only about £12,000 had been spent on research since 1948 when expenditure under this heading was authorized by statutory authority. And he continued: 'I acknowledge straight away that this is quite unsatisfactory' and he uttered the promise that 'on this vital question of research [it is] my intention of giving it a first priority in the administration of the prisons throughout England and Wales'. By 1955–6 the total expenditure was still only £2,500 a year. It is remarkable how many voluntary researchers up and down the country had shown courage, devotion and perseverance in embarking upon intricate and frequently very tedious investigations in the dire circumstances then prevailing. I recommend a perusal of Appendix B of the White Paper, *Penal Practice in a Changing Society*, which catalogues these efforts.[15] Many of those explorers have passed away but some are still alive and active. They all deserve even more recognition than they have received up till now.

This neglect of support for research was not to reoccur: that was beyond doubt. 'It is now', stated the White Paper most emphatically, 'widely recognised that in this field research is as essential as in the fields of science and technology.' For a minister of Butler's status the easiest thing would have been to urge the Treasury to authorize larger funds for this purpose. But this would have been a palliative, of a more or less transitory nature, hiding or ignoring the much more fundamental and enduring principle involved in the matter. There was a gap in the very structure of the Home Office in terms of organization and administration, indicative of a certain lack of vision, which called for remedy. This no doubt was in Rab Butler's mind when in May 1957 he announced the formation of the Home Office Research Unit. It then consisted of two research workers and four civil servants with a total budget

---

14 *Parl. Debates*, HC, vol. 566 (1956–7), col. 1141.
15 Cmnd 645 (1959), pp. 29–32.

of a few thousand pounds a year. By 1959 the Unit was carrying out some eighteen inquiries. At that time it was a truly pioneering initiative, perhaps not the first of its kind, but certainly one of the first. My notes, imperfect as they are, suggest that an important centre was already then functioning in the Ministry of Justice of Japan.

Its first head was T.S. Lodge. He was neither a sociologist, nor a criminologist or penologist, but an actuarial statistician. This may appear strange, but it worked out satisfactorily. He was aware that he might be regarded as a wolf with sharp teeth playing a guitar trying to prove the superiority of statistical methods over precedents, wider knowledge and common sense. By nature, as well as by reasoning, he was cautious, hesitant, tactful, over-humble. He was also inherently bureaucratic. His integrity and high sense of duty could not be impugned even by those who were likely to become impatient with his much too long suspended decisions. But at this stage of this unusual and bold departure he was in many ways the right kind of man. Perhaps he may have stayed too long, but in the course of the tenure of his office he did a lot of good. The solidity of the man was transparent in the two pieces he wrote, one in the volume of essays in my honour,[16] and another in Lord Longford's book, a rare occasion when he went 'public' and gave his views on criminal statistics as an instrument for assessing trends in crime.[17] Alongside him, Leslie Wilkins provided the vital energy, ideas and expertise that were necessary to launch a significant programme of research. At the age of eighty-two, he is still busy and the publication of a Festschrift, edited by Don Gottfredson and Ronald Clarke, gave much pleasure to his many admirers.[18]

Later on, when the Unit had grown considerably, John Croft became its head. Cultivated (Christ Church, Oxford), with the attractive hobby of painting, his vision was wider and his approach more subtle than that of Lodge. He was also a successful empire builder in extending the size and facilities of the Unit. A faithful conservative with a strong liberal bent, he continued on his retirement in the Isle of Man to expound his views on a variety of penal matters.[19] With both of them my relations were steady and friendly and on

---

16 'The Founding of the Home Office Research Unit', in Roger Hood (ed.) *Crime, Criminology and Public Policy* (1974), pp. 11–24.
17 See 'Letter from T.S. Lodge, Home Office Statistical Adviser', appendix to Lord Pakenham, *Causes of Crime* (1958), pp. 183–93.
18 See Don M. Gottfredson and Ronald V. Clarke (eds) *Policy and Theory in Criminal Justice: Contributions in Honour of Leslie T. Wilkins* (1990).
19 While at the Home Office Croft published five reports in the *Home Office Research Studies Series*, beginning with *Research in Criminal Justice*, Research Study no. 44 (1978) and ending with *Concerning Crime*, Research Study no. 75 (1983). Since then he has published privately a number of papers, such as *Croft on Crime: Reflections on Conservative Policy* (1990) and *Managing Criminal Justice* (1991).

more than one occasion they took me into their confidence when they felt the need to obtain an outside view of somebody with no axe to grind about some of their objectives.

The Unit was expected to fulfil nine objectives. First, to carry out any *ad-hoc* research and present its findings in response to the Home Secretary's requirements. Second, to provide data needed by the Home Secretary for answers to Parliamentary Questions. Third, to do the same when asked by the other ministers assigned to the Home Office. Fourth, to do the same when proposed by a senior member of the Home Office staff, or more precisely by a head of one of the departments concerned with an important issue which needed some further factual elucidation. Fifth, to supply information to a Royal Commission, departmental committee or advisory body – a request which usually had to be approved by the Home Secretary or senior officials. Sixth, to advise the latter when they themselves were called upon to appear before such external bodies. Seventh, to help the Home Office in taking up positions in national or international conferences, seminars, or in their dealings with international organizations. Eighth, on its own initiative to explore a subject which the Unit felt called for a more systematic, thorough elucidation: these initiatives, however, as a general rule required approval from the Head of the Criminal Department of the Home Office, of which the Unit was an administrative part. Ninth, to enlist the interest of some external centres (usually academic institutions or individual researchers) and to provide them with financial support as well as accessibility to needed material. Initially it was anticipated that the research funds would be shared on a fifty-fifty basis between in-house and external projects, but as the years have passed by a radical shift towards internal officially sponsored research has taken place and I shall have more to say about it later on (pp. 458–459).

Tremendous changes have taken place in the life of the Unit since Rab Butler's initiative, taken some four decades ago. To start off its very title has changed in a significant way: it now goes under the name of the Home Office Research and Statistics Directorate. Its expansion has been truly stupendous. By 1995 it consisted of 81 social researchers, scientists and statisticians supported by 165 other staff. The total budget for 1995–6 amounted to nearly £14 million, of which over £4.5 million was allocated for research projects. Of this, 40 per cent (£1.9 million) was for inquiries conducted internally by members of the Unit; 33 per cent (£1.5 million) for external research; 10 per cent (£462,000) for the British Crime Survey; and the remainder for computer capital and other expenses.[20] Today, in 1998, when I cast my eyes at the shelves of my library, I can see at least 185

---

20 I am very grateful to Christopher Nuttall, Director of Research and Statistics at the Home Office, for providing me with this information in 1995.

documents originating from the Unit, and this is by no means everything that has been published.

They are diverse in content and presentation and easily fall into distinctive types. Those with a more durable substance from which a deeper impact is expected; those prepared with the view to making certain aspects of criminal matters more easily assimilated and understood; those calling attention to, or emphasizing, the topicality of certain issues or options in criminal policy; those recording the findings of an *ad-hoc* research project; those monitoring specific problems deserving some further elucidation. And quite recently yet other regular publications were added, the *Research Bulletin* and *Research Findings*, which present in the simplest possible manner and a non-technical, attractive language the findings of some of the investigations carried out or supported by the Unit. This was no doubt launched in the hope that some of the senior civil servants in the Home Office burdened by the unending weight of their administrative duties, and indeed some of the ministers themselves, much less interested in criminal policy than in policy *tout court* and often with preconceived views of, and a deeply ingrained impatience with, the 'criminology thing', may yet find time to glance at these more popularized and simplified attempts to convey the essence and importance of the research findings.

Today unquestionably the Unit is the leading institution of its kind in the world, if its appraisal is based, as it should be, on its size, scope, quality of output and financial resources put at its disposal. But since its inception so much has changed in criminological thinking, in the state of crime, and in the directions taken by criminal policy, that the Unit is ripe for a major informative and critical stock-taking of the first fifty years of its existence.

The grounding of independent criminological research and teaching

The initial step

This initiative calls for a special comment. An influential bureaucrat would be inclined to keep the whole field of research, where there is so much to hide and so little to boast about, within the orbit of his exclusive determination. This, however, was not in the making of Mr Butler and he went out of his way to stress how vital it was to secure the independence of outside criminological research, and so did his senior Home Office advisers.

> Research [it was declared in the White Paper] is not necessarily best conducted by official agencies. The outlook, training, and environment of the academic worker give him advantages in some kinds of research over the staff of a Governmental Department. On the other hand, a Department in daily practical touch with the realities of

penal treatment, and with contacts and access to data not available to outside workers, has its own distinctive contribution to make. The work that is being done and planned is therefore being shared between academic and official agencies working closely together. In this new advance, the Home Office has taken a lead. It has set up a Research Unit and assists from its own vote research work being done elsewhere.[21]

I do not wish in any way to appear to diminish the role played by Mr Butler in bringing criminology into the Home Office. It was a remarkably innovative development. But it was not one which a Home Secretary of his national stature would have found particularly difficult to put into effect, providing he sincerely and firmly believed in it. It would have been very difficult indeed for the Prime Minister or the Treasury to block it. It was an altogether different matter to introduce criminology into the academic world. The universities of Britain guarded jealously their independence and looked with a particularly vigilant, if not hostile, eye at any interference from outside, however benevolent and disinterested the motivation might happen to be. And the more influential a minister of the crown was, the more stringent and concentrated would be the suspicion aroused by his intervention.

There was a strong case for governmental intervention, but it had to be deployed with utmost tact and delicate touch. Fortunately, in this instance, the first public step came from an unmistakably unofficial quarter, and yet one well qualified to take it up. At that time the Howard League for Penal Reform was at the height of its influence, being led by Margery Fry, George Benson and Hugh Klare. It seized the moment. Its proposal relating to the development of criminology was postulated in a letter from Hugh Klare, in his capacity of Secretary of the League, addressed to Mr Butler on 25 June 1952. It was a good letter, well constructed, persuasive and dignified. Its objective was to promote the establishment of a chair of criminology and of an Institute of Criminology. 'We are encouraged to approach you in this matter because of the interest you are showing in criminological research, and because of your past service to education. No one could speak with greater authority than yourself.' There was a pointed urgency about it because the subject was 'in some danger of disappearing with the actual or eventual retirement of a few well-known criminologists'. The critical condition prevailing in Britain was contrasted with 'most continental countries [which] have one or more Institutes of Criminology, and even small universities have chairs in criminology'. The letter, characteristic of the then

---

21 *Penal Practice in a Changing Society*, Cmnd 645 (1959), para. 18, p. 5.

prevailing climate of public opinion, evoked immediately favourable comments in the leading national newspapers, such as *The Times* (1 July 1957), *Manchester Guardian* (1 July) and *Observer* (30 June).

Barely three weeks after the publication of the Letter a meeting was arranged for Miss Fry and Lord Drogheda to see the Home Secretary. It may well be that this was the first time that Lord Drogheda had heard of criminology, but it was a wise move on the part of Miss Fry to ask him to come along. As both Chairman of Committees of the House of Lords and Chairman of the Home Office Advisory Council on the Treatment of Offenders, he naturally inspired much public confidence. Mr Butler's response was most encouraging. He recognized that 'in a matter of this importance the initiative ought perhaps to come from Her Majesty's Government' and he promised to give it his 'fullest and careful consideration'. And in November he 'went public' on this subject in a most emphatic manner. He appeared at the League's annual general meeting in London, paid tribute to it for having taken up this matter, and declared:

> I intend through various contacts to see that this proposal will be obviously considered, not just by the Government, because it was not primarily our business, but by the Universities. Crime and its treatment seems to me to be no less suitable as a subject for study and teaching by the Universities than a number of other social phenomena.

To emphasize the importance he attached to this proposal he asked Sir Charles Cunningham, the Permanent Under-Secretary of State, and Francis Graham-Harrison, the Assistant Under-Secretary in charge of the Criminal Division, to undertake all the necessary explorations and to report to him regularly about the progress made. With a high-powered reforming Home Secretary at the helm of an exceptionally strong department and a favourably disposed public opinion, conditions seemed to be ripe for a speedy and effective implementation of new ways to study crime and criminal justice within the academic context, and at a proper level. But it took no time, however, to see how erroneous and optimistic such assumptions would prove to be.

The first hurdle

From the very beginning of the discussions up to their very end, the Howard League's spokesmen and their many friends linked the idea of having an institute with its being located in London. 'When I visited Margery Fry,' wrote Lady Inskip to Mr Butler at the Home Office,

> a few weeks before her death [she died in 1958] the future Institute of Criminology was very much on her mind. She visualized such a

Centre in London, serving the world in a way neither Oxford nor Cambridge could do. She urged me to see you and press the claims of London. I promised to do so.

The advantages of London were obvious, undeniable and many. The reality of crime and its raw or digested material were there and would always be there. I was more than ready to concede that, at that time, the only crime for which Cambridge was nationally known was the theft of bicycles. The entrance doors to my house at Cranmer Road were usually left unlocked by day and very frequently by night. The metropolis, to recapitulate the well known, was the seat of the Home Office, with its statistical branch and the recently set up Research Unit; of the Lord Chancellor's department; of the office of the Director of Public Prosecutions; of the largest police force; of high courts, of magistrates' courts; of remand homes; of prisons of several kinds; and it was there that the parliamentary or public inquiries, relating to penal matters and criminal justice, as a general rule originated. The resources that could perhaps be mobilized by the powerful University of London for the study of the phenomenon of crime in its many aspects, through the Institute of Psychiatry, departments of sociology and demography, of psychology and medicine, of criminal and public law, were enormous. Nor was criminology unknown. Over a period of several years its foundation had been laid at the London School of Economics by Dr Hermann Mannheim, the first Reader in the subject, and a group of his pupils, still young but gifted, enthusiastic, and eager to continue, indeed to expand, the good work.

It was contended, and with a large measure of justification, that what Cambridge was able to offer stood in deprecatory contrast. It was true that the Department of Criminal Science, in spite of its record, not to be lightly ignored, did not yet have very much empirical work to its credit. Also it was an integral part of a Law School which deservedly enjoyed a high reputation, both scholastic and pedagogical, but was fundamentally a highly traditional, conventional body, which was bound to look upon criminology with distrust, if not with enmity. An Institute of Criminology, grafted upon the department, could not be expected to throw off these deeply rooted impediments and its future work could not fail to reflect a prominently juridical imprint. And, on top of it, there were no academic centres in Cambridge dedicated to social sciences or psychiatry. This was before Noel Annan (afterwards Lord Annan), the Provost of King's College, marshalled his forces to seed the roots for a modest advent of sociology. These were all very serious misgivings and apprehensions.

Hugh Klare, in his already quoted letter to the Home Secretary, had it all well planned. London was the appropriate place and if it were decided that 'London would be appropriate, then presumably the Institute would be part of the University of London. In such a case, representatives of Oxford, Cambridge, and other Universities interested in criminology would presumably be on the Board of Management.' The menu was smoothly settled but without the chef and hosts in sight. And, when after some rather embarrassing and unexplained delay in responding to Mr Butler's letter, the representatives of the Home Office were invited to meet the Vice-Chancellor, the Vice-Chancellor Designate, the Principal of the University and the Professors of Psychology and Psychiatry, it became abundantly clear almost at once that from the point of view of the University of London the project, to put it rather crudely but correctly, was an absolute non-starter. The two crucial documents are reproduced in my already quoted report on the Cambridge Institute.[22]

The arguments against it were forcefully stated by the Principal, Dr Logan (afterwards Sir Jack Logan), his central reservation being that institutes

> which cut across existing academic disciplines were extremely difficult to establish on a firm and living basis and had little, if any, prospect of success unless a really outstanding man could be found to serve as the first Director . . . Unfortunately, however, even if other obstacles could be overcome, it did not appear that any suitable person could be found among those at present engaged in relevant fields of study in London University. Dr Mannheim, who had recently retired, might be willing to return for five years, but it did not seem that he had the necessary qualities of personality for this post.

The contrast of Cambridge's response to an identical letter from the Home Secretary could not have been more striking. This was reflected in the attitude taken up by Lord Adrian, then the Vice-Chancellor of the University, Dr Harold Taylor, the Secretary-General of the Faculties (who played so prominent a part in establishing Churchill College), by Robert Rattenbury, the Registrary, and by Trevor Thomas, the Chairman of the Committee of Management of the Department of Criminal Science. I was asked to present a detailed memorandum on how I would envisage the establishment of an Institute of Criminology in the setting of Cambridge and in the light of the experience gained through the Department of Criminal Science. My memorandum was examined by the above-mentioned members of Cambridge University and, of course, the Home Office. On several occasions, I was also asked to appear before them to elucidate further some of my proposals or to answer supplementary questions connected with it. It would be tedious and unprofitable to record the exchange of correspondence or the series of meetings which followed, but I am bound to acknowledge that my memorandum

---

22 See Leon Radzinowicz, *The Cambridge Institute of Criminology: Its Background and Scope* (HMSO, 1988), pp. 8–10 and Appendices 2 and 3 at pp. 133–7.

emerged from this grilling surprisingly unscathed. The way was clear for a final ratification and reciprocal commitment. This took place in a meeting convened by Lord Adrian in Cambridge and followed by yet another exchange of views soon afterwards at the Home Office. 'We have made excellent progress in our discussions with Cambridge,' reported Sir Charles Cunningham to the Home Secretary, and Dr Taylor echoed the feeling of satisfaction and confidence, declaring that the necessary university legislation could be passed by October 1959. In reply to a question by Montgomery Hyde, MP (obviously prearranged), Mr Butler reported briefly, but most warmly and appreciatively, about the progress made in Cambridge.[23] 'You will see', stated Graham-Harrison in his note to Sir Lionel Fox, 'that it looks as though Cambridge would probably win the race.' And Sir Charles Cunningham was right in his report to Mr Butler: 'it seems clear, however, that if there is to be an Institute at all for some time to come it will have to be in Cambridge'.[24] Yet he underestimated the strength of dissatisfaction which would surface if this solution were adopted by describing it as 'some criticism'.

The disapproval could hardly have been more accentuated and more vociferous. Sir George Benson who, following Miss Fry's death, came to the forefront in these exploratory discussions, wrote to J.E.S. Simon (afterwards Lord Simon of Glaisdale), then at the Home Office, in a state of obvious despair: 'I am coming to the conclusion that you will have to look inside the Home Office, for I don't know where else you will find the necessary combination of academic experience, administrative ability and common sense. I have someone like Graham-Harrison in mind – and others as well.' And in a private note to Butler he said: 'I am sorry about the attitude of London University. But it cannot be helped.' In the course of an important debate in the Lords on 'Crime and Penal Practice' when references were made to a Criminology

---

23 Written Answers, *Parl. Debates*, HC, vol. 592, cols 178–9, 31 July 1958.
24 Professor David Garland states: 'Eventually the ISTD's emphasis on psychoanalysis, and its open hostility to much official penal policy, ensured that it remained essentially an outsider body, operating at arm's length from the Home Office and the Prison Commission. This outsider status forms an important background to the later decision of the Home Office to establish a criminological institute at Cambridge, rather than under ISTD auspices in London.' See his article 'Of Crimes and Criminals: the Development of Criminology in Britain', in M. Maguire, R. Morgan and R. Reiner (eds) *The Oxford Handbook of Criminology* (2nd edn, 1997), pp. 11–56, at p. 40. This statement needs to be corrected. First, the Institute was not 'established' by the Home Office. It was established as an independent academic department by the University of Cambridge after careful consideration in response to the initiative taken by the Home Office and with the decisive support of the Wolfson Foundation. Second, it would have been fatal to establish the first Institute of Criminology under the umbrella of the ISTD, an organization, as Garland himself acknowledges, so committed to the psychoanalytic approach. The views of members of the ISTD on penal policy, whatever they may have been, were never a factor in the discussion of where it would be best, at that time, to try to establish an Institute.

Institute at Cambridge, Lord Chorley (Professor of Law in the London School of Economics, editor of the *Modern Law Review*, and also a Justice of the Peace and Chairman of the Institute for the Study and Treatment of Delinquency (ISTD)) minced no words in damning the projected Cambridge enterprise: 'I could go into that matter at considerable length', he said, and although he did not, what he said was quite enough. 'What the Department at Cambridge has been largely doing is historical work, and work into the substantive law. As to criminological work it has not so far done a great deal.' The book on *Mental Abnormality and Crime* (which was praised by Lord Birkett in the course of the debate) 'is very good from certain points of view, but it has been severely criticised in other aspects'. And he concluded with this sombre prophecy: 'it is in fact going to be exceedingly difficult to get adequately good work done in Cambridge during the next few years'.[25]

Dr Hermann Mannheim, though by then retired, proved to be a most energetic opponent. Anything that happened to come from Cambridge was insignificant, flawed, indeed often glaringly erroneous and hence damaging to the cause of criminology.[26] But perhaps the most unfair was the attitude adopted by the *British Journal of Delinquency* (later *Criminology*) when the White Paper on *Penal Practice in a Changing Society* appeared containing a substantial paragraph on the projected Cambridge Institute. A single sentence of twenty-five words was devoted to it: 'in the same section', the *Journal* stated, 'there follows a paragraph on the Institute of Criminology to be established at Cambridge and on the advantages expected from it'.[27] As I stated a few years later in my *Report*: 'No examinations of its scope and purposes, no word of encouragement. It was as if it were an episode happening in a far away, hardly known country.' A sad finale, particularly because, at that stage, the future of criminology largely depended on what Cambridge would be able to make out of the opportunity which had come its way. Lord Birkett correctly assessed what would happen if this attitude of negation and isolation were to prevail. 'This Institute of Criminology,' he stated during the debates in the Lords, 'if it is to do any good at all must wish the co-operation of every kind of worker in the field of criminal administration or penal reform. The Judiciary, the Executive, the medical profession, the psychiatrists, the social psychologists, the Prison Commissioners, the Probation Officers, must all be brought into the great work which the Institute can do.'[28]

---

25 *Parl. Debates,* HL, vol. 215, cols 399–558, at cols 512 and 513, 8 April 1959.
26 See, for example, what he often described as his 'Critical Notes', 'Comparative Criminology', vol. 1 (1965), p. 173 and vol. 2 (1965), p. 657; *British Journal of Delinquency*, vol. 9 (1958–9), pp. 68–70, and *British Journal of Criminology*, vol. 3 (1962), pp. 187–92.
27 *British Journal of Delinquency*, vol. 9 (1959), pp. 241–4, at p. 243.
28 Lord Birkett, *op. cit.*, cols 440–1.

Dr Mannheim's acerbated and distorted criticisms should in no way detract from the scholarly and pioneering contributions he made, in difficult circumstances, to the development of British criminology. I do not believe that he was ever an easy-going man with much generosity and tolerance, but there can be no doubt that his bitterness was intensified, and very justifiably so, by not having been made at the final stage of his career a professor. It is, if I may say so, very much to the credit of his pupils and of the London School of Economics that the new criminological centre there was named the Mannheim Centre – as a tribute to this in many ways unusual man. I was very happy and very moved to have been asked by the *Dictionary of National Biography* to write a piece about him. I only regretted that I was not given room to be more expansive.[29]

The second hurdle

The matter was still further in the balance because there was still another hurdle to clear, not as emotionally tense and embarrassing as the preceding one, but nevertheless crucial: the funding of the projected innovations. This experience brought home to me, a novice in the game, how tight the control of the Treasury was, how restricted the discretionary powers of the University Grants Committee in fact were, and in consequence how exceedingly difficult it was to bring into being something new which did not slot into a quinquennial programme, planned well ahead and firmly fixed. Nor could one avoid seeing how delicate and painful was the task the Grants Committee was called upon to discharge in assessing the competitive (and often conflicting) aspirations and needs of so many academic centres, given the restricted means at their disposal. Nor did Britain resemble the United States, even to a modest extent, in the number of rich individuals, guided by generous impulses and substantial tax reliefs, who were willing to give away their money for worthy objectives of philanthropy, nor in the very many foundations, small and large, ready to spread their bounty to diverse fields of endeavour in need of support and encouragement.

The University Grants Committee offered a sum of money, primarily to help in the building up of the library, and made it clear that no more would be forthcoming in the quinquennium ending in 1961–2. There could be no firm promise of further support. The university generously reaffirmed that it would continue to honour its commitment to the department as hitherto discharged and would transfer the funds to the Institute should an institute be established. However, under no circumstances would it go beyond it. Indeed, it would approve the establishment of the Institute and of the Chair

---

29 Hermann Mannheim in *Dictionary of National Biography 1971–80* (1986), note by Leon Radzinowicz, pp. 543–4.

only if adequate funds from outside were made available. In such financial negotiations with outside bodies the university was not involved at all. These were expected to be conducted by the Home Office representatives. Nevertheless the Cambridge University authorities were kept informed and, not surprisingly, the Secretary-General of the Faculties soon stated in a letter to Charles Cunningham that 'the financial picture presented by your letter is not very encouraging'. Indeed, after four and a half months of concentrated efforts, the prospect of a stable and satisfactory financial existence for the Institute seemed as remote and uncertain as ever. With this partial, but nevertheless substantial, setback we faced the danger that the interest and support expressed by Cambridge might well evaporate. In the circumstances a successful appeal to a foundation became imperative and urgent.

The Nuffield Foundation had just given two grants, one to Lady Wootton and another to Lord Pakenham, to assist them in producing two books concerned with problems of crime, and was therefore the obvious first source to approach. A meeting was arranged with the Director of the Foundation, Leslie Farrer-Brown, and I was invited by Charles Cunningham and Francis Graham-Harrison to join them because this first 'informal and exploratory' discussion was to centre on the kind of Institute which was under consideration. We were facing a man with hardly any knowledge of our subject, but who nevertheless had strong opinions about it and strong authoritarian leanings. He was not prepared to listen. Before Cunningham and Graham-Harrison had any chance to make a statement he tried to overpower us all by his views. The only *raison d'être* for an Institute could be if 'it were able to show in scientific terms how the mind of a criminal ticked' and the way to achieve this is to pursue 'the biological approach' in research and in the direction of the Institute as a whole. I did not deny that work into certain biological aspects of criminal behaviour might properly find a place within the general programme of the Institute's research, providing that these aspects were most carefully defined and that ample financial means were made available. But to assign to them a dominant part in the planning and direction of the entire work was scientifically unsound and politically undesirable. I remember well how bewildered and depressed we all were on leaving Mr Farrer-Brown's office. This was our first and last meeting with him.

We then saw a badly needed ray of hope when the representative of the Home Office was informed that the Treasury had decided 'for other reasons' to revise the amount of money at the disposal of the University Grants Committee, with the result that Cambridge was offered for the projected Institute a further limited amount of assistance, amounting to £21,000, to meet expenditure spread over the remaining three years of the quinquennium. This was welcomed because of the tangible indication it contained concerning future regular commitments, but it stood in no relation to the capital needed to bring into being a Chair and an Institute. And then suddenly, a bolt out of the blue, a breakthrough appeared, real and conclusive. Asking for money, small or big money, even for the most noble of causes, is not always a smooth and amiable exercise, but this experience could hardly ever be excelled. It happened thirty-nine years ago and it was so agreeable that I would not mind being a party to it all over again.

On 7 January 1959 Mr Butler brought the project, to which he 'attached the greatest importance', to Lord Nathan, then the Chairman of the Wolfson Foundation, in the hope that he and his trustees would be sufficiently interested in it to consider sympathetically a request for help. The aim was to establish the Institute on a firm basis, and to ensure its future stability, by raising an endowment of £150,000 (which in present-day values would broadly speaking amount to about £2 million). And he mentioned the two senior Home Office officials whom he had asked to take care of the project. Three weeks later General Sir Harold Redman, the Director and Secretary of the Foundation, got in touch with them and the three reviewed the matter in greater detail. When the matter was discussed by the Board of Trustees, Lord Nathan called upon Lord Birkett and Professor Arthur Goodhart (Hon. KCB), who were both trustees, to give their advice. No two people could have been more competent to discharge this task in a balanced and unprejudiced manner. The sense of the meeting was decidedly favourable and the decision of the board was taken with unanimous concurrence.

One evening in mid-February Lord Nathan called on Mr Butler in his private room at the House of Commons. Mr Graham-Harrison and Mr David Renton (afterwards Lord Renton and Minister of State, but who at that time was Butler's private secretary) were also present. An agreement in substance was easily reached and it was decided that the next stage should be a meeting between Lord Nathan and the Vice-Chancellor, Lord Adrian, including those members of the university most directly concerned in the project. On 3 March Lord Nathan was entertained by Lord and Lady Adrian in the Lodgings at Trinity. This was preceded by a meeting arranged by Lord Adrian, at which the university was represented by five members. The proposal was to endow a Chair of Criminology ('perhaps to be called the Wolfson Chair'), another senior post besides, and a contribution to the establishment of a first-rate library, to be kept up to date, which the trustees also felt to be a pressing and important requirement. The adequate and regular maintenance of the Institute, once set up, was to be the responsibility of the university as well as the provision of a suitable building.

As it happened, on 8 April 1959, Lord Pakenham put forward a motion in the Lords for a debate on 'Crime and Penal Practice' arising out of Mr Butler's already quoted White Paper, and Lord Kilmuir, the Lord Chancellor, was to reply on behalf of the government. Lord Nathan was quick to seize the occasion to give to the event a much greater panache. He obtained the consent of Mr Butler and agreement from Lord Kilmuir to speak somewhat earlier in the debate, indeed before Kilmuir rose to make his speech. His statement was restrained and concise, and he ended on the following optimistic and eloquent note:

> I feel sure that your Lordships will share the hope of the Wolfson Trustees that the Institute may by this means be established on a firm, durable and appropriate basis, and may become a centre of teaching and research and a focus for ideas and action which may make a useful and continuing contribution to the solution of the problems of crime in all the varied aspects.

Nothing succeeds like success. At last some of those opposed to Cambridge seemed to be impressed if not pacified. 'The magnificent donation', stated Lord Chorley, 'for the new Institute of Cambridge positively makes one's mouth water, when one has been thinking in terms of tens, or hundreds of pounds, at the outside, over so many years.' Lord Pakenham, who initiated the debate, in concluding his speech said: 'we must congratulate him [Lord Nathan] on a record that is likely to stand through all time'.[30]

The official response from the University of Cambridge followed swiftly. By Grace 4 of 7 February 1959, the recommendation of the General Board proposed 'the establishment of an Institute of Criminology' and this was approved by Grace 1 of 31 October 1959. The report of the Council of the Senate on 'the establishment of a Wolfson Professorship of Criminology, containing a recommendation for appointment of Leon Radzinowicz' followed. In both instances no voice of dissent was raised in the Senate where, in accordance with the ancient procedure, the proposals were put up for a discussion in which any member of the university was entitled to participate and have the right to vote. Thus, some twenty years after the Faculty Board of Law at Cambridge set up a committee to inquire whether wider initiatives should be taken to promote research and teaching in criminal science, and ten years after the establishment of a Department of Criminal Science, the highest academic recognition within the context of the university was accorded to criminology by one of the leading universities in the world.

I am pretty certain that this was the first innovation of its kind adopted by any Faculty of Law in the English-speaking world. The Roscoe Pound Professorship at Harvard Law School was established in honour of their eminent Dean, and at that time there had been two incumbents: Sheldon Glueck and Livingstone Hall. Both had a particular interest in criminal law, but only Glueck was a criminologist. Moreover there was nothing in the regulations to prohibit the appointment to the Roscoe Pound Chair of a professor who had altogether different interests, and at no stage was an institute of

---

30 *Parl. Debates*, HL, 'Crime and Penal Practice', vol. 215 (1958–9), cols 400–558, at cols 433–4, 509–10 and 556–7, 8 April 1959.

criminology brought into existence. At the time I was also inclined to maintain that there were hardly any chairs specifically devoted to criminology in any of the sociology departments of the universities and colleges of the United States, although, of course, there were many sociologists who chose to specialize in criminology. And soon my suspicion was to be confirmed by my inquiries carried out on the spot.

The advance in Britain was yet to be tested by actual achievements, but it swiftly acquired the characteristics of a public event. The press took it up on a large scale; not only the leading national newspapers, but also the 'popular' ones in London as well as in the provinces.[31]

I resisted as much as I could the very many invitations to give interviews, make speeches and appear on television. But, of course, I could not refuse them all and the very few which I undertook taught me a lot about public attitudes towards crime, their evaluations and their expectations, and how widespread was the tendency to express definite views about some of the most obdurate aspects of crime and its control in utter disregard of hard, solid evidence. The insistence was on experience and common sense. Nor could I fail to notice the extent of suspicion that the study of crime and its control if left in the hands of academics would most likely turn out to be soft and sentimental in harmony with the French saying 'tout comprendre c'est tout pardonner'. The reaction in professional circles was of course much more sober, balanced and encouraging and the University of Cambridge was frequently congratulated on moving boldly in this innovative direction. But there was also an undercurrent of doubt about how easy it would be to set up a vigorous Institute of high quality discharging so many functions. How durable would its influence be, once the initial *élan* and enthusiasm had inevitably subsided? With a directness that could not fail to produce uneasiness Professor Aubrey Lewis (afterwards Sir Aubrey Lewis), a member of the University of London delegation convened to express their views on the desirability of adopting Mr Butler's proposal, stated: 'he was against setting up an Institute, which would only waste the time of people who would otherwise be engaged on useful research in existing institutions'. He could speak with special authority because he happened to be the Head of the famous Maudsley Institute of London. Yes, we reached the summit of our

---

31 See especially 'Broad Structure for Institute of Criminology. Dr Radzinowicz outlines his aims', *The Times* (15 June 1959); 'Study of Crime', *The Times* (18 August 1959); 'Seeking for Causes of Delinquency', *The Times* (28 December 1961); 'Classifying Young Offenders', *The Times* (29 December 1961); 'Cambridge Institute of Criminology', by Colin Mars, *Manchester Guardian* (4 May 1961); 'Home Office may start a University of Crime', *Evening News* (15 July 1957); 'Study as a Weapon against Crime', by H. Montgomery Hyde, MP, *Birmingham Post* (5 August 1958); 'Institute of Criminology in Britain – First Chair in Britain', *The Scotsman* (6 August 1958); 'Studying Crime', *Liverpool Post* (8 August 1958); 'Causes of Crime', *Observer* (23 August 1959); 'Nobody Has Had This Man's Job Before', by Anthony Lejeune, *Daily Express* (2 November 1959).

hopes and received its glittering prizes, but we would have deserved a verdict of unforgivable naïvety if we were to ignore that the road before us was still bumpy, and indeed with some dark, potentially lethal, corners.

The course still bumpy

Three episodes went far to reveal the truth of this apprehension. And significantly all three happened when the authoritative seal of approval was about to be affixed to the project. All three were rather colourful, but by clearly expressed intent hostile and potentially harmful.

First, on 6 September 1958 an article appeared in the *Sunday Dispatch* entitled 'Sherlock Holmes Chair Mystery' in black capitals right across page 3 of the paper. It claimed to have been written in consultation with several senior officers of Scotland Yard. It was an incoherent amalgamation of distorted or plainly fictitious information about the Institute and the Chair. Its standard can best be judged from the way it ended: 'Final comment from a Scotland Yard man: personally I think Isaac Wolfson has wasted his money.' It was signed by Jacques Reid, unknown to us. It is only fair to state that no one in Cambridge, nor anyone in the Home Office, was in the least disturbed by this cheap performance, but the Wolfson family, especially Isaac Wolfson (afterwards Sir Isaac Wolfson), were rather unhappy. This was understandable, for to put it rather crudely the Home Secretary had asked the Wolfsons to give a lot of money to establish a Chair and an Institute and then his police warns old Isaac that his money has gone down the drain. How could this give pleasure to him, his family, and for that matter the Wolfson Foundation? At first it was thought that a letter from Mr Butler or Lord Adrian should put the matter right, but a little later much wiser counsels prevailed. 'We must be careful', declared Leonard Wolfson (afterwards Lord Wolfson of Marylebone), 'not to overdo things.' Sir Charles Cunningham wrote to General Redman assuring him that the Home Office had no knowledge of the statements attributed to police officers. Before dispatching his letter he had shown it to Sir Joseph Simpson, Commissioner of the Metropolitan Police, asking him whether he would accept the above-quoted passage. The latter expressed his 'entire agreement' with the letter and capped it with a comment which I did not like very much: 'and I am sorry', the Commissioner said, 'if one or more of our officers were in fact caught in an unguarded moment'.

The episode was interesting but with no durable negative effects. As a matter of fact our collaboration with the police over the years could not have been more pleasant. We were given ample facilities for our inquiries into the condition and trends of crime in England in the last half-century, and large portions of the archives at the Scotland Yard Library were made available for our historical studies. I often asked a senior member of the Institute's staff to go to the Police College in Bramshill to give a lecture or two and conduct a seminar, and senior police officers from that college would come to Cambridge to share with us some of their experience. I was invited there on 1 August 1968 to deliver the Fourth Frank Newsam Memorial Lecture and I chose as my topic 'The Dangerous Offender'.[32] At some stage the Commandant of the college, General R.W. Jelf, and Professor John Stead, in charge of the academic programme, came to Cambridge for consultations with respect to their plans to reorganize the college and with particular reference to matters of criminology and criminal policy. John Steed in 1972 was invited to join the John Jay College of Criminal Justice in New York and became a very popular and respected Professor of Criminal Justice. An Oxford man, highly civilized with wide interests, I spent many happy times in his company. I was very pleased when they made me an Honorary Fellow of the college (with a proper tie of course).

The second episode was much more disconcerting. On 18 August 1959 a leading article in the *Daily Telegraph* subjected the whole projected Cambridge venture to ironical, offensive and distorted comments. 'The Department may well make illuminating contributions to the philosophy of law. It may also provide agreeable summer schools.' What was really needed is 'to inspire a detestation spreading from the very top throughout society of the shoddiness of mind from which crime springs'. The Institute was envisaged as completely free from any political affiliations or allegiance. Nevertheless, its impact would have been affected if its *raison d'être* was rejected outright by a major political party. Crime and its control have political and ideological implications which cannot be ignored. Did this mean that from the very outset there would be an estrangement between the Cambridge Institute of Criminology and an important segment of the Conservative Party? Soon afterwards I was able to discover the author of this pernicious piece. It was Mr M.J. Cowling (Fellow of Peterhouse and then Lecturer in History in the University of Cambridge) who, unsolicited, told me about it in the course of a casual encounter. I was rather sad that a scholar and thinker, endowed with an original and incisive mind, could so easily descend to such cheap travesties of such grave and complex problems.

But here also in the long run no damage worth mentioning was produced. I hasten to mention that soon afterwards William Deedes (later Lord Deedes of Aldington), a major figure on the *Daily Telegraph*, joined the Advisory Council of the Institute, served on it from 1962 to 1972, and proved to be a valuable and constructive member. And indeed the point of view of the Institute as reflected in its publications and activities always received a fair and thoughtful hearing in the columns of the *Daily Telegraph* even if disagreements in substance or emphasis should appear. The two letters which

---

32 Published in *Police Journal*, vol. 41 (1968), pp. 411–72, with a foreword by Professor John Stead.

appeared in the paper, following Mr Cowling's leading article, provided an illuminating footnote to it. One by A.W. Hart (8 August 1958) contained suggestions how 'to destroy this bestial Institute of Criminology' by stimulating the growth of moral philosophy and social anthropology, and another by N.H. Pannell, MP (the same date) advocated a sharply raising scale of punishments settled 'by a small body of judges, justices of the peace and members of the general public' which would be the required remedy for crime and would render the setting up of a permanent Institute unnecessary.

Mr Cowling's Leader produced an occasion when Rab Butler's well-known amiable disposition deserted him. 'Perhaps,' he wrote, commenting upon the piece, 'such views, and others favouring heavier deterrents, as a more speedy remedy than research, were to be expected for, of course, it was precisely this approach which I hoped in the long run would be counteracted by the educative impact of the Institute.' As the first Professor of Criminology, and as the head of the first Institute of its kind, I could never be far away from the controversial penal issues of the moment, or from certain public inquiries of a delicate nature. I could never be sure whether or when a label would be attached to me, with little regard to the likelihood of it containing a germ of truth. Thus, for example, even some thirteen years after the establishment of the Institute, a piece appeared in the *Daily Telegraph* suggesting that 'a secret organization' was planning violent or at least trouble-making action within prisons and that 'some are working for the Cambridge Institute of Criminology – unknown to Professor Leon Radzinowicz, its director'.[33]

The third episode was of a predominantly domestic nature, but in effect its overall repercussions could have been grave and lasting. It related to the selection of the first holder of the Wolfson Professorship of Criminology. It could have been a simple and smooth matter; instead it became a source of embarrassment throwing severe doubts as to whether Cambridge really wanted to have criminology after all. The university had two options for proceeding. One, applicable to all kinds of professorships, was for the professor to be selected by the Board of Electors set up for the purpose, the post to be advertised, stating in the advertisement the essential requirements. But the university had also the discretionary power in certain cases, especially when there was to be a replacement of an existing post by a professorship, to ignore the usual procedure and to invite a named person to be the holder of the chair in question. For this, the consent of the faculty concerned was naturally required. When the Law Faculty was asked by the General Board 'whether the Wolfson Professorship of Criminology should be established for a named person in replacement of the existing office' the vote revealed that

---

33 Peter Gladstone-Smith, 'Academics Link Up with Prisoners to Force Reform. Outsiders Plot Prison Protest', *Daily Telegraph* (14 May 1972). This 'insurrection' died almost as soon as it was noticed.

the proposal was carried by seven votes to nil, but with six abstentions and a similar division was displayed with respect to the post of the Director of the Institute to be held jointly with the professorship.

This was significant and confirmed several things. A muted opposition to criminology was always there though its intensity varied in the course of time. It had been apparent when the first proposal, advanced some fifteen years earlier, to establish an Assistant Directorship of Research to promote criminology, was thrown out by the faculty. It was active when, seven years later, an attempt was made to set up a Department of Criminal Science with the Assistant Directorship, by then established, being upgraded to the post of the Director. The most recent spectacular support from outside evoked on the one hand admiration, but on the other some degree of envy and apprehension. The faculty had never had an Institute and it was by no means clear that, when set up, it would not operate in competition with the acknowledged basic needs of the faculty. At that time there were only five professorships in the faculty and there were some who wondered why criminology should be pushed to the very top.[34] They also continued to question the academic worth of criminology and felt that its proper place belonged in the social sciences. Throughout its long existence the faculty had hardly ever had any senior posts filled by scholars of foreign extraction and, at that time, there were already two of them, a professor and a lecturer. There also came into play, as is often the case, the not always clearly definable element of personal like or dislike. And, last but not least, persistent rumours were circulating that a distinguished Professor of Criminal Law already established in Cambridge could be attracted to fill the post of the Director.

The whole episode of this rather unsavoury volte-face caused some embarrassment in Cambridge, but even more importantly it provided the right kind of ammunition to those outside Cambridge who never believed that there could be a genuine supportive atmosphere to give criminology in Cambridge a truly meaningful chance.

I have often asked myself the question: how could the Institute achieve a substantial measure of success if, from the outset, strong doubts were evinced towards it in so many influential quarters of London? To gain their goodwill and, if possible, their participation in the projected work figured prominently in my early endeavours. This task appeared hazardous and the sheer effort of deploying those persuasive initiatives was quite considerable. And now it would appear that, rather late in the day, there also remained the task of conquering the distrust, of counteracting the prejudice of one's own

---

34 The Cambridge Law Faculty (according to the *Faculty Handbook for the Years 1997–98*, p. 6) now consists of fifteen professors, seven readers and nearly sixty other university, faculty and college teaching officers.

faculty. I am not usually put off by challenges, but I must confess that those undercurrents caused me some distress. Fortunately this was not the time for indulging in such feelings or reflections. Forging ahead was the order of the day.

9

MAKING IT WORK: INFUSING REALITY INTO AN IDEA

Some false assumptions

Today if criminology proves to be a flop in a particular place and setting it is, of course, regrettable and should be remedied. It would, however, be restricted, manageable damage, because much valuable work is being done in so many other places across Britain and by so many other gifted individuals. But in those days conditions and attitudes were very different.

Nor can it be denied that the enterprise of promoting the development of criminology was launched in exceptionally impressive circumstances. Expectations were running high and how could this be different? The fact that the initiative was taken by a national political figure of Rab Butler's stature; that from the start it had enthusiastic support from the senior staff of the Home Office; that it gained financial backing of considerable magnitude from a highly respected foundation; and that a university as prominent as Cambridge had expressed its willingness to give criminology a permanent home. Yet, in spite of all these favourable circumstances the enterprise was still regarded by many as controversial in its basic premises and anticipated benefits. Should the results turn out to be poor these very factors would become the kernel of gravely incriminating evidence that the experiment had never deserved to be attempted at all. No solace or justification could have been advanced that inadequate means had been made available to launch properly the Cambridge development and make it prosper.

I was very aware of all this. Nor could I ignore the fact that my detailed memorandum on the projected Institute was endorsed by the university, the Law School and the Home Office, and that I had been given a considerably free hand in bringing it about. This included the shaping of its basic structure, the selection of the staff, the programme of teaching and research, and several other initiatives which, taken together and speedily implemented, should give a decisive impetus in putting criminology on the national map. I had expressed confidence at a very early stage that this could be achieved and I had been believed. I had no illusion that my own reputation was perilously at stake. I do not believe that I would have continued (very much

MAKING IT WORK: INFUSING REALITY INTO AN IDEA

to my regret) to reside in Cambridge, if the University of Cambridge, like the University of London, had responded negatively to Mr Butler's initiative. I had made this clear, though on occasions my intentions were misunderstood.[1]

Yet it had to be acknowledged that, even under the most favourable of circumstances, it is exceptionally difficult to establish 'institutes' and even more difficult, once they have been set up, to make them function in an imaginative and fertile manner. This remark, as well as those which follow, relates to 'institutes' as such, irrespective of their type or location. It is on the whole more realistic to expect them to lapse into bureaucratically minded units where appearances overshadow the real things that should be done. There can be no denying that creative work is *par excellence* individual work. An organizational framework, kept in strict balance, can be of help, indeed sometimes of considerable help, but it can never be a substitute for creative individuality. The continuing discharge of many administrative functions which the organizational side of an institute inevitably requires, can in the course of time draw too heavily upon the energies and the resourcefulness of the director and the senior staff with a deadly effect on their innovative intellectual vitality. And this can easily, again under the impact of time, lead to a stagnant, mechanical existence.

To assign to an institute but a very few functions, in the hope that thereby depth and reputation will be achieved, may give birth to a thoroughly uninteresting, parochial structure. To burden it with too many tasks may foster superficiality and pretentiousness. But perhaps the most dangerous thing of all is to assign to criminology – and to an institute which is to serve its development and enhance its credibility – purposes which it will not be able to achieve under any circumstances. The outline of what the Wolfson Chair and the Institute intended to accomplish presented in the White Paper provided a faithful summary of the plans which I had formulated at an initial stage of our discussions in Cambridge, at the Home Office and at the Wolfson Foundation. They were, I concede, rather ambitious, but I did not feel that in order to achieve our ultimate objectives we could have settled for less.[2] However, its last proviso, namely that the Institute will also be

---

1 In the course of my research for this book I came across a note of a conversation I had had with a Home Office official. It conveyed the impression that I intended to leave Cambridge if the Institute were not established there. This is certainly not what I recall having said. Indeed, I distinctly remember saying that I would do whatever I could to support an institute, even if it were established elsewhere.

2 Paragraph 22 of the White Paper, *Penal Practice in a Changing Society* (1959), stated:

> The Institute would be broadly based; and it would be closely linked with all the faculties concerned in any aspect of the study of delinquency. It would necessarily have to keep itself informed of all that is being done in the furtherance of that study, both at home and abroad. Its purposes would be various. It would teach criminology, especially on the post-graduate level; and it would

concerned with 'the general problem of the criminal in society, its causes and its solution', was not included in my memorandum and I was surprised to see it in print. I went out of my way to make my position clear. I was against it and I felt that if this purpose were taken literally and found its articulation in some of our dominant activities this would produce negative effects on our enterprise as a whole. I did not expect at this early stage to secure unanimous concurrence with my point of view, and I was content, indeed gratified, to note that I would not be expected to adhere to it without a further full-scale and well-timed discussion. In view of its importance, I shall return to this subject in my last chapter when I expand on my views concerning the scope and potentialities of criminology at this stage of its evolution (see p. 449).

There was still another issue which could have easily become a subject of acute dissent. Namely, how much profit could we derive from the experiences and criminological achievements of others, primarily in Western Europe, when promoting the development of criminology in Britain? In view of my background, I was only too aware of this concern: it had been in my mind long before Mr Butler appeared with his innovative plans. And I had been fully conscious that, if we in Cambridge were asked to take up his initiative, I should have at my disposal up-to-date extensive information of the European scene effectively supported by inquiries carried out on the spot. This concern had been made so much more compelling because in their letter to the Home Secretary, the Howard League for Penal Reform bluntly contrasted the inadequate situation in Britain with that prevailing in Europe. 'Most continental countries', they stated, 'have one or more Institutes of Criminology, and even small universities have chairs in criminology.'[3] My view that I could hardly avoid the issue was most emphatically confirmed by the Home Office and by Cambridge. I was granted leave of absence to assess the condition of criminology abroad. The expenses involved in carrying out this exercise were graciously shared by the university and the Home Office.

I have passed in my life through many periods of exceptional concentra-

---

      undertake and encourage research on the highest academic standard. It would therefore not only itself contribute to our knowledge of criminology; it would help to produce the teachers of that subject, and the highly qualified research workers, who are at present so scarce. It would also, it may be hoped, be able from time to time to bring together groups of those concerned with the administration of justice and the treatment of offenders. By doing so it would help to keep them abreast of current thought and findings of research; and it would at the same time strengthen its own contacts with those doing the practical work of which it would study the results. Finally, the Institute should be able, as no existing agency is in a position to do, to survey with academic impartiality – in the light of the results of the research effort as a whole – the general problem of the criminal in society, *its causes and its solution* [my italics].

3 They derived encouragement for making this statement from a report published by UNESCO, *The University Teaching of Social Sciences: Criminology* (Paris, 1957).

tion, but this one was undoubtedly the extreme specimen. In a period of four months I went to Italy, Austria, the Federal Republic of Germany, France, Belgium, The Netherlands, Denmark, Norway and parts of the United States of America (California, New York, Philadelphia, Boston and Washington DC) where I visited many leading centres, no fewer than fifteen. Altogether I had interviews and discussions with one hundred and twenty-five people who directly or indirectly were involved in some of the aspects of the subject of my inquiry. In addition I received or collected some forty-five memoranda. The end product was a book: *In Search of Criminology*. The interest it evoked was most pleasing.[4]

Its findings were alarming and painful. Criminological studies and criminological teaching, with very few exceptions (such as Oslo or Utrecht), were in a state of definite stagnation. They paraded under high-blown titles, but in vain would one look for real substance. My Institute of Criminology of Rome, founded by Enrico Ferri – the first of its kind in the world and for so long so inspiring – was academically in ruins. The Institute of Paris, in contrast to the brilliant heritage of French criminology, was no more than an empty shell. The Institute of Vienna had hardly developed beyond the stage of 'scientific police' developed by Hans Gross at the turn of the century, while the Institute of Graz had embarked upon the highly questionable conception of 'Criminal Biology' developed by Adolf Lenz and taken up by an influential group of German prison doctors. The Criminal Biology Society, which met in Graz, Vienna, Munich and Dresden, produced several volumes of reports and discussions which gravitated towards a reformulation of crime as a product of individual predestination. Through skilful, though often gravely flawed, use of constitutional, endocrinological, genetic and twin studies, it had supported a neo-Lombrosian revival of the etiology of crime. All this had been welcomed by the emerging fascist and Nazi leaders and their accommodating criminological entourage.

The bulk of the academic schools of criminology in Belgium no doubt performed useful functions, but they lacked well-qualified staff, a meaningful curriculum and adequate funds for research and library facilities. Many other centres, including those located in the Federal Republic of Germany, were no more than seminars usually conducted by the Professor of Criminal Law with wider interests in criminal science; no doubt useful as far as they went, but far removed from what a proper Institute of Criminology should stand for. The means put at the disposal of virtually all of them were utterly inadequate

---

4   It was published by Heinemann in 1961 (in the series of *Books on Sociology*, general editor Donald Gunn MacRae); by Harvard University Press in 1962; in Italian, translated by Professor Franco Ferracuti, with a preface by Professor Silvio Ranieri of Bologna in 1964; in a French translation with an introduction by Marc Ancel, in 1965; in Spanish, translated by Professor Rosa del Olmo, in 1970.

and one cannot but have admiration for those who tried to keep them alive, in face of humiliating and seemingly never-ending adversity.

The situation in the United States in this respect was also not encouraging. The School of Criminology in the University of California, Berkeley, was one of the first pioneering enterprises in North America and had a decent record of achievement within the limits imposed upon it by the organizational and financial resources made available. As I stated at the time, in the setting of a great university, with a forward-looking school of law and several major departments concerned with the study of human personality and society, in a region well known for its reforms and experiments in the penal sphere and beyond it, a small but well-organized and properly endowed criminological centre of real academic standing would have been a natural development. But there was very little there when I visited it.

In the period between the two wars the Rockefeller Foundation became interested in the project of establishing an Institute of Criminology and Criminal Justice conceived on a large and proper scale. Before a decision was reached, a Professor of Criminal Law and Procedure and a Professor of Philosophy – both of Columbia University – were invited to survey the work which had already been done by criminologists, to assess its value and to set out their opinions on the desirability of founding an institute dedicated to the subject. In 1933 Jerome Michael and Mortimer J. Adler's report was published under the title *Crime, Law and Social Science*. This was the era of great expansion in sociological and criminological work across the country, which produced much material of permanent importance. But it also fostered in some quarters an attitude which is often associated with a sudden advance in a hitherto neglected branch of knowledge. In this case, extravagant claims were made that criminology would identify the causes of criminal behaviour and would discover a plan for the ultimate prevention and control of crime. While the authors had many salutary comments to make about the limitations of criminology, they themselves did not escape deadly criticism. Their vision of a criminological institute amounted to a wild metaphysical construct in irreconcilable opposition to experience and common sense. It took no time to reveal it. Optimism gave way to scepticism, support fell off and the entire project foundered.[5]

---

[5] For an authoritative confirmation of my impressions, see Edwin Sutherland, 'The Michael–Adler Report', in Albert Cohen, Alfred Lindesmith and Karl Schuessler (eds) *The Sutherland Papers* (1956), p. 229, *passim* and the editor's note (*ibid.*, p. 230) which stated that out of a committee of twenty-one members set up by the Bureau of Social Hygiene of New York City to reply to three questions relating to the report, only one of the eighteen members who replied supported the conclusions of the report on the first two questions and only one on the last two points. 'In all other cases, where the questions were directly answered, the conclusions of the report were opposed on all these points, with minor qualifications in several instances.'

Not surprisingly, Dr Hermann Mannheim subjected my book to the full blast of a merciless critique. Much more to the point, Marc Ancel, with no axe to grind and at the height of his international reputation as the Director of the Section of Penal Law and Criminal Science of the Paris Institute of Comparative Law, in a lengthy introduction to the French edition of the book which he had sponsored, bestowed upon it much warm praise and expressed his virtually unqualified support.[6] This I found most agreeable, but it did not make our task less daunting: why should we succeed when so many others had failed?

Added to this, a further rather basic consideration should be stressed. All this took place in the spring of 1960 when I was fifty-four years old. I could not divest myself of the reminiscences of my youth of some thirty years earlier when, with restless activity, I had set out on my European pilgrimages 'in search of criminology', full of enthusiasms and beliefs. But soon afterwards, having witnessed the very grave injustices and no less great illusions which had demolished so many national and individual existences throughout the world, I might well have become cynical. Happily I had not. Instead I grew into a realist and a pragmatist, much more critical and indeed often much more suspicious, especially of all-embracing ideologies and doctrines of widely stretched expectations.

By 1936 I had ceased to be a positivist, but I never ceased to be proud to have been one at an early stage of my criminological formative years.[7] I had also become disappointed and irritated by the superficiality of some of my early writings. This was not an abrupt rejection but a revaluation of several aspects of the positivist school which I had pursued in the light of what I continued to observe and to learn. I had always been aware that it is not difficult to find holes, big or small, in doctrines evolved a century ago; indeed it seemed to me rather childish to indulge in such clever-by-half exercises. The positivist doctrine of criminal law and criminology, although still possessing some very important and fecund elements, has been played out a long time ago and for good. But the contribution the early positivists had made outweighed by far the criticisms mobilized against them. Criminology as a virile academic discipline and as an acute socio-political construct owes its birth to them and they, in turn, deserve our deep respect and not cheap derision.[8]

---

6 See Marc Ancel, 'Introduction', in *Où en est la criminologie?* (Paris, 1965), pp. ix–xvi.
7 In 1956 I was invited to a congress in Mantua to celebrate the centenary of Ferri's birth (attended alas by a very thin contingent of Italian admirers). I spoke on the weaknesses, indeed unrealities, of Ferri's positivist doctrine. My address was received with respect but not with enthusiasm.
8 In his book *The Mismeasure of Man* (1981, pp. 122–43), Professor Stephen Jay Gould lends his considerable critical, literary and polemical gifts to reveal the fatal flaws of Lombroso's criminal anthropology. Such onslaughts have been made by scholars and investigators on

The impact of growing older had naturally had a substantial share in my own evolution and so had the rich and diversified wealth of accumulated knowledge and experience. But it is England which helped me enormously to evolve and to hold on to this healthy process of emotional and intellectual maturation. I was (and still am) at a loss to comprehend why the epitaph of 'positivist' is still hurled against me or against the research programme of the Institute which I proposed or approved of. Unless, of course, it is crudely applied to any kind of quantitative criminological research. There is nothing in my books, articles or public pronouncements that follow or express approval of the positivist doctrine of social defence. The same can be affirmed, without any hesitation, with respect to my collaborators and colleagues in the Institute. The tendency amongst a number of criminologists to attach labels to each other is rather widespread, though by no means always fair or correct.[9]

At the very beginnings of our discussions concerning the functioning of the projected institute, with reference to its programme of research, I laid down six directives which should regulate the adoption and launching of the investigations carried out by senior members of the staff. No topic of inquiry should be imposed on us by the Home Office, or by any other source from which the financial support for the particular topic was expected to come. No topic should be imposed by me or the governing bodies of the Institute on any member of the staff. Special consideration should be given to any proposal brought forward by a member of the Institute's staff. Any project of research had to be in the final instance approved by me in my capacity as the Director of the Institute. In case of difference of opinion between the Director and the Researcher the latter should be given unfettered opportunity to put his or her case before the Committee of Management, the Director being present or absent as desired. Under no circumstances should the Director have the right to launch an inquiry, even if all the preliminary requirements

---

very many occasions and in many countries. I could not have been more emphatic when I stated in my James S. Carpentier Lectures at Columbia University in 1966 that: 'The Lombrosian doctrine has now been relegated to the status of myth, and can safely be placed, together with the theories of his forerunners, in the historical repository of criminology. His writings are no longer read and indeed are hardly readable. If you were to embark upon them, you would feel as though you were moving about in a bewildering, fantastic antique shop, out of this world.' But Professor Gould missed a point of considerable importance. Long after so many of us have been utterly forgotten or hardly remembered, Cesare Lombroso will continue to stand out as the originator and creator of the discipline of criminology. See Leon Radzinowicz, *Ideology and Crime* (1966), pp. 48 and 56–9.

9   The most recent example of such a generalization is provided by Professor David Garland when he refers to 'the positivism and "correctionalism" associated with the Home Office and Cambridge Institute at that time'. See 'Obituary F.H. McClintock', *British Journal of Criminology*, vol. 35 (1995), pp. 134–7, at p. 136.

connected with it had been settled satisfactorily, until he had put the selected topic on the agenda of the Committee of Management's meeting for information and discussion and obtained their broad agreement. He also had to inform the Advisory Council of the Institute.[10]

I have scrutinized my memory, checked my notes and talked to two members of the Institute of long standing, and I have no hesitation in making it clear beyond any qualification that, throughout my directorship, I scrupulously observed these six self-imposed directives. Nor do I remember any instance in which the Committee of Management or the Advisory Body, directly or indirectly, conveyed the view that these directives (or any one of them) had been disregarded or bent in any way.[11]

The subject of crime and its control contains a highly sensitive and volatile political component and I was, therefore, particularly anxious that, from the very outset, the Institute should not be identified with any of the political parties or affiliations. Our duty was to examine the many aspects of the subject-matter in a manner as dispassionate and objective as possible, leaving the political *coloratura* to those called upon to make the appropriate decisions. Whenever I happened to be invited to present a report on the condition of crime and the ways of dealing with it to House of Commons Committees concerned with penal matters, whether Conservative or Labour, I scrupulously practised the gospel that I preached. I went so far that, within the Institute, I consistently abstained from engaging in conversations of a political nature with my colleagues, and the views even of those with whom I collaborated over very many years remained unknown to me. In this context, I cannot resist the temptation to recall an episode which I cherish very much. Once I invited to Trinity a US General to dine with me in Hall and I put him next to George Trevelyan. This happened to be the day of elections in England. With the spontaneity so characteristic of the Americans, which however can be rather embarrassing, my guest said: 'Master, how did you vote?' 'By ballot, Sir,' came the terse reply.

---

10 For further comments on the subject of research see pp. 220–224
11 In one instance, the Home Office inquired whether the Institute would like to carry out a full-scale inquiry into violent criminality. I had my doubts about it, but asked two senior members to express their views. After some preliminary investigations, they were not attracted to undertake it and the matter was dropped. In another instance, I regarded a topic proposed by a senior member of the staff as unrealistic because of the inaccessibility of essential sources of information. As he disagreed with me I encouraged him to state his case to the Committee of Management. They endorsed my view. He continued to be unconvinced and wrote to the Home Office, who also confirmed my view. Whereupon he pursued another subject which we approved of and in due course presented an original and important report. He decided not to have it published in our Cambridge Series.

The Cambridge Institute of Criminology

Only once during the twelve years of my directorship did I write about the Institute and even then only in the sixth year of its existence and because I was expected to do so as part of a wider inquiry carried out by me in New York (1966). I felt strongly that the Institute should, if I may put it this way, speak for itself and its worth should be assessed by the work it was expected to discharge. I retired from the Wolfson Professorship in 1973 and from the directorship in 1972, but I continued to be silent on the subject for the next sixteen years. By then I had become increasingly conscious how rapidly and how substantially memories tend to fade. I was, therefore, becoming increasingly receptive to the idea that I should attempt to provide a full account of the initial crucial period of the Institute's functioning and of its role within the context of the penal and criminological developments of that time. In consequence I greatly appreciated the encouragement and help I received from Sir Brian Cubbon (then the Permanent Under-Secretary of State), from David Faulkner (then the Deputy Under-Secretary of State), and from Mrs Mary Tuck (then the Head of the Research and Planning Unit of the Home Office) to undertake this task. As I stated in my preface, 'I embarked upon this venture with certain misgivings, with a sense of embarrassment. And yet, reliving these years has been an exciting experience.' My report of 190 pages, including 20 appendices, is available for those requiring a detailed picture.[12] Here no more is needed than a digest of its essential and durable features of wider applicability.

Inter-disciplinary foundation

What should be the place of a criminological institute in relation to the university? In some instances it could be argued that it should stand apart so as to more securely guarantee its independence and identity. This was the advice which I gave when I was asked to come for consultations in Australia and New York. But for England this would have been the wrong advice. For criminology to stand alone might well lead to its isolation, to a position of an orphan in need of a parent. The objective of gaining recognition for criminology as a full-blooded academic discipline would be acutely weakened. Partnership with a Law Faculty should be the first option, and in the conditions then prevailing in Cambridge this was by far the best solution. Whatever the connection it was vital to define and to guarantee the unfettered development of the Institute while at the same time securing a genuine and constructive association with the 'host' institution.

---

12 See Leon Radzinowicz, *The Cambridge Institute of Criminology: Its Background and Scope* (HMSO, 1988).

The steps taken by us in this respect, I venture to say, were unique. A wide foundation was laid down bearing no resemblance to the structure of the Department of Criminal Science, or for that matter of any criminological centre in the world: a foundation which cut across the legal aspects of the phenomenon of crime and its control and which aimed to foster close links and exchanges with several non-legal disciplines basic to criminology. However, the Law Faculty was strongly represented on the Committee of Management of the Institute: the Chairman of the Faculty Board of Law was to be an ex-officio member and the faculty was also to appoint from amongst its members three further representatives. This I thought highly desirable not only because criminology should not be arbitrarily cut off from law, but also because it would indicate a strong willingness on the part of the lawyers to get involved in the work of the Institute and to care for its well-being. But this also meant that, more than ever, it was imperative to counterbalance, or rather to supplement and to enrich, the legal component by other wider influences. The Regius Professor of Physic, the Professors of Experimental Psychology, of Social Anthropology and of Human Ecology – all agreed to become members of the Committee of Management. The committee was also given the right to co-opt two residents of Cambridge from outside the university. And this provision was used later on to bring in two non-legal members. The committee was expected to meet every term of the academic year and to receive beforehand a detailed report from me, as the Director of the Institute. It was also understood that I would regularly share information and consult with the Chairman of the committee and the Secretary.

In addition an Advisory Council was brought into being. It consisted (in addition to the members of the Committee of Management) of up to twelve members, at least half of whom would not be persons resident in Cambridge, or officially connected with Cambridge University. They were of undisputed high standing in public or academic affairs. We felt that it would be of great advantage to be able, from time to time, to survey the work of the Institute from a higher plane, without being overburdened by the details of everyday administration. And this would also help us to forge valuable links with the wider outside world. In contrast to the Committee of Management they held their meetings in London, usually in the House of Lords. It was easy, just glancing at the list of the members making up the two bodies, to see that – although well disposed towards the Institute – these were not placid and easy-going bodies but vigilant and critical, expecting constant high quality.

The Wolfson Professor of Criminology was ex-officio a member of the Faculty Board of Law, which added to his status and influence. It was regarded as highly desirable that he should also be the Director of the Institute, but to provide for all kinds of eventualities a separate post of Director was set up. But whereas the Professor was appointed to the retiring age, the Directorship (even if held by the Professor) would be appointed for a definite term of years (as a general rule five years) which could afterwards be extended to the retiring age. (Perhaps I may be allowed to mention that when the directorship is held by the Wolfson Professor, the latter draws no remuneration at all for holding and discharging his heavy tasks as Director – a stipulation which invariably evoked great surprise, especially from our American visitors.)

We believed that the principle of diversity built into the governing centres of the Institute should also be reflected in the vitally important process of appointments and reappointments of its senior staff. The Assistant Directors of Research, as they were initially called, were selected by a Committee which comprised, in addition to the Vice-Chancellor (or Deputy) and two members chosen by the General Board, the Chairman of the Committee of Management of the Institute, and all its members. They were to be appointed for an initial period of five years, with the possibility of reappointment for further periods of up to five years at a time.

To make certain that none of these arrangements would be of a transitory nature, but all become part of the permanent structure of the Institute, they were approved by the central authorities of the university and embodied in statutory provisions.

A word about terminology. I well remember the many anxious hours spent by those of us who were responsible in 1948 for launching of the subject in the university in finding a suitable name by which it should be known. We had finally settled on 'criminal science'. I also vividly remember how Lord Adrian, in spite of his strong support for our endeavours, shook his head and murmured in obvious desperation: 'There is no such a thing as the science of crime, unless one is concerned with the most effective way of committing it.' And, in his pleasing autobiography, Sir Ernest Barker, one of the most distinguished residents of Cranmer Road, wrote in reference to my house, 'Cranmer Road is not what it used to be since "Criminal Science" moved into it'.[13] It took the university a very long time to get accustomed to this ambivalent and somewhat pretentious term. And then, after ten years, and with hardly any notice, it suddenly disappeared, to be replaced by 'Criminology'. The Central Administration was obviously disconcerted. 'What reasons', it asked, 'underlie the proposal to refer to the Department of Criminal Science in future as an Institute of Criminology?' It was obvious that the article I had published with Turner, 'The Meaning and Scope of Criminal Science' (mentioned on p. 145), had escaped their attention, but nevertheless the change was duly accepted.

The postgraduate course

It has always been clear to me that one can produce a valuable work in criminology and play an important role in its development without having

---

13 See Ernest Barker, *Age and Youth: Memories of Three Universities* (1953), p. 10.

been a criminologist to start with. This sounds somewhat paradoxical but nevertheless is utterly true. To take a few examples at random: Lombroso was a medical man, Ferri was a criminal lawyer, Tarde was a sociologist and Burt was a psychologist. This does not hold true in respect to mathematicians, physicists, biologists or astronomers. It is to be explained by the very nature of criminology, and I shall say more about it in one of the subsequent chapters. But in order to avoid any misunderstanding, I hasten to reaffirm the elementary truth that the examples I have given are unusual, operating within the context of exceptional circumstances, and they do not invalidate the no less elementary truth that in the long run the scholarly worth of criminology and its utility to criminal policy and administration of criminal justice depend on criminological training and more specifically its quality and availability.

I had been reflecting on the relationship between the teaching of criminology and research for a long time, drawing upon my own training and teaching and the situation prevailing in this field in many countries of the world. In consequence I was especially gratified to be invited to act as General Rapporteur on 'The Teaching of Criminology, Theme No. 5' of the International Colloquium on Criminology held in Mendoza, Argentina, 22–8 January 1969. My report of forty-seven pages was made available to the Colloquium in a mimeographed form, leading to a lively discussion which I found very instructive. I was hardly surprised that the establishment of a postgraduate course in criminology was from the very outset, and by everybody, regarded as one of the central objectives in setting up an Institute of Criminology.

In November 1959 I began to collect my thoughts upon the subject and presented an internal memorandum in which I tried to delineate some of the essential issues involved in this projected development. My formula was endorsed by Cambridge and by those from outside whose collaboration in the teaching I was eager to enlist. I reiterated it seven years later in my report to the Advisory Council of the Institute at the meeting held on 18 May 1966, when I surveyed the functioning of the postgraduate courses in criminology during the first five years.[14] I was pleased to have it reaffirmed and even more pleased when, thirty-five years later, it was endorsed by the current Wolfson Professor of Criminology and Director of the Institute (Anthony Bottoms) though naturally the substance of the course had undergone significant changes. This is how I viewed its purpose:

> The Course was not intended to provide professional training for those entering the services connected with the administration of

---

14 See my report (p. 26) to the Advisory Council of the Institute (18 May 1966), where I surveyed the functioning of the course during the first five years. Mimeographed copy in the Institute's library.

justice or the enforcement of law (such as probation officers, police officers and prison staff). Since special instruction for this purpose was available in colleges and training centres, the original object of the Diploma Course was to impart a sound knowledge of criminology in its various aspects; to form an aptitude for teaching and research of a high academic standard; and to train a critical mind towards basic problems of the administration of criminal justice.

On 24 November 1960 there appeared in the *University Reporter* a comprehensive report of the Faculty Board of Law on the establishment of a Diploma in Criminology. With no objection raised by the Senate it was approved by Grace 12 of 11 February 1961. And 15 October 1961 was the day which made us feel proud, for it was then that we enrolled the first contingent of men and women from Britain and abroad to be trained as criminologists in the first Institute of Criminology under the auspices of the University of Cambridge. It was my great privilege, as the Director of the Institute, to take part in the direction of the course for the subsequent ten years. The syllabus of the postgraduate course, as it was initially constructed, fell, broadly speaking, into seven major subdivisions:

1 The development of criminological thought
2 The development of penological theory and practice
3 Methodology of criminological research
4 Conditions of criminal behaviour
5 Enforcement of criminal law and its administration
6 The treatment of offenders
7 Prevention of crime.

In each of these we tried to promote instruction which departed from the traditional approaches. Thus, for instance, in Section 3 we were fortunate to enlist the collaboration of Professor C.A. Moser of the London School of Economics (afterwards Sir Claus Moser, Warden of Merton College, Oxford). An authority on methodology in social sciences, he had the advantage of not being a criminologist and in consequence his methodological dissection, with no axe to grind on his part, of several major criminological inquiries of the last half-century, continued to evoke the intense interest of the course. Especially valuable also was the contribution of Dr A.N. Oppenheim (also from the London School of Economics) on the socio-psychological aspects of questionnaire design and response.

With respect to Section 5, I approached Lord Parker, the Lord Chief Justice, to ask whether a High Court judge and the Recorder of London could conduct seminars in which concrete cases (but without names) which they had tried and sentenced would be discussed with the course. He gave his support and Mr Justice Lawton (afterwards Lord Justice Lawton) and His Honour Judge Carl Arvold, the Recorder of London, joined us, and for many years continued to take part in this stimulating innovative adventure.

Initially the course consisted of 145 lectures and 109 seminars, yielding an average of 6 lectures and 4 seminars a week in the first term, proportionately reduced in the second and third terms. We soon discovered that there were too many lectures in relation to seminars and that more opportunities should have been provided for independent work by the postgraduate students and we went quite far in remedying it, by cutting them at least by one-third. That a prominent place should be given to the individual work of the students is all to the good, but I would be very unhappy if a coherent and thorough programme of instruction through lectures and seminars were to be too drastically reduced – still worse – virtually abandoned and replaced by the other alternative. Teaching and seminars should remain the core of a good postgraduate course.

Altogether our course was supported by twenty-three lecturers and twenty-five conductors of seminars, though in several cases the two were combined. The whole senior staff was engaged in teaching and many of their assistants, as well as some members of the Committee of Management, of the Advisory Council and the Law Faculty. It was particularly engaging and rewarding to note, in spite of the initial doubts, the very large number of distinguished experts from outside Cambridge who became associated with the course: over the first five years as many as forty came to our help and contributed greatly to the scope and quality of the teaching. Every one of them was expected to forward to us in good time his or her programme and bibliography to see to what extent it satisfied our total needs and in order to avoid repetitions or overlapping. Full bibliographies were included for each topic, but those items regarded as basic and essential were marked with an asterisk. A total syllabus was composed (consisting of sixty-five pages) and it was put in the hands of each admitted student. A special area was set aside in the library of the Institute where all the material in seven copies was assembled for the unhindered use of the participants of the course.

A distinctive post was created, that of Director of Studies of the Postgraduate Course, a post held in rotation by a senior member of the Institute's staff for a period between two and three years, and a modest remuneration was attached to it. Dr (later Professor) John Martin was the first incumbent and for several years he proved to be an outstanding leader of the course. Every accepted student became a member of one of the Cambridge colleges, and was thus given an opportunity to participate in the life of the college and derive support or advice from their college tutor in addition, of course, to remaining in close touch with the Director of Studies. The course evoked very considerable interest and literally hundreds of applications came in from many parts of the world. We had decided to limit the number of admissions to the first course to eighteen students and we found that this was the optimum size. We kept it at this level during the entire period when I was the Director of the Institute. Foreign students were admitted, but their number was kept restricted.

A very good degree from a good university, and strong and reliable recommendations, were required. One of the recommendations I would remember, even if I were to lose my memory: 'and to give you a proof of the exceptional interest evoked by Mr. —— in the subject and in having a chance to be admitted to the Cambridge Course', a Vice-Chancellor of one of the leading universities of India wrote to me in full earnest, 'was that we have at last discovered that the very many books which we were regularly losing from our library were being taken by Mr. —— to be able to learn about the subject in the quietness of his home.' I understand from the present librarian of the Institute's library that books continue to be stolen at an alarming rate and I console myself with the thought that perhaps the present day thieves are actuated by similar noble motives.

We had the power to admit a candidate who had no university qualifications. We made use of it in three cases during my directorship and they proved to be outstanding successes. The course of three terms and part-time 'observation work' in the Easter vacation ended with an examination for the Diploma in Criminology comprising five papers plus a short dissertation. A strong contingent of outside examiners was a permanent feature. A mark of distinction could be given but was awarded only exceptionally.

Later we came to feel that a diploma was not a sufficiently formal recognition for such a sophisticated and thorough course. With the support of the Law Faculty and the Central Administration it was agreed that a master's degree was much more appropriate. I am not embarrassed to state that the course was soon regarded as one of the leading postgraduate courses of any kind in Britain and that it was generally looked upon in the well-informed and influential international circles as the best course of its kind in the field of criminology in the world at that time and for many years to come. The first three courses produced one professor each, and between them two readers, one senior lecturer and five or six who held lectureships of one kind or another. At least four Cambridge graduates held similar senior posts abroad and as the years passed by more and more were added to the list. I felt (and so did Dr Martin) that it was important to foster a regular assessment of what was being done and how it should have been done. Accordingly, arrangements were made to send out a succinct, and yet specific, questionnaire a few months after the students left the course. And we did so again, usually two years later. The information thus gathered was carefully analysed by the Director of the course and discussed by the senior staff of the Institute under my chairmanship at meetings held for that purpose. And, in a more informal way, reactions from the outside teachers were strongly encouraged.

Doctorates in criminology

There was, however, still another dimension to criminological training which we aimed to secure, namely doctorates in criminology. It cannot be questioned that a substantial doctoral dissertation requires concentration, depth, selectivity and marshalling of material. On its satisfactory completion it may mark an important, decisive stage in one's career. But it should not be assumed that one who has obtained a PhD in criminology is likely to make better use of it than the man or woman who has passed successfully through a tough postgraduate course with a good master's degree in criminology. The two experiences are not comparable, but they can supplement each other in an intellectually satisfying manner.

A transition from one to the other should be allowed, indeed encouraged. A good director of the course ought to be able to discover those who have a potential for writing a worthwhile book on an important criminological topic and should tempt them to do so. But, of course, it was left open to a student to proceed straight to a doctoral degree, bypassing the postgraduate course. Three years' research was the requirement for a doctoral degree. It was a handsome compliment to the Institute's standing that our proposal that, in suitable cases, the postgraduate course could be counted for one year, and thus the doctoral requirement could be reduced to two years, was supported by the Faculty Board of Law, adopted by the University and embodied in a proper statutory instrument of 11 May 1967.

It would, however, be unfair and incorrect to assume that we were inclined to expand the award of doctorates. Nothing was further from our thoughts than to become a kind of PhD factory of criminological dissertations. Our doctoral programme was selective and vigorous, 60 per cent having already completed the postgraduate course. Within the ten years of my stewardship no more than thirteen doctorates were conferred. Two came from Canada, one from the United States and one from Australia – the rest from Britain. But for two who followed different paths, they all became academics of high repute; they made, and continue to make, a distinguished contribution to a variety of important criminological concerns. Virtually all their dissertations were published either by the Institute or elsewhere. This was an impressive list and they all made us feel proud.[15] A not negligible pleasure was added by the fact that so many of them continued to maintain close links with the Cambridge Institute for many years to come.

---

15 The list which I described as 'The First Ones who Aimed High' comprised Roger Hood, Duncan Chappell, T.B. Hadden, Richard F. Sparks, A. Keith Bottomley, Keith O. Hawkins, John Hogarth, P.C.E. Moodie, K.D. Kemper, Eric Colvin, R.A. Ryall, Irvin Waller, Richard Ericson and Seán McConville.

Undergraduate teaching

I have always held that criminology should have an integral part to play at the undergraduate level in Faculties of Sociology and Social Sciences, in Departments of Political Science and in the curriculum of a Faculty of Law. It cannot, however, be the same kind of criminology, for it must be drastically remodelled to suit the ethos and purpose of such diverse centres and the kind of student body they are expected to instruct and to guide. This has not always been fully appreciated by some criminologists who have been given the chance to 'preach the gospel' beyond their customary abodes. And this has frequently been the main cause of their failure to integrate criminology into fields seemingly far apart and yet on closer scrutiny containing so many pivotal points of cross-fertilization. Most desirable in this context would be an arrangement in which the invited criminologist would construct a course in consultation with a distinguished professor of the particular faculty known for his or her endorsement of the idea. And a further suggestion, down the line, would be if, in addition to the course given by the criminologist, that person would also be given a chance to conduct a seminar in collaboration with one of the 'ordinary' professors.

I was anxious to transplant criminology into the regular teaching of the Law Faculty not only because, after all, we were part of the Law School, but also because of some wider considerations. From amongst law students come the future judges, the public prosecutors and many key functionaries concerned with criminal justice and law enforcement. Lawyers still produce a strong contingent of legislators and politicians. They play an important part in many sectors of social affairs. This varies in different countries, but is always prominent. It is when they are young that their minds are most open and most susceptible. Criminology needs to be put on the doorstep of their intellectual curiosity. This is easily said, but not easily done. Amongst university departments the law schools practically everywhere are the most conservative, the most traditionally minded. In effect the more conservative and traditional a law school is, the less inclined it will be to accept criminology as part of its programme of instruction. As I have so often said, specificity, consistency, precision, durability, legitimacy, neutrality and practicality are the outstanding features of the intellectual equipment of a legal mind. But the assumptions, involvements and conclusions of a criminological approach often do not display such characteristics. Indeed it often does not aspire to acquire them and to promote them. This criminology shares, to a large extent, with many other disciplines concerned with the study of the individual and of society. Yet it was so important to catch lawyers when they were young and our Institute was the place to experiment with this delicate relationship on a larger and more durable scale. If successful it would have a great impact on the law schools across the country.

I was by no means certain how our Cambridge students would respond to such an innovation and I was most anxious to avoid the risk of academic rebuff. The extraordinary publicity extended to the efforts of Mr Butler, of the Wolfson Foundation and ultimately of Cambridge University, to put criminology on the national map, all acted as a natural attraction to take up the subject and strengthened our hands considerably. But lawyers, by and large, are a phlegmatic and suspicious lot, anxious to get on with their future professional specialization, and all this noise could well have produced a negative attitude. The wise thing to do was to stage an experimental trial and, in the light of it, to assess the likelihood that criminology would prove to be attractive to law students.

In October 1961 there appeared in the *University Reporter* a 'Notice by the Wolfson Professor of Criminology' in which I reported that a series of weekly lectures on 'Aspects of Criminology' would be given in the Michaelmas and Lent Terms at 5 p.m. on Fridays in the Mill Lane Lecture Rooms. There would be seven lectures in Michaelmas Term and six in Lent Term. The series had a predominantly criminal policy bent, but not without a substantial criminological component. The team of lecturers consisted of the three senior members of the Institute's staff, the Visiting Fellow, two members of the Committee of Management and myself. The series proved to be an immediate hit and continued to be so to the very end. Mill Lane was packed and the audience consisted primarily of young men and women displaying throughout a keen interest. The first lecture was attended by about 275, and the second by about 400. The largest room was then assigned to the series and the level of attendance remained very high. The signals to go ahead were clear and bright.

A few months later the Faculty Board of Law approved a 'Syllabus of the Course on Criminology at Undergraduate Level'. Criminology identified as 'Subject No. 13. 40 Lectures' became part of the Law Tripos of the Cambridge Faculty of Law. It was a composite course: it started off with five lectures by me and was followed by thirty-five lectures given by eight senior members of the Institute and persons associated with it. It was rounded off by a series of visits to penal institutions and other centres and by a number of seminars. As with other subjects in the Tripos fortnightly supervisions in small groups (usually not exceeding four), and for which essays were prepared and discussed, were also organized by the student's college but mostly given by the Institute's staff. And, like in all other subjects, the instruction led to a written examination requiring the candidate to answer five questions. External examiners were frequently enlisted.

A few figures will suffice to show the response to this innovation. In June 1963, 90 of the 246 students taking Part II of the Law Tripos chose criminology as one of their subjects. In 1964, 111 out of 214 students took the paper, and in 1965, 100 out of 207 did so. In the years to follow the numbers dropped because some other new subjects were introduced, for example, 'family law' and 'labour law'. But criminology continued to hold its own. Indeed, in 1972, the last year of my directorship, the number went up from about 90, a decade earlier, to 120 – over 40 per cent of all those studying law. At no time did I hear a criticism that criminology was regarded as a 'soft' examination subject and in the light of our careful comparison with the results obtained in other topics, no such an aspersion could in fairness be sustained. I knew only one director of studies in a college who discouraged his undergraduates from selecting criminology as an option.

Much more characteristic of the prevailing attitude was the resolution adopted by the Faculty Board at its meeting on 15 July 1963 as recorded in the minutes:

> the Board agree to request the General Board to allow the Institute a grant . . . to cover the travelling expenses of groups of undergraduates to prisons and other institutions in connection with the course on Criminology for Part II of the Law Tripos, in response to a request from Professor Radzinowicz.

Such a decision in the Law School of Cambridge would have been unthinkable only a few years before, and I could not refrain from reflecting that at none of the major European law schools, which I had had the privilege of attending or visiting, were such opportunities ever provided for. The status accorded to criminology at the undergraduate level, the scope of its teaching and its pedagogical support in Cambridge, produced a situation which was unique even when compared with virtually all major law schools of the United States or of the British Commonwealth. Criminology began to make inroads in the European law schools, but even there – where, after all, criminology was born – it would have been very difficult to find a place where the subject was taught by a highly specialized, yet diversified and full-time, group of teachers following an integrated and carefully thought-out pattern. In most of the places, a fragmentary and rather haphazard expansion was annexed to the teaching of criminal law proper and usually discharged by a professor with a primary and predominantly juristic background.

I wish to conclude this section by recording with great satisfaction that in 1968 the Institute was approached by the university sub-committee which was considering teaching arrangements for the emerging Social and Political Sciences Tripos and asked to take part in their programme. It was concluded that it would be appropriate for students taking sociology to come to our eight lectures on sociological aspects of deviant behaviour and thus about a hundred students taking the new Tripos attended this segment of the course. In the natural course of events it is the sociologists who are expected to come to help lawyers to extend their perception of social matters. That in Cambridge this should have occurred the other way round was a compliment which gave us much pleasure.

MAKING IT WORK: INFUSING REALITY INTO AN IDEA

Building bridges with the practical world: the Advanced Course in Criminology

In order to preserve its *raison d'être* criminology must be able to respond to the reality of crime. From this basic interconnection several concrete consequences flow. To ignore it is to condemn criminology to sterility. But this cuts both ways. Criminologists should not cut themselves off from practitioners, nor should practitioners cut themselves off from criminologists. And thus, like so many other things of this world, it all largely depends in what form and how far this affinity of concerns should in practice be carried out.

Here also the Cambridge Institute was expected to make a beginning. To some extent the two worlds were already meeting in the postgraduate course and also in the consultative committees appointed to review the various projects of research undertaken by the Institute. This had proved to be useful to both sides, but manifestly it was not enough: the points of contact appeared somewhat accidental, haphazard and were diluted by other purposes. The Home Secretary was much more explicit about it. In his letter to Lord Adrian, Mr Butler also expressed the hope that, amongst the functions the Institute would discharge, would be

> to consider how best to develop the teaching of criminology for those outside the Universities (such as magistrates, police, members of the prison service and probation officers) who are concerned with the administration of justice and the prevention of crime . . . These are all functions for which there is a growing need that ought to be met.

I was strongly against it and made my views known to Sir Lionel Fox, who was particularly interested in this aspect of our programme. I felt (and still feel as strongly as ever) that an essential distinction should be drawn here between two types of instructional arrangements. There are training schemes for people working in the field of criminal justice. Courses of various duration operate under the auspices of police colleges, prison staff colleges, probation and parole departments, or judicial studies centres. Their aim is to provide regular professional training and refresher courses for substantial numbers and in rather constant and regular ways. Criminologists in their individual capacity and under proper conditions should be ready to give a hand. But meritorious and indeed indispensable as this mode of professional instruction is, it is not, and should not be, part of proper university activities.

And yet I felt, and so did the Committee of Management and the Advisory Council, that there was also a clear need for a special type of course which would cater for a small, but carefully selected, group of people who were likely to play an increasingly important role in the administration of criminal justice at various levels. It should widen the outlook of those attending it, and show them something of the relevance of research to their own specific work, and it should bring them up to date with the most recent research findings. It should raise them above and beyond their own valuable individual – yet necessarily restricted – experiences and should prompt them to reflect upon big issues, dominant trends or shifts of emphasis, in the concerns of criminal justice and of the public in general. It should not lead to any examination or degrees, and should not be convened too frequently. I also felt that such a course would foster a two-way traffic. Criminologists, whether teachers or researchers, are, and in many ways must remain, theoreticians. But theoreticians who deal with so real and so tangible a subject need contacts with practitioners. Through their involvement in such a course, academics would gain many vital insights, and be spurred to many fruitful initiatives.

There are two forms such a course can take. It may consist of participants from a homogeneous group, such as police, or prison or probation officers. Or it may be planned for a group which brings together members from all the major services. It was my contention that the composite course was likely to prove particularly interesting because different experiences, views and even conflicts would inevitably come to the fore. And there could be no doubt that, from the point of view of the Institute also, a composite course would prove much more stimulating because many criminological problems acquire a different meaning when tested against diverse experiences. In close consultation with Arthur Armitage (afterwards Sir Arthur Armitage), at that time Chairman of the Committee of Management, I prepared a memorandum on the structure of such a course and we left it with Sir Lionel Fox and his colleagues to probe further and deeper into the scheme's feasibility and desirability. Between June and October 1959 we held several meetings with the Home Office committee set up for that purpose. With an improved scheme in our hands Arthur Armitage and I had still to appear twice before the General Board of the Faculties to reply to their searching questions so as to chase away for good any suspicion that a door was being opened to something in fundamental conflict with an academic vision of things. We convinced them. In 1961 the Advanced Course in Criminology became an integral part of the Institute's structure.

Six groups were to constitute the core of the course:

1   Police: inspectors and chief inspectors
2   Prison and Borstal services: governors and assistant governors
3   Children's services: Heads and deputy heads of approved schools
4   Probation Service: principal probation officers and other supervisory officers with relevant experience
5   Prison doctors and psychologists
6   Magistrates and justices' clerks.

MAKING IT WORK: INFUSING REALITY INTO AN IDEA

The total number of participants was limited to forty-five and the various services were, as far as possible, to be evenly represented. It was to last three weeks, with three short weekend breaks. A course was announced by circulars issued by the Home Office and the Lord Chancellor's Department, specifying the qualifications required for admission. A most rigorous three-tier process of selection was set in motion. Short-lists were composed and presented by the relevant departments with recommendations for a selection by a special committee of the Home Office. These were then submitted to Cambridge's selection committee consisting of the Chairman and Secretary of the Committee of Management, the Director and Deputy Director of the Institute. And finally a joint committee, assisted by assessors from each of the departments, selected those to attend. Nominations had to be made at least six months in advance of the opening of the course. A very considerable effort went into this selection mechanism, especially if account is taken of the number of applications. Already over 200 applications were received for the first course in 1961. But it was an essential sorting out process and the crop which emerged out of it went very far to guarantee the success of the experiment.

The form the course took, I venture to affirm, was as novel as the organization of the course as such. There were to be no lectures and seminars of the usual kind, but instead the course was to centre around four sessions sharply focused on particular, well-defined major issues. The four topics chosen for the first Advanced Course in Criminology of 1966 consisted of:

1 Psychological factors in juvenile delinquency
2 Some aspects of law enforcement and the sentencing of recidivists
3 Social consequences of conviction
4 New developments in the treatment of offenders with respect to non-institutional methods and institutional methods.

A different senior member of the Institute was in charge of each of these topics, and each was joined by two or three distinguished experts from outside. It was the responsibility of each senior member in charge of the sessions to assemble and to edit well in advance essential up-to-date material relating to each of the topics for which he was responsible. The substantial sourcebooks were dispatched to each admitted member on the day of his or her admission, that is, six months before the opening of the course, so as to give everyone enough time to read and reflect upon it. While attending the course they were given an additional syllabus which contained some very exceptional pieces to peruse. Effective steps were taken to prevent the repetition of the topics in subsequent courses. The residential work started with a detailed statement by a representative from each of the six participating groups on their work and responsibilities within the system of criminal justice followed by an uninhibited and lengthy discussion.

MAKING IT WORK: INFUSING REALITY INTO AN IDEA

A few 'independent' lectures and colloquia were added to the agenda of the course, but they were very much in the background. Thus, in the first course, there was an opening lecture by me on the 'Study of criminology and criminal policy in Cambridge'; on the 'Justification for punishment' by Professor H.L.A. Hart; 'On current social interpretations of crime', by Dr (later Professor) Terrence Morris; 'The mentally abnormal offender and the penal system', by Dr (later Professor) Nigel Walker; 'Considerations in sentencing', by the Hon. Mr Justice Fenton Atkinson (as he then was); 'The aims and uses of criminological research', by T.S. Lodge; and 'The work of the Police Research and Planning Unit', by N. Bebbington, the former Chief Constable of Cambridge. There were a number of colloquia in which members of the staff reported to the course about the pieces of research they had been carrying out, and a discussion of a topic or two prepared by a member of the course. At the very end of the course a symposium was held devoted to a subject of exceptional topical interest. For the first course 'The Family Service and Family Courts' was chosen, under the chairmanship of Lady Rothschild, JP (Chairman of the Cambridge County Juvenile Court) and Lord Kilbrandon (Chairman of the Scottish Law Commission and the author of the Scottish Social Work Legislation). They were joined by three other speakers, Professor Monrad Paulsen of Columbia University (an authority on the subject) being one of them.

At each course, there were two observers, one from the Home Office and one from the Scottish Home Department. They were expected to present reports to the appropriate authorities on the course, and I was expected to do the same for the benefit of the Committee of Management and the Advisory Council. I also held a meeting or two to reassess the strong or weak parts of each course with those who ran it. Participants were encouraged to send comments directly to me if so desired or to the Director of the course.

The course gained so high a reputation that inquiries from many Commonwealth countries came in to ascertain whether admission from those distant parts would be considered. At some stage the Home Office approached us to ask whether the advantages which the course offered could not be spread wider by holding it annually rather than biannually. Realistically, we refused this flattering suggestion. The Institute was too small: our responsibilities in so many directions already widely stretched; and there was the fear that too many encounters of this kind might rob them of their refreshing spontaneity – a rather unusual experience might become a somewhat routine exercise. And we were determined that this should not be allowed to happen.

The members of the course were fortunate to stay at Caius College, living in the attractive new quarters of the college, so very close to the Institute, and it all added to the style and atmosphere of this enterprise. A formal black tie dinner in the magnificent Hall of my college marked the end of the course. It was usually attended by a Minister of State and the Permanent

Under-Secretary of State. Speeches by them as well as by participants of the course, the Director of the Course and the Director of the Institute were part of the occasion. And I still remember how thrilled they were when their former chief, now Master of Trinity – the father of the Institute, as he most properly may be referred to – came down to Nevile's Court to greet them all, and to remain with them for a while.

Another bridge: the Cropwood Fellowships

Fruitful as the Advanced Course proved to be, I felt that there were still other ways of fostering the two-way traffic of ideas and experiences between criminology and the outside practical world. But I also felt somewhat uneasy about it because here we were entering a largely uncharted field with no precedents whatsoever to guide us and with an impending criticism that our designs might well be labelled as belonging to the semi-academic world, which, by definition, was condemned to remain outside the academic world proper. In this case, the plan would be to stimulate a few carefully selected practitioners to embark upon an active and critical stocktaking of their own work in the field of criminal justice, or to pursue in depth a significant topic which was of special interest to them. I had no doubt that such a scheme would meet a need long felt amongst those involved in the day-to-day enforcement of the criminal law and the control of criminal behaviour. They had few opportunities to stand back and consider the implications of their experiences. It also would help to disseminate amongst them a keener appreciation of the problems encountered in research as well as to direct the attention of the Institute to some of the most sensitive or topical issues in criminal justice and criminal policy.

I shared these views, still rather vague, with R.D. Fairn (Assistant Under-Secretary of State, Prison Department), one of our lecturers, who stated that this project would greatly appeal to a Quaker foundation, and he being a Quaker himself would be pleased to act as our ambassador. An encouraging response from the secretary of the foundation followed and no time was lost; in friendly consultations with them and the Committee of Management of the Institute, a Cropwood Scheme was brought into being. 'It appealed to Paul Cadbury, the Chairman,' wrote Anthony Wilson, the Secretary of the Barrow and Geraldine S. Cadbury Trust, 'on both counts: it combined the proper demands of research and publication, with a whole-hearted respect for the experience of people working at the coal face'.[16]

---

16 Paul Strangman Cadbury (chairman), who died on 24 October 1984 at the age of 88, was, as *The Times* (31 October 1984) stated in its obituary notice, 'a deeply concerned Quaker whose success in the family firm was equalled only by his commitment to philanthropy and public service'.

MAKING IT WORK: INFUSING REALITY INTO AN IDEA

In June 1967 we were happy to announce that we were in a position to offer occasional short-term fellowships, henceforth to be known as Cropwood Fellowships. The object was to enable practitioners to have a kind of 'sabbatical' from their normal duties. They would be attached to the Institute for a period of study concentrating on a definite purpose. This might involve: undertaking a specific piece of research (or completing an inquiry already begun) and presenting the results in the form of a short monograph or article; preparing special lectures; or intensive reading on a subject of practical and topical concern. Fellowships would normally be tenable for a period of six weeks, three months or six months, their exact duration depending on the kind and scale of work which was proposed. Fellows would have full use of the Institute's library and accommodation for study would be provided. A senior member of the Institute's staff would be invited by me to be available for frequent consultation and guidance. The amount of the award was fixed, in each Individual case, so as to be sufficient to cover travel and living expenses in Cambridge, and any reasonable expense involved in their work. Members of services falling under the jurisdiction of the Home Office who were successful in obtaining a fellowship would be granted leave with pay for the period of study.

As in the case of the postgraduate course, the doctorate programme, or the advanced course, I was determined that the scheme should be carried out in a selective and cautious manner. The first announcement produced nearly a hundred applications. The procedure for determining who should be admitted was rigorous. The applications were carefully scrutinized by the senior staff of the Institute, and a small number of candidates were short-listed. They were not automatically selected: they had to appear at the Institute and were subjected to a lengthy interview by all the senior members of the Institute deliberating under my chairmanship. Perhaps one figure will suffice to characterize the selectivity of the appointment process. Ultimately, out of the hundred applications, five candidates were chosen to become the first Cropwood Fellows. Brief reports about their progress were expected from their advisers at regular intervals.

The launching of the programme in 1967 proved to be a successful and happy experience. The first batch of Cropwood Fellows took full advantage of these unusual opportunities, and completed their tasks speedily and well. Fellowships for 1969 were advertised in September 1968. There were seventy-six applicants and I was able to report to the Advisory Council and to the Committee of Management of the Institute that 'in terms of formal qualifications and experience, the general standard of candidates for 1969 was higher than in 1968'. But again we aimed at the very best and only six were selected. The publications of the Cropwood Fellows who passed through the Institute since 1966 have evoked much interest. Between 1968 and 1973 their number amounted to twenty-four, covering many sensitive aspects of the criminal justice system. Two further encouragements came our way. The Home Office, no doubt by a decision of Sir Philip Allen, agreed to add a grant sufficient to meet the cost of two additional fellowships each year. And the Barrow and Geraldine S. Cadbury Trust expanded its initial generosity by deciding to support the benefaction for an indefinite period of time.

Yet another bridge: Cropwood Round-Table Conferences

The 'Cropwood Round-Table Conferences' were again a rather unusual departure, but their utility, I stated at the time, was obvious. This is still as true today as it was when I first formulated it. Crime, attitudes towards it and the ways of controlling it are not static phenomena; they often change and rapidly so. This is particularly true of democratic societies, because crime and punishment are debated within the context of open public exposure. Topics and solutions emerge constantly and many of them rapidly attract public approval, rejection or severe scrutiny. There is a need to assess whether they have real substance or are of more than transient topicality. At their inception they often do not need to be the object of a long-term exhaustive investigation, but rather of a rapid preliminary, and yet expert, assessment of their worth and potentialities. Thus, a round-table conference consisting of a small but highly qualified number of participants, guided by specialists and leading to specific conclusions, can be very useful.

I can do no better than to give a brief description of one or two such conferences launched in the period 1968–72 and the way we went about running them. The conference on 'The Disposal and Treatment of Psychopathic Offenders' was convened by a senior member of the Institute. Meetings took place in the library of the Institute and the participants were entertained at Darwin College. There were fifteen participants, including lawyers, doctors, civil servants and academics. Thirteen papers were prepared and circulated well in advance and fully discussed. They were all edited and published by the Institute with an introduction by the convenor. They were sent for review to leading journals and the press. Two hundred copies were sold at once and a substantial reprinting was arranged. At some later stage, I had the pleasure to act as a convenor for a conference on the 'Suspended Sentence' – at that time an intensely disputed and controversial issue. In addition to a number of papers from Britain, I asked Marc Ancel of the Supreme Court of Justice of France to prepare and to put at our disposal a comprehensive report on the European experience with this type of sentence. Other topics were 'The residential treatment of disturbed and delinquent boys', 'Community homes and the approved school system', 'Criminological implications of chromosome abnormality' and 'The security industry in the United Kingdom'. The latter, directed by two institute convenors, drew twenty-five participants including executives of the main companies, senior police officers, senior civil servants and criminologists, supported by eight substantial papers, fuelled by a rich discussion probing several aspects of this complex problem, and again duly published.

During my directorship six Cropwood Round-Table Conferences were set on foot and as years passed by they progressed from strength to strength.

Visiting Fellows to the Institute

Soon after the Institute had been established we were successful in convincing the General Board about the desirability of attracting scholars and experts from outside Cambridge to join the Institute for a fixed period of time to participate in, and contribute to, its work. They would substantially add to the role of the Institute as a centre for the interchange of ideas, and last, but not least, while in Cambridge they could be 'lent' to other growing centres in the country, to share with them their knowledge and experience. We stated that, in view of the growing prestige of the Institute, we had good reason to believe that we would be able to attract persons of real distinction. On 1 June 1960 the General Board presented a report to the university embodying this idea and shortly afterwards it was formulated and embodied in ordinances.

This required but a few organizational provisions, all of them straightforward and easy to administer. Appointments and reappointments to visiting fellowships were to be made by the Committee of Management of the Institute for periods not exceeding one year at a time. There were to be no more than four Visiting Fellows at any one time. Visiting Fellows during the term of their fellowship were not allowed to hold any established university office or post in Cambridge, but would become members of the university. More often than not they would also be attached to one of the colleges, though this, of course, was not stipulated in the published provisions. They would be required, under the general supervision of the Committee of Management, to take part in the teaching and research programme of the Institute; in practice they would be expected to undertake any other duties that would be regarded as advantageous to the work of the Institute, and be compatible with their formal position as a Senior Visitor to the Institute. Their stipend, if any, was to be determined by the Committee of Management, with the approval of the Financial Board and the General Board on the occasion of each appointment or reappointment; this applied also to the grants to meet travelling or other expenses incurred in connection with the fellowship.

The implementation of this promising scheme hinged on the provision of adequate funds from outside: the General Board made it clear that the University would not be involved in any additional expense. They even expressed the hope that 'some Visiting Fellows may indeed be willing to receive nothing other than the reimbursement of their expenses'. In effect this expectation proved to be correct with respect to our first two Visiting Fellows from

England. In the case of American Visiting Fellows, who were of vital importance to us, the Ford Foundation came forward and assigned a portion of their generous grant to us to serve this purpose for a period of five years.

Sir Lionel Fox was the first Visiting Fellow from England. He accepted our invitation to join us, on his retirement as the Chairman of the Prison Commission, on 1 October 1960. He moved to Cambridge with Lady Fox and we installed him in the Institute. He was as keen and eager as ever and we were looking forward to a most fruitful collaboration. Alas, he died about a year later. But even during this brief period he rendered us great service in the planning of the Advanced Course in Criminology, and in some of our activities abroad where his reputation stood so high. It was my melancholy duty to deliver his lectures and conduct the seminars which he had prepared with so much enthusiasm and thoroughness for our first postgraduate course. I lost a good friend and a wise adviser. But I have never forgotten the brave, kind-hearted man, with his high sense of duty, his faithful adherence to principles, his never faltering belief in the necessity of keeping alive the dignity of English criminal justice (I shudder to think how he would react to the present fashion of selling off parts of the penal system as yet another ordinary commodity to be made available in the open market), his unshakeable conviction that penal reform and penal discipline can be made to work in productive harmony. He is best remembered in penological circles for his book *The English Prison and Borstal Systems* (1952).[17]

Dr Manuel López-Rey was the second Fellow to belong to this category. He took up residence in this country and was elected by the Committee of Management as from 1 October 1966. As the Chief of the Social Defence Section of the United Nations, which was primarily concerned with penal matters, from 1952 to 1961, and afterwards as an Adviser to the United Nations, he had acquired considerable experience and knowledge of criminological developments in many parts of the world. His association with the Institute continued to our mutual satisfaction virtually until his death in 1987. We were deeply moved when his widow, following his will, presented the Institute with a benefaction used to reward the best student of the postgraduate course. A Festschrift was presented to Dr López-Rey by criminologists from many parts of the world at the Seventh United Nations Congress on the Prevention of Crime and the Treatment of Offenders in Milan in August 1985.[18]

---

17 See also his earlier book, *The Modern English Prison* (1934). For an exceptionally good account of Lionel Fox, an outstanding man in so many ways, see his obituary in *The Times* (9 October 1961) and Lord Butler's note on him in *Dictionary of National Biography 1961–70* (1981), pp. 386–7.

18 *Crime and Criminal Policy* edited by Professor Pedro R. David. My successor in Cambridge, Professor Nigel Walker, was the author of a brief but well-informed and warm obituary in *The Times* (17 December 1987), p. 189.

MAKING IT WORK: INFUSING REALITY INTO AN IDEA

Lack of funds cut short any further appointments from Britain and the Commonwealth. In contrast, we were able to exploit to the full the generous facilities accorded to us by the Ford Foundation. The sheer enumeration of the American experts shows how fortunate we were in enlisting their dedicated collaboration. The late Professor D.R. Cressey, from the University of Los Angeles, was the first Fellow from the United States to join the Institute (July 1961–July 1962). He was followed by Professor A.S. Goldstein (afterwards Dean of the Law School and Provost of Yale) who stayed with us from July 1964 to August 1965; Professor S.H. Kadish (afterwards Dean of the Law School) from the University of California, Berkeley, who made me aware of certain aspects of sentencing policies in the United States and put some valuable material into my hands; Judge R. Tyler, at that time a Federal Judge; Professor Marvin E. Wolfgang from the University of Pennsylvania; followed in the period 1965–6 by Professor Peter Low from the University of Virginia (afterwards Provost and Vice-President of the university); Professor A.K. Cohen from the University of Connecticut, the author of the unusual and elegantly written book *Delinquent Boys: The Culture of the Gang*, appointed a Fellow for 1972–3, was the last of them while I was Director. I was a fortunate convenor of so eminent and diverse a group of scholars.

Their activities while at the Institute were many and manifold. My policy was to take fullest possible advantage of their particular expertise. They taught (lectures and seminars) in the postgraduate course; in the advanced course, both as part of the regular syllabus, and by conducting seminars on a subject of their own choice; they presented reports to the National Conference on Criminology, which at that time was convened by the Institute on a regular basis; they lectured on important subjects in the Faculty of Law, or in their college, or in other centres such as the British Society of Criminology, the Institute of Advanced Legal Studies, the London School of Economics, at Oxford and Edinburgh; they did their own research, especially when in its final stages, or still better joined hands with some of the senior members of the Institute in undertaking a piece of research. They engaged in informal contacts with the senior staff of the Institute, and with others from outside interested in the promotion of criminology and in the comparative patterns of its evolution. They often left behind them important written work which found its way into learned journals or monographs. They brought prestige to the Institute and enriched the contents of our work. It had become clear to us, already when the Fellowships were in the middle of their deployment, that an Institute which aspires to be more than a local, parochial department cannot effectively discharge its functions without them.

Programme of research

The task of launching and carrying out a significant programme of research was regarded as no less important and topical than the organization of a diversified programme of instruction of an academic and practical nature. And it was no less intriguing because hardly anywhere at that time was a diverse programme of criminological research expected to be carried out simultaneously under the same roof. What arrangements should be made and what rules should be observed to insure as far as possible that this task should be discharged in an effective and fair manner to everyone concerned with it? And how should they fit in with the purposes and the role assigned to the Institute as a whole? I feel that I went far in answering these questions in the previous section of the chapter, but I also feel that more details should be added to round off the picture.

It was expected that each senior member of the Institute would undertake substantial projects of research. This was regarded as an essential, irreplaceable condition of the appointment and throughout the tenure of the appointment. No less categorical was the responsibility of the Institute. Once a project was agreed upon and launched the Institute was bound to provide all reasonable financial assistance and all the other facilities essential to the successful and speedy completion of the work. Often the cost involved would be assessed beforehand on the basis of a pilot study. In addition to ample secretarial help, research officers and assistants (whose number depended on the nature of the projected inquiry) would be appointed by me, with the chief investigator playing an essential role in the process of selection. Their appointments would be made in order to provide maximum help to the inquiry, but also with a view to giving a chance to young researchers to develop their potentialities and stimulate them to devote themselves in the future to criminological work.

As the main inquiry was progressing the chief investigator was encouraged to publish papers, mainly in professional journals, which could be defined as the by-products of the main inquiry. Sufficiently important not to be forgotten, they related usually to detailed methodological aspects, or covered ancillary themes which emerged in the course of the main work. Frequent references to the investigation in progress were expected to be made by the chief investigators in all their teaching activities in the Institute and elsewhere, and reputable and effective occasions were seized to make the central findings of the investigations known to the wider public, through lectures, the press, or the media. The researchers would be given the guarantee that the fruits of their labours would always be published, and that no attempt would be made, neither by the Director, the Home Office nor anybody else, to change any of his basic views and conclusions. The end product would be published under the auspices of the Institute in a criminological series promoted by a publishing house of high repute. Yet the chief investigator would have the choice to take the book to some other publisher if he were to feel, and be able to prove, that conditions of publication offered by the latter were better than those offered by the series.

Though launched, supported and published by the Institute, the book belonged to the researcher in chief, and it was he, and he alone, who would sign the contract with the publishers of the series and be the recipient of the royalties and any other emoluments arising out of it. The function of the Director, at this final stage, was to do all he could to ensure that the publication would turn out to be as gratifying and rewarding as possible to the author. The role of the research assistants would be acknowledged on the title page, or in the preface, as was appropriate. Often the Director, in his capacity as the editor of the series, would welcome the new publication in a brief foreword. The launching of the volume would as a general rule be marked by a dignified reception held in London, sponsored by the publisher.

Inquiries varied in size and complexity. The larger projects imposed a great strain upon those conducting them. They employed several research assistants, extended over several years and were always in danger of becoming unwieldy. The medium-sized or smaller inquiries could be better focused, were less overweight and more pliably tuned to get more specialized and significant findings. Nor should it be forgotten that, as a general rule, the chief investigator, as a senior member of the Institute's staff, had many other functions to discharge within the Institute in addition to research. What I have described as the question of strategy in the distribution of criminological research calls for the most careful consideration. I firmly believed that as a general rule the chief investigator should carry no more than one project at a time. Whenever an ambitious long-term piece of research is launched, interim reports should be issued and made widely available. After two years' duration any such project should be subjected to the strongest possible reassessment with the view to determining whether it should be continued. It should be the responsibility of the Director to set this in motion and bring it to a definite conclusion, to be settled in its turn by a decision of the Committee of Management. Once an inquiry was set in motion it was assumed that the chief investigator would keep in close and regular touch with the Director throughout the progress of the research and would be receptive to any ideas and suggestions which might emerge out of this relationship.

I strongly felt that this connection was not sufficient to give to the chief investigator the fullest expert assistance, nor to the Institute as a whole or to those who financed the project, a conviction that satisfactory progress was being made. In consequence, I proposed that each project should have a consultative committee, as a general rule with independent members enlisted from outside Cambridge. I was an ex-officio member of all such committees, but never a chairman of any one of them. They were exceptionally well-qualified advisory bodies which met regularly from the very beginning of an inquiry until it was completed and ready to appear as a publication. The chief investigator and the assistants and consultants (if any) were always part of the meetings which usually were held in London. The members discharged the duties without any remuneration, except reimbursement of the expenses of travel and subsistence. Their deliberations were recorded and made available to the Committee of Management if so desired. There were, on average, six or seven such consultative committees active each year, each meeting twice a year. I never missed one.

Naturally, there is no such thing as one kind of criminological research to be pursued to the exclusion of others. Indeed, advances in and the standing of criminology depend on a diversity of approaches and interpretations. But there is such a thing as one kind of research being pointedly suited to a certain set of circumstances. This concern may well appear irrelevant to scholars working on their own, but had to be regarded as of prime importance within the framework of an Institute, projected some forty years ago, as a pivotal part of an attempt to put criminology on the national map. I was fully aware of it and felt most reluctant to encourage complex, long and expensive investigations with the self-assigned purpose of unravelling the origins of crime and constructing broad, flamboyant 'theories', with vague pretensions. This was a real danger then, and to some extent it is even now. I was very fortunate that my Committee of Management, the Advisory Council and our friends in the Home Office, all gave me their unflinching support in taking this seemingly negative attitude. Unavoidably I had sometimes to bear stoically epitaphs of stodginess, anti-intellectualism, theoretical retardedness and even of narrow-mindedness which were, much too often, attached to me.

One inquiry in particular, the Cambridge Study in Delinquent Development (formerly known as the Family Delinquent Study), did throw some valuable insights into the controversial and tortuous question of the role of individual disposition versus social environment in the production of crime.[19] It was also one of the first inquiries in the world to lay down the foundation for long-term cohort studies. However, the core of our programme of research and reassessment centred upon certain specific, well-defined, criminological and penological problems, plucked out, as if it were, of the vast field of crime and its control. They dealt with the incidence, distribution and trends in crime; the quantitative and qualitative indices of crime; the classification of offences; the characteristics and *modus operandi* of several categories of offender; the dark figure of crime and chances of impunity; the cost of crime; police personnel problems; the reorganization of the courts; sentencing processes and disparities; the extra-legal social consequences of conviction; the shortcomings of some penal sanctions; the crisis of the prison system; the limitations of treatment within a captive society; patterns of relapse into crime.

The inquiries carried out during my directorship were mostly contained in

---

19 For a view in sharp contrast to mine, see Professor Stanley Cohen, *Against Criminology* (1988), pp. 76–7.

some twenty volumes of our Cambridge Series, attractively published and properly launched in many parts of the world. A few found their way to other publishing houses. To this should be added some twenty shorter mimeographed reports or papers largely grounded on research carried out in the Institute. The total research output, under any criteria of valuation – providing that it was fair and competent – was very impressive; and again much more so if a fair and competent account were taken of all the other regular activities of the Institute in which the chief investigators invariably played so prominent a part. A further, no less striking, fact was that not one of the topics has lost its significance in methodology and substance, indeed each of them is as relevant now as it was some thirty or forty years ago.

A word about finances: the chief investigators drew no remuneration additional to their university stipends for the work involved in the inquiries. But the research fund proper, including the stipends of the research assistants or consultants, as well as the expenses entailed in secretarial help and all kinds of incidental expenses (quite considerable), was provided by the Home Office and was usually fixed in consultation with the Research and Planning Unit of the department. From £9,400 in the first year (1960–1) it rose through various fluctuations to an annual maximum in the period 1971–2 of £37,000. Taking the programme as a whole, the annual average during the ten-year period of my directorship was £22,000, which meant that no more than between 15 and 20 per cent of the total 'outside' Home Office Research Budget was taken up by Cambridge. Translated into 1995 terms, it would amount to around £250,000, a modest budget by current standards.

Miscellaneous but connected activities

A note is necessary on what I would describe as miscellaneous but connected activities for lack of a better description. There were very many such activities undertaken by the senior staff and by me, sometimes at first sight appearing divergent and having little in common, but which, when more closely looked upon, soon revealed a common purpose, namely that of promoting more sophisticated criminological methods of inquiry or a greater emphasis on central, yet somewhat neglected, issues. What follows is not a full inventory but a series of selective characterizations.

Between 1967 and 1971 papers were presented by four members of the senior staff to the Conferences of Directors of Criminological Research Institutes organized by the Council of Europe Committee on Crime Problems. A report on 'Research on the Effectiveness of Punishment and Treatment' presented to the Council of Europe in 1967; 'Interaction between Types of Treatment and Types of Offender' was the topic in 1969; yet another on 'The Effectiveness of Measures of After-Care, Probation and Parole' in 1970; and still another on 'The Dark Figure' in 1971. They all evoked exceptionally great interest amongst penal administrators and criminologists across

Europe. I was present in Strasbourg when they were delivered and proud to listen to them all.

On several occasions sophisticated help was given in a consultative capacity to important domestic inquiries. Such, for instance, as the 'Special Statistical Survey' presented to the Royal Commission on Assizes and Quarter Sessions 1966–9 by G.N.G. (Gerry) Rose, a member of the Institute and an undisputed expert in statistical methods; or by Richard F. Sparks, as the author of the 'Appendix C' to the Report of the Advisory Council on the Penal System on *The Regime for Long-Term Prisoners in Conditions of Maximum Security* in 1968. Derick McClintock, a senior member of staff, was appointed to sit as a magistrate in Cambridge. He also played a welcome role in the work of the Magistrates' Association and became a member of the departmental committee on the subject of Criminal Statistics (the Perks Committee). Two members, Donald West and Roger Hood, served, at different periods, on the Parole Board at the critical time when this new institution was feeling its way and its place within the penal system of the country. Donald West acted as an honorary consultant psychiatrist, mostly assessing offenders for Cambridge Courts, as a member of the Home Office Advisory Council on Child Care, and was also invited to lecture to the course for newly appointed judges set up by Lord Parker, the Lord Chief Justice. Many of these collaborative links were not just episodic occurrences, but extended over long periods of time.

At irregular, but thoroughly prepared, occasions I communicated essential information and perspectives to the Home Affairs Committees of the Conservative and Labour Parties when concerned with problems of crime. This led to informal discussions and exchange of views in one of the committee rooms in the House of Commons. Responding to invitations from the international press to comment upon the state of crime on the occasion of the publication of the *Annual Criminal Statistics* also became a regular fixture.

On another occasion, a cumulative and extensive report on the 'Young-adult offender' was submitted to the International Society of Social Defence for its Congress in Stockholm in 1964 and became a central part of the *Proceedings of the Congress*. Sometimes I urged comparative exchanges of views 'on the spot' such as the 'Anglo-Scandinavian seminar' held in Norway, when a delegation of some twelve criminologists from Britain, which I brought together, in consultation with my colleagues, met their colleagues from Denmark, Finland, Norway and Sweden for a well-planned discussion of criminological problems of common or contrasting interests supported by intensive reports. This was made possible by a generous grant from the British Council. Two years later we met together in Cambridge.

I have no difficulty in picking up some twenty-five occasional papers, articles and critical notes, published by the senior staff during my directorship in leading periodicals or independently, as well as influential books, such as Donald West's *The Young Offender* (1967) and *Homosexuality* (1968), or Roger Hood and Richard F. Sparks's *Key Issues in Criminology* (1970). They also have lost nothing of their intrinsic significance and topicality over these many years.

I tried hard not to be left behind. I continued to pursue historical studies and during these years a number of pieces appeared in several journals, pieces which soon were to form part of the forthcoming volumes of my *History*.[20] Among the lectures, in addition to the one already mentioned on 'Sir James Fitzjames Stephen, 1829–1894, and his Contribution to the Development of Criminal Law', it is perhaps worth mentioning, primarily because of the occasion, 'Changing Attitudes towards Crime and Punishment and the Devices to Control it'.[21] Amongst other lectures on non-historical themes, I would like to single out five: 'The Study of Criminology in Cambridge', *Medico-Legal Journal*, vol. 29 (1966), pp. 122–33; 'The Criminal in Society' (Peter Le Neve Foster Lecture with Lord Parker, LJ, in the chair), *Journal of the Royal Society of Arts*, vol. 112 (1964), pp. 916–29; 'The Dangerous Offender' (Fourth Frank Newsam Memorial Lecture, Police College, Bramshill, 1 August 1968), *Police Journal*, vol. 41 (1968), pp. 411–47; 'Them and Us' (lecture given under the auspices of the New Bridge at the Mansion House with Lord Butler in the chair), *Cambridge Law Journal*, vol. 30 (1972), pp. 260–79; and 'The Criminal Law Explosion – Can it be Controlled?' (public lecture, Columbia Law School), *Columbia Journal of Law and Social Problems*, vol. 9 (1972), pp. 88–130.

In 1967–9 I had the pleasure of collaborating with Professor Marvin Wolfgang of Pennsylvania University, one of the foremost criminologists, as the result of which (with the valuable assistance of Joan King of the Institute's senior staff), we produced a three-volume collection called *Crime and Justice* which was used in forty universities across the United States. At the time Fred Graham, in his review in the *New York Times*, referred to it as 'the Bible of Criminology'.[22] In 1956 the second and third volumes of my *History* appeared and in 1968 the fourth.[23] By then I needed and – I venture to say – I deserved a prolonged and decent holiday.

---

20 Such as 'First Steps Towards Government Control over Police Forces before Peel', *Law Quarterly Review*, vol. 70 (1954), pp. 88–108; 'The Radcliffe Murders', *Cambridge Law Journal*, vol. 14 (1956), pp. 39–66; 'New Departures in Maintaining Public Peace in the Face of Chartist Disturbances', *Cambridge Law Journal*, vol. 18 (1961), pp. 53–80; 'Introduction' to Sidney and Beatrice Webb, *English Prisons under Local Government* (1963 edn).
21 Selden Society Lecture (1957); Discourse to the Royal Institution of Great Britain, delivered on 28 February 1958 and reprinted in *Law Quarterly Review*, vol. 75 (1959), pp. 381–400.
22 *Crime and Justice*, 3 volumes (Basic Books, 1971; 2nd revised edn, 1977), vol. 1, *The Criminal in Society*; vol. 2, *The Criminal in the Arms of the Law*; vol. 3, *The Criminal in Confinement*.
23 Leon Radzinowicz, *History of the English Criminal Law and its Administration*, vol. 2, *The Clash between Private Initiative and Public Interest in the Enforcement of the Law* (1956); vol. 3, *Cross Currents in the Movement for the Reform of the Police* (1956); vol. 4, *Grappling for Control* (1968).

MAKING IT WORK: INFUSING REALITY INTO AN IDEA

National Conferences of Research and Teaching in Criminology

The desirability of bringing together criminologists on a broader national basis was strongly stressed by all of us involved in the initial planning of the Institute. The National Conference of Research and Teaching in Criminology, held in Cambridge (8–10 July 1964), was the first of its kind in Britain. From its initiation it was not perceived as an event which might or might not occur again. Rather, it was to be the beginning of what I expected to become a permanent fixture in the life of the British academic criminological community. They were not to be loosely structured gatherings. They were planned as a scientific congress should be, working through sections recording and exploring the latest happenings and thinking. Emphasis was put on the contemporary scene and contemporary concerns. Comparative developments were expected to be strongly emphasized. Several stringent rules were laid down to ensure, as far as possible, the high quality of these gatherings.

The procedure I followed in relation to each of the conferences was as follows. I started by sending a note to all my senior colleagues in the Institute asking them to reflect about subjects which should be put on the agenda and to share with me their preliminary opinions. I followed this up by two lengthy meetings in the Institute in order to give more precision and emphasis to our views. The next very important step was to send an invitation to several leading criminologists and social scientists from outside Cambridge, and to a few Home Office experts, to meet us in London to discuss the agenda and to constitute an *ad-hoc* organizing committee. I found these discussions invariably fruitful and an agreed agenda for the conference emerged out of them. The number of topics selected to make up the scientific programme of a conference varied between five and nine. A senior colleague from the Institute was asked to be responsible for organizing the details of the conference and for making sure that it ran smoothly. He was assisted by the librarian. Although I was always invariably involved in every aspect of the conference, from the time of its inception to its closing, my formal involvement would usually be a brief speech of welcome and a few summarizing remarks before its dispersal. Only once did I assume the chairmanship of a section: at the Third National Conference in July 1968 when the two distinguished rapporteurs from abroad happened to be my old friends, Professor Herbert Wechsler and Monsieur Marc Ancel. The holding of the conference was made known well in advance. Anyone could apply to attend, and those who decided to come received an invitation. The press was admitted to all deliberations and could take part in the discussions. Usually a press conference was held before the opening to focus attention on the issues selected for examination. On each occasion the participants enjoyed the hospitality of Caius College and the three days allocated to the conference passed quickly. Concentration during the day happily blended with informal exchanges at dinner in Hall, and more often than not for many hours afterwards.

Each topic was to be tackled by at least one rapporteur and two commentators. The latter, as far as possible, represented different points of view. The three statements were embodied in fully written up and mimeographed documents which were in the hands of each participant of the conference at least two weeks before the meeting in Cambridge. A discussion which followed the presentations by the rapporteur and the two commentators was conducted under the chairmanship of an eminent person. No resolutions (or recommendations) were adopted and no vote on any propositions taken, although naturally the degree of consensus or dissent was duly noted by those in charge of the conference.

As an example may I reproduce the agenda of the First Conference (8–10 July 1964)? The six sessions were taken up by the following topics: 'Ways of classifying offences for criminological research', 'Interviewing in criminological surveys', 'Family patterns in delinquency', 'Prognosis in young criminals', 'Research into probation', 'Research in penal institutions' and 'Research in criminology'. And there were two special communications from abroad: 'Study of criminal law in America' and 'Criminological studies in Canada'. The conference was covered by seven chairmen, seven rapporteurs, and sixteen commentators. Some twenty-four reports were submitted. The programme of the last conference (8–10 July 1970) over which I had the honour to preside was possibly even more thought-provoking and certainly more controversial. It included 'The contribution of the labelling and social interactionist school to criminological thought' (with two subsections), 'Aspects of violent criminal behaviour' (with four subsections) and 'Research on police' (with two subsections). Eight chairmen, twelve rapporteurs and fourteen commentators came forward to shoulder the work of the conference and they all discharged their tasks splendidly. The progressive Permanent Under-Secretary of State, Sir Philip Allen (now Lord Allen of Abbeydale), came to visit us and delivered the opening address.

Altogether thirty-nine topics were covered by the Conferences and some eighty-seven chairmen, rapporteurs, commentators and visiting lecturers were involved. The records of the first four conferences contained in four substantial volumes were deposited in the Institute's library. I regret that we were unable also to preserve the stream of sometimes intense, but always very refreshing, discussions which constituted an important part of what I described as 'criminologists in concert'. It was my fervent hope that a beginning had been made which would not be allowed to disappear, and that perhaps one day the initiative of the 'Cambridge parents' and their supporters would not continue to be identified with Cambridge alone, but would be given a wider national scope. This did in fact happen. The National Conferences of Research and Teaching in Criminology have been peacefully taken over by the British Society of Criminology and have become an integral and central part of its activities. My only regret is that when in 1989 they met in Sheffield they failed to mention their predecessors and happily awarded to themselves the label of having been the first national conference. Criminologists, not unlike some criminals, should sometimes make better use of their memories and try not to forget events of the past.

To preserve the quality of this development I recommended that the conferences should not take place annually, but every two years. Even so, a certain, rather serious, weakness was creeping in – a counterpart of the success which accompanied our initiative. The difficulty of reconciling the quality of work discharged by a conference and its increasing size was becoming a problem. And there was the growing appetite for criminology evinced by the younger generation of students and scholars which undoubtedly the conferences were satisfying, an appetite which should not be cut off by arbitrary and bureaucratic limiting interferences.

The first conference was attended by seventy people from all over the country; and the second by a good hundred. As criminology itself expanded, and as interest in its findings spread, the numbers expanded too. Thus at the fourth conference in 1970 the hall was overflowing and a thorough discussion was severely limited. On this occasion we had the privilege of welcoming nearly two hundred and fifty. In my closing statement I suggested that the time had come to reconsider the form of future meetings, and I proposed that a planning committee should be set up to prepare a report for the conference in 1972. In his vote of thanks to the Institute the late Professor T.C.N. Gibbens endorsed my proposal and it met with unanimous support. My recent visits to the Criminological Conference in Cardiff (1993) and much more pointedly to the meeting of the American Society of Criminology in Miami (1995) have made me acutely aware that the problem was still there, awaiting for a constructive solution.

I do not wish to end this account without mentioning a rather amusing episode. Right in the middle of the Third National Conference, taking place in Cambridge in July 1968, a group of seven young social scientists and criminologists, participants of the conference, met secretly and decided to establish an independent 'National Deviancy Conference' and soon afterwards they duly met in York. At the time, it reminded me a little of naughty schoolboys playing a nasty game on their stern headmaster. It was not necessary to go 'underground' because we were not in any way opposed to discussing new approaches to the sociology of deviance. Indeed, the subjects of 'Social reaction to deviance and its effects on crime and criminal careers' as well as 'The contribution of the labelling and social interactionist school to criminological thought' formed the agenda of the first section of our Fourth National Conference (July 1970) with Laurie Taylor, David Downes and Paul Rock as rapporteurs, and four commentators, all under the chairmanship of Professor T.H. Marshall. Although not invited to their conference in York I asked one of my senior colleagues in the Institute to go there as an observer.

My attitude was by no means hostile or patronizing. As I stated at the time and later, movements in ideas, like life in general, often lead to seemingly unexpected, baffling results. Those were the years of dissent, protest and ferment in the United States, with their unmistakable echoes in Britain. They affected not only the ways people acted, but also their thinking on many matters relating to social life and its reinterpretations. But it was also a reaction, to some extent inevitable and to some extent misguided, of the new generation of British criminologists against what appeared to them to be the stolid establishment of criminology as personified by the Cambridge Institute and probably also by its first Director. As regards 'interaction' and 'deviance' let us not make a mistake: these are fertile and revealing concepts provided that they are not over-laboured and overemphasized.

Cambridge Studies in Criminology

Today, as I mentioned in my speech in Cardiff in 1993, the situation with respect to publication of criminological texts has changed drastically. Though criminological texts do not as a general rule breed best-sellers they now present, on the whole, a sound financial proposition which might lead to other attractive ventures. A new animal has emerged in our field and is galloping fast and far: I refer to the tempting publisher of short texts, general books and collected articles.[24] In the days when we started, publication was not an easy matter. At that time I was asked to subsidize the first edition of *Penal Reform in England* and for several years Cecil Turner and I were expected to cover a variety of expenses entailed in our efforts to promote criminological publications. And yet it was vital that each of our chief investigators, as well as those in an auxiliary capacity, should have had the certainty that the end-product of their efforts should see the bright light of day and be properly published as part of a distinctive series. It was also highly desirable that, in order to stimulate work carried out by others not belonging to the Institute, we should be in a position to invite them to become contributors to the series.

Already at an early stage, the Department of Criminal Science had established a promising relationship with Macmillan. We had obtained an initial guarantee that it would publish the results of all our investigations, and a promise that it would give the most careful consideration to the works of other researchers and authors whom we desired to promote. This is how, in 1946, *English Studies in Criminal Science*, edited by L. Radzinowicz and J.W.C. Turner, came into being and its connection with the Department of Criminal Science of the Faculty of Law of the University of Cambridge was established.

---

24 Leon Radzinowicz, 'Reflections on the State of Criminology', *British Journal of Criminology*, vol. 34 (1994), pp. 99–104, at pp. 102–3.

I had been in touch about all this with Daniel Macmillan, then in charge of the firm. He was a very attractive person, a lover of books, a friend of authors, with an eye on profit no doubt, but also with a conviction that new departures deserved support and patience. And, after all, the bookshop of Bowes and Bowes facing the Senate House in Cambridge was Macmillan's original bookshop after it left Scotland and before it moved to London in splendour and prosperity. Within twelve years the series amounted to ten volumes, evoking much interest in Britain and abroad.

Following the death of Daniel, Harold Macmillan became the head of this major publishing house. The apparent inability of the Series to capture a wider market, while the investment it required continued to be heavy and the immediate financial returns rather unexciting, began to cause him concern. Cuts of one kind or other were hinted at. I noticed a change in attitude (the lack of interest in penal matters by Harold Macmillan has already been referred to, see p. 167) on the part of the new regime, so markedly different from the earlier enthusiastic support. I felt that the time had come to make a change.

Through a senior colleague at the Institute I got acquainted with Alan Hill, the Chairman of Heinemann Educational Books, and I was not wrong to feel that a fruitful friendship was struck almost at once. It marked the beginning of a collaboration which extended over fifteen years and was to continue for another five years with his son, David. I had a deep respect for his publishing instincts, for his shrewdness and imagination, for his drive and compulsion to launch or support new developments. As a publisher he fitted admirably into the period of English history which witnessed the establishment and the growth of the welfare state, and of the expansion, not to say explosion, of social and sociological studies. In this sense he was a publisher for the period and an outstanding one. Furthermore, as a Cambridge man, he was particularly gratified to be associated in this way with his old Alma Mater.

The first eighteen volumes, edited by me and J.W.C. Turner, ran under the title of *English Studies in Criminal Science* and were published by Macmillan. Afterwards the series became known as *Cambridge Studies in Criminology* and was published by Heinemann and continued under my editorship. The establishment of the Institute of Criminology stimulated its scope and quickened the pace of publications. When I retired as the editor, the series consisted of fifty-two volumes. Inevitably it was uneven, and naturally a criminological series today would be quite different but, in the prevailing circumstances, our series helped enormously to achieve the broader objectives which had animated us when we launched it nearly half a century ago. I was deeply touched to find a niche in Alan Hill's memoirs.[25] It was a rather colourful,

---

25 See Alan Hill, *In Pursuit of Publishing* (1988), pp. 190–1.

but basically accurate and very pleasing, account of our encounter and the initial stages of our collaboration. We continued to remain in touch following my retirement and in writing this book I was greatly encouraged by the interest he took in it. As late as 1992–3 he read some early chapters and offered a number of valuable suggestions. His sudden death, while still active and as stimulating as ever, was a heavy personal loss.[26]

Building an international library of criminology

Already at the first meeting in 1961 of the newly formed Advisory Council to the Institute, Lord Nathan emphatically stated that the Wolfson Foundation (he was their Chairman) regarded the creation of a library as of the first importance. And Lady Wootton reinforced it by 'expressing the hope that the Library should be made available to scholars from all over the world'. This was very stimulating to hear but it was also very frightening when contrasted with what we had to start off with. When we ceased to be a Department of Criminal Science and became an Institute of Criminology we virtually had nothing but a few empty shelves. We brought with us from our one room at the Squire Law Library to the house at Scroope Terrace, our first temporary new home, no more than a hundred miscellaneous items relating to criminology. To build up a library to fit the needs of the Institute and beyond was under any circumstances a formidable undertaking.

Because criminology is a composite discipline, we had to develop several bibliographical component parts of it, each of which covered a very wide area. The library, in order to be useful, had also to be international in scope. The American segment of it was vital, and European works were becoming more and more so, though of course on a much smaller scale. In addition to books, pamphlets and offprints, there were the numerous regular reports recording the state of crime and the working of the administration of criminal justice, as well as important debates and public inquiries. The Cambridge Criminological Library had also to be conceived to serve a combination of needs which, from a bibliographical point of view, were by no means identical: the undergraduates, the postgraduates, the doctorates, the Advanced Course, the Cropwood Fellows and Round-Table Conferences, the Visiting Fellows, the national conferences, and, last but not least, the Institute's research staff and the many different demands from the outside world, official or scholarly.

And then, of course, there were the periodicals and, with respect to many of those of long standing, continuity was highly desirable. In many cases, and this applied to the entire material, the items, though recent, or relatively so, were out of print and photocopies had to be substituted for them. Crimi-

---

26 See his obituary notice in *The Times* (23 December 1993), p. 17.

nological texts were usually published in small numbers and went quickly out of print. To proceed in an ordinary way in order to acquire very old, but essential, material was a hopeless undertaking. Here I did not hesitate to make use of a somewhat unusual approach. Thus, to build up a collection of material retracing the development of criminal policy in England in the past two centuries, we drew up a list of a few hundred items, checked and identified their availability in some major libraries of the country, especially the British Museum, and asked and obtained permission to install a xeroxing unit in a quiet corner. The material duly photocopied was then made into books or pamphlets as the case might be. A senior colleague in the Institute, who had strong bibliographical leanings, graciously came forward and gave me a hand in this rewarding but tedious operation. To beat any foreign competitors who might be casting their envious eyes on the libraries of deceased professors offered on the market, I made special arrangements to receive their catalogues by express air mail and I ordered by long-distance telephone or by telegram the needed items. Fully aware that this might be regarded as a rather unusual way of building up acquisitions, I asked for permission from the Committee of Management to allow me to cover the expenses of these operations out of my own personal budget.

Substantial funds were needed and a lot of it had to be readily available if the chase was to be effective. My efforts were deployed simultaneously in several directions. They called for much perseverance, energy and tact. In spite of its very cautious approach to the whole idea of an Institute, the University Grants Committee went out of its way to make a non-recurrent grant of £4,000 earmarked towards the building up of a library. The Home Office followed with £1,000 for each of three succeeding years. The Barrow and Geraldine S. Cadbury Trust again made its generous presence felt by a contribution of £600 for each of three years. For several years we received a welcome gift of £300 per year from the Smith Memorial Fund to help to build up a Commonwealth section of the library. The Wolfson Foundation assigned a portion of its benefaction for the development of the library. Armed and strengthened by all this noble help I made an approach to the Ford Foundation with one specific object: the United States had made (and continues to make) a lasting contribution to criminology and it was therefore vital that the first Institute of Criminology taking root in Cambridge would need help to lay the foundation of a representative American section. A grant of £10,000 followed. I feel that I ought to remind anyone taking cognizance of this total information that I refer to events taking place in 1962–3, and that in consequence all these grants, if they are to be compared to present-day conditions, should be multiplied at least elevenfold.

I cannot fail to mention two gifts. To mark her enthusiasm following the establishment of the Department of Criminal Science, Mrs Keynes (a respected Justice of the Peace sitting in Cambridge), the mother of Lord Keynes and of Sir Geoffrey Keynes, had sent us a bundle of her books and papers. And nearly a quarter of a century later (in November 1966) Lord Adrian (the former Chancellor of the University and Master of Trinity) passed over a hundred books from the collection of the late Lady Adrian to mark her long connection first with the Department of Criminal Science and then with the Institute of Criminology. These were indeed two very special gifts.

It would have been erroneous to use the money raised for the library by plunging enthusiastically into this exceptionally vast area without first trying to lay down a purchasing policy which, although substantial, would still need to be highly selective, basic and representative. To achieve it I invited Professor Thorsten Sellin (who at that time was spending part of his Fulbright Fellowship with us) to join me in drawing up an 'outline' of the field covered by the 'sociology of crime' and a 'penological survey'. The first was broken down under seventy-five and the second under ninety-four interrelated and yet specific headings. I also asked a senior member of the Institute, with a wide and solid medical background, to help in mapping out the much more hazy and far-reaching field which we described as the 'psychiatric and psychological aspects of crime'. The aim of this exercise was to indicate the topics in which regular bibliographical support might be needed. These were rough and ready indicators, but they proved to be of great help, especially in the initial stages of the formation of a library from which so much was expected.[27]

In 1962, about three years following the establishment of the Institute, we placed 4,000 volumes on freshly constructed shelves. A year later I was able to report that nearly 5,000 books and 2,550 pamphlets and articles formed the nucleus of the library, to which was added an important selection of leading periodicals. Twelve months later, in 1964, the number of books and bound volumes of periodicals amounted to 10,000. The number of pamphlets and offprints was doubled to nearly 5,000. To this we added 2,000 official publications of one kind or another. We took out current subscriptions to 87 periodicals of which 40 were British and 47 foreign. About 36 periodicals were, on arrival, put immediately at the disposal of the senior staff, because of their particular relevance to the research or teaching carried out by them. In 1975, which may be regarded as the end of the formative period, which was also its peak point, the library consisted of 17,500 books, 8,000 pamphlets and offprints and 6,500 volumes of periodicals. The library subscribed to about 200 periodicals of which about 60 were received free of charge – a recognition of its standing in the world. In 1980 it consisted of 23,000 books, many in languages other than English, of 11,000 pamphlets and offprints and of almost 200 current periodicals

---

27 The first two documents are included under Appendix VII, 1 and 2, in my report to the Advisory Council for their meeting of 16 March 1961.

as well as runs of many others which had ceased publication (making up 8,500 volumes).

Accession lists were issued on a regular quarterly basis, and redesigned in 1966. The average list consisted of ten pages and the acquisitions were grouped under fifteen headings, some of which were still further broken down under a number of subheadings. In 1967 we launched a new Bibliographical Series, which at once proved to be a most welcome development. During my directorship eight titles appeared and were all eagerly acquired by many bibliographical or criminological centres throughout the world. Yet another subsidiary publication was launched, namely the *Review of Current Periodicals*, which also immediately proved its utility as a tool for research and teaching. Several of such developments owed their inception to the initiative of the librarian, Martin Wright (Dr Martin Wright has since branched out and made his name in the field of victimology as relating to crime). Already, by 1967, I was able confidently to assert that 'the Library is now regarded as the leading centre of its kind, not only in this country, but in the world'. In 1979, G.K. Hall & Co. of Boston published at their initiative a massive collection of our holdings under the direction of Miss Rosina Perry, our imaginative and devoted librarian – a worthy successor to Martin Wright.[28]

The growing use of the library was truly spectacular. In 1964 we could record about 1,300 loans to serve the needs of the Institute and demands from outside Cambridge (including abroad). In the year 1967–8 they reached the 2,000 mark. No fewer than sixty written inquiries were directed to the library from Britain and from abroad every year, many of which required closer investigation on the part of the librarian and colleagues. Criminological libraries in the process of being set up elsewhere started to ask for advice on how to proceed. Freshly recruited members to the staff of other libraries were being attached to the Institute's library to gain experience and knowledge. Four times a week the library was also open in the evening until 10 p.m., and on Saturday morning. Except for a very brief period, it was fully accessible during the summer months.[29]

It is hard to believe that it took seven years before the combined post of Administrative Secretary to the Institute and Librarian was abolished: it was only in 1967 that the duties were separated and a permanent post of librarian was at last established. It is, I venture to say, no less hard to believe that at no time during the entire period was the truly dynamic increase in the size and

---

28 See *The Library Catalogue of the Radzinowicz Library*, Institute of Criminology, University of Cambridge, England, 6 volumes (G.K. Hall & Co., Boston, Mass., 1979).
29 On the life of the Cambridge Library see the perceptive paper by Rosina Perry, 'The Radzinowicz Library of Criminology', *Law Librarian Bulletin of the British and Irish Association of Law Libraries*, vol. 7, no. 1 (1976), p. 43.

use of the library matched by any meaningful increase in the size and rank of the staff. Throughout the period I was Director it remained virtually the same: in addition to the librarian, it included one qualified graduate assistant librarian, one clerical assistant and an evening invigilator. The year of 1969 was truly memorable. I was at last able to announce proudly that we had received permission from the central administration to carpet the floor.

Concluding remarks

The initiatives taken by us aimed to make it possible for the Institute to achieve the essential objective for which it was created: of demonstrating why there was a need for criminology and why it should be put on the national map. Seemingly these initiatives moved in different directions but in reality there was a close interconnection between all of them, indicating that it would be advantageous to launch them simultaneously so that they could stimulate and reinforce each other. Indeed none of them had been launched in a haphazard, improvised way. In each case they were preceded by a careful weighing up, in close consultation with people both from inside and outside Cambridge, of the available resources; of the extent to which these could be mobilized; of the needs which were required to be met and of their relative priority; of the experiences, both positive and negative, originating from abroad. Once launched, all of these developments were expected to become permanent features of the Institute's activities – the essence of its life. In effect this durability was proven already during my tenure as Director. It is gratifying to note that nearly all of them continued to be deployed long after I had gone. Yet I was also anxious to provide effective mechanisms for the periodical review of each of them, with the object of improving their quality and style. The fourth point to make within these general concluding remarks, and one in which I take particular pride, was the pace and the rhythm of these implementations – so many of which called for especially sensitive, diversified and time-consuming efforts. Virtually all were put into effect and made operative within two years of the formal establishment of the Institute. One or two activities had to be somewhat postponed, but not because of hesitancy or tardiness on our part.

As I was coming close to retiring from my post as Wolfson Professor and Director, I was being made acutely aware of the incipient but rapidly growing weakness of the Institute. Even if conditions had allowed it, I would have been categorically against creating a really large institution. The drawbacks would by far have outweighed any advantages. Yet to restrict growth while expecting the Institute in the long run to maintain its quality and its drive was to ask for too much while providing too little. A quarter of a century after it had been established, the permanent research and teaching staff of the premier Institute of Criminology in England was virtually the same as when it had been set up. Again, an identical situation was also evident in the funding and equipment of the Library.[30] It is difficult to escape making a dispassionate comparison with the stupendous expansion of the Home Office Research Unit over the same period (see pp. 172–175). But in the mean time each day in the life of the Institute was crowded, was different, was exciting. It was worth living through it and looking forward to the next day.

Welcomed recognitions

The Cambridge Institute was regarded as the first Institute of its kind in the world, and its activities continued to be watched with respect in very many academic circles as well as governmental departments. In view of the initial scepticism of whether Cambridge could do it, responses at home were particularly important.

The minutes of the very first meeting of the Advisory Council of the Institute recorded that 'Lord Nathan expressed his gratification and amazement at the achievements of the Director and his staff during the short period the Institute had been in existence, and expressed his congratulations to the Director'. Professor Sir Aubrey Lewis, another member, declared that he 'wished to associate himself with Lord Nathan's remarks'. Lord Nathan further intimated that he would report to his colleagues on the Wolfson Foundation 'the useful and far-reaching developments that had already taken place within the Institute'.[31] The Foundation's satisfaction seemed to continue undiminished. Six years later it was stated in their internal memorandum that the Institute 'has flourished greatly ... and now has a world-wide reputation, and is undoubtedly doing excellent work for the country in this field'.[32]

The White Paper, *The War against Crime in England and Wales* (1964), regarded the developments which were taking place in the Cambridge Institute as 'making a most important advance in the study and teaching of criminology'.[33] And two years later a report issued by the Conservative Political

---

30 I am glad to say that in more recent years a considerable expansion has taken place. At present (1997–8) the Institute consists of two professors, one honorary professor, two readers, seven university lecturers, three senior research associates, one half-time assistant director of research and the librarian and her staff. It is almost certainly the largest University Criminological Institute in Europe and it will soon have a fine new building.
31 See Lord Nathan in the *Minutes of the Proceedings of the Advisory Council of the Institute* (16 March 1961), p. 3. 'One institutional grant in which Nathan took an especial interest', wrote his biographer, 'made possible the establishment of a chair and an Institute of Criminology in Cambridge. Hitherto Criminology had received little attention in academic circles in England.' See H. Montgomery Hyde, *Strong for Duty: The Life of Lord Nathan of Churt* (1968), pp. 239–40.
32 *Note for Viscount General Monckton* (29 June 1967), Isaac Wolfson Foundation Archives, File on the Cambridge Institute.
33 Cmnd 2296 (1964), para. 25, p. 8.

Centre, under the chairmanship of Peter Thorneycroft (afterwards Lord Thorneycroft), praised the start made by the Home Office Research Unit and the Cambridge Institute, 'both of which had produced notable results'.[34]

Perhaps particularly rewarding was the view expressed by the Longford Report for the simple reason that the committee was largely composed of people who at the time constituted the core of the initial and persistent opposition to the establishment of the Institute in Cambridge. 'The Institute of Criminology in Cambridge', they stated in their unanimous report, '. . . which started work only some four years ago, has already justified its existence.'[35] No less significant was the view of Hugh Klare, the Secretary of the Howard League and the author of the letter to the Home Secretary (quoted on pp. 176–7 and 194). He was not a member of the Longford Committee, but he too changed his attitude and acknowledged the Institute with uninhibited and graceful generosity. 'Butler and Radzinowicz', he wrote,

> both wanted policies in the field of crime prevention to be increasingly influenced by facts and research findings. Of course, they were not the only ones. But if we are now gradually beginning to move in that direction, it is largely because a far-seeing Home Secretary created a tide in the affairs of criminology which Radzinowicz lost no time in taking at the flood.

And he referred further to 'the enormous dynamism' which was needed to put the idea of the Institute into effect. 'I am now grateful', he concluded, 'for the Cambridge style of criminology.'[36]

Yes, these were important testimonials and I could easily multiply them. But it seems to me no less important to put on record the feelings and views of Rab Butler himself. In the context of the vast and rich panorama of his activities, whether achievements or failings, criminology was a very modest and circumscribed topic indeed. But his involvement in it was strong and it occurred when for all practical purposes his active career had come to an end. This was his last initiative and it would have been an embarrassing blow to his self-esteem if, after all that fanfare and publicity, his initiative would have been regarded as of no great worth. This was not so, and this gave him very great pleasure which he wanted to be known and shared by others.

---

34 *Crime Knows No Boundaries* (Conservative Political Centre – A Policy Study Group, 1966), p. 38.

35 See *Crime: A Challenge to Us All*, Report of the Labour Party's Study Group (1964), pp. 11 and 72. It recommended that two more institutes should be established and that a criminological adviser should be appointed by the Home Office.

36 See Hugh J. Klare, 'Crime, Criminology and Public Policy' (a review of the Festschrift in Honour of Sir Leon Radzinowicz, edited by Roger Hood), *Justice of the Peace* (14 December 1974), pp. 689–90, at p. 690.

'Undoubtedly,' he wrote in the opening piece to the Festschrift in my honour,

> it is to the credit of the Institute in Cambridge that criminology has now been firmly established as a subject of vital academic importance in so many universities. I count my involvement in its foundation as one of the most significant acts of my term as Home Secretary: perhaps in the long run it will prove the one I shall be remembered for. It has given me great pleasure to have the opportunity to write this article as a tribute to Professor Sir Leon Radzinowicz. He was chosen, as I have noted, as the first Wolfson Professor because of his drive and imagination. That drive and imagination ensured a national and international reputation for the Institute of Criminology within only a few years of its establishment.[37]

To this has to be added his warm personal satisfaction that the new departure took place in Cambridge, with which his family has been associated since the early nineteenth century. He conveyed this satisfaction to Lord Adrian (then the Chancellor of the University) in a special letter. Butler's own book *The Art of the Possible* and Anthony Howard's biography, *RAB: The Life of R.A. Butler*, contain many delightful references to his Cambridge ancestral connections.[38] He joined Pembroke College, read history and French literature and was elected into a Fellowship. He did not stay long there and went for politics, but he always regarded Cambridge as a precious and living part of his life. By a pleasing coincidence, at the time of the establishment of the Institute he was appointed to the ancient office of High Steward of the University. In 1964 he was appointed Master of Trinity, was re-elected in 1973 and remained there until 1978. This, in its turn, made it so much easier for him to follow at close quarters the criminological adventure which owed so much to his inspiration and commitment, and for us to turn to him for further guidance should the need arise. In effect, he was invited to join the Advisory Council of the Institute in 1966; a year later he was elected its Chairman and continued in this capacity until 1972.

Essential acknowledgements

In his article in my Festschrift, Lord Butler had said some very nice things about me and I was (and still am) greatly moved by it. It was an unusual

---

37 Lord Butler, 'The Foundation of the Institute of Criminology in Cambridge', in R. Hood (ed.) *Crime, Criminology and Public Policy: Essays in Honour of Sir Leon Radzinowicz* (1974), pp. 1–12, *passim*.
38 Butler, *op. cit.* at pp. 1–2 and 13–19; Howard, *op. cit.* at pp. 11–12 and 341, *passim*.

privilege to have met him and to have been associated so closely with his initiative. For somebody who had come from so different a background and from so far away, as I had done, to have been given a chance to have a hand in building something new in an old place was a very rare privilege – a product of many circumstances, some carefully planned but others utterly unexpected. And now, because I have grown so old, I can enjoy the fascination of witnessing the exploits of the first and second generation of home-grown British criminologists. Absorbed by the present and intrigued by the future, they have naturally shown little inclination to retrace and reflect upon the past. But when they do, I sometimes wish that their perceptions and interpretations would be less one-sided, less hasty and less categorical. Yet no doubt similar thoughts had sometimes been passing through the minds of my old professors of Paris, Geneva or Rome. You just cannot ignore natural laws and their effects.

A director must inspire, direct and fully participate in the work of an institute. But the good name of the institution ultimately depends on the *équipe* as a whole. I would be hard pressed to point to disappointments, but I have no restraint in praising my colleagues' manifold contributions. I continue to remember the surprise of the many visitors to the Institute on seeing how very much has been accomplished by so very few. The initial nucleus of the senior staff consisted of four members. They were all recruited by me from other universities: they were young (between their thirties and mid-thirties) and they were not easily intimidated or discouraged by the novelty of the environment in which they were expected to live and to work. Also they differed in their approaches to the subject-matter of criminology and in their individual styles of functioning. This diversity served the Institute well. They were conscious that they had not joined an established enterprise, but an adventure, the future of which largely depended on them. They formed a team, which in their cumulative impact would have been hard to match in the criminological world at that time. Many of them have since gained well-deserved reputations and enjoyed a high academic standing far beyond Cambridge. And this applies equally to several of their collaborators. None of them needs an introduction from me any more, but it is I who am most anxious to reaffirm how fortunate and privileged I feel to have led them.

I mention them in alphabetical order: Joan King, John Martin, Derick McClintock (all of whom I deeply regret to say have passed away) and Donald West. At a later stage, they were joined by Roger Hood, G.N.G. Rose, David Thomas, R.L. Morrison and Richard F. Sparks, the last two of whom, I am very sorry to say, have also passed away. Nor should some of their collaborators, assistants or advisers be forgotten: N. Howard Avison, Anthony Bottoms, David Dodd, David Farrington, Hazel Genn, Monica Walker and Paul Wiles. In addition to his many research and teaching activities, Roger Hood was appointed Secretary to the Institute and as such played a major role in the life of the Institute as a whole. I have already mentioned our very great debt to the two librarians, Dr Martin Wright and Miss Rosina Perry.

The role of the Wolfson Foundation and of Lord Nathan, the Chairman, was decisive and the way it was discharged was in keeping with the highest standards of academic independence. But the part played by the Ford Foundation, the Rockefeller Foundation, the Barrow and Geraldine S. Cadbury Trust and the Smith Memorial Fund was by no means negligible, each of them helping to launch and to sustain initiatives which otherwise could not have seen the light of day.

Lord Adrian, the Vice-Chancellor, and Lady Adrian (a distinguished person in her own right and deeply interested in penal matters) never failed to guide gently the sometimes delicate discussions. The Central Administration of the university, especially Dr Harold Taylor, the highly respected and influential Secretary-General of the Faculties, was continually supportive.

The Faculty Board of Law acted in the same manner, respecting the independence of the Institute but also emphasizing throughout the common links. There were a few instances when I felt rather disappointed. As, for example, when at some early stage of the Department of Criminal Science's existence the Law Faculty Board were asked by the University Grants Committee whether they needed funds for promoting some newer approaches to the study of law. Their laconic answer was 'nil' and they conveyed this message without communicating with us. Nor were they more co-operative in their response to Lord Heyworth's Committee on the Social Sciences, with Dr Glanville Williams being the only member appearing before the committee – we having been left out of it altogether. But it would be mean to leave it at that, for apart from one or two such early episodes I do not remember any clash in interests, or any difference of principle between us. I was proud to be a member of the Law School and of the Institute.

The disinterested and always effective help given to the Institute by Arthur Armitage (afterwards Sir Arthur Armitage, president of Queens' College, Vice-Chancellor of the university and later of Manchester University) exceeds all tribute that can be paid to him. Other devoted allies included Patrick Duff (Regius Professor of Civil Law), Professor R.M. Jackson, Robert Jennings (afterwards Sir Robert Jennings, the President of the International Court of Justice), Trevor Thomas (Chairman of the Faculty and subsequently Vice-Chancellor of Birmingham University) and David Williams (afterwards Professor Sir David Williams, the Vice-Chancellor of Cambridge University).

The Committee of Management and the Advisory Council added considerable weight, not only because of the high standing of their members, but also because of the scrupulous way they discharged their voluntary duties. Oliver Zangwill, FRS (the Professor of Experimental Psychology), was outstanding as the Chairman of the committee for many years, and Meyer Fortes, FBA (the Professor of Social Anthropology), in this respect came close to him.

I would blatantly expose myself to the justified charge of meanness if I were not to seize this opportunity again to express my gratitude to so many distinguished people from outside Cambridge who extended to us their fruitful and sustained collaboration in so many of the Institute's most important activities. There were some sixty of them during my directorship, and they included an appreciable number of those who initially held the view that Cambridge should not be the place to have the first Institute of Criminology in the country.

This section of my account would also be flagrantly distorted without a reference to the Home Office. From the start, to use a much abused term, there was a special relationship between the Home Office and the Institute, I am proud to say, and it continued as such while I was the Wolfson Professor of Criminology and the Director of the Institute. Its involvement in so many of our activities such as the postgraduate course, the Advanced Course in Criminology, the Cropwood Fellowships and Cropwood Round-Table Conferences, the participation in many of our consultative committees in respect to projects of research, and in the national conferences, was very valuable indeed. And yet I do not remember one single instance when an attempt was made by any official of the Home Office, directly or indirectly, to interfere in any matter, big or small. I would particularly like to pay my respects and to express my gratitude to Sir Charles Cunningham, Francis Graham-Harrison, Sir Lionel Fox, Sir Arthur Peterson, Sir Philip Allen (afterwards Lord Allen of Abbeydale) and Sir Brian Cubbon for the role they played and the attitude they displayed in harmony with the most scrupulous regard for the unfettered academic independence of the Institute.

Lord Butler: a few scattered reminiscences

Lord Butler added enormously to my pleasure when dining at the High Table of Trinity, when taking port in the Combination Room, and when ending the evening in the Lodge with a glass of whisky. He would often invite me to sit next to him in these sumptuous surroundings and engage in conversation. He was proud to be Master of Trinity, appointed by the Crown in the first instance, but re-elected unanimously for the second period by the Fellows. He was pleased that he could get on with the dons – a species not particularly renowned for its capacity (or willingness) to form and maintain easy, relaxed relationships. He was simply enchanted that he could have proved to be, almost effortlessly, so successful in his dealings with the undergraduates at a period when the solid English customs of social subordination were being so severely tested and re-examined (see Plate 9).

As time passed by I easily discovered that the very centre of his captivations was not so much the world round him, but the events big and small which had crowded his intense political life in the past. These inevitably grew to become much more remote or even alien to others, though not to him. He was *par excellence* a political animal, but he was much more than a politician. He belonged to the ranks of statesmen. However, he was not a leader in the true meaning of this word, but an exceptionally fecund, resolute and imaginative promoter. I was one of several in college who would suddenly be asked by him 'why did I not become a Prime Minister?' – causing an acute embarrassment and an intense desire to find quickly a safe escape route from the Lodge. It is pretty certain that he would have been a distinguished Prime Minister. He was convinced that he was not fairly treated by his own party, and he regarded it almost as a personal rejection. This generated a pain which remained with him to the end of his life.

He was generally regarded, and frequently castigated, for being indiscreet and sometimes even tactless. But this, it seemed to me, was very often a deliberate, studied *faux pas* deployed to reaffirm his own personality when he felt hurt or unfairly treated. Sometimes it slipped into a form of excessive relativism in assessing events or personalities, a relativism which on other occasions came close to a civilized, philosophical scepticism. He respected achievement in its various manifestations and those who reached the top. But he despised ruthlessness and marked, uninhibited arrivism. He abhorred vulgarity. He was a thoroughly cultured human being. For a man of the world, of ample personal means, of wealth of experiences and influence and of many recognitions, he was conspicuously shy, indeed gauche. He lacked grace and panache but he was impressive in so many other ways and the epitaph 'enigmatic', so often bestowed on him, was an undeniable asset.

I do not know – and, anyhow, how could I be expected to know? – how wide and genuine was the circle of his friends. 'Friends', 'friendship' are a coin which politicians are particularly prone to use freely and to exchange no less freely. Butler was not an exception to this kind of licence. In his memoirs friends appear, disappear and reappear with disconcerting velocity. That he needed and appreciated true friends it cannot be doubted. Whether there were many of them in his life is another question. He often struck me as fundamentally a very private person and a lonely man. He must have been in his younger days acutely sensitive. He was, I venture to say, in need of love and supportive affection. I wonder whether he ever got them from his family. The few Butlers I had the privilege to meet struck me by their worth as much as by their aloofness. He did get much affection from his wife, Molly (Lady Butler), and he thoroughly enjoyed it. In emotional terms she made his life so much richer and instinctive. But this came his way rather late. It was a pity that, particularly in the last few years of his life, he allowed himself to neglect his appearance. He was getting increasingly bored and increasingly introspective. This may have been because the illness, which ultimately dragged him to his death, had been progressively sapping the springs of his life.

Lord Butler died on 8 March 1982 in his eightieth year.

10

THE AWKWARD QUESTION OF CAPITAL PUNISHMENT

It was not unrealistic to expect that at some stage, sooner rather than later, the authorities would call upon me to take part in official deliberations bearing upon some aspects of criminal policy and the working of the criminal justice system. After all, criminology was perceived by its promoters not only as an academic discipline but also as a rich and evolving body of empirical knowledge and ideals which could be of some use in the practical business of enforcing the criminal law. The first Director of the first Department of Criminal Science in Britain ought not to be left on the side solely as a neutral, external observer and registrar of steps taken. He ought also to be involved to a certain degree in the happenings or not-happenings within the criminal sphere. Yet I never expected that such participation would start off in so memorable a way. On 28 April 1949 the Prime Minister, Clement Attlee (afterwards Earl Attlee), rose in the House to announce that it had been decided to set up a Royal Commission on Capital Punishment, making known, as was usual, its terms of reference and its Chairman. Sometime later, the names of the commissioners were made public. I had the great honour to be included amongst them.[1]

The six inconclusive but revealing stages

It occurred to me that my first task should be to refresh my memory by trying to retrace the parliamentary history of capital punishment over the preceding two decades. Its most significant stages and episodes should provide an instructive background to the decision to set up the Commission and the role it might aspire to play in discharging its terms of reference. This history seems to fall neatly into six stages, making up a story which sometimes appears to be monotonous, but is quite frequently fascinating and even dramatic. It also sheds light on some aspects of the contemporary debate on capital punishment which has by no means ceased to be topical and controversial.

---

1 *Parl. Debates*, HC, vol. 460, col. 330, 20 January 1949.

THE AWKWARD QUESTION OF CAPITAL PUNISHMENT

A deep-rooted schism disclosed

The first stage commenced in late 1929 when Ramsay MacDonald, the Prime Minister at the head of a Labour administration, promoted the establishment of a select committee of the House of Commons 'to consider the question of Capital Punishment in cases tried by Civil Courts in time of peace, and to report whether any penalty, and if so, of what nature, should be substituted for the sentence of death in such cases where that sentence is now prescribed by law'. It was composed of six Labour MPs, seven Conservatives and two Liberals. They reported swiftly in 1930. Their report was easy to read and revealed a refreshing approach to the whole problem. But the document was not considered by Parliament nor was its evidence published. The select committee recommended that the death penalty should be abolished for an experimental period of five years and that there should be substituted for it 'the penalty now attached to reprieved murderers, interpreted and administered in the same way as at present'. This central recommendation, however, was not adopted unanimously: only eight of the committee's members endorsed it. Still worse, the Conservative contingent walked out, took no further part in the proceedings and refused to sign the report. The seeds of a fundamental discord were there which made its paralysing effect felt for very many years to come.[2]

A glimmer of hope

The second stage was linked with Neville Chamberlain's Conservative administration. More specifically, it emerged in connection with the Criminal Justice Bill of 1938 which was piloted through Parliament with great skill and vigour by the then Home Secretary, Sir Samuel Hoare (afterwards Viscount Templewood). The abolitionists urged that a clause be included in the Bill to suspend capital punishment experimentally for five years. He resisted on three grounds. First, because capital punishment was too important an issue to be smuggled, as it were, into a much wider and varied Bill, it required to stand on its own and be considered independently on its merits. Second, because his position, already made precarious as the result of his resolve to abolish the punishment of flogging, could well be made untenable if he were to inflame the controversy by also disposing of the death penalty. Third, he warned the abolitionists that if they did not follow his advice the fate of the entire Bill might well be jeopardized. Indeed, it might be thrown

---

2 The Chairman, the Revd James Barr, a sturdy Scotsman, was a deeply religious and faithful member of the Labour Party. After a few months, owing to illness, he was replaced by Sir John Power, Bart, best remembered as the founder of the Institute of Historical Research and of the Royal Institute of International Affairs, a Conservative MP of long standing, highly respected and liked.

out altogether for two to three years without any guarantee of being ultimately adopted at all. The abolitionists desisted, but they nevertheless secured a most encouraging advance when they succeeded, on a free vote (114 to 89), in having a motion passed that the House would welcome legislation which would suspend capital punishment in time of peace for a five-year experimental period. The government refused to endorse it, but obviously the question was bound to be resurrected on the first propitious occasion.

A painful rebuff

The war and subsequently several complex and urgent issues halted the tempo of the abolitionist movement. But the situation seemed to change radically when, in 1947–8, a new Criminal Justice Bill, similar to the abandoned 1938 Bill, was taken up in earnest. In this third stage it appeared to many that the adoption of the motion for experimental suspension was a foregone conclusion. After all, this was the time when Labour had been returned to power with a triumphant absolute majority in the Commons. A further dose of optimism was injected by the fact, well remembered, that this time the new Home Secretary was Chuter Ede, who in 1938 had voted for a similar motion.

He was soon presented with a significant, though somewhat embarrassing, gift: a memorial containing the results of a canvass of all members of the House of Commons (except ministers) which revealed that 187 of them urged the adoption of the clause. On closer scrutiny it appeared that out of the 187 as many as 171 were Labour, that the Conservatives numbered but 6, while the remaining 10 were made up by 2 National Liberals, 3 Liberals, 1 Communist and 4 Independents. It was thus apparent that the abolition of capital punishment was a cause primarily embraced by the Labour Party, and, in effect, not at all by the other major party. The echo of the 1930 select committee reverberated portentously. Capital punishment was both a penal and a humanitarian issue, but it was also a socio-political issue with a deep and clear-cut split along the traditional lines of party allegiance. The final blow occurred when the Bill, piloted by Chuter Ede, ready to be turned into the law of the land, emerged enriched by several new progressive clauses on other matters, but not the one the abolitionists had hoped for and thought they were fully justified to expect – the suspension of the death penalty.

I have not made special inquiries to ascertain what the decisive reasons were which led the government to reach this negative decision. But it seems to me that the scenario I have construed was not far removed from the calculations of its political tacticians. There might well have been a number of Conservative parliamentarians who, on the spur of the moment, or even upon more sustained reflection, would have joined the Labour abolitionists. But they would number at most some 10 or 15 per cent of their party. And, in the last analysis, when it came to the crunch, not all of them could be counted as consistent allies. Even more to the point, a good 90 per cent of Conservative voters across the nation were firm, uncompromising retentionists who would not hesitate to express their view in their votes.

The configuration on the Labour side was much more tenuous and perilous. The number of Labour parliamentarians who would cast their votes in favour of abolition would be much higher, no less I guess than 70 per cent, amongst which the left-wing and the intellectual group would be quite substantial. But, more importantly, 70 or 80 per cent of rank-and-file faithful Labourite voters would prove to be retentionists. In these circumstances was it really prudent and justified to get identified with an issue of this unpromising nature? Moreover, the number of abolitionists in the House of Lords at that time hardly exceeded the fingers of one hand. To produce, on top of everything else, a collision between the two Houses on an explosive issue of this nature, when it was the Tories in both Houses and not Labour who represented the preponderant feeling of the nation and of the electorate, would come close to embracing a flight into lofty romanticism in flagrant disregard of the bread and butter of ordinary politics. Any kind of rebuff is painful, but a rebuff from the leadership of your own party is particularly so. At the time it produced a lot of bad feeling, indeed of bitterness, amongst Labour abolitionists.

A resurgence of abolitionist pressures

Attempting to appease the widespread dissatisfaction, but at the same time underestimating the intensity of abolitionist feelings, the government allowed a free vote on the suspension of capital punishment at the report stage of the Bill, though not for ministers. As a result, tactical and arithmetic calculations were simply swept away. Group psychology often turns out to be something different from the sum of individual psychologies. Sometimes a group, like a forest caught by fire, surges forward to break down the defences erected by the forces of the status quo; 14 April 1948 was such a day. It marks the fourth stage, in many ways the most dramatic in the story. The debate lasted till late evening and some twenty-three speeches were delivered. Chuter Ede, the Home Secretary, in a forceful speech opposing the amendment urged by so many members of his own party and, in a later debate Winston Churchill, forgetting his early Liberal image when Home Secretary, castigated the government for impotence and for leaving 'this grave decision on capital punishment to the casual vote of the most unrepresentative and irresponsible House of Commons that ever sat at Westminster'. Yet a big surprise was round the corner: the clause was adopted by 245 to 222.[3]

---

3 *Parl. Debates*, HC, vol. 449, cols 949–1098, 14 April 1947.

A further scrutiny of the vote brought to light some significant indicators. There were still 75 Labour Members who were against the amendment, though three times more, 215, cast their votes in favour. And this proportion would have been statistically significantly higher if several members of the government had not felt it desirable to abstain. The clause enlisted the meagre support of 14 Conservatives in contrast to the 134 who voted against – a proportion of one to ten. The schism between the two parties on this topic, already noticed in 1930, appeared some two decades later to be unbridgeable. Yet the debate also provided enough hard evidence that, in parliamentary terms, the issue was not dead nor could it be shelved for much longer. And the evidence coming from outside, supported by reliable polls and well-qualified interpreters of trends of public opinion, still revealed the troublesome fact that no less than 60 to 70 per cent of the population favoured no change at all.

Followed by a humiliating rejection

On reaching the House of Lords (1 and 2 June 1948) the 'suspending' clause was confronted by a wall of stone. Viscount Jowitt, the Lord Chancellor, made no bones that he profoundly disliked it; the Marquis of Salisbury, the venerable patriarch of the House, was simply horrified; Viscount Simon displayed his considerable dialectical powers to condemn any attempt to devise a reasonable alternative to the system in force; even Viscount Samuel, the devoted veteran penal reformer, raised his emphatic voice against experimenting with the capital law as it stood. And of course no one could be more fierce and uncompromising than the formidable Lord Goddard, the Lord Chief Justice. Insisting that all twenty judges of the King's Bench Division were behind him, he recited to their Lordships a string of atrocious cases of all kinds of murder which deserved the full rigour of the law, but which under the projected changes were likely to escape the gallows. From the benches occupied by the bishops, the highly charged moral voice of Archbishop Temple was no longer to be heard. His successor, Dr Fisher, was ambivalent on the subject of capital punishment. He was not likely to take the initiative in doing away with it and, if hard pressed, would perhaps meticulously try to secure a moderate compromise. One of the bishops, known as an abolitionist, warmly blessed the clause, but another, in a most categorical way, insisted on the eternal moral precept of 'eye for eye'. I can still see Lord Templewood, a staunch fighter for the clause, yet in no doubt that his intervention would be of little avail – a lonely, pathetic figure.

The attendance was exceptional: some 200 peers clocked into the chamber. The debate was intense: it was sustained by some forty-five speeches and lasted until 7:45 p.m. Naturally somewhat uneven and repetitive, it nevertheless remains as one of the most outstanding debates of its kind to have taken place anywhere in the world at any time. The vote was crushing: 181

to 28.[4] The Bill was sent back to the Commons, but without the clause which led to this passionate contest. I have defined this fifth stage, not unfairly I hope, as 'the stage of humiliating defeat'.

The government in the dock

Stage six witnessed the government in the dock, with little if any sympathy shown by anyone, and widely blamed for having brought this shapeless mess upon itself. People on the point of being drowned are hardly ever capable of saving themselves by their own efforts; yet in politics such efforts can hardly ever be abandoned. The government cooked up a new clause which acknowledged degrees of murder: one class of murders, comprising five types of killing, would still carry capital punishment, but the other class would be non-capital murders, punished with imprisonment for life.[5] The Royal Prerogative of Mercy was still retained. Sir Hartley Shawcross (afterwards Lord Shawcross), then the Attorney-General – a skilful and lively debater – took charge of the measure only to encounter apathy and derision. At the same time, to increase the confusion and the frustration, another respected Labour politician presented his own separate Bill for a total suspension of capital punishment for five years with the Home Secretary to order when that period should begin.[6]

The Conservative side of the House, fortified by their victory in the Lords, was determined to tear the new clause out of the Bill or to force the abandonment of the Bill altogether. The old lion, Winston Churchill, woke up and thundered against Attlee's administration with abundant use of adjectives such as 'dangerous' and 'absurd'. The Lord Chief Justice, Lord Goddard, intimated that if such a Bill were to pass he would strongly consider resigning. In a widely quoted letter to *The Times* Lord Simon elegantly dissected the proposal with irony and contempt. Thus, a husband who, because he hated his wife, or because he wanted to marry another woman, deliberately

---

4 See 'Criminal Justice Bill', *Parl. Debates*, HL, vol. 198, cols 19–75, 102–78, 1–2 June 1948.
5 The five types of murder for which capital punishment was to be retained were: murder incidental to certain grave crimes, including robbery, housebreaking or rape; a murder of a police officer or helper in resisting arrest or escaping from custody; a murder of a prison officer by a prisoner; a murder by a person who has been convicted of murder before; a murder committed by means of, and in the course of the systematic administration of poison or any other noxious substance. See leading article 'The Death Penalty', *The Times* (9 July 1948), p. 5.
6 In his autobiography Lord Shawcross refers to this debate with an emotional emphasis as fresh as ever. He produced some interesting information about the attitude of Attlee and Morrison to the topic. He points to his constant opposition to capital punishment, but he adds: 'To-day I am not quite so confident about it.' See *Life Sentence: The Memoirs of Lord Shawcross* (1995), pp. 167–70 and 30.

plotted to drown her and did so, would come under the second category of non-capital murder and not be hanged. A ruffian who made plans to waylay a child and deliberately killed the child could not be sentenced to death unless there was evidence to satisfy the jury that he was aiming at a sexual offence. Lord Simon who asked 'if it were permissible to joke on so grave a matter', nevertheless dragged Shakespeare into the debate. If a man poisoned his wife by deliberately giving her one single dose which killed her, he would go to prison, but if, on the contrary, his method was to kill her by a series of small doses this would be 'systematic administration of poison', and he would be liable to capital punishment. Until now the murder of Duncan by Macbeth and his wife was a particularly heinous crime; under the government's proposal it would only be a second-class murder and no death sentence could be pronounced upon them.[7]

This time there was to be no free vote, but three-line whips were issued to all members of each of the contesting parties. Sydney Silverman, naturally disheartened, urged members to support the government's degrees of murder amendment, not because he liked it but because there was no alternative left and it was better to have less executions than more. He estimated with ingenuity, but not with wholly convincing evidence, that if such a Bill had been in force since 1945 the lives of twenty-eight murderers would have been spared.

I met Mr Silverman on only one or two brief occasions, but I heard him speaking and of course I read his many pronouncements on the subject. He struck me as an aggressive, combative man, with a lively intellect and great energy: ready to simplify complex issues if the case was one he happened to care for. He was impatient, not to say hostile, with the traditional establishment and well on the left wing of his party. He was not immune from indulging in political phraseology, but when there was a real need he had at his disposal an exhaustive and meticulous file for acting, or abstaining from acting, as the case may be. He had strong convictions and firm principles and the courage and style to fight for them. He was recognized as a highly visible figure in the abolitionist movement, and indeed as its respected, devoted and resourceful leader.[8]

By a vote of 307 to 209 the Commons agreed with the Lords to abandon the suspending clause, but at the same time urged the adoption of the government's new compromise clause of degrees of murder. No one expected that the latter would fare better in the Lords and it was knocked out by 99 to

---

7 Lord Simon, letter to *The Times* 'Two Classes of Murder: Some Anomalies' (10 July 1948), p. 5.
8 For a fine and fully deserved notice, see Silverman (Samuel), Sydney (1895–1968), *Dictionary of National Biography 1961–70* (1981), pp. 941–4; his obituary in *The Times* (2 October 1968), p. 10; and Emrys Hughes, *Sydney Silverman, Parliamentary Rebel* (1969).

19. The Criminal Justice Bill travelled back to the House of Commons, much thinner by the elimination of the clause.

Resisting, very wisely, the temptation to introduce a new Bill in the next session, the government advised the Commons to drop the issue of the death penalty altogether in any shape or form. In the then prevailing atmosphere of despondency and weariness this advice to capitulate was accepted – with obvious relief by many and bitter dismay by others. Parliament had proved unable to evolve an acceptable solution. An altogether different approach was needed and a Royal Commission was perhaps the instrument to break the impasse and tackle this tortuous and obdurate topic with renewed confidence and creative imagination.

The Royal Commission on Capital Punishment 1949–53: a new departure or a move 'to delay' and 'to postpone'?

The terms of reference assigned to the Royal Commission on Capital Punishment when it was set up in 1949 read as follows:

> 'to consider and report whether liability under the criminal law in Great Britain to suffer capital punishment for murder should be limited or modified, and if so, to what extent and by what means, for how long and under what conditions persons who would otherwise have been liable to suffer capital punishment should be detained, and what changes in the existing law and the prison system would be required; and to inquire into and take account of the position in those countries whose experience and practice may throw light on these questions . . .' And at the request of the Prime Minister '. . . we have considered [stated the Report of the Commission] whether any change should be made in the method of execution, although this question was not included in our terms of reference.'

This is quite a mouthful and while pondering upon this assignment I was reminded of a poem about Royal Commissions in general. A.P. Herbert was its author.[9] The opening stanza reads:

I saw an old man in the Park:
I asked the old man why
He watched the couples after dark;

---

9   It appeared first in *Punch* (27 June 1934) and was included in his collection *Mild and Bitter* (1937). It was reproduced by H. McDowall Clokie and J. William Robinson, *Royal Commissions of Inquiry* (1937), appendix, pp. 236–8. Their book still deserves a careful reading.

He made this strange reply:–
'I am the Royal Commission on Kissing.
Appointed by Gladstone in '74;
The rest of my colleagues are buried or missing;
Our Minutes were lost in the last Great War.
But still I'm a Royal Commission
Which never has made a Report,
And acutely I feel my position,
For it must be a crime (or a tort)
To be such a Royal Commission.
My task I intend to see through,
Though I know, as an old politician,
Not a thing will be done if I do.'

My apprehension, not to say anxiety, would have risen much higher if the book by K.C. Wheare (afterwards Sir Kenneth Wheare) – a book full of ripe wisdom and most attractively written – had already been published at the time our Commission was set up.[10] Next to the three types of inquiries, wrote Sir Kenneth, patronized by governments with the objective either 'to pacify', 'to nullify', or 'to camouflage', there is also sometimes the no less pressing desire 'to delay' or 'to postpone'. The last mentioned category, he stated, 'is not necessarily wicked . . . The Government may want to delay until action is possible, or until action is unnecessary . . . Indeed in the period of delay, the public may be given an opportunity to educate itself and form its opinion on the subject.' This was the case of the Royal Commission on Marriage and Divorce in 1951, 'where the Government appreciated that something might have to be done, but wished to postpone it for as long as possible' and the Royal Commission on Capital Punishment of 1953, 'where the division of opinion within the parties meant that delay would be appreciated by both sides if it could be obtained'. But he also hastened to warn that 'the use of Committees of Inquiry in order to delay can be bad, for delay sometimes makes things worse'.[11]

There was certainly a case for taking the issue of capital punishment out of the turmoil of changing governmental strategies, of emotionally charged and inevitably repetitive parliamentary debates, of aggressive and confrontational pressure groups, of sensational commentaries by the press. The lowering of the temperature all round could thus be justified on many grounds. But there was even more to it than that. Whenever the question of capital punishment

---

10 K.C. Wheare, *Government by Committee: An Essay on the British Constitution* (1955). On his full and distinguished life see Wheare, Sir Kenneth Clinton (1907–1979), *Dictionary of National Biography 1971–80* (1986), pp. 894–6, by Max Beloff (afterwards Lord Beloff).
11 *Op. cit.*, pp. 68–95, *passim*.

is raised and becomes an acutely controversial topic it is the retentionists who remain calm, indeed reticent to justify their point of view, putting their trust in the static strength of the status quo as such. In contrast, it is the abolitionists who make most of the noise and sometimes become quite belligerent and self-righteous about their cause. The books, pamphlets, essays, articles and circulating pronouncements which appear usually originate from the abolitionist side and, with the best will in the world, many of these (often the most persuasive ones) cannot avoid becoming one-sided, generalizing or simplifying. And deprived, as they often are, of sufficient means or proper authority to be able to collect and interpret a vast amount of diversified evidence, domestic and foreign, they frequently cannot escape justified criticism for taking too restricted a view of a complex subject. These remarks should not be interpreted in a deprecatory manner, nor should abolitionist material be rejected off-hand as fatally flawed, although undoubtedly at the time there was a pressing need for a solid, dispassionate and spacious inquiry, both national and international, of the subject in its contemporary setting.[12]

The Chairman and the Secretary

When the other day, in order to refresh my memory, I looked at the composition of the Royal Commission, I could not help reciting to myself the well-known saying of Lord Keynes that 'in the long run we are all dead'. Of the twelve members, I am the only one still alive. And a fascinating human cocktail it was. Sir Ernest Gowers was our star. It would have been very difficult indeed to make a better choice to chair a Royal Commission on Capital Punishment in the then prevailing circumstances. The son of an eminent doctor of international reputation (Sir William Gowers, FRS), he was educated at Rugby and Clare College (first class Classical Tripos) of which he was in time to become an Honorary Fellow. He was also a barrister of the Inner Temple. He had joined the Civil Service in 1902, was at some stage the Principal Private Secretary to Lloyd George when the latter was Chancellor of the Exchequer, and ended his Civil Service career as Chairman of the

---

12 Of the books which in this context should be regarded as a 'must' I include the following: E. Roy Calvert, *Capital Punishment in the Twentieth Century* (1st edn 1931; 5th edn 1936), with a preface by Hugh Klare; Arthur Koestler, *Reflections on Hanging*, with a preface by E. Cahn and afterword by Sydney Silverman (1937); Viscount Templewood (Sir Samuel Hoare), *The Shadow of the Gallows* (1951); Sir Ernest Gowers, *A Life for a Life?* (1956); Terence Morris and Louis Blom-Cooper, *A Calendar of Murder* (1964). Elizabeth Orman Tuttle's *The Crusade against Capital Punishment in Great Britain* (1961), with a foreword by Dr Edward Glover, and James B. Christopher's *Capital Punishment and British Politics* (1963), are extremely useful as an analytical record of events leading to the abolition of capital punishment.

THE AWKWARD QUESTION OF CAPITAL PUNISHMENT

Board of Inland Revenue (1927–30). Soon afterwards in his retirement Sir Ernest became known to the public as the chairman of a host of select and departmental committees of inquiry relating to an exceptionally wide range of topics. But he became much better known to a much wider public when he made his persuasive and elegant appeal for greater care in the use of the English language.[13]

He was sixty-nine when he accepted the invitation to lead the Royal Commission, still enjoying good health and, though slow moving, very alert and observant. With his impressive appearance, perfect manners, imperturbable patience, tactful and yet persisting probing of witnesses, and with a gift for assimilating swiftly the central parts of an issue, he could hardly be equalled, and certainly not surpassed. His matter of fact approach and refreshing economy of language made him no less valuable in our internal meetings and informal exchanges of views. But he was also basically withdrawn, rather cold and very much aloof. A top professional type of chairman, he was equally involved in *Admission of Women to the Foreign Service* (1945), *Shops Acts* (1946), *Preservation of Historic Houses* (1949) and *Foot-and-Mouth Disease* (1952–3). He never said foolish things, but equally hardly ever uttered profound or arresting remarks. He had not much of a sense of humour and was invariably solemn.

Not unlike the Chairman, the Secretary of the Commission, Francis L.T. Graham-Harrison, came from a distinguished background and had the privilege of what today is often called elitist education. His father, Sir William Montagu Graham-Harrison, had been elected a Fellow of All Souls College, and later became a KC and was awarded an Oxford DCL for a thesis which went far to lay down a foundation for the study of administrative law in England. He discharged his intricate and important duties as Parliamentary Counsel with widely acknowledged distinction.[14] Francis went to Eton, was a Scholar there and then proceeded to Magdalen College, Oxford, graduating with first class honours in Greats (Classics and Philosophy). He entered the Home Office in 1938, reached the rank of Assistant Under-Secretary of State and retired in 1963. Still alive, he preserves lively recollections of our experiences on the commission. He discharged the duties which, as a general rule, are assigned to and expected from a Secretary of a Royal Commission, but our concerns were exceptionally complex and he invariably satisfied them with exceptional competence and imagination. Lord Butler, when talking about his Home Office years, frequently referred to Graham-Harrison, never

---

13 Sir Ernest Gowers, *The Complete Plain Words* (1962 edn), was 'a reconstruction of my two previous books, *Plain Words* and *ABC of Plain Words*' (Gowers). A classic of its kind and a delight to read and to reread.
14 Sir William Montagu Graham-Harrison (1871–1949), *Dictionary of National Biography 1941–50* (1959), pp. 314–15, by Sir Cecil Carr.

forgetting to add: 'Francis's brain is like the engine of a Silver Rolls-Royce.' I knew what he meant by it, because I could not help watching him at close quarters running the Commission and bringing its work to fruition with flying colours. I also had the pleasure of many personal conversations with him about a wide range of matters.

In my long and crowded life I have met no more than four or five men endowed with Francis Graham-Harrison's quality of mind. And this quality of mind went hand in hand with equally exceptional integrity, fairness, loyalty and a kind of rare hesitancy which made his whole personality so very attractive and challenging. He was a civil servant and an intellectual, a rare species, that was sometimes encountered in the Foreign Office at the turn of the century, but a species rather rare at the core of the Home Office dealing with criminal matters. This combination could hardly be expected to operate harmoniously, certainly not in our days. I often wondered whether in the long run it really worked to his advantage. His wider literary and artistic interests and expertise have been recognized: he was a member of the Advisory Committee of the British Library and a trustee of the Tate Gallery as well as of the National Gallery. And again, his rather exceptional gift of weighing things up, and sifting arguments for and against, made him a splendid adviser, though one reluctant to take speedy and drastic decisions – an essential quality for those operating in the very top executive posts. He quietly proved to be the pillar of the commission. Not only did he prepare all the questions the Chairman was to ask our multitude of witnesses but also, anticipating many of their answers, he frequently put at the Chairman's disposal a neatly typed set of follow-up questions. He played a major role in drawing up our lists of witnesses and many institutions likely to be interested in the topic and able to make useful contributions to it. He drew up an elaborate and sophisticated questionnaire to be sent to many governmental departments and leading experts in several foreign countries which we were expected to visit, but well in advance of our journeys so as to make them more profitable. He analysed the very many memoranda submitted to the Commission.

Surprisingly the Chairman was not a good draftsman, at least not in our line of business, and on one occasion when he tried his hand at it we had to send the draft back to our Secretary for redrafting. Because of Sir Ernest's linguistic reputation it was sometimes assumed that it was he who wrote the report. 'The Royal Commission's Report was written with the clarity and plainness of style of which Sir Ernest Gowers is both a master and advocate'. Thus wrote Professor James B. Christopher, who in the course of composing his book visited Sir Ernest on several occasions. As a matter of fact this was the only mistake I have discovered in this excellent book.[15] Except

---

15 See James B. Christopher, *Capital Punishment and British Politics* (1963), p. 85.

Plate 1 Enrico Ferri (1856–1929)

Plate 2 Paul Logoz (1888–1973)

Plate 3 Louis Vervaeck (1872–1943)

Plate 4 Paul-Émile Janson (1872–1944)

Plate 5 Comte Henri Carton de Wiart (1869–1951)

Plate 6 Henri Donnedieu de Vabres (1886–1968)

Plate 7 Cecil Turner (1886–1968)

Plate 8 H.A. Hollond (1884–1974)

Plate 9 Lord Butler (1902–82) (photograph graciously provided by Lady Butler)

Plate 10 Herbert Wechsler (photographed in 1975)

Plate 11 Roger Hood (photographed in 1992 by Rob White)

Plate 12 Marc Ancel (1902–90)

Plate 13 Cambridge Institute of Criminology (photographed in 1968)

Plate 14 G.M. Trevelyan (1876–1962)

Plate 15 Sir Leon Radzinowicz
(photographed in 1953)

Plate 16 Sir Leon Radzinowicz
(photographed in 1965)

for Chapter 13 ('Methods of execution') the entire report was written up by Francis Graham-Harrison.[16]

Some of its members

The composition of the Commission was an exciting human cocktail. I can still recollect a few of the responses of some of the members. It was, for instance, not difficult to detect that for the two dedicated trade unionists of the old type, Dame Florence Hancock and John Mann, the equation between murder and capital punishment was natural and deeply embedded, not to be lightly disregarded. At the same time, should flaws in the existing system of enforcement be convincingly proven they would wholeheartedly welcome changes to remedy them. It was, however, also not unfair to say that on occasion the problems and discussions were somewhat over their heads. Thus, at the conclusion of taking evidence for two days from a group of high-powered psychiatrists, Mr Mann approached me quietly suggesting that we should have a drop of whisky. After we sat down with our drink he said: 'You seem to know quite a lot about this psychiatric stuff, tell me please what is a psychopath?' 'This is rather complicated,' I replied, 'but, for instance, to give you some idea, I am a psychopath.' 'Oh yes, this may be so, but I would not hang you' came the reassuring comment.

The position of Mrs Elizabeth Cameron was different. A distinguished literary figure, better known as Elizabeth Bowen, she could hardly have been at ease with a Royal Commission probing into the modes of imposing and enforcing the penalty of death. As far as I am aware, murder never entered into the exquisite delicacy and imagery of her many novels and essays. It was compelling to look at her as she gazed with gripped amazement at the crowd of our witnesses coming from a world so far from her own. And this became even more obvious when, like all of us, she had to face at close quarters Mr Albert Pierrepoint, the officially accredited hangman of England, and listen to his callous, impertinent and bombastic testimony.[17] She came closer to the

---

16 On this Professor Terence Morris's information was much more exact when he states: 'Graham-Harrison's ... outstanding grasp of the issues undoubtedly contributed to the stature of the report which in both language and scholarship is easily the equal of any of the great Victorian "Blue Books".' See his *Crime and Criminal Justice since 1945* (1989), p. 87, fn. 25.
17 In the documents issued by the Commission he is referred to as 'Mr Pierrepoint. Executioner'. His evidence given in the twenty-eighth session of our deliberations was heard 'in private' and was not published, but he himself was not reluctant to publish an exceptionally dull, crude and obviously disingenuous book *Executioner: Pierrepoint*, by Albert Pierrepoint (1977). He took offence to my question when I ventured to ask him whether he was paid by head or was in receipt of a regular stipend. When asked how did it happen that several members of the family chose the same profession, he replied with no hesitation 'Tradition,

world of crime when the Governor of Sing-Sing politely, but categorically, refused her desire to visit the prison on the grounds that she could be grabbed by the prisoners and held ransom. 'Our clients', he said, 'are well aware of what is going on in the world at large and are anxious to be involved in happenings which may again bring them to public notice. The visit of a Royal Commission from England provides such an opportunity.'

Dr Eliot Slater was the only medical man on the Commission. It was a blessing and a joy to have him as a colleague. Mental problems, directly or indirectly, play a major role in the anatomy of murder and the ways of dealing with it. To have at our elbows an expert highly regarded in his profession, both in Britain and abroad, who did not make exaggerated claims from particular perspectives (not only psychoanalytical), and who combined a solid knowledge of psychiatry and psychology with common sense and a vivid perception of the specific needs of criminal justice and of so often rudimentary public prejudices, was a precious acquisition for all of us. Gifted in explaining complex mental concepts (not to say enigmas) in jargon-free, lively and attractive English, he had wide interests extending to Shakespearian studies and a contagious sense of humour – something not too often regarded as a characteristic of his profession.

He could make some of us see his point of view and share his enthusiasm for some changes, but he could make little impact on Mr Norman Fox-Andrews, QC, barrister of Lincoln's Inn, Recorder of Bridgwater, Bournemouth and Bristol. He was the only practising lawyer from Britain on the Commission, and he was a classical embodiment of the traditional English lawyer of the period. He was instinctively proud of things as they were. Almost invariably, not to say automatically, when proposals for change were advanced (even if minor ones) he would say (I quote his own words): 'I do not say that their application has never led to an undesirable result, but if this has occurred it has occurred rarely, and only provides an example of the truism that no rule can be perfect.' It was his signature tune.

There was on the Commission a member who knew more about specific cases of murder, where the perpetrators had been found guilty and sentenced to death, than anybody else in the country. This was Sir Alexander Maxwell. An Oxford man (Christ Church), he had spent his entire working life in the Home Office. He entered the department in 1904, at the age of twenty-four, passed through various posts, including the chairmanship of the Prison Commission and Deputy Under-Secretary of State, before being appointed in 1938 head of the department. During his ten years as Permanent Under-

---

Sir'. I was thrilled to find when working on the first volume of the *History of English Criminal Law* that several of his predecessors in the bygone ages were themselves executed and a few had found their way into the *Dictionary of National Biography*: see vol. 1 (1948), pp. 187–90.

THE AWKWARD QUESTION OF CAPITAL PUNISHMENT

Secretary of State (1938–48) he was the closest adviser to the Home Secretaries of the day when they were called upon to discharge their awesome responsibility under the Royal Prerogative of Mercy in deciding whether the death penalty as imposed by the courts should ultimately be put into effect. Yet, during the four long years when we sat as commissioners or in our individual encounters, he never referred, either directly or indirectly, to any of these cases. Perhaps, as a justification of his attitude, I may quote the following story told by André Maurois, who combined his admiration for the English with an effective temptation to tease them. An elderly couple, married for forty-two years, appeared before a judge to ask him to grant them a divorce. Surprised, the judge first turned to the husband and asked him for reasons after so long a conjugal life. 'During all these years she never talked to me', said the husband. The wife in turn, when asked, confirmed the truth of his statement, but added: 'Your Honour, during the forty-two years he never asked me a question.'

No less surprising was the fact that at no time during these four years did any member give the slightest hint whether, in the light of our proceedings and inquiries, he or she was moving in the direction of endorsing the abolitionist or the retentionist cause. I would be hard pressed to single out any country in the world, other than in England, where such reticence would be kept up and such a scrupulous faithfulness be shown in observing terms of reference which, under any fair interpretation, could not fail to be regarded as somewhat strained, not to say artificial, or even unreal – certainly not in North America, though perhaps in China. As our report emphasized, 'the natural construction [of our terms of reference] precludes us from considering whether the abolition of capital punishment would be desirable'. And yet at the same time

> we have not thought it necessary on this account to exclude all evidence tending to establish or to refute the proposition that capital punishment should be abolished: evidence relevant to this issue may often also be relevant to the question whether the existing scope of capital punishment should be restricted, and we have not attempted to draw nice distinctions in this field.

This was a priceless dialectical jump over potentially threatening hedges, but it was also not deprived of some salutary admonitions.

We also felt encouraged when, after our report had been printed, each of us refrained from giving any interviews, in the press or on the radio, or making any other pronouncements. The report was our collective effort and we believed it should speak for itself and for us. Sir Ernest was the only one who 'went public' on the issue. He granted interviews to one or two organizations known for their abolition views and he published a book, *A Life for a Life?*, a skilful but rather pedantic *résumé* of the evidence and of the report.

He also announced his conversion to the abolitionist cause, but at the same time safeguarded his position with the correct wording of a well-seasoned civil servant.[18] I felt that it would have been gracious of him (and fair) if, once he had decided to make known his views, he had informed us all about it and thus made clear to his colleagues on the Commission that they, any one of them, should not be restrained from going beyond the terms of reference which all of us from the outset had agreed to observe. He kept the secret of his book exclusively to himself and I bet even Graham-Harrison knew nothing about it.

The search for solutions

I was not unaware of the early grumblings emanating from influential outside quarters that we were rather slow in settling down to begin our work, and also of subsequent grumblings that we had taken rather a long time to come forward with a report. I was not disturbed in the least by either. I was clear in my mind that our main task was to produce an outstanding report – in substance, composition and presentation – containing the results of a thorough, exact, spacious and objective investigation and thus filling an obvious gap. This was urgently needed for the benefit of the government, Parliament and public opinion, who needed to come to grips with the essential as well as detailed elements of the question. To achieve this objective the exploratory foundation had to be ambitious and the effort could not be other than exacting and time consuming.

A few pieces of information will illustrate the magnitude of our task. For England and Scotland we had a list of 118 witnesses comprising a wide and diverse group of people with a direct involvement in the field of criminal justice in general and capital punishment in particular, as well as a significant number who at some time or other had had indirect connections with aspects of the subject. Thus there appeared before us four former Home Secretaries, two from the Liberal and two from the Conservative Party, each of whom was expected to speak freely, unencumbered by departmental briefs. There was the Lord Chief Justice of England, accompanied or followed by a group of the most senior of the judges, and their counterparts from

---

18 Before serving on the Royal Commission I, like most other people, had given no great thought to this problem. If I had been asked for my opinion I should probably have said that I was in favour of the death penalty, and disposed to regard abolitionists as people whose hearts were bigger than their heads. Four years of close study of the subject gradually dispelled that feeling ... when I say that I think capital punishment 'ought' to be abolished, I must not be thought to be expressing any opinion on the question whether it would be prudent or practicable to abolish it without some further education of public opinion. I do not know. That is a question of politics, and I am not a politician.
(Gowers, *A Life for a Life? The Problem of Capital Punishment* (1956), pp. 8 and 134)

THE AWKWARD QUESTION OF CAPITAL PUNISHMENT

Scotland, led by the Lord Justice General of Scotland. All were anxious to retain their custom of putting on a black cap when passing the death sentence. And all were against assuming the responsibility for choosing whom among the convicted murderers should ultimately suffer death. There was the Archbishop of Canterbury, already known to be ambivalent about changing the status quo, surrounded by bishops, several of whom were more anxious than ever to find harmony between ethics of punishment as derived from religion and the imposition of the death penalty by temporal and legally constituted jurisdiction.

We had made available to us the impressive, so efficiently and so monolithically collected, contributions of the executive organs of machinery of justice – as exemplified by the representatives of the Home Office, the Prison Commission, the Scottish Home Department, the Director of Public Prosecutions and the Crown Agent, down the line to the two under-sheriffs and the executioner. There were spokesmen of all ranks from the agencies and institutions engaged in the front-line of prevention and control of criminal behaviour: constables and police officers from England and Wales and Scotland, prison governors, medical officers and chaplains, and representatives of the Prison Officers' Association. There was the Magistrates' Association, the after-care organizations, and the Probation Officers' Association. And one could hardly ignore the divisive but very important contributions which came from the British Medical Association, the Royal Medico-Psychological Association, the Institute for the Scientific Treatment of Delinquency and the Institute of Psycho-Analysts. Delegates from societies known and respected for their uncompromising abolitionist platform, such as the Howard League for Penal Reform (one member of which was soon to become the Lord Chancellor) and the Society of Labour Lawyers, were accorded a proper place. The views and recommendations of nearly thirty departments, associations, societies and institutions were elicited and carefully recorded. Four foreign authorities were invited to come from abroad to give evidence in London on particular topics prior to our own inquiries carried out abroad. In very many cases a memorandum prepared by the witnesses preceded or accompanied the evidence. Often witnesses would be invited to have lunch with us and continue discussions in a more informal way. Sometimes evidence was given in private at the request of a witness, if and when we found the request justifiable. Not infrequently, written statements were sent at the initiative of the interested individuals themselves (George Bernard Shaw being one of them): these were not printed but as a general rule were put at our disposal by the Secretary. Otherwise everything was published. With very few exceptions evidence was given in public.[19]

---

19 See *Minutes of Evidence taken before the Royal Commission of Capital Punishment* (HMSO, 1949–52), pp. 1–678. For the list of witnesses see appendix, 'Lists of Witnesses and Correspondents', in the *Report*, Cmd 8932 (1953), pp. 289–92.

THE AWKWARD QUESTION OF CAPITAL PUNISHMENT

To carry out our foreign inquiries properly we proceeded simultaneously at several levels. A questionnaire covering the whole field of our inquiry was addressed to the governments of the countries of the Commonwealth (six states of Australia, Canada, Ceylon, India, New Zealand, Pakistan, Southern Rhodesia and the Union of South Africa); to eight European countries (Belgium, Denmark, France, Italy, the Netherlands, Norway, Sweden and Switzerland); to the United States government and eight states (California, Connecticut, Massachusetts, Michigan, Missouri, New Hampshire, New York and Wisconsin), and to fourteen states with respect to methods of execution. In addition to eleven penal institutions in Britain, we visited fifteen institutions in five selected European countries and in the United States. Altogether we heard, on these visits, evidence from thirty-eight witnesses, official and non-official. We spent another three weeks taking evidence (in September–October 1950 and in June 1951) in Washington DC, Cambridge (Massachusetts), New Haven (Connecticut), New York and Philadelphia (Pennsylvania). During these fascinating and exhausting investigations we heard evidence from forty-one witnesses and visited four representative institutions for those undergoing imprisonment for life. This most valuable and many-sided material was not published in its entirety. However, part of it can be found in the *Minutes of Evidence* and the report.[20] The whole of it was collated and very ably digested by our Assistant-Secretary, E.U. Elliott-Binns, and was very carefully studied by all of us and made good use of in our deliberations. At our invitation, about twenty memoranda were contributed by foreign experts of recognized international reputation;[21] the commission set up a special sub-committee to deal with all the aspects of our foreign inquiries. I was very pleased to serve on it. Finally, we ordered the preparation of brief but authoritative reports on a number of topics which, by their very nature and topicality, needed to be marked out in this way. These were reproduced as appendices to our report. There were thirteen of them and none has ceased to be instructive and significant.[22]

We were all fully aware of the problem of the size of the final document which, if pushed too far, would undermine its accessibility and hence its public usefulness. We were most anxious that the end product should be compact, succinct and as far as possible easily digestible. We were proud and

---

20 See Minutes of Evidence, 'Questionnaire', pp. 681–3; replies from the *Commonwealth*, pp. 685–734; from *United States of America*, pp. 735–89; from *Europe*, pp. 797–868.
21 Such as Mr Justice Felix Frankfurter (Washington, DC), Thorsten Sellin (Philadelphia), Louis Schwartz (Philadelphia), Herbert Wechsler (Columbia), Wilfred Overholser (Washington, DC), Marc Ancel (Paris), Paul Cornil (Brussels), Stephan Hurwitz (Copenhagen), Donnedieu de Vabres (Paris), Johannes Andenaes (Oslo), Ivar Strahl (Uppsala), Jean Graven (Geneva), I.M. van Bemmelen (Leiden), W.P.J. Pompe (Utrecht) and George Dession (Yale), all friends and colleagues of long standing.
22 See report, Appendices 2–16, pp. ix–x and 298–497.

relieved that everything was covered in only 287 pages. The very substantial and absorbing material collected as evidence was made available to the public (through the Stationery Office) in one massive volume of 868 pages. This was indexed in the main body of the report so as to facilitate its full use, if and when so desired. I was particularly pleased when, a few years later, Sir Kenneth Wheare, a disinterested and highly competent person, singled out our evidence as an example particularly conducive to the formation of enlightened public opinion.[23]

Reaching the end of the road

I went along with the eighty-nine recommendations and conclusions adopted by the Commission. They were obviously and necessarily a very mixed bag of varied importance. But taken together, they left virtually nothing out that was part and parcel of the complex and many-sided issue of capital punishment. Perhaps more should have been added and integrated into the body of the report on the crime of murder as such, or on categories of murderer. But, on the other hand, our document was expected to be primarily a product within the province of criminal policy and not of criminology proper. There were also considerations of time and what can reasonably be expected from a body such as a Royal Commission, which should not be confused with a research institute.

I differed from the majority of the Commission (six against five) about raising the age limit from eighteen to twenty-one, although I fervently shared 'the natural desire to spare a young life whenever possible and recognise that a youth who commits a murder at the age of nineteen or twenty may be capable of reform and, if he is reprieved, may live to become a useful and law-abiding member of the country'. But I felt that no category of offender aged eighteen or over should a priori be excluded from the operation of capital punishment as long as the latter is part of the criminal justice system of the country. Each case should be considered individually on its own merits and not on the basis of a rigid and necessarily arbitrary rule related to a particular age. Ample place should be accorded to the mechanism of extenuating circumstances and considerations of mercy through the recommendations of the jury and the use of the Royal Prerogative of Mercy. The two points of view were fairly and clearly stated in the body of the report.

There was an issue about which perhaps I felt more strongly, so strongly as to ask for the inclusion in the report of a 'Note of Dissent'. It related to the question of insanity and criminal responsibility. The majority of the

---

23 See K.C. Wheare, *Government by Committee: An Essay on the British Constitution* (1955), p. 55, '[the evidence] played a valuable part in the education of public opinion'.

Commission felt that there was a strong case for the enlargement of the M'Naghten Rules rather than to leave them as they were. But they would have much preferred to abrogate the rules altogether and to leave the jury to determine, without being bound by any formula, whether at the time of the act the accused was suffering from disease of the mind or from mental deficiency to such a degree that he or she ought not to be held responsible. I strongly felt that a formula was essential and that there was enough reputable knowledge and experience available to undertake such a reformulation. However, I was able to enlist the support of only two colleagues.[24] Nevertheless, we had the satisfaction of seeing the majority proposal failing to evoke any decisive response. Indeed, the overwhelming majority of our witnesses (both legal and medical) and the large majority of criminal codes from all over the world, as well as the American Model Penal Code, all adopted a regulating formula. If asked today, I would still be as firmly convinced as I was some forty-five years ago that this is the right solution.

One could easily, and at some length, make comments about the shortcomings of some of the adopted recommendations, or still worse the lack of proposals for urgent action. But this could become a rather petty exercise overshadowing what was at the very core of the Commission's report and its significance in the then prevailing ferment of opinion. We were expected to ascertain whether there was an effective and acceptable proposal which, if fully implemented, would lead to a substantial limitation or modification of the liability under the criminal law of Britain to suffer capital punishment for murder. We pitched our imagination as high and wide as we could; we pushed our investigations at home regardless of where they were likely to lead us; and we explored the foreign comparative material with all due attention but also with no less desirable circumspection. Of four possible solutions we categorically rejected the first three (reframing the statutory definition of murder, dividing murder into degrees, empowering the judge to substitute a lesser sentence), but we were also fully aware of the traditional and practical flaws inherent in the fourth: namely to empower the jury to decide in each case whether a lesser sentence than the death penalty should be imposed. Yet it was still the only one which could provide the more radical solution searched for. 'The present system', we stated, 'is open to obvious objections, and a remedy must not be dismissed merely because it too is open to objections: it may nevertheless be on balance preferable.'

I felt that to limit ourselves to signalizing the only remaining possible alternative would deprive our report of its final unmistakably indicative seal that the search for a significant reconstruction of our capital system in accordance with the emerging concerns of contemporary English society had,

---

24 See 'Note of Dissent' by Dame Florence Hancock, Mr Macdonald and Mr Radzinowicz in the *Report, op. cit.*, pp. 285–7.

THE AWKWARD QUESTION OF CAPITAL PUNISHMENT

to put it bluntly, reached the end of the road. This feeling must have been shared by several members, because a sentence to this effect which I proposed was accepted with easily reached unanimity. It is this sentence which has proved to be the one most frequently quoted whenever references are made to the conclusions reached by our Report. I hope that, after so many years, I shall not be criticized for being indiscreet. The passage and the sentence in question, printed in italics to be more easily identified, reads as follows:

> the proposal to give discretion to the jury to decide in each individual case whether there are such extenuating circumstances as to justify the substitution of a lesser sentence for the sentence of death ... involves a fundamental change in the traditional function of the jury in Great Britain and is not without practical difficulties. For these reasons its disadvantages may be thought to outweigh its merits. *If this view were to prevail, the conclusion to our mind would be inescapable that in this country a stage has been reached where little more can be done effectively to limit the liability to suffer the death penalty and that the real issue is now whether capital punishment should be retained or abolished.*[25]

The report's clear indication that the Commission's very terms of reference, which were trying to secure a workable compromise between the abolitionist and retentionist camps, could not be achieved, meant that the document was not likely to satisfy fully either camp. It was therefore particularly encouraging when Sydney Silverman, a man difficult to satisfy under any circumstances, and particularly in respect to this issue, welcomed the report in flattering terms. 'It was', he wrote, 'a most influential Commission and, after four years of exhaustive enquiry in Great Britain and in many other countries, it produced what is almost certainly the most exhaustive and comprehensive investigation into the subject ever made.'[26] Perhaps even more weighty is the view expressed by Herbert Hart, well known as a severe critic:

> Within the confines of this report, there is a far more comprehensive, dispassionate, and lucid evaluation of the arguments both as to questions of fact and to questions of law and principle relevant to murder and its punishment, than in any of the many books published in

---

25 See *Report of the Royal Commission on Capital Punishment 1949–1953*, Cmd 8932 (1953), 'Final Conclusions' (610), p. 214, and 'Final Conclusion on Main Issue' (46), p. 278.
26 Sydney Silverman in an afterword to Arthur Koestler's *Reflections on Hanging* (1957), pp. 205–14 at 209–10.

either of our countries [Britain and the United States] on this subject. Certainly the publication of this report in England introduced altogether new standards of clarity and relevance into discussions of a subject which had too often been obscured by ignorance and prejudice. The value of this most remarkable document was not diminished by the fact that the Commission's terms of reference postulated the retention of the death penalty.[27]

And I felt confident in presuming, from a generous dedication of their book *A Calendar of Murder* to our Chairman, that both Terence Morris and Louis Blom-Cooper (afterwards Sir Louis Blom-Cooper) thought highly of our report. A penetrating opinion was expressed by the US scholar Professor James Christopher:

> If a Royal Commission is to be judged by the extent to which its recommendations are quickly adopted as official policy, the Gowers Commission must be termed a failure. But if such a body is to be judged by other, more subtle standards, this particular Commission looms larger and takes on importance as an element in the process by which British opinion on the value of capital punishment was changed. By its very existence – and, one might add, in spite of its terms of reference – the Gowers Commission helped keep alive public interest in one of the seminal questions of the state's approach to crime and punishment. Its chief recommendations were for change and by forcing the government to consider the consequences of revising the law of murder the Commission helped ensure a revival of the time-worn controversy that had been in cold storage for five years. Finally, simply by amassing a body of data in the way they did, the Gowers Commission provided a treasure chest with which abolitionists could dip freely and hopefully in preparing for a resurgence of Parliamentary interest.[28]

The response from the leading foreign authorities cannot be described otherwise as invariably full of admiration. The report was welcomed as a major document of its kind and tributes were paid to the thoroughness and scope of our analysis as well as to the way in which the enormous mass of material had been marshalled and presented. I am fully aware that, as a

---

[27] See H.L.A. Hart, 'Murder and the Principles of Punishment: England and the United States', *North Western University Law Review*, vol. 52 (1957), pp. 433–61, at p. 436. Reproduced in Hart's *Punishment and Responsibility* (1968), pp. 54–80, at p. 58.

[28] James B. Christopher, *Capital Punishment and British Politics* (1963), p. 92.

member of the Commission, I should regard myself as an 'interested party' and refrain from expressing an opinion. Yet I feel that the many years I have spent inquiring into Blue Books, covering a period of two centuries, perhaps allows me not to remain absolutely silent. In looking at the report, as one amongst very many in this remarkable series, I have no hesitation in stating that it ranks alongside the half-dozen best reports on penal problems which have been published in the course of the nineteenth and twentieth centuries. I will go further and say that, as long as the issue of capital punishment is considered within the wider context of criminal policy or penal history, this report should continue to be regarded as indispensable by all those to whom quality is not an empty word.

Inevitably, not all abolitionists were inclined to appreciate the more subtle aspects of the Commission's work and of its impact. Gerald Gardiner (subsequently Lord Gardiner, the Lord Chancellor), the then Chairman of the Society of Labour Lawyers and a prominent member of the Howard League, acknowledged that the Commission had made several useful recommendations, but he could not bring himself to say more than the report 'appears to the lawyer to be a careful and competent piece of work'. To Hugh Klare, who took so prominent a part in mobilizing public opinion against the continuation of capital punishment, the report 'made a number of vague and often minor recommendations'. Dr Edward Glover, the Head of the Institute for the Study and Treatment of Delinquency, while recognizing that some parts of the report were 'brilliantly written and marshalled with skill, judgement and a patent regard for reason', but nevertheless criticized it for falling short of being an important investigation into the mind of the murderer and the nature of the crime of murder. Dr Hermann Mannheim commiserated with the Commission for having 'been placed by their terms of reference in an awkward and unenviable position', but, with sublime condescension, he observed 'it is no reflection on its work to say that to the serious student of the problems of Capital Punishment the Minutes of Evidence are probably more important than the Report itself'. Nevertheless, all three concluded that the Commission produced much evidence in favour of total abolition 'and represents nothing but another step towards this final goal'.[29]

I was proud to have been appointed a member of the Royal Commission and

---

29 See Hugh Klare's introduction to E.R. Calvert's *Capital Punishment in the Twentieth Century* (5th edn, 1972), pp. vi–xx, at p. viii; Gerald Gardiner, Edward Glover and Hermann Mannheim, 'A Symposium on the Report of the Royal Commission on Capital Punishment 1949–1953', *British Journal of Delinquency*, vol. 4 (1953–4), pp. 157–72, *passim*. In an earlier article Mannheim had stressed the necessity of a full-scale inquiry into the etiology of murder. See 'Capital Punishment: What Next?', *The Fortnightly*, vol. CLXIV (1948), pp. 213–21 (included in his collection of articles *Group Problems in Crime and Punishment* (1955)).

I always regarded my appointment as a gesture of undiluted liberalism. The assignment was almost always an arduous task and always a grim one. I tried hard to be useful to the Commission as a whole, though whether I succeeded is not for me to say. But I do know for sure that I profited enormously from this unusual experience. It taught me a great deal, not only about the attitude of contemporary English society towards capital punishment but also towards crime and punishment in general. In addition I was so very fortunate that the slender plant of friendship developed between Francis Graham-Harrison and myself, a friendship which, in the course of nearly fifty years, has never faltered and never given rise to misunderstandings. This rare gift, if I may say so, also extended to Carol Graham-Harrison, a distinguished woman in her own right.

I well remember the last, late afternoon meeting of the Commission. We dispersed in virtually complete silence, no shaking of hands, no goodbyes, certainly no *au revoir*. Everyone followed his or her destination by underground, bus, cab or on foot, as if we had never met before, or possibly only on one or two furtive occasions. This, in spite of what Maurois might have insinuated, was not characteristically English. The English love valedictory dinners, providing that there is ample drink of quality and the speeches are few and very brief. Our almost unreal dispersal was in harmony with our Chairman's temperament and style of life. A few days later we received a letter asking us to return the red attaché-box given to us when we started work to carry papers and documents relating to our investigation. The request, I hasten to add, did not come from the Chairman, but originated with the Treasury.

Yet a further period of equivocation

A speedy and clear cut response from the government to the Commission's report was widely anticipated but this hope had to be swiftly put to rest. Instead the report was greeted by a silence so prolonged and so scrupulously observed that a suspicion began to gain ground that perhaps, after all, the government was motivated by some other considerations than a legitimate desire 'to postpone and to delay'. Perhaps the Commission was set up just 'to pacify'. 'A committee', wrote Mr Gladstone in 1865, 'keeps a Cabinet quiet.' Perhaps, and this would be more serious, this had been a Commission merely 'for appearance's sake' (the government decides on its policy, or is fairly certain what it will be. It sets up a committee to secure approbation for its policy or perhaps to demonstrate the futility of the conflicting interests or to show that it has done its best). Perhaps, and this would have been worst of all, this would prove to be a Commission brought into being with the object of 'killing a proposal either by reporting against it, or by revealing so great a divergence of opinion that no action is possible, or by keeping it out of sight so that public interest ceases to be concerned with it. By smothering, strangling, drowning or tearing to pieces the proposal is killed.'[30] This, the most ominous explanation, could not be excluded without the government revealing at least some of its intentions.

When they at last surfaced they did not look so innocuous. After almost a year had passed by, Viscount Simon moved a resolution in the Lords stating that 'in the opinion of the House it is not desirable to cast upon the jury which has convicted the accused of murder, the further duty of answering questions which may determine his punishment'. The resolution was not brought to a division because Lord Simon withdrew his motion, saying that the important thing was what their Lordships thought, not to 'merely count heads'. But 'the heads' were there because, except for Lords Templewood and Chorley, virtually everyone else was in agreement with him.[31] The purpose of this move might well have been to stir up the past decades' division of opinion, as if nothing else relevant had since occurred to justify a change, and to utter a warning to the Commons to tread very gently because the question of capital punishment might lead to a grave constitutional crisis in the relationship between the two chambers with respect to the promotion and ultimate determination of legislative measures. If this is what the government intended to indicate, Lord Simon's motion could have hardly been more obliging.

A year later, and under pressure, the government (Sir Anthony Eden's administration) reluctantly agreed to allow time for a debate on the report and with a free vote. I would be hard pressed to cite a Royal Commission which had been kept waiting for two full years before the Commons had been given an opportunity to consider it. The debate took place on 10 February 1955.[32] It was introduced by Gwilym Lloyd-George (afterwards Viscount Tenby). At that time he held the office of Home Secretary, combining it with the Ministry of Welsh Affairs. 'He had', stated Kenneth O. Morgan, 'a far happier and more fulfilling career than do the sons of many great men. He also avoided the storms that beset his father's political and personal life.'[33] This may be so, but it seems to me that as Home Secretary he was one of the most mediocre of the period.

On the subject of capital punishment he glaringly reversed himself. In 1948 he had been a determined abolitionist but now he declared himself to be most firmly opposed to its abolition. He singled out what he regarded as the three central issues of the report and rejected them all outright. But this was not very relevant, for whatever the recommendations of this or any other

---

30 See K.C. Wheare, *Government by Committee, op. cit.*
31 'Juries and Capital Punishment', *Parl. Debates*, HL, vol. 185, cols 137–88, 16 December 1953.
32 'Capital Punishment (Royal Commission Report)', *Parl. Debates*, HC, vol. 536, cols 2064–183, 10 February 1955.
33 See 'Lloyd-George, Gwilym (1894–1967)', a note by Kenneth O. Morgan, *Dictionary of National Biography 1961–70* (1981), pp. 664–6, at p. 666.

Commission might have turned out to be, Sir Anthony Eden's government was against any change in the existing system of capital punishment. This negative or evasive attitude was pursued with varying degrees of emphasis, of course, by all governments of the period. At some point the government expressed the desire to bring forward a Bill, rather surprisingly based on the Commission's report with respect to constructive murder, provocation, and being an accessory to a suicide pact. But events and pressures directed towards abolition, or at least suspension, had moved too far. We were constantly witnessing radical Bills, promoted by the seemingly inexhaustible Sydney Silverman, accompanied by tactically ingenious manoeuvres. The debates which only a few years earlier had been vivacious and provocative, bringing out not only the central arguments but also the clash of personalities, became damp, pedantic, repetitive beyond endurance, just hopelessly boring. The perorations were more and more frequently delivered to empty benches. And as soon as a Bill with some tangible degree of hope left the Commons the guillotine of the Lords was set in motion and that was the end.

One such episode prompted the leading left-wing weekly the *New Statesman* to observe:[34]

> The House of Lords may have delayed the abolition of hanging; but it has hastened its own abolition. From the hills and forests of darkened Britain they come: the halt, the lame, the deaf, the obscure, the senile and the forgotten – the hereditary peers of England united in their determination to use their medieval powers to retain a medieval institution.[35]

This piece provoked much criticism, even amongst the most ardent of the abolitionists such as Sydney Silverman and Viscount Astor. It was not only intemperate but also politically flawed. I rather suspected that Kingsley Martin, the editor of the paper, was its author. If the passage in question intended to characterize the political situation prevailing with respect to the retention or abolition of capital punishment, the diatribe was dangerously

---

34 See 'Death Penalty (Abolition Bill)', *Parl. Debates*, HL, vol. 198, cols 564–842, 9 July 1956. Characteristic of the exceptional interest evoked by the debate is the rather colourful fact of a professor of philosophy reassessing the debate by classifying their lordships into three categories: 'Draconians', 'Tolstoyans' and 'Spinozists'. See W.B. Gallie, 'The Lords' Debate on Hanging, July 1956, Interpretation and Comment', *Philosophy*, vol. 32 (1957), pp. 132–47. I was fascinated by it, but of course was not competent enough to express an opinion. Hart described it as 'illuminating philosophical analysis'. See his 'Murder and Principles of Punishment: England and the United States', *North Western University Law Review*, vol. 52 (1957), pp. 433–61, at p. 446, fn. 39.

35 See 'Government from the Backwoods', leading article in *New Statesman and Nation*, vol. 52 (14 July 1956), p. 29, quoted by Elizabeth Orman Tuttle, *The Crusade against Capital Punishment in Great Britain* (1961), p. 120.

misconceived. It was true that about 90 per cent (if not more) of the members of the House of Lords opposed the abolition of capital punishment, although perhaps some 25 per cent (while in favour of retaining the death penalty) might have favoured a few changes in the system as enforced, providing the changes would be rather circumscribed. It was also true that no less than 90 per cent of Labour Party members in the Commons would have welcomed the abolition of capital punishment, or at least its suspension for an experimental period of five years. But again, it was also true that the number of peers who would favour a change was steadily increasing, and very significantly some of Silverman's amendments were seconded by highly respected Conservative Members of the House of Commons. Yet the commanding fact which stood out, seemingly impervious to the passage of time, was the attitude of the population as a whole. If it were taken 'in the raw' there would be a firm 90 per cent in favour of keeping the death penalty as part of the English system of criminal justice. The politicians of either party could hardly fail to take notice of this electoral reality which in its turn goes far to explain the hesitancy, the evasiveness, the circumvolution which they so often displayed when attempting to confront the real issue at stake.

At last the government decided to take the initiative, although nearly three years had to elapse before this move was devised. On 7 November 1956 – when a change of leadership took place (Harold Macmillan succeeding Anthony Eden as Prime Minister) – the Homicide Bill was introduced. Sir Reginald Manningham-Buller, the Attorney-General, and Viscount Kilmuir, the Lord Chancellor (formerly Sir David Maxwell Fyfe), took charge of it. I certainly had no hesitation then, nor do I hesitate now, to endorse the characterization of the Bill by the Archbishop of York and of the Bishop of Chester as 'morally shocking'. But I would supplement it by saying that to moral shabbiness the epitaph of professional incompetence should be added. Hardly any one of our very many witnesses suggested that a scheme of degrees of murder followed or not followed by the imposition of the death penalty should become the basis of a revised system. Not satisfied by the scarcity of evidence favourable to this solution we had also undertaken a detailed inquiry into how it worked in those states where it had been adopted in the United States, starting with Pennsylvania in 1794.[36] The government's Bill was an opportunistic attempt to try to rescue for a moment a ship definitely doomed to go down.[37]

---

36 See *Report of the Royal Commission on Capital Punishment*, pp. 167–89 and section 41, p. 278.
37 Under the Homicide Bill, capital punishment was maintained for murder in the course of furtherance of theft; murder by shooting or causing an explosion; murder in the case of resisting arrest or escaping from legal custody; murder of a police officer or a prison officer; repeated murders. For other types of murder the penalty was life imprisonment. The attractive feature of the Bill was the introduction of the concept of diminished responsibility, which if accepted in a particular case would reduce the charge of murder to manslaughter.

The Bill, which passed into law as the Homicide Act 1957, distinguished 'capital' from 'non-capital' murder. The abolitionists supported it because they realized that, for the moment, they could not expect to get more. The retentionists felt that this was the only way to preserve capital punishment in Britain, while allowing time for the grave limitations of this solution to be revealed. The unbridgeable contradictions inherent in the measure soon became apparent and were subjected to a devastating critique on the part of experts.[38] More importantly, three *causes célèbres* had appeared on the stage: Ruth Ellis – Timothy Evans – Derek Bentley. Ruth Ellis was a young woman (twenty-eight years of age) put to death for what was a *crime passionnel*, not a very nice one, but a crime of passion nevertheless.[39] Timothy Evans was exonerated of the murder of his baby daughter. In all probability she had been murdered by John Christie, who lived in the same house and had given evidence against Evans at his trial. Derek Bentley, aged nineteen with a history of epileptic fits and a mental age of about ten or eleven, was an accomplice in a burglary which led to the fatal shooting of a police officer by Bentley's companion, sixteen-year-old Christopher Craig, at a time when Bentley was already in police custody. The latter escaped capital punishment because of his age, while the former was put to death in spite of strong recommendation to mercy by the jury and similar advice from the Permanent Under-Secretary of State.[40] Three different cases, but ones which by their cumulative weight produced a deep and disturbing effect on public opinion.

---

38 I particularly refer to the articles by J.E. Hall Williams, 'The Homicide Bill', *Howard Journal*, vol. 9 (1956), pp. 285–99; J.E. Hall Williams, 'Developments since the Homicide Act, 1957', published as an appendix to E.O. Tuttle, *The Crusade against Capital Punishment* (1961), pp. 149–65; J.Ll.J. Edwards, 'The Homicide Act 1957: A Critique', *British Journal of Delinquency*, vol. 8 (1957), pp. 49–61; Arthur Armitage, 'The Homicide Act 1957', *Cambridge Law Journal*, vol. 15 (1957), p. 83; Barbara Wootton, 'Diminished Responsibility: A Layman's View', *Law Quarterly Review*, vol. 76 (1960), pp. 224–39 (Seventh Biennial Lecture in Criminal Science under the auspices of the Cambridge Institute of Criminology, 12 February 1960).

39 See the report on French views of this case in *The Times* (13 July 1955), p. 6e, where it was pointed out that in a similar case in France a woman had received a sentence of two years' imprisonment which was suspended so that she was released immediately on probation.

40 Among the very many publications devoted to these cases I would like to mention: R. Hancock, *Ruth Ellis: the Last Woman to be Hanged* (1963); L. Marks and T. van den Bergh, *Ruth Ellis: a Case of Diminished Responsibility?* (1977); M. Endowes, *The Man on Your Conscience* (1955); L. Kennedy, *Ten Rillington Place* (1961); D.A. Yallop, *To Encourage the Others* (1990); F. Francis, *Gangland: the Case of Bentley and Craig* (1988); *Trial of Christopher Craig and Derek William Bentley* (1954); R.T. Taget and S.S. Silverman with an epilogue by Christopher Hollis, *Hanged and Innocent?* (1953). The tragic aspects of the Bentley case have recently been made still more painful by the statement of Lord Bingham, the Lord Chief Justice, when the Court of Appeal quashed Derek Bentley's murder conviction. He declared that Lord Goddard's 'summing up of the case was such as to deny the appellant that fair trial which is the birthright of every British citizen'. Reported in *The Times*, 31 July 1998.

THE AWKWARD QUESTION OF CAPITAL PUNISHMENT

No objective and competent observer could fail to note that the tortuous question of capital punishment in Britain was reaching its final stage.

When the end came it came peacefully and with dignity. In 1964 a Bill to abolish capital punishment was introduced by a Private Member in the Commons. The government gave the measure parliamentary time and allowed a free vote. The Bill was accepted by both Houses and became the law of the land as the Murder (Abolition of Death Penalty) Act on 8 November 1965. It was to be in force for an initial period of five years, after which it had to be affirmed by Parliament. This meant that on 31 July 1971, the Act would expire unless Parliament determined otherwise by affirmative resolution of both Houses. And this is exactly what happened.[41]

In 1861 the equation between the crime of murder and the punishment of death had been recognized by Parliament as pretty much sacrosanct. The passionate speech in the Commons by the great liberal John Stuart Mill when he was a Member of Parliament in 1868, in which he stressed how essential the preservation of this equation was for the moral and social cohesion of English society, can be regarded as faithfully representing the prevailing opinion of the time.[42] This was considered as the ultimate limit beyond which the abolitionist movement should not attempt to trespass. 'The storm which once seemed to be gathering', wrote *The Times*, 'has subsided and has been followed by a great calm . . . The abolition of capital punishment had ceased to have a place among the real questions of the day.'[43]

It took 104 years for this equation to be swept away. But the issue was by no means dead. Within a year of Parliament voting for abolition, more exactly on 23 November 1966, a Private Member asked for leave to introduce a Bill restoring capital punishment for the murder of police and prison officers, though the Commons on a free vote refused it. As Lord Windlesham has rightly observed, 'Dormant though the possibility of legislative change may be for the duration of one more Parliament, the intensity of interest in capital punishment shows little sign of abating, and the merest spark can set passions ablaze once more . . . Strong feelings lie latent and from time to time are activated. Events are the spur.'[44] Also, the British government has made no moves to sign and ratify the international instruments prohibiting

---

41 The death penalty was abolished by the Crime and Disorder Act 1998 for treason and piracy with violence. It can still be imposed for certain military offences in time of war under the Naval Discipline Act 1957, Army Act 1955 and Air Force Act 1955.
42 L. Radzinowicz, *History of English Criminal Law and its Administration* (1968), vol. 4, pp. 326–43, and especially see L. Radzinowicz and R. Hood, *The Emergence of Penal Policy* (1986), vol. 5, pp. 685–8.
43 Leading article, *The Times* (14 March 1878), pp. 9b–c.
44 See Lord Windlesham, *Responses to Crime* (1987), pp. 152 and 157. His Table 8 is revealing: 'Votes in the House of Commons on Capital Punishment since 1955', pp. 158–9. So far there have been thirteen motions in thirteen years by Private Members to reintroduce capital punishment for certain types of murder.

the use of the death penalty. Indeed it strongly opposed the recommendation adopted by a majority in the Parliamentary Assembly of the Council of Europe which called on countries to abolish the death penalty for all crimes, including treason and espionage.[45]

My further unexpected involvement in the subject

I had hoped that having just been involved in the subject for four years I would at last be able to concentrate on some other more novel questions – and so I did. Nevertheless, rather unexpectedly, I had to return to the question of the death penalty on four further occasions, though in a different capacity and in an altogether different set of circumstances.

A major issue still left in the balance because of lack of direct empirical evidence, and one which could still swing public opinion one way or another, was to ascertain with all necessary precision and impartiality whether, since the abolition of capital punishment, the incidence of violent criminality, and especially of murder, had gone up to a significant extent. This, as might have been expected, led to a fierce battle over the interpretation of criminal statistics. It led me to remember a saying which I uttered in a frivolous moment in reply to being asked what I thought about criminal statistics: 'Criminal statistics are like a bikini: what they reveal is suggestive and what they hide is vital.' Soon after I made this flippant remark I noticed that a High Court judge of New York was found guilty of an identical utterance. I still continued to believe that I can claim authorship, for what it is worth.

Harold Evans, then the editor-in-chief of the *Sunday Times* of London (and until recently President and Chief Executive of Random House), invited me early in September 1969 to express my opinion on this delicate and complex subject, either in the form of a lengthy article or in a detailed interview. I selected the latter alternative and I was fortunate because my interviewer, a young member of the newspaper's staff, proved to be so very effective in probing me. It was for the first time that virtually the entire page of this important newspaper was devoted to a penological subject, including an impressive graph splashed across it.[46] 'The criminal, it must be admitted, does not help us.' By that I meant that since the death penalty was suspended in Britain for an experimental period of five years, those murders that would, in theory at least, have merited the supreme punishment had increased, indeed they had more than doubled. Capital murder prior to abolition – 71; post abolition – 161. Because these absolute figures for murder were rela-

---

45 See Roger Hood, *The Death Penalty: a World-wide Perspective* (2nd edn, 1996), pp. 15–16.
46 See 'Hanging – Has Abolition Worked? Professor Leon Radzinowicz of the Cambridge Institute of Criminology talks to Lewis Chester', *Sunday Times* (London, 12 September 1969), p. 13.

tively small it was tempting to mention that, while the figures might look disquieting, they were not statistically significant. I disagreed with this point of view. The increase was too large to be accidental. It must have had a cause or causes. Incomparably more accurate light could be thrown on the problem if capital murder, instead of being examined in isolation, were seen in the context of trends in criminality in general and of violent criminality in particular. It then appeared that all kinds of crimes were increasing and indeed were increasing more substantially and more speedily than the murder rate. During this very period there was a five-fold increase in crimes of violence (short of murder), which was more than three times the increase in the number of murders. We were therefore confronted with a burgeoning crime wave accompanied by several factors which indicated that a much higher rate of crime all round was soon to become a permanent feature of our communal life. I tried to point out that a dozen or so executions per year were irrelevant one way or another to our social cohesion, public morality, or protection against crime; to indicate the negative broader social effects of a drastically increased level of executions; to warn of its effect on the substitute penal alternatives and on the unbearable pressures it would place on the Royal Prerogative of Mercy. My piece had at the time evoked much interest, and I am glad to say was received by many with due consideration as to its reliability.[47]

I felt rather strongly that much more was needed than my own evaluation, and that the voice of criminologists should be heard and authoritatively expressed. I was therefore particularly glad to be informed in December 1969 by Dr Terence Morris (Professor of Social Institutions and Criminology at the London School of Economics) that criminologists and academicians of allied interests were feeling that, in view of the impending consideration by Parliament whether to affirm the abolition of capital punishment, they should express, if possible, a collective view on the subject. This was done and I had the honour to lead a letter to the editor of *The Times* supported by thirty-four signatures. It read as follows:

> Sir, – Now that Parliament is being required to consider the final abolition of capital punishment we feel compelled to point out that there is nowhere in any of the voluminous statistical material about murder and the death penalty any conclusive evidence as to its special deterrent value. On the contrary, such evidence as there is suggests that the rate of murder in society is a function of other

---

47 I was surprised (but glad) to see my article reproduced in several provincial papers. See, for example, 'Hanging: an all or nothing solution?' by Professor Leon Radzinowicz, *Burnley Evening Star* (10 December 1969).

infinitely more complex social and psychological factors. We further believe that to return to the situation as it obtained under the Homicide Act, 1957, or any other system of degrees of murder – a state of affairs which the Royal Commission on Capital Punishment 1949–53 predicted would be shot through with unjust anomalies – would be the most unfortunate compromise course that Parliament could take.[48]

The last two interventions took me back to the United States. The prestigious Bar Association of the City of New York decided to devote one of its fixed public meetings to the subject of capital punishment. Abe Fortas, a former Justice of the Supreme Court of America, and Professor Ernest van den Haag were expected to confront each other: the former a radical liberal so closely associated with the decision in *re-Gault*, and the latter a stern conservative, author of the commanding book *Punishing Criminals: Concerning a Very Old and Painful Question*. I was brought over for the occasion by the Ford Foundation to deal with the subject from an international comparative perspective. The foundation also most generously put at my disposal a small grant which enabled me to bring my material up to date. Two hundred copies of my report were mimeographed and put at the disposal of those present. I well remember how excited the audience became when I produced the evidence provided by an eminent Cambridge mathematician (Professor Sir Peter Swinnerton-Dyer, FRS, Fellow of Trinity College) who regarded with utter suspicion the basis on which Professor Isaac Ehrlich had tried to estimate how many people would have had their lives saved if capital punishment had been in force in the United States.[49] Since then Professor William Bowers of Northwestern University and several others have expressed strong

---

48 'Capital Punishment: View of Criminologists, Letter to the Editor from Professor Leon Radzinowicz and other Criminologists', *The Times* (15 December 1969). L. Radzinowicz (Institute of Criminology, University of Cambridge); N. Howard Avison (Edinburgh); M. Banton (Professor, Bristol); A.E. Bottoms (Sheffield); S. Box (Kent); W. Carson (Bedford College); D. Chapman (Liverpool); S. Cohen (Durham); P. Didcott (LSE); T.C.N. Gibbens (Professor, Institute of Psychiatry, London); J.E. Hall Williams (LSE); F. Heidensohn (LSE); R. Hood (Cambridge); H. Jones (Professor, Cardiff); J. King (Cambridge); R. King (Southampton); F.H. McClintock (Cambridge); J. Mack (Glasgow); J. Martin (Professor, Southampton); J. Mays (Professor, Liverpool); P. Morris (Borough Polytechnic); T.P. Morris (Professor, LSE); R. Parker (Professor, Bristol); C.M. Philipson (Goldsmiths' College); P. Rock (LSE); G.N.G. Rose (Cambridge); R.F. Sparks (Cambridge); W.J.H. Sprott (Professor, Bedford College); L. Taylor (York); P. Tomlinson (LSE); G. Trasler (Professor, Southampton); D. West (Cambridge); P. Wiles (LSE); T. Willett (Reading).
49 Isaac Ehrlich, 'The Deterrent Effect of Capital Punishment: A Question of Life and Death', *American Economic Review*, vol. 65 (1975), pp. 397–417, and 'Deterrence. Evidence and Inference', *Yale Law Journal*, vol. 85 (1975), pp. 209–27.

reservations.[50] It was a fascinating occasion and the beautiful auditorium was filled with a distinguished audience. But if a vote were to be taken I would be hard pressed to guess in what direction it would have gone.

Another occasion, a solemn one, took place on 20 March 1968. It was an invitation from a highly respected Senator, the late Philip A. Hart of Michigan, to appear and give evidence to the Judiciary Committee of the Senate (of which he was the Chairman), at that time considering 'A Bill to Abolish the Death Penalty under the Laws of the United States, and for other Purposes'.[51] In this instance I had the floor to myself and I was expected to concentrate on the English experience with particular emphasis on developments which had taken place in the previous three decades. As a guide to what I wanted to say and how I intended to say it, I took the well-known French saying: 'Je ne suppose rien – Je ne propose rien – J'expose.' I tried to 'transport' the senatorial committee to England to see for themselves the legal, penal, social, political and moral issues involved in the question as confronted by English society and its governing centres, and not as part of a doctrinal programme connected with a particular school of thought, retentionist or abolitionist, as the case may be. At the time I spoke, some thirty years ago, the respect in which the English system of criminal justice was held had made the abolition of capital punishment an international event, especially in the English-speaking world. It is no doubt to this that I largely owed the invitation.

It was an exhilarating event, though strenuous and demanding. It took close to two hours. I was more than compensated by the brief and very much to the point exchange of views which followed and by the gracious and succinct remark of Senator Hart when he brought the meeting to an end by saying: 'Professor, you have been exciting as well as helpful, and we are grateful.' This was a time when a strong and confident movement to abolish or at least to restrict the scope of capital punishment in the United States was in the ascendancy. Today I would not expect to be invited to appear before a judiciary committee, for thirty-eight states of America have the death penalty and its scope has been greatly expanded under federal criminal law.

---

50 See, for example, W.K. Bowers and G.L. Pierce, 'The Illusion of Deterrence in Isaac Ehrlich's Research on Capital Punishment', *Yale Law Journal*, vol. 85 (1975), pp. 187–208; P. Passell 'The Deterrent Effect of the Death Penalty: A Statistical Test', *Stanford Law Review*, vol. 28 (1975), pp. 61–80; J.A. Fox and M.L. Radelet, 'Persistent Flaws in Econometric Studies of the Deterrent Effect of the Death Penalty', *Loyola of Los Angeles Law Review*, vol. 23 (1989), pp. 29–44. And, generally, Roger Hood, *The Death Penalty: a World-wide Perspective* (2nd edn, 1996) (Chapter 6, 'The Question of Deterrence', pp. 186–212 at pp. 196–210).

51 'To Abolish the Death Penalty. Hearings before the Sub-Committee on Criminal Law and Procedures of the Committee on the Judiciary, United States Senate', Nineteenth Congress, Second Session on S. 1760, 20–21 March and 2 July 1968, pp. 55–68.

A very high potential for ferocity

In this somewhat incongruous postscript may I share with the readers of this book a piece of information about the history of capital punishment in Britain which it took me a long time to ascertain and have confirmed from other sources. I was anxious to know who was the youngest offender ever executed in England and who was the last person found guilty of high treason who suffered death accompanied by some of the aggravations in its enforcement prescribed under law for this kind of crime.

As to the first (1620):

> It is believed that the youngest person who was ever executed in this country was a boy between eight and nine years old, named Dean, who was found guilty of burning two barns at Windsor, and it appearing that he had malice, revenge, craft, and cunning, he had judgement to be hanged, and was hanged accordingly.[52]

As to the second (1817):

> A particularly striking example of such proceedings is provided by the execution of the sentence for high treason passed in 1817 on Jeremiah Brandreth, William Turner and Isaac Ludlam. This execution is only briefly mentioned by the *Annual Register* but the Rev. Charles Cox gives a detailed and trustworthy account of it:

> 'On November 1st, the Prince Regent signed the warrant for the execution of these three misguided peasants, remitting that part of the sentence that related to quartering, but ordering the hanging, drawing and beheading ... Two axes were ordered of Bamford, a smith of Derby ... On the morning of Friday, November 7th, the three prisoners received the Sacrament ... The hurdle or sledge was then brought within the gaol ... A horse was attached to it, and each of the three condemned men was dragged round the gaol-yard, their hands being held to prevent their being jolted off ... They hung from the gallows for half-an-hour. On the platform, in front of the gallows, was placed the block and two sacks of sawdust, and on a bench two axes, two sharp knives, and a basket ... The body of Brandreth was first taken down from the gallows, and placed face downwards on the block. The executioner, a muscular Derbyshire

---

52 'This case was tried before Whitlock, J., at the Abingdon Assizes, 1620, and is reported in Emlyn's Edit. Hale's Pleas of the Crown', p. 25 (n.). Quoted by C.S. Kenny, *A Selection of Cases Illustrative of English Criminal Law* (1901), p. 43.

coal miner, ... was masked, and his name kept a profound secret. Brandreth's neck received only one stroke, but it was not clean done, and the assistant (also masked) finished it off with a knife. Then the executioner laid hold of the head by the hair, and holding it at arm's length, to the left, to the right, and in front of the scaffold, called out three times – "Behold the head of the traitor, Jeremiah Brandreth". The other two served in like manner ... The scaffold was surrounded by a great force of cavalry with drawn swords, and several companies of infantry were also present. The space in front of the gaol was densely packed with spectators. "When the first stroke of the axe was heard, there was a burst of horror from the crowd", says an eye witness, writing to the *Examiner*, "and the instant the head was exhibited there was a terrifying shriek set up, and the multitude ran violently in all directions, as if under the influence of a sudden frenzy".'[53]

The potential for cruelty inherent in capital punishment is unlimited.

---

53 Revd Charles Cox, *Three Centuries of Berkshire Annals* (1890), vol. 2, pp. 41–3; Shelley, *An Address to the People on the Death of the Princess Charlotte* (first issued in 1817 and reprinted in 1843); apparently Shelley was present at the execution. See also for the full account of the trial W.B. Gurney, *The Trials of Jeremiah Brandreth, William Turner, Isaac Ludlam, George Weightman and Others* (1817), 2 vols. Quoted by L. Radzinowicz, *History of English Criminal Law and its Administration* (1968), vol. 1, pp. 226–7.

11

AN ISSUE WHICH REFUSES TO GO AWAY

The persistency of the death penalty in so many parts of the world has prompted me to reflect on the issue within a wider historical and comparative context.

'All arguments in favour or against capital punishment have been stated, and stated well, some hundred years ago', I have been told many times, by many people in many countries. I had suspected that this was so when I embarked upon my inquiries into the death penalty more than half a century ago. Consequently, I was not disappointed when more systematic research and publicly oriented work showed how true it was.

But I soon discovered that it would be an oversimplification to draw the conclusion that the arguments of today are identical with those used in the past. Many of the arguments used today are much more sophisticated, the emphasis put on different considerations is far from being the same, and the methods employed to present them are now much more refined.

A bolt of lightning

There have been many writings and pronouncements against capital punishment throughout the centuries. As an outstanding French historian of the subject observed, they are no less ancient than capital punishment itself. Confucius, Plato, Saint Benedict, Saint Augustine, Sir Thomas More come to one's mind, and there are very many others of unquestionable eminence and authority. But these were isolated individual expressions of view, which more often than not failed to evoke any wider and sustained response. Capital punishment acquired the status of a question only when Cesare Beccaria took it up in his book *Dei Delitti delle Pene* in 1764, a book which overnight gained him immortality far beyond Italy, indeed in the world at large Beccaria, then a young man of twenty-six years of age, suddenly became the most celebrated *porte-parole* of a rapidly growing movement which gave birth to a crusade.

The way in which he did it is significant for more than one reason. *Of Crimes and Punishments* contained no public opinion polls, no statistics, no historic excavations, no comparative illustrations. One would almost be tempted to say that it was a *cri de cœur* of unusual eloquence and persuasiveness in the service of what had been felt to be a deep, compelling cause which was bound to engage the human conscience everywhere. The appeal was instant, not only because it was so effectively discharged, but also because it was faithful to the premises and ideas of the Enlightenment and later of the French Revolution, both of which shook the existing order to its very roots.[1]

Its appeal was part and parcel of the ethos of the period, nourished by beliefs which had been erected into dogma: in the right of every individual to enjoy freedom and happiness; in the necessity of restricting the power and the interference of church and state; in the general and uninterrupted progress of humankind.

The prevailing practice of administering criminal justice was singled out as one of the central targets of his violent onslaught against what was soon to become known as the *ancien régime*, which was commonly indicted for its arbitrariness, cruelty and corruption. Capital punishment was an integral part of it. It was appointed for a great variety of crimes of varying degrees of gravity. It was often accompanied by terrifying aggravations in its modes of enforcement and in the legal consequences flowing from capital convictions. It was carried out in public with ruthless and barbarous forms of exposure of the body in order to maximize and spread the terror which it was expected to inspire. Thus a radical, if not total, expurgation of capital punishment from the criminal law was regarded by Beccaria and his many ardent and influential followers as a condition *sine qua non* for a radical reconstruction of the criminal justice system as a whole. Only ten pages of his book were dedicated to the subject of the death penalty, yet they became the rallying kernel of an agitation which sought to remodel the system and endow it with a new moral and social justification. In some ways this emphasis on capital punishment diverted attention from other vital areas of the system of criminal justice, but it was a distortion with an exceptionally high emotional and imitative potential.

The crusade against capital punishment originated in Europe, then regarded as the centre of the world. In consequence the abolition of capital punishment was not conceived in strictly national or even regional terms. It should take root, so it was declared, in the world at large. It should suffer no territorial restrictions, indeed no restrictions of any kind. The question of the death penalty thus had its status raised still higher. It became a universal

---

[1] It was the French Revolution which propelled him on to the world stage and fuelled his message with immediate potency. But he himself was not so much its direct product, but rather a product of the Enlightenment and the Encyclopedists. One of the first to study their impact on the development of criminal law and procedure was Alfred Freiherr Von Overbeck, *Das Strafrecht der Französischen Encyclopaedie etc.* (1902). But a modern full-scale study still remains to be done.

question, an almost transcendental, absolute issue to be agitated for and put into effect without regard for time, place, ethnicity or political system.

As the galvanizing impact of the Enlightenment began to recede, as the large hopes postulated by the French Revolution were being chastised by the enormity of its excesses, and as the heavy Napoleonic handling of law and order reflected by his Code of 1810 became imitated far and wide, the abolitionist crusade inevitably lost much of its spiritual purity. It began to reveal a naïvety, indeed even shallowness.[2]

Inspirations for change: humanity, religion, politics

From the 1850s until the early years of the twentieth century concrete changes were under way throughout Europe in the scope of capital punishment, the extent of its enforcement, and in ways of carrying it out. A significant indicator of this trend was the decision of the British government in 1881 to publish *Reports on the Laws of Foreign Countries Respecting Homicidal Crime*, and even more significant was the inclusion of an extensive survey of the *Penalty of Death* on the agenda of the Congress of the International Penitentiary Commission held in Washington in 1910.[3] Points of view and angles of approach could now be identified with much greater precision and the universal question of the death penalty started to present a much more complex and variegated picture than the early crusaders had ever contemplated. Three layers of opinion and feelings had come to the forefront: the humanitarian; the religious; the political.

The humanitarian approach was possibly the simplest. No arguments

---

2 Here are a few instances which I liked to quote as an example of the disparity between the ethos of the Enlightenment and the sombre reality. In Russia, Catherine the Great suspended the use of capital punishment in 1767, and homage was paid to her by all the philosophers of the period. But an English visitor to that country noticed the alternative that had been substituted for the death penalty. Offenders were subjected to 333 lashes of the knout instead. Joseph II of Austria abolished capital punishment in 1787, and he, too, was singled out by philosophers as a great liberal luminary of the period. But again a contemporary traveller recorded the following condition of prisoners, who instead of being put to death were manning galleys: 'A Danube vessel towed by human beings is so repulsive a spectacle that even an executioner who has become familiar with breaking upon the wheel will turn his eyes away.' The great American criminal law codifier and reformer Edward Livingstone (a contemporary of Jeremy Bentham and strongly influenced by him) was very much in advance of his time when he proposed the abolition of capital punishment in his system of penal law for the state of Louisiana. But the substitute that he proposed, permanent solitary segregation, was frightening in its inhuman physical and soul-destroying regime.
3 See *Reports on the Laws of Foreign Countries Respecting Homicidal Crime,* C 2849, *Parliamentary Papers* (1881), vol. 76, p. 197 and *Further Reports,* C 2913, *ibid.*, p. 267. See also 'Capital Punishment', in *Actes du Congrès Pénitentiaire International de Washington, 1910* (Groningen, 1913), vol. 1, pp. 326–408, and vol. 5, pp. 3–97.

needed to be marshalled in its defence and no arguments could be of much avail to shake its premises. It was based on an almost saintly truth that human life should not be taken away under any circumstances and by anyone, certainly not by a state expected to be the repository and the guarantor of individual rights. Such an approach could not fail to command respect, but it was never a factor of real influence in undermining the foundations for capital punishment or in substantially reducing its scope. It was a marginal factor. And when advanced it was often relegated by its critics to the sphere of lofty philanthropy rather than sturdy criminal justice.[4] Since the Second World War humanitarian concerns have been strengthened and institutionalized through the international human rights movement. This has embraced the concept of 'the right to life' which in its turn has been used as an argument against capital punishment. So much so, that optional protocols have been included in the International Covenant on Civil and Political Rights to encourage abolition of the death penalty and several states have abolished capital punishment through the instrumentality of their constitutions.[5] Furthermore, the United Nations has promulgated standards and safeguards in a laudable effort to try to ensure that where the death penalty is in existence it is carried out in a decent manner.[6] Thus the humanitarian approach has taken on a new and more potent guise.

The religious strand was, of course, of altogether different magnitude. But it was by no means a factor of coherent, uniform gravitation. The Judaic and Islamic religious canons – to proceed by necessarily generalized observation – acknowledged and indeed justified the fundamental necessity of capital punishment, on redemptive, moral and social grounds. At the other extreme was the Protestant religious heritage, much more pliable and tolerant. The Catholic creed and doctrine lay somewhere in between the two. On the one hand, its lofty infusion of compassion militated against the use of capital punishment as far as possible. On the other, its avid insistence on individual

---

4 This point of view, or rather this belief, is thus expressed by Baroness Wootton (an agnostic) – its fervent adherent:

> First and foremost is a profound sense of the value of human life and of human personality. This can hardly be surprising. Those who believe that this life is all that we can expect to have naturally hold it dear. To me at least, except in a few extreme cases of mercy killing, it is unthinkable to contemplate taking the life of another human being. On this ground alone, I am irrevocably opposed to capital punishment in any circumstances, even apart from the cogent arguments as to its ineffectiveness, and I am very proud that it fell to my lot to introduce into the House of Lords the Bill which has, I hope, finally abolished this barbarous practice in this country.
> (Barbara Wootton, *In a World I Never Made* (1967), p. 173)

5 For a useful account of this movement see William A. Schabas, *The Abolition of the Death Penalty in International Law* (1993).
6 Economic and Social Council Resolutions 1984/50, annex, and 1989/64.

responsibility and accountability were an unhedged justification for imposing penalties, including capital punishment – but again within a scrupulously defined code of conduct.[7]

No one could ignore the fact that societies, especially those of Western Europe, were becoming increasingly secular, hence more independent in reaching decisions affecting their existence or destiny. Such a divide seemed to have occurred when the universal question of the death penalty was placed within the political compass, or more precisely within the political surround. The emergence of great political parties, cemented by close alignments, gave fresh directions to the question. The religious and humanistic substratum were still there (and indeed would always be there) but by then it had become a strongly coloured political issue. Its abolition, retention or modification was to be decided in political terms and frequently in an open public arena fermented by parliamentary battles, by explosive confrontations, and by carefully planned strategies or improvised opportunistic tactics. The question began to figure prominently on the agenda of the great political parties of our times and was assiduously kept there throughout all the vicissitudes of political change. It began to be dissected through the prism of the ideologies and programmes of the Conservative, Liberal and Social-Democratic parties. It was certainly not ignored or neglected by the Fascists, Nazi and Communist parties, and it was kept alive by the authoritarian regimes of the vast and troubled Third World.

The socialists in Europe and the labourites in Britain needed time to organize themselves into powerful permanent political parties, and so for quite a long time the divide on criminal matters continued to be between the Conservatives and the Liberals. With respect to the impact of liberalism, a distinction has to be drawn between its European and its British brand. Generalizations are usually perilous, especially when retracing the movement of ideas and preoccupations in the field of capital punishment. Nevertheless, one cannot be very wrong in stating that the total and immediate elimination of capital punishment was a unanimous desideratum of European liberals. Not so in the case of their English counterparts. They remained in favour of retaining capital punishment for the crime of murder (in addition to high treason and connected offences) and would acquiesce in an experimental period of suspension for five years only as an initial step towards

---

7   The fluidity of attitudes towards capital punishment as shaped by religious beliefs can be retraced in the major article by Paul Savey-Cassard, 'L'église catholique et la peine de mort', *Revue de Science Criminelle et de Droit Pénal Comparé*, new series, no. 1 (1961), pp. 773–85; and by Harry Potter, *Hanging in Judgement. Religion and the Death Penalty in England* (1933). For a widely noted categorical abolitionist statement by Dr William Temple (Archbishop of Canterbury) see his 'The Death Penalty', *Spectator* (25 January 1935). For general observations, well presented, see *Report from the Select Committee on Capital Punishment* (1930), 'Scriptural Considerations', pp. 61–4.

abolition. The already quoted stand taken up by John Stuart Mill was not exceptional but solidly representative. A similar view, adopted with firm consistency some eighty years later by Viscount Samuel – a leading Liberal and former Home Secretary, whose zeal for penal reform in general cannot be questioned – serves as another eloquent illustration of this divergence between European and British liberals.

In two other, by no means insignificant, respects the Europeans developed an approach that remained foreign to the British. The European liberals looked upon murder committed within the context of an intimate sexual relationship as a quasi-distinct species of killing and, supported by the romantic tradition, they clothed it in the attractive terminology of *crime passionnel*. With the help of recommendations to mercy profusely dished out by the jury, the concept of *crime passionnel* almost always nullified a capital conviction and indeed frequently led to a dramatic acquittal. The second exception was political crime. Here also, it was claimed, the motivation differed so profoundly from that which prompted the commission of all other crimes, that for humanitarian, moral and social reasons, political murder should be removed from the catalogue of crimes carrying the supreme penalty. The statesman and historian F. Guizot may well have been the first to advocate the recognition of this departure as early as 1822 in his widely acclaimed book *De la peine de mort en matière politique*. But he was soon followed by a host of others and the criminal code was changed to give effect to this approach. On both these accounts Britain continued to be criticized, but with no effect whatsoever. As long as capital punishment was appointed for murder, it was believed that *crime passionnel* and *crime politique* should be part of the commanding catalogue and that no distinction was justified under the law, or in practice, between them and other kinds of murder. If exceptions were to be made they should express themselves through recommendations to mercy made by the jury and by a flexible use of the Royal Prerogative of Mercy.

Only after very many efforts and laborious discussions did a consensus emerge to remove capital punishment for that other rather special species of murder, the crime of infanticide. But it was not until 1922 that the law was changed in England.

Once socialist parties were formed and became a parliamentary force, they overtook liberals on the subject of capital punishment as they did on a number of other social and economic controversial issues. This is revealed by a cursory reading of the histories of some of the major socialist parties of Western Europe, by the agendas of their national conferences, by the formulation of their programmes of intended action, and by the pronouncements of their authoritative spokesmen. I have been struck how often the demand for a total, immediate and universal abolition of capital punishment evoked a fervent emotional resonance and a distinctive resolve to implement it. Jean Jaurès, the leader of the French socialist party, who himself was soon to become the victim of political murder, stated with pride and certitude:

'Nous sommes tous solidaires de tous les hommes même dans le crime.' The death penalty was regarded as one of the instruments used by capitalistic regimes to keep the labouring classes down, and socialists were confident that in the socialist order, which was bound to come, capital punishment would be relegated to a museum of historical curiosities and abominations.

The lot of conservatives, squeezed on this issue between the moderate liberals and the radical socialists, was by no means enviable, though they had the advantage over all their opponents of representing on this matter the views of a great and constant majority of the population. True, it was Sir Samuel Romilly and his Whig friends and successors who started the crusade against the criminal code of England, bristling with some two hundred capital offences. However, it was also true that it was Sir Robert Peel, an orthodox and cautious Tory if ever there was one, who finally purged the laws of England of this largely symbolic, but still cruel and irrational, burden. But again, it is also fair to say that the bulk of the Tories were unhappy with the 1861 Act which restricted capital punishment to murder, and many of their successors were even more unhappy with the Act of 1965 which, in effect, disposed of capital punishment altogether.

I use the word 'bulk', but I am also inclined to think that, by that date, not only had some 25 per cent of Conservatives in Parliament reached the conclusion that a change had become necessary, but also many of them had become partners in the abolitionist cause. Finally, once the Act had been passed there was no concentrated planned effort on the part of the leadership of the Conservative Party to dislodge the decision, though the revival of the issue proved more than once a topical and deeply felt issue at the national conferences of the party. And, as already pointed out, there has been no shortage of Conservative Private Bills urging a move back to the past, at least partially.

Totalitarian distortions

At the opening of the twentieth century the outlook seemed to be very promising. The belief was widely shared that crime in general had reached its peak and that there might in future be even less of it, especially violent criminality. Indeed, with the advance of capitalism and progress of civilization, violence would be replaced by offences against property. True, it was the time when juvenile delinquency and recidivism caused grave concerns, but these were not the forms of criminality for which even the most extreme supporters of the death penalty advocated capital punishment. There was also a lot of confidence in the political and constitutional stability of the leading countries. All these factors strengthened the cause of the abolitionists. War, any kind of war, is never a propitious period for penal reform in general and the reduction of capital punishment in particular. The scope of the latter is usually enlarged, and in these circumstances it is not always enforced with due respect for procedural guarantees of fair, thorough trial by independent courts, prosecutorial circumspection and ample availability of defence counsel of high quality. Summary and emergency jurisdictions tend to become fashionable. The First World War was not an exception and short-cuts and abuses of this nature were recorded in several of the combatant countries with varying frequency and intensity.

Any hope that a vigorous abolitionist movement would come to the forefront again was already shattered in the period leading up to the outbreak of the Second World War, and even more so in the fateful years of 1933–43. Fascism, Nazism and Communism were the three political forces of the twentieth century which brought havoc to the universal question of the death penalty. The role of fascism in the actual use of the death penalty was secondary, but its ideological impact was important. Italy, true to Cesare Beccaria's heritage, was amongst the first major European countries to abolish capital punishment (1889), but it became the first to reinstate it (1930). And in doing so, Benito Mussolini and his powerful Minister of Justice, Arturo Rocco, laid down the doctrine according to which capital punishment not only was an indispensable instrument for the protection of society and of the state – hence an irreplaceable device of practical politics – but also represented an unchallengeable right of the state when regulating its relationship to the individual.

Nazism proclaimed or assumed the permanency of capital punishment. It was expected to operate against dissenters, political offenders, inferior or dangerous races, deviant or marginal strata, and several categories of ordinary criminals. The net for the applicability of capital punishment thrown out by Communism when in power was also extremely wide and elastic. There was no criminal lawyer or political writer of repute who could define with necessary precision the concepts of 'counter-revolutionary', 'social danger' or, still worse, 'enemy of the proletariat'. But in contrast to the Nazi doctrine, it was claimed that the institution of capital punishment was bound to die when a socialist society had been firmly established, and the very concept of state had withered away.

The details of the inhuman fury with which Nazis and Communists decimated masses of innocent humanity are by now all too well known. Suffice it to observe that the criminal justice of the *ancien régime* of the eighteenth century bears no comparison with the experience of the twentieth century. This, in its turn, prompts the embarrassing question whether, in penal matters, there is such a thing as progress and how it can be measured in valid scientific terms.

To expect that, in face of this unleashing of forces – so formidable, so primitive and so fanatical – criminological thought could exercise any restrictive influence on the death penalty would be to indulge in unforgivable naïvety. A few criminologists remained silent, some conveyed their disagreement in genteel, diplomatic terms, but the great majority put their criminological knowledge (or rather a revised version of it) in the service of justifying the new criminal policy and a new usage of capital punishment. This was particularly noticeable in Germany, in spite of its splendid criminological heritage. But this should only be said by those fortunate to have lived outside the totalitarian hell, not as passing a verdict of guilt and denigration, but as a soberly recorded historical fact with sensitive understanding of the tragic predicaments and pressures of the then prevailing situation.

Largely as a reaction against the criminal policy of the totalitarian states, capital punishment as a means devised to deal with certain categories of criminals acquired a much wider meaning. It came to be regarded as a sensitive and representative indication of a liberal way of thinking and living. And even further, the extent to which democratic ideals were being pursued, both in theory and in practice, could be related to the place assigned to capital punishment in a country's system of criminal justice. The universal question of the death penalty was thus invested with a new characteristic: the universal question of the death penalty and its democratic significance. But in its reformulation there seemed to be one glaring exception – the United States – so often referred to as the greatest democracy of all. The point is too important to be left without further comment.

The deadly weight of the United States

There was a time when capital punishment was assiduously examined by scholars of high reputation from all over Europe. The old books, such as those of Lucas, Mittermaier, Von Holtzendorff, d'Olivercrona, Lacassagne, Tarde, Liepmann, Von Hentig, are by now regretfully covered with thick dust.[8] I well remember reading them and deriving so much profit and pleasure from the fullness and integrity of their approach. I would still recommend them to the present generation of criminologists as part of their wider criminological education. It is instructive to note that some of them, though opposed to capital punishment, nevertheless found it justifiable to retain it in restricted and narrowly defined instances. The influence of Social Darwinism upon their thinking was apparent.[9]

At present European criminology no longer has much to say about the topic, largely because Western Europe has become almost totally abolition-

---

8 See J.M.C. Lucas, *Du système pénal en général et de la peine de mort en particulier* (1827); C.J.A. Mittermaier, *Die Todesstrafe* (1862); F. von Holtzendorff, *Das Verbrechen des Mordes und die Todesstrafe* (1875); L.R. d'Olivercrona, *De la peine de mort* (1893); Gabriel Tarde, *La Philosophe pénale* (1907 edn), pp. 520–67; Alexandre Lacassagne, *Peine de mort et criminalité* (1908); M. Liepmann, *Die Todesstrafe* (1912); Hans von Hentig, *Die Strafe*, vol. 1, *Frühformen und Kulturgeschichtliche Zusammenhänge* (1954), pp. 206–380.

9 See on this interaction Leon Radzinowicz, *The Roots of the International Association of Criminal Law and their Significance* (1991), Chapter 7, 'The Impact of Social Darwinism', pp. 26–31.

ist. While on the subject I should not fail to notice an *aperçu* in the best French tradition, elegant, precise and erudite by a French historian,[10] nor the very rare occasion when the Faculty of Law of the celebrated University of Coimbra organized an international colloquium on the status of capital punishment across the world as a tribute to the fact that Portugal had been the first European country to have abolished it (1867). This led to the publication of three volumes dedicated to the subject.[11]

Today the centre of academic interest has shifted from the Old to the New World. This is primarily explained by the truly dramatic return of capital punishment as a practical proposition in legislation and enforcement. It has rapidly expanded across the United States with the decisive support from Republican and conservative forces – the traditional supporters of a widely appointed and energetically enforced death penalty. Yet it is also increasingly supported by Democrats, including President Clinton himself.

The stubborn scholarly endeavours of scholars such as Thorsten Sellin and Hugo Bedau to refute the belief that capital punishment has an extra capacity to prevent crime and to refute the moral and social justification put forward by retentionists are too well known to be retold here. Nor should the contribution made by Professors Michael Meltsner and Charles Black be ignored.[12] Furthermore, what is sometimes not fully appreciated is the continuous and numerous appearance in leading legal, sociological and criminological periodicals of inquiries and essays bearing upon the subject. I could easily cite some eighty of them and I would still be reluctant to maintain that my list is exhaustive. The philosophical, moral, political and social arguments are still important but there is also a strong emphasis on the impact that capital punishment has, or is likely to have, on the working of the criminal justice system of the United States.

What are the trends in criminality in general and in violent crime and murder in particular over a certain period of time? Do they provide convincing

---

10 See Paul Savey-Cassard, *La Peine de mort* (1968) with a preface by François Perroux.
11 See the unusual and rather impressive publication *Pena de Morte*, 3 volumes (1967), an international colloquium under the auspices of the Law Faculty of the University of Coimbra in celebration of the centenary of the abolition of capital punishment in Portugal (1867) which took place in Coimbra (11–16 September 1967). The first two volumes contain reports presented. The colloquium was packed by abolitionists and the discussion upon the resolution submitted in vol. 3 reflects it. The tendency to ignore or to simplify some of the basic aspects of capital punishment is much too apparent. A similar criticism can be made of the contributions to the international conference on the Death Penalty, held at Syracuse, Italy, 17–22 May 1987, under the auspices of L'Insitut Supérieur International de Sciences Criminelles, the *Proceedings* of which were published in *Revue Internationale de Droit Pénal*, vol. 58 (1987).
12 See Michael Meltsner, *Cruel and Unusual: The Supreme Court and Capital Punishment* (1973) and Charles Black, Jr, *Capital Punishment: The Inevitability of Caprice and Mistake* (2nd edn, 1981).

evidence for retaining, abolishing or reintroducing the death penalty? How much of the crime, and which kinds of it, escape being brought to justice and thus remain a part of the crime usually described as 'the dark figure of crime'? What are the main categories of murderers most likely to suffer capital convictions? Are the criminal careers of capitally convicted offenders characterized by a progressive acceleration (quantitative or qualitative) reaching a ripeness which brings them within the purview of incapacitation or even elimination? What guarantees, constitutional and procedural, are provided in bringing capital offenders to justice to secure a fair trial, and to what extent are these guarantees respected in practice? What has been the incidence of wrongful convictions in capital cases? How far (if at all) are the sentencing determinations influenced by factors such as race or socio-economic background? What are the variations and disparities in sentencing processes of capital cases across the country and in relation to certain strata of society, and how can they be explained? What alternative (if any) is provided to the imposition of the death sentence and how is its regime and functioning organized? What is being done (or not being done) to secure a fair and reasonably speedy appeal in capital cases? What is the state of public opinion regarding capital punishment and its alternatives?

The almost invariable conclusion reached by the authors of all such inquiries is that the impact of capital punishment on the criminal justice system as at present administered in the United States is messy and indeed in very many ways pernicious. And it cannot be denied that the evidence adduced is solid and convincing. These observations originate as a general rule from the abolitionists. The academic case for capital punishment is less often made. An article which gained much notoriety largely because of its author's eminence as a cultural and literary critic; a significant statement in justification of capital punishment by a distinguished conservative professor; an entire book, well conceived and thorough by a legal scholar – are three instances from the other side which occur to me as particularly deserving to be read and reflected upon.[13] In practical terms this paucity of academic support is of no significance. The tide urging more capital punishment and its more vigorous enforcement now sweeping across the United States is so pervasive that it can ignore its opponents and needs no allies.[14]

---

13 See Jacques Barzun, 'In Favour of Capital Punishment', originally published in *American Scholar*, vol. 31 (1962), pp. 181–92, and reproduced in several collections of essays on the subject by others. Also Professor Ernest van den Haag, 'In Defence of the Death Penalty: A Legal–Practical–Moral Analysis', *Criminal Law Bulletin*, vol. 14, no. 1 (1978), pp. 51–68; Walter Berns, *For Capital Punishment: Crime and the Morality of the Death Penalty* (1991).

14 The book by Herbert H. Haines, *Against Capital Punishment: the Anti-Death Penalty Movement in America 1972–1994* (1996), retraces the unsuccessful attempts to stop the expansion of the death penalty and makes painful reading. Since 1994 there have been further accretions to capital statutes and to their enforcement. The pressure for further extension continues.

Criminology has thrown invaluable light on the subject of capital punishment. Its approach today is fundamentally different from that which was prevalent half a century ago. To this extent it has played a fruitful and scientifically rewarding role. But when it comes to an individual's decision whether to be an abolitionist or a retentionist its impact is much more restricted. For as Professor Marvin Wolfgang has so astutely observed, 'The death penalty is fundamentally an ethical issue ... and criminological research ... is often purposively selected to buttress with reason either what is believed or is ethically held.'[15]

Forces of resistance

There is no question that the movement towards total abolition has made considerable strides. This fact comes out clearly from Professor Hood's latest survey of the subject. But should Cesare Beccaria and his eminent followers come back to life and look at the map of capital punishment across the world they would hardly be able to control their disappointment. It is true that Western Europe has moved decidedly away from capital punishment. But even there a few countries still preserve the supreme penalty for the most serious crimes against the state as well as for military offences in times of war. Britain joined the abolitionists and Canada, Australia and New Zealand are the other most notable abolitionist English-speaking countries. The dissolution of the Soviet empire has brought with it the effective abandonment of capital punishment in Russia and its total abolition by several countries which gained independence from the Soviet Union.

There is no sign that China, India, Pakistan, Afghanistan, Japan or any of the Middle Eastern states will join the abolitionist camp. The heaviest blow to the abolitionist cause has come from the United States, which has resolutely rallied behind the retentionist cause.

The Council of Europe first, and then the United Nations, have set up a kind of regular monitoring of the state of the questions amongst their members. The reports by the late Marc Ancel, by Norval Morris and now by Roger Hood, on behalf of the Secretariat of the United Nations, have produced documents of integrity and precision.[16] They reveal a remarkable steady and significant fact: 80 per cent of the retentionist countries simply refused to answer the questionnaire addressed to them by the Secretariat of the United Nations. Indeed capital punishment is maintained by some

---

15 Marvin Wolfgang, 'The Death Penalty: Social Philosophy and Social Science Research', *Criminal Law Bulletin*, vol. 14, no. 1 (1978), pp. 18–33, at p. 18.
16 See Marc Ancel, *The Death Penalty in European Countries* (Council of Europe, 1962); Norval Morris, *Capital Punishment Developments 1961 to 1965* (United Nations, 1967); Roger Hood, *The Death Penalty: a World-wide Perspective* (1989; rev. and updated edn, 1996).

eighty-five member states, with a further twenty-nine having it on their statute books, even if not put into effect.

As Amnesty International, with its unquestionable authority, regularly brings to light, there are still many countries in which capital punishment is carried out 'in the dark', outside the regularly constituted machinery of justice by administrative or executive organs with hardly any public accountability. Nor should the vital information gathered by Human Rights Watch (composed of five Watch Committees) be ignored. The fact that in a number of countries the imposition of the enforcement of the supreme penalty has become less strict should not be ignored, but this does not alter the basic world-wide statistical distribution and interpretation of the picture as a whole.[17] Indeed, to clinch the essence of the picture as a whole, one cannot escape noticing that no less than four-fifths of the total population of the world still live in conditions which sanction the appointment and the use of capital punishment.[18]

Among the obvious major factors in support of the retention of capital punishment is the widespread intensity of retributory and expiatory feeling in respect to crimes of exceptional gravity or perversion;[19] the still not insignificant belief in the effectiveness of deterrence in spite of it not being proved statistically; a conviction that, should it not prove to be sufficiently deterrent, the potential for increased deterrence is there and could be easily achieved by expanding the scope of capital punishment, by raising the rate of

---

17 See Peter Hodgkinson and Andrew Rutherford (eds) *Capital Punishment: Global Issues and Prospects* (1996). One of the most dramatic reversals of the retentionist pattern has been provided by the new South African Republic. For a very long time it headed the list of countries with the highest rate of capital convictions and of the ratio of executions to convictions. The simultaneous hanging of two or three offenders was a frequent occurrence. See Roger Hood, *op. cit.* (1996), pp. 28–9 and John Hatchard and Simon Coldham, 'Commonwealth Africa', in Peter Hodgkinson and Andrew Rutherford (eds) *op. cit.*, pp. 155–91, at pp. 161–2 and 171–2.
18 The total population of the entire world amounts to 5,544 million. The total for Europe amounts to 726 million. These are estimates for 1993 and 1992 respectively. See *World Total Population. Estimate by the United Nations Demographic Year Book*, UNS (New York, 1995).
19 Stated the formidable Karl Binding (perhaps the greatest criminal lawyer of Germany): 'The offence is the reason and retribution a purpose of punishment' and 'the idea of retribution is perhaps the deepest in world history'. Connected with it is the instinct of vengeance. States Ernest van den Haag: 'The motives for the death penalty may indeed include vengeance. Vengeance as a compensatory and psychologically reparatory satisfaction for an injured party, group, or society, may be a legitimate human motive – despite the biblical injunction. I do not see wherein that motive is morally blameworthy. When regulated and directed by law, vengeance also is socially useful: Legal vengeance solidifies social solidarity against lawbreakers and is the alternative to the private revenge of those who feel harmed.' 'In Defence of the Death Penalty', *op. cit.*, pp. 64–5. On this subject see the attractively and interestingly presented four volumes edited by Raymond Verdier, *La Vengeance. Études d'ethnologie, d'histoire et de philosophie* (Paris, 1980).

capital convictions, by a more stringent imposition of the death sentence, and by more speedy executions;[20] the insistence that penal reform can be achieved without the abolition of capital punishment, the former being so much more complex and wide in scope, and bearing no relation to the number of criminals put to death; the insecurity and frustration bred by the upward trend of crime in general, and of crimes of violence in particular; the terroristic aspects of political crime, with its indiscriminate aims; the unsatisfactory nature of imprisonment for life as an alternative to capital punishment and its very substantial and steadily increasing cost; the defects inherent in the parole system; the use of the issue of capital punishment in party politics and electoral battles as a proof of liberal softness; the sheer numerical influence of authoritarian or semi-authoritarian states across the world which do not endorse capital punishment as a 'universal' or 'international question' but *par excellence* as a 'national question' which is to be shaped by the national tradition and needs of each particular country; the deeply felt objection to a solution being imposed on them by ideological manifestos, castigating monitoring, or international conventions and maintaining that it is they who faithfully express the view of a vast majority of their citizens. And in this field, like in so many others, the expansive retentionist trend exemplified by the United States weighs heavily and persuasively.

There is no room in the contemporary world for a Cesare Beccaria to emerge and find an attuned powerful public echo. I well remember the wise warning of George Eliot that 'among all forms of mistakes prophecy is the most gratuitous', and yet I am inclined to state that I do not expect any substantial further decrease in the appointment and use of capital punishment in the foreseeable future. In my opinion most of the countries likely to embrace the abolitionist cause have by now done so. However, there remains a recalcitrant group of states which, for a combination of reasons – religious, political or social – proclaim their right to keep the death penalty and they are unlikely to change. They are particularly unlikely to be sympathetic to the argument that capital punishment is 'cruel and unusual' or that it should be rejected on the grounds that it violates the right to life of every individual.

Capital punishment has displayed throughout its chequered and frequently repellent history a truly exceptional degree of durability. This is a fact of deeply rooted and exceptional complexity which cannot be ignored or disposed of by hazy dialectics or confusing generalizations.

---

20 In 1955, at the height of parliamentary debates in Britain for or against capital punishment, twenty-five persons were sentenced to death of whom nine were executed. In the United States in 1995, at an expansionist and confident stage of capital punishment, the number convicted of capital murder was five hundred and the number executed was fifty-six. But there were over three thousand on 'death row'.

12

A PRISON SYSTEM IN CRISIS

A great escape

On 3 May 1961 a dramatic trial was concluded at the Central Criminal Court in London. George Blake, alias George Behar, born in Rotterdam on 11 November 1922, pleaded guilty to five counts under Section 1 of the Official Secrets Act 1911 and was sentenced by the Lord Chief Justice of England, Lord Parker, to a total of forty-two years' imprisonment. As far as I am able to determine this was the longest determinate sentence ever imposed. The trial was held largely in camera but Lord Parker in passing the sentence said: 'Your case is one of the worst that can be envisaged in times of peace.'

It was an exceptional sentence because George Blake was an exceptionally wicked major spy. As a double agent he betrayed several of his trusting *confrères* and sent them to atrocious deaths. Perhaps still worse he betrayed his own country which on his own volition he had adopted as his own, duly becoming a naturalized British subject, following his father who had applied for and obtained British citizenship. Under the shadow of forty-two years' detention he could either die in prison, or be set free as an old man when he would be of no further use to his Soviet masters.

On 22 October 1966 the case took on an even more dramatic aspect. On that day, 'D' Wing of HM Prison, Wormwood Scrubs, where Blake was undergoing the fifth year of his detention, was on 'Free Association' from 4:15 p.m. until locking-up time at 7 p.m. This was the time when the inmates could either watch films in the recreation hut or mix freely within the wing, watching television, playing cards and table tennis, or visiting each other on all four landings. When a roll-call was taken, at about 7 p.m., the prison officer in charge found that Blake was not in his cell. His second check at about 7:20 p.m. found Blake still missing. In accordance with standing instructions, he then notified it to the main gate of the prison.

The voluminous material recording the efforts deployed by the authorities to recapture George Blake makes breathtaking reading, close to a gripping thriller. What about the knitting-needles used to reinforce the rungs of a rope ladder? 'It has been ascertained that 485 shops in England and Scotland stock them. All these have been circularised, through local Police Forces, in an endeavour to trace any person buying an abnormal number of size 13 needles.' This was followed by the melancholy conclusion: 'To date this enquiry has met with no success.' What about the wrapping paper surrounding the pot of flowers found in the grounds, most probably to indicate to Blake the spot where he could look for the ladder? 'It is indicated that F. Meyers Limited, Head Office, Gypsy Corner, W.C. . . . were the florists concerned. Enquiries revealed that five branches of the firm stocked these pots of Chrysanthemum at the material time.' And again: 'All of these have been visited but nothing positive has been learned which could assist.'[1] And thus it went on and on for quite a long time with similarly disappointing conclusions and with many new puzzling points emerging. I understand that, on escaping from Wormwood Scrubs, Blake did not leave the country at once but stayed well hidden for a few weeks in the Paddington area of London, and then, unmolested, moved to Moscow for good via Berlin.

When the Court of Appeal considered Blake's appeal against the sentence they most emphatically endorsed it: 'It had a three-fold purpose. It was intended to be punitive, it was designed and calculated to deter others, and it was meant to be a safeguard to this country.' Blake and his accomplices had done a job which exceeded their wildest expectations. Through their bold initiative the sentence *de facto* has been shortened by nearly 90 per cent and with no restrictive conditions attached to it whatsoever. Now, after more than thirty years, it is impossible to describe the sensation which this defeat of criminal justice created and the humiliation and ridicule to which it gave rise throughout Britain and abroad.[2]

On 20 August 1963 a prisoner serving a sentence of eight years' preventive detention had escaped from Nottingham Prison. He succeeded in leaving the country and went to East Germany. On 12 August 1964 Charles

---

1 See the memorandum from the Metropolitan Police, Shepherd's Bush Station, 'F' Division, 11 November 1966, CO 63/661/478.
2 'British prisons', stated Roy Jenkins, 'became something of an international joke, with cartoons by Faizant in the *Figaro* and columns by Art Buchwald in the *Herald Tribune.*' See his *A Life at the Centre* (1991), p. 204. Strange letters found their way on to the desk of Lord Mountbatten, like the ones from Mme A. Gathier (from Paris) describing herself as a *Radiesthésiste* (the Cassell French Dictionary renders it into 'Radio-electric detection') informing his Lordship that 'En ce qui concerne l'espion Georges BLAKE, je suis assuré qu'il est actuellement *à Londres, dans une clinique de chirurgie estétique*. Il me faudrait un plan de Londres par arrondissement . . . pour que je puisse vous donner l'adresse exact de son asile.' But sometimes the information offered was of a much more sombre nature as when Chapman Pincher (Security Correspondent of the *Daily Express*) reported in his paper: 'Many British agents were successfully pulled out of East Germany, Poland and Russia in 1961 after it was discovered Blake was responsible for the liquidation of more than 40 of their colleagues by revealing identities to Moscow.'

Frederick Wilson escaped from Birmingham Prison where he was serving a thirty-year sentence for his part in the great train robbery. On 8 July 1965 Ronald Arthur Biggs – a participant in the same crime – who was serving a sentence of thirty years' imprisonment, escaped from Wandsworth Prison together with three other prisoners with records of violence. On 25 May 1966 a party of thirteen prisoners, also with heavy records of violence, while being conveyed by coach between Winchester and Parkhurst, succeeded in overpowering their guards and regained freedom. On 5 June 1966 six prisoners escaped from 'D' Wing of Wormwood Scrubs. And soon after Blake had gone missing, Frank Mitchell, sentenced to life imprisonment, escaped on 12 December 1966 from the outside working party on Dartmoor. This was not his first escape and during his periods of freedom he embarked upon several daring and damaging exploits. He was described by the police and prison officers as 'the most dangerous and violent criminal in captivity'. The full list of escapes, attempted or successful, was much more numerous: I have singled out some of the most notorious and disturbing instances. But it was undoubtedly George Blake's escape and the failure to recapture him which touched an explosive nerve, causing wide public and official concern.

A swift response from Parliament was inevitable. A debate took place two days after the escape was formally notified and another was held a week later.[3] I listened to both debates and I must confess that I found them particularly unedifying. There was the inevitable attempt by the Conservative Opposition to make political capital, with the threat that they would call for an account giving 'the number of escapes from prisons which occurred during the thirteen or fourteen years that the Conservative Party was in office'. There was the usual noisy bickering emanating from the uncontrollable but often so incisive Mr Emmanuel Shinwell (afterwards Lord Shinwell of Easington), from the pedantic, but often so well meaning, Mr Edward Heath, and from the flowery but rapidly evaporating questioning of Quintin Hogg (afterwards Lord Hailsham, the Lord Chancellor, but at the time the Shadow Home Secretary). The Opposition went too far and arranged for a vote of censure. This, as might have been expected, embittered the relationships between the two parties and indeed the relationship of old parliamentary colleagues and even friends. 'Ted Heath,' wrote Roy Jenkins, 'I regret to say, took the outcome [of the debate] badly. Despite our then more than a quarter of a century of relationship [now more than half a century] he wrote me a constituency-case letter that week beginning unbelievably "Dear Jenkins", and in the following week he flapped around like an affronted penguin in order to avoid speaking to me at the French Embassy.' The Home Office papers are full of pedantic, often petty, exchanges in internal memoranda, or statements to the

---

3 See 'George Blake (Escape from Prison)', *Parl. Debates*, vol. 734 (1966–7), cols 649–56, 24 October 1966. See also *ibid.*, vol. 135, cols 41–4, 31 October 1966.

press, between Lord Brooke (the former Home Secretary), Roy Jenkins and other participants of inferior rank.[4]

Fully aware of the gravity of the moment, Roy Jenkins came well prepared, in full command of the situation but visibly tense and under pressure. He correctly assessed that no statement from him or any immediate review within the department would satisfy the House, but that an independent inquiry was called for. In consequence, to quote his own words: 'I have asked Lord Mountbatten to head such an enquiry and he has most generously agreed to undertake this important task. He had also expressed the hope that his report will be available in a few months.' Considering Lord Mountbatten's background and his style of life in public matters, it was not unrealistic to expect that the Blake affair was bound to reach yet another dramatic configuration.

The perplexing concept of security

I am not a professional and seasoned prison inspector but it took me very little time to make up my mind that the level of security provided for certain types of criminals in certain prisons in Britain at that time (in the 1960s) was blatantly unacceptable and bound sooner or later to lead to a series of daunting escapes. And I had reached this conclusion without any help from or knowledge of the Mountbatten Inquiry. I do not know, for example, of any penal institution in the world where a prisoner of George Blake's calibre, only forty-two years old with powerful and dedicated support outside, virtually sentenced to the end of his life expectancy, would be detained in a prison like Wormwood Scrubs with the kind of regime made accessible to him. My only surprise was that he stayed there so long, but possibly this was calculated patience on his part. Later Blake wrote: 'It was clear to me from the very beginning that if I wanted to escape I had first of all to create the firm impression that I had no intention of doing so. This was no easy task.'[5] He had been removed from the 'escape list' and, in fairness to the governor then in charge, it has been noted that Blake was singled out by him as one of the three prisoners who should not stay in Wormwood Scrubs for security reasons. His recommendation was ignored. My conclusion was identical with respect to the other cases already mentioned. Even without a radical and detailed change in the regime for dealing with dangerous offenders, hardly any one of these escapes would have occurred if the precautions directly or indirectly built into the existing prison rules had been diligently and

---

4 See a memorandum of D.E.J. Dowler (Private Secretary to the Home Secretary) with eight appendices of 8 November 1966, in the Home Office Papers relating to George Blake's escape.
5 See George Blake, *No Other Choice* (1990), p. 217.

intelligently observed. A penal system, like any other social institution, does not stand still but evolves, for better or for worse, over periods of time. This was obviously a particularly unfortunate patch in a phase which was in urgent need of a robust shake-up.

It is, however, easy to simplify or even to distort the problem of escapes from prisons. This is not the only institution from which those connected with it may have the desire at one time or another to escape. Schools, military units, enforced labour camps and mental establishments bring to light many such attempts. One may even try to escape from oneself for long periods of time; indeed suicide can in many ways and instances be viewed as a form of escape from the seemingly unbearable pressures of life. As a general rule, it can safely be assumed that cemeteries are the only places which effectively ensure the non-recurrence of escapes.

It is therefore unsound to examine prison escapes in absolute terms and it is much more realistic to talk about 'tolerable escape rates', and even more specifically about different escape rates for different categories of offender in different kinds of institutions – which in turn leads to the definition of 'security risk'. On this account a thoughtful memorandum from the Prison Department deserves to be quoted:

> We do not really know the size of the problem [of prison security] which is incapable of scientific evaluation. We have had widely differing estimates from governors, police, and our own professional advisers on the definition of security risks. The views of certain police officers and of the security working party were that every prisoner was a security risk but that some were greater risks than others.

The memorandum then drew attention to a 'variety of reason' which prompts prisoners to attempt to escape: domestic anxiety; indebtedness in prison; a sense of grievance over the sentence; inability to stand imprisonment any longer; an easy opportunity presenting itself; a self-determination to escape at all costs. The fact that the population now entering prison 'is much more tool-conscious, has much more mechanical "know-how" than that of a generation ago' also tended to make conventional methods of security less adequate. But there could also be a confusion of motives if due account were not taken of the make-up of the personality of the escapees and their social and criminal backgrounds. The escape of a youngish offender sent to prison for the first time, isolated and disorientated, and that of a seasoned professional criminal who can count on powerful outside support from his associates, stand as far apart as the most vivid imagination can afford to stretch. The suggestibility and the imitation which permeates so many prisoners' reactions to their prison environment also come into play when star criminals succeed in becoming star escapees. To the confusion of motives should be added the impact of differences in the physical fabric of penal institutions. In a prison constructed to give full effect to a system of solitary confinement rates of escape sink to their lowest level, but this could well be accompanied by an increase in suicides (attempted or carried through) and much more frequently by grave mental and emotional regressions. It is also significant whether an escape took place at the beginning of detention, in its middle, or just before the prisoner was about to be discharged. The circumstances in which the escape was planned and set in motion, the length of the illegally gained freedom, the conduct displayed and the damage inflicted, are some further important aspects of the problem.

However, prison security cannot be left in trust to the enlightened and relaxed deliberations of academic seminars devoted to penal matters in search of perfect, or close to perfect, solutions. It should be accepted as elementary that, in the penal system of any civilized country, the regular study of escapes should be accorded a prominent place within the central penitentiary organization. The findings and recommendations of how they might be controlled should diligently be reported for internal discussion and appropriate action to those at the very top of the system as a whole. It should also be recognized that a healthy penal system must provide and ensure that the level of security is unquestionably satisfactory throughout the entire spectrum of penal and corrective detention. No purpose, or purposes, assigned to a penal system can be effectively pursued and gain firm public support unless due attention is paid to these two preconditions. A penal system loses its *raison d'être* if it fails to keep in safe custody all those sent forcibly to it by courts which have deprived them of their liberty in accordance with sentences duly imposed under the authority of the law.

Lord Mountbatten takes command

The choice of Mountbatten imbued high hopes that the inquiry would be properly launched and energetically pursued.

> Mountbatten may have been no great strategist, as Pownall's despairing diaries show, but he was a genius when it came to public relations. He was a far better handler of men than of ships or armies and when dealing with press, propagandists and cameramen he showed an ability amounting to brilliance. His troops too responded well to the plucky spontaneous vitality. He had not watched *In Which We Serve* twelve times for nothing.

This was stated by Andrew Roberts who could hardly be accused of taking a gentle view of Mountbatten's personality and achievements.[6] Lord

---

6 Andrew Roberts, *Eminent Churchillians* (1994), Chapter 2, 'Lord Mountbatten and the Perils of Adrenalin', pp. 55–136, at p. 73.

Mountbatten revealed identical qualities in this instance. He criticized but did not castigate; he tried to mend but not to demolish; he relentlessly pursued his central objective, but let no occasion pass by to show that he had an open, receptive mind to various options. It is indeed enticing to read the records of the conferences which he promoted – I hate to use the too well-known American expression of 'marketing his product'. Thirty-two London daily and weekly editors; twenty provincial editors;[7] a gathering of a hundred and two governors plus six assessors provide a splendid illustration of his art.[8]

Far be it from me to detract in any way from the contribution made by Lord Mountbatten – an utter novice to the subject – to the ultimate version of the report; indeed, I have been told on good authority that he made a sizeable impact on it. But the role played by his two principal assessors was of the very first order. I have recently read virtually the whole of the bulky background material to the Mountbatten Inquiry, and this is the impression which is persistently conveyed. Robert Mark (afterwards Sir Robert Mark) and Philip Woodfield (afterwards Sir Philip Woodfield) were both exceptionally gifted men. Both were endowed with an energetic mind and perspicacity in observation, and they had an attractive way of expressing themselves. Sir Robert was at the time of the inquiry Chief Constable of Leicester and afterwards became the Commissioner of the Metropolitan Police and the author of two well-received books, *Policing a Perplexed Society* (1977) and *In the Office of Constable* (1978), as well as the outspoken and incisive Dimbleby Memorial Lecture (1973). Sir Philip had an outstanding and varied career in the Home Office.

Except for one section relating to the escape of Frank Mitchell vividly reconstructed by Sir Robert, the whole report was written by Sir Philip – an admirable piece, concise, direct and persuasive. Lord Mountbatten, even long

---

7 'I am writing as Secretary to the Inquiry into prison escapes which Lord Mountbatten has been appointed by the Home Secretary to conduct. Lord Mountbatten thinks it might be helpful if he were to meet London Editors of Provincial Newspapers for an informal non-attributable discussion. At this meeting Lord Mountbatten will indicate the way in which he proposes to undertake his task, and he would also be very glad to consider any suggestions which they might like to put to him at the meeting. Lord Mountbatten would be very pleased, therefore, to see you, or your representative from the Editorial staff, at 10:30 am on Thursday, November 3, in Room 245, 70 Whitehall.' There was present the elite of the journalistic world. The *New Statesman* was the only one to decline. By a stroke of cruel irony the report was leaked extensively in the *Daily Express* a month before its publication.

8 At the meeting with the governors there was to be no provision for the press; to avoid any possibility of discussions being overheard, back-stage and projection room doors must be locked; no special messing, understood that menu now reduced to either sweet or cheese and biscuits, not both; no wine but Catering Officer to be on hand in case it is asked for; no planned top table, but top table must be reserved and Lord Mountbatten will on the day ask various governors to sit at the top table.

after the appearance of the report, used to go out of his way to pay warm compliments to the two assessors whenever a suitable occasion presented itself. Impressive also was the energy displayed in the discharge of the task: on 24 October 1966 Lord Mountbatten was appointed to conduct the inquiry and on 22 December his report saw the light of day.

Some ambiguity became transparent immediately the Home Secretary announced the setting up of the inquiry. It was the escape of George Blake which had prompted it and naturally there was a general and agreed insistence that his case should be thoroughly examined: 'to look into the circumstances of this particular escape and to report anything which Lord Mountbatten thinks should be reported on that.' No sooner had the Home Secretary stated this than questions were raised about other escapes and there were calls for these to be included in the inquiry as well. 'Lord Mountbatten and his inquiry can look into any matter including the escape of Blake, which they think is in any way relevant' – came the reassuring response from Roy Jenkins. But a while later, with soothing smoothness, he took the House into his confidence by declaring that 'what I am primarily concerned about, and what I believe the House will be primarily concerned about, is to improve our prison security'. Again, a little later, he went further: 'what I think is required at present is an enquiry into our prison security as a whole'. Jeremy Thorpe's enquiring appetite did not seem to be easily satisfied: 'can the Mountbatten Committee', he asked, 'go into the general problem of security in relation to long-term prisoners?', which he disarmingly acknowledged 'presents a rather different problem'. This remarkable extension of the inquiry did not seem to worry the Home Secretary in the least. 'Certainly,' he replied, 'the inquiry can look into matters of custody of long-term prisoners.' And like a seasoned criminologist, with major empirical material to back his views, Mr Jenkins added: 'There really is no distinction here except in so far as the Leader of the Opposition is trying to make one.' His concluding sentence 'I am anxious for the inquiry to look as fully and as deeply at the facts of this case as it can' was utterly disconnected from the preceding question and answer.[9]

This brief but intense exchange of views could not fail to have a stimulating effect on Lord Mountbatten's expansive nature. The bulk of his recommendations was useful, or to quote Philip Ziegler: 'Most of the Report was sensible if undramatic . . .'[10] And the Home Office, with the energetic support of the beleaguered prison staff, were feverishly set about putting them into effect. Lord Mountbatten, however, believed he had a mission not only to mend but also to reconstruct. Hence his classification of all prisoners into four security categories; the adoption of the principle of concentration of

9 See *Parl. Debates*, vol. 734 (1966–7), cols 650–5 and vol. 735, cols 42–4, *passim*.
10 See Philip Ziegler, *Mountbatten* (1985), p. 650.

those declared to be the most dangerous – Category A; and the architectural projection of a maximum security prison ready to receive them. It was to be an entirely new building designed with panache on the Isle of Wight. Though still not born it was baptized in glamorous terms as 'Vectis'.

Still more to the point it was not to remain isolated: already at this early stage Lord Mountbatten was busy dispatching a building expert to find another appropriate site for a second maximum security establishment grounded upon similar principles and with similar objectives.[11] It was the 'recommendation which he felt to be the most significant and also likely to be achieved' but it was also the recommendation which 'generated a storm of abuse so violent that it is hard for an outsider to understand'.[12] I must confess that I did not notice a reaction as strong as the one conveyed by this description, though perhaps I was not observant enough. What I did observe was a deep concern, expressed in strong terms in certain quarters, that too much had been read into the series of escapes and that this was too narrow a basis for attempting to bring into operation changes of disproportionately wider scope, if not immediately, in the not too distant future.

Lord Mountbatten's 'policy', stated a writer who could hardly be accused of a propensity to indulge in 'violent abuse', 'may well have re-assured the public but it has probably set back the advance to a humane and sensible prison policy some twenty-five years'.[13] Similarly the late Dr Pauline Morris, who together with her husband had published the notable study *Pentonville* in 1963, had no hesitation in saying (as quoted by Philip Ziegler) that 'his [Lord Mountbatten's] name has become synonymous with the imposition of restriction and an almost obsessional concern with security'. In an important article following the publication of the report, Hugh Klare, the Secretary of the Howard League for Penal Reform, although seemingly endorsing the idea of maximum security prisons, nevertheless expressed, in restrained but unequivocal terms, his uneasiness that the total impact of the new policy with respect both to prison staff and prisoners might go too far in its 'human consequences'. Indeed the caption to his piece read: 'Since the Mountbatten

---

11 'Dear Lord Mountbatten' – this is how the letter of 8 November 1966 from Admiral Frank Hopkins, KCB, DSO, DSC, to Lord Mountbatten starts – 'when we met at lunch the other day you asked me to look into the possibility of an island suitable for use as, or conversion into, a top security prison. My staff have prepared the attached paper which shows that . . . there are three which might be suitable, and the Calf of Man seems to be the most attractive for the purpose.' Then follows a detailed memorandum of nearly four pages entitled 'Staff Paper to Consider Possible Islands for Use as Top Security Prisons'. Home Office Papers relating to Lord Mountbatten's Inquiry.
12 Ziegler, *Mountbatten*, p. 650.
13 Tom Clayton, *Men in Prison* (1970), p. 222. Also quoted by Ziegler. The chapter of Clayton's book (pp. 215–26) is full of thoughtful remarks.

Report on prison security there has been a spectacular fall in the number of escapes. But constructive penology is suffering in the process.'[14]

At that time I knew nothing about the prevailing climate of opinion within the Home Office on the subject, but it is significant that some fourteen months after the publication of the Mountbatten Report, more exactly in February 1967, Roy Jenkins asked the Advisory Council on the Penal System to undertake an inquiry with similar but not identical terms of reference. Having gone rather thoroughly through the papers relating to the Mountbatten Inquiry I got the impression that the new Home Secretary, James Callaghan (afterwards Lord Callaghan of Cardiff), was sensitive to the wider, more fundamental issues involved in the report. Thus, following the appearance of Hugh Klare's article, the Home Office papers record that Mr Callaghan had asked a group of senior members of his staff to prepare memoranda on the observations contained in the article and furthermore had convened a meeting to discuss the situation with them. Indications soon surfaced that the advance in the blitz offensive envisaged by Lord Mountbatten was wavering, close to tottering. Sir Kenneth Younger, the Chairman of the Advisory Council, complied with the Home Secretary's request and a sub-committee was set up to inquire into and report on 'The Regime for Long-Term Prisoners in Conditions of Maximum Security'.[15]

The situation was rendered even more tense. Considering the unusual topicality of the subject, it was extraordinary that a long time had passed by with no proper notice being taken of the central recommendation of Lord Mountbatten's report. And then, still worse, another train had been set in motion. No one could predict whether it would follow the same route, and more importantly, whether it would arrive at the same station.

Challenging Mountbatten's solution

I was asked by Sir Kenneth to be the Chairman of the sub-committee. Hardly ever in my long academic and public life had I been more acutely aware of

---

14 In an article published in *New Society* entitled 'Prisons since the Mountbatten Report'.
15 The terms of reference of the Mountbatten Committee read as follows: 'To inquire into the recent prison escapes, with particular reference to that of George Blake, and to make firm recommendations to assist you (Mr Roy Jenkins, the Home Secretary) in deciding what needed to be done.' The Advisory Council was asked 'to consider the regime for long-term prisoners detained in conditions of maximum security and to make recommendations'. Immediately following the publication of Lord Mountbatten's Inquiry the Home Secretary was asked in Parliament 'why the details of loose security in Her Majesty's Prisons recently uncovered by the Mountbatten Inquiry were made available as news to the general public, including prison inmates' (Parliamentary Question by Mrs Jill Knight, *Parl. Debates*, HC, vol. 739, Written Answers, col. 324, 26 January 1967). It appears that it was decided by the Home Office that 'prisoners who wish to buy a copy of the report are allowed to do so, but they are not permitted to keep it in their cells after they have read it'.

how heavy and far reaching was the responsibility that I had to discharge. The peak of the heat had perhaps gone, but the tension had by no means subsided. There were three other members of the committee: the Bishop of Exeter (The Right Revd R.C. Mortimer, DD), Dr Peter Scott, the distinguished psychiatrist, and Mr Leo Abse, MP. I found my collaboration with the first two unassailably fruitful and trustworthy. Our two assessors, Mr H.J. Taylor (then Chief Inspector of Prisons) and Mr W.N. Hyde of the Prison Department, were of inestimable value to us. Their readiness to help and their tact could not have been excelled. Furthermore Mr Hyde's draft of the report could not be improved upon, and Major L. Snowden proved to be a most diligent Secretary.

This was not an ordinary committee of inquiry and under any circumstances it was bound to draw wider public interest. But as one following so closely in the path of an investigation carried out under the forcible imprint of 'Admiral of the Fleet, the Earl Mountbatten of Burma' it could not fail to be the focus of persistent attention. Telephone calls from the press (even from abroad), invitations to meet them and a variety of other people, Questions in Parliament – all were inimicable to calm deliberation. Sometimes 'Questions' would emerge from utterly unexpected quarters. Thus, Mr Norman St John Stevas (afterwards Lord St John of Fawsley and Master of Emmanuel College, Cambridge), known as a student of the British Constitution and an eminent expert on Bagehot, asked the Home Secretary 'when is the Radzinowicz Report due to appear?' Or, on another more pointed occasion, 'what progress has been made on implementing the Mountbatten Report on Prisons?' and, probing still harder,

> has the Right Hon. Gentleman [Mr Callaghan] abandoned the project for a maximum security prison in the Isle of Wight, as has been reported to have been recommended by the Radzinowicz Committee? To borrow a phrase from my Right Hon. and Learned friend [Mr Hogg], is it the intention no longer to put all the bad eggs in one basket, but to distribute them around several areas?[16]

Mr Hogg could not be expected to remain silent.

> Would the Right Hon. Gentleman recognise that despite the conflicting advice which I understand he has now received about the treatment of maximum security prisoners, this is one of the cruxes of the matter. Will he assure us that he will not allow the difficulty of reaching a decision to delay it beyond the earliest possible moment?

---

16 He was rebuked by Mr Speaker: 'Order. Questions would be briefer without borrowed phrases.' See *Parl. Debates*, HC, vol. 761, cols 1708–9, 25 March 1968.

The Home Secretary kept calm, but obviously a leak, a fatal leak, had occurred. 'The plans for the maximum security prison have been deferred but I propose to look at them again in the light of the Report from the Advisory Committee on the Penal System which will be published next week. I will then reach a conclusion and inform the House.' This was not the only leak, but it was certainly the most grievous one.

It has always been my deeply anchored conviction that no public inquiry should be treated lightly, and that if for any reason the job cannot be done thoroughly and impartially, it should not be done at all. No investigation deserved to be carried out in conformity with this elementary premise more than ours. Even Lord Mountbatten, firmly as he came out in favour of concentration, candidly acknowledged the relativity, if I may put it in this way, of either solution. 'There are', Philip Ziegler informs us, 'strong arguments against a maximum security jail, as Mountbatten privately admitted to Philip Woodfield, but in advancing the idea he was seeking to achieve the same objective as that aimed at by his critics.' I venture to say that we went further than that because we publicly declared at the very opening of our report:

> The manner in which the prison service of this country meets the challenge of containing long-term prisoners in conditions that combine security and humanity will have a lasting effect on the service as a whole ... We have to consider difficult problems. We have no perfect or simple solutions to offer, but we hope this report will make a contribution towards their solution.

Here is the path which we followed to gain insights into, and to collect evidence on, a broad and comparative basis and the kind of information we endeavoured to gather. In England we visited six institutions directly relevant to the nature and scope of our inquiry, in the course of which we took evidence from about sixty people. In addition, written evidence on certain selected points was elicited from six witnesses. Nineteen experts of one kind or another gave further evidence combined with written statements. Nine people gave only oral evidence. Seven more supplied evidence either generally or on a certain specific point. We requested help from the police and five senior officers from the Metropolitan area and from certain provincial forces appeared before us. We lost no time in hearing the views of twenty maximum security prisoners detained in several of the institutions we visited and always with no prison staff present.

We were, of course, particularly eager to obtain a full and incisive picture of the developments which had taken place abroad. We visited two institutions in Denmark, two in Sweden, one in Germany, two in France and six in the United States of America. We took evidence from a substantial number of leading administrators and penological and medical experts. In all we visited twenty institutions, saw nearly two hundred people and met together as a committee on forty-six days. The whole sub-committee participated in all these exercises and so did one of our assessors, Mr W.N. Hyde. Major L. Snowden, our Secretary, was of great help to us throughout, by providing exact summaries of the evidence we amassed.

We asked for and received 199 papers. Research work was carried out and reports presented on six topics by the Prison Department; on two topics by the Home Office Research Unit under the direction of Mr Lodge; on two topics by Dr Donald West and Dr Richard F. Sparks of the Cambridge Institute of Criminology; on four topics by Dr Peter Scott and on conjugal visits from six sources. On two occasions the sub-committee sent a note to the Home Secretary on certain matters of great urgency and on one occasion I asked for a meeting with him. Twice I gave a detailed account of our activities and trends of thinking to the Chairman of the Council, Sir Kenneth Younger. At the final stage, the sub-committee accepted my invitation to meet in Cambridge for three days to settle the main issues. Copies of all formal minutes were regularly issued and copies of all important letters sent to Sir Kenneth Younger and the Secretary of the Council.

At the plenary meeting of the Council I was invited to introduce our report. A written nine-page statement was put in the hands of every member of the Council. I felt strongly that I should emphasize that I had regarded it as a privilege to be the Chairman of this particular committee, that I had learned a lot from my colleagues, and that grim as our business had been, we had tackled it with enthusiasm and with the consciousness that we were accomplishing something of importance. I also stated how happy we had been to have Mr Taylor and Mr Hyde as our assessors. We had worked together so harmoniously and there had never been any disagreements between us. On several occasions in the course of the inquiry I had to appeal to Sir Philip Allen, then the Permanent Under-Secretary of State, and always found a ready and effective response. I would have been delighted to acknowledge this in our report, but with characteristic modesty he protested because, as he put it, he was doing no more than his duty. I found it particularly reassuring that Sir Philip Woodfield, the 'engine' of the Mountbatten Inquiry, found it desirable to be present at our final presentation.

These deliberations, as might have been expected, moved around what the Chairman of the Council called 'the most important and contentious issue', namely, concentration versus dispersal. At first, several members expressed their doubts concerning the principle of dispersal. But at the second meeting – in the light of further memoranda received from some of the members of the Council, as well as important clarifications added by the Bishop of Exeter, Dr Peter Scott, Mr Leo Abse and by one of our assessors, Mr W. Hyde – they closed ranks. Dispersal was recommended unanimously by the sub-committee and by the Council. Nevertheless all along we had had a clear understanding that dispersal could not be expected to be problem-free and that concentration was a concept much easier to live with. Dispersal had to be combined and supported by a regime specially devised to supply the needs, administrative and humanitarian, of this *sui generis* penitentiary configuration. I have a persistent feeling that this element of our recommendation was never fully put into effect. As a consequence the concept of dispersal was distorted due to the general shortcomings of the penal system as a whole. In practice the regime for 'dangerous offenders' could hardly be expected to be on a higher plane than regimes which catered for 'ordinary prisoners'. And, if the latter happened to be of poor quality, the former's quality would have to be no higher. The famous and fatal principle of 'lesser eligibility' would come into play and an explosive response could be expected.

The recommendation which proved divisive was the proposal to have armed guards in watch towers on or outside the perimeter of the prison. A veritable 'hue and cry' was raised against it. Our own member, Dr Peter Scott, wrote an impressive and moving dissenting note and seven members of the Council (as against nine) rebelled against it. This aspect of our deliberations could easily have been avoided if our recommendation on the topic had been more carefully worded. In effect it had little significance in the light of the crucial and most aptly expressed statement made by the Chairman of the Advisory Council. Even the members of the Council who were in favour of this recommendation, he stated in his letter to the Home Secretary,

> are unanimous that before a decision to introduce firearms is made it would be essential for further consultations to be held with the prison service at all levels and for the authorities professionally charged with security to examine in detail how the necessary degree of perimeter security should be achieved. If these authorities were to advise you that adequate security can be attained either now or in the future without resorting to armed guards both the sub-committee and those of the Council members who wholly support its findings would be happy to accept that conclusion.[17]

Moving towards a British Alcatraz?

It would be erroneous to suggest that support for the principle of concentration should be laid exclusively at Lord Mountbatten's doorstep. It was the result of a process of interaction with public opinion made deeply uneasy by

---

17 See 'The Regime for Long-Term Prisoners in Conditions of Maximum Security' (1968), Letter to the Home Secretary from Kenneth Younger, pp. v–vi, and *Report*, pp. 23–4 and 80. Also, Minutes of the Meeting of the Advisory Council of 29 January 1968, in HCPS (M) 4, pp. 5–6.

the epidemic of escapes and receptive enough to accept radical, unusual solutions. In this trend towards penal regression the extraordinary prestige of Lord Mountbatten was a priceless asset. There was nothing in his report to indicate the unfolding of a deliberate all-embracing oppressive policy, but the dynamics of the situation unmistakably pointed towards it. We are told by Philip Ziegler that Mountbatten had visited Kumla Prison in Sweden 'and had been struck by the way it vindicated his ideas'. I also visited Kumla but I was deeply depressed by the mercilessly impersonal, mechanical and electronic pervasiveness of the whole fabric and regime of this prison. Following our visit I convened a brief meeting of our sub-committee to register our views, while they were still fresh and specific. On the one hand, the Swedish authorities were proud of Kumla and apparently were planning maybe four or five similar institutions. On the other, a senior official of the Swedish Prison Department had confidentially shared with me his hope that Kumla would not be the model which our committee would aspire to import into Britain. Whether the prisoners detained in Kumla needed maximum security was irrelevant to several of our Swedish colleagues so long as the factory there kept working. Industry was the sacred cow and the rest was geared to it. We reached the very important conclusion that 'some 85 per cent of the prisoners in Kumla could be tackled in Vridsloselille in Copenhagen without a qualm and without the need for maximum security'. And, not surprisingly, we also agreed that 'the danger was that it was easier to build four or five more Kumlas than to get rid of them'. (All quotations are extracts from the minutes of our *ad-hoc* committee as recorded by our Secretary, Major Snowden.) In general we found hardly anything attractive in any of the major maximum security institutions which we visited and got acquainted with.

While conducting this inquiry I was made painfully aware how very little first-hand knowledge our own prison staff possessed about what was going on in the penitentiary scene outside Britain, and of the virtually non-existent opportunities to be able to gain at least a smattering of this comparative knowledge. I was therefore particularly pleased when Mr F.G. Castell, then the General Secretary of the Prison Officers' Association, agreed to accept a travelling and study fellowship in the United States should I be able to arrange one. I was successful and the Ford Foundation made a generous grant for this purpose. Mr Castell scrupulously honoured my condition that, on completing his inquiry, he would neither orally nor in writing communicate with me on the subject, but he did thank me handsomely for my initiative.

There was nothing sacrosanct about Category A. Once accepted, it could easily be restricted, but it was more likely to be expanded by wholesale administrative policy or even by the individual decision of a prison governor, simply because the line of lesser resistance is so often taken to smooth the arduous and often intractable tasks involved in running penal institutions. An exceptionally instructive document was handed to me in Washington by the then Director of the Federal Bureau of Prisons. From this it unmistakably transpired that when the top maximum security prison in the United States, the famous Alcatraz, was closed and its inmates dispersed to a few other much less secure institutions, they soon lost their label of being the most dangerous and intractable prisoners and were smoothly integrated into the much more humane and relaxed penal environment.

There is a hint in Philip Ziegler's book of the undesirable elastic potentialities of the concept. 'If', wrote Lord Mountbatten to Sir Philip Allen on 2 September 1972, 'the criticism was that Category A prisoners were not necessarily the most likely to escape, then a new sub-category could be introduced for prisoners who needed to be isolated in a special prison even though not *prima facie* a menace to the public or the state.'[18] I do not know how far Gresham's Law in economics still holds good (or even if it ever held good) that bad money has the tendency to drive out good money, but certainly penitentiary history seems to provide credible evidence for such a trend. Even stronger evidence is available to indicate that radical changes in prison structure should not be conceived and put into effect in an atmosphere of 'panic', 'bitter disappointment' or 'frustration' – all terms frequently used in the memoranda by prison staff of the period. The urgently needed shake up had already produced most encouraging results. The number of escapes from closed prisons had gone down from 114 in 1961 to 87 in 1966. The downward trend continued and in the 1970s or thereabouts the number was authoritatively described as 'minimal'. It was a good time to pause and reflect and not to jump ahead.

Penitentiary organization and structure by their very nature and objectives are predominantly static. In this sphere of public administration it is extremely difficult to retrace steps hastily taken, especially when they have taken shape in bricks and mortar. The penal history of Belgium, for example, provides a fascinating illustration of how, almost at one stroke, the country was covered by a network of institutions based on extreme solitary confinement (see pp. 53–54). The available English example is not so dense but it is none the less also instructive. It was a report from the 1811 Parliamentary Committee on Prisons, influenced by the 'new' institutions of Gloucestershire and Nottinghamshire, that caused the government to launch the building of Millbank Prison on sixteen acres of marsh bought from the Marquis of Salisbury for £12,000. The construction was subsequently described by Sidney and Beatrice Webb as a 'monument of ugliness' and

> was at any rate, one of the most costly of all buildings that the world had then seen since the Pyramids of Egypt, the total expense from first to last amounting to not far short of three-quarters of a million

18 Ziegler, *Mountbatten*, p. 651.

sterling. It may be doubted [the Webbs concluded] whether the Taj at Agra, the Cloth Hall at Ypres or the Cathedral of Chartres, had cost anything like this sum.[19]

Millbank itself proved to be a disaster but in its place there emerged a network of thoroughly repressive penal institutions across the country. *Comparaison n'est pas raison* we are taught by a French saying. This does not mean however that glimpses into the past should be ignored altogether. And significantly from Europe, or at least from its leading countries, came a timely warning: 'Consensus of opinion emerged in the select committee favouring dispersal rather than centralisation.'[20]

Mountbatten's report in abeyance

By March 1968 the chances of the principle of concentration being accepted were visibly receding. Thus, when Mr Callaghan was asked in a Parliamentary Question how much progress had been made in implementing the recommendations of the Mountbatten Report, he replied 'a good deal', and enumerated some of them. But when pressed to say whether he had abandoned the project for a maximum security prison on the Isle of Wight he replied rather ominously that 'the plans have been deferred but I propose to look at them again in the light of the report from the Advisory Council on the Penal System'. In April the horizon was clearly obscured by heavy clouds of increasing doubts. In response to yet another Parliamentary Question asking the Home Secretary whether he had received the report of the Council and whether he would make a statement, Mr Callaghan confirmed 'that in fact it is being published today' and concluded:

> Before finally deciding the important issues raised by this report, I shall obtain the views of the prison service and of the staff associations with whom I have initiated urgent consultations. I would like to take this opportunity of thanking the Advisory Council, and in particular the members of the relevant sub-committee, for having prepared this comprehensive report, and for their careful study and analysis of these difficult problems.

---

19 See Sidney and Beatrice Webb, *English Prisons under Local Government* (1922), reprinted with a new Introduction by Leon Radzinowicz (1963), pp. 48–9. Also Sir Louis Blom-Cooper, *The Penalty of Imprisonment* (1988): 'fashion often has more to do with penal policy than reason or experience, let alone humanity', p. 7.
20 See *Custody and Treatment of Dangerous Prisoners*. Recommendation no. R(82)17 adopted by the Committee of Ministers of the Council of Europe on 24 September 1982 and Explanatory Memorandum (Strasbourg, 1983), at p. 16.

Lord Mountbatten, not surprisingly, was becoming impatient and in a speech at the National Association for the Care and Resettlement of Offenders (NACRO) Annual Conference did not mince his words in voicing criticism of the delay in taking a decision. In May 1971 the zero hour of the crisis was reached: the Home Secretary was to be asked whether he 'will make a statement on the progress made to date in implementing the Mountbatten Report on the Prison Service'. On 10 May 1971 the Parliamentary Under-Secretary of State at the Home Office, Mark Carlisle (afterwards Lord Carlisle of Bucklow), was briefed by the department and this is the answer he gave in reply:

> Forty of the fifty-two recommendations made by Lord Mountbatten have been implemented in whole or in part; two have led to changes in practice, though not precisely on the lines proposed; and ten (nine of which related to the proposal to establish a special maximum security prison) were not accepted.

Graciously, a little later (24 July 1968) the Home Secretary wrote a letter to Sir Kenneth Younger as well as to me (we had not met before) briefly informing us of his decision to accept our recommendations for dispersal. The next day, again in reply to a Question, he made it public through an announcement in the Commons. It was a decision of courage and wisdom.

It might sound patronizing, perhaps even in bad taste, to say that one cannot help feeling rather sorry for Lord Mountbatten. Retired, covered with innumerable honours but still dreaming that incessant public admiration would continue to come his way – he was not looking for a job in the ordinary sense of the word.[21] But as Lord Zuckerman, who knew him so well, observed, 'he was impulsively interested in almost any suggestion that looked as if it might lead him back to the national stage'.[22] He was a man born for action and in need of continued acclaim. He was not a man who, even in the advanced years of his life, could be content to reflect and enjoy his past. He was too much absorbed by the present. He responded with genuine enthusiasm to Mr Jenkins's invitation to infuse a new resistance into the seemingly crumbling walls of prisons and thus redress the prestige and credibility of the system of criminal justice as a whole. He was intrigued by the novelty of his mission and he was so imaginatively kept on his toes by his two

---

21 Mountbatten was associated with 189 organizations ranging alphabetically from the Admiralty Dramatic Society to the Zoological Society. In some of these his role was formal, in many more it was not. See 'Mountbatten, Louis Francis Albert Victor Nicholas, first Earl Mountbatten of Burma (1900–1979)', *Dictionary of National Biography 1971–80* (1986), pp. 605–16, by Philip Ziegler.
22 Quoted by Andrew Roberts, *Eminent Churchillians* (1988), 'Lord Mountbatten and the Perils of Adrenalin', p. 134.

co-adjutors, Sir Philip Woodfield and Sir Robert Mark. This, of course, did not escape the vigilant and perceptive eye of his biographer. 'He [Mountbatten] took great pride in it [the report], and at Christmas sent a copy to each member of the Royal Family. It was a curious choice for festive literature, but only the Queen Mother is said to have announced firmly that she had no intention of reading it.' We are further told that he never gave up his battle for the maximum security prison and even as late as six years after the publication of his report (in 1972) he tried to gain the support of the new Conservative Home Secretary, Robert Carr (afterwards Lord Carr of Hadley), but with no success. And then, five years later, it was the turn of the Labour incumbent, Merlyn Rees (afterwards Lord Merlyn Rees of Morley and Cilfynydd) – again with no success. Dreary humiliation was replacing the exuberant fanfare of the 1960s.

In June 1971 the *Observer* bluntly declared that Lord Mountbatten had been 'betrayed'. This prompted Nigel Spearing, MP, to write a lengthy letter to the Home Office urging them to clarify the situation of the apparent 'antithesis' between the two reports. In his reply Mark Carlisle went out of his way to assuage any possible misunderstanding (the more pliable word to use in this context would be the French expression *mal entendu*).

> May I start [wrote Mr Carlisle in a tempting way] by clarifying the position about the two reports which you mention in the third paragraph of your letter? These were reports dealing essentially with different matters, and it is a mistake to treat them as if they were in some way putting forward rival philosophies. Lord Mountbatten was asked, in the aftermath of several sensational escapes, to enquire into prison escapes and security. Although he made important and valuable recommendations on aspects of prison treatment, with a view to reducing motives for escapes, it was not his concern to look in depth into the regime for any one class of prisoner. The other report you have in mind is the report prepared by the sub-committee of the Advisory Council of the Penal System on 'The Regime for Long-Term Prisoners in Conditions of Maximum Security'. This was a study in depth of the conditions and regime which should be provided for such prisoners. It dealt with some security matters but went much wider.

This subtle interpretation (Mark Carlisle was a barrister and a recorder) might have pacified Mr Spearing but I doubt very much whether it satisfied Lord Mountbatten.[23] He might well have been justified in suspecting that he had primarily been used just to provide an exceptionally protective political

---

23 See Home Office Papers, Document 8 June 1971 and July 1971, PDG/66; 1/10/46.

shield to keep an embarrassingly cornered and threatened Home Secretary out of an enveloping mess.

On 27 August 1979 Lord Mountbatten was assassinated in circumstances too well remembered to be repeated, circumstances which bore an ironical twist. He who had shown such remarkable alertness to security problems in prisons had himself shown a strange indifference to his personal security and of those close to him. And here belongs an enigmatic epitaph, so delicately and so movingly expressed, that it cannot be retouched:

> To die with no time for fear or regrets, doing what he enjoyed most with the people who were above all precious to him, escaping the horrors of increasing decrepitude or senility, to an end not with a whimper but with a bang that reverberated around the world – that truly was the fate Mountbatten would have chosen for himself.[24]

To the nefarious protagonist of one of the absorbing penal dramas of our century, fate continued to be kind. He seemed to have escaped the turbulent anguish of Philby or of the other elitist spies. Blake has lived in Moscow, undisturbed throughout these many years, an uneventful middle-class existence. In November 1997, he was seventy-four years old and – judging from a recent photograph in the London *Times* – looked well and relaxed. He has remarried and has a son who made him a grandfather.

In April 1966 an English court decided that he should be allowed to put into his pocket the £90,000 he had made from the publication of his book by Jonathan Cape in England. Here too there is a leaf of irony floating. The extremely liberal regime of Wormwood Scrubs presented him thirty years ago with the sweet gift of freedom. This had now been rounded off by a seemingly no less liberal (legal purists will say 'strict') judicial decision which made him financially so much better off.[25]

The zigzags of Mr Roy Jenkins

Naturally one cannot help speculating what would have been Roy Jenkins's attitude if, still the Home Secretary, he had had before him the option of choosing between the solutions offered by the two reports. In May 1961 George Blake was sentenced to undergo forty-two years' imprisonment; in October 1966 he succeeded in escaping; in 1966 Lord Mountbatten reported

---

24 Philip Ziegler, *Mountbatten* (1985), p. 700.
25 See George Blake's book *No Other Choice* (1971); *The Times* (12 April 1996). He frankly admitted passing to the KGB the names of communist bloc agents retained by MI5. In fact, he said he did not betray 42 agents but 'more likely 400'. But he insisted that the KGB killed none of them, that they promised him not to do it and he believed them. See Philip Knightley's introduction to *No Other Choice*, at p. x.

on the case and its wider implications; in April 1968 the Advisory Council on the Penal System presented its report; in July 1968 the government decided its course. The atmosphere was still tense and heavy and the prospects of how the crisis would ultimately be resolved were still very much uncertain.

But the prevailing currents and cross-currents of 1968 bore no resemblance to the terrible autumn season of two years earlier. For 1966 was the time when a politician, barely forty-nine years old but already with an exceptionally solid and varied record of public service to his credit, and with no less exceptional drive and ambition, was at a crucial stage of his career and acutely aware of it. To quote his own words: 'Aviation was beginning to lose its charm [he was Minister of Aviation 1964–5]. It was not unreasonable in view of my January conversation with the Prime Minister to cast my mind towards a high office, and the one which beckoned, for a variety of reasons, was the home secretaryship.'[26] Roy Jenkins started with aplomb to put into effect his 'personal agenda'.[27] The passage of events was by no means always smooth, but like the radiant actor in *Oklahoma!* he could let himself go and chant, uninterrupted, 'oh, what a beautiful morning'. And then, unexpectedly, one evening Lady Jenkins gave him the 'glad tidings' just received from David Dowler, his principal private secretary, about Blake's escape. He immediately telephoned the Prime Minister and he acknowledged in his book that Harold Wilson 'behaved thoroughly well to me. He sounded calm, with no hint of recrimination, although not underestimating the seriousness of the event.'[28] This support, however, was more than counterbalanced by the remark Harold Wilson made to Richard Crossman about George Blake's escape: 'That will do our Home Secretary a great deal of good. He was getting too complacent and he needs taking down a peg.'[29]

In terms of parliamentary duels and skirmishes and the responses from the press, the young Home Secretary performed remarkably well. And he was unashamedly proud of it. 'It was by far the greatest parliamentary triumph that I ever achieved. It provided most welcome and even glorious relief.' This strange piece of self-indulgence reappears as far away as Chapter 10 ('The Liberal Hour', p. 213) which ends with a reference to 'the Blake triumph'. But of course Mr Jenkins is a far too intelligent and perceptive a personality not to distinguish between appearance and substance. 'Yet', he lost no time in observing,

> it was all rather ludicrous and showed that debating (for it was that rather than oratory) really is the harvest of the arts . . . I had merely

---

26 See Roy Jenkins's autobiography *A Life at the Centre* (1971), p. 174.
27 *Ibid.*, p. 180.
28 *Ibid.*, p. 202.
29 Recorded by Richard Crossman in his thoroughly indiscreet *Diaries of a Cabinet Minister*, vol. 2 (1976), p. 87, and retold by Jenkins, *op. cit.*, p. 198.

effectively deployed the art of *tu quoque*: everything I had done Henry Brooke had done worse ... I had not become a better Home Secretary as a result of that debate.

Most reluctantly I have to confess that I was not very impressed by the general attitude the Home Secretary adopted and pursued in this matter. He sounded like a man anxious to disassociate himself as quickly and as persuasively as possible from this threatening mess. To start with, the choice of Lord Mountbatten was a gimmick. It was suggested by David Dowler. 'This was a bold idea, which I accepted with some enthusiasm.' He was then to discover that the atmosphere on the back benches on the Labour side was 'glacial' and 'uneasy'. Indeed Mountbatten appeared more as a gimmick than a coup. 'I was saved from a substantial Parliamentary disaster only by ineptitude on Ted Heath's part.' This was of all times a time to lower the temperature. Lord Mountbatten was the last person in the world to generate this effect, and there were several others in Britain with high prestige and proven expertise who could have undertaken this task without neglecting the necessary sharpness and directness of their probing. When the Mountbatten Report appeared, in vain would one have looked for Roy Jenkins's opinion concerning its crucial proposal; he did not go further than observing that the document turned out to be 'less critical of the Home Office than we had feared'. I understand that at some very early stage Roy Jenkins offered his resignation to the Prime Minister, but this, of course, was a theatrical gesture, perhaps another gimmick.

Concerning the complex and delicate issue of the extent to which a Home Secretary is ultimately responsible for a grave dysfunction in the penal system, he was more than vague, he was perfunctory. 'In fact,' he comments in his autobiography,

> it was as foolish to pretend before the debate that I had any real responsibility for who goes over a wall in W12 as it was to suggest that I had suddenly become a superman whose ability to deflate leaders of the opposition more than compensated for my inability to find absconding spies.[30]

The beleaguered Society of Civil Servants Prison and Borstal Governors' Branch attempted to develop an argument, but from a diametrically opposite angle:

> Essentially, the controversy about the escape of the spy Blake is a political one. The conditions of custody in which such a man, or any similarly dangerous prisoner, should be kept, are decided upon by

---

30 *Ibid.*, p. 203.

the use of criteria which are unconnected with problems of custodial treatment for more ordinary criminals. No prison governor can make free decisions about a State prisoner of this calibre and decide where he is to be located. Nor can a governor, unless specially instructed, keep such a prisoner in conditions which are different from those allowed for other prisoners in the same prison. To do this would contravene the prisoner's rights. Unless the political and the penological issues in the case are kept separate, the community and parliament will find that politically motivated decisions have determined for many years ahead penological practices of this country. It will give little genuine satisfaction at some future date to be able to use the prison service once again as the community scapegoat.[31]

Those of us who have some knowledge and some experience of penitentiary matters and who, far away from the scene of those tormenting events, can take a more detached view, need hardly any convincing that the problem of ultimate ministerial responsibility in the penitentiary sphere calls for an incomparably more sophisticated, operational and parliamentary approach than either of these two statements seem to be willing to comprehend.

In the course of our inquiry I felt that the possibility of further serious disturbances could not be ruled out and firmly believed that the Home Secretary, who after all had brought our sub-committee into being, should be informed about it. We sent him a letter and with hardly any delay, almost by return of post, I was invited by Mr Jenkins to have lunch with him at Brooks's – the Club he was so fond of – although a good menu and excellent wine lost their tempting significance because of our lengthy and grim discussion. Our letter of 14 May led to his reply of 9 June. I was naturally very pleased to be told: 'I found the discussion which we had about the matter at luncheon yesterday of the greatest interest and value', but more cogently we were all relieved to hear about the variety of steps taken on the 'Wings' to ensure, at least for a while, there would be no explosion.

But when this threat of a fresh crisis subsided, the prisons seemed to regain some of their habitual lethargy. Perhaps more importantly than anything else, the opposition could not, after the two reports had been published, be a source of irritation and embarrassment. Roy Jenkins's interest in the penal controversies of the period then rapidly declined. He did say with attractive frankness:

---

31 See *A Paper Submitted by the Secretary etc., to The Earl Mountbatten's Inquiry into Prison Security and The Secretary of State for the Home Office Department* in Home Office Papers relating to the Mountbatten Inquiry, pp. 1–12, at p. 12.

in general I over-reacted to this ephemeral public (or press) hysteria about escapes, and tilted the emphasis of prison regimes too much towards security and away from training and work. I ought to have been steadier under fire, but it is easier to say this in retrospect than it was to sustain it during the barrage of daily bombardment.

This was written in 1991 and Lord Mountbatten had by then been dead for nearly twelve years. Lord Jenkins's attractively expressed self-confession, if Mountbatten had been able to read it, would have added a further heavy load to his disappointment. But at least his contribution to penal affairs had not been forgotten. He pops up in Lord Jenkins's autobiography on several occasions and always approvingly. In contrast the Advisory Council on the Penal System and its sub-committee cannot claim even this transitory satisfaction. Lord Jenkins has completely forgotten us, or perhaps he did not bother to remember. This is the more remarkable because it was Mr Jenkins who, as Home Secretary, asked the Advisory Council on the Penal System to look afresh at the problem. So perhaps it was no more than a tactical move to make sure there was no new embarrassment. I wonder whether Lord Mountbatten was informed about it at the time, and if so, what form the *démarche* took. This *volte-face*, to which also no reference is made in Lord Jenkins's autobiography, clearly called for an elegant escape of the kind Lord Jenkins is so good at supplying. I have also the feeling that although Roy Jenkins was deeply, and sometimes even passionately, involved in the many matters which came within the purview of his department, his intellectual and aesthetic pulse did not vibrate in the direction of the strictly penological sphere. And yet it is the penal system (in addition to public order and sentencing processes) which constitutes the hard core of the Home Office's permanent business.

I would be very sorry indeed if the tenor of my comments were to be construed to imply that I do not hold Lord Jenkins in high regard as a Home Secretary. He cannot fail to be placed amongst the distinguished holders of this office within the past half-century. He contributed greatly to repainting in much stronger colours the human and liberal projection of the Home Office. He was one of our most civilized keepers of the Department – an epitaph by which, I venture to assume, he would like to be remembered.

Roy Jenkins came back to the Home Office for a second term in 1974–6 and again he had to face another frustrating penological miscarriage. This time it was not set in motion by a rather sordid spy affair and its aftermath. With vastly enhanced experience he was able to stand on firmer ground and he was fortified by a remark his predecessor Sir Frank Soskice (afterwards Lord Stow Hill) had minuted on one of the Home Office files: 'We are not always wrong, but we always get the blame.' How he reacted, if at all, is a question which I certainly cannot fail to raise.

Rules of fairness to be observed when passing judgment on an inquiry

Our report continued to be controversial long after it had been published and so was Lord Mountbatten's. This was inevitable. It would have been naïve in the extreme to expect otherwise. Sometimes I regretted that the 'other side' insisted too emphatically that the 'truth' was on their side to be picked up and categorically proclaimed as such. The more controversial an issue appears to be the greater should be the tolerance for the divergence of views. Only twice have I noticed a deviation from rules of interpretation which should be respected in discussions of this nature. It is because these episodes have a significance which goes far beyond the particular issue that I have decided to devote some space to it.

'The Radzinowicz sub-committee', stated Professor Rod Morgan,

> consisted of five members. Unlike the other sub-committees during this period it is alleged that it worked in virtual seclusion from the remainder of the Council. It circulated no minutes or discussion papers to other committee members. Indeed two Council members have informed me that they had no idea as to the sub-committee's recommendations until January/February 1968, when the full Council was suddenly presented with the final report.[32]

Every statement contained herein is incorrect or grossly misleading. To start with, the sub-committee did not consist of five members but of four with two assessors. All sub-committees of the Council worked separately from each other, otherwise no inquiries could have been carried out and no reports published. No sub-committee circulated minutes or discussion papers to all the members of the Council, but every member, should he or she so wish, could call upon the Secretary of the Council (through the Secretary of the sub-committee – if more convenient) and ask for the minutes of evidence or discussion papers, which were scrupulously kept by our Secretary in an easily accessible form.

The two members of the Council who apparently informed Professor Morgan that they had no idea as to our sub-committee's recommendations until January/February 1968 were correct in saying this, but they were misguided in judging this to have been wrong. To have done otherwise would have been fatal for the status and the effectiveness of the Council. The proper procedure was to forward the completed report to the Chairman of the Council and for him to decide how to proceed. The last stated assertion that the 'full Council

---

32 Rod Morgan, *Formulating Penal Policy: The Future of the Advisory Council on the Penal System* (1979), p. 8.

was suddenly presented with the final report' is particularly hurtful. In fact the report once completed was dispatched by the Secretary to every member of the Council and it should have been understood by every member acting in good faith that the report was far from being considered as 'final'. It would have become final only when accepted by the Council as a whole, but the Council, indeed any of its members, had the undisputed right to propose changes to it, to record his or her dissent in the final text, indeed to reject it altogether. The very fate of our report shows the correctness of my statement and any impression that consideration of it was distorted into a hurried affair should be most categorically dispelled.[33] In his introductory letter to the Home Secretary our Chairman, Sir Kenneth Younger, whose strictness on this point had been almost pedantic, stated: 'The Sub-Committee's report has been *fully* discussed by the Council at meetings held on 29 January 1968 and 15 February 1968.' The copious minutes of the two meetings deposited amongst the Home Office Papers amply corroborate his statement.[34]

A no less distorted interpretation is given by Professor Morgan with respect to the two reports submitted to us in response to our invitation by Dr Donald West and the late Dr Richard F. Sparks. We asked the first to re-examine for our benefit the empirical basis for the classification of prisoners, especially the most dangerous ones, in Category A. We asked the latter to give us a summary of the leading American criminological literature on the dynamics of the prison environment with particular reference to long-term prisoners. I had made it clear that we could not guarantee that their papers would be included in our report, but that we would certainly refer to them. They would be free to publish their papers in their entirety or in any way they might decide to be proper and convenient. As it turned out, we considered Dr West's report to be of the very first importance and we published a large part of it in an appendix and drew several conclusions from it in the body of our report. Dr Sparks's paper, although not deprived of interest, proved to be distinctly marginal for our purposes. Even so we referred to it in

---

33 See Progress Report drawn up by Major Snowden, 3 November 1967. AGPS /N /27; ACPS / PR /1, 12 pages.
34 See *Advisory Council on the Penal System*, Minutes of the 4th Meeting held at the Home Office on Monday, 29 January 1968, ACPS (M) and *op. cit.*, Minutes of the 6th Meeting held on Thursday, 7 March 1968, ACPS (M) 6; also Kenneth Younger's letter to the Home Secretary introducing the report, see *The Regime for Long-Term Prisoners in Conditions of Maximum Security* (1968), pp. v–vi. In addition to oral discussions, six written statements from several members of the Council also became part of our deliberation. And not to forget: the draft of a weighty letter written by the Chairman to the Home Secretary, dispatched to all members of the Council for their comments at the meeting.

the introduction to our report.[35] Worse was still to come when Professor Morgan insinuated the nature of our evidence, 'a subtle evidence' was 'apparently gleaned from a review of the literature on maximum security prisons commissioned by the Council and undertaken by Dr Richard F. Sparks'. It is sufficient to glance at the value of the evidence we received, its quantity, quality and diversity, to see the utter emptiness of this allegation.

I sincerely hope that these remarks will not be interpreted as affecting the high regard in which I hold Professor Rod Morgan. I remember vividly when, many years ago, he came to visit me in Cambridge, wishing to establish a postgraduate course in criminology at the University of Bath, where he was at the time. He was anxious to take note of our experience gained at the Cambridge Institute. When he wrote his report on the Advisory Councils relating to penal matters (1979) he must have been no more than thirty-five years old and already full of promise. Since then he has grown in stature and I regard him as one of the leading criminologists of his generation. I am pretty certain that today he would have approached this subject with greater circumspection.

I have used rather a lot of space on this episode, not only to put the record on our report straight, but also because this episode can perhaps be viewed as a case study of wider and more permanent significance. When an inquiry is in the process of being completed (or immediately following its completion) should members belonging to this particular committee express their views to an outsider, leaving him or her at liberty to make views publicly known according to their wishes or whims? And if they do, is it correct and fair that they should remain anonymous and hide behind the foggy designation of 'certain members'? And if they are anxious to act in this way is it not correct and fair to keep their chairman or the Chairman of the Council informed about their misgivings? And now I come to the point which perhaps impinges upon the crux of the matter: if the inquirer or interviewer (whether an academic or a journalist) collects these kinds of obviously disapproving comments and wishes to write about them, should he not, before doing so, take the trouble of seeing the Chairman of the committee without divulging his sources of information? He may well hear an altogether different version of events.

I can be very brief about the other episode. In an important symposium held in Cambridge, Professor Roy King, referring to our report, wrote about 'the rhetoric of Radzinowicz'. To put it bluntly, this is a disparaging dismissal of the efforts of a group of people of unusual distinction, experience and ripeness of judgement, who reached the dispersal conclusion not with

---

35 See *The Regime for Long-Term Prisoners in Conditions of Maximum Security*, Appendix C, 'Records of 138 Category A Prisoners', pp. 90–2, and 'Report on a Study of the Prison and Home Office', pp. 2, 53–4 and 57–61.

high-handedness but after an exemplary many-sided study and still with anguish in their hearts and minds.[36]

Public service in the cause of penal progress is hardly ever a rewarding, fulfilling occupation and to stick as closely as possible to rules of fair play should be regarded as a compelling ethical duty.

---

36 See Professor Roy D. King, 'New Generation Prisons, the Building Programme, and the Future of Dispersal Policy', in A.E. Bottoms and R. Light (eds) *Problems of Long-Term Imprisonment* (1987), pp. 115–39, at p. 115. The Council's members were Rt Hon. Kenneth Younger, Rt Hon. Lord Justice Widgery, Leo Abse, MP, Louis Blom-Cooper, Mark Carlisle, Lord Delacourt-Smith of New Windsor, Bishop of Exeter, Mr W.L. Mars-Jones, QC, Mr R.E. Millard, Mr T.A.F. Noble, Lady Rothschild, Revd the Rt Hon. Lionel Sandford, Dr Peter Scott, Baroness Serota of Hampstead, Mr George Twist, Baroness Wootton of Abinger, and myself. Mr A.E. Corben of the Home Office acted as the Secretary to the Council.

13

A FRUITFUL APPROACH TO PENAL REFORM

Setting up an advisory council

On 3 August 1944 Herbert Morrison (afterwards Lord Morrison of Lambeth), then the Home Secretary in Clement Attlee's administration, announced in the Commons the setting up of the Advisory Council for the Treatment of Offenders, which soon became known in interested circles as ACTO.[1]

There was nothing novel or unusual about the concept of an advisory council in governmental practice or parliamentary parlance. Quite to the contrary, it was an old, firmly established and well-respected organizational device of a wider public character set up to provide help and advice to major departments of state: ministers could create an advisory council whenever they considered it desirable.

At the very time that ACTO was brought into being by the Home Secretary, advisory councils (official and non-official) were built into and associated with no fewer than sixteen departments of state.[2] When, in 1949, Mr Attlee was asked how many central or national committees had been set up to advise government departments, he stated that they numbered about seven hundred. While the Lord President of the Council had nearly a hundred such bodies, not including the fifty-five committees which advised the Department of Scientific and Industrial Research which was also under his direction, the Treasury had thirty-one and the Commonwealth Office only one. Writing in 1955 Sir Kenneth Wheare estimated that their total number was not greatly different, but that it could fluctuate.[3]

The Home Office had thirty-one such bodies and a few of them related to

---

1 Oral Answers, *Parl. Debates*, HC, cols 402, 1598–9, 3 August 1944.
2 See the solid study emanating from the Political and Economic Planning (PEP): *Advisory Committees in British Government* (1960), pp. 198–212 and summary, pp. 23–4.
3 See his *Government by Committee* (1955), pp. 45–7.

certain aspects of criminal policy, such as the Probation Advisory and Training Board, the Police Council, the Advisory Council on Child Care and the London Juvenile Courts Consultative Committee.[4] But the Advisory Council on the Treatment of Offenders was the first one to be established with such wide terms of reference and such high expectations.

There were (and I suppose still are) two types of councils – those which derive their birth certificate from statutory authority and those which originate from a minister's directive. A department would be obliged by an Act of Parliament to set up the first type of council and consequently could not wind one up without repealing the relevant statute. The birth, existence and demise of the second type depended on the minister's administrative decision, and ACTO belonged to this second category. The chairman and the members were invited to undertake their duties by the minister. There was no limit of service fixed for the chairman but the period assigned to members was usually a two years' term which could be renewed, but not necessarily with an indication of for how long it would be extended. The only Home Office member of the Council was the Permanent Under-Secretary of State, who would often be vice-chairman. The Council had one or two secretaries selected from the younger civil servants in the department with the particular abilities needed to discharge such functions.

The Council often worked through two sub-committees, each in charge of a particular topic. These were, as a general rule, proposed to the Council by the Home Secretary, but the Council had been granted the power to use its own initiative to suggest to the Home Secretary topics which it considered should be inquired into.

Each inquiry when completed was submitted by the Chairman for discussion and final acceptance by the Council as a whole. It was then forwarded to the Home Secretary by the Chairman with a brief introductory note and speedily published by the Stationery Office. Members were allowed to present their dissent or reservations, which were published as part of the report in the usual way.

The Council had, of course, the right to call witnesses, and to have their evidence recorded; to ask the Home Office for additional material or help from the Home Office Research Unit; and, should the effective implementation of their terms of reference so require, it would receive financial or any other assistance from the Home Office. Not only the Council as a whole but also any of its sub-committees would be provided with a secretary – again a member of the Home Office staff. Neither the Chairman of the Council nor its members were remunerated for their services, although their travelling expenses and subsistence were covered according to generally accepted

---

4   See PEP, *op. cit.*, pp. 204–5.

governmental rates. The Haldane Committee on the Machinery of Government stated:

> we have come to the conclusion, after surveying what came before us, that in the sphere of civil government the duty of investigation and thought, as a preliminary to action, might with great advantage be more definitely recognised. It appears to us that adequate provision has not been made in the past for the organised acquisition of facts and information, and for the systematic application of thought, as preliminary to the settlement of policy and its subsequent administration.[5]

This was postulated in 1918, but the atmosphere in the 1940s was still very receptive to it. *Ad-hoc* advisory bodies, set up to deal with a particular issue, could go far towards satisfying this need, and so of course could a departmental or select committee. But standing advisory councils had certain advantages, real and visible, which should not be minimized. Because it was already in existence, it was easy for a Home Secretary to instruct the council to explore any topic he regarded as urgent. The council could approach the subject in less formal and more flexible ways than other bodies. Furthermore, its deliberations and conclusions could be kept at a safer distance from immediate political pressures.

An influential and dedicated group

The effectiveness and usefulness of an advisory council largely depended on whether it was genuinely needed and welcomed by the department concerned, or whether it had been imposed on it by outside unfriendly criticism. It also depended on who was selected as chairman and members. Another obvious consideration was the kind and range of topics entrusted to it and the extent to which its recommendations were acted upon. Considered under each of these headings the prospects of ACTO seemed to be propitious and the start could not have been more promising. The Home Secretary was strongly in favour of endowing the department with such a body and so were the senior members of the department. Mr Morrison made no secret that he considered himself 'as having been fortunate in obtaining the services of Mr Justice Birkett as Chairman of the Council'. Sir Norman Birkett (afterwards Lord Birkett) was then at the height of his reputation, a truly remarkable, widely respected and popular personality. A liberal, but with his feet firmly on the ground, an idealist gifted to inspire and yet a realist who, holding firm to principles, recognized the usefulness of wise and timely compromise:

---

5 *Report of the Machinery of Government Committee*, Cd 9230 (HMSO, 1918), para. 12.

and, of course, with deep interests in penal matters.[6] The Council then consisted of twenty people. It was a distinguished group of varied experience. It consisted, amongst others, of Sir Alexander Maxwell (acting as Vice-Chairman), the Bishop of Bristol, Margery Fry, Lady Allen of Hurtwood, Dame Lillian Barker, Mrs Walter Elliot (afterwards Baroness Elliot), Lady Inskip, George Benson (afterwards Sir George Benson), Geoffrey Crowther, Professor Harold Laski, Leo Page (afterwards Sir Leo Page) and H.W. Shawcross (afterwards Lord Shawcross).

The Home Secretary's intention was not only to nominate persons with specialized knowledge of the subject but also 'to include men and women with other outlooks who will bring to the human problems confronting the Council experience gained in varied walks of life'. At that juncture an unexpected interjection occurred: Mr James Callaghan (afterwards Lord Callaghan of Cardiff) asked whether his suggestion had been considered 'that an offender who had later made good should be included in the Council'. This must have been Lord Callaghan's *Sturm und Drang Periode* for when he became Home Secretary in the years to come he did nothing about it. Mr Morrison, as the son of a London police officer, no doubt felt that he could speak with greater authority on the subject, He replied: 'I did consider it. It was not without its attraction, but I would not have been able to find a suitable offender.'[7] Miss W.M. Goode of the Probation Department and Francis Graham-Harrison were appointed Secretaries to the Council.

The Chairmen under whom I had the honour to serve in the course of many years were Sir Patrick Barry, Sir Granville Ram, the Earl of Drogheda and Sir Kenneth Younger. Baroness Serota took charge of the Council after I had retired from it. Sir Patrick was the son of Redmond Barry, the Lord Chancellor of Ireland, and he followed this legal career. He left a mark as a barrister, joining the Northern Circuit and becoming a KC in 1938. Two years later he was appointed a judge of the King's Bench Division and in this capacity, both in civil and criminal cases, was regarded as outstanding, 'handsome and distinguished, always well dressed, very courteous and soft spoken and always expressing himself in careful and perfect English. He was a fair and kind man and had a gentle sense of humour.' This reference to him in his obituary notice in *The Times* described him perfectly and this is how I

---

6 A fine note on Lord Birkett was composed by Lord Devlin for the *Dictionary of National Biography 1961–70* (1981), pp. 110–12; also *The Times* (12 February 1962), p. 15, and H. Montgomery Hyde, *Norman Birkett* (1964). Educated at Cambridge (Emmanuel College) he was a good friend to the Department of Criminal Science and then of the Institute of Criminology.

7 I would be against the inclusion of former offenders in advisory bodies of this kind. But I would be no less emphatic that thorough and undiluted evidence should be enlisted from well-selected former and actual offenders whenever their experiences would be relevant to a penal inquiry at hand.

remember him. He was the Chairman of ACTO from 1958 to 1966 and we could not have had a better chairman in the formative years of our existence. Sir Granville Ram's personality and experience were different, but no less valuable. As the first parliamentary counsel he had played a crucial role in the preparation of many major statutes such as the Education Act 1944 and the Criminal Justice Act 1948. 'No man ever did more to produce order out of chaos', stated Lord Jowitt, the Lord Chancellor. As the Council hoped that some of its recommendations would become law, his seasoned expertise was of great value. He was always concise in his interventions from the chair and effective.

The Earl of Drogheda's acceptance to lead the Council was another feather in our cap. Chairman of committees and Deputy Speaker of the House of Lords, he was a highly respected public figure with important and varied work behind him. He was still alert and influential, invariably anxious that the Council should prove to be a productive and stimulating body. At some stage he rallied behind Margery Fry, urging the establishment of an Institute of Criminology in London. Sir Kenneth Younger, who joined the Council as Chairman, was not a novice in penal matters. He was Parliamentary Under-Secretary of State at the Home Office 1947–50 and Minister of State 1950–51. He was the Chairman of the Howard League for Penal Reform in the years 1960–73. But he was also, amongst many other things, at some stage a Minister of State at the Foreign Office. He joined the Labour Party and was the Member for Grimsby for many years. When Labour went out of office in 1951 he became a member of the Shadow Cabinet and a front bench opposition spokesman on foreign and home affairs. At the end of 1958 he announced that he would not be seeking re-election for Grimsby and his political career came to an end. Successful as he had been in many political undertakings he did not have it in him to reach the very top of the political ladder. He soon became Director of Chatham House – the Royal Institute of International Affairs. The Younger Report of 1972 – an outcome of the Committee of Inquiry into Privacy – was an important document. His involvement in the work of the Council was exceptionally intense and throughout he acted in striking contrast to the traditional concept of a chairman. Under a mild and charming appearance there was an effective stubbornness: to see him change his views was a very rare occurrence indeed. His premature death in 1976 at the age of 67 came as a shock to all of those who knew him. I happened to disagree with him on a few occasions, but like everybody else I had a great respect for his concerns for the public good and for fairness in social and human relations.[8]

---

8   For more details of their careers, see the obituary of Sir Patrick Barry, *The Times* (8 May 1972); of Sir Granville Ram, *The Times* (27 December 1952) and *Dictionary of National Biography 1951–60* (1971), pp. 832–3; of the Earl of Drogheda, *The Times* (23 November 1957); of Sir Kenneth Younger, *The Times* (22 May 1976) and *Dictionary of National Biography 1971–80* (1986), pp. 934–5.

With time the composition of the Council was broadened, very much to its advantage, both in substance and prestige. Lord Widgery, the Lord Chief Justice, Mr Justice Griffith, Mr Justice Waller, Sir Norman Skelhorn, the Director of Public Prosecutions, Mark Carlisle (afterwards Lord Carlisle), Colonel Sir Arthur Young, T.A.F. Noble (afterwards Sir Thomas Noble), Dr Peter Scott, Professors Nigel Walker and Gordon Trasler, Louis Blom-Cooper (later Sir Louis Blom-Cooper), Lady Rothschild and Baroness Wootton accepted the invitation to serve on the Council. The attendance at sub-groups was good, but these were people with many commitments and inevitably it was very difficult to ensure their regular participation in the plenary sessions of the Council. Sometimes such meetings had to be convened twice to secure an adequate quorum, which even then often proved to be unsatisfactory.

A twenty-year involvement

The Advisory Council for the Treatment of Offenders was in existence for twenty years, more precisely 1944–64. ACTO was then discontinued because of the appointment of a Royal Commission on the Penal System in England and Wales (1964–6). Following its dissolution (on which more will be said in Chapter 14) a new Advisory Council on the Penal System (ACPS) was set up in 1966 and it functioned for twelve years until 1978. Altogether the two Councils covered a period of thirty-two years. I was invited to join ACTO in 1950 and served on it to the end of its existence (1964). In 1966 I was reinvited to join ACPS and served until 1972. Thus my association with the first two Advisory Councils extended over a period of twenty years. I wanted to retire earlier but was urged by the Home Office to stay until the inquiry carried out by Sir Kenneth Younger on Young Adult Offenders had been completed. On my retirement I received a very nice letter from the then Home Secretary, Robert Carr (afterwards Lord Carr of Hadley). Twenty years is a big slice of one's professional life, but my work with the Councils was as fruitful and agreeable as one could hope for in this sombre field of criminal justice where, as a general rule, disappointments by far exceed rewards. It was a very civilized and congenial grouping. Our disagreements were few and they were always voiced in an atmosphere of mutual tolerance and courtesy. In those days I would go to London quite frequently and often I would have a drink or luncheon with some of the members of the Council – occasions which invariably turned out to be friendly and useful.

What follows is a list of reports issued by the two Councils.

1 *Proposal that a Special Institution Outside the Prisons should be provided for Offenders with Abnormal Mental Characteristics* (1949)
2 *Report on Dartmoor Prison by Mr George Benson, M.P.* (1952)

3 *Suspended Sentences* (1952)
4 *Alternatives to Short Terms of Imprisonment* (1957)
5 *The After-Care and Supervision of Discharged Prisoners* (1958)
6 *The Treatment of Young Offenders* (1958)
7 *Corporal Punishment. Cmnd. 1213* (1960)
8 *Non-Residential Treatment of Offenders under 21* (1962)
9 *Preventive Detention* (1963)
10 *The Organisation of After-Care* (1963)
11 *Interim Report on Detention of Girls in a Detention Centre* (1968)
12 *The Regime for Long-Term Prisoners in Conditions of Maximum Security* (1968)
13 *Detention Centres* (1970)
14 *Non-Custodial and Semi-Custodial Penalties* (1970)
15 *Reparation by the Offender* (1970)
16 *Young Adult Offenders* (1974)
17 *Powers of the Courts Dependent on Imprisonment* (1977)
18 *The Length of Prison Sentences* (1977)
19 *Sentences of Imprisonment* (1978)

The terms of reference assigned to ACTO read as follows: 'To be a Council to assist the Home Secretary with advice and suggestions on questions relating to the treatment of offenders.' The second set of terms, assigned to ACPS, was somewhat different and the difference was significant. They were covered by the more generic term of 'penal system' of which the 'treatment of offenders' was but a part. The objective of 'prevention of crime' was also introduced. This is reflected to a certain extent in the type of inquiries undertaken.

The first ten documents emanated from ACTO and the last nine from ACPS. Taken together, as they should be, they represent an impressive record of inquiries into several central and constantly topical issues of criminal policy and the administration of criminal justice. It is no less remarkable that the recommendations of virtually all of them were adopted unanimously by the relevant sub-committee and the Council as a whole. The most striking exception was the sixteenth report in my list, on *Young Adult Offenders* (1974). This was the pet project of Sir Kenneth Younger. He identified himself with it, brain and heart, almost forgetting that he was not chairman of this particular sub-committee alone but the Chairman of the Council as a whole, thus giving himself hardly any elbow-room to draw up viable alternative solutions should a really deep division of opinion within the Council come to the forefront. And this was at the time when criminal policy in thought and practice, both in Britain and abroad, was changing gear. He was, however, determined to follow his projected course without any deviations from it. The effects were disastrous. The final report bristled with notes of dissent (five of them) or reservation (one). Two of the dissenting notes carried the signatures of as many as four members of the Council.[9] The report was still very useful as an introduction to an important but exceptionally complex subject and one of its recommendations found its way into legislation. But as a practical document on which coherent and systematic action could be taken it was in tatters.

Another instructive episode was provided by the vicissitudes encountered when an attempt was made to introduce into criminal legislation a new measure: the suspended sentence. Twice, in 1952 and again in 1957, ACTO was asked to inquire into it and make recommendations. On both occasions the Council concluded that it should be rejected. Yet evidence in favour of it continued to be produced and was submitted for example to the Royal Commission on the Penal System by the Magistrates' Association, by the Law Society, and by several other respectable organizations.[10] I turned against it in most categorical terms.[11] I tried to show that a suspended sentence was largely used on the continent of Europe *faute de mieux*, simply because they did not have probation or conditional discharge; that in comparison the suspended sentence was definitely inferior; and if added to probation and conditional discharge it would harm their basic distinctiveness and in practice confuse both the offenders concerned and the courts. To strengthen my case I invited Monsieur Marc Ancel, the noted French penologist and judge of the Supreme Court of France, to present a report on the suspended sentence in a comparative continental perspective. At my suggestion Joan King, an Assistant Director of Research in the Cambridge Institute and my close literary collaborator, capably translated it into English and I included it as a volume in our series, *Cambridge Studies in Criminology*.[12]

I seemed to have made little progress in my attempt to clarify the issues involved. Lord Chorley was my constant and severe opponent. The Council was not asked for further advice but the proposal found its way into the Criminal Justice Bill of 1967 and soon passed into law. Nevertheless I stuck to my guns and I restated my position in an article which, at the time, was widely quoted.[13] Soon afterwards the innovation proved to be an unmistakable and irrefutable failure and sank into oblivion. But I continued to be

---

9 With much regret I felt compelled to join Mr Justice Waller, Mr Richard Lowry, QC, and George Twist, CBE, QPM, in a note of dissent because a basic principle was involved.
10 It was the well-known Metropolitan magistrate Sir Leo Page who in 1950 proposed that the suspended sentence should be introduced as a new method of treatment and it was Lord Oaksey who mentioned it in his address to the Magistrates' Association that year. See *Suspended Sentence*, Report of the Advisory Council for the Treatment of Offenders (1952), reproduced as Appendix D in the report on *Alternatives to Short Terms of Imprisonment* (1957), pp. 26–32.
11 See Leon Radzinowicz, 'A Foreseeable Failure', *Sunday Times* (24 January 1971).
12 Marc Ancel, *Suspended Sentence* (vol. 29 of *Cambridge Studies in Criminology* (1971)).
13 See Leon Radzinowicz and Lewis Chester, 'Prisons: The Reform that Went Wrong – A Foreseeable Failure', *Sunday Times* (24 August 1978).

mystified about where this idea had come from and why it had drawn such strength. A few years later Baroness Wootton of Abinger opened my eyes: 'the Labour Government ... had become greatly alarmed at the continual rise in the prison population and widely hoped that this might be checked by the imposition of suspended, in place of immediate, sentences of imprisonment.'[14] In view of her very close association with the Labour Party, this explanation should be regarded as authoritative. The history of criminal policy followed in many countries and by many major political parties is, alas, full of episodes where simplistic, opportunistic anticipations or solutions have been fostered to serve immediate political objectives. But the history of criminal policy is equally rich in showing how short-sighted and damaging the consequences of such short-cuts have invariably proved to be.

I was somewhat unhappy about our report on *After-Care*. It certainly did mark a significant step forward in strengthening the system of after-care for adult offenders which was still very inadequate in face of the formidable tasks confronting it. But in a modern society after-care of convicted offenders cannot be effectively organized and directed unless it becomes part of the processes of general industrial activity, taking into account any relevant differences between the ordinary working population and those who have just emerged from prison. Integration of the latter, however fragmentary and restricted, could not be put into effect without the firm support of the trade unions. But the opposition of organized Labour, remembering the depression years and the danger of employers exploiting unskilled workers, was formidable. Indeed it was unwilling to make the slightest of concessions. On listening to the statements made by the leaders of the trade unions to our committee with respect to the employment of ex-prisoners, Karl Marx's exhortation that criminals like all workers are the victims of the capitalist system and as such deserve understanding and support, appeared to be very far away from the feelings of the rank and file of the proletariat and their representatives. The further vitally important impediment was the problem of building a proper after-care system within the context of a society already acutely affected by economic decline. Yet a vision of an effective after-care organization, however remote, should have found its place in a report produced in the twentieth century. It was this lack of vision and the reluctance of the Council to supply it, that compelled me to present a memorandum of dissent, although only two members of the Council thought fit to support me.[15]

---

14 See Baroness Wootton of Abinger, 'Official Advisory Bodies', in Professor Nigel Walker (ed.) *Penal Policy-Making in England* (1972). Papers presented to the Cropwood Round-Table Conference, December 1976, pp. 13–24, at p. 16, Cambridge Institute of Criminology.
15 See *The Organisation of After-Care*, Report of the Advisory Council on the Treatment of Offenders, Home Office (1963), Memorandum of Dissent by Professor Leon Radzinowicz, the Hon. Lady Inskip and the Revd E. Shirvell Price, *ibid.*, pp. 83–6.

In contrast I was particularly happy with the report of the sub-committee on *Preventive Detention* which was so effectively chaired by Dr Mortimer, the Bishop of Exeter, which I had been invited to join. Our report unanimously recommended the abolition of preventive detention and this was unreservedly endorsed by the Council as a whole.[16] The second attempt, in the Criminal Justice Act 1948, to erect a special barrier against habitual and persistent offenders had proved, like its predecessor, the Prevention of Crimes Act 1908, highly controversial in theory and useless in practice. We recommended that the courts should have the power to extend the sentence of an habitual offender, but that the amount by which it could be extended would depend on the maximum penalty for the offence of which he had been convicted. If the maximum was five years the sentence could not be extended beyond that point and no sentence could be extended beyond ten years. In addition we tightened the criteria for receiving an extended sentence.[17] Yet I was quite convinced that the new experience, assuming that our recommendations were to be adopted, would soon reveal that a truly satisfactory solution was still far away. It is indeed very awkward to acknowledge to one's self and to convince others that there are problems in crime control as intractable and as elusive as the crime problem itself.

No need for apology

No doubt some of the reports of the Advisory Council would have certainly gained in substance if more research had gone into them before the final recommendations were reached. Often, as has already been noted, the full weight of the Council might have been more effectively deployed if the participation of its members had been more regular. But there is no perfection in this world of ours and in fairness a broad and dispassionate assessment of the work accomplished by the Advisory Council should produce nothing but high praise. And, not for the first time, I beg to be allowed to draw upon my comparative experience. Casting my mind back over the past seventy years I can cite no country in the world where an eminent group of people have put at the disposal of the government their knowledge, motivated largely by a disinterested desire to help to raise the standards of criminal justice. And a particularly valuable lesson which emerged from their endeavours was the realization that much good can be achieved in promoting progress and readjustments in the penal system not so much by putting on the agenda of reform huge, ambitious schemes of 'reconstruction', but by coming to grips

---

16 *Preventive Detention*, Report of the Advisory Council on the Treatment of Offenders (Home Office, 1963).
17 *Ibid.*, sections 63 and 75, pp. 25 and 29.

with a series of much more limited and much more precisely defined topics in response to certain obvious, yet not adequately satisfied, needs.

This lesson will emerge with unquestionable acuteness in Chapter 14 when an enterprise mounted on diametrically opposed premises crashed irretrievably and in rather humiliating circumstances.[18] And again, to be realistic, whether an Advisory Council if set up in the late 1990s could work as effectively as its predecessor is open to doubt, because the broad consensus in the penological sphere has given way to contentious and divisive attitudes.

---

18 I was naturally very pleased to note that the role of our advisory councils has not been ignored. Compliments were paid by Professor Rod Morgan in his study *Formulating Penal Policy: The Future of the Advisory Council on the Penal System* (1979); by Professors David Downes and Rod Morgan, 'Hostages to Fortune: The Politics of Law and Order in Post-War Britain', in M. Maguire, R. Morgan and R. Reiner (eds) *The Oxford Handbook of Criminology* (1994), pp. 183–232, at pp. 209 and 224. Following the dissolution of the Royal Commission on the Penal System, Mr Harold Wilson, then Prime Minister, announced that the Advisory Council would be resurrected and so it was for a few years. The new Conservative administration led by Mrs Thatcher made it pass away almost imperceptibly. For the reasons which might have influenced the decision see Lord Windlesham, *Responses to Crime*, vol. 2 (1993), pp. 104–5, 150, which includes a trenchant letter from Sir Louis Blom-Cooper. By then I had been 'unemployed' by virtue of my resignation in 1972 and would have regarded it as undignified and unproductive to have anything more to do with the subject.

14

THE DEATH OF A ROYAL COMMISSION

My early misgivings

In this chapter I shall give, as objectively as I can, an account of a very sad experience and indicate the major lesson which emerges from it. It is an account of an episode in the political and penal history of England which I understand had no precedent and one which I sincerely hope will not serve as a precedent in the future.

An investigative commission under the seal of Her Majesty (which means a Royal Commission) was set up. It was entrusted with a truly heroic mission, not only to illuminate the present but also to project the future in a manner which would leave a deep and lasting impact on society at large and on the evolution of the subject which constituted the essence of its investigations.

And yet within barely two years of its appointment this exhilarating enterprise lay in ruins. It was engulfed by its terms of reference. It ceased to be effectively directed by its Chairman. It divided itself into sub-committees, each pursuing its own path leisurely and with little profit. It sapped the enthusiasm of several of its members. It produced on occasions embarrassing tensions amongst them. It exposed the whole body to undesirable political pressures, which led to discreet but nevertheless critical confrontations between the commission, the Home Office, and the government of the day. Ultimately the commission found itself sliding into a languid cul-de-sac. Instead of boldly producing progress in the penal sphere, it hindered it. If it had continued to exist, it would have led to much confusion and postponed constructive alternative options which were emanating from other quarters.

The Royal Commission on the Penal System broke up disillusioned and in pieces. No initiative, however sagacious and influential, could have revived it. The epitaphs hurled at it from many quarters were frequently acid, merciless and contemptuous. It is very much to the credit of those members of the Commission who felt strongly that it should not be dissolved but reconstructed, that they refrained with dignity from any public recriminations.

The main stages of this story are firmly engraved in my memory, but I have also consulted bulky Home Office papers relating to the Commission. They were graciously made available to me by the Home Office and an official kindly photocopied all the pieces which I selected for further consultation when writing up this account. This was a very considerable amount of material, not easy to handle, yet indispensable.

Around the middle of 1964 rumours were circulating in interested and usually well-informed circles in London that the government was planning to set up a 'super star' investigative body which, in the light of a close and many-sided scrutiny of the prevailing penological situation, would provide an authoritative and detailed projection of what the system for dealing with criminals should be in this country in the century ahead. A case did not have to be made. It was envisaged almost as an inescapable natural necessity by the aggressively titled White Paper *The War against Crime in England and Wales* issued under the authority of the then Home Secretary Henry Brooke (afterwards Lord Brooke of Chinnor).[1] The other, exceptionally energetic, spur was the determination of the Labour Opposition to make penal reform an electoral issue.

Mr Harold Wilson, the Leader of the Opposition, asked that a committee be set up within his own party to survey the whole penal field and prepare the Labour Party's programme. Penal reform, as I stated at the time, occupied one of the Earl of Longford's *Five Lives*. He was appointed Chairman of this very influential committee which included several other prominent members of the Labour Party and one or two able and versatile criminologists (Dr Terence Morris amongst them).[2] On 27 April 1964 the Commons was informed by Miss Alice Bacon (later a Minister of State at the Home Office) that if Labour came to power the new government would act upon the committee's recommendations and that in a few weeks' time it would be ready with its report.[3] And so it was: *Crime: A Challenge to Us All* was the end product. I do not know whether, in witnessing all this, Mr Brooke was

---

1 It was affirmed in *The War against Crime in England and Wales 1959–64*, Cmnd 2296 (1964), p. 13:

> The fundamental review of the whole penal system for which, in the Government's view, the time is now ripe, is of such importance and magnitude that it needs to be carried out by a Royal Commission. There has been no comprehensive study of this kind since the Gladstone Committee of 1895. A purpose will be to reassess the value of our penal system as it has been built up until now – but much more than that. With that as the background, it is the time for a deep study of the philosophy underlying the system – to determine afresh what we ought to be seeking to achieve, to examine how far, and in what manner the results of our present practice fall short, and to sift new ideas in order to judge which of them appear both constructive and practicable in operation.

2 Subsequently four members of the committee joined Mr Wilson's government in important positions: Lord Gardiner, Lord Longford, Lord Elwyn Jones and Mr Greenwood.

3 'Juvenile Delinquency and Hooliganism', *Parl. Debates*, HC, vol. 694, cols 31–97, at col. 85, 27 April 1964.

reminded of the song in the American musical *Annie Get Your Gun* with the memorable refrain 'Anything you can do I can do better'. He was much too serious and grave a man for that, but he was too much of a seasoned politician to let the moment pass without a response. As it happens, the two considerations, though originating from different motivations, strengthened each other and produced the desired effect. On 15 August 1964 Sir Alec Douglas-Home, the Prime Minister, announced in the House of Commons the establishment of the Royal Commission on the Penal System in England and Wales.[4] Mr George Brown, in the proper and customary terms usually uttered on such occasions, welcomed the decision on behalf of the Opposition but expressed so strongly his regret that the setting up of a commission had 'been delayed for quite a long time' that it should be taken as a reproach. And he coupled with his welcome the ominous warning that the existence of the Commission would not inhibit any 'incoming' government in undertaking reform in this sphere. 'I do not anticipate any incoming Government other than the one I lead' was the Prime Minister's confident retort.

Viscount Amory was to be the Chairman, and the Commission was composed of sixteen members. The terms of reference were to inquire into and to make recommendations

> in the light of modern knowledge of crime and its causes and of modern penal practice here and abroad to re-examine the concepts and purposes which should underlie the punishment and treatment of offenders in England and Wales; to report how far they are realised by the penalties and methods of treatment available to the courts, and whether any changes in these, or in the arrangements and responsibility for selecting the sentences to be imposed on particular offenders, are desirable; to review the work of the services and institutions dealing with offenders, and the responsibility for their administration.

I had played no part in these intricate, sensitive and high-powered deliberations. But my views on the essence of the subject were widely known. I had expressed them for a long time and on many occasions in books, essays, statements, and through the criminological programme of the Institute. As late as May 1964 when I was invited to address the Howard League for Penal Reform by Lord Gardiner and Hugh Klare, the Chairman and Secretary respectively, I made no bones about my deeply felt misgivings. I cannot resist reproducing here extensive extracts of my speech for, alas, not only have they proved correct in relation to the specific circumstances accompanying

---

4 See 'Penal Policy (Royal Commission)', *Parl. Debates*, HC, vol. 693, cols 601–5, 16 April 1964.

the appointment of the commission but also, I venture to maintain, are still relevant to contemporary developments in criminology and criminal policy.

> This Commission will have no reason to complain of any narrowness in its terms of reference. On the contrary it may suffer from an *embarras de richesse*. The Prime Minister, moreover, has assured the Commons that nothing – certainly not its terms of reference – need inhibit it in re-examining the causes of crime. I wonder how many of the Commissioners will prove eager to fish – I will not say to drown – in these troubled and treacherous waters. The White Paper makes it clear that this new Commission is envisaged as being in the tradition of the Gladstone Committee of 1895, with its revolutionary impact on the penal system. But is the comparison a just one? The enquiry carried out by the Gladstone Committee was certainly fundamental, but it was restricted in scope. Its task was to examine the prison system evolved and directed by Sir Edmund Du Cane. Its great achievements were the affirmation of a new attitude to offenders in custody and specific suggestions for particular categories. In the comprehensiveness of its objectives it would be perhaps more relevant to compare the Royal Commission to those earlier Criminal Law Commissions of the 1830's and the 1840's who were charged with the gigantic task of reviewing the whole criminal and penal law and reducing it to a single logical and coherent structure. They produced some of the most impeccable reasoning on first principles that has ever been seen. They applied it to their codification but the great design never became law. They made their most immediate impact on the penal system when asked by the government to turn aside to consider such specific issues as the treatment of young offenders and reduction in the scope of capital punishment. I sometimes wonder how far, in this sort of context, we should pursue arguments about the principles of punishment . . . It is not, at least nowadays, arguments about first principles that influence the strength or direction of public opinion or awaken public response to the need to cope with crime and criminals.[5]

With my very serious doubts so clearly articulated how could I bring myself to serve on the Commission? Yet, as the first and at that time the only Professor of Criminology in the country and the Director of the first Institute,

---

5 Leon Radzinowicz, *Criminology and the Climate of Social Responsibility* (W. Heffer & Sons, Cambridge, 1964), pp. 18–19 and 20–2.

I considered it my duty, if invited, to accept this responsibility and to do all I could to help to salvage as much as possible. Thus, when I accepted the invitation I was pretty certain that this would be a stony path to follow, and one very likely to be met by bitterness and sadness at the end of it.

Trying to avoid a catastrophe

At first the Chairman made a move which seemed to indicate that a sense of realism would, after all, emerge and make its influence felt on the subsequent evolution of the Commission's work as a whole. On 22 October 1964 Lord Amory, already uneasy about the first part of the terms of reference, arranged to meet Sir Charles Cunningham, then the Permanent Under-Secretary of State at the Home Office, to discuss how far the Royal Commission would be expected to inquire into 'the causes of crime'. He was reassured by Sir Charles that 'it would be right and feasible for the Commission to acquaint itself, in the words of the terms of reference, with "modern knowledge of the causes of crime" rather than to conduct aetiological research of its own'. And most properly 'he did not wish to suggest particular matters with which the commission should concern itself'. This clarification still left a daunting task. To acquire proper knowledge of the available material concerning the causation of crime was, in itself, a formidable undertaking. Anyhow, any good that might have resulted from this exchange of views soon evaporated simply because, instead of trying to build upon this restricted basis, the commission, with hardly any loss of time, set about trying to reach the peak of an unassailable mountain and, still worse, galloped at accelerated speed towards the very brink of an abyss.[6]

The Commission decided to break up into three sub-groups for an unspecified duration. Such a course is almost always accompanied by grave dangers. It can undermine any coherence there may be in the terms of reference. It may distort the role of the Chairman, undermining his influence and effectiveness. It brings to the fore two or three chairmen of sub-groups who, with the passage of time, may act as shadow chairmen, each of whom may have a different outlook and mode of conducting the inquiries in hand. It may isolate members of the Commission from each other: confining them to only one segment and so losing sight of the centrality of the problem. It may

---

[6] It is only fair to observe that the Prime Minister in announcing the setting up of the Commission added to the confusion. 'I think', he stated, 'that the terms of reference include an inquiry into the causes of crime. This may lead the Royal Commission to make recommendations. The field', he added approvingly, 'is very wide.' And a little later he re-emphasized: 'the Royal Commission must take into account the causes of crime.' He read out to the House the relevant part of the recommendations and confidently concluded: 'I should have thought that that gave the Royal Commission very wide terms of reference indeed.' *Parl. Debates*, HC, vol. 693, cols 603 and 605, 16 April 1964.

also produce an artificial, mechanical demarcation between the topics entrusted to the sub-committees as well as undesirable overlapping. Royal Commissions with subdivisions can be cited which have provided satisfactory results, but hardly any of them were burdened by terms of references so vast and so vague as those of the Royal Commission on the Penal System.

The dangers inherent in subdividing the work of a commission increase or decrease in accordance with the selection of the topics assigned to the sub-committees. I became painfully aware that the first committee, regarded as the most important one, was the epitome of what a commission would do if it wanted to prove to be a total failure. Its very title was already indicative of the imminent débâcle: 'Concepts and Purposes Committee'. You had to be present, or read the material coming within its orbit for speedy assimilation and subsequent reflection by the members, to see that the strong expressions which I am using are unfortunately a realistic assessment of the crisis in perception and planning which was soon to bring the committee down, thus inflicting a destructive blow to the morale of the Commission as a whole.

A call to arms was sounded to members of this committee, indeed to all members of the Commission, to the secretariat of course, and to outside experts in, and observers of, the penal and social sciences, to come forward and share with the committee their information, their knowledge, their ideas and indeed, frequently their dreams. Hundreds of pages converged on the committee in an uninterrupted flow, producing a well-intended but hopelessly disorientating pseudo-seminar in which 'concepts and purposes' were atomized, cross-directed, moved backwards and forwards, expressed in terms detached from reality, or in ponderous pseudo-philosophical language, often accompanied by eulogy or by virulence in presentation.

I used the term 'pseudo-seminar' but to avoid any confusion I hasten to record that at some stage the committee had decided that it would be useful to set up a 'seminar'. It agreed that the seminar 'on penal philosophy ... might better take the form of a confrontation between philosophers and social scientists than an attempt to reconcile conflicting views of philosophers themselves', and a curious list of possible gladiators was drawn up.[7] However, the committee also concluded very wisely that 'it would be premature to arrange this until members had more fully acquainted themselves with the relevant literature, including writings of the possible invitees, and had satisfied themselves that these were questions which could usefully be pursued in a discussion of the kind contemplated'. The Secretary was asked to circulate a reading list. This extraordinary idea was thus put to rest for a

---

7 'Possible invitees to Seminar: Professor H.L.A. Hart, Lord Devlin, Professor A.R.N. Cross, Professor A.J. Ayer, Dr Nigel Walker, Dr Hall Williams, Professor W.J.H. Sprott, Mr R.D. Fairn. And Mr R. Hare, Sir Aubrey Lewis, Professor Gluckman.'

while. Nevertheless at another meeting 'The Committee agreed that it would be useful if its members, so far as necessary, acquainted themselves with the views expressed ... by controversialists such as Lord Devlin and Professor Hart.'

It is fair to notice that even as late as 26 October 1965 the committee seemed still to be disorientated about the crucial two words of their terms of reference. 'The Committee', state the records of one of its meetings, 'noted that the Commission's terms of reference referred to both "concept and purpose". They agreed that the Home Office should be asked whether these words had been included with any clear distinction between them in mind.' Sir Charles Cunningham advised the committee that it is not necessary to make any distinction between these two expressions. I wondered at the time what Wittgenstein's response would have been to this! In case there might occur some oscillation amongst some members of the commission, a letter to the Chairman from one of the members (an academic, Professor J.N. Morris) certainly could not be accused of failing to raise the atmosphere and expectations:

> I agree entirely that we must now [1 February 1965] get down to hard work and would rather we attempted too much than too little, not worrying too much meanwhile about tidiness, overlapping etc. Thus, it might be a good idea to set up the *high-power consultative group on the philosophy of the penal system straightaway*; this would give them a full year to produce a report in good time for the rest of us to study when we get round to attempting a modern restatement of concepts and purposes. I would also like to see a small study group exploring the problem of the young adult ... I think that we need a very active working party (again with co-opted members) on the 'prison' problems outlined in para. 4(B) of the Secretary's note; there is two years' work or more for such a working party, and I am sure that they will need to have sub-groups. Several other subjects in N/28 also lend themselves for *ad hoc* treatment, but further general discussion on this is probably necessary. However, a specialist group on psychiatric-penal problems might well be started now ... These are some ideas I would have put were I pressed on Wednesday. In short: full steam ahead ... P.S. I will try to have a word with Professor Radzinowicz before I leave for Newcastle, and if unsuccessful will send him a copy of this letter.

The enumeration of documents submitted to the committee (and the Commission) which follows is not exhaustive, but it is amply sufficient to serve as an illustration of my preceding remarks. To start with the 'heavy guns', Dr Mortimer, the Bishop of Exeter, wrote a four-page paper on 'Retribution' and Lady Wootton a somewhat longer paper on 'Criminal law and morality' (with a promise to 'return to the subject'). There was a note by Professor J.N. Morris on 'Some questions for discussion with social scientists', only two pages long but enumerating nine topics of simply encyclopaedical scope. The Secretary of the Commission, who already had produced a lengthy paper on the many different problems one encounters while attempting to get acquainted with the available criminological knowledge, followed it up by a short paper on 'The principle of lesser eligibility' as it operated in the penal sphere and yet another one on 'Concepts and purposes', which offered advice on what this formulation presupposed and what it aimed at. Soon he was also instructed by the Chairman to put material into members' hands so as to encourage them to educate themselves. He responded with vigour and diligence and at some moments it looked as if he were running an introductory course in criminal science under the auspices of an Open University. Photocopied lengthy extracts were sent to each member of the commission from a book entitled *The English Prison and Borstal Systems* (1952) by Sir Lionel W. Fox (eleven pages); an extract from a book entitled *The Future of the Law* (1964) by David Yardley (seven pages); from the Archbishop of Canterbury, Dr William Temple's (1934) address 'The Ethics of Penal Action' (almost the whole); twelve pages containing extracts from the Gladstone Committee of 1895 and the Departmental Committee on Persistent Offenders of 1932; a document describing the use of 'Indeterminate sentences in the English penal system' by the Home Office; a bulky collection of papers from the Departmental Committee on Criminal Statistics 'dealing with matters of general importance'; another no less bulky assemblage of twenty-one papers, speeches, rules, articles, book reviews, etc. And the net seemed to be getting wider and wider: two photocopies of papers were circulated, one by the noted criminal lawyer Professor Johannes Andenaes of Oslo on 'Punishment and the problem of general prevention', another by Professor Eryl Hall Williams on 'Must criminal justice be either punitive or preventive?' – both of which had been read at a Congress in Montreal; quite an extended list of books and pamphlets, which members were recommended to read, found its appropriate place amongst the parcels of materials made available to the commission by the secretariat. At the same time several meetings were devoted to 'taking evidence' from a group of distinguished experts. Thus, for instance, Mr Justice Lawton (as he then was) kindly agreed to share with the committee his views on the expected responses of the criminal law towards crime; Dr Nigel Walker spoke on the nature and functions of punishment; Professor W.H. Sprott gave evidence on social aspects of crime and the principal investigations into them; Sir Aubrey Lewis discussed psychiatry and criminal law; Dr Manuel López-Rey gave his views on the English prison system. Each of them also obliged the commission by presenting its members with, quite often extensive, memoranda relating to what they proposed to say or to discuss.

Visits to penal institutions, it is widely acknowledged, are under any circumstances of limited value. They can, however, shed some useful and revealing light if the investigative body knows what it wants to find out; if its members are well prepared in advance; if they have already made some notable progress in their connected inquiries. If they visit the institutions they should not, as a general rule, do it singly but as a committee so as to elicit wider and more diversified views. Last but not least, they should be accompanied by a particularly well-qualified secretary, keeping a precise and detailed record. None of these essential requirements was observed, and when one looks at the table recording the visits undertaken, one has the impression of someone going to a concert which has been selected to satisfy his or her own curiosity and leaving it at that. No wonder that the copious records of the Commission do not contain a single major document which summarizes the views and the experiences of the Commission as a whole about the structure, organization and functioning of the prison system, its strengths, its weaknesses, and its most acute needs for improvement and subsequent development. From time to time the committee devoted part of its regular meetings to exchanging views in agreement or disagreement about a central theme of their remit. They were usually aptly summarized by the Secretary in a page or two and their fatuity and pretentiousness were embarrassing. I could not help casting my mind back to the Royal Commission on Capital Punishment, hardly believing that I found myself in the same country and within such a short period of time.

On a collision course with the Home Office

I can be much more brief about the other two committees. First, they were, from the point of view of the objectives of the Commission as a whole, much less important. Second, they exhibited similar failings in their approach and in their deliberations. One dealt with 'Treatment of Young Offenders' and the second with 'Aspects of Treatment of Adult Offenders'. The subjects were more tangible but it is not clear, and it had never been made convincingly clear, why they and not several other topics had been selected for close scrutiny by the Commission. And they were still immensely wide.

The deadly blow that these two committees had to suffer came this time not from their own performance (it was still a little too early to pass a final verdict on it) but from an unexpected and yet very potent quarter – the Home Office itself. On 26 July 1965 Lady Adrian, a leading and highly respected member of the Commission, wrote a letter to Lord Amory, the last passage of which read as follows:

> There is one other point I meant to ask you about – I believe that last autumn and again in January you were assured by the Home Secretary that the Commission would be kept informed of the

Government's thinking on proposed reforms. Have we in fact been given any idea of their thinking . . . If not, ought we to remind the Home Secretary of this promise in his letter to you on January 12th to 'see that the Commission are informed at the earliest possible stage of our legislative proposals'?

The Chairman must have given an unsatisfactory answer to this pertinent question (I cannot find a copy) because a month later (25 August 1965) Lady Adrian felt compelled to comment in this way:

> As to the Home Secretary's undertaking to keep us informed, I cannot feel that the circulation, a bare two weeks before publication and in the middle of August, of a summary of the Government's proposal in the White Paper on Young Offenders really amounts to keeping the Commission informed of their thinking about legislative reforms. Further it is clear, from an article in *The Observer* only two days later, that much of the information in the summary was already available to the political correspondent of that paper . . . It still seems very likely, in view of Lord Stonham's somewhat vague reply [in the House of Lords], that this Commission will be put in a similar position with regard to other proposed reforms, such as those concerning sentencing and parole. I feel, therefore, that the whole matter ought to be discussed by the Commission at its next meeting on October 8th . . . I continue to be very doubtful about the wisdom of the Commission undertaking work on proposals for the solution of complex problems in such circumstances.

A crucial piece of information affecting the work of the Commission should not have been imparted by a member to the Chairman. It was the latter (or the Secretary) who should have made it known in good time to all the members. Once appraised of it (Lady Adrian's letter was circulated) the decision of the Commission was that the Chairman, as a matter of urgency, should get in touch with the Home Secretary, to ask for clarification and report back to the Commission as soon as possible. This started another painful and humiliating episode in the tormented existence of the unfortunate commission. Sir Frank Soskice (afterwards Lord Stow Hill) was then the Home Secretary in Harold Wilson's second administration. He was ineffective, indecisive, suspicious to the point of being afraid of his own shadow. I met him on two or perhaps three brief occasions but these characteristics were so transparent that longer periods of observation were unnecessary. The description of him by Lord Jenkins is rather drastic but I am afraid that it is totally faultless. He was of Russian origin and his father had been close to Kerenski, being his trusted Secretary. It is perhaps from both of them that Sir Frank Soskice inherited some of his indecisiveness. Lord Jenkins, with a touch of too visible snobbishness, did acknowledge that Soskice 'appeared entirely English'.[8] The fact stands out that Sir Frank Soskice must rank as one of the worst Home Secretaries the Labour Party has bestowed upon the United Kingdom in the past sixty years. I can understand why it might be said that he was no worse than Lord Brooke. I am inclined however to give a higher grade to the latter. He was in many ways much better put together than Soskice. And there was always Baroness Brooke to pep him up.

The discussions and exchange of views between the Home Secretary and the Chairman of the Commission provided a perfect reflection of Soskice's characteristics. What emerged in the end was an intolerable impasse. The government would proceed with promoting one or two Bills on matters which the committees had started to inquire into. Indeed, there was no guarantee that the government would refrain from a larger legislative programme in the penal sphere before the commission had reported. The Home Secretary said he would fully understand if, in the circumstances, we were to abandon the agenda of the two sub-committees. He would have nothing against the Commission tackling another subject and the field of 'Adult Imprisonment and Alternatives Thereto' was singled out. The Chairman went out of his way to reassure the Home Secretary that 'we are giving consideration to the question as to what notification to potential witnesses may be required as a result of this change of sequence'. 'We may need', he added, 'your help in this matter and if we do I will, if I may, write to you again.' The Home Secretary certainly did not wish to put a nail in the Royal Commission's coffin, but he had certainly made this event more likely to happen when he expressed his view 'that the Commission shall proceed with the fundamental and comprehensive review which it was appointed to undertake'.

In a move which could be described as self-destructive, the Chairman and those who rallied behind him agreed to give priority to 'The Treatment of Adult Offenders and in particular to the Prison System'. A detailed note (1 February 1965) from the Secretary followed, and this was followed up again by the Commission. This, in its turn, was supplemented by a list of several problems which needed to be inquired into in order to produce a report on the 'Alternatives to Imprisonment'. Even the most cursory look at these documents would convince anyone that this was a formidably complex task. To the 'Criminological Encyclopaedia' there had now been added a 'Penological' one. Another gargantuan edifice built on dissolving sand was in the offing.

---

8 See Roy Jenkins, *A Life at the Centre* (1991), p. 175. But note that he also said several personable and very amiable things about Lord Stow Hill as a human being.

Moving towards disintegration

In his letter to the Home Secretary the Chairman at last alluded to the crisis in delicate but revealing terms:

> Some of our members still feel some doubts whether a period of major active legislation is an opportune one for conducting the kind of assessment and philosophical appreciation envisaged in our terms of reference. In the light, however, of the opinions you have expressed and the request you have made to us, the Commission have decided to proceed with our task. Those to whose reservations I have referred hope that any misgivings they may feel may be allayed in the course of our work.

I do not know from which sources the Chairman derived his benign optimism. As a member of the House of Lords he surely must have been aware of a brief but pointed exchange of views which took place in the Lords when Lord Brentford wanted to know 'whether the two White Papers, *The Child, the Family and the Young Offender* and *The Adult Offender*, are being submitted to the Royal Commission for its consideration?' And that, after having heard a totally unsatisfactory answer from Lord Stonham (Minister of State at the Home Office), Lord Brentford had persisted: 'is it not extraordinary that the Government have not asked for the views of the Royal Commission on the contents of these two Reports which, as the noble Lord has said, have been made quite independently?'[9]

All indications pointed in the opposite direction. At some stage suggestions were made that a vice-chairman should be appointed. This was so inimical to the very concept of a Royal Commission and to the role of Chairman that reluctantly I felt it necessary to present a brief paper recording my definitive opposition. The proposal was abandoned, but the fact that it was put forward at all was significant. Another stage was reached when, what might perhaps be described as 'the ticking away of time', began to make an impact. For how long did we have to meet, to read, to listen, to journey until we finally crown all our travail with a worthwhile report? The Commission acknowledged that it 'was receiving a great deal of written evidence much of which was unsupported opinion and of little value. This mass of evidence was at present tending to control the Commission's pattern of work, and members felt that the Commission should take more initiatives in directing its own progress.'[10] And after this salutary comment came the inevitable: 'It

---

9 See 'Royal Commission and Penal Reform', Question asked by Viscount Brentford, *Parl. Debates*, HL, vol. 272, cols 965–8, 15 February 1966.
10 From the strictly administrative point of view (or, as the Secretary has described it, 'A number of small points mainly affecting domestic administration') this would be smoothly

was, on the other hand, pointed out that the phase of receiving and considering written evidence was probably inescapable and that the bulk of this evidence should have been received by the end of the year.' But for how long should the Commission sit?

> Some members thought that a definite term, say of two or three years, should be set to the Commission's work, and that the Commission should be prepared to divide its forces to enable it to work within this time limit. Other members doubted whether it would be possible to report on the whole of the very wide terms of reference in less than five years.

It was left at that, but I distinctly remember how shocked several of the members had been when confronted with the latter, much more realistic estimate.

I was surprised to receive one day a letter from the Chairman expressing the hope that in view of my 'vast experience' I would agree to address the Commission on its future work. It was a nice letter but it was a letter dispatched very late in the day. I felt, however, that it was my duty to accept this embarrassing invitation. If I can remember correctly I had asked in advance that this meeting (or part of it) should take place in private, that is without the secretariat being present, and that I should be allowed to deliver it orally without presenting a written statement. My diagnosis and prognosis could be summed up in a few sentences. From the very start the chances for the Commission to accomplish the task assigned to it were very slender indeed. Since then, because of the wrong directions taken by the Commission, coupled with an unfavourable (though fully understandable) turn of events in the Home Office, even these very slender chances had faded away. A speedy and radical extinction of the Commission was now the only viable option. Not to follow this course of action would foster confusion and embarrassment to everybody concerned and, more importantly, would have an adverse and frustrating effect on penal progress itself. My deep regret and sadness

---

solved. We were informed that the Stationery Office would supply duplicating paper in six primary colours, viz., White, Pink, Green, Orange, Blue and Yellow. The Commission accepted the Secretary's proposal to allot the colours as follows: White: Commission Minutes and Agenda Notes, Evidence; Pink: Sentencing Minutes, Notes and Agenda; Blue: Concepts and Purposes Minutes, Notes and Agenda; Green: Treatment – ditto; Yellow: Research Minutes, Notes and Agenda; Orange: Spare [an alternative is to allocate the colour to the covering sheet to pieces of evidence]. The Secretary of the Commission Mr A.J.E. Brennan (the future Head of the Criminal Department of the Home Office) worked hard and patiently to make the Commission a success. His role was extremely delicate and often could not fail to be painful and unrewarding. Yet his demeanour throughout was dignified and courteous.

while I was saying all this must have been very visible, because throughout my statement, which lasted forty-five minutes, irreproachable courtesy and full consideration was shown to me by all present. There was a feeling that we were coming to the end of the road or at least the parting of the ways.

The need to 'revise' Lord Windlesham's account of how the end came about

I hesitate to disagree with Lord Windlesham because I have found his account of recent penal policy and legislation highly informative and reliable.[11] Nevertheless it is necessary to correct his account of how the dissolution of the Royal Commission on the Penal System came about. He first asserts that Barbara Wootton and I were of the opinion that 'any thorough re-examination of the concepts and purposes underlying the punishment and treatment of offenders in the light of modern knowledge of crime and its causes was worthless without systematic research, in doing field-work by qualified staff, taking anything up to four years to complete'.[12] I can speak only for myself and I can briefly dispose of his remarks by repeating that I was against the re-examination of 'the concepts and purposes' from the very start and that therefore the amount and quality of research needed with respect to this particular topic was not a question which even entered my mind. I have also been known to hold the view that a great number of very important penological developments could be evolved and put into practice or rejected on the basis of common sense and experience without the need for research. But, of course, a commission composed largely of non-professionals, expected to review critically the vast field of penal legislation and practice, should have at its disposal a research centre of high quality to illuminate as far as possible through empirical studies the many dark corners of the enforcement of criminal law. In this respect, as I pointed out, the commission was not at all well served.[13]

To pass to a more important point. According to Lord Windlesham, 'Professor Radzinowicz and Barbara Wootton, both strong characters unaccustomed to taking no for an answer', were the two figures leading to an irretrievable situation. It is true that I was the first to sound the alarm that we were going nowhere; that in addition to our suicidal terms of reference we were becoming increasingly handicapped by a Chairman (a very kind, conscientious and publicly minded man) who was losing his grip; that we were a

---

11 Lord Windlesham, *Responses to Crime* (1981), vol. 1, and *Responses to Crime: Penal Policy in the Making* (1993), vol. 2.
12 *Ibid.*, vol. 2, p. 101.
13 Leon Radzinowicz, *Criminology and the Climate of Social Responsibility* (1964), pp. 25–6.

much too numerous body (sixteen members), with a few who, despite being well intentioned and dedicated, were overwhelmed by the task; that the Home Office increasingly regarded the Commission as a garrulous assemblage of people, the goodness of their intentions being more than matched by their incongruity. Lady Wootton, a respected friend of mine, like a few other members of the Commission, was at first reluctant to draw appropriate conclusions from the situation.

For a Labour government to dissolve a Royal Commission set up by a Conservative government (or vice versa) is a move which should be avoided as far as possible, and in this instance several members of the Commission had long and devoted affiliations with the Labour Party. The two members who were first to reach a conclusion similar to mine, although a little later, were Dr Mortimer and Lady Adrian. I was greatly reassured and encouraged when two people of this calibre and prestige joined me. Still later, Beatrice Serota (afterwards Baroness Serota of Hampstead), Baroness Wootton of Abinger and Professor T.C.N. Gibbens joined us. We dissenters would sometimes meet at my suggestion either at lunch or for a drink at Brown's Hotel (not a bad place to meet) on the days of the Commission's meeting. At some stage I proposed that Dr Mortimer, the Bishop of Exeter, should be asked to prepare a memorandum which would express our views and propose the dissolution of the Commission. This was agreed and so was the suggestion that I should help Dr Mortimer, if necessary.

I put him up in Trinity for the weekend and we had an agreeable time together. I had taken to him almost at once when we had met at the Advisory Council many years earlier. He was rather remote and withdrawn and lacked an easily communicated kind of warmth. But he was a man of deep and well-matured convictions. He was impatient, impatient I suspect with himself, but also with the world at large. He was a tough realist, not wedded to the ideas or dreams of an uninterrupted progress in human and social affairs, but quite to the contrary someone who acknowledged the inevitability of dark and long periods of regression. This, however, in no way weakened his belief in and resolve to promote gradual changes. He hated pomposity of phraseology in any form and under any circumstances. He was precise and concise. I was very proud that over many years together on the Advisory Council and at the critical phases of the Royal Commission we happened to see eye to eye on virtually all the problems.[14]

He was a superb draftsman and my role was substantially reduced. The statement, accepted by our group without any changes, was forwarded to the Chairman and put at the disposal of all the members to be considered at our

---

14 See the authoritative note about Dr Mortimer by J.R. Porter in the *Dictionary of National Biography 1971–80* (1986), pp. 595–6, and the obituary notice in *The Times* (13 September 1976).

next meeting (Tuesday, 1 March 1966). What follows is the text of the document:

> The Royal Commission was appointed with the widest terms of reference, to review the whole penal system, the concepts and purposes of punishment, the causes of crime, the methods of punishment available to the courts, the sentencing policy of the courts, the recruitment and administration of the prison services and so on. The terms of reference in fact are:
>
> 'In the light of modern knowledge of crime, and its causes and of modern penal practice here and abroad to re-examine the concepts and purposes which should underlie the punishment and treatment of offenders in England and Wales; to report on how far they are realised by the penalties and methods of treatment available to the courts, and whether any changes in these, or in the arrangements and responsibility for selecting the sentences to be imposed on particular offenders, are desirable; to review the work of the services and institutions dealing with offenders, and the responsibility for their administration: and to make recommendations.'
>
> This means that the Royal Commission is expected to produce the kind of report which might have come from a 19th century Commission, that is, a comprehensive review, in great depth, of the whole penal system and the firm outline or blueprint of the direction in which it should move in the next fifty years. Such an expectation is dangerous. It could be an excuse for delay in putting into effect certain urgent reforms for which there is widespread support. 'Let us wait until the Royal Commission reports.' It could sustain the dangerous illusion that there is a comprehensive solution to the problem of crime, waiting round the corner, for the Royal Commission to find and enunciate.
>
> We are convinced that this is an illusion. The comprehensive solution – if indeed there is one at all – will only be reached as a result of long, painstaking and expertly-guided research and experiment. This is not the kind of task which any Royal Commission, constituted as this is, or indeed constituted in any way, is a suitable body to undertake. Meanwhile there are certain reforms or experiments which the Government feels it is urgent to put into effect at the earliest possible moment, without waiting for the report of the Royal Commission. The Government has issued two White Papers: one on juvenile and one on adult offenders. These two papers cover a substantial part of the field which the Royal Commission has been asked to investigate.
>
> We welcome the initiative the Government has taken in these matters. It is an initiative which we believe reflects a widespread

agreement in the country as to the general principles which should govern the development of the penal system in England and Wales. We are in no position to express any opinion about the wisdom of the ways in which these principles are applied in the two White Papers: for we have not been able to give them adequate consideration. Nor can we possibly produce a report, in any way commensurate with our terms of reference, before at least one of the Bills contemplated in the two White Papers is drafted or indeed actually before Parliament. We have considered the possibility of issuing an interim report dealing only with the two White Papers, and giving our opinion on their specific proposals. But for the Royal Commission, charged to review the whole field, to isolate one or two subjects and to deal with them outside the general context of the penal system is difficult and might be misleading.

We are convinced that in these days of rapid and urgently needed changes in the penal system the necessarily somewhat leisurely approach of a Royal Commission, composed of persons heavily engaged in other occupations and unable to devote more than a small portion of their time to the work of the Commission, is unsuitable. What is needed is not a slow deliberate survey of the field by a body which reports its conclusions at an arbitrarily chosen moment. For by then both the penal system itself and the society in which it operates will have changed. What is needed is a continuous survey of the penal system by a body in continuous existence.

We therefore recommend that the Royal Commission be discharged and that there should be constituted a permanent Advisory Council to the Home Office on the penal system. It should be the duty of this Council to keep the penal system in all its aspects under continuous review. It should be empowered to investigate any part of the field as and when it thinks fit, without waiting, as the old Advisory Council for the Treatment of Offenders had to, for specific matters to be referred to it by the Home Secretary. It would at all times be at the disposal of the Home Secretary to undertake any task which he might wish to lay upon it.

The Council which we envisage would be an independent body of not more than 10 or 12 persons of considerable standing in the country. They would not be, or not all of them would be, experts in the criminological field, for we recognise the value, which Royal Commissions have, of bringing in 'lay' opinion on matters of great social importance. The duty of the Council would be to hold the penal system under continuous review, to order enquiries or research into particular parts of the field and to co-ordinate the various enquiries and researches which are going on at any one time. We recommend that this strongly constituted Advisory Council should have, working under it, a number of sub-committees, perhaps permanent, perhaps *ad hoc*, dealing with specific parts of the field, e.g., the Police (i.e., enforcement of law), Treatment in Custody, Probation and After-care, Sentencing Policy and Authority and so on. These sub-committees should be composed of experts in their own field. Their purpose would be to give to the Advisory Council the best, most expert, advice available on whatever part of the field the Advisory Council thought investigation and possible changes was needed, or to which the Home Secretary had drawn the Council's attention.

It is essential, if this Council is to do its work adequately, that it be supplied with a strong secretariat and that sufficient funds are put at its disposal. We have become more and more aware that, in spite of many experiments and changes which have been introduced in recent years at home and abroad, there has been remarkably little expert research into their results and efficiency. So much of the evidence we have received relies on opinions and hopes of what any particular new experiment will achieve or is achieving. We therefore recommend that in every experiment and change to be made in the penal system there should be included in-built machinery for evaluating its efficacy. It should be the duty of the Advisory Council to see that in every case such machinery is created and the results of the research in due course evaluated.

The Royal Commission has been at work for 18 months. Its members have learnt much. But our work has convinced us that the cause of penal reform and of the diminution of crime in England and Wales should be best served by the creation, as soon as possible, of the Advisory Council which we have suggested.

The brief exchange of views which followed revealed again a deep split in the Commission. A vote was taken. Six members of the Royal Commission tendered their resignation.[15] Two subsequently resigned on the grounds that a Commission thus reduced would not be able to discharge its task.[16] Eight members wished to continue and shortly afterwards the chairman expressed the hope that those who had resigned would be replaced.[17] This was confirmed by Roy Jenkins, who returned to the Home Office in 1974 and

---

15 As confirmed by Mr Roy Jenkins in response to a question raised by Mr T.L. Iremonger, the six who resigned were Lady Adrian, Professor T.C.N. Gibbens, Bishop of Exeter, Professor Leon Radzinowicz, Mrs Beatrice Serota and Baroness Wootton of Abinger.
16 The two who subsequently resigned were the Hon. Silva Fletcher-Moulton and Mrs Eliot Warburton, JP.
17 The eight who did not resign were the Chairman, Rt Hon. Viscount Amory, Mr David Bassett, Hon. Mr Justice Edmund Davies, Mr T.L. Iremonger, MP, Mr R.E. Millard, LLB, Professor J.N. Morris, Mr S.C. Silken, QC, MP and Rt. Hon. Lord Wheatley.

remained there until 1976.[18] It was a sombre day when we all assembled in Room 240 of the Home Office (if my memory does not mislead me), the two groups sitting separately in complete silence and listening to a few amiable words uttered by the Home Secretary, who registered his deep regret.

The final lesson

On 27 April 1966 the Prime Minister, Harold Wilson, rose in the Commons to announce that the Queen on his recommendation had approved the dissolution of the Royal Commission on the Penal System in England and Wales. The brief debate which followed revealed some latent but fundamental differences and some incorrect affirmations. It was not correct to state that 'no fundamental differences within the Commission on philosophy and principles have manifested themselves' (Mr Wilson), though it was correct to observe that the members who resigned

> felt increasingly that the time is not opportune for a single review of the penal system, leading to a comprehensive report, which could set the direction for a generation.

It was also fair to point out that perhaps it was the fault of both the Conservative and Labour administrations to have given birth to the Commission.

> One of the fundamental questions here is whether, looking back on it, we were not all wrong — it was the present government who appointed the Royal Commission, but we all commented on the terms of reference — in thinking that, in this field, what was wanted was a once-for-all look, as it is the manner of Royal Commissions, at something which is changing so rapidly and whether, perhaps, we were not all wrong as well, all of us, in feeling that a Commission could do a job with such wide and far-reaching terms of reference.

In spite of all the differences, Mr Wilson stated, the government and both sides of the Commission 'are in agreement that the permanent machinery of government should now be strengthened by the establishment of a body exercising a continuous review of development in the penal field'. And he promised that a further announcement, giving the membership and terms of reference of a new Advisory Council, would be made as soon as possible. This, however, was not the view of the Opposition. On its behalf Edward Heath emphasized that the dissolution of the Commission in itself 'is a

---

18 See Written Answer, 'Royal Commission on the Penal System', *Parl. Debates*, HC, vol. 727, col. 74, 4 May 1966. It is surprising that the 'Recidivist Home Secretary', to use his own designation, made no reference whatsoever to the Commission in his autobiography.

THE DEATH OF A ROYAL COMMISSION

matter for widespread regret' and he asked whether 'it would not have been possible to avert quite such a serious situation developing if, after the resignation of the six members, the Prime Minister or the Home Secretary had said firmly that they would appoint others to take their place thus enabling the Royal Commission to continue?'[19] This remained an unanswered question simply because the right decision to the contrary had been taken.

For me, who had spent several years of my life in studying the British Blue Books, who had derived so much profit from them and developed so deep a respect for this so peculiarly English instrument of government, this was an exceptionally bitter experience. I remember having tried at the time to ascertain whether there were any precedents for dissolving a Royal Commission in the past and I had reached a pretty firm, though not definitive, conclusion that there was none. The *Report of the Departmental Committee on the Procedure of Royal Commissions* examined many aspects of the work of such bodies big and small, but the possibility of the dissolution of a Royal Commission had not even been mentioned.[20] The two volumes of Alpheus Todd, which contain so much information on English Commissions of Inquiry of one kind or another, are equally silent on such a possibility.[21] Similar absence is noticeable amongst modern writers such as Hugh McDowall Clokie and J. William Robinson; K.C. Wheare; and the edited collection by Richard A. Chapman.[22] This saddened me still further.

But for those who are willing to learn by experience, however painful it turns out to be, a lesson had emerged that could no longer be rebutted. The complexity and the relativity of penal matters in our type of society preclude designs of appraisal and reformulation conceived on so vast and all-embracing scale. Thus the conclusion reached by this chapter may in some ways be regarded as confirming the message of Chapter 13. As such it should acquire a permanent place in the penal history of Britain.[23]

---

19 See 'Royal Commission on the Penal System (Dissolution)', *Parl. Debates*, HC, vol. 729, cols 703–8, 27 April 1966.
20 Cd 5235 (1910), known as the Balfour Report.
21 See Alpheus Todd, *On Parliamentary Government in England*, 2 vols (Walpole edn, 1892).
22 Royal Commissions of Inquiry: *The Significance of Investigation in British Politics* (1937); *Government by Committee: An Essay on the British Constitution* (1955); *The Role of Commissions in Policy-Making* (1973).
23 There are however some who are not convinced. See the open letter to *The Times* (3 July 1996) from Professor Seán McConville and others under the title 'Penal Philosophy for the 21st Century', followed by a response from Professor Nigel Walker, 'Dubious Value of Royal Commissions', *The Times* (10 June 1996), in which he referred to the signatories as 'naïve'. This seems to be an inappropriate characterization of Lord Allen of Abbeydale and several other signatories of great experience in penal matters. It should also be pointed out that Lord Bingham and Lord Woolf seem to favour a Royal Commission.

15

SEEKING INTERNATIONAL SOLUTIONS

At some stage the Committee of Management of the Cambridge Department of Criminal Science, which preceded the establishment of the Institute of Criminology, asked me whether I would be interested in undertaking a study, the purpose of which would be to retrace the early stages of international collaboration in criminal matters and to review some of the controversial issues that might have emerged. I welcomed this invitation with enthusiasm. From the very beginning of my criminological studies I had developed a vivid interest in the comparative aspects of the subject, both theoretical and practical. As the years passed by my interest became more intense and more widely spread. The windows in Poland, from whence one could cast one's eye on the world at large, were rather narrow. And yet, like many other young men and women of my generation, I developed a natural fascination for Western European history and culture. Once I left Poland my studies at the Sorbonne, Geneva and Rome brought me into direct contact with the currents and cross-currents of penological thought and of many other subjects. This, in its turn, prompted me to undertake studies on the spot in countries where such ferments were at their height. I was fortunate to be endowed with some linguistic gifts and thus was able to read and discuss matters in five foreign languages (in addition to Polish) – an immense advantage, but alas something I can no longer do. I was also fortunate in having the financial independence to indulge in many scholarly pursuits in an unrestricted atmosphere, going, staying, and doing whatsoever I wished to do. Conscious of this privilege, I tried to make maximum use of my time. Comparative studies in criminal science can be disappointing or tedious, but they can also considerably help to open many closed doors. Undoubtedly they widen one's perspective enormously.

Out of my inquiries came the article 'International collaboration in criminal science', which was accepted for the *Law Quarterly Review*, subsequently published with some changes in the *Toronto Law Review*, and finally as a chapter in *The Modern Approach to Criminal Law*.[1] It was, as far as I know, the first attempt, in English legal literature or abroad, to retrace the evolution of the topic within its comparative context. It is perhaps because of this that the editors of the two periodicals so warmly welcomed the piece, although it was written in less than perfect English and the material was badly organized. Since then I have deepened my knowledge of the subject and have had the advantage of learning more about it through my involvement in comparative work in various international settings.

The big issue out of the way

My essential view, which it took me some time to formulate, was quite simple and can be, I hope, unpretentiously expressed. It is true that differences between the systems of criminal justice in force in various countries, differences which at first seem substantial, and even unbridgeable, are often found on deeper investigation to be much less important than initially suspected. Indeed, when embarking upon comparisons there is nothing more misleading than to insist only on noting the differences. Nevertheless differences do exist. Many of them are so deeply embedded that a complete international unification (which in practice would have to be equivalent to the adoption of one code of criminal law, one code of criminal procedure, and identical systems of criminal justice administration) has no chance of being brought into being in any foreseeable future. Such a universal system would be nothing but an artificial, tottering construction.

There were, however, scholars of undisputed reputation who had raised their voices in favour of such an ultimate goal and were confident of it becoming a reality. Thus Baron Raffaele Garofalo, a High Court judge and next to Enrico Ferri the most distinguished exponent of the positivist school, ended his memorable treatise *Criminology* with an appendix entitled 'Outline of principles suggested as a basis for an international penal code'. In this he formulated principles of criminal liability and enumerated the main categories of offenders, a system of penalties to be adopted to combat crime, and some basic rules for bringing offenders to justice.[2] Franz von Liszt, the leading authority on criminal science at the end of the nineteenth century and the beginning of the twentieth century, in his introduction to two massive

---

1 See Leon Radzinowicz, 'International Collaboration in Criminal Science', *Law Quarterly Review*, vol. 58 (1942), pp. 110–39; also in *University of Toronto Law Review*, vol. 4 (1942), pp. 307–37; and in L. Radzinowicz and J.W.C. Turner (eds) *The Modern Approach to Criminal Law* (vol. 4 of *English Studies in Criminal Science*) (1945), pp. 467–97.
2 See Raffaele Garofalo, *Criminology*, pp. 405–16 (1st Italian edn, 1885; 2nd edn, 1891; French edn, 1905); translated into English and published in *Modern American Criminal Science Series* (1914; reprinted 1968).

volumes surveying the criminal legislation of the major European countries, eloquently proposed that it was 'possible and often desirable to establish unified general principles and even a unification of criminal legislation as a whole'.[3] But it is only fair to observe that he supported this far-reaching conclusion primarily by limiting his claim to the general part of criminal law and with respect to countries such as France, Germany, Austria and the Netherlands. Also he made no reference to criminal procedure, to the penal system, and to the administration of criminal justice as a whole.

Professor Maurice Travers, the author of a monumental five-volume opus on international penal law, had a similar, perhaps even bolder, vision. His argument was rather subtle. International codification of the civil and commercial law, he maintained, presented formidable intrinsic difficulties because harsh and persistent competition between the powerful economic interests of different countries could not be avoided. In contrast, in the criminal field rivalry between states did not exist: 'seule subsiste l'identité des intérêts. Tous pays a avantage à voir diminuer la criminalité dans les autres'.[4] An international integration of certain efforts could undoubtedly have a beneficial effect on making the commission of some kinds of criminal activities much more difficult. Extradition treaties or preventive measures against terrorism were the best known and rather elementary examples, but problems involved in unification proper were infinitely more complex.

In this sphere, as in several others pertaining to international relations, many political scientists and well-intentioned politicians and leaders of public opinion have regularly tended to underestimate the static, but formidable, impact of what – in the absence of a more appropriate definition – I will call the 'national component'. I refer to the fervent desire to assert and preserve a separate cultural identity, and the not infrequent and quite virulent animosity towards neighbours. The establishment of an international, or even of a truly unified regional, construct is neither feasible nor desirable. However, the rejection of the radical programme should not mean that other modalities of penal collaboration should not be energetically pursued. Yet one should constantly be aware that at every stage formidable restraints of an historical, political and social nature will be encountered. And this warning applies even to issues which, in a too light-hearted manner, are disposed of as being of a purely 'technical' nature.

Let me give what to my mind is an illuminating example. For years

---

3   See Franz von Liszt, introduction to *Die Strafgesetzgebung der Gegenwart in Rechtsvergleichender Darstellung* (1895), vol. 1, pp. xxiv–xxv.
4   See Maurice Travers, 'Les effets internationaux des jugements répressifs', in *Académie de Droit International*, Recueil des Cours (1924), III, vol. 4 (Paris, 1925), p. 465.

International Institute of Statistics, helped by a group of outstanding statisticians in charge of criminal statistics in several leading countries of Europe, tried to standardize definitions of crimes so as to make comparisons of the incidence and trends of crime meaningful. At that time it was widely felt that such comparisons might play a major role in ascertaining the causes of criminality and its fluctuations. The *Proceedings* of the Institute's congresses in Brussels (1853), Paris (1855), Vienna (1857), London (1860) and Florence (1866) bear witness to the importance attached to the subject, and yet no tangible results were forthcoming. Nevertheless these efforts were never totally abandoned. The topic was put on the agenda of the International Penal and Penitentiary Commission at its congress in Prague (1930) and a recommendation was adopted that it should be taken up by a 'Mixed Committee' composed of members of the International Statistical Institute and the Commission. The committee presented two documents which were to serve as a basis for international unification of criminal statistics. In the end those dedicated and highly competent promoters had to content themselves with one criminal entity, the crime of murder, and even then several substantial reservations and stern warnings had been attached to the 'unifying' text. Parallel to these disappointing developments steps had been taken to unify penitentiary statistics, but here also no tangible results can be recorded.

Yet there are abundant instances where crime policies in different countries have been grounded on identical penological principles. But a point of cardinal importance – much too often ignored in international comparative studies – is that it is essential not only to examine the origins of penal solutions and the way they are implemented, but also to try to explain the reasons why they fall into disuse. For example, the triumphant expansion of many types of security measures in Europe and beyond was soon followed by their virtual disappearance. What was baptized as progressive was soon chastised as regressive. I shall return to this significant point in Chapter 17. International comparative investigations, and indeed international collaboration in criminal matters, run the risk of being branded as naïve and misleading unless critical vigilance of the first order is meticulously observed at every stage of a projected inquiry.

In weighing up the pros and cons of international criminal integration I came close to endorsing the conclusion reached by the International Penal and Penitentiary Congress held in Prague in 1930, which while approving a progressive unification of certain general parts of criminal law nevertheless recommended realism and moderation. A citation of the kernel of this recommendation is an apposite way to end this section.

> L'éffort d'unification a pour limite le point où commence le risque d'enlever au droit pénal, dans les divers pays, les forces indispens-

ables qui lui viennent du dévoloppement historique de chaque pays et des racines profondes qu'il a jetées dans le coeur du peuple.[5]

First steps towards penal co-operation

Imitations, mutations and cross-fertilization of all kinds of institutions and measures in response to crime can be traced in abundance throughout the world, and certainly with much more precision within the generally more homogeneous regional constellations. Such developments did not, of course, appear all at the same time or with similar aplomb. But there was effervescence enough to captivate the attention not only of scholars and administrators but also of social reformers, philanthropists, the press, indeed of public opinion in general. Penal history shows that there was a continued ferment of varying intensity, often preceded by invigorating hopes but also no less frequently followed by damping disappointments. The seeds go back to the middle of the nineteenth century,

The first international gathering took place in Germany, at Frankfurt am Main (28–30 September 1846). The event owed its origin to the initiative taken by the already noted (see pp. 53–54) Edouard Ducpétiaux, the well-known Belgian social and penal reformer, and to Whitworth Russell, the highly regarded English prison inspector. Professor C.J.A. Mittermaier of Heidelberg University, whose European reputation came close to that enjoyed half a century later by Von Liszt, was elected President. The second international congress followed closely on 20–3 September 1847; this time it was convened in Brussels. It was hoped that the third assembly would take place either in Switzerland or in the Netherlands in 1848. But 1848 was the year of the European 'spring' – a revolutionary awakening, not exactly the most propitious of seasons for penological explorations. A rather longish gap followed before the third congress was convened in Frankfurt on 14 September 1857.

I was fortunate to get hold of the *Proceedings* of all three congresses published in German and French, and I enjoyed reading the five volumes and making extensive photocopies of their contents, not as a record of more or less incongruous relics of a remote past. I owed this treat to the courtesy of the library of the Law School of Minnesota while I was there in 1977 as a Distinguished Professor in the recently established Chair in memory of the late Senator Hubert Humphrey.[6]

---

5 'The limit of the effort towards unification comes at that point where it starts to incur the risk of removing from the criminal law, in the various countries, the indispensable strengths which it derives from the historical development of each country and the deep roots the law has established in the heart of the people.' See *Proceedings of the International Penal and Penitentiary Congress of Prague* (1930), vol. 1b, p. 47.
6 See *Verhandlungen der ersten Versammlung für Gefängnisreform, etc.* (Frankfurt, 1847); Debats du Congrès Pénitentiaire (Brussels, 1847); Congrès International de Bienfaisance de Francfort-Sur-Le-Mein, Session de 1857 (Frankfurt, 1858).

The debate on how to handle 'political offenders' revealed differences of approach and solutions which have a strikingly modern ring. The perception that solitary confinement as the mode of enforcing imprisonment was a logical consequence of the classical school of criminal law was no less startling. And so was the proposal that recidivists sentenced to imprisonment who failed to be reformed and whose discharge would present a danger to society should be subjected to a 'supplément de détention' – not exceeding twice the length of the originally imposed sanction. This, it seemed to me, was one of the earliest anticipations of the 'double track' system (punishment and security measures) which some eighty years later made its triumphant entry into the leading criminal legislations of Europe.

In general, the scope of the proceedings was rather restricted and the exchange of views rather superficial. The self-satisfaction, not unknown in many of our contemporary international penological gatherings, was already there glaringly present. 'We believe', declared Whitworth Russell (at the 1847 Congress), 'that the experience gained in England with respect to prison reform . . . "est à peu près achevée" . . . and the solitary confinement which corresponds to the needs both of society and of the criminal himself . . . "mérite d'être adopté exclusivement et universellement".' This comforting statement, we are told, was met by the Congress with 'manifestations multipliées d'un assentiment général'.

The pioneering cycle had come to an end in 1857. Apparently on this last occasion Professor Mittermaier remarked that 'while he would like to see universal agreement upon penal matters, he entertained little hope that this could be achieved within a foreseeable future due to the wide differences of opinion expressed and cherished'. Professor Negley Teeters was inclined to attribute the lack of future initiatives to 'this note of pessimism from one of Europe's outstanding students of penal affairs'.[7] I hesitate to accept this judgement. The wider environment, national and international, was simply not yet ripe for the movement of international collaboration in penal matters to take root, to develop and to be accepted. Yet it was bound to come.

It was not until later in the nineteenth century that a change in attitude towards the penal system occurred in conjunction with changes in many other social developments. The growing vision of the state assuming new responsibilities and powers in many sectors of social life; the progress of commerce between nations, bringing them closer to each other; more extensive travel and spreading of news; rising standards in education and in many other facets of civilization; a strong desire to be better informed about patterns of crime and a no less fervent hope that by some refined methods crime

---

7   We owe a debt to Professor Negley K. Teeters for a most useful reconstruction of these proceedings. See his 'The First International Penitentiary Congresses 1846–47–57', *Prison Journal*, vol. 26 (1946), pp. 190–210.

could be brought under better control; a firm resolve to ensure that advances in urbanization and industrialization should not be unduly threatened by anti-social elements, the perceived dangerous classes; the necessity to create a healthy, law-abiding workforce and to get to grips with inferior demographic stock as circumscribed by the precepts of Social Darwinism; the continued contrast provided by the regularity and universality of crime and the glaring limitations in the effectiveness of steps taken to control it revealed with increasing precision by criminal statistics and criminological studies.

These were some of the major factors which provided the spur and energy to deal with crime and punishment on a larger scale across frontiers: to throw reflective light upon the phenomenon of crime and its prevention and punishment and to plan proposals for legislative, judicial and administrative initiatives. And besides this there was an international growing desire which my old and respected friend, the late Marc Ancel, described in a noteworthy essay as the 'climat de curiosité, attention et de sympathie pour les institutions et les expériences étrangères'. And he quoted, with warm approval, Laboulaye, the founder of the Société de Législation Comparée who, in his speech opening the first Congress, observed that 'désormais chacun ressent le besoin de connaître la législation et les manières de vivre de ses voisins'.[8]

The first breakthrough into the field of international collaboration in criminal matters occurred in 1872 and it was the International Penitentiary Commission which became its full-blooded embodiment. But this commission also revealed certain grave, indeed almost chronic, shortcomings which seem inherent whenever these internationally orientated objectives are pursued in earnest. These features appear to me persuasive enough to reflect upon the commission at some length.

Governmental sponsorship of an international commission

I would be very hard pressed to cite another association of any kind which had been launched with more aplomb, lustre and vast expectations. In 1869 Count Vladimir Alexandrowitsch Sollohub ('a man of vigorous intellect and broad sympathies' – to quote Dr E.C. Wines), Director of the House of Correction and Industry in Moscow and President of the Commission for Penal Reform in Russia, published a paper in the annual report of the Prison Association of New York in which he submitted a proposal:

> to all who are interested in the future of prisons, to convene an international reunion of specialists ... who under the patronage of

---

8   See Marc Ancel, *Utilité et méthodes du droit comparé* (1971), p. 15.

their respective governments should be charged with the duty of giving penitentiary science its definitive principles.

The Reverend Dr Enoch Cobb Wines, a noted American social philanthropist and penal reformer, was very attracted by this idea and submitted it to the Prison Association of New York, of which he was the Secretary. After having failed to convince them he submitted the proposal again, but this time to the famous American Prison Congress held in Cincinnati in 1870, and there he obtained unanimous support. The congress passed a resolution affirming that the time had come when an international gathering might be convened and Dr Wines was invited to take charge of this mission. He could not have moved with greater energy and imagination.[9] He enlisted the interest of Rutherford B. Hayes and Ulysses S. Grant, successive Presidents of the United States of America, of the US Congress and of Hamilton Fisch, the Secretary of State. With an official introduction he crossed the Atlantic to Europe in 1871. He met with a most encouraging welcome and national committees were formed in almost every European country. The English committee was presided over by Sir Walter Crofton, the well-known reformer of the Irish prison system, who was asked to lay the foundations for a congress. The event took place on 3 July 1872 in the splendid Hall of the Middle Temple and was presided over by the influential Earl of Carnarvon.[10] Twenty-two states were officially represented. It was attended by a hundred official delegates and a further three hundred interested people. It lasted ten days and its *Proceedings* were published in 1872 and reissued in 1912.[11]

On closer scrutiny the *Proceedings* did not amount to much. It is true that there were many questions on the agenda which related to important aspects of penitentiary theory and practice. But the delegates responded with an uncoordinated exchange of views or experiences rather than exploring the topics in depth through a series of carefully prepared reports. The final text adopted unanimously by the congress, which followed a flamboyant lengthy statement presented by the American delegation, reads like an idealistic manifesto. It proclaimed the sacrosanct duty of states throughout the world

---

9 On the early stages of the International Penal and Penitentiary Commission see E.C. Wines, *The State of Prisons and Child-Saving Institutions in the Civilised World* (1880; reprinted 1968), pp. 49–56; C.D. Randall, *The Fourth International Prison Congress* (1891), pp. 33–4; Sir Evelyn Ruggles-Brise, *Prison Reform at Home and Abroad* (1924); Negley K. Teeters, *Deliberations of the International Penal and Penitentiary Congresses: Questions and Answers* (1949).

10 On Lord Carnarvon's role in Victorian penal history, interestingly portrayed, see S. McConville, *English Local Prisons 1860–1900: Next Only to Death* (1995), pp. 64–148.

11 See David Pears (ed.) *Prison and Reformatories at Home and Abroad – Being the Transactions of the International Penitentiary Congress held in London, July 3–13, 1878* (reprinted, HM Prison Maidstone, 1912).

to regard the principle of reformation as the primary and decisive aim of all kinds of punishment and in designing their penitentiary systems. There was hardly a reference to the formidable difficulties which such an approach would inevitably encounter because of the nature of crime and its threat to society, the characteristics of certain categories of criminals, the sceptical attitude of public opinion, and the frustrating, not to say dead weight, of opposing traditional forces. But it was this almost religiously conceived ameliorative creed which made this congress so memorable. It was, in many ways, the European replica of its predecessor, the famous Congress of Cincinnati, which amidst uncontrollable enthusiasm had laid down the premises for the implementation of a similar utopian vision. The leading lights of the Congress of London were united in their ultimate objective. They were not to be satisfied by a single congress, however significant it had proved to be. They aspired to an international movement through which important information could be exchanged and penal standards could everywhere be raised.

The response to this initiative was so spontaneous, so widely spread, so effectively set on its course under so high a patronage, that the speedy implementation of this aspiration had been regarded at first as a foregone conclusion. Yet subsequent events indicated disturbing shifts in attitude and resolve. Although the commission was established and started to function it took a further two decades before all the major states joined it. The stages in this process, as related by the commission itself, had frequently been embarrassing and painful.[12] Some of the governments suddenly turned against the establishment of the commission; some declared their adherence but soon afterwards withdrew it; while two states, at first opposed, later embraced it. As late as 1885 the commission was compelled to state, with dignity but also with sadness, that 'most of the great nations of Europe and America kept aloof'. It was only in 1895, following the Congress of Paris, that Britain and the United States – the two sponsoring states – joined the commission without any reservation. These equivocations and retardations were not a bureaucratic ploy but had a real significance as will be described a little later. In 1900 the commission consisted of official representatives of fifteen countries. On the eve of the First World War, in 1914, it included twenty-two countries, and on the eve of the Second World War, in 1939, the number had jumped to thirty-one.

A rapid indication of a few organizational details is needed. Once fully established the commission fixed itself up speedily, effectively and economically. Every country was represented in the commission by one or several delegates, but each delegation had one vote only. It was composed

---

12 See the account prepared by the Permanent Bureau of the Commission, 'Work and Activities of the International Penal and Penitentiary Commission 1872–1942', in *Recueil de Documents en Matière Pénale et Pénitentiaire*, vol. 10 (1942–3), pp. 61–90, at pp. 62–5.

exclusively of official delegates of the governments and as a general rule they were high functionaries of the criminal justice system or university professors. The judiciary was not part of it. The President of the commission was elected by this body at the end of each congress and the post was filled by one of the delegates of the country in which the next congress was to be held. There was one full-time highly qualified Secretary-General of the commission. A little later a bureau of the commission was formed and consisted, besides the President and the Secretary-General, of two additional members. In 1929, to give a formal expression to its wider range of concerns, the commission changed its name to the International Penal and Penitentiary Commission. Its budget was covered by an annual subscription paid by each member-state calculated according to the size of their respective populations. At a later stage permanent headquarters of the commission were established in Berne where the Secretary-General and his small staff were expected to reside. A centre of documentation and a library of the commission were steadily built up. The well-known publishing house of Staempfli & Cie of Berne served well the needs of the commission.

Its first task was the organization and the direction of its penal congresses and the publication of the *Proceedings*. Eventually the congresses were held at five-yearly intervals. Twelve such gatherings took place.[13] The preparation and the deliberations of the congresses followed a carefully thought out pattern which helped enormously to avoid overlapping and sharpened the focus on the issues to be examined. The agenda of each congress was divided into four sections, such as penal legislation, preventive measures, children and minors. A section would on the average contain between four and seven questions. A question would be usually covered by between seven and ten reports – thus leading to about two hundred reports. Each section had a chairman and every question had one or two rapporteurs. All questions discussed in every section would ultimately find their way to the meetings of the general assembly to be presented there and accompanied by carefully worded recommendations. A vigorous debate, with votes clearly recorded, took place.

The second activity was taken up much later, in the 1930s. It consisted of selecting a specific topic, entrusting it to a small group of experts, but with the commission by no means relinquishing its involvement, with a view to presenting a report, or a model, as the case may be. The end product was to be published and communicated to the member states with a recommendation to act upon it. There can be no better way to give a precise idea of this

---

13 London (1872), Stockholm (1878), Rome (1885), St Petersburg (1890), Paris (1895), Brussels (1900), Budapest (1905), Washington (1910), London (1925), Prague (1930), Berlin (1935) and The Hague (1940). All, except the *Proceedings* of the Washington Congress, were published in French.

SEEKING INTERNATIONAL SOLUTIONS

activity than to reproduce the titles under which initiatives made their appearance. Repatriation of foreign discharged prisoners; the setting up of juvenile courts; vocational training of prison officials and inter-state meetings of senior prison staff; preparation of a model draft of an extradition treaty; elaboration of a dossier for the scientific examination of prisoners to be used by centres of criminal biology and anthropology in penitentiary establishments; report on the treatment of habitual offenders; rules for drawing up criminal statistics, including a model for a general assimilation of criminal statistics for comparative purposes; a model for the definition of the crime of murder to be adopted in international numerical records of crime; a model for covering the essential items in penitentiary statistics; participation with other centres in those inquiries which attempted to regulate under the rule of law guarantees against abuses by prosecutorial organs of criminal justice in interrogations and in detention pending trial and similar protective measures of witnesses – against the use of violence and any other forms of physical or mental restraint; preparation of a set of standard minimum rules for the treatment of prisoners; launching of a survey describing penitentiary systems of twenty-two countries.[14]

The third undertaking was a regular publication at first called *Bulletin* and then under a more apt title *Recueil de documents en matière pénale et pénitentiaire*. It contained accounts of some of the most significant penological developments within the member states; of legislative and administrative texts; of articles by the leading members of the commission and its Secretary-General and of brief reviews of recent publications.

It is not an easy task to evaluate the impact of an international body of this rather unique type, brought into being in such extraordinary circumstances, prolonging its existence from the mid-Victorian period up to the First World War, resuming its activities with seemingly increased vigour in the years between the two wars, attempting to prevail as the leading internationally recognized centre at the conclusion of the Second World War, but soon afterwards suffering a deep humiliation and going out of existence for good.

With reference to the first activity, I do not know of any *Proceedings* of any congresses in the field of history, social or political sciences or comparative law which were superior to this aspect of the commission's performance. The prevailing tone, it is fair to say, was cautious, restricted, conservative, but by no means invariably favouring the status quo. I have been the lucky owner of the whole set of *Proceedings*, consisting (if I remember correctly) of no fewer than forty hefty volumes. At the risk of appearing inhuman I must confess to having read all of them and to have continued to consult separate volumes from time to time. Inevitably they vary in quality but unquestionably when

---

14 For the exact location of all these documents see the report of the commission quoted in note 12 above (p. 361), at pp. 83–8.

taken *in toto* they represent a unique record, drawn upon a vast comparative scale, of the evolution and dilemmas of criminal policy covering a vital period of its sixty years' history. They constitute material of the first order which should become an integral part of the scholarly and professional knowledge of anyone working in the field. The *Proceedings* of the many contemporary penal or criminological congresses bear no comparison to this achievement of the past. In addition, the separate publication of the resolutions adopted by the congresses is invaluable.[15]

The second activity sponsored by the commission was ingenious and fruitful, deserving a full mark of approval. It sprang from the growing realization that there is, and always will be, a cluster of important problems which call for special inquiries centred round one precisely defined topic. If tackled properly this would lead in good time to the issues being formulated in a way which could be made use of by the authorities concerned. The problems addressed were of a practical and scientific kind which could be much more effectively and expeditiously inquired into in this way rather than through the channel of large, inevitably diffuse congresses. This technique is virtually absent in the deliberations of contemporary criminological societies or of those with related interests. But it is a solid approach which deserves to be revived and firmly supported.

The third activity calls for only a brief comment. The *Bulletin* of the commission was not particularly exciting, but nevertheless useful as a reliable source of penological information in a period when so much was happening. It still deserves to be consulted.

Cracks and collapse

The commission was soon to become the object of acute controversy, but I do not believe that my laudatory comments would be seriously questioned by any expert acting in good faith. The picture becomes much more problematic when one tries to assess to what degree the commission fulfilled the mission initially assigned to it. I am afraid when this issue is raised I become a critic. I deeply regret it because several of the leading members of the commission over the course of many years became my valued friends. The

---

15 See *Questions et Résolutions. Traitées et votées dans les Neuf Congrès Pénitentiaires Internationaux 1872-1925* (1926). See also Sir Evelyn Ruggles-Brise, *Prison Reform at Home and Abroad* (1924). The resolutions of the last three congresses (Prague, Berlin and The Hague) are included in the *Proceedings* of these congresses. For an up-to-date collection admirably arranged see N.K. Teeters, *op. cit.* There was also a German version edited by Rudolf Sieverts. Even more than the resolutions adopted by the International Association of Criminal Law (see also note 18 below) they represent a vital and living record of criminal policy and as such are an important source for students of penal history.

commission itself seemed to be disarmingly unrealistic and self-satisfied as the following passages reveal.

> From the very onset it has been the aim of the Congresses and the Commission to form gradually, by the joint efforts of official representatives, men of penal practice and science, and philanthropic organisations, a universal conscience, as it were, regarding the problems of crime and prison, and thus to arrive at the internationalisation of certain principles or standards, by submitting proposals to the governments who should examine them and introduce them by degrees into their legislations.
>
> The characteristic feature of its [the Commission's] mission thus seems to us to be its aspiration towards a progressive assimilation of the penal law of the various nations, without prejudice to their particularities in that a certain minimum of guarantees on an international basis be more and more ensured in the various domains of penal and penitentiary practice.

When it came to providing tangible evidence of the commission's impact, its pronouncements were evasive.

> The limited scope of the present publication does not permit us to give even a short account of the *effects* [original italics] by the numerous recommendations and suggestions issued by this organisation, and of the direct and indirect influences which can be attributed to its activities, and also we must abstain from giving a statement of the positive results in the legislation and in the practice of the different countries.

A more objective evaluation reveals many disturbing facets. The commission failed to become the powerful catalyst of world-wide penal renovation, which its early promoters expected it to develop into when they laid its foundation and enlisted so much official encouragement. Yet, in fairness, the factors which contributed to these failings cannot be exclusively put at the doors of the Commission in Berne. They are of quasi-permanent nature, inhibiting the activities of any international organization likely to hide penal reality behind more or less theoretical, idealistic, and often even sentimental, propagandist perorations. The shrewd Dr Wines put his finger on probably the most delicate point when he declared at the very beginning of the enterprise: 'if ever true and solid penitentiary reform is made, it must in the end be through the action of governments.' This, he added, was 'the keynote of my work'. But governments of any country have hardly ever been the leading initiators of changes in the sphere of criminal justice. They expect, before making any decisive move, firm support from public opinion, a support which is not often forthcoming. In addition, governments as a general rule regard with utmost suspicion any moves emanating from an international body as an unwelcome threat to national sovereignty. The already noted length of time that it had taken before the commission was firmly established is largely to be explained by the schism between national sovereignty and international scrutiny.

What should be the role and the functions of the commission in relation to its member states? And how should this be expressed in the charter of the commission and be accepted by all the participants? These questions were intensely debated at the Congress of Paris in 1885 and continued to be discussed (usually behind closed doors) for some time to come. It was finally agreed that several of the considerations and observations raised during these exchanges of views should be reflected in a statement and communicated to governments. This explanatory memorandum determined the exact sense and meaning of the general rules governing the commission as contained in the original charter of the commission: 'It laid stress on the purely consultative role of the Commission, which was not meant to impose rules and whose deliberations, communications and action could lay no obligation on the Governments.'[16]

On another point Dr Wines's perception was again dead right:

> it seemed equally clear that a Congress composed wholly of representatives of governments would have a character too exclusively official, and therefore it was determined to combine a non-official with the official element, so as to give greater freedom and breadth to the discussions.

He was obviously delighted with the outcome so strikingly visible at the first congress of the commission:

> The union of these two elements in the same body stamped a character of originality on the Congress of London [in 1872]. There had been international congresses of Governments and international congresses of private citizens, the one official, the other wholly non-official; but the London Congress was unique, in that it combined both these elements.

---

[16] Section 1 of the Regulations declared: 'The purpose of the International Penal and Penitentiary Commission is to collect documents and information regarding the prevention and repression of crime, and prison administration, in order to advise Governments on the several measures to be taken to prevent violation of the penal law and to provide for the repression of crime, and at the same time to reform criminals.'

Yet seventy years later the commission quoted Dr Wines and tried to convey the impression that this happy blending had been preserved and made fully active ever since. I have participated in several congresses and I cannot agree. In a good position to observe, I noticed that the role of the non-official element has been progressively squeezed out with very severe restrictions on the time and occasions when they could present their views to the assembly. They had been given no part in the drawing up of recommendations and had little visible presence in any of the many smaller but important gatherings of the congresses. It was regrettable, especially as penal history abundantly shows that ultimately decisive permanent changes in criminal legislation and penal practice rarely start in the ministries of justice, or even in parliaments, but in crusades imposed on a reluctant or hostile world by magnetic individual figures made in an exceptional mould.

Furthermore, the commission grew inwards, cutting itself off from independent influences. The key position of the Secretary-General was shaped to promote and preserve this attitude. His tenure was not intended to be short but on the other hand it should not degenerate into quasi perpetuity. Dr Guillaume, the Swiss delegate, discharged these functions from 1875 until the congress in 1910. Professor Simon van der Aa, the representative of the Netherlands who succeeded him, kept the office until 1938, and he resigned only for reasons of health. Professor Ernst Delaquis, who followed him, was also expected to continue without any time limit. This was clearly wrong and indicative of the static and bureaucratic nature of the institution.

Moreover, the commission seemed, throughout its privileged existence, to display an evasive attitude towards controversial but central issues of the moment. Thus only once had the subject of the death penalty been introduced into the proceedings of one of its international congresses, but even then there was no debate and no recommendations were made. It was simply a matter of conveying straightforward information to confirm that the commission was not unaware of the problem.[17] It is significant that the commission never took the initiative to inquire into any important sector of criminal justice where there was evidence that remedies were called for. At best it joined in such efforts when others had advocated an intervention. The only major instance which might seem to contradict my view was the inquiry launched by the commission into the penitentiary systems of twenty-two countries.[18] Hopes were raised that the many grave defects from which so

---

17 See *Actes du Congrès Pénitentiaire International de Washington,* October 1910 (1913); 'L'enquête relative à la peine de mort', vol. 1, pp. 326–408 and 'Le rôle de la peine de mort dans les différents pays', vol. 5, pp. 13–97.

18 See 'Aperçus des systèmes pénitentiaires' (and the 'Cadre arrêté par la Commission pour l'élaboration des aperçus des systèmes pénitentiaires') in *Recueil de Documents en Matière Pénale et Pénitentiaire,* vol. 4 (spécial) (July 1935).

many prison systems suffered would be objectively recorded and remedial measures proposed. Yet I can record no instance in contemporary penal history when such hopes were dismantled so completely and convincingly. The commission's survey was a dreary, flat, pedantic inventory of administrative machinery, utterly disjoined from the human material it was expected to control and to inspire. Even the English account appeared embarrassingly uncritical and flat.[19] Indeed, to get a proper perspective on the prison system and its dilemmas one would do much better to read a survey of prison life described by imprisoned conscientious objectors,[20] or the accounts of their imprisonment given by literary and political figures interpreted with skill and sensibility by a professor.[21] At some later stage, no doubt to eliminate the deadly effect of this survey, Sir Alexander Paterson suggested that further responses should be elicited about 'extraordinary' or 'special' features in the systems; some responses followed but they hardly affected the general impression conveyed by the 'surveys'.

Still another disturbing occurrence: the continued acceptance of the fascist governments of Italy, Germany and Spain as permanent members of the commission, without any qualifications or reservations, presented a painful affront to the ideas proclaimed by the commission as its guiding inspiration. For instance, at discussions held at one of the most important sections of the commission's Penitentiary Congress, convened in Berlin in 1935, Dr Goebbels, Dr Bumke and a numerous group of Nazi 'experts' attempted to impose the Nazi criminological and penal doctrine on the congress.[22] The bureau of the commission did not dissolve itself during the Second World War but seemingly continued to vegetate in its headquarters in Berne. I understand that it continued to accept financial contributions from all member states in the usual way.

The end of the war and the establishment of the United Nations heralded the advent of the most serious crisis in the commission's existence. Once the war was over the question arose whether the commission should be recognized as the central and leading body entrusted with discharging the functions inherent in penal reconstruction, or whether this directing task should be entrusted to the United Nations' organization, with the commis-

---

19 Nor did the survey or the general introduction to it give any critical consideration to four issues which were hotly debated at the time: namely, the value of the 'progressive system' as the basis of penal regimes; the utility of criminological laboratories within the prisons; the practicability of involving the judiciary directly in the administration of penal sanctions; and the advantages of having a Code of Penal Enforcement in addition to the Criminal Code and the Code of Criminal Procedure.
20 Such as S. Hobhouse and A.F. Brockway, *English Prisons Today* (1922).
21 See Rudolf Sieverts, *Die Wirkungen der Freiheitsstrafe und Untersuchungshaft auf die Psyche der Gefangenen* (1929).
22 See on this note 26 below (p. 371).

sion playing a consultative role, if at all. As already pointed out, I have dealt with the subject of the commission at this rather extended length not only because of the exceptional place it occupied in the modern movement for international collaboration in criminal matters, but also because the predicament that the commission suffered was, and still largely is, present whenever organized efforts are set in motion to gather reliable information about standards of criminal justice across the world.

A plethora of voluntary initiatives

This is how Dr Wines introduced Chapter 26 of his book, *The State of Prisons and Child-Saving Institutions in the Civilised World*, which was devoted to 'International Prison *Congresses* which owe their origin to the combined action of the family of States and communities':

> International Congresses, whatever the subject of their study, show the comparative condition of nations as regards intellectual and social development, in the same manner as international industrial exhibitions show the comparative results of their material and economic development. Hence the necessity for their existence. Hence their great and acknowledged utility. Hence their wide and growing popularity – very nearly 100 of them having been held last year.

And this is how a few years later the eminent Belgian criminologist, Adolphe Prins, the co-founder of a new and prestigious international penal organization, tried in an eloquent manner to capture the alluring feature of such initiatives:

> It is being said that there are many Congresses, indeed that sometimes there are too many. One should not, however, forget that Congresses are one of the modern forms of scientific activity. The exchange of ideas has become as frequent and as necessary as the exchange of goods . . . Scientific progress, which in the past was primarily of an individual nature dependent on the efforts of an isolated thinker, has become collective receiving its impulse from the great currents which direct the whole of humanity. Yes, gentlemen, it is the glory of the nineteenth century that it embraces a collective conscience . . . Our Congresses, gentlemen, are the expression of the collective conscience of criminal law scholars.

This is an extract from a response addressed to the Minister of Justice of Hungary by Adolphe Prins on behalf of the International Association of Criminal Law at the opening of their congress held in Budapest in 1890. Its establishment in 1889 marks the second memorable stage in international collaboration in criminal science. In contrast to the International Penal and Penitentiary Commission, it was a voluntary organization established by three highly regarded personalities of the period: the famous German Professor Franz von Liszt, the versatile and exceptionally gifted Adolphe Prins (Professor at the University of Brussels and Inspector General of Penal Institutions) and the Dutchman, Professor G.A. van Hamel, a noted expositor of the criminal law of his country and a respected parliamentarian. Their organization also differed from the former by being less ponderous, less structured and more intellectual. They recognized that the onslaught of the *Scuola Positiva* was to a large extent justified, but at the same time that its conclusions were much too radical, monolithic and anti-historical. Their aim was to blend the best of the positivist and classical schools into a system of criminal justice more in harmony with the political and social climate of the twentieth century. They proved to be excellent at this job of ideological fusion.

The *Proceedings* of their congresses,[23] their *Bulletin* and the edition of the leading Criminal Codes and Draft Penal Codes of the period left an indelible stamp on the evolution of penal thought primarily, but by no means exclusively, of Europe. The contribution of German criminal science to the activities of the Association was of the first order, both in continuity and quality. Their collective work of comparative presentation and analysis of the German and Foreign Criminal Law was truly majestic. Although not initiated by the Association (but by the German Ministry of Justice) it added immensely to the Association's prestige – a prestige that remained high.[24] Members from 17 countries, their total number exceeding 200, participated in the first congress. In barely nine years (by 1897) the number of countries had jumped to 24 and the members to 590. In 1913, 26 countries with a total membership of 1,150 kept the Association fully alive.

On 4 January 1914 a banquet took place in the leading hotel of Berlin, the Kaiserhof. The three founders of the Association and a splendid group of eminent members and guests from all over Europe, exceeding 100, met to

---

23 During this period the following twelve congresses took place: Brussels (1889), Berne (1890), Copenhagen (1891), Paris (1893), Antwerp (1894), Linz (1895), Lisbon (1897), Budapest (1899), St Petersburg (1902), Hamburg (1905), Brussels (1910) and Copenhagen (1913). Very important is the publication containing 'Résolutions votées dans les neuf derniers Congrès de l'Union Internationale de Droit Pénal' (edited by Ernst Rosenfeld), *Bulletin*, vol. 13 (1906), p. 46, *passim*. The resolutions of the other congresses can be easily traced in the volumes of the *Bulletin* relating to the time of the congress held.

24 First a publication in two volumes of comparative criminal law in European states and non-European states entitled *Die Strafgesetzgebung der Gegenwart in Rechtsvergleichender Darstellung*, vol. I (1894), ed. by Franz von Liszt; vol. II (1899), ed. by von Liszt and Georg Crusen. These were followed by the fifteen volumes (which appeared in the period 1905–8), a product of collaboration between forty-eight German scholars covering the general part, a group of major offences and some key problems of criminal policy. *Vergleichende Darstellung des deutschen und ausländischen Strafrechts* was its title.

celebrate the twenty-fifth anniversary of the Association. And as an eloquent testimony of reigning optimism it should be noted that at the same time the bureau of the Association met to draw up the programme of work which was to be pursued in 'the next twenty years'.[25] Eight months later the First World War broke out and the Association was in ruins. At the conclusion of hostilities, in painful circumstances, the German and Austrian branches refused to be part of the former pre-war organization and formed their own group, keeping the old name. The remainder, and by far the most numerous, continued independently.

The difference was in their stability. Whereas the 'French side' continued undisturbed, indeed gaining somewhat in prestige – especially when led by Comte Carton de Wiart and Jean-André Roux, the President and the Secretary-General respectively – the independence and credibility of the German group was increasingly undermined by the Nazi legal establishment. On 8 March 1935 the eminent Professor Kohlrausch (holder of Von Liszt's chair in the University of Berlin), then the President of the German branch, resigned in pursuance of a resolution adopted by the governing body. The occasion was made even more dramatic when the legacy of Von Liszt was handed over to Dr Hans Frank, the notorious Nazi Minister of Justice and the President of the recently established Academy of German Law (he was to become the no less notorious *Generalgouverneur* of Poland). Nevertheless, at the conclusion of his resignation speech Kohlrausch – the liberal expositor of criminal science in the best Von Liszt tradition – stated: 'The national-socialist state demands a total surrender of the individual to the state and to the community . . . we recognize this requirement unconditionally and wish to co-operate in achieving this great, wonderful goal which the Führer has set out for us. We thank you Mister Minister for having given us this opportunity.' On 26 November 1937 the verdict of death was duly confirmed and the Association ceased to exist.[26] This experience teaches us that progressive penal movements are, in the final analysis, ineffective in the face of intense and unscrupulous political pressures. It illustrates the endemic frailty of international collaboration in criminal matters.

The Association, neither the old one nor the two which followed upon the outbreak of the First World War, could hardly be accused of aggressive pronouncements or tactless interference with organs of criminal justice. The Association was primarily concerned with theoretical issues and remained

---

25 See 'Das neue Arbeitsprogramm der I.K.V.', Minutes of Records of the meeting held by the Governing Body on 4 January in *Bulletin*, vol. 21 (1914), pp. 447–52 (German version) and pp. 453–58 (French version).
26 For Kohlrausch's servile address to the Minister of Justice see 'Internationale Kriminalistische Vereinigung', *Zeitschrift für die gesamte Strafrechtswissenschaft*, vol. 57 (1938), pp. 666–74.

remarkably aloof from any practical controversies affecting the reality of crime and punishment. An exceptional instance occurred in 1894, but even then there was little enthusiasm and an obvious reluctance to get more closely involved in it. The question had been raised at the International Congress of Antwerp in 1894 of whether the prison system was not too lenient with respect to offenders undergoing short-term imprisonment. The rapporteur informed the congress that in seven European states no aggravations in the enforcement of this type of sanction had been introduced, but, that apart, 'we witness in Europe a recurrence on forty-three occasions of a truly daunting list of aggravations, pliable enough to be used as the instrument of arbitrariness and torture'.[27] Nevertheless, although regretting it, the section concluded (no vote having been taken) that 'in principle, aggravation in the enforcement of deprivation of liberty could not be avoided'. This highly questionable stance was subsequently approved by the congress. It is true that at some stage Von Liszt presented a recommendation that aggravation in the enforcement of deprivation of liberty by administrative action should be unconditionally rejected. But this took place sixteen years later, not at an international congress followed by a proper resolution, but at the meeting of the German section held in Munich, and no more was heard about it.

In the period during which the Association was split a similar evasive attitude towards the realities of criminal justice can be observed. Only once had the French branch shown an interest in such matters, namely when its Secretary-General, Professor Jean-André Roux, carried out an inquiry with the aim of ascertaining to what extent and in what form conditional discharge had been adopted by the member states. Even then it was not the working and effectiveness of the measure which had been reviewed but its legal and administrative requirements. The *Proceedings* of the German branch fail to reveal any sign of a different approach. They may be fairly characterized as criminal jurisprudence, but not criminology or penology in action.

Four years before the Association had been set up, a new development, stirred by the positivist school, attempted to leave a mark on the tide of collaboration in criminal matters. I refer to the International Congresses of Criminal Anthropology, of which seven took place between 1885 and 1911.[28] Nearly two hundred subjects jostled for a space on the crowded agenda of these meetings. Their range was fantastic: virtually nothing connected with criminal behaviour was omitted. And yet, hardly ever was a

---

27 The grim enumeration comprised: 'régime du pain et de l'eau'; 'couche dure'; 'cachot sombre'; 'travail forcé dur'; 'confinement'; 'châtiment corporel'; 'ferrage avec chaînes ou avec boules'; 'catorga'; 'pilori'. See Dr Felish, report on the Fourth Question in *Bulletin*, vol. 5 (1896), pp. 146–56 and 177–80.
28 I refer to the International Congresses of Criminal Anthropology (which became known as the ICCA) of which seven took place: Rome (1885), Paris (1889), Brussels (1893), Geneva (1896), Amsterdam (1901), Turin (1906) and Cologne (1911).

thorough report produced on any subject. As a general rule very brief communications were hastily thrown together. Amongst them there were a number which made good points or led to refreshing hypotheses, but they were buried amidst a bewildering mass of uneven assertions and unwarranted conclusions. And hardly any thorough references were made to the working of the system of criminal justice. The congresses died a natural death.

After a long interval, in 1934 a group of interested people, mainly French and Italian, reached agreement that an International Society of Criminology should be formed.[29] Four years later in 1938, the first mammoth congress was held in Rome with a participation of over a thousand people from forty-six countries.[30] In 1949 the next similarly mammoth gathering of the society was held in Paris.[31] The latter went even so far as to provide an event which cannot be traced in any criminological congresses of the past, nor since: a duel was fought on the stairs of the premises of the congress between two participants. I hasten to add with no fatal outcome and furthermore the two combatants came from South America and as far as I am able to ascertain differences of opinion relating to criminological matters were not the cause of this theatrical performance. It is just impossible to assess to what extent these huge gatherings contributed to the development of criminology as a discipline, simply because what was of value has been submerged, not to say obliterated, by the disjointed, slight and often pretentious mass of the accumulated material.

The holding of regular international conferences is still regarded as one of the Society's major activities. Between 1939 and 1993 eleven have taken place.[32] Again it is very difficult to form a balanced view of the totality of these endeavours. No doubt the Congress of London organized by Dr Denis Carroll and Dr Hermann Mannheim, though of a rather restricted scope (one topic only, i.e. recidivism), was worth holding and the Congress of The Hague was excellent both in scope and depth. But unfortunately the full proceedings of the bulk of the congresses have not been published and this makes it impossible to undertake a meaningful evaluation. This, of course,

---

29 See Jean Pinatel (one of the guiding minds of the Society), 'International Society of Criminology', in Elmer H. Johnson (ed.) *International Handbook of Contemporary Developments in Criminology* (1983), pp. 37–62, *passim*. Another guiding spirit was the Italian Benigno di Tullio, my former professor at the Criminological Institute of Rome and the author of the treatise *Principi di Criminologia Clinica e Psychiatria Forense* (3rd edn, 1963): a stimulating work, but gravely imperilled by many of its unsubstantiated comments and conclusions.
30 See *Atti del 1 Congresso Internazionale di Criminologia* (Rome, 3–8 October 1938), 5 vols (1939).
31 See *Actes du 2 Congrès International de Criminologie, Paris, Sorbonne* (September 1950), 6 vols (1952).
32 Rome (1938), Paris (1950), London (1955), The Hague (1960), Montreal (1965), Madrid (1970), Belgrade (1973), Lisbon (1978), Vienna (1983), Hamburg (1988) and Budapest (1993).

should not be construed as a failure to recognize the role that the Society has played in keeping alive an inquiring interest in criminology through national and regional colloquia, publication of a *Revue*, or awarding coveted prizes for meritorious books dedicated to the subject.

The excitement generated by the first two congresses, in spite of their many limitations, was encouraging in as much as neither the demise of positivism nor the distortions brought about by Nazi criminology, or for that matter Soviet criminology, seemed to succeed in extinguishing a genuine desire, spread over many parts of the world, to support the recognition that criminology should be pursued with vigour in the changing political atmosphere of the times. Yet, what I cannot otherwise describe as a tendency to run away from the reality of prevailing criminal justice, can be observed in the International Society of Criminology just as it has been already registered with respect to other international groupings.

This is a convenient moment to take notice of the International Society of Social Defence, which similarly has a predominant Franco-Italian component. Its history is rather unusual. Filippo Gramatica, a young Italian count and a *Dozent* at the University of Genoa, published a book in 1934 in which he proposed the establishment of an international society dedicated to worldwide penal reconstruction.[33] The sincerity of his beliefs was undeniable and so was his naïvety. My venerable maestro, Enrico Ferri, even at the height of his *Sturm und Drang Periode*, would not have had the audacity to entertain a similar dream. The programme, if put into effect, would have meant a total erasure of the system of criminal justice and criminal legislation as known and practised in the civilized world. The episode proves how difficult it is to become a Cesare Beccaria and how much more is needed than pure revolutionary spirit if one is to leave a real mark on penal history. The author and his book were doomed to disappear had it not been for Marc Ancel, who took a fancy to the idea.[34] He drastically revised its programme,[35] enlisted influential and devoted collaborators, and launched the freshly baptized child into the big world of wide ideas in the invigorating expectancy that it would make good.[36] International conferences were set on foot and continued at

---

33 *Principi di Diritto Penale Suggettivo* (1934).
34 It appeared in a French translation under the title *Principes de défense sociale*, with a preface by Marc Ancel (1964).
35 See 'Minimum Programme of the I.S.S.D.' and 'Addendum' presented by Marc Ancel, both reproduced in *Cahiers de défense sociale* (1996), pp. 167, 169 and 169–72. See also Marc Ancel's eloquent (but to my mind not convincing) article 'Les doctrines nouvelles de la défense sociale', *Revue de Droit Pénal et Criminologie*, vol. 32 (1951–2), pp. 47–60.
36 The late well-known Professor Pietro Nuvolone was one of the energetic supporters, and Adolfo Beria di Argentine (a highly respected former Procurator at the Supreme Court and the author of the fascinating book *Giustizia: Anni Difficili* (1985)) continues to be the guiding light. In France there is a distinguished team which includes Madame Simone Rozès (First Hon. President of the Supreme Court).

regular intervals.[37] Regional and national colloquia followed. A *Revue* was established to monitor the various initiatives of the Society. Imagination was shown in selecting topics for its deliberations and resolutions were adopted by a ballot of members. Ancel, who succeeded Gramatica as the President of the organization, fervently believed that birth had been given to a new school of thought and action embodying a coherent and original approach to criminal matters. He in turn wrote a book *La Défense Sociale Nouvelle* and was anxious, because of his deep respect for the English-speaking legal heritage, that the ideas he expounded should be made known to English readers. He asked me whether it could be published in English. I was very happy to arrange this and wrote a brief preface. It saw the light of day in 1965 and was launched by a respectable publishing house.[38] But as I anticipated, it failed to make an impact. It was regarded as too abstract, too dry and too doctrinaire. And the British were put off by the term 'Social Defence'. I was of course delighted to see that more recent editions, thoroughly revised and expanded, have met with a much better response. More informative and wider in scope, these editions nevertheless revealed on closer scrutiny what some of us had felt from the start, namely that the basic programme of the International Society of Social Defence (ISSD) was an elegant and skilful rendition of the programme of the International Association of Criminal Law. The time for the emergence of 'Schools' in criminal law, criminal policy and criminology has passed, and I shall return to this point in the last chapter of this book (see pp. 455–456). These reservations of course leave intact the stimulating role the ISSD continues to discharge for all of us to profit from. And in the rather static condition of criminal policy in France and the definitely grim conditions in Italy, it is particularly pleasing to have an open window to convey opinion and hope.

On one cardinal matter the International Society of Social Defence could have made an important difference. In his Addendum Marc Ancel declared that one 'of the three fundamental requirements' of modern Social Defence is 'a critical study of the present system that might at times go as far as to question its value'.[39] I am afraid I have found it impossible to come across, in the *Proceedings* of the Society, pronouncements directed towards existing systems of criminal justice in any country which effectively expressed this declared concern.

The international movement for collaboration in criminal matters faced

---

37 The thirteen congresses are as follows: San Remo (1947), Liège (1949), Antwerp (1954), Milan (1956), Stockholm (1958), Belgrade (1961), Lecce (1966), Paris (1971), Caracas (1976), Thessalonika (1981), Buenos Aires (1986), Paris (1991) and Lecce (1996).
38 Marc Ancel, *Social Defence*, with a preface by Leon Radzinowicz (Routledge & Kegan Paul, London, 1965).
39 See Ancel, 'Addendum' (quoted above in note 35).

stagnation and sterility unless an altogether different approach could be devised and successfully launched. What was needed was a wider non-technical appeal to make public opinion aware of (and possibly embarrassed or even feel guilty about) the frequency and seriousness of abuses in some of the most sensitive sectors of criminal justice. Scholarly and abstract reports richly supported by an apparatus of footnotes were not enough. Something that would disturb consciences and stir the imagination was required. The International Penal and Penitentiary Commission could not do it because it had become part of the establishment and officialdom. The International Association of Criminal Law was too intellectual, too academic. The International Society of Criminology, with a few exceptions, lost itself in the cul-de-sac of etiological vagaries. The International Society of Social Defence apparently lacked the will.

Penal standards and the League of Nations

The Howard League for Penal Reform proved to be the catalyst. It was free of all these limitations and constraints and being British it was down to earth, practical, observant, critical and yet ready to accept reasonable compromises. That brilliant woman, Miss Margery Fry (ably helped by Gertrude Eaton), became the *porte-parole* for a fresh initiative in the 1920s. In fairness it should be acknowledged that in her efforts she found discreet but firm support from three forward-looking British penal administrators: Sir Alexander Paterson, the eminent penal reformer; Sir Maurice Waller, the Chairman of the Prison Commission for England and Wales; and Lord Polwarth, the Chairman of the Prison Commission for Scotland. Of this remarkable campaign a few central events have to be mentioned, however briefly.

The start was a draft convention produced in collaboration with the Society of Friends. This affirmed among other postulates that all prisoners, irrespective of the criminal proceedings against them, should be entitled to a minimum of rights, to a public trial within a reasonable period, to legal help and to security from torture. Political prisoners should not be treated worse than ordinary prisoners and no one should be executed in secret. A little later (in 1928) an appeal to the League of Nations was published which documented many abuses in penal institutions for delinquents with illustrations, the veracity of which could not be questioned. Though the chances of adopting an international convention were dim, further steps were taken which met with increased interest and support. A survey of world prison populations was launched which showed wide discrepancies in the rates of penal detention which called for justification, or at least for explanation. This was followed by an inquiry into the treatment of prisoners detained before trial which was highlighted by a pamphlet *For All Prisoners*. Another inquiry revealed extraordinary variations in the ratio of persons awaiting trial. Still another made proposals aimed to reduce the number of prisoners. Yet another

SEEKING INTERNATIONAL SOLUTIONS

reviewed measures to protect witnesses and persons awaiting trial from violence or other forms of physical or mental constraint. And in 1930 the first of the many subsequent reformulations of Standard Minimum Rules for the Treatment of Prisoners was prepared and circulated to governments and specialized agencies. As with a number of other initiatives, the International Penal and Penitentiary Commission joined with the Howard League and proved its usefulness and competence, but it was the League which acted as the spearhead. Particularly important was the fact that several respected international groupings which had nothing to do with penal matters, such as the Federation of League of Nations Societies, the National Council of Women of Norway and a number of organizations in Britain, appealed to the Howard League to take action to promote penal progress and reveal abuses in the field of criminal justice.

The pressure was intensifying. The support of the Cuban delegate to the League of Nations was secured: his name was de Agüeroy Bethancourt. After a few setbacks his proposal, preceded by a three-page statement, was adopted by the Council of the League of Nations.[40] In vain did I search the *Proceedings* of the United Nations Congress on the 'Prevention of Crime and Treatment of Offenders' held in Cuba in 1990 for a tribute to this pioneer in international collaboration in criminal matters. At the time of his intervention Cuba was under the strong influence of the positivist school and its Criminal Code of 1930 embodied many of Enrico Ferri's ideas. Ferri was strongly in favour of an extended role for the League of Nations in the penal sphere. On 14 January 1930 the Council of the League passed the following resolution:

> In view of the fact that the improvement of penal administration is at present occupying the attention of many peoples of the world and that there are certain international aspects to the question, the Council requests the Assembly to place the question on its agenda with the object of deciding the best way in which the League of Nations can co-operate with the International Prison Commission and other interested organisations in their efforts to assist in the development of prisons in accord with modern economic, social and health standards.

The Cuban delegate made a further proposal which was also accepted. The International Penal and Penitentiary Commission and the Howard League for Penal Reform should be invited to present a memorandum which would contain more detailed recommendations to give effect to the Council's resolution. An indirect, but very fruitful, approach to juvenile delinquency had

---

40 See for his intervention: 'League of Nations. Improvement in Penal Administration. Report of the Delegate of Cuba', C. 51, 193.

already been made by the League of Nations through the activities of its Child Welfare Committee. But now a principle of much wider import was affirmed, namely that the upholding of proper standards in the penal sphere should be recognized as a matter of direct concern to the comity of nations at the highest level of their organization. However, the universality of this commitment was still restricted by the very composition of the League of Nations. It did include the European states (though not all of the defeated states) and the British Commonwealth. But only very few states from the Asian and Latin American areas were members. And most significantly the United States and the Soviet Union had not joined.

The resources assigned to penal issues within the organization of the League of Nations were still very modest – one official with a secretarial assistant – but the subject was placed on the agenda of the Fifth Committee of the League. The League was authorized to initiate or even to carry out specific inquiries. It was also expected to encourage international organizations concerned with problems of crime to undertake inquiries and several such centres were declared to be 'technical' organizations which were expected to collaborate with the League. Under the League's auspices a regular publication was issued with a significant subtitle *Penal and Penitentiary Questions – Improvements in Penal Administration.* It was envisaged that resolutions or draft conventions would be prepared for possible adoption by the Assembly of the League on subjects such as illicit trafficking in dangerous drugs, prostitution, or trafficking in obscene publications.[41]

The way was opened up for a new phase in international penal collaboration and it would have been a mistake to underestimate its potentialities. But it would also have been imprudent not to perceive the great difficulties which loomed ahead. It took no time for these to appear in full strength. Thirty-seven governments had replied to a questionnaire that the *Prison Rules* had been observed in their countries. Nevertheless, in spite of great pressures, the Fifth Committee in 1934 did not propose to the Assembly of the League that the *Rules* should be embodied in a convention, but only that they should be recommended to governments as a standard to which their penal institutions should conform. The only steps the League thought proper and feasible to take were to publish a statement enumerating some violations of

---

41 Appendix 4 of A.G. Rose's *The Struggle for Penal Reform* (1961), pp. 314–21, gives a good account of the Howard League's role. For an insight into the League of Nations' activities in this sphere, see the documents issued by the League between 1939 and 1929: A.20. 1939. IV; A.70. 1938. IV; A.24. 1938. IV; A.62. 1937. IV; A.23. 1937. IV; A.70. 1936. V; A.V/16. 1936. IV; A.25. 1936. IV; A.63. 1935. IV; A.21. 1935. IV; A.45. 1934. IV; A.14. 1934. IV; A.44. 1933. IV; A.37. 1933. V; A.26. 1933. IV; A.23. 1933. IV; A.7. 1933.V; A. 58. 1932. IV; A.6 and A.6 (a). 1932. Extract No. 1; A. 70. 1931. IV; A.25 (a). 1931. IV; A.25. 1931. IV; C.620. M.241. 1930. IV; A.64. 1930. IV; A.26. 1930. IV; C.564. M.215. 1929.

the *Rules* in a number of unnamed countries and to adopt a resolution by the assembly citing several practices as contrary to the *Rules*.[42] This was an all too familiar weakness, already so blatantly conspicuous in the work of the International Penal and Penitentiary Commission. The League was not ready or not willing to face a clash, a bitter and divisive clash, not only within itself but also with other centres of power and influence. What was at stake was the traditional concept of unfettered national sovereignty, an apprehension that this would be infringed and ultimately violated by interferences which, whatever their motives, should be avoided. This was also a convenient shield behind which those who clung to the status quo or who were inimical to penal progress could hide.

The very last initiative taken by the League of Nations in the penal sphere was to convene a meeting of representatives of all the 'technical organizations' with a view to drawing up a joint document on measures to prevent violence and intimidation of witnesses and persons held for trial and to guarantee that preventive detention should not be abused. I had the honour to be invited by Miss Margery Fry to represent the Howard League for Penal Reform on this vitally important topic. We had a very useful and pleasant meeting at the impressive Palais des Nations in Geneva, where some years earlier I had pursued my legal and criminological studies. We made good progress at this initial stage, but I also remember that the atmosphere was heavy and strangely unreal. Not surprisingly, because two months later the Second World War broke out. I was relieved to be back in England.

There was a tremendous will and a vibrant hope to build a better world once the war had come to an end, feelings that usually follow the conclusion of hostilities, but which in view of the exceptional barbarity displayed in the Second World War were exceptionally deeply felt. The preamble to the Charter of the United Nations stated that its purpose was

> to reaffirm faith in fundamental human rights, in the dignity of worth of the human person . . . to promote social progress and better standards of life in larger freedom, and for these ends . . . to employ international machinery for the promotion of the economic and social advancement of all peoples.

An Article of the United Nations Charter boldly proclaimed as one of its objectives:

> To achieve international co-operation in solving international problems of an economic, social, cultural, or humanitarian character, and

---

42 See the League of Nations: Documents A.45, 6 September 1934; *ibid.* A.45, 24 September 1934.

in promoting and encouraging respect for human rights and for fundamental freedom for all without distinction as to race, sex, language or religion.

Consideration of penal matters on a world scale fitted neatly into these contagious idealistic projections. And there was certainly no lack of volunteers to join in this forward march. The already quoted pronouncements in Dr Wines' book in 1880 and of Adolphe Prins in 1900 (see p. 369) might well have appeared, at that time, to be at variance with reality. But by 1950 reality proved to be faithful to their anticipations. Eleven organizations reaffirmed their deep interest in problems relating to the 'prevention of crime and treatment of offenders'.[43] Furthermore three specialized agencies connected with the United Nations reiterated their interest in certain aspects of the problem and confirmed their readiness to help.[44] At last, it seemed that a voice of high authority would acknowledge that the maintenance of proper penal standards everywhere should be an integral part of the wider political, social and humanitarian advances expected across the world.

The signposts to the road ahead were clearly marked but there was still considerable uncertainty about how best to proceed. The various organizations were content to make their contributions under the aegis of the United Nations if they were granted consultative status. There was only one exception: the International Penal and Penitentiary Commission maintained that, because of its long service and meritorious contributions, it should be called upon to discharge a much more elevated function. But all its drawbacks and past failings could not be overlooked. It would require a lot of good will, imagination and patience to resolve this complex and delicate issue. I never suspected that I might one day get involved in it, but this is what in fact did happen.

Lending a hand at the United Nations

Towards the end of 1947 I was invited by the United Nations in New York to become the first Chief of the Social Defence Section. The invitation came out of the blue. No informal approaches were made beforehand and no specifications of the job were provided. A further discussion (over the telephone)

---

[43] International Association of Criminal Law, International Bureau for the Unification of Criminal Law, International Penal and Penitentiary Commission, International Criminal Police Commission, International Law Association, International Union for Child Welfare, Nordic Association of Criminologists, International Statistical Institute, Howard League for Penal Reform, joined a little later by the Benelux Crime Commission and the International Society for Social Defence.

[44] International Labour Organization (ILO), World Health Organization (WHO) and United Nations Educational, Scientific and Cultural Organization (UNESCO).

made it clear that I was expected to help to stabilize the Section, to make a few appointments, to launch an attractive programme of research, and to assist in promoting constructive relations with international organizations working in this field. The flattering hope was also expressed that I might perhaps at a later stage decide to make this work my permanent and exclusive concern. To avoid any future misunderstanding I made it as clear as possible that I would not leave Cambridge, and that as much as I appreciated the significance of the invitation I would be unable to stay longer than a year at the most. This clarification was generously accepted, but even so the timing was rather awkward. I had just been appointed Assistant Director of Research and was eager to embark upon my duties. Moreover the first volume of the *History* was in the process of being printed and I felt strongly that I should not be so far away from it. Nevertheless I felt, and I was reinforced in this by advice I received from my Cambridge friends, that the appeal from the United Nations could not be rejected. The university granted me leave of absence for two terms and I set off on my first journey to America.

This was still the romantic phase in the life of the United Nations. It was not located like today in the prestigious building in the heart of Manhattan on the site given by the Rockefellers, but in a former war factory building with pokey little rooms, long and dull corridors, very low ceilings, a modest restaurant and a still more modest cafeteria. The address, most appropriately, was Lake Success, Great Neck, some thirty miles from Grand Central Station. The organization, if my memory does not desert me, consisted of some 55 member states as against the 185 of today. There was a lot of postwar excitement, as echoed in the already quoted Preamble and First Article of the Charter, mixed with an increasing realization that there was a huge gap between these lofty, almost poetic, proclamations and the rough and edgy realities of international relations.

The Social Defence Section was built into the Division of Social Activities (which subsequently became part of the Department of Social Affairs) along with several other sections. There was a Director at the head of the division and a Deputy Director. At the highest level the division fell within the jurisdiction of an Assistant Secretary-General. There was also a senior officer indirectly connected with the division who was expected to look after all kinds of private or semi-public international organizations which cooperated with the United Nations. I was puzzled on what grounds Sir Raphael Cilento could have been made the Director. He must have done something important in his native Australia to have been knighted, but from the first moment I met him he struck me as a narrow, arrogant, cynical and lazy man. I am sorry to say that, as time passed by, I saw no extenuating circumstances to change my view. His most notable achievement was to be the father of the attractive and talented actress Diane Cilento. Monsieur Henri Laugier, the Assistant Secretary-General, was a former Professor of Neurology at the Faculty of Medicine in Paris, well liked in the liberal political circles of the capital, cultured, highly intelligent and witty.[45] To him at this stage of his life the United Nations presented a dignified and convenient form of retirement. I formed an instantaneous respect for Martin Hill, who was in charge of international organizations co-operating with the United Nations. He was a former English civil servant who had developed into an almost perfect international civil servant. He was not an eagle, but he was always well informed, effective in finding constructive compromises, proud to serve the United Nations and most anxious to contribute to its reputation. I had met the Deputy Director, Monsieur Adolphe Delierneux, as a young man when I was inquiring into the penal reform of his country (Belgium). He was then the Governor of Merxplas, the institution for young offenders, and I was deeply impressed by his work there (see pp. 63–64). Since then he had become the Director of the prison in Ghent, the regime of which was based on solitary confinement, no doubt with the object of eliminating this repressive system. He was a born penal reformer and as such he had his strong and weak points. He was emotional, indeed passionate, he was realistic in dealing with his young delinquents but unrealistic in his view that penal reform potentialities had no limits, providing that there was a will to attain them. He had the courage of his convictions. At the Congress of Berlin in 1935 he had spoken out against the Nazi attempt to distort the debates in favour of their dwarfed penological doctrines and inhumane practices.[46]

My position, though respectable, was not on the top of the United Nations' ladder of appointments and my role was mainly regarded as being of a technical and advisory nature. Nevertheless it was a rather exposed role simply because the decision about whether the United Nations or the Penal and Penitentiary Commission should have the final responsibility for promoting international co-operation was still in flux.

---

45 Late one evening, when I was about to leave the building to go home, Monsieur Laugier emerged out of the restaurant and said: 'What are you doing here at this late hour?' 'I am busy organising dust,' I replied. Whereupon came his remark: 'Is it you who have uttered this or Proust?'

46 His firm counter-attack on the first question, the purpose of which was to get acknowledged by an international congress that there is no room for humanitarian and reformative initiatives within the penal system, and his continued opposition in the course of discussions within the section, were truly impressive. The Berlin Congress with the perorations from Dr Goebbels (fourteen pages long), of Dr Gürtner (the Minister of Justice), of Dr Roland Freisler (Secretary of State in the Ministry of Justice) and the sending of a sleazy telegram to Hitler by Dr Bumke (President of the Congress) on behalf of the congress, and his servile appeal to the congress soliciting their consent (eventually given) that the telegram should be associated 'à la salutation que la nouvelle Allemagne à l'habitude d'adresser à son Führer: "Der Führer und Kanzler des Deutschen Reiches Adolf Hitler, Sieg Heil!"' have all effectively contributed to present the Berlin Congress as perhaps the darkest page in the history of the international collaboration. See *Actes du Congrès Pénal et Pénitentiaire International de Berlin* (August 1935), *passim*.

First, there was the name given to the section which raised doubts about its focus. To those familiar with the development of criminological thought and up-to-date literature the term 'Social Defence' was not unknown. It was frequently used by Enrico Ferri, it had been adopted by Adolphe Prins in the title of his well-known book and used throughout. Indeed an organization had been formed which with enthusiasm had decided to be known as the International Society of Social Defence (see pp. 374–376). It signified an approach towards crime and its control from which expiation and retribution would be expunged. This raised a multiple of controversial, indeed divisive, questions and obviously was an inappropriate term to identify the work in the penal sphere which the United Nations aspired to perform. What was needed was a much more neutral and more widely accepted designation. I lost no time in making a rather lengthy statement on the subject which was favourably received except by Monsieur Delierneux, but it was not accepted on the grounds that the section already figured under the heading of Social Defence and any change would be likely to lead to confusion. Several years had to pass by before my point of view was vindicated. The section was known for a long time as the United Nations Crime Prevention and Criminal Justice Division. It has now been given the title of The Center for International Crime Prevention in the United Nations Office of Drug Control and Crime Prevention.

Second, the Section existed, but largely on paper: it had no qualified and permanently employed staff. Enticing competent people to join the secretariat was (and still is) under any circumstances a difficult and delicate task. People of high calibre with stable positions in their own country would hesitate seriously to become part of a different world, with different work, indeed a different way of life, with the feeling of insecurity which an organization such as the United Nations inevitably conveys. Relatively high remuneration makes an offer much more attractive, but not to the extent of neutralizing the other features connected with such a radical transfer. And then there are all the pressures exercised by member states to have their favourites installed, often in disregard of their intrinsic qualifications. I made it clear that I would, of course, be most willing to receive suggestions from those quarters and carefully consider them, but at the same time I would regard it as my prerogative to initiate extensive searches, indeed go out of my way to find suitable candidates. We received the authority to make two appointments as soon a possible. It was, however, a long and tedious process. Ultimately they were my choices, found and selected by me. Both were very young (about thirty), from two countries as different as South Africa and Denmark, and both were at the very beginning of their criminological careers. I was aware of the risk I was taking, but I was so attracted by both of them that I was ready to take the plunge. They arrived at Lake Success almost at the same time, eager to face the adventure.

The next important tasks were to formulate a programme of research, to get it accepted and launched. I had two subjects in mind, but before initiating any discussions to ascertain whether they would evoke a sufficiently strong interest from the two research officers, I had to clarify my own thoughts and draw up extended terms of reference for each of them. The subjects I chose were 'The condition, trends and penological consequences of crime in the immediate post-war era' and 'Probation and allied measures' as an alternative to imprisonment for certain categories offenders, its legal and penological framework within the existing system of criminal justice, its strength and weaknesses.

The aim of the first inquiry was to make both the United Nations and its member states aware of the nature and trends of crime in both the victorious and defeated countries, as well as the deficiencies inherent in the available statistical resources to keep these issues under regular and adequate review. The aim of the second inquiry was to accentuate as far as possible the resolve of the United Nations to explore the possibility of new approaches to the punishment and treatment of offenders instead of simply following traditional penal responses. I had no difficulty in securing the consent of the United Nations' authorities, but even more importantly both researchers were eager to start without any further delay. I directed the work of both of them and I cannot recollect a more pleasing experience. Every fourteen days I had at least a two-hour meeting with each of them and shorter exchanges of views whenever they or I felt the need. The report on probation was completed in barely eight months and published.[47] It was at once acknowledged to be an outstanding document of theoretical and practical value, quoted and used in many parts of the world. The report on crime, using replies to a detailed questionnaire but also special investigations by the researcher, was not published but mimeographed and circulated. It also evoked considerable interest and laudatory comments.[48]

I had great hopes for both of my young colleagues, but unfortunately fate did not turn out to be kind to them. It is true that on his return to Copenhagen, Karl Otto Christiansen gained rapidly a deservedly high reputation. He became a close collaborator of Dr Stephan Hurwitz, the well-known Professor of Criminal Law and the Ombudsman of Denmark, and became himself Professor of Criminology in Copenhagen. His published scholarly work, particularly his study of the concordance of criminality amongst monozygotic as compared with dizygotic twins, was highly valued. However,

---

47 See United Nations, *Probation and Allied Measures* (Department of Social Affairs, New York, 1951).
48 The idea of providing such surveys was later on taken up by the United Nations in an expanded and much more sophisticated manner. For the latest in the series see *Results of the Fourth United Nations Survey of Crime Trends and Operations of Criminal Justice System*, A/CONF 169/15 (20 December 1994). But the difficulties of drawing valid comparative conclusions are as formidable as ever.

he died suddenly, only fifty-three years old. In Klaas Pansegrouw's life something very serious must have gone wrong for he simply disappeared. Soon after I left the United Nations I tried to find him and to help him if I could, but I was not successful.

There remained the delicate and complex question of the role of the International Penal and Penitentiary Commission in the emerging new set up. I was asked to assess the quality and the usefulness of all the many existing organizations, including the commission. That there should have been so many organizations pursuing activities in this field was to a large extent understandable and desirable for the simple reason that there are so many and different facets to the problem of crime and punishment: the legal, the judicial, the police and the prosecutorial, the penal and penitentiary, the etiological, the preventive, the after-care and the economic aspects. But the experience which I had gained when I had been a member of two such organizations (the International Association of Criminal Law and the International Society of Social Defence), and later confirmed when I became an honorary member of their governing bodies, led me to conclude that the contribution of such organizations would be substantially greater if their number were reduced, their resources pooled and overlapping avoided.

I voiced my concern about this multiplicity of effort and presented specific projects for fusion, but with hardly any success. I was reinforced in my views by the fact that so sociable and clubbable a personality as my professor and subsequently my good friend, Henri Donnedieu de Vabres of the Paris Faculty of Law, had expressed similar misgivings with similar lack of success fifteen years earlier when there were fewer such groupings in existence.[49] Those who brought such organizations into being or had a prominent hand in promoting their activities often had a very inflated ego. They were afraid that the identity of their enterprises would be distorted or even lost. And they believed that the formal separateness and distinctiveness of each organization would act as a stimulant to competition and innovation. All such considerations should not be ignored, but in practice excessive multiplicity in this sphere is bound to lead to negative results. However, I thought it undesirable to get involved further in this matter. To do so would have been to lose sight of what was the central issue, namely the ultimate role of the International Penal and Penitentiary Commission in relation to the United Nations.

The British government suggested a compromise, but its proposal failed to appeal to the other member states. In the mean time the American interest

---

49 In terms very relevant to our present situation in international collaboration he deplored the 'double emploi', the 'deperdition de forces', the 'inévitable empiétments' produced by too many 'diverses sociétés scientifiques'. See *Mitteilungen der I.K.V. Neue Folge*, vol. 6 (1933), p. 141.

in the commission was declining. They looked upon it as a kind of elitist penological European club, whereas they wished the subject to be taken up on a vast international scale. In contrast to the attitude they had adopted to the League of Nations, they were anxious to expand the activities and responsibilities of the new world organization far beyond regional frontiers. And American backing, political and financial, was in this field as vital as in so many others. Within the United Nations' secretariat a strong wing led by Delierneux wished to eliminate the commission altogether. The tender child baptized at the Congress of London in 1872, which had been expected to grow into a sturdy adult with influential parents from so many governments of the world, began to look much like an abandoned geriatric. The fatal warning *rien ne va plus* was to seal its fate at the meeting of international organizations concerned with the prevention of crime and the treatment of offenders convened by the secretariat of the United Nations which took place in the Palais de Chaillot in Paris from 15 to 16 October 1948.

There had been no necessity to prolong my stay at the United Nations through the summer months to go to the Paris meeting, for the pattern of business to be concluded there had been fixed beforehand in informal consultations and no great surprises were to be expected. I was thus able to return to Cambridge in July. Martin Hill expressed the hope that the United Nations might continue to take advantage of my interest and advice in the years to come. I assured him that the activities carried out by the United Nations in this sphere were close to my heart, and I was anxious to give it as much support as I could within my modest means.

In the light of the detailed account I received and the *Minutes of Proceedings* adopted by the meeting in Paris, it is not difficult to describe the final denouement. The commission was squeezed between the eleven other already mentioned international organizations and the three specialized agencies.[50] Its potential contribution was defined in the *Minutes* in these shabby terms:

> [to be consulted by the Secretary-General of the United Nations] on problems of applied criminal law (practical questions of criminal law and penitentiary science), and the collection of data regarding specific problems.

That Sir Lionel Fox and Professor Delaquis, representing the commission, should have remained silent in face of this embarrassing degradation in status was characteristic of the sombre adversity which had become the steady companion of the commission. The meeting reaffirmed the leading role of the United Nations in the field of prevention of crime and treatment of offenders, but was remarkably evasive in laying down in tangible terms how

---

50 See notes 43 and 44 above.

the United Nations' responsibility would be discharged. The meeting lamely recorded that

> it is desirable that the Secretariat of the United Nations should: (a) Publish an annual report on its own work and on that of the interested institutions and organisations, on the progress made with problems under study, on results achieved and future plans in the field of prevention of crime and treatment of offenders in pursuance of the present resolution; (b) Consider the possibility of asking the various Governments for reports of their activities and experiences in these fields.[51]

One would have expected that once the leading role of the United Nations had been affirmed it would declare its intention to build up the Social Defence Section into a Department along the lines of the Commissions on Human Rights or Narcotic Drugs, but nothing of this kind was said or intimated. Nor was there any inclination by organizations present at the meeting to raise and press the point. In 1950 its functions were transferred to the United Nations.[52] The Penal and Penitentiary Foundation continues to carry out some restricted activities and hold colloquia. Thus a memorable chapter in the history of international collaboration in criminal matters came to a close. It is true that a centre within the United Nations was established to keep the heritage alive, indeed with the intention of expanding it substantially. But in effect that centre was set up on a scale which was glaringly inadequate to discharge the vast tasks expected from it.

New congresses – old problems

The United Nations was expected to organize regular international congresses on the lines of those which the commission had so successfully carried out over so long a period of time. The first United Nations Criminal Congress was to take place in Geneva in 1955 from 22 August to 3 September. It is only fair to acknowledge that the preparatory steps taken to ensure a high standard of proceedings, deliberations and constructive conclusions could not have been more thoughtful and elaborate. In addition to several regional seminars and consultative groups a number of colloquia were sponsored to precede the Geneva meeting. One of these organized by the United Nations in collaboration with the World Health Organization and entitled 'Cycle

---

51 See Paper no. 12, 'Resolution adopted by the Meeting', pp. 3 and 4.
52 By General Assembly Resolution 415 (V) on 1 December 1950. On the role the IPPC expected to play see their Memorandum of 1945, reproduced in *Recueil de Documents en Matière Pénale et Pénitentiaire*, vol. xii (1946–7), pp. 67–90.

européen d'études sur l'examen médico-psychologique et social des délinquants' took place in Brussels from 3 to 15 December 1951. Each of the European states was invited to appoint a delegation consisting of five experts chosen from the universities, the magistracy, psychiatric medicine, penitentiary organizations and after-care. Eighteen countries were represented at this unusual gathering. Naturally Britain was amongst them and the Home Office chose the delegation. In a courteous letter Sir Frank Newsam, the forceful, effective and in some ways controversial Permanent Under-Secretary, asked me to be a member of it. I accepted with alacrity because the subject was of great interest to me; it renewed my contacts with the United Nations and I regarded it as a privilege to be part of a delegation headed by Sir Lionel Fox, who as a penal administrator and penologist was nationally and internationally respected.

It was generally acknowledged in the European literature that one of the major contributions of the positivist school and the International Association of Criminal Law was the recognition of the necessity to take more fully into account, in all stages of criminal justice, and especially in the course of the sentencing process, not only the seriousness of the crime committed, but also the personality of the convicted person when assessing his guilt and choosing the appropriate punishment. In Europe this notion took a long time to gain ground because of the traditional suspicion nurtured by the abuses of the *ancien régime,* which had always been ready to use the 'personality' of the offender as justification for arbitrary and frequently cruel punishment. But with the growing acceptance of the premise that society should be governed by the rule of law, the principle of individualization of punishment became more acceptable in the field of criminal policy. It is only when viewed within this wider political and social context that a proper understanding can be gained of the notable volume first published in France in 1898 by Raymond Saleilles, an eminent Professor of Criminal Law in the Faculty of Law at the University of Paris. It was later translated into English.[53] In time similarly enthusiastic support for this principle was evinced by the leading criminal codes of Europe.[54] But in vain would one look for an empirical study, however

---

53 See Raymond Saleilles, *The Individualisation of Punishment*, with an introduction by Gabriel Tarde and Roscoe Pound (1911).
54 See, for instance, Italian Penal Code of 1930 (Article 54), Polish Code of 1932 (Article 64) and Swiss Code of 1937 (Article 69). The formulation of the principle varied greatly. Thus in the Swiss Code it was defined in two dozen words: 'The Court shall not mete out penalties in accordance with the guilt of the offender, considering the motives, previous conduct and the personal situation of the convicted person.' Under the Italian Code there is no definition but a descriptive enumeration which does not seem to come to an end. After having affirmed that the Judge 'must take into account the quality of the offence', it continues: 'The Judge must likewise take into account the guilty person's capacity of delinquency as inferred from – (1) The motives to commit delinquency and the character of the offender. (2) The criminal antecedents and, in general, the conduct and life of the

modest, to see to what extent and how this principle was put into effect when concrete cases were tried. Here again it was revealed that the gap between theoretical formulations and practical applications in the criminal sphere tends to be wide and persistent.

From the very start our colloquium took several stringent steps to avoid, or at least to minimize, these empirical limitations. At the beginning of the conference, the chairmen of the delegations presented overall reports of the procedure followed in their own countries. We then identified the issues which constituted the essence of the problem and broke up into four sub-groups with specific agendas attached to each. What kinds of inquiries should be carried out into the personality and social background of the offender? By whom should they be conducted and what status should they have in the proceedings to follow? At what stage should the inquiries be initiated, before or after proceeding to conviction? Should the findings of the inquiries be communicated to the accused and the defence counsel as well as to the prosecuting organs? What steps should either party be entitled to take to challenge the report and at what stage of the proceedings? Which categories of criminals and of crimes should call for an obligatory pre-sentence examination, and who should determine this? The examination of these basic issues was assigned to one or other of the sub-groups and reports were drawn up at the end of the discussion. This was followed by plenary sessions of the whole colloquium and the adoption of a further substantial report.

This experience provided further evidence that comparative collaboration in criminal matters gains enormously if well thought out and properly organized efforts are deployed with respect to specific, clearly defined topics which can be reflected upon without haste in relatively small and compact groups. But this is not enough if empirical material is still lacking, as it was on this occasion.

The British delegation was naturally pleased when the head of the Swiss delegation, Professor François Clerc, summarizing the views of the colloquium, stated: 'On devine que la solution anglaise a emporté un grand succès.' He was referring to the English practice of presenting a report on the personality of the accused after finding the person guilty and before the choice of sentence.[55] Similarly, on another occasion, a

---

offender prior to the offence. (3) The conduct contemporary with or subsequent to the offence. (4) The individual, domestic and social conditions of life of the offender.' In recent years, with the resurgence of the neo-classical approach emphasizing 'just deserts', the principle of individualization of punishment has been under attack.

55 See François Clerc, 'L'examen médico-psychologique et social des délinquants', *Revue Pénale Suisse*, vol. 67 (1952), pp. 40–61, at p. 51. This article is not only a very lively and informative account of the Brussels Colloquium but also a piece of intrinsic value as a contribution to the subject as a whole. Even today its translation into English would be worthwhile. The bulk of the material relating to the commission was published with an introduction by Paul Cornil (who acted as its Director) in *International Review of Criminal Policy*, no. 3 (January 1953).

distinguished Belgian judge and criminal law professor most emphatically declared:

> il faudrait reconnaître au système anglo-saxon et diviser la procédure de jugement en deux phases; la première se terminerait par un jugement sur la culpabilité, la second par une décision sur la nature et sur le taux de la peine.[56]

Sir Lionel Fox, not surprisingly, displayed his great gift for preserving the 'united front' of our delegation and yet he did not prevent us from making individual contributions even when on occasion they happened to differ from the 'official' line.

Some time in March 1955 our Department of Criminal Science in Cambridge received a note from the United Nations' secretariat informing us about the Geneva Congress and expressing the hope that we would take part in it. I was delighted to be informed that the University of Cambridge had decided that two official delegates should be dispatched to Geneva for this occasion: Arthur (afterwards Sir Arthur) Armitage, one of my dearest friends and at that time the Chairman of the Committee of Management of the Department, and I, in my capacity as its Director. We divided our time so that between us we could participate in the deliberations on all five major topics. It was hard but worthwhile work and it also allowed us to establish new and valuable contacts from many parts of the world. Arthur Armitage (subsequently Chairman of the Law Faculty, President of Queens' College, Vice-Chancellor of Cambridge University, of Manchester University and Chairman of the Vice-Chancellors' Committee) was an impressive person. He was very intelligent and had a lot of common sense. He was conservative but anxious not only to preserve but also to innovate. Profoundly humane and fair, he had a robust sense of humour. We became close friends and it was (and still is) a very personal and professional blow to have to say farewell to him when he passed away in 1984 at the age of 68.

The Second United Nations Crime Congress was set to take place in London in 1960, from 8 to 20 August. Sir Lionel Fox was to be Chairman of the congress, but alas he was struck by a fatal and painful illness. There was no question that he could undertake the congressional duties which under any circumstances were onerous and demanding. Sir Charles Cunningham was the natural alternative choice to replace him, but very much to my surprise I was asked to be co-Chairman. I moved to London for nearly three weeks, as the congress required me to participate fully all day followed by

---

56 See Jean Constant (Avocat Général à la Cour d'Appel and Professeur at the University of Liège), 'A propos du dossier de personnalité', *Revue de Droit Pénal et Criminologie*, vol. 32 (1951), pp. 202–21, at p. 203.

long and varied social evenings or unexpectedly late deliberations. It was a great honour but also one which I accepted with great trepidation. The co-chairmanship turned out to be a most pleasant experience which I continue to cherish. It was the beginning of a firm and rewarding friendship which remained as strong as ever. Sir Charles, who died in 1998, was by any account an exceptional man. He was endowed with a mind and character of the first order. He could be incisive and was always quickly aware of the central points of virtually any issue. He needed a lot of evidence to change his mind, but once he changed it he followed the new course with firmness and constancy: a most agreeable mixture of conservatism and liberalism. He was a gifted draftsman. Under a somewhat severe and reserved appearance I discovered a lot of warmth, loyalty and dedication. We were both so very happy that Lionel Fox could at least attend the opening of the congress, and when he appeared in a wheelchair the whole congress stood up and saluted him with respect and emotion.

The number of people attending the congress was twice as large as that of the preceding one: over eleven hundred persons. Seventy governments and fifty non-governmental organizations were represented. The agenda was a rather mixed bag and some of the topics were not defined with necessary precision and clarity. This was not of our making, for the agenda had been decided at the headquarters of the United Nations in New York and handed over to us.[57] But it was a good congress and one of its attractive features was the small part played by crude political considerations and antagonisms which have nothing to do with the cause of penal reform. In addition to my duties as a co-Chairman of the congress I was also invited by the Chief of the Social Defence Section, Professor López-Rey, on behalf of the secretariat of the United Nations, to address the congress. The subject assigned to me was 'Criminological and penological research', a fascinating but intricate theme. It was, I venture to say, a constructive but critical exposition. I worked hard to prepare it and was more than compensated by the interest it evoked.

I thought that by then I had done my bit and deserved to remain in the background. I attended the subsequent congresses (they were held at five-yearly intervals), was once named one of the honorary vice-chairmen – a pleasing but primarily decorative distinction which did not prevent me from enjoying my relative anonymity. But a great surprise came in 1970 when the Fourth United Nations Crime Congress was due to take place in Kyoto from

---

57 The programme was made up of the following six topics: New forms of juvenile delinquency; their origin, prevention and treatment. Special police services for the prevention of juvenile delinquency. Prevention of types of criminality resulting from social changes and accompanying economic development in less developed countries. Short-term imprisonment. The integration of prison labour with the national economy, including the remuneration of prisoners. Pre-release treatment and after-care and assistance to dependants of prisoners.

17 to 26 August. I was asked by William Clifford (then the head of the section concerned with prevention of crime and the treatment of offenders) on behalf of the secretariat of the United Nations to act as *Rapporteur Général* at the closing plenary session of the congress. It was a distinct honour because never before had a person in their private capacity been called upon to discharge this task. It was a daunting and delicate task. Eighty-five countries were represented at the Kyoto Congress and twelve hundred persons participated. Four complex topics were selected for deliberation.[58] A lot of material had come in already before the congress started and an increasing flow of papers emerged every day from the work of the sections of the congress. I had to digest it all so as to be able to take into account the latest contributions to any of the major topics. I was given a convenient office on the premises of the congress and an efficient secretary with a good command of Japanese, French, German and English. I stayed on the premises every day from 9 a.m. up to 10:45 p.m. Lunch was served in my office or I had it with some of the delegates in the restaurant of the congress, and a little more than an hour was spent in my hotel for dinner. I found Japanese food incompatible with my regular tastes and Japanese wine the surest way to commit suicide. I was driven from and to my hotel at a frightening speed in a luxurious Mercedes put at my disposal by the government. A very nice thing that the congress did was to elect as one of its honorary vice-chairmen Hermann Mannheim, but he was not present at the congress and had by then retired from his university post at the London School of Economics.

Without any previous notice, a few days before I was expected to present my report (26 August), the Soviet delegate expressed his objection, at a meeting held by the organizing committee, to the final report being entrusted to a private participant of the congress, and stated that it was not too late to find an 'official' replacement. Obviously he never expected that this late proposition would be accepted. He simply wanted to be obstructive and did not press his point in the face of opposition. On the appointed day when I was about to address the assembly, a senior member of the Soviet delegation approached the podium and whispered to me: 'I hope Professor that you will confirm that there are now hardly any criminals in the Soviet Union.' I was able to whisper back: 'Perhaps, but I assume you do have recidivists.' 'Yes,' he said, 'we have no criminals, but we have recidivists.' Obviously, the instructions he had received failed to include some other alternatives besides a straightforward idiotic lie.

I have never before nor afterwards addressed so vast an audience and in

---

58 'Prevention of crime; public participation by citizens in crime prevention and control; research progress with causation and effectiveness of social defence measures; standard minimum rules for the treatment of prisoners.' Here again I would have welcomed a much greater specification in formulating some of the topics.

such an impressive conference building. I was told that fifteen hundred people were there. The text of my report (in English) was made available on the eve of its delivery to every participant who wanted to have it. I could not have wished for a more courteous and attentive audience. It would be improper for me to add any observations concerning the quality of my report. But perhaps I may say that it found its way into several publications.[59] It was a tough assignment and I felt justified in spending a few days in Japan after the end of the congress to appreciate more fully the delicate beauty of Kyoto and a few other places, but avoiding the sombre, brutal-looking Tokyo.

I remained concerned about how the secretariat of the United Nations would fare in discharging its expected role in the penal sphere. And I had good reasons to be concerned. Promotion of an enlightened international criminal policy and of independent and solid criminological research, as I am never tired of repeating, requires firm and widely spread political support. Everyone could see that such support was not going to be forthcoming. It was sad to witness the aggressive hostility of the Soviet Union's delegates to the United Nations. They and their subjugated bloc of partners almost automatically opposed any measure likely to raise penal standards anywhere in the world. It was depressing to observe the regular alliances between the Soviet bloc and the very many countries of the 'third or developing world' with the same objective in view. Indeed, one could not help giving up hope altogether when witnessing the scenes so often prevailing at international crime conferences. There you would hear the heads of official delegations reading out speeches prepared beforehand at home, ignoring what transpired during subsequent discussions and voting according to already arranged alignments, with independent experts having hardly any chance to contribute to the debates, let alone to influence their outcomes. And on top of this there was the mountain of resolutions, sonorous and interminable, so effectively excelling in evasive language. In these circumstances the role of non-governmental organizations was crucial and much was expected of them. But here too there was a tendency to keep aloof from the sombre reality which characterized so many contemporary systems of criminal justice.

This is an opportune moment to pay a tribute to Eduardo Vetere and his small band of colleagues in the Crime Prevention and Criminal Justice section of the United Nations for showing, and continuing to show, resourcefulness and dedication in this difficult atmosphere. Their work over the past fifteen years reveals notable advances in sophistication and diversity.

---

59 See, for instance: 'Some Current Problems and Future Prospects of International Collaboration in Penal Matters', in *Liber Amicorum in Honour of Professor Stephan Hurwitz, LL D* (Copenhagen, 1971); 'Rapport de Synthèse présenté au IV Congrès des Nations Unies etc. (Kyoto, 17–26 août 1970)', *Revue de Science Criminelle et de Droit Pénal Comparé*, no. 4 (1970), pp. 766–86.

Controversial topics have been raised; earnest efforts at securing solid documentation deployed; and energetic steps taken to establish closer links in many countries of the world with relevant organizations, academic centres and individual experts. But it should never be forgotten that in the penal sphere, perhaps more than in a number of other fields, the scope and boldness of the initiatives likely to be propelled by the secretariat of the United Nations are severely circumscribed by the interests of the member states. The section has from the very start been accorded much too low a status within the structure of the UN Organization and has been critically under-staffed for several decades. In contrast, its tasks have become much more complex and extended, while the international significance and perception of crime problems across the world have become so much more acute. The time has come to redress this balance.

The general expectation in well-informed quarters close to the United Nations is that the new Secretary-General Kofi Annan will narrow the scope of some of the organization's initiatives, reduce its supporting bureaucracy and, at the same time, try to increase all-round efficiency. I very much hope that in this process it will not always be the knife which will be wielded, but that reasonable expansion will in the case of the Crime Prevention and Criminal Justice division be regarded as long overdue.

More than twenty years had passed since my last involvement with the United Nations. It was therefore a great surprise and a great pleasure when one day in 1992 the following document came through the post.

> This Testimonial is awarded to
> Sir Leon Radzinowicz (United Kingdom)
> In Grateful Recognition of Dedicated Service
> In Support of the United Nations
> Programme on Crime and Justice
> Dated 15 April 1992
> Secretary-General
> Boutros Boutros-Ghali

Lending a hand at the Council of Europe[60]

The Council of Europe was established in 1949, four years after the setting up of the United Nations. Already then the condition of Europe, indeed of the world at large, was changing rapidly. However, the vision and the

---

60 What follows is based on my recollections and notes and on my analysis of the archives (unpublished) relating to the European Committee on Criminal Problems (ECCP) deposited in the Library of the Council of Europe, Legal Division, in Strasbourg.

expectations (or shall I say dreams?) which propelled the birth of the Council were virtually identical to those which gave birth to the United Nations. Extracts from 'The Statute of the Council of Europe' make this abundantly clear:

> Convinced that the pursuit of peace based upon justice and international co-operation is vital for the preservation of human society and civilisation; Re-affirming their devotion to the spiritual and moral values which are the common heritage of their peoples and the true source of individual freedom, political liberty and the rule of law, principles which form the basis of all genuine democracy; Believing that, for the maintenance and further realisation of these ideals and in the interests of economic and social progress, there is need of a closer unity between all like-minded countries of Europe.

Criminal laws, or more precisely criminal codes and their modes of enforcement, were an integral part in this bold compact. The decision by the Committee of Ministers of Justice of the Council of Europe taken in September 1957 to set up the European Committee on Crime Problems (ECCP) followed logically from the premises which brought the council into being. It proved to be a strong and influential body with several sub-committees, each of which tackled a specific topic leading to the elaboration of a convention, or adoption of resolutions or the issuing of interesting reports. But what about criminology? Would it be ignored, or included, and if so, in what form?

It appears that by the end of 1959 the ECCP on their own volition was moving in the direction of recommending the establishment of a generously equipped European Criminological Institute with several far-reaching functions assigned to it. This should not have come as a surprise to any one who knew Sir Lionel Fox, Marc Ancel and Paul Cornil, all three of whom enjoyed exceptional prestige within the ECCP. But wisely, to make their ideas as convincing as possible, they recommended that a small committee of 'expert consultants' should be convened to give further thought to the idea and to embody the gist of their deliberations in a formal document which would include an outline of a model to which such an institute should aspire.

Five people were invited to join the committee as expert consultants: Professor J. Andenaes (Norway), Professor J. Graven (Switzerland), Monsieur J. Pinatel (France), Professor W.P.J. Pompe (Netherlands) and myself. The invitation addressed to me stated that importance was being attached to the contribution which I could make to the deliberations because 'Apart from being the Director of the Cambridge Institute of Criminology, you know better than any one how different institutes work and the difference between Continental and English attitudes towards criminology and criminological research.' Three members of the ECCP were also expected to take part in our deliberations and to take turns in chairing the meetings: Lionel Fox, Marc

Ancel and Paul Cornil. The two Secretaries, A.T. Adam and Hugh Klare, proved to be exceptionally helpful. The first meeting, held in Paris, took place on 29–30 July 1960, and the second in London followed swiftly. Our unanimous memorandum entitled *Experts' Report on the Proposed Establishment of a European Criminological Centre* reached the ECCP on 23 September 1960.

According to the initial plan the European Criminological Institute was to comprise four departments: sociological; legal, including penitentiary questions; medical and psychiatric; and statistical – each to be led by a chief with a scientific assistant. There was to be a further chief responsible for the publications of the institute and a chief of internal administration responsible for the general organization, eight executive and clerical staff, plus a number of bilingual shorthand typists. At the head of this permanent staff there would be a director (with a personal assistant) who would co-ordinate the activities of the institute's departments; look after the institute's external relations; and secure regular contacts with the Scientific Advisory Committee, the bureau of the European Committee on Crime Problems, the Secretary General of the Council of Europe, and the representatives of member states.

The Scientific Advisory Committee was to consist of between five and seven persons, each appointed for five years. Membership would reflect as far as possible the various branches of criminology and the need for adequate geographical distribution. It would determine the scientific policy of the Criminological Institute under the supervision of the bureau of the ECCP. It would express opinions on the findings of criminological studies. It would meet three times a year, elect its chairman and define its rules of procedure, subject to the approval of the bureau of the ECCP.

The ECCP consisted of high officials of the ministries of justice and chiefs of penal administration from all the member states of the council. Through its bureau it was expected to exercise top-level supervision of the Criminological Institute. It would also appoint members of the Scientific Advisory Committee on the advice of the Director of the Criminological Institute. It would also be expected to submit for the approval of the Secretary-General of the Council of Europe the appointments of the higher officials of the Criminological Institute.

At first prospects seemed promising. It is true that the Secretary-General did not go out of his way to acclaim the proposal as a whole. Nevertheless the tenor of his lengthy memorandum (of 1 August 1961) was sympathetic to what he described as the 'Extension of Criminology Programme'. Soon afterwards the Conference of Ministers of Justice, through their deputies, passed a resolution in favour of it. Yet three months later ominous signals emerged. When the plan in all its details was put on the table for detached and scrupulous dissection, its spread and breadth and its financial implications generated grave concerns. This was implied, though never openly stated, in two documents – one emanated from the secretariat of the council: 'Une Note à l'attention de Monsieur le Secrétaire Général Adjoint sur le projet d'extension des activités de la section de criminologie', and another 'memorandum' with a similar heading was submitted by the Deputy Secretary-General.

This is perhaps a good moment to define where I stood on this issue. It seemed to me that the envisaged organization would be out of context and out of proportion in relation to the other centres of the Council of Europe and that this would present truly formidable difficulties in ensuring its effective operation. Some functions clearly should not be assigned to it at all, particularly carrying out independent projects of research or even participating in projects of research carried out by other agencies. The recruitment of numerous top chiefs of departments and their deputies – all expected to be of truly high quality – and ensuring their prolonged retention would be a source of chronic anxiety. The connections and relations between the Criminological Institute and the Scientific Advisory Committee appeared to me to be precariously vague, indeed confusing. Avoiding overlapping and friction with the United Nations Centre for the Prevention of Crime and the Treatment of Offenders was bound to pose delicate and often intractable problems. I would have needed to be in receipt of many more weighty arguments to persuade me that an International Institute of Criminology was a necessary and viable proposition. I tried delicately to utter the warning that 'il ne faut pas au départ être trop ambitieux' and that 'Il faudrait prévoir un comité scientifique petit mais fort'.

However, this note of caution and hesitation failed to make much of an impact. It would have been insensitive on my part to make a stand against the committee's exuberant overtures, especially as I was totally convinced that a scheme on the lines proposed would ultimately have no chance of being accepted. I was quite happy to convey my misgivings privately to one or two leading members of the committee and leave it at that. I do not know who did the killing, but by 1962 the 'criminological expansion programme' had become for all practical purposes a stillborn product with no chance of being revived at any foreseeable time.

A revision of the scheme was undertaken, and it proved to be quite drastic and very much to my liking. The Scientific Advisory Committee – a pretentious and undefinable creation – was swept away and replaced by the Criminological Scientific Council, the tasks of which were perceived in an altogether different light.

The Criminological Scientific Council (CSC) was expected to discharge its functions as a self-contained body without special departments staffed by directors, deputy-directors and a director-general. It was to work in close consultation and collaboration with the ECCP. It was to consist of seven members, 'representative of the criminal sciences', of acknowledged competence and linguistic abilities, taking into account geographic distribution. The candidates were to be nominated by the national delegations which made up the ECCP and each delegation could nominate three candidates. The Secretary-General of the Council of Europe would have the right to make observations on the list of candidates. At its plenary session the ECCP would appoint the seven members out of the submitted lists. Once constituted the CSC by a majority vote of its members would select a chairman for a term of three years. The Chairman would represent the CSC at the plenary sessions of the ECCP and would be expected to present a report on its activities. In order to fulfil their objectives the bureau of the ECCP and the CSC would be expected to make all the necessary arrangements for keeping themselves informed of the activities of the other body, including joint attendance at the meetings of either of them. Meetings of the CSC were to be convened by the Secretary-General of the Council of Europe after consultation with the two chairmen. This much more realistic structure offered a real chance for criminology to prove its worth at a European level.

Somewhere near the end of 1962 (the exact date escapes me) I was invited to become a member of the CSC. And at our first meeting (30 May 1963) I was elected its Chairman. This gave me much pleasure, particularly because I was chosen unanimously by the other six members, and also because the proposal came from Professor Andenaes – a leading and highly respected Professor of Criminal Law in the University of Oslo with a solid international reputation. I needed no time to register that the atmosphere in the secretariat of the council was receptive to criminological initiatives. The Secretary-General, Sir Peter Smithers, and Dr H. Golsong, the Director of the Division of Legal Affairs, went out of their way in promising their unequivocal support, and they kept their promise. But our recommendations or proposals had to be well thought out and piloted with great circumspection through several organs of the council: the Secretary-General, the bureau of the Committee on Crime Problems, the Committee of the Ministers of Justice or Deputy Ministers of Justice acting on their behalf. I regarded myself as privileged to have been asked to preside over a council consisting of a group of experts of quality, such as E. Altavilla, M. Ancel, J. Andenaes, P.H. Bean, F. Ferracuti, J. Pinatel, R. Sieverts, K. Waaben, D. Wiersma and several others of similar calibre who at one time or another served as members. They were certainly not the kind of people who would be short of suggestions. The collaboration with the ECCP, first through its Chairman, Paul Cornil, followed by Thorsten Erikson and then by Louk Hulsman, could hardly have been better. Sir Arthur Peterson, who succeeded Sir Lionel Fox on the ECCP, was always ready with wise advice. The two members of the secretariat, Norman Bishop and Aglaia Tsitsoura, proved to be very effective. My duties required two visits of two full days each per year and in addition there was a substantial amount of work to be done while in Cambridge. Quite a lot of wear and tear was involved in all this but I enjoyed it thoroughly and still regard it as one of my happiest experiences in international collaboration.

This was, I thought, an opportune moment for all of us to get out of our shells and turn an inquisitive eye on what kind of criminological work was being done in the leading European criminological centres; what kind was especially needed to support a more effective and humane system of criminal justice; and what resources have been made available to criminologists to help them to attain these objectives. A European Conference of Criminological Research Institutes seemed to me to be an appropriate point of departure, providing that it was well organized and carried out in style. Our proposal was endorsed by the ECCP and the secretariat of the Council of Europe. I was anxious that we should move fast and the first conference took place at the premises of the Council of Europe in Strasbourg on 9–12 December 1963.

The conference proved to be so invigorating that we had no difficulty in obtaining authorization from the Council of Europe to regard such conferences as a fixture in our programme of activities and to assign to them a prominent place. During my chairmanship seven such conferences at yearly intervals took place, growing from strength to strength. But throughout I kept a vigilant eye on the size and composition of the enterprise. These were not to be mass congresses with dozens of topics like so many of the meetings set on foot by national or international societies of criminology, but carefully selected gatherings of people representing distinctive approaches to criminological theory and research. There were hardly ever more than fifty participants. I also made it a firm point of our policy, while not neglecting established figures, to go out of our way to solicit the collaboration of the young eagles, those in their late twenties or early thirties. They were sometimes not easy to handle but they always proved to be the source of constructive ideas, of challenges to orthodoxy, or refreshing imagination. It would be tactless on my part to produce a list of names, but no surprise will be caused if I single out the Norwegian Nils Christie (now a professor and a member of the Norwegian Academy) as an outstanding exemplar of this breed. I also brought along a number of talented young English colleagues.

The pattern of organization of these conferences can be summed up as follows. The criminological members were selected by our council and participated in the gatherings by invitation from the secretariat of the Council of Europe. The choice of topics was also made by us but had to be approved by the ECCP, who also could make proposals and indeed were expected to take an active part in the conference, with a member often presiding over some of the sections. The number of topics for a conference was limited – an average of three or four – and only once were there five. As a general rule each topic was dealt with in a separate session with different chairmen and rapporteurs.

Observers from states which were not members of the Council of Europe were invited to attend the conferences and there were no rules preventing them from intervening either through questions or comments. I did not expect at the time that one of the most distinguished amongst them, Madame Inkeri Anttila – Professor of Criminal Law, Director of the Helsinki Institute of Criminology and a former Minister of Justice – would some twelve years later choose to contribute an article to the Festschrift in my honour on my work in Strasbourg in these critical early years.[61] Representatives from the leading international organizations pursuing activities in the penal sphere were also invited and could participate in discussions should they so desire. Usually the conference was opened by the Secretary-General of the Council of Europe or by his deputy. It ended with a press conference and a jolly reception. In addition to the part that I was expected to play in planning the conference, I sometimes made oral presentations in the sections. But much more frequently I was asked at the end of a conference to sum up and comment upon the gist of the deliberations and present tentative recommendations for further action. On other occasions I submitted my views to the next meeting of the CSC and the ECCP.[62]

During this period we put on the agenda of the conference thirty-two topics and in addition asked for fifteen stock-taking reports in reply to a questionnaire. We enlisted the collaboration of forty-one experts and welcomed six reports from scholars from non-member states. A list of the topics discussed at the conferences is useful, first because it reveals the kinds of problem which, a generation ago, were regarded as significant in the evolution of criminological thought and research; and second, because they were acknowledged by the Council of Europe as valuable in 'providing information for the guidance of Council of Europe member states' criminal policies and the planning of Council of Europe activities in the sphere of crime problems'.

- Organization and administration of criminological research
- Programmes and methods in fundamental research
- Programmes and methods in applied research
- Research into juvenile delinquency
- Ways and means of instituting co-operation between the institutes and the Council of Europe
- What senior officials, judges and others expect from criminological research
- Causation research in criminology
- Research into methods of crime prevention
- Research on the effectiveness of punishment and treatment

---

61 See Inkeri Anttila, 'The Foundation of Co-operation in European Criminological Research: Sir Leon Radzinowicz and the Criminological Scientific Council at the Council of Europe', in Roger Hood (ed.) *Crime, Criminology and Public Policy: Essays in Honour of Sir Leon Radzinowicz* (1974), pp. 25–32.
62 They are usually to be found in the *Proceedings* of the Conferences of Directors of Criminological Research Institutes. The *Proceedings* were first issued in mimeographed form, widely asked for and distributed. Later on they were included in the published volumes of *Collected Studies in Criminological Research*.

- Status of prisoners as individuals
- The prison community
- Problems and possibilities for the future
- Criminological aspects of road traffic offences
- Research concerning the characteristics of motoring offenders
- Desirable developments in the administration of justice
- Forecasting research in the social sciences, with special reference to demography
- Forecasting the volume and structure of future criminality
- Forecasting the trend of criminality in Finland
- Criminality of migrant workers
- Relationship between types of offenders and types of treatment
- Survey of such research in France
- Survey of such research in England
- Scandinavian research reports on the subject
- The dark figure of crime
- Model for the organization of corrections in a modern state
- Legal, judicial and administrative aspects
- Organization of a system of corrections
- Sociological and criminological aspects of correctional systems
- Methodology of criminological research
- The identification of key problems in sociological research within the field of criminology
- Fundamental psychological problems of contemporary criminological research in European countries
- Identification of the problems in criminological research, the lawyers' point of view
- Identification of key problems in penological research
- Identification of key problems in criminological research
- Six special reports on criminological research in certain member states and six reports relating to non-member states.

The success already achieved by the first conference was noteworthy, but it would have been a great mistake to exaggerate its potentialities because many of the criminological centres still lacked depth and influence. Yet the discussion at the conference was projected to centre upon the following complex topics: problems of organization and administration of criminological research; problems and methods of fundamental research; means of co-operation between institutes and the Council of Europe. In these circumstances I regarded it my duty at the first conference in 1963 to make a frank, indeed a blunt, statement on the prevailing state of criminological institutes, many of which, in my view, were no more than seminars. I was delighted to read much later that Professor Inkeri Anttila, in her already quoted article written in 1973, described it as a 'realistic observation' and that 'his comments, now twenty years old, still retain their accuracy and relevance'. She also remarked most wisely, in reference to the initial period of my presidency, that 'The first years are the most important, because then the goals and methods of a new organisation are determined.' I was fortunate to lead a council which fully shared my resolve to draw up a plan of immediate action which would go far beyond the purely ceremonial exercise which in the field of international collaboration much too often superseded urgently needed real work.

We decided to deploy, in addition to regularly held conferences, the following six initiatives:

1   Small meetings of research workers
2   Exchanges of research workers
3   Criminological research fellowships
4   Study visits on the spot
5   Regular biannual records of current criminological research
6   Serial publication of studies in criminological research and related matters.

It was encouraging to note the indispensable support we received from the ECCP and the secretariat of the Council of Europe. We had to put into effect some of these initiatives by stages and on a more restricted scale.[63] Nevertheless it was very rewarding to watch the activities of our Criminological Council in the period following our initial labours. In spite of the changes imposed by the impact of new circumstances and requirements, our basic approach remained intact. Nor could I personally remain unmoved by the tribute paid to me when, after the expiration of the three-year period of tenure, I was invited, again by unanimous vote, to continue as the Chairman for a further three years. At the closing of the Seventh Conference on 4 December 1969, which coincided with my retirement as Chairman, Professor Louk Hulsman, the Chairman of the ECCP, made a gracious speech emphasizing 'the important contribution' which I had made to the Council of Europe.

Summing-up

In my last year as Chairman of the Criminological Council I presented a report in which I tried to bring out some of the salient characteristics of the

---

63   For a more detailed enumeration of the initiatives taken, see the three following publications: *Council of Europe: Activities in the Field of Crime Problems. 1956–1976*; introduced by P.G. Pötz, Chairman of the ECCP (1977); Aglaia Tsitsoura, 'Un quart de siècle d'activités dans le domaine des problèmes criminels. Comité européen pour les problèmes criminels, Conseil de l'Europe', *Revue Internationale de Criminologie et de Police Technique*, no. 3 (1981), pp. 253–68; and a piece by Norman Bishop which I cannot put my hand on.

work in the international penal field. Professor Inkeri Anttila, who was again present, described my report as 'a frank and penetrating evaluation of the activities of the European Committee on Crime Problems' – a compliment which again gave me great and enduring pleasure.[64] I presented the following observations:

> International activities in the penal sphere were of course fraught with difficulties and disappointments. The working tempo is inevitably sluggish. Considerable circumspection is necessary. Only limited projects could be tackled, while more important issues often had to be shelved. The financial support continued to be meagre and difficult to secure. There are very frequent difficulties stemming from the differing approaches of research workers and administrators. There is no immediate visible result and the real influence of research on decisions taken by political, judiciary and administrative organs is still transient. But in the long run (very often much too long) in spite of all its flaws and imperfections the international work has a beneficial influence on the progress of criminal science and on the shaping of an improved criminal policy throughout the world. Patience is called for, but patience matched with enthusiasm.[65]

Some fifty-five years ago I concluded my survey of international collaboration in criminal matters (see p. 353) by stating that a proper solution to penal problems would not only benefit the stability of each country individually but also greatly improve international relationships between them. It seems to me that this conclusion is today as firmly warranted as ever. But I was also made acutely aware throughout these many years that an exceptionally tactful and sensitive approach is an essential ingredient in any undertaking pertaining to international collaboration in criminal matters. I have been convinced that in this field a moral responsibility should direct us not to avert our eyes or close our ears when degradations of human personality are practised by a fraudulent and distorted use of the term 'criminal justice'. The defence of society against crime is a grave international responsibility which derives justification from the very existence of the phenomenon of crime and from the disturbing manifestations it has assumed in so many parts of the

---

64 See Inkeri Anttila, *op. cit.*, p. 30.
65 A thorough and critical analysis of the material accumulated by international collaboration in criminal matters is still missing. A daunting task, if ever there has been one, and one which may never be satisfactorily discharged. But, for a few points of departure, the following should be noted: B.S. Alper and J.F. Borens, *Crime: International Agenda* (1972); Roger S. Clark, *The United Nations Crime Prevention and Criminal Justice Program* (1994); M. Cherif Bassiouni (ed.) *The Contributions of Specialised Institutes and Non-Governmental Organisations to the United Nations Criminal Justice Program* (1995).

world. But another aspect of our responsibility is not always given the predominance it deserves, and yet the reality behind it is in many ways more grim than the reality of crime itself. When John Howard's book on the *State of Prisons* appeared, Sir Samuel Romilly (the future crusader for the reform of the criminal laws of England) read it at once, and thus summed up his deep emotions in a letter to his brother-in-law John Roget dated 23 May 1781:

> Howard's *State of Prisons* is not a book of great literary merit; but it has a merit infinitely superior; it is one of those works which have been rare in all ages of the world – being written with the view only to the good of mankind . . . What a singular journey! – not to admire the wonders of art and nature – not to visit courts and ape their manners – but to compare the misery of men in different countries, and to study the acts of mitigating the torments of mankind![66]

It is our duty to recognize that the 'misery of men in different countries' is still with us. This is how I finished my report to the assembly of the Fourth United Nations Congress on the Prevention of Crime and the Treatment of Offenders in Kyoto on 26 August 1970. And this is where I stand today.

---

66 *Memoirs of the Life of Sir Samuel Romilly* (ed. by his sons, 1840), vol. 1, pp. 169–70.

16

SOME FORAYS ABROAD AND AT HOME

Consultative work

Australia

In Kyoto I had the good fortune to get to know the Hon. J.C. Maddison, the Minister of Justice of New South Wales (NSW). He was an impressive man, genuinely committed to developing proper standards in criminal justice, a liberal with a firm grip on reality, an attractive human being. I took to him at once. Three years later, in 1973, after he had visited me in Cambridge, I received an official invitation from him to go to Australia as the Consultant to the Minister of Justice, NSW, and the National Institute of Criminology for a period of five weeks. I had no hesitation in accepting.

The Minister was concerned about the condition of criminological research within his own ministry and about the status and prospects of the recently established National Institute of Criminology in Canberra. In more general terms he wanted me to give a stimulus to the increasing interest in criminology being taken by influential judges as well as amongst the wider public.

With help from the Minister a seminar was convened, composed of researchers in the department and senior officials. In a series of twelve longish sessions, I asked them to provide me with a detailed account of the research that they were undertaking or proposing to initiate. I followed this by an account of the main directions that research was taking in Britain, continental Europe and the United States of America. We then tried to draw up priorities for research which would be applicable to conditions prevailing in New South Wales. In doing so we critically reviewed the methodological and administrative problems which would be involved in this kind of research. The Minister himself was present at some of the sessions and sometimes a few outside experts would be invited to join us. As a general rule the meetings did not exceed twenty people and a three-hour session was *de rigueur*.

The second purpose of my visit was a lecture tour which required much moving about and many social encounters. Sometimes my lectures and addresses were given to the wider public but often they were directed to specifically convened meetings of judges, penal administrators, senior police officers and practising lawyers. I covered quite a range of topics, the subject being agreed with the organizers in good time ahead of each meeting. The cycle ended in Melbourne when I was invited by J.H. McClemens, Judge of the Supreme Court of New South Wales, to address the biennial conference of the Australian Crime Prevention, Corrections and After-Care Association (of which he was the Chairman) in the presence of the Governor-General, an impressive galaxy of dignitaries, and a large group of interested and knowledgeable people. I remember noticing in the audience with great pleasure Professor Norval Morris, who, after his academic studies in the London School of Economics under Dr Hermann Mannheim, did a lot of important work in Australia with Sir John Barry, a respected judge, before he moved to the University of Chicago Law School, where he left a distinctive mark on American criminology. The topic of this, concluding lecture was 'Some international trends in criminal policy and their relevance (if any) to the needs and aspirations of Australia'.

The third objective of my mission was the most delicate: the presentation of a report on the National Institute of Criminology in Canberra. At the time it was regarded as controversial. In consequence, I shall confine myself to a summary of its essentials. The Institute had been set up as an independent entity. It was hoped that it would establish and cultivate good relations with the academic world as well as with the Federal Ministry of Justice. But in practice the connection with the ministry was becoming dominant. The person in the ministry responsible for relations with the Institute was the Attorney-General. This arrangement did not seem to be working as smoothly as had originally been anticipated and there was concern in several influential quarters. I was expected to report on this central issue and on the directions that the Institute should follow in the future.

I had taken extensive evidence and made a few short investigations of my own. A judge had agreed to act as temporary head of the Institute and he was chosen to accompany me on some of my journeys. Judge Muirhead was a very amiable man, well disposed to my inquiry, and I derived much pleasure from his company. In my report I tried to indicate how fruitful the connections with a ministry can be if they are sustained in a sensitive and liberal manner, but also how negative, indeed how destructive, this influence can be if exercised in an interfering, intolerant and narrow way. I drew upon my experiences in England and abroad. The supportive yet non-interfering stance of the Home Office towards the Cambridge Institute of Criminology never failed to evoke great admiration.

For obvious reasons I made an oral statement about the relationship between the Ministry of Justice and the Institute. As regards the role of the Attorney-General, I felt I should be brief but unequivocal. He appeared to me to be a man of high and fertile intelligence, unusual in many ways. But he also struck me as impetuous, impatient, strong-willed and dogmatic. He was not the kind of man who should have been the *de facto* head of a National Institute of Criminology. Indeed, the Attorney-General, whoever he happened to be, ought not to direct the work of an academically independent institute, although he might well be invited to become a member of its advisory committee.

I strongly recommended that Mr William Clifford should be appointed as the Director. He was not a criminological star and he could be somewhat pedantic. But he had a solid appearance and many solid qualities which were badly needed at this stage of the Institute's life. He had wide experience and a gift for establishing good relationships and useful contacts. I am glad to say that my recommendation was accepted. He proved to be very good at the job. Several other suggestions were also endorsed and I concluded that the Institute had a bright future. It gave me particular pleasure when Dr Duncan Chappell, who had obtained his doctorate at the Cambridge Institute, was appointed a few years later as the Director of the Canberra Institute.

It was a principle in my consultative work that once my mission had been completed the file – to put it figuratively – was dead. If the subject needed to be re-examined I felt that someone else should have a fresh go at it.

I enjoyed my mission to Australia enormously. I was struck by the wild beauty of the country. I was exhilarated by the vitality of the Australians, even on occasions when it was carried somewhat too far. I was fascinated by their instantaneous, frank and robust responses even to most awkward questions. Because of their curiosity, hospitality and the distance from Europe, visitors are well advised to expect an exacting schedule. If my newly acquired Australian friend, the Minister, had still been alive I know I would have returned one day.

South Africa

My earlier visit to South Africa in 1970 bore little resemblance to my Australian journey. On the very day of my arrival I was struck by the tense, explosive and poignant atmosphere and felt repelled by the many glaring iniquities of the existing regime. But the terms assigned to me were more detached and more restricted. I was to advise whether an Institute of Criminology at the University of Cape Town should be part of the Law Faculty or whether it should be situated in the Department of Sociology within the Faculty of Social Sciences. I was also expected to stir up greater interest in criminology and an enlightened criminal policy through a series of public lectures and private meetings with the judiciary and the Bar. I made it clear that I expected my freedom of expression and movement to be guaranteed; that I should be able to visit penal institutions; and that I would be able to talk not only to the supporters of the regime but also to some of its leading opponents. I specifically expressed the hope that suitable arrangements would be made for me to visit Nelson Mandela in prison. I informed the

Foreign Office about my impending visit and our Ambassador elegantly entertained me on two occasions with important personalities who had been invited to meet me. It may well be that one or two of the distinguished guests have since appeared before Archbishop Desmond Tutu's Truth and Reconciliation Commission to unload their more or less guilty conscience relating to the past. I had read a lot about the fascinating and agonizing history of the country and I had revealing conversations with well-informed experts on the South African scene before I left, such as Sir Robert Birley, the former Headmaster of Eton, Meyer Fortes, Professor of Social Anthropology at Cambridge, and Bob Hepple, the Cambridge law don and now Master of Clare College.

The promoter of my visit and my principal host was Professor Edward Batson, the Dean of the Faculty of Social Sciences and Professor of Sociology at the University of Cape Town, whom I had met previously at an international congress in Mendoza, Argentina. He was a progressive (he came from the London School of Economics) and appeared to me to have an exceptionally well-organized mind. Fundamentally withdrawn, he nevertheless formed strong personal loyalties. There was a certain veil of sadness about him: he did not seem to be happily disposed towards his own life. I spent several most pleasing evenings in his company and also with Professor Bronhilda Helm, a formidable and very intelligent woman. Furthermore, I was very grateful for the welcome extended to me by the Hon. J.H. Steyn (the scion of a distinguished South African family) and at that time Judge of the Cape Provincial Division of the Supreme Court of South Africa, who was keenly interested in penal reform. James Midgley, a young lecturer in the Department of Sociology and Social Administration at Cape Town, was assigned to help me move about and to keep records of the information which I gathered. A pupil of the inspiring Richard Titmuss at the London School of Economics, he inherited from his teacher a conscience in social matters and considerable discernment. Of course, his career has not stood still. He has since been a lecturer in the London School of Economics, a Dean and Professor of Social Work in the University of Louisiana and is now Professor and Dean of the School of Social Welfare in the University of California at Berkeley. He is the author of one of the early pioneering pieces on the condition of capital punishment in South Africa – which is still an important contribution to the subject. I am very happy that we continued to be in touch.

I took some time to reflect upon the central issue, namely in what faculty the Institute should be situated. I asked for two meetings to be convened, one with representatives of the Law School and another with members of the Faculty of Social Sciences. I also took evidence from several witnesses from outside the university. I reached the conclusion that, especially in the prevailing political atmosphere in the country, it would be better to anchor the Institute in the Law School where it was more likely to enjoy a higher standing and exercise a wider beneficial influence. But I also strongly emphasized that there should be close and regular links with the Social Sciences Faculty as well as some other departments of the university. A further vital requirement was that the Head of the Institute, who would presumably be a Professor of Criminal Law, should be someone with a good understanding of and deep sympathy with the wider concerns of criminology and criminal policy. This solution was accepted and I was particularly happy because it also met with Professor Batson's consent. I was pleased but not surprised because he was not an empire builder, but a man who put the public good before personal ambition. I was not asked to recommend who should be the Director.

Following my public lectures, I was frequently asked to give a press conference in the course of which I was not reluctant to express my views about delicate and divisive aspects of criminal policy. Capital punishment was the issue which gave rise to the most passionate responses. I did not hesitate to express my grave misgivings about the South African system. I was greatly impressed by the quality of several High Court judges and eminent barristers, but I noted their unhappiness in being involved with a system of criminal justice which so openly violated basic human rights. I was very uneasy about both the civil and military police, the heavy-handed and secretive way in which they functioned and the lack of accountability for their actions. With a very few exceptions the penal system was atrocious. The cages filled with forty or fifty convicts haunted me long after I left the country. My demand to visit Polsmore Prison on Robin Island, where Nelson Mandela was detained, and to meet the most illustrious political prisoner of the twentieth century (beating Gandhi on this score), was only partially implemented. I was given a thorough and long tour of the place and had a useful two-hour discussion with the governor. But I was informed that I could not meet Nelson Mandela because he was not in the prison at the time of my visit. Needless to say, I did not believe it.

I was struck by the fact there was no fair and well-informed text dealing with the South African penal scene. Taking advantage of my presence there, a foundation was laid for such an endeavour through my discussions with James Midgley and Mr Justice Steyn. I left it in their capable hands and, as a result, a substantial book was produced by twenty collaborators. It was composed of three parts, each with an introduction: 'The Crime Solution', 'The Criminal Justice System' and 'Social Welfare in Correctional Work'. The twenty chapters gave a vivid and highly informative account of the condition of crime and punishment in the country at that time, although for understandable reasons they could not go as far as they might have wished.[1] I was

---

1 James Midgley, Jan H. Steyn and Roland Graser, *Crime and Punishment in South Africa* (1975).

asked to write an introduction but I refused because I felt strongly that no impression should be created that it was not a 'genuine local product'. But a gracious reference to me in the preface naturally gave me much pleasure.

The moral and social misery of the country has been laid bare by many gifted hands. But to see it directly operating at so many levels, and usually with such relentless inflexibility, is an altogether different experience. The position appeared to me untenable in the long run. It also seemed to me that the attitude of Britain had not been sufficiently robust. A vigorous implementation of economic sanctions should have been set in motion much earlier. But all this is already history. Today, the Republic of South Africa, like so many other newly born states, presents, at least in the criminal sphere, a disjunction between aspirations and practice. The recently adopted Constitution, which aims to inculcate a 'human rights culture', is firmly grounded on what I have described as the socio-liberal doctrine in criminal policy (see pp. 115–119). Capital punishment was abolished even though murder, violent criminality and many other forms of serious criminal activities have all risen drastically. Indeed, the maintenance of public order is fragile. I believe it will take some twenty years – providing that political and economic circumstances evolve in the right direction – before the new republic is endowed with a system of criminal justice faithful to the spirit of the new Constitution.

A few years later I was invited to pay another visit to South Africa to give a series of lectures. Unfortunately my already fixed commitments prevented me from going. I was delighted to hear that Professor Nigel Walker, my distinguished successor at Cambridge, was able to take up this invitation. These are connections which should not be allowed to die out.

New York

In 1963 the prestigious New York Bar Association expressed its readiness to sponsor the launching of a survey, the purpose of which would be 'to suggest how the City of New York could marshal its resources to provide new knowledge and a better mechanism for continuing improvements in criminal justice'. Mr Henry T. Heald, the President of the Ford Foundation, and his senior advisers, particularly William Pincus, evinced an immediate interest in such an undertaking and offered the necessary financial support. Swift action followed. The Hon. Herbert Brownell (the powerful and highly respected Attorney-General in President Eisenhower's administration), at that time the President of the New York Bar Association, set up an advisory committee, to be known as the Special Committee on the Administration of Criminal Justice. The Chairman was Mr Justice Charles Breitel, the Chief Judge of the State of New York. He was a prominent Republican, a man of wide interests with an acute analytical mind. There were five other members, all of them well known and of varied experience.[2] A month later, in July 1963, I had the honour of being invited by Herbert Brownell to come to New York to conduct the investigation under the auspices of the committee.

It was a fascinating assignment but also complex and forbidding. In New York one feels that at any turn one might step on a landmine. Its perplexing and disturbing diversity of population, its seemingly unbridgeable disparities, its tensions and conflicts, inexhaustible dynamism, fierce and often ruthless competition, its brutal reality but also surges of inspiring idealism, its abject poverty and dehumanization of a number of ethnic groups, but also its bewildering embrace of a never ending philanthropy, corruptive practices of unusual audacity and inventiveness, insatiable needs for novelty, for glamour, for promising the unattainable, of rejecting the past and yet often being so insecure of the future. These were some of the features which struck me forcibly. Although it is true that one may encounter many of these characteristics, including a similar level of criminality, in many of the big cities of the world, in New York they are displayed on a stupendous scale. On no account could my inquiry be detached from these considerations.

It was clear that I had to attack my task from many different angles and on many different levels. And it was no less obvious that I had to carry out my investigations by stages, to have sufficient time to absorb the accumulated information. The members of the committee, all exceedingly busy people, made no secret that they wished to have speedily in their hands a concise document and – to facilitate its wider circulation – one which would be free of professional jargon, menacing statistics and elaborate projections.

I carried out my work in three stages, starting on 1 September 1963. In consultation with the chairman of my advisory committee and several of its members, I drew up a list of ninety-three leading New York authorities on criminal justice and its wider social context. They represented the judiciary, public prosecutors, attorneys, city administrators, police, penal and rehabilitative agencies, psychiatrists, social workers and professors. All of them agreed to engage with me in frank and thorough discussions and allowed me to keep a record of our encounter. I also made an attempt to get acquainted with the major pieces of research on the state of crime, the machinery of justice, the treatment of offenders and the general prevention of crime which were being carried out in the New York area. I also went to see how criminal law, criminal policy and criminology were taught in the Law Schools of the area, and I also investigated criminological studies in some Departments of Sociology, Schools of Social Work, and psychiatric establishments. I visited the leading centres for the training of personnel involved in the many law enforcement agencies. I endeavoured to learn more about the working of

---

2 Timothy N. Pfeiffer, Harris B. Steinberg, Bethuel M. Webster, Herbert Wechsler and David S. Worgan. Roland W. Donnem was the Secretary.

judicial conferences and tried to assess their impact, as well as that of the leading Bar Associations in the city. I could not help being fascinated by several major scientific institutions, such as the Brookhaven National Laboratory or the Rockefeller Institute (now Rockefeller University). Although I spent most of my time in New York, I went to Harvard, to Yale, to Philadelphia and to Washington, to seek further information on certain points of wider concern. And as I went along I accumulated all kinds of material, again from a wide range of sources, published and unpublished. At the end this amounted to a small and very revealing library. I also drew upon my experiences in Cambridge as well as upon my criminological connections in Europe and certain parts of the Commonwealth.

Dean Eugene Rostow of the Yale Law School kindly made me a member of the Yale Club, situated in the heart of Manhattan, and I stayed there while carrying out the inquiry. I was also fortunate to have my headquarters at the Bar Association on 42nd Street. Opposite was the landmark hotel and restaurant of New York, the Algonquin, where I was given a small table, tucked into a corner, so that I could draw strength from their excellent cuisine and reliable martinis. Six weeks after I had begun work I submitted to my committee a few preliminary, rather tentative, findings. On 15 April 1964 I gave them an outline of my impending report. On both occasions I had the benefit of a lengthy, thorough and frank exchange of views. The final draft of the report was completed following a meeting of the committee on 30 October 1964 and received their 'unanimous endorsement'. Judge Breitel submitted it to the Hon. Samuel J. Roseman, Herbert Brownell's successor as the President of the Bar Association, who warmly encouraged the committee to pursue the project to its conclusion. Roseman was a democrat, best remembered as President Roosevelt's adviser on the Home Front – the man who 'invented' for the President the term 'New Deal', which Roosevelt used as his signature tune when unfolding his vast plan of social reconstruction. The executive committee of the Bar Association in its turn transmitted my report to the Ford Foundation. Published under the title *The Need for Criminology* (1965), it was out of print a few months after publication.

As to the main recommendation, no one could articulate it with greater precision and conviction than Judge Breitel in his foreword to the report. I can do no better than reproduce the relevant passage:

> The fact is, as demonstrated in the annexed report, that there has been no continuing, permanent organisation or institution for the study of crime in all its phases in this country. Instead there have been only isolated curricula associated with university or professional schools, largely subordinated to vocational training (and vocational biases) in the field of criminal law administration, ranging from police science and administration to the education of lawyers in criminal prosecution and defence . . . The obvious need for a continu-

ing center or institute for basic criminological study and for the practical application of criminological research has for one reason or another gone unmet despite this country's rich institutional and educational resources. Such an institute or center of criminology should be an institution of educational quality and standing. In the first place, it should be a home of basic or pure research in the field of criminology following the pursuit of knowledge wheresoever it might lead and without commitment to the achievement of a particular, practical result which might otherwise introduce bias into the research. Secondly, it should provide practical programs for the application of knowledge and techniques developed by its basic research. Thirdly, such an institute or center should embrace within its program all the disciplines which may contribute to the understanding of the nature of crime, its effects and its control. These would include disciplines varying from psychology through sociology, anthropology, and economics to the law itself. Fourthly, in addition to providing a home for research, such a center or institution should be the source and home from which, either experimentally or on a continuing basis, there can be offered or developed advanced training programs for future experts in the field of criminology and its several larger branches ... [T]he Committee found itself in complete agreement with its reporter that the kind of criminological center ... contemplated should, as a matter of strong preference, not be associated with any particular university, professional school, government or private organisation devoted to other purposes ... It must be free to do advanced work untrammelled and it must also have the prestige associated with an elite institution of advanced study ... The Committee and its reporter are deeply aware that what is being projected in this report by Professor Radzinowicz is a grand institution on a grand scale ... The Committee, particularly its Chairman, are very grateful indeed to Professor Radzinowicz who by reason of his unique knowledge, ability, and experience in this field has been able to articulate for us what we earnestly hope and pray, will provide a memorable plan for a magnificent contribution. This country, blessed with resources, yet conscious that its civilisation is circumscribed with an insidious and under-mining rise of criminal anti-social conduct crossing all economic, social and ethnic classifications, would do well to give this contribution its serious consideration.

the report had an influence on what President Johnson's Commission on the Challenge of Crime in a Free Society had to say about proper training in criminology. It also had an impact on the establishment of the highly respected School of Criminal Justice in Albany, which owed so much to the efforts of Elliot H. Lombard, at that time Special Assistant Counsel for Law Enforcement in the New York Executive Department.

A towering figure was needed to put the whole plan into effect, someone utterly devoted and willing to act for the first five or even ten years. And in my view it had to be an American with a well-grounded knowledge of the situation in New York and of the wider national scene. There was no such person then available. Today the rhetoric of criminal policy in the United States is dominated by more and more calls for the use of the death penalty and for stringent enforcement of the crude slogan 'Three strikes and you're out'. In this climate an Advanced Institute of Criminal Science and Administration of Criminal Justice would have no chance of getting off the ground.

Washington

Yet another American initiative, this time launched from the White House, deserves at least a brief mention, because it provides a classic illustration of what Americans mean by a major commission and how they make it move forward in an incredibly brief span of time. What follows can be looked upon as a 'case study' and lessons of some significance may be derived from it. I had the honour to be the only foreigner invited to become consultant to the commission, and as such one of the six members of the advisory panel.

On 10 June 1968, by executive order, President Lyndon B. Johnson established a commission 'to undertake a penetrating search for the causes and prevention of violence – a search into our national life, our past as well as our present, our traditions as well as our institutions, our culture, our customs, our laws'. The charge to the commission, to quote the President's words, was 'simple and direct'. This had a typical Johnsonian ring about it. The commission respectfully added that 'it was also demanding'. The Chairman was Dr Milton S. Eisenhower, President Eisenhower's brother, a noted educator who had been president of three universities. The commission consisted of thirteen members, all public figures of high standing and varied experience. Four of them had special assistants to help them. Two assisted the Chairman and Terence Cardinal Cooke, Senator Philip Hart and Senator Roman Hruska each had one special assistant at their elbow. Lloyd N. Cutler was the Executive Director of the commission and close to him there was a deputy director, a general counsel, a senior administrative officer, a director of information, and last but not least two co-directors of research, Professor Marvin E. Wolfgang and James F. Short Jr – both at the height of their reputations as scholars and researchers in the field of criminology, including the phenomenon of violence.

Then there was the commission's staff consisting of five people engaged on editorial, research and writing tasks, five administrators and ten executive secretaries. There was also a network of experts connected with task forces and study teams covering seven different areas of inquiry. Each had an extensive staff consisting in total of nearly two hundred people. These task forces were supplemented by five special investigative reports, carried out by seven researchers and by several dozen shorter commissioned papers. A Student Report Panel composed of fourteen students was set up. The advisory panel of consultants to the commission has already been mentioned.

While the commission was sitting, forty-seven academic conferences and twenty-nine conferences on 'Youth and Violence' were held in many parts of the country. The views of twenty university presidents were solicited and duly obtained. And detailed evidence was taken from close to ninety witnesses at public hearings. The commission itself spent sixty days in closed session debating the issues. After eighteen months the report was published in December 1969 under a title borrowed from the Constitution *To Establish Justice, to Insure Domestic Tranquility*. Its less dramatic official title was the National Commission on the Causes and Prevention of Violence. It was a document of about three hundred pages, written in a fluent, plain and concise manner, free of jargon, forceful, and carrying great conviction. Fourteen volumes of supportive material were published, all of them highly readable, constantly informative and well constructed.[3] I was, however, surprised that this enthusiasm for publication did not stretch to a volume containing the oral evidence which had been gathered from so many quarters.

I know of no comparable enterprise in any country in the world and, even in the United States, the only two which came close to it were the National Commission on Law Observance and Enforcement (known as the Wickersham Commission, 1931) and the President's Commission on Law Enforcement and Administration of Justice, which had reported in 1967.[4]

There can be no doubt that any progressive and affluent society should regard such a critical stocktaking as a commitment to be regularly undertaken. But as an instrument for immediate political action a commission of this kind is too cumbersome, too diffuse and too potentially divisive to have an immediate and tangible effect on the reality of its subject-matter. Moreover the emphasis of this commission was not so much on violence as a reflex of individual behaviour but rather as a phenomenon conditioned by historical, economic, socio-psychological and political forces. By its very nature such an approach was unlikely to lead to recommendations for immediate changes which could affect the level of violence in society. Also, sometimes a

---

3 See *Assassination and Political Violence*; *Law and Order Reconsidered*; *Crimes of Violence* (3 vols); *Violence in America: Historical and Comparative Perspectives* (2 vols); *Firearms and Violence in American Life*; *Shut it Down! A College in Crisis*; *Rights in Concord*; *The Politics of Protest*; *Shootout in Cleveland*; *Violence and the Media*.

4 The *Report of the Commission on Obscenity and Pornography* (1970) came close to the Violence Commission as regards its scope and supportive research, but it did not primarily deal with crime and the commission was acutely divided in its final recommendations.

particular factor may be overlooked by an inquiry or its importance not sufficiently recognized at the time. Soon afterwards this very factor may turn out to be so important that, had it been taken into account, the findings and interpretation of the inquiry would have had to be drastically recast. In the case of the Commission on Violence, illegal drugs proved to be such a factor. Hardly any reference is to be found to its impact on the phenomenon of crime and violence, either in the volumes of supportive material or in the report itself. In any case, a commission of this complexity would have been hard pressed to rearrange its priorities at short notice.

Finally, it would be highly desirable, both from the academic and practical points of view, if a decade or two after a significant investigative body had reported, it or some other well-qualified group were to be asked to reassess the recommendations in the light of subsequent experience.[5]

I had a marvellous time acting as a consultant. I was hoping that my connection would be primarily with Lloyd Cutler, the Executive Director, rather than with the commission itself. And this is how it developed. I used to send him my observations on the incoming reports and sometimes he would ask me to submit a more lengthy memorandum, for example a paper on the connection between economic conditions and crime. On a few occasions we met informally for a drink or dinner in Washington to exchange views on some of the problems. It was a great privilege to have had this association with Lloyd Cutler. A prominent Washington lawyer, counsel to two presidents (Carter and Clinton), Lloyd Cutler is a man who one cannot forget. Formal and reserved, maybe somewhat withdrawn, concise and precise, with a high capacity for getting rapidly to the crux of complex problems, a gift for balanced judgement, a proven loyalty in personal and professional relations, a critical mind but combined with a subtle understanding of human frailties as well as of social vicissitudes. Politically I would have the temerity to describe him as a Democrat of the centre. I was touched when I heard that he was one of those who urged the American Law Institute to make me an Honorary Foreign Member. I was no less flattered when he expressed an interest in the project which led to the publication of this book by introducing me to Judge Patrick Cudahy, and thus securing the support of the Patrick and Ann M. Cudahy Foundation.

Preaching the criminological gospel

I like teaching and lecturing very much but I have not been involved with it at every stage of my academic career. For many years there was not much

---

5 I was pleased to note that a similar suggestion was made (but with much greater authority) by Mirva Komarowsky (ed.) *Sociology and Public Policy: the Case of Presidential Commissions* (1975), which includes an illuminating piece by Robert Merton.

teaching worth talking about: one or two courses in Geneva, a little more over a longer period in Warsaw, hardly ever when engaged in research abroad, and in Cambridge, as an Assistant Director of Research, one course a week for one term in the LLB programme. When the Institute of Criminology was established the situation changed but, as a result of my deliberate decision, not very drastically. I used to give the opening part of the course in criminology to undergraduate students and lectured on 'The development of criminological thought' to the postgraduate course. I also gave opening lectures to the various specialized programmes launched by the Institute. I would have liked to lecture more but I was anxious (and in this I was firmly supported by the Committee of Management) that the maximum possible opportunities for lecturing should be given to the young and enthusiastic assistant directors of research.

My major involvement in teaching took place in the United States between the period 1962 and 1979. It was an involvement on a very large scale as the following list reveals:

Walter E. Meyer Research Professor, Yale Law School, 1962–3

Adjunct Professor of Criminal Law and Criminology, Columbia Law School, 1964–77

Visiting Professor, Criminal Law and Criminology, Virginia Law School, 1968–75

Professor of Criminology, Rutgers University (Camden) Law School, 1968–72, 1979–81

Visiting Professor, Department of Sociology, University of Pennsylvania, 1970–4[6]

Visiting Professor of Criminal Justice, John Jay College, City University of New York, 1978–9

Visiting Professor, Criminal Law and Criminology, Benjamin N. Cardozo Law School, Yeshiva University, New York, 1979–81

Visiting Professor of Criminology, University of Minnesota Law School, 1979[7]

Often the adjective 'distinguished' was added to make me feel better. I had to take these commitments seriously. There was no binding contract of any kind, merely a yearly appointment which could be easily revoked.

---

6   Later (1979–82) I became an Overseer of the University of Pennsylvania Law School and an Associate Trustee.

7   I also had the privilege of being appointed (for short terms in all instances) a Visitor to the Princeton Institute of Advanced Study in 1975, a Visitor to the Rockefeller Center in Bellagio in 1976, and to the Max Planck Institute (criminological section) in Freiburg in 1990.

On one occasion, during a period of student unrest, I entered the lecture room to be confronted by a notice emblazoned on a banner: 'We have enough local reactionaries. Do we need a British knight?' The class, calm and silent, was waiting to see how I would react. When I said, 'Yes, you do need me, but it may take quite a long time for you to realize it', they burst into laughter and applauded. Early on, when there were still few women in the Law Schools of the country, the competitive and aggressive attitude of the male students inhibited women from participating in the seminars as fully as they wished. Two of them came to see me to ask whether it might embarrass the men if I were to run one or two parallel seminars exclusively for the women. I agreed to this suggestion and it worked well. The 'women's seminar' presented me with a luxurious wallet and the aggressive male students began to behave better. Today, I suppose that I might be accused of sexual discrimination in reverse. On yet another occasion, when I was in Cambridge expecting to receive examination papers from Columbia Law School, an airline strike broke out. I managed through the courtesy of our embassy in Washington to receive them through the diplomatic bag. My students were greatly excited by it. Almost everywhere at the end of my course the Dean and the faculty would give a farewell party, but perhaps I appreciated it even more when a similar gesture was forthcoming from the students.

My headquarters were in New York at the then exquisite Stanhope Hotel opposite the Metropolitan Museum. Studio 215 was my regular abode. I was allowed to leave the bulk of my papers and part of my wardrobe there so as to make the flight across the Atlantic as convenient as possible. As I love the sea I would, in the early days when it was still possible and the pressure of time was not too great, return to Britain on one of the great ocean liners.

The teaching was exhilarating but also very exacting. Neither its shape nor its contents followed a uniform pattern. In some places I would give a course of lectures and seminars; in another only a series of lectures; in yet another, seminars only – but sometimes two in parallel when there were more than twenty candidates.

The seminars were organized in two stages. During my autumn visit I would convene a meeting usually lasting a full two hours in which I would expound the plan of the seminar which I had in mind and consider any comments and suggestions from the students. I would then interview each participant and discuss with him or her the chosen topic. One of the class was asked to act as secretary to the seminar, to keep in touch with the other members and with me while I was in Cambridge. Their reports had to be in the hands of the secretary before my arrival so that all of us could read them. I based my marks on the quality of the written report, the way in which it was presented, and on the contribution the student made to the discussions in the seminar as a whole. The librarians played their part to the full. A selective and up-to-date criminological section was built up in the law faculty library.

I was never short of very good and keenly interested students. The reports and discussions were always lively and direct (as may be expected from Americans), but always courteous. Each session lasted two hours ending with a brief summary from me of the major conclusions. At the end of the entire series of seminars I made a lengthy survey of what had been achieved.

Giving a course of lectures presented different problems. There is a core of criminological knowledge which must find its place in any worthwhile course, but adaptations need to be made when teaching in a law school. There are many approaches and issues which have to be handled in a rather subtle manner if the interest of law students in the subject is to be maintained. I quickly appreciated, when teaching simultaneously at two, three or even four law schools, how the emphasis of the course had to be readjusted to fit the traditions of each particular school. Its style of operation, the cultural and social background of the student body, even the location of the school, had a subtle but pervasive influence on the aspects of criminology which the students were likely to be interested in. However, sometimes it was a good pedagogical stimulus to redirect their attention into corners of the subject which they professed not to be interested in.

I followed the American way of lecturing, allowing, indeed encouraging, interruptions, questions, disagreements or appeals for further clarification or amplification. But I was rather severe with a small but persistent group of students who tried to monopolize the discussions. I called them the 'Besser Wissers' ('knowing better than anyone else'). I used to give the class a selected reading list and sometimes I prepared a handout entitled 'Hundred questions in criminology and criminal justice' which I left with them for further reflection.

I am fully aware that this rather exceptional programme of preaching criminology in places not previously known for being attracted to it was, to some extent, due to the glamorous adoption of the subject in the ancient, illustrious and traditionally orientated University of Cambridge and the international reputation so rapidly gained by the Institute of Criminology. But the main reason is to be found in the spirit animating the period. It was a stage in American domestic history when the liberal ideology was still vibrant. I do not believe that today, even if I were as young as I was then, that I would have the slightest chance to embark upon a similar adventure. Times have changed. That is the simple answer.

In addition to regular teaching I was frequently invited to give public lectures. In responding to such invitations I had a guiding principle. One should not do too much of it. Otherwise there is the danger of repetition and eventually of superficiality. And when time is precious one should conserve one's energy for occasions when one can say something really worthwhile. In a long career such as mine I could not always be faithful to this principle, but I tried. Particularly in the field of criminal policy, one is often asked to address questions of the moment, and inevitably a lot of what one has to say turns out in the long run to have been rather ephemeral. Looking back, only a few of my public addresses stand out in my mind, such as the Selden Society Lecture on 'Sir James Fitzjames Stephen'; the three Carpentier Lectures at Columbia, published as *Ideology and Crime*; the Frank Newsam Memorial Lecture on 'The Dangerous Offender'; 'Criminology and the Climate of Social Responsibility', given to the Howard League for Penal Reform; the Peter Le Neve Foster Lecture 'The Criminal in Society' sponsored by the Royal Society of Arts; 'Them and Us' given under the auspices of the New Bridge; and my contribution to the bicentennial celebrations in Turin of the publication of Cesare Beccaria's *On Crimes and Punishments*.

My crowded teaching commitments in the United States required great concentration. Nevertheless I made time to enjoy the many attractions of New York, Washington and other cities. The splendid museums, intriguing art galleries, lavishly staged operas, erratic but often so fascinating plays and shows, were a source of constant pleasure. Nor shall I ever forget the personal side. I was constantly the beneficiary of the renowned American hospitality and spontaneous friendliness, which often grew into real friendships: Paul Freund, Walter Gelhorn, Harvey Goldschmid, Abe Goldstein, Joseph Goldstein, Erwin Griswold, Paul Hayes, Louis Henkin, Alfred Hill, Daniel Maier-Katkin, Peter Low, David Rockefeller Jr, Abe Rosenthal, Thorsten Sellin, John Stead, Telford Taylor, Marvin Wolfgang, to name only a few. I was impressed by the Deans of all the law schools and institutes at which I taught: Eugene Rostow at Yale, William Warren and Michael Sovern at Columbia, Monrad Paulsen at Virginia and later at Cardozo, Russell Fairbanks at Rutgers Camden, Carl Auerbach at Minnesota and Gerald Lynch, President of John Jay College. They were different in background and diverse in their interests, but they had in common a resolve continuously to raise standards in their institutions and to promote interesting innovations. It was my good fortune to forge firm friendships with all of them.

I was lucky to get a glimpse of the old lions of the past, especially Felix Frankfurter and Judge Learned Hand. My closest friends in the United States were, and still remain, Herbert and Doris Wechsler. Herbert did more than anybody else to lay the foundation for the modern study of criminal law in its various aspects (see Plate 10). He is justly famed as the architect of the American Law Institute's Model Penal Code.[8] The time of his lectures at Columbia Law School coincided with mine and we invariably lunched together. Only much later did I hear the student witticism, paraphrasing a well-known Boston saying ('The Lowells talk to the Cabots and the Cabots

---

8   See the tribute I paid to him at a meeting especially convened for that purpose by the Correctional Association of New York in 1982. Leon Radzinowicz, 'Herbert Wechsler's Role in the Development of American Criminal Law and Penal Policy', *Virginia Law Review*, vol. 69 (1983), pp. 1–10.

talk only to God'): 'Radzinowicz talks only to Wechsler and Wechsler talks only to God.'

Helping to transplant a foreign institution into English soil

This describes a proposal I put before the Lord Chief Justice, Lord Parker, in the 1960s. I had the great satisfaction to see it adopted almost at once. I had outlined the wider background which activated me to take this initiative in an article published in *The Times*.[9] What follows is a summary of it, but one should be aware that many things have changed since I wrote it in 1964.

As dispensers and maintainers of law, English lawyers are unrivalled, but it was said many years ago that they did not begin to consider matters connected with punishment 'till after they are judges, and then only cursorily and at odd times'.

Before the beginning of the nineteenth century a blind reliance on crude deterrence had not encouraged scrutiny of penal legislation, of sentencing practices or their effects. Sir Samuel Romilly showed remarkable foresight when, in 1817, he hailed Bentham's famous treatise on punishment with the comment: 'Penal legislation hitherto has resembled what the science of physic must have been when physicians did not know the propensities and effects of the medicines they administered.' The pressure for reform in the first part of the nineteenth century brought a wider recognition of the need to consider such issues. But the judges were rarely in the van of progress. In the 1840s the Select Committee of the House of Lords asked the judges for their views on the relative effectiveness of punishments. In the 1880s the Home Secretary, at the suggestion of the head of the prison administration, drew the Lord Chancellor's attention to the great disparities in the sentences imposed by different judges. This provoked a vigorous reaction from that untamed lion, Sir James Fitzjames Stephen, who objected to the idea of trying to secure uniformity in sentencing as unconstitutional, impracticable and unnecessary. 'It is unavoidable', he concluded, 'that the judge should have his attention more strongly directed to the crime, and that the officials of the prison department should think more of the criminals.'

The next significant stage was marked by full-scale debates in both Houses of Parliament on sentencing practices. Striking evidence was again brought forward of 'inequality and irregularity' in sentences passed in all kinds of courts and it was proposed that a Royal Commission be appointed to explore the whole field. The proposal was rejected, though both the Home Secretary and the Lord Chancellor acknowledged the reality of the problem and expressed their intentions to deal with it. As the result of a second

---

9   'Sentencing Policy in Criminal Cases', *The Times* (30 May 1964).

debate, initiated by Lord Herschel, the Lord Chancellor, in 1890, the judges came together in a series of informal conferences with the intention of clarifying the principles that should regulate the selection of sentences for certain groups of offences.

In my article I stressed that these early initiatives were of more than historical interest. The principles and attitudes were still relevant. There had however been a subtle shift of approach. Concern was still expressed about disparities in sentencing, but the issue was not only uniformity but also the utility of sentences. Hence the demand for more information about offenders and about the effectiveness of the available ways of dealing with them. The report of the Streatfeild Committee marked a new sense of urgency in facing the problems of sentencing as well as recognizing their increasing complexity. Brian Cubbon, then a young civil servant, served the Committee with remarkable efficiency and sensibility. Some years later he became the Permanent Under-Secretary of State at the Home Office, where I got to know him well. He became a valued and dear friend.

The report contained many wise reflections and many useful recommendations, all inspired by the contention that 'sentencing is, in a sense, an emergent branch of the law'. The Home Office booklet *The Sentence of the Court* (1964), which was the direct product of the committee's work, immediately proved to be a valuable practical instrument in assisting the courts to discharge their duties.

I went on to say that society must give support to the judges who, like surgeons in an emergency, had to use the instruments ready to hand. As criminologists themselves still knew too little about the effects of sentences it was perhaps not entirely fair to expect judges to know a lot. It was, however, perfectly fair to expect those who imposed sentences to show a genuine interest in all major aspects of this intricate business; to share and examine their common experiences; and to encourage and take advantage of any knowledge, however modest, accumulated in the course of the enforcement of the criminal law and through criminological studies. Those engaged in devising new approaches for dealing with offenders as well as those engaged in criminological research would be greatly encouraged if they knew that what they were trying to do was considered important by the judiciary.

During my many trips to North America I often wondered whether I might come across a development which, if carefully transplanted, might help the English judges to evolve to more consistent sentencing policy. 'Sentencing institutes' for judges struck me as being likely to make such a contribution.

On three occasions I had been invited to attend such sentencing institutes held in the New York area, to witness their activities at close quarters and to follow this up with prolonged conversations with some of the leading judges in charge of them. Some fifty to sixty judges would convene together for a two-day conference, usually in an attractive place outside New York. They would break up into five or six syndicates, each chaired by a senior judge. Each of these syndicates received identical details of between ten and fifteen cases, each raising important and controversial issues. All the judges were asked to consider the cases and to say what sentences they would impose, and why. The outcome of each syndicate was carefully recorded and compared at a plenary session. These comparisons were very illuminating. Apart from the influences judges could have on each other, there were frank discussions with experts from outside the judiciary: academics, psychiatrists, probation officers and prison officials. Often a highly qualified social statistician would extrapolate the essential findings in as scientifically reliable and yet acceptable form for the benefit of all those involved.

It is this experience that I brought to the attention of Lord Parker on my return to Britain. I showed him the article which I was then preparing for *The Times*. His response was immediate and most encouraging. His mind was soon made up that a similar scheme should be set on foot in Britain. The first one-day conference was held on 30 September 1963. On the day that my article was published in May 1964, *The Times* announced that Lord Parker had called for the setting up of a working party to organize 'more and longer conferences for holders of judicial office'.[10] It was composed of judges only, but Lord Parker asked me whether I would like to continue to advise him or join the committee. In view of my many commitments I preferred the former alternative. I was soon asked to propose 'outside experts' to participate in a two-day conference for High Court judges to be held in January 1965. I ventured to suggest Dr Walter Hammond of the Home Office Research Unit; Dr Lindsay Neustatter, the Senior Physician in Psychological Medicine at the Royal Northern Hospital; Dr Nigel Walker, then Reader in Criminology at Oxford; and Dr Donald West, at that time Assistant Director of Research at the Cambridge Institute of Criminology. I was delighted to be informed afterwards by Lord Parker and several of the other participants that their contributions were of the first order and exactly what was needed. The conference was described as 'the most comprehensive of its kind ever held' in England.[11] It was followed by others held at regular intervals, the scope of which was extended to include other ranks of the judiciary. In reality this was a rather modest beginning, but it was significant because it marked the first stage of a more systematic and concentrated approach to an issue of immense importance to society as a whole. I felt honoured to have been initially associated with it and I continued to follow with great interest the developments which in due course led to the establishment of the Judicial

---

10 'Uniformity in Sentencing. Lord Parker calls for Study Group' and leading article 'Unequal Punishments', *The Times* (30 May 1964), pp. 8 and 9.
11 *The Times* (9 January 1965), p. 6.

Studies Board in 1979. My satisfaction has been greatly increased because a senior member of the Cambridge Institute of Criminology, Dr David Thomas, has been so successfully engaged in building these bridges.[12] But an enormous amount of truly innovative work in this sphere still needs to be done, and there is a need for further openness in approaching sentencing problems through solid research and dignified public discussion.[13]

A surprised co-midwife

One day, somewhere towards the end of 1959, Dr Francis Camps, the distinguished forensic scientist, rang me up in Cambridge to say that he would like to come to see me. I knew, of course, who he was. We had never met and his courteous telephone call made me very curious. I asked him whether he would like me to invite a few guests to welcome him at lunch or dinner. His answer was categorical: he would like to talk with me about a confidential matter of some importance. A few days later he came to my home in Cranmer Road for lunch and we had a long and interesting talk. The gist of what he said may be summarized as follows. A lot of valuable work had been done by experts in forensic medicine both individually and within the orbit of the British Association for Forensic Medicine and the time had now come to recognize this nationally and internationally by establishing a British Academy of Forensic Sciences. I fully agreed with him. Forensic medicine and legal medicine were subjects not entirely unknown to me. In contrast to the English and American law schools they are in continental Europe often part of the legal curriculum. They were strongly represented in the Law Faculty at Rome, especially so in its Criminological Institute, and I was fortunate to be able to profit from these arrangements. They have close links with criminal science proper. They teach us a lot about the *modus operandi* of criminals, which can throw valuable light on their motivations. And in many cases they play an important part in the discovery, identification and determination of the culpability of offenders. I was proud to have encouraged Dr John Havard, a young and very able medical man, who was later to become President of the Academy, to write an important book on a crucial aspect of the subject – *The Detection of Secret Homicide* (1960) – which was published in the series *Cambridge Studies in Criminology*.

But when Dr Camps said that he had come to see me to ascertain whether I would accept an invitation from him and his colleagues to become the first President of the Academy I was astonished. I told him that, although I had

---

12 His *Principles of Sentencing* (1st edn, 1970) was vol. 27 of *Cambridge Studies in Criminology*, with a foreword by me.
13 However, as Professor Andrew Ashworth has shown in his *Sentencing and Criminal Justice* (2nd edn, 1995), the principles and practice of sentencing are in need not only of exposition but of constant critical re-evaluation.

always been interested in the subject and recognized its importance, I was too far removed from the field to be President. It was he who, according to authoritative opinion, was 'one of the best known and respected experts in forensic medicine this country has ever produced', who should fill the post. He could not be moved and I felt bound to accept.

It was fascinating to work with Dr Camps and a few of his colleagues in sub-committees to formulate the aims of the Academy, its rules and procedures, its attempts to raise still further the status of the discipline, and to enlist disinterested but firm support from outside. There seemed to be no difficulty which could not be overcome and the spirit of camaraderie and goodwill seemed to be inexhaustible. For my first presidential address I selected the topic 'Criminal law, criminology, and forensic science'; for my subsequent address 'Public opinion and crime'.[14] Francis Camps – in the best British tradition of 'the power behind the throne' – continued as the Secretary-General until 1963 when he agreed to become President.

The British Academy of Forensic Sciences has proved its vitality and its usefulness. As I am writing this piece I am looking on my desk at the issue of the Academy's journal, *Medicine, Science and the Law*, for July 1998, which is part of volume 38. It is as informative as ever. The Academy occupies a prominent and respected place amongst similar institutions across the world. It is a great pity that the inspirer of this enterprise is no longer amongst us to see this blossoming of his efforts. He died in 1972 at the age of sixty-seven.[15] I, the fortuitously adopted co-midwife of the enterprise, am grateful for the opportunity I had to work alongside this remarkable and lovable man.

---

14 See *Medicine, Science and the Law*, vol. 1 (1960–1), pp. 7–15; and *ibid.*, pp. 24–32.
15 For a delightful account of his personality and work, see the entry by J.M. Cameron (a forensic authority in his own right) in *Dictionary of National Biography 1971–80* (1986), pp. 120–1, and the obituary in *The Times* (7 October 1972).

17

A GRIM PENAL OUTLOOK

I cannot claim to have been in all parts and corners of the world, or to have studied them all in depth. But I have travelled enough, observed enough, recorded enough, and read enough, to be able to characterize their predominant philosophies and practices.

In very many parts of the world, including parts of Europe, the system of criminal justice is amorphous, disjointed and stagnant. In many countries it is torn by chronic turmoil and punctuated by savage convulsions, the inevitable consequences of recurring political and social upheavals. Often there are pious proclamations of goals to be pursued which are flagrantly contradicted by ugly realities; or else brutality is openly paraded in the hope of maximizing deterrence and fear. Often the system of criminal justice is perceived and enforced as a self-perpetuating bureaucracy, a self-contained machine deliberately cut off from wider influences and reliable reassessments. I am aware that these are harsh statements, but they simply reflect harsh realities. The exceptions to such strictures are very few, accounting for a very small proportion of the countries of the world. At least four-fifths of the world's population of over 5 billion people are as hungry for elementary criminal justice as they are for everyday essential commodities.

The annual reports of Amnesty International and of Human Rights Watch – terrifying but authentic accounts of violations of human rights across the world – are as important, if not more so, as the accounts which reveal the working of criminal justice as a whole. Indeed, one of the most disturbing interconnections brought out since the early 1970s is the one between human rights and penal standards. They condition and influence each other and neither can achieve satisfactory fulfilment without the other.

The authoritarian model [1]

In the field of criminal justice, political considerations rather than crimino-

---

[1] This section is largely based on my article 'Penal Regressions' *Cambridge Law Journal*, vol. 50, 1991, pp. 422–444.

logical knowledge increasingly hold sway. Indeed in several parts of the world they have become predominant. The authoritarian model of criminal justice is a natural outcome of this tendency and its many features are closely interconnected. They are as follows.

1. Criminal codes lack precise definitions of crimes. The number of acts classified as criminal tends to increase, while, at the same time, the limits of what is permissible are often left deliberately vague. This leaves the door wide open to arbitrary interpretations and retroactive decisions.
2. The police act in flagrant violation of the requirements of legality. There is no emphasis in police recruitment on personal integrity and social responsibility, no independent investigations of complaints, indeed hardly any public accountability. Police forces operate primarily as agents of those who hold the supreme power and not as organs of criminal justice based on the rule of law.
3. Use and abuse of physical or mental pressures to achieve the objectives of the criminal process is common.
4. The system of prosecution, trial and sentence lacks a general commitment to openness. The rights of the suspect and the accused to keep silent, not to be forced to confess, and to have independent legal representation, are non-existent or neglected.
5. Strictly enforced rules of evidence, strictly interpreted and inspired by the principle of the presumption of innocence, are absent or neglected.
6. There are inadequate guarantees and provisions for appeal against conviction and sentence.
7. The judiciary is committed to following the wishes of the political rulers and is weak in maintaining its independence and impartiality: public prosecutors and the Bar display a similar attitude.
8. The criminal is primarily seen as an anti-social individual, in revolt against the laws of the state, a malevolent force to be broken or annihilated. Crime is not perceived as a social phenomenon, society is not thought to bear any share of responsibility for producing it. Criminal justice, utterly divorced from social policy, is essentially punitive, even when given the gloss of 're-education'.
9. The concept of insanity is crudely and capriciously interpreted and hardly any regard is paid to the mental state of prisoners.
10. Retribution, intimidation and elimination are regarded as the dominant functions of penal sanctions. Belief in, and a widespread use of, capital punishment are essential ingredients of criminal policy. The reformative function, although usually admitted for juveniles, is, in practice, grossly restricted.
11. The entire system of punishment, in sentencing and in enforcement, is consistently harsh and rigid. The general bent of criminal policy is strikingly anti-humanitarian.

12 Not even lip-service is paid to the rights of prisoners and no effort to protect them is deployed. Independent inspection of penal institutions is fiercely discouraged.
13 Hardly any worthwhile initiatives are taken to evolve a humane system of alternative measures, outside the scope of traditional penalties.
14 The courts are not the only body to enforce the criminal law. It can be, and often is, also exercised by the executive through administrative and police organs, and frequently through the secret police of the ruling party, which runs its own coercive confinement centres. This hidden jurisdiction relates to a large area of behaviour vaguely described as anti-social, deviant or parasitic.
15 Independent public investigations of the working of the system as a whole, or any part of it, even when abuses and inefficiency are glaring, are hardly ever set on foot. Governmental authorities are extremely reluctant to publish any significant facts or accounts about what is going on in any field of criminal justice.
16 The entire system is protected not only by secrecy at home but also by isolation from abroad. Developments in other countries are either ignored altogether or presented in a very distorted way.
17 And finally, independent criminological research is not tolerated. Any research permitted is kept under very strict official supervision. Its mission is to endorse and justify the existing system, its own output hardly ever going beyond shallow and tedious reports.

It is the former Soviet Union and Nazi Germany which are entitled to claim the credit for evolving and practising the most perfect (and cruel) examples of the authoritarian model. China now leads the way and in at least two-thirds of the member states of the United Nations (and there are 185 of them) criminal justice is administered very much according to this model, although not always in a form so monolithic and so extreme as to embrace all my seventeen points. Attenuations and adaptations take place to fit particular local traditions and socio-political mutations. A leading student of terrorism commented, a few years ago, that 'far from being a fortunately rare exception in an otherwise civilised world, the *coup d'état* is now the normal mode of political change in most member states of the United Nations'. 'There are now', he continued, 'many more military dictatorships in existence then Parliamentary democracies . . . during the last fifteen years there have been some 120 military coups.' These military regimes are a mixed bag, but their effects on human rights and systems of criminal justice are uniformly devastating, reducing them to the lowest common denominator of arbitrary repression.

In sharp and unbridgeable contrast to this authoritarian pattern stands the socio-liberal model of criminal justice which I have described earlier in this book (see pp. 114–119). Its ideology can easily be reconstructed by virtually reversing each of the seventeen leading characteristics of the authoritarian model. On the other hand, it is much more difficult to identify with precision what it is that constitutes the conservative model. It stands somewhere between the socio-liberal and the authoritarian, containing elements of both. It can never be assimilated with the former: the areas of contradictions between them are too basic and too striking. It can, however, in certain political and social circumstances, move much closer to the authoritarian formula.

Tensions and dilemmas in democratic societies

It is no mystery why criminal justice is passing through a crisis in many democratic countries, why their penal standards have stagnated or fallen. The factors responsible can be easily identified but they have rarely acted independently. Usually there has been a forceful and continuous interaction between them, which makes any attempt to weigh up their relative significance a rather futile exercise. They have varied in intensity and duration in different countries and at different times.

The condition of crime – as expressed by its amount, quality and trends – is everywhere a decisive element in the shaping of criminal policy. And when it is regarded as ineffectively controlled, major socio-psychological effects flow from it. Sheer inconvenience, frustration, humiliation, damage and losses of all kinds, apprehension about what the future might bring, curtailment of freedom of movement, and often – especially with respect to the older strata of the population and those who are compelled to live in run-down neighbourhoods – an ever present feeling of fear. These reactions are accentuated when the more dangerous and repulsive forms of criminal activity – such as serial killing, multiple rapes, abduction and sexual abuse of children and random terrorism – appear to become more threatening or more successful in evading capture and exemplary punishment.

No great service is rendered by alarmist hyperbole. Indeed it is positively harmful to a rational discussion of the problem. The press and other media would render a greater service to society if they were to keep crime in perspective instead of constantly raising the temperature by the amount of space they devote to it and the sensational way in which they often report it. It is still worse when politicians, particularly ministers responsible for the maintenance of public order and justice, play on public fear of crime for political ends.

Yet fluctuations in the amount of crime are 'eternal' in the sense that they occur in every era and in all parts of the world. But very rarely are we in a position to identify convincingly the determining causes of such fluctuations because of the multiplicity of circumstances and factors which shape crime as a mass phenomenon. Often, in disagreement with several of my distinguished colleagues, I firmly maintained the view that, following the end of the Second World War, we would be confronted for a long time by severe accretions of crime in virtually all its main forms.[2]

Now, after more than fifty years, the United States – which was leading in this expansion of criminal activity – seems to be breaking this mould. Abundant statistical data are coming in recording an encouraging amelioration in the totality of crime across the country and especially in several of the vast conurbations, leading to an outburst of contagious national relief. An intense search has begun to find valid explanations or at least ones that can provide some reassurance that this vastly improved crime picture will prove to be durable. These efforts are still in their infancy and indeed may never produce truly conclusive answers.[3]

In the mean time there is a danger that this decrease in recorded crime may be used directly, or often sub-consciously, to legitimize the prevailing exceptionally low standards of the criminal justice system in general and the inordinate expansion and stiffening of penal repression in particular. Such a distorted simplification should be resisted.[4]

Connected with this is the amount of crime which escapes criminal justice. In my judgement this 'dark figure' has grown more rapidly than officially recorded crime and continues to do so with serious negative effects. It tends to foster an atmosphere of impunity which increases the temptation to take risks in breaking the law; it weakens the preventive and deterrent utility of punish-

---

2   See my 'Les crises repetées de la justice pénale' in the Festschrift *Aspects nouveaux de la pensée juridique: recueil d'études en hommage à Marc Ancel* (1975), vol. 2, pp. 230–9. On a broader and more extensive plane see Chapter 1, 'The Relentless Upsurge of Crime', in Leon Radzinowicz and Joan King, *The Growth of Crime* (1977), pp. 3–30. According to the United Nations (*Results of the Fourth United Nations Survey of Crime Trends and Operations of Criminal Justice System*, A/CONF 169/15, 20 December 1994), 'although rates differ each year, stated the report of the Secretariat, crime increases on average by about 5 per cent per year, controlling for population growth' (*ibid.* at p. 10). (I am reluctant to endorse this generalization.)

3   For a lively account of these trends see the articles and leading articles in the *New York Times*, 28 September, 5, 12, 14 and 27 October 1997. Their titles are characteristic: 'Crime Keeps on Falling but Prisons Keep on Filling'; 'Serious Crime has Declined for the Fifth Year, FBI Says'; 'Property Crimes Steady Decline Led by Burglary'; 'Little Evidence of Gang Violence Seen'; 'The Keys to Cutting Crime'; 'Crime Down All Over'; and 'Drop in Homicide Rate Linked to Crack's Decline'. However, authoritative revelations of extensive manipulations of police statistics so as to give an impression of lower crime rates have recently come to light. See Fox Butterfield, 'Crime Falls, Pressure Rises to Alter Data', *New York Times* (3 August 1998), pp. 1 and 16.

4   Such an impression is conveyed by Professor James Q. Wilson in his paper (summarized) read at the Stated Meeting of the American Academy of Arts and Sciences, 216 Annual Meeting (8 May 1996) entitled 'Crime and Justice in England and America'. Professor Wilson was probably drawing upon the important article by David Farrington and Patrick A. Langan, 'Changes in Crime and Punishment in England and America in the 1980s' *Justice Quarterly*, vol. 9 (1992), pp. 5–46. The book by William J. Bennett, John J. Dilulio Jr and John P. Walters, *Body Count-Moral Poverty: And How to Win America's War Against Crime and Drugs* (1996), draws similar inferences, fiercely and categorically stated.

ments; it reflects and intensifies a lack of confidence in the apparatus of criminal justice, and generally undermines the respect in which the law is held.

Yet again discrimination is needed in interpreting the figures. The bulk of 'hidden crime', as reported to victimization surveys, is still of the less serious kind. More of it has come to light because citizens are more sensitive than they used to be to certain violations – such as domestic violence – and more ready to think of them as crimes.

A high volume of crime has deleterious effects on the machinery of criminal justice as a whole. All its major sectors suffer – police, prosecutors, courts and correctional agencies. The system works more slowly, is less efficient, more inclined to have recourse to short cuts, and more likely to violate the basic rules of justice.

In these circumstances attempts to remove traditional safeguards for the accused in order to increase the chances of conviction are particularly dangerous. The system of criminal justice in reality is already heavily stacked in favour of the police and prosecutorial agencies of one kind or another. The myth that the innocent citizen has nothing to fear from the criminal justice system has been shattered by tragic cases of wrongful conviction.

The more acute public concern becomes about the condition of crime and its effects, the more pressure there is to do something drastic about it, and swiftly. There has never been a complete consensus about what the purposes of punishment should be. But when lack of confidence in criminal justice grows it brings with it a greater degree of uncertainty about the goals of the system. We witness a 'penological no man's land' in which forward-looking objectives connected with the treatment or rehabilitation of offenders give way to retributive objectives which look back to the nature of the crime and the punishment it deserves. Repressive elements gain the ascendancy: deterrence, incapacitation, condign punishment and, in some countries, even elimination.[5]

Ironically these reactions were fuelled by criminological research which showed that the 'rehabilitative ideal' had not been translated into reality. A blast occurred in 1974 when an article appeared in a widely read and respected American periodical.[6] Although later the author and several others somewhat redressed the gloomy picture it conveyed, the basic conclusion remained intact, leading to widespread pessimism expressed by the slogan 'nothing works'.

---

5   To quote an exceptionally well-informed observer, this 'can lead . . . to a coarsening of standards not only of debate but also of criminal justice itself', see David Faulkner, *Darkness and Light. Justice, Crime and Management for Today* (1996), p. 3.
6   R.M. Martinson, 'What Works? – Questions and Answers about Prison Reform', *Public Interest*, no. 35 (1974), pp. 22–54. The full report was published as a book: R.M. Martinson, D. Lipton and J. Wilks, *The Effectiveness of Correctional Treatment* (1974).

A GRIM PENAL OUTLOOK

In the natural disappointment created by such statistical revelations sight was too often lost of the fact that, irrespective of whether the penal system succeeds or fails to reform its detainees, the entire system of criminal justice should be organized from top to bottom so as to conform to the standards expected from a civilized state. In this sense the famous utterance of Winston Churchill in 1910 – 'the mood and temper of the public in regard to the treatment of crime and criminals is one of the unfailing tests of the civilisation of any country' – is as pertinent as ever. Indeed, in the light of the barbarities committed in the name of criminal justice since the 1930s in so many parts of the world, his statement has enormously gained in significance.

There has also been much concern about the state of the prisons. It became widely recognized that, by and large, penal institutions could not discharge the often proclaimed function of turning out better men and women than when they went in, as many prison authorities had confidently hoped for.[7] The cluster of circumstances which has contributed to the deep and chronic penitentiary crisis is well known. The dilapidated fabric of so many of the prisons, the steeply rising prison population,[8] the increasing length of detention, an inmate culture replete with intimidation and violence, affecting staff as well as prisoners, the pernicious circulation of drugs, the far too limited opportunities for productive work and other incentives for good conduct, have led to an almost exclusive concentration on the maintenance of order and security at the expense of other objectives.[9] Prisons, with very few exceptions, have become at best 'humane warehouses', at worst, and all too often, dens of despair and iniquity. The prison of today is ripe for a John Howard to set out on a heroic journey to draw its ugly portraiture for posterity. In many countries the standards are so low that I doubt very much whether their prisons can be rescued.

And yet it has to be recognized that a substantial use of imprisonment is a necessary evil. It will continue to be demanded as punishment for a variety of serious crimes and for the purposes of deterrence and incapacitation. Total abolition is a pipe dream. It would probably lead to even worse alternatives and inevitably produce penological anarchy. Neither is the privatization of prisons an acceptable solution. It flagrantly violates what I consider to be a fundamental principle. Detention, control and care of prisoners should not

---

7   The most recent rendition of this objective reads: 'The purpose of the training and treatment of convicted prisoners shall be to encourage and assist them to lead a good and useful life.'
8   As of June 1997 the total number of Americans detained in prisons and jails amounted to 1,725,842. The national incarceration rate was 645 per 100,000 persons, more than double the 1985 rate of 313 per 100,000. In England and Wales the prison population per 100,000 people increased from 95 in 1985 to 100 in 1996.
9   See Richard Sparks, Anthony Bottoms and Will Hay's valuable study, *Prisons and the Problem of Order* (1996).

be parcelled out to entrepreneurs operating according to market forces, but should remain the undiluted responsibility of the state.[10]

The idea of finding alternatives to prison is not new. It started to make headway at the end of the nineteenth century but it was then mainly directed towards first offenders serving very short terms of imprisonment – usually less than six months – who in those days accounted for a very considerable proportion of the prison population. Fines, discharges – absolute and conditional – suspended sentences and probation, all played a major role in bringing about a drastic reduction of this class of inmate.

Today, the problem of diverting offenders from custody is much more complicated and much more difficult to achieve. In order to reduce the prison population further, there is a desire to go beyond the short-term prisoner and find alternatives for those serving medium terms, perhaps even as long as three years. Are there any alternatives that would satisfy the judiciary and public opinion, especially when crime and fear of crime cause so much public concern? Various substitutes for custody are being developed and experimented with. Intensive supervision, electronic monitoring, curfews, different forms of community service, payment of compensation and victim–offender reconciliation, are being imposed in varying degrees and in various combinations. And there is a growing security industry manufacturing new technological devices, some of them gruesome, for controlling offenders in the community. However, the available evidence suggests that the extent to which they will reduce the number of medium-term prisoners is likely to be modest. I would be surprised if it were to exceed 15 per cent. Furthermore there is a danger that these measures may be applied to a much wider range of less serious offenders and develop into an instrument of surveillance and control with undesirable wider social consequences.

Very little progress has been made in dealing with persistent offenders. The bulk of them, those who regularly commit less serious forms of crime, have in recent years been increasingly dealt with by non-custodial measures. We now witness a growing impatience and irritation with this chronic contingent. There appears to be a greater readiness to regard continued repetition, in itself, as a justification for the imposition of imprisonment of longer duration. It is, however, those who have repeated very serious offences – such as homicide, grievous violence, rape, child sexual abuse, armed robbery and aggravated burglary – who cause the greatest concern.

---

10 See my letter to *The Times* (22 September 1988) 'Principles at Stake in Prison Reform'. But my opposition to privatization does not mean that regular consultations between prison authorities and outside experts from other fields should not be pursued in order to obtain advice on a variety of matters relating to the efficient and economical management of penal institutions.

Again, there is nothing new in the idea of taking special measures against persistent offenders. Around the turn of the century it was widely believed that a solution had been found through the indeterminate sentence in North America and elaborate systems of security measures in European countries, similar to preventive detention in Britain.[11] The goal was to deprive recidivists of their liberty until they had been reformed and, failing this, to keep them out of circulation for a long time. In Europe, apart from Nazi Germany, this approach never really took root, partly because its rehabilitative pretensions were revealed as a sham, but largely because of the opposition of the judiciary. The judges detested imposing sentences out of all proportion to the crime committed and were deeply suspicious of passing control over the length of time to be served in custody to parole boards or other administrative organs. In the United States, the indeterminate sentence was attacked on similar grounds and with increasing virulence.

From the 1970s onwards these approaches began to lose ground to the 'justice model', according to which primary consideration should be given to the seriousness of the last offence committed, with much less emphasis on the offender's previous convictions. In European criminological language this was described as a return to neo-classicism and in the English-speaking world as the principle of 'just deserts'.

This may well have given greater confidence in the fairness and legality of the system but it fostered a feeling that society was being insufficiently protected against those who were not restrained by the proportionate punishments they received for each offence taken alone. And it is this feeling which lies behind increasing support for extra-special measures to deter and incapacitate recidivists of all kinds. The new arsenal, contemplated or implemented, includes mandatory minimum sentences of imprisonment following a third conviction – made popular by the slogan 'Three strikes and you're out' – and automatic life imprisonment for repetition of a wider range of very serious offences, sometimes without the possibility of parole.[12]

---

11 On the United States see George K. Brown, 'The Treatment of the Recidivist in the United States', *Canadian Bar Review*, vol. 23 (1945), pp. 640–83, reprinted from the *English Studies in Criminal Science Pamphlet Series* (Cambridge, 1945). On Europe see B.V.A. Röling, *De Wetgeving Tegen de Zoogenaamde Beroeps- en Gewoontemisdadigers* (The Hague, 1933). On the early period in England, L. Radzinowicz and R. Hood, 'Incapacitating the Habitual Criminal: the English Experience', *Michigan Law Review*, vol. 78 (1980), pp. 1305–89.

12 For valuable commentaries on these developments in the United States see David Schichor and D.K. Sechrest (eds) *Three Strikes and You're Out* (1996), Franklin E. Zimring and Gordon Hawkins, *Incapacitation: Penal Confinement and the Restraint of Crime* (1995) and Lord Windlesham in volume 3 of his very informative series *Responses to Crime* (1996), pp. 246–58. For an English contribution to the debate see R. Hood and S. Shute, 'Protecting the Public: Automatic Life Sentences, Parole and High Risk Offenders', *Criminal Law Review* (1996), pp. 788–800.

I cannot reconcile myself with such extreme, emotionally loaded, measures. Penal history amply demonstrates that unjust levels of punishment in democratic societies break down sooner or later. On the other hand, I do not deny the justification for increasing the punishment in cases involving persistent and reckless criminality. But the law should set reasonable limits and the judges should be left free within these limits to consider each case on its merits, subject to appeal by the defence or prosecution.[13]

All these developments have led to the questioning of the judge's role in sentencing. Proposals have been advanced to control, to restrict, and even to eliminate their discretion altogether. And here again an historical reference is helpful. In order to avoid the evils of arbitrariness and to ensure that the law should be both determinate and equally applied, the French Penal Code of 1791 – a product of the Revolution – gave no latitude to the judge to choose the penalty. It was fixed for each crime in the Code. This reduction of the function of the judge to a bare minimum was regarded as a major achievement. Le Peletier de Saint-Fargeau, one of its draftsmen, expressed this in these memorable words: 'Il faut qu'il [le juge] ouvre la loi et qu'il y trouve une peine précise applicable au fait déterminé; son devoir est de prononcer cette peine'.[14] But such an artificial system could not be maintained and soon the Code Napoléon had gone far to extend the discretion allowed to judges, leading to the establishment of a flexible system which recognized a wide variety of mitigating and aggravating circumstances.

In our own times the movement to restrict judicial discretion was at first motivated by the desire to eliminate unjustifiable disparities in the sentences imposed for more or less similar offences. But the idea that punishment should be made as certain and determinate as possible particularly appealed to those traditionalists who believed that this would sharpen the deterrent impact of the law. This led, especially in the United States, to the setting up of Sentencing Commissions which laid down narrow guidelines within which the judges were allowed very little room for choice of sentence. Alternatively, some jurisdictions have, as already noted, enacted mandatory sentencing provisions, again with hardly any room for judicial discretion. The danger of all such approaches is to confuse the fundamental differences between the proper role of the executive and that of the judiciary.[15]

---

13 One would be well advised to study with care what the American Model Penal Code has to say on this subject. See American Law Institute, *Model Penal Code and Commentaries*, part 1 (1985), pp. 170–8, 240–60.
14 See Leon Radzinowicz, *A History of English Criminal Law*, vol. 1, *The Movement for Reform* (1948), pp. 294–5.
15 Roger Hood and I drew attention to this danger in 1981: see 'The American Volte-Face in Sentencing Thought and Practice', in C. Tapper (ed.) *Crime, Proof and Punishment: Essays in Memory of Rupert Cross* (1981), pp. 127–43.

The juvenile justice system, once the pride of the socio-liberal approach, is also under attack. There have always been inherent in it contradictions between the aims of welfare and of punishment. In the 1960s the pursuit of the welfare model was criticized for extending the tentacles of the law into the lives of too many children and young persons, in practice punishing many of them 'in their own interests' with interventions out of all proportion to the harm they had done. The system was indicted as discriminatory and stigmatizing, too often removing the children of the poorer classes to institutions which were corrupting rather than correcting, with little regard paid to the requirements of due process.

As a result of these criticisms policy shifted. To take England and Wales as an example, fewer and fewer juveniles were brought before the court and were cautioned instead, sometimes over and over again. Those that were convicted mostly escaped penal detention, the network of reformatory institutions having gone out of existence. Now this approach is under fire for appearing in practice to grant immunity to young offenders who continue to commit serious crimes. There are calls for tougher action. In the United States, where an increasing number of serious young offenders are in any case transferred to the jurisdiction of the adult court, there is growing pressure to abolish the juvenile court altogether. In a nutshell, if this view were to prevail, the guiding principle would no longer be the welfare of the young person. Juveniles would be dealt with in the same way as ordinary adult criminals, except that their age might be taken into account.

The operation of juvenile justice has undoubtedly revealed a number of flaws, but the tension between welfare and punishment when dealing with young people is inevitable. What is required, every so often, are readjustments to strike the right balance. To get rid of the system altogether would be retrograde and another specimen of dangerous oversimplification.

The nineteenth-century principle of 'lesser eligibility' continues to haunt modern penal systems. Under the New Poor Law of 1834 in England, it was proclaimed that the conditions offered to a pauper who entered the workhouse (and there was to be no out-relief) should be less eligible than those of the lowest paid free worker, otherwise the poor would be encouraged to forsake work for the comparative comfort of the workhouse. Consequently, it was held as a matter of elementary logic that conditions for those who had been convicted of crime should not be better than those offered to honest paupers. Otherwise they would forsake the workhouse for the prison. There was a difficulty in all this. It had to be recognized that the physical conditions and the diet in workhouses and prisons could not be made as bad as the conditions under which the masses of the urban and rural poor continued to live. The authorities compensated for this by making the disciplinary regime of these custodial institutions especially severe – the prison more severe than the workhouse. To Karl Marx there was a much simpler solution to the problem. From the fact that convicts worked less and were better fed than agricultural labourers he implied not that the former were too well fed, but that the latter had too little to eat.[16]

The principle of lesser eligibility is neither defined nor applied in such a crude way today. Nevertheless, it permeates public attitudes towards the priority that should be accorded to expenditure on penal reform and improvements in conditions for prisoners in comparison with expenditure on education, health and public welfare. Nevertheless, there is public support for policies which increase the number of prisoners and inevitably add to the costs involved in the maintenance of the penal system.

Cutting across, invading and distorting the traditional penal scene is the phenomenon of the trade in, and consumption of, illegal drugs. It is a major factor in increasing the level of crime in general and particularly amongst certain ethnic minorities, in pushing up the scale of punishments, in increasing the size of the prison population, in making prisons incomparably more difficult to manage, in fuelling organized crime across national frontiers, and in spreading the microbe of corruption far and wide. One thing is certain. The present approach is not working – 'the war against drugs' cannot be won through the crude application of criminal sanctions.[17] Other measures are needed if this tragic scourge is to be kept under better control. The time has come to search for, and experiment with, more effective solutions outside the crude penal sphere, while at the same time pursuing initiatives designed to deal with those who trade in drugs on a large scale for lucrative purposes.

Penal reform has traditionally been espoused by Liberal and Social Democratic parties. As these parties have, by and large, shifted to the political centre (and in several instances close to the right) so has their attitude to criminal policy. Thus penal reform is in danger of losing many of its supporters as they follow the dominant trends of public opinion.

There was a time when many countries looked towards the United States for inspiration in penal matters but this was a long time ago. Taking the end of

---

16 See his 'Inaugural Address to the Working Men's International Association, 28 September, 1964', in Karl Marx and Friedrich Engels, *Articles on Britain* (Moscow, 1975), pp. 338–9.
17 For a brief but muscular exchange of opposing views on this very controversial and complex subject, see Milton Friedman (a Nobel Prize Winner and Senior Research Fellow, Hoover Institution, Stanford University) – a man of unblemished conservative views – 'An Open Letter to Bill Bennett', *Wall Street Journal* (7 September 1989) and William J. Bennett (at that time Director of the National Drug Control Policy) 'A Response to Milton Friedman', *Wall Street Journal* (19 September 1989). Also Milton Friedman's even more emphatic and persuasive article, 'There's No Justice in the War on Drugs', *New York Times* (10 January 1998).

the Second World War as a point of departure I have reluctantly reached the following six conclusions. First, at no time during this half-century is it possible to point to a stage, however brief, when I could confidently assert that the machinery of justice was discharging its major functions in a satisfactory manner. Second, the system has been constantly declining, its basic defects and flaws becoming more and more accentuated with hardly any redeeming features. Third, the pace of regression has quickened since the late 1970s, has turned from bad to worse, and has now reached its nadir. This has led to a massive application of distorted and distorting devices, such as the use of plea bargaining in nearly 90 per cent of cases. Fourth, this has been exacerbated by crude legislation such as 'Three strikes and you're out'. Fifth, even the undoubted juridical advances in refining the substance of the criminal law have failed to have a practical impact on the operation of the system of criminal justice. Sixth, I am well aware that a comparative rating of a particular criminal justice system involves, in the final analysis, a subjective element. Nevertheless, I do not hesitate to affirm that the US system now belongs to the lowest category amongst the democratic countries of the world.[18]

It is sad that the British system also cannot be regarded as a model worthy of inspiration as it once was.[19] It would however be misleading to compare it with the situation in the United States. The challenges that it faces, the flaws that it exhibits bear no comparison with the American predicament. Nevertheless the fact stands out that British criminal justice is passing through a grave, widely spread crisis and one which, if decisive action is not taken, threatens to become permanent. The promising provisions of the Criminal Justice Act 1991 have not led to a reduction in the use of imprisonment as many had hoped they would. On the contrary, a higher proportion of offenders are now being sent to prison and the more stringent alternatives introduced by the Act have failed to stem the tide. Another ray of hope was the outstanding report by Lord Justice Woolf in 1990 arising out of the

---

18 The proposals advanced by Chief Judge Richard Posner, the eminent legal writer, to reform the US system of criminal justice (except for his recognition that some of the drug laws call for revision) seem to me to be wholly inadequate. His conclusion that 'the practical futility of the rehabilitative approaches [has] largely discredited criminology as a discipline' bears hardly any relevance to the contents of criminology as a fertile and well-sustained academic discipline. See Richard Posner, 'The Most Punitive Nation', *Times Literary Supplement* (1 September 1995), pp. 3–4.

19 A leading article with the pointed title 'British Justice, No Longer a Beacon', *New York Times* (27 February 1994), stated that there has been 'a dangerous retreat for a nation that pioneered the concept of individual legal rights, but has in recent years steadily eroded these rights'. And that: 'The already perilous state of civil liberties in Britain is going to get worse.' A somewhat exaggerated verdict perhaps, but nevertheless one which contains a large kernel of truth.

savage riot at Strangeways Prison in Manchester. His conclusion was that if serious disturbances were to be avoided in the future, a 'compact' would have to be forged between prison authorities and prisoners based on a more enlightened balance between security, order and justice. A White Paper with proposals for implementation soon followed. This could have been the point of departure for wider innovative initiatives in penal reconstruction.[20]

But the pendulum swung in the opposite direction under a new Home Secretary, Michael Howard. His programme aimed to sharpen the teeth of criminal justice throughout. The reduction of crime by drastic means was his main objective. The list included abolition of the accused's right to silence; more police and with wider powers, including those relating to the maintenance of public order; a restriction on the amount of cautioning of young offenders; closed institutions for young recidivists between the ages of twelve and fourteen; more stringent prison regimes, guidelines aimed further to restrict the granting of parole; severe mandatory prison sentences for repeated housebreaking and drug dealing, and automatic life sentences on second conviction of a wide variety of serious offences, thus drastically restricting the discretion of the judges. Prisons were no longer regarded as 'universities of crime'; the Fabian slogan 'The most practical and the most hopeful of prison reforms is to keep people out of prison altogether' was cast aside. The new rallying call was 'prison works'. Symptomatically, the funding of outside criminological research by the Home Office was in danger of being brought to an end. But I am glad to say that the change of government has brought a change of attitude with regard to the funding of research.

Many of these measures have been introduced in response to perceived public concern about crime. But the way in which they have been pushed through, often without careful deliberation and consultation, was part and parcel of a resolve to push the control of crime up the political agenda for electoral advantage. This may be an understandable party strategy but it is not the way to formulate a wise and just penal policy. The new Labour administration has also promised to reduce crime. It remains to be seen whether they will be successful and, if so, how they will achieve it.[21]

---

20 A further illuminating footnote to Lord Woolf's penal philosophy is provided by his discourse to the New Assembly of Churches on 'Crime, Punishment and Rehabilitation', 12 October 1993, reported in *The Times* (13 October 1993). See also his letter to *The Times* (23 October 1993), 'Lord Woolf: Reflections on Treatment of his Crime Lecture'.
21 'I do believe there would be less crime under Labour – I believe that absolutely sincerely', Tony Blair, *New Britain: My Vision of a Young Country* (1996), p. 248.

18

A BRIEF FOR CRIMINOLOGY

This 'barbarous neologism'

There is no mystery about the parenthood of 'sociology', indeed no controversy, no incertitude. It was Auguste Comte who invented the term and it was Durkheim who referred to it scornfully as this 'barbarous neologism'.[1] It is also true that much earlier John Stuart Mill had described the term sociology as a 'convenient barbarism' and this most likely prompted Enrico Ferri to refer to criminology as a 'barbaric term joining a Latin word to a Greek one'. As a matter of fact, Ferri hardly ever made use of the term, preferring 'criminal sociology'. It was only in the very last phase of his academic activity that he most generously acknowledged my criticisms that 'criminal sociology' conveyed the impression that crime was solely a social phenomenon whereas its study involved several other branches of inquiry. Consequently 'criminology' was by far the most appropriate characterization of the subject-matter as a whole.[2]

This still leaves open the question: who was the first person to use the term? Baron Raffaele Garofalo — next to Ferri the most prominent expositor of the *Scuola Positiva* — selected *Criminology* for the title of his book, which first appeared in 1885. It gained instantaneous international notice, was translated into several foreign languages, and went through several editions. Its success was immensely influential in facilitating the adoption of the term criminology into the academic vocabulary throughout the scholarly world and it also familiarized the wider public with this strange, but fascinating, new subject.[3]

---

1 Anthony Giddens (ed.) *Introduction to Positivism and Sociology* (1974), introduction by Giddens at p. 1.
2 Enrico Ferri, *Sociologia Criminale* (5th edn by Arturo Santoro, 1930), vol. 2, p. 555.
3 Raffaele Garofalo, *Criminologia* (1st edn, 1885; 2nd edn, 1891; French edn, 1905), translated into English and published in the famous *Boston Modern American Criminal Science Series*, (1914; reprinted 1968).

Yet William Bonger, the Dutch criminologist, stated that the first scholar to use the term 'criminology' was the Frenchman P. Topinard, who was not a criminologist but an anthropologist. However, Bonger failed to provide a reference.[4] I turned to Thorsten Sellin in the hope that with his vast historical knowledge of criminological thought he might be of some help, but in his letter to me of April 1990, he was unable to confirm that Topinard was the first. I went carefully through Topinard's published works, and the only paper I could find in which he used the term 'criminology' is the one which he presented to a congress in 1889, four years after the appearance of Garofalo's book.[5] At this point, I decided that it was rather fastidious to attempt to track down this terminological query. Suffice it to say that, by the last quarter of the nineteenth century, 'criminology' had gained world-wide acceptability, though different views continued to be held about its scope and its relation to other branches of criminal science.[6] No more is needed to confirm this than to recall the session held under the heading of 'Criminologie' at the memorable International Congress of Comparative Law held in Paris from 31 July to 4 August 1900 and the several reports presented by some of the leading figures of the period.[7]

There is no comprehensive and authoritative work retracing the history of criminology. The intense discussions which accompanied its birth, the multitudinous directions in which it soon branched out, and the diverse, rich and controversial harvest of knowledge it brought into being are such that the task of exposition and analysis demanded by the discipline would exceed by far the capabilities and the determination of one single author, however exceptionally gifted he or she might turn out to be. Even a composite work would require careful planning, a team of highly qualified experts, considerable time, and very substantial resources. And it would still present a formidable challenge to bring it to a successful completion.[8]

The sterile search for the causes of crime

The 1950s was a time when there were high hopes that a rich harvest would soon come to fruition. It was also a time which inevitably generated a lot of

---

4 William Adrian Bonger, *Introduction to Criminology* (1936), p. 1. 'It was the French anthropologist P. Topinard (1830–1916) who gave this science the name of criminology.'

5 See P. Topinard, 'Criminologie et anthropologie', *Actes du deuxième Congrès international d'anthropologie criminelle* (Paris, 1889), pp. 489–96.

6 See L. Radzinowicz and J.W.C. Turner, 'The Language of the Criminal Science', *Cambridge Law Journal*, vol. 1 (1940), pp. 224–317. See also above, pp. 144–145.

7 *Congrès International de Droit Comparé tenu à Paris du 31 juillet au 4 août 1900. Procès Verbaux des Séances et Documents* (1905), vol. 1, *passim*.

8 What we can hope for however are national histories of the subject, an encouraging example of which is the collaborative book written under the direction of Laurent Mucchielli, *Histoire de la criminologie française* (Paris, 1994).

excessive enthusiasm and lofty expectations. It was therefore a time when a detailed evaluation of criminological potentialities was needed more than ever. Moreover, because it was likely that Cambridge might be drawn into R.A. Butler's plans, a clarification of the kind of criminology which should be encouraged was certainly likely to be useful for me personally.

My early continental experiences had, under the impact of time, matured and fresh ones had been added, though with very different emphases. Also I had naturally acquired more knowledge and been given, in the contemplative atmosphere of Cambridge, the opportunity for dispassionate reflection. The Department of Criminal Science had been in existence for nearly ten years and through its work and its wider contacts had accumulated a lot of comparative information. Furthermore my ideas could be put to the test amongst those in Cambridge who shared the responsibility for promoting an expansion of the subject. And such a clarification also made it easier to ascertain whether and to what degree my perspective might meet with a supportive response from the wider academic community as well as from the Home Office.

A particularly suitable occasion for this kind of 'ideological ventilation' was provided when I was invited by the Secretary-General of the United Nations to address a plenary session of the Second United Nations Congress on the Prevention of Crime and the Treatment of Offenders.[9] This invitation to speak on 'Criminological and penological research' was transmitted to me by the late Professor Manuel López-Rey, then the Head of the Social Defence section of the United Nations. I have reached the conclusion on reading again my statement that several of the points raised in it are still very relevant to the subject-matter of this chapter, in which I survey the contemporary condition of criminology. Yet one should be clearly aware that such a survey can never be objectively tested for its validity. However impartial and detached one is, or appears to oneself to be, the conclusions, indeed the very premises, of such a stock-taking inventory will always reflect the subjective imprint of the personality of the interpreter. But I venture to say that there would be more progress in criminology if more frequent attempts were made to clarify what the subject should seek to achieve.[10]

I did not need much time to ascertain that 'the causes of crime' stood at the top of the agenda at that time. As a matter of fact it has never been off the agenda, for it had preoccupied humankind long before criminology came

---

9 See Leon Radzinowicz, 'Criminological and Penological Research', Address to the Second United Nations Congress on the Prevention of Crime and the Treatment of Offenders, London, 15 August 1960. Mimeographed and summarized in the *Report* presented by the secretariat, (United Nations, New York, 1961), pp. 54–5.

10 An excellent example of such an undertaking was Ian Taylor, Paul Walton and Jock Young's *The New Criminology* (1973), followed up recently by Paul Walton and Jock Young (eds) *The New Criminology Revisited* (1998). See also Ezzat Fattah, *Criminology, Past, Present and Future: A Critical Overview* (1997) with a Preface by Professor Paul Rock.

into being. It can be found in the corpus of religious and moral disquisitions, philosophical inquiries and social investigations into the human condition and the nature of society. But at the turn of the century it got a fresh and potent impetus from the nascent and expanding criminology. Advances in the anthropological, biological and medical sciences, in psychology and psychiatry, in social sciences and statistics, all contributed to an increasing confidence that it would be possible to unravel, exhaustively and precisely, the causes leading to anti-social and criminal conduct. The spread of the ameliorative creed, culminating in the ideology of socialism in its extreme modes, and more persuasively in the notion of the welfare state, also helped to promote this current of thought.

Another factor which pushed 'the causes of crime' to the forefront was primarily of a fiscal nature. The early expectation that social progress, at least in the leading countries of the world, would be accompanied by a decrease of crime, both violent and acquisitive, was being refuted by the reality of experience and confirmed by criminal statistics. Consequently the cost of crime, direct and indirect, was becoming an important item in the steadily increasing national and local expenditure. Many leading criminology textbooks of the period, as well as reports, reflected this preoccupation by including laborious chapters with detailed estimates of the cost of crime. In these circumstances it was widely believed that a scientifically grounded unravelling of the causes of crime would, in its turn, lead to the formulation and adoption of effective preventive measures and thus to an appreciable reduction in the general expense entailed in coping with crime.

In Britain this preoccupation with the causes of crime was not as intense, confrontational or dramatic as it was in Europe. It would, for example, be very difficult to find in Britain an instance like that which took place on the continent of Europe when an entire delegation of one country boycotted a scientific congress because an eminent member of another foreign delegation had failed to keep his promise to undertake a comparative study of a criminal and non-criminal group to ascertain to what extent the difference in their behaviour was caused by differences in their individual make-up and to present a report for expert discussion.[11] Or to take a more telling example: two scholars from the same country and at the same time each providing a hefty volume of several hundred pages surveying critically the attempts made over two centuries to elucidate the role played (or assumed to have been played) by economic factors and conditions in the causation of crime.[12]

Nevertheless, it would be a mistake to believe that the objective of finding the decisive causes of crime had not been pursued in Britain. Sir Thomas

11 See Leon Radzinowicz and Roger Hood, *A History of the English Criminal Law and its Administration*, vol. 5, *The Emergence of Penal Policy* (1986), pp. 19–20.
12 Joseph van Kan, *Les Causes économiques de la criminalité* (1903); W.A. Bonger, *Criminality and Economic Conditions* (1916; reprinted 1967 and 1969).

More would be the first to stand up to deny it. And it is curious to observe how many of the 'causative' researchers into crime have not been able, or willing, to throw off the mantle of utopianism. This certainly meant a lot to those in the nineteenth century who disputed the role of nature versus nurture. And certainly the question of causation moved into a central position as steps were taken to establish criminology as an academic discipline.

In 1934, the Archbishop of Canterbury, Dr William Temple, was one of the first to express the hope that 'it may not be long before we see established not only one but several professors of criminal jurisprudence'. He did not go into the details, but it can be safely inferred from several of his writings and from his endorsement of the welfare state, that he regarded the search for the causes of criminal behaviour as part of the prescription.[13] Two years later, in March 1936, Miss Margery Fry sent a memorandum to Sir Alexander Maxwell at the Home Office pleading for action to start research, a memorandum which, according to T.S. Lodge, 'made a case in a remarkably topical way'.[14] The Home Office has been unable to unearth her document, but I understand that she strongly endorsed the need to study the causes of crime. Sir Cyril Burt did not accept the idea of a single cause, but endorsed the concept of 'multiple causality'.[15] Hermann Mannheim provided an erudite, though somewhat convoluted, piece on the subject although his own attitude remained rather ambiguous.[16] In contrast, Leslie Wilkins, who made so outstanding a contribution to prediction techniques, minced no words on the subject: 'simple models of "cause" and "effect" will not be adequate to explain social phenomena'.[17] The few and rather scattered remarks about causative factors in Baroness Wootton's methodologically very important book shows that she cannot be accused of having embraced any specific 'causative' doctrine of crime commission.[18] But this cannot be said about her *confrère* Lord Longford (formerly Lord Pakenham) who, like she was, is an eminent member of the Labour Party. As he himself freely acknowledged, he was neither a sociologist nor a criminologist. His publication was not so much a coherent book as a lively and skilful series of interviews. At that time he enjoyed high

---

13 William Temple, 'The Ethics of Penal Action' (1934), p. 17.
14 T.S. Lodge, 'The Founding of the Home Office Research Unit', in Roger Hood (ed.) *Crime, Criminology and Public Policy: Essays in Honour of Sir Leon Radzinowicz* (1974), pp. 11–24, at p. 11.
15 Cyril Burt, *The Young Delinquent* (1st edn 1925; 4th edn 1944), pp. 590–608. 'Crime is assigned to no single universal source, not yet to two or three: it springs from a wide variety, and usually from a multiplicity of alternative and converging influences', at p. 590.
16 Hermann Mannheim, *Comparative Criminology* (1965), vol. 1, *The Causal Approach*, pp. 5–12.
17 Leslie Wilkins, *Social Deviance* (1964), p. 133.
18 Barbara Wootton, *Social Science and Social Pathology* (1959), pp. 173–4 and 323–4.

public visibility as an ardent penal reformer and supporter of criminology and in his book he tirelessly chased after causes of crime in individual behaviour and social environment, attempting to catalogue and grade them in accordance with their assumed impact. At no time did he reflect whether in fact this goal could ever be achieved if rigorous rules of methodology were observed; and still further whether this kind of approach, if continued, would not in the final analysis adversely affect the healthy development of criminological thought and practical action. Yet the fact that parallel to the expansion of the welfare state there was a sharp increase in recorded crime of all kind, provided an additional pressure to look for and identify the causes of criminality. In this respect Lord Longford's approach was illuminating, for it raised a question which was being raised in all sections of society. He wrote that he 'dated his connection with criminology' to 1 December 1952 when he had read an article in *The Times* describing and analysing the ongoing increase in crime.

> I became imbued ... with the desire to discover the reason why the increase had occurred, and if possible to solve what at first sight seemed the paradox of a declining standard against a background of material improvement. Here, it seemed to me, lay the next great task for the social reformers of our generation; to find out what had gone wrong or was still missing in the Welfare State. How otherwise could we ensure that the Welfare State did after all realise our cherished hope? How otherwise could it provide a material jumping-off ground for a widely expected elevation of our national character and conduct?[19]

This causative preoccupation figured prominently in the efforts of leading penal administrators, noted parliamentarians and Home Secretaries, whenever they pressed for financial support for criminological research and for other developments related to the field. In 1948 it was firmly endorsed by two Members of Parliament, Major Wilfred Vernon and Mr Victor Collins (afterwards Lord Stonham, a Minister of State in the Home Office) when they introduced a clause into the Criminal Justice Bill providing for regular financial governmental support for criminological research. Indeed, they affirmed that the expense incurred would be easily recovered through the considerable reduction of crime which would be achieved through the application of the findings of such research. Those who believed in this hypothesis often referred to the 'enormous savings' which would be secured in the long run. The cost of research into crime, and the profit to be derived from it,

---

19 Lord Pakenham (afterwards Lord Longford), *Causes of Crime* (1958), pp. 17–18.

were thus brought into a more attractive equation with much wider public appeal. 'We are all aware', stated Collins,

> there is a great deal of glib talk as to the cause of crime of various kinds. People attribute it, no doubt rightly, to bad housing conditions, unemployment, drink and poverty, but there is no real, solid knowledge based on research into these matters. I commend this Clause – in the hope that it will provide a valuable insurance policy which will produce very big dividends.[20]

Particularly instructive was Vernon's Memorandum. 'The great sums of money spent on administering the Criminal Code' was singled out as a major argument and he estimated that 'the direct monetary cost to the country of crime was unlikely to be less than 26 million pounds' per year. It included money wholly spent on dealing with crime (£4,355,000 for prisons, borstals, Broadmoor, approved schools and remand homes, probation service and public prosecutions and Court of Criminal Appeal) and partly spent on dealing with crime (£11,846,000 for police forces and administration of justice). Furthermore, one should not lose sight of the cost in human suffering to the victims, the criminals and the relatives of the criminals, in lost and damaged property and the not inconsiderable loss in industrial personnel. Special importance was attached to research into 'the origins and causes of recidivism' because statistics revealed that not only had half the persistent offenders been in prison before but nearly a quarter had been there at least six times. Statements from Sir Alexander Carr-Saunders, Sir Cyril Burt and Sir William Norwood East were included in the Appendix and Section 82 of the Education Act 1944 and Section 16 of the National Health Service Act 1946 were reproduced for further support.

It was the last-mentioned provision providing that 'the Minister may conduct, or assist by grants or otherwise any person to research into any matters relating to the causation, prevention, diagnosis or treatment of illness or mental defectives' which was recommended to be used as the precedent for a Clause in the Criminal Justice Bill and in effect was adopted.

The widely noted Home Office and Ministry of Education Joint Circular of 1953 acknowledged that 'informed opinion varies as to the immediate reasons for the recent increase of juvenile delinquency'. But nevertheless they were as emphatic as one could be in a governmental document of this

---

20 See Collins in *Parl. Debates*, Standing Committee Session 1947–8, vol. 1, cols 1342–3, 4 March 1948, and Major Vernon's *Memorandum on the Needs for a New Clause in the Criminal Justice Bill making Provisions for Research*. Appendices A and B. *Ibid.*, 11 February 1948, pp. 2 and 3–4.

nature that 'the main and deep-seated causes of juvenile delinquency are hardly in doubt'. They distinguished what they described 'as long-term causes [which] stand out' from a few other influences which could be described as less fundamental but not transitory. Even more important was the following, so often quoted, passage of Mr Butler's path-breaking White Paper:

> Research into causes and prevention of delinquency is confronted with problems which are immense both in range and complexity. The causes of crime are varied: heredity, environment and unpredictable influences to which the individual may be subjected all play their part.

And the necessity for their systematic investigation was stressed.[21]

It was also very characteristic for the prevailing climate of opinion that when, at some later stage, the Nuffield Foundation was approached by the Home Office as to whether it would support criminological research and an Institute, members of the Foundation made it clear in a definite manner that, in their view, and even under the most propitious of circumstances, only very limited progress was likely to be made in the special field of criminology 'until we have come much nearer to understanding the wider problems of human behaviour as a whole, since criminal conduct is only one form of human behaviour'. And in a subsequent communication they went further and declared that 'because the problem of crime is a problem of human behaviour, it is most important that biologists should play a leading part in the planning and conduct of the work of the Institute' (see above, p. 183).

As late as 1966, in his opening speech at the Second National Conference on Research and Teaching in Criminology in Cambridge (29 June to 1 July 1966), the Home Secretary, Roy Jenkins (afterwards Lord Jenkins of Hillhead), distinguished three main fields in which he wanted the help of research – 'research into the causes of crime being one of them'. 'Perhaps,' he observed,

> [it] is more academic and more remote from immediate administration. But in the long term this is the field in which lies potentially the greatest benefit. In a sense, everything else is a matter of palliatives, but here is the fundamental problem, the solution to which could vastly civilise our society.[22]

---

21 *Penal Practice in a Changing Society*, Cmnd 645 (1959), para. 19.
22 Roy Jenkins's opening speech. Second National Conference of Research and Teaching in Criminology, Cambridge (1966). Mimeograph available at the Radzinowicz Library of the Institute.

Two years later, on a similar occasion, in July 1968, his predecessor at the Home Office, Mr Henry Brooke (afterwards Lord Brooke), referred to 'the part that research can play in illuminating the causes of crime'.[23]

It is instructive to go back in time for a while. In 1889, when defining the leading objectives of its future activities, the International Association of Criminal Law declared: 'The purpose of the Association is the scientific study of criminality, of its causes and of the proper means to combat it.' And yet in 1914 on the occasion of their twenty-fifth jubilee Professor Van Hamel, one of the three founders of the Association, bluntly declared in his speech at the banquet that it cannot be denied that

> criminal aetiology, the search for the cause of criminality, has certainly failed so far to provide results which I expected twenty-five years ago to be made available . . . This has to be acknowledged, but why should further knowledge in the future be ruled out.[24]

In 1920 the even more authoritative voice of E.H. Sutherland, at that time widely regarded as the doyen of American criminology, confidently proclaimed:

> In fact there are several indications that we are approaching the time when a central principle of causation will be discovered. This principle would be immensely valuable of course as a means of promoting and directing research.[25]

Limitations and prospects

The question of causation is not the only issue which needs to be clarified. What follows is a list of other issues which need to be addressed if criminology is to be of durable value.

Criminology is not a primary and self-contained discipline but enters into the provinces of many other sciences which treat of human nature and society. Indeed, many advances made in research into crime arise out of advances achieved in these other basic departments of knowledge.

---

23 Henry Brooke's opening speech, Third National Conference (1968). Mimeograph available at the Radzinowicz Library of the Institute.
24 See 'The Statute of the IKV', *Bulletin of the International Association of Criminal Law*, vol. 7 (1899), p. 2; G.A. van Hamel, 'Zur Erinnerung und zum Abschied' ('Reminiscences and Farewell'), *Bulletin*, vol. 21 (1914), pp. 440–5, at p. 445.
25 E.H. Sutherland, 'The Report', in Karl Schlessler (ed.) *On Analysing Crime* (1973), pp. 229–46, at pp. 234–5.

In spite of many illuminating ideas, the unilateral approach, which is based on the assumption that crime is the outcome of one single cause, or can be encapsulated in a self-contained theory, must be abandoned. Even if the hypothesis is a very broad one – such as the concept of sub-cultures or differential association, or *anomie* – this is still not a primary cause but a complex of influences, which, at the best, can provide only a partial explanation.[26]

The very attempt to elucidate the causes of crime would be better put aside altogether. The most that can be done is to throw light upon the combination of factors or circumstances likely to be associated with crime. And even then it must be recognized that these very factors or circumstances can also be associated with other forms of social maladjustment, or indeed often with behaviour accepted as normal. Nor should it be forgotten that, as it was so judiciously noticed by a young but perceptive student, Arthur E. Fink: 'The use of cause and causation is governed by the usage of the period under consideration. It will be seen that much of what passed for cause in the nineteenth century would be termed correlation today.'[27]

The factors and circumstances themselves acquire a different meaning with the advances of research and the growing realization of the complexity of human personality and of the structure of society. For example, 'economic conditions', as factors influencing the state of crime, no longer mean what they meant a number of years ago. It may mean relative deprivation or even excessive expectations. Similarly the concept of the 'broken home' has been expanded beyond the criterion of physical separation to include all the emotional relationships between parents and children. It would be easy, but unnecessary, to provide further illustrations of the constantly changing substance of very many vital influences. Nor should their variable interactions be ignored.

This restrictive approach should in no way eliminate, but on the contrary should stimulate, systematic studies in depth of particular groups or sub-groups of crimes or criminals of which there is a great variety within each of the conventional classes lumped together as offences of violence against the person, against property, against sex, against the state or by the state, and the group of self-inflicted offences. The differences between offenders within

---

26 See on this my comments in *Ideology and Crime* (1966), pp. 89–96. Robert Merton, who did so much to make the concept fashionable and attractive, has returned to the topic, with further interesting observations. See his 'Opportunity Structure: the Emergence, Diffusion, and Differentiation of a Sociological Concept, 1930–1950', in Freda Adler and William Laufer (eds) *Advances in Criminological Theory* (1995), vol. 6, pp. 3–78.
27 See Arthur E. Fink, *Causes of Crime: Biological Theories in the United States 1800–1915* (1938), p. ix.

these sub-groups, in social background, in individual make-up, in motivation and in criminal history, are often greater than the differences between the groups themselves.

There is still the need for mental readjustment on the part of researchers in sorting out the often deep schism between those attaching a greater weight to individual disposition and those emphasizing environmental conditioning. These two influences are in fact interconnected, constantly interacting: a complex relationship varying not only between broad categories of offences, but even within particular offences. However, the controversy of nature versus nurture affects too many vital issues of social and educational policy ever to die out.[28] And whatever is done or said there will also be individuals with instincts and appetites potentially apt to express themselves in anti-social or criminal behaviour. It is perhaps what Bertrand Russell had in mind when one evening, very many years ago, he asked me to accompany him to dine in Hall. As we entered the parlour of Trinity College one of the Fellows – rather sure and full of himself – turned to Bertrand Russell and said: 'Bertie, what do you think of the Ten Commandments?' The old wizard replied: 'Ten Commandments? I would regard them as an examination paper and try no more than three.'

The methods used in criminology are almost as diverse as its pursuits. Most frequently one method only is used, but very often several methods have to be combined simultaneously. There are fashions in methods, as in so many other things. There are times when an exaggerated expectation is attached to a particular method, only to be followed by its virtual eclipse. One cannot too strongly emphasize the necessity for discrimination and caution in their choice and use, and for the realization of their intrinsic limitations. What they all have in common is that they are predominantly inductive and not deductive, they are not speculative but empirical. The empirical approach – testing, checking and, whenever possible, projecting the reality of crime, of criminals, and of the processes of criminal justice – must and will remain the major direct concern of criminologists. I subscribe as firmly as ever to the dictum already quoted in the White Paper, *Penal Practice in a Changing Society*, 'that in this field research is as essential as in the fields of science and technology'. But all these methods are not experimental in the true sense of the word: the phenomena of crime and punishment cannot be isolated from

---

28 For a more recent attempt to attack the problem again see James Q. Wilson and Richard J. Herrnstein, *Crime and Human Nature* (1985). It is irreproachable in its methodology but inconclusive in substance. But this cannot be said about the book by Richard Herrnstein (since deceased) and Charles Murray, *The Bell Curve* (1994), the methodology and conclusions of which have been authoritatively challenged by many experts.

other phenomena, cannot be transposed into another environment, cannot be manipulated like subjects in laboratory experiments.

One of the conclusions which is sometimes drawn from the growing realization of the complexity of the phenomenon of crime, and of the need to utilize the resources of several branches of knowledge, is that progress can be made only by means of what is sometimes described as an interdisciplinary approach: a psychiatrist, a social psychologist, a penologist, a lawyer, a statistician, joining together in a combined research operation. A closer liaison, leading to a more productive exchange of views concerning methods and objectives, is needed. There can be no doubt that a particular project of research undertaken by a penologist, for instance, could gain in richness and depth if some parts of it could be reviewed by a social psychologist. But I cannot help thinking that, except in very rare instances indeed, an inquiry embracing several disciplines from the start, and depending on the coordination of their individual methods and distinctive terminologies, would carry the seeds of its own failure and would inevitably fall apart into as many undertakings. This interdisciplinary fusion breeds centrifugal confusion. Yet at the conceptional and consultative stage it undoubtedly contains great advantages.[29]

The connection between criminological research and penal reforms should not be too dogmatically insisted upon. Treatment through probation, the Borstal system, the juvenile courts, and several other innovations, were not devised on the strength of fresh and precise criminological knowledge. They can be shown to have evolved, on the whole, under the influence of growing social consciousness, of religious movements and philanthropic stimulus, from some temporary measures, or just from straightforward common sense supported by experience. But once they have taken root and developed, criminology should make its entry, because it is primarily through the aid of its

---

29 In his book *Against Criminology* (1988, p. 71) Professor Stanley Cohen states: 'Again let me start with an assertion from Radzinowicz to the effect that progress in criminology can be made only by the interdisciplinary approach "A psychiatrist, a social psychologist, a penologist, a lawyer, a statistician joining together in a combined research operation".' He refers in his footnote (16) to my book *In Search of Criminology* (1961, p. 177) where the passage occurs, *but quotes only part of it*. The passage begins with the words 'one of the conclusions which is being drawn from the complexity of the phenomenon of crime is'. The words quoted by Professor Cohen are not *my* conclusion, quite the opposite, as can be seen from what follows: '*But I cannot help thinking that, except in very rare instances indeed, an inquiry embracing several disciplines from the start, and depending on the co-ordination of their individual methods and distinct terminologies, may well carry the seeds of its failure and inevitably fall apart into as many undertakings.*' I have a great admiration for Professor Cohen's intellectual distinction, yet I cannot but deeply regret that it should be so conspicuously divorced from a modicum of fairness.

methods and accumulated knowledge that their proper evaluation can be ensured. This applies not only to institutional measures. One of the most promising ways for criminologists to maintain an empirical and realistic attitude is to cultivate close contacts with those engaged in the administration of criminal justice and the penal system.

There is the method of direct observation and interviewing; the method of clinical and psychological examination; the statistical method; the historical method; and the comparative approach. Each of these five methods and approaches has gained a prominent place in contemporary criminological investigations and each is likely to yield encouraging results as progress is achieved by the basic disciplines from which they draw their impetus and imagination.

The statistical method is inextricably linked with the origin and subsequent evolution of criminology. It was, after all, Adolphe Quetelet, who laid the foundation for the social study of crime and of the emergence of 'criminal sociology' as a branch of criminology. The immense indebtedness of criminology to social statistics continued throughout the nineteenth and the beginning of the twentieth centuries.[30] Since the mid-1940s there has been a truly remarkable upsurge of statistical interpretation, especially in the United States, but not only there. There are 'criminological' journals, studies and monographs which virtually contain nothing, or very little indeed, which is not statistical and, more often than not, of a very sophisticated kind. It would be ungracious and erroneous not to recognize the valuable part that the statistical method has played (and continues to play) in illuminating so many hitherto dark sectors and corners of our knowledge of crime. I would deserve severe castigation if I were not to mention three major developments which owe so much to the deployment of advanced statistical techniques: prediction studies, cohort studies and studies of incapacitation. But criminology is more than the application of statistical methods and I fear that this statistical expansion may be carried too far and become monotonous. I would also urge that the authors of this type of article or monograph attempt at the end of their pieces to summarize in plain English their main findings and conclusions. I also hope that the editors or sponsors will use their influence to bring this about. And a warning must still be uttered: however valuable all such studies can be (and frequently are) no firm inferences for criminal policy

---

30 See the *magnum opus* by the leading social statistician of the nineteenth century, Georg von Mayr, *Moralstatistik mit Einschluss der Kriminalstatistik* (1917) and several of his other monographs and articles. I had always hoped that a similar volume relating to the twentieth century would one day see the light of day.

should be drawn from them in isolation from moral, social or political considerations.

Within this methodological context the truly remarkable upsurge of the historical approach since the 1950s should not pass unnoticed. Indeed it should be warmly applauded. I particularly refer to the contributions made by the younger generations of general historians, legal historians and social historians (including, of course, several criminologists) in France, Britain, Canada and in several other parts of the world.[31] Their investigations often relate to periods as distant as the sixteenth, seventeenth and eighteenth centuries. My old and respected friend, the late Sir Lionel Fox, taught me a French saying: 'Rien n'est nouveau que ce qu'on a oublié' ('Nothing is new but what has been forgotten'). These retrospective studies extend our comprehension of the contemporary penal scene, add a new exciting perspective and allow us to preserve a better balance in assessing bewildering current problems.

There was a time when the universal application of criminology and criminal policy was widely believed in and fervently hoped for. The 'French Revolution' was French because it was there that it originated, but its apostles and architects had no doubts that this was to be a world revolution. A new religion of politics was born and sooner or later it would be adopted everywhere and so would be their Penal Codes – specimens of the new criminal legislation. Indeed, earlier, the European Enlightenment was also confidently expected to serve as the enlightenment of many other places in the world. As already noted, Cesare Beccaria's celebrated book was destined to be the binding authoritative text regulating the concepts of crime and punishment far beyond Italy. Even seven decades later a highly experienced jurist and eminent positivist like Raffaele Garofalo had no hesitation in regarding the adoption of a binding international code of criminal law and criminal procedure as a highly desirable objective and one not particularly difficult to put into effect. In 1903 a young Dutch scholar had shown the remarkable foresight and clarity of mind to cut to size those lofty generalizations prevailing in the field of criminal science, insisting that, in spite of its universality, crime (and even economic crime) should still be regarded 'comme un produit loco-historique', and he emphasized the necessity of giving full weight to this quasi-permanent characteristic.[32] This, however, was an exceptional voice of caution and to some extent still is.

---

31 See a report presented to the Council of Europe by Professor Nicole Castan on 'Historical Research on Crime and Criminal Justice', *Collected Studies in Criminological Research*, vol. 22 (Strasbourg, 1985). But it is already in need of being brought up to date.
32 See Joseph van Kan, *Les Causes économiques de la criminalité* (1903), pp. 476–7. These two pages could constitute a remarkable point of departure for a richly rewarding seminar.

Contemporary criminologists (especially criminologists of the younger generation) take much more notice than did many of their predecessors of the profound contrasts in the cultural, moral, social, political and economic textures in the world at large and of their resistance to change. The setting up of a Section on 'comparative criminology' within the American Society of Criminology is an encouraging step, and so is the increasing number of publications bearing the comparative stamp.[33] I use the term both in its traditional sense of carrying out an investigation of a topic in more than one country, and in the more restricted sense of an investigation carried out in one country but by a scholar belonging to another.[34] All such inquiries yield valuable results though they can prove to be exceedingly difficult to undertake over long periods of time with respect to a wider range of countries – especially when they differ deeply in their basic structure. It is also highly desirable for the criminological comparatist to have a good knowledge of the foreign languages involved and of the general conditions of the countries concerned.

There are moral problems of the first order in the subject-matter of criminology and criminal policy, especially with reference to guilt, responsibility and punishment. Philosophers and moralists in very many countries and for a very long time have reflected upon and written about these subjects, often with passion and always with deep concern. And they continue to do so. The traditional expositors of the classical or neo-classical school were in the habit of paying utmost attention to the philosophers and moralists and widely drew upon their writings in defining the foundation of criminal legislation and indeed of the system of criminal justice in general. The textbooks of those luminaries reveal in their 'General Part' this close interaction.

Closer to the contemporary scene, significant lines of demarcation have emerged. The positivists, as might have been expected, turned against the bulk of philosophers, criticizing them for their abstract and speculative bent which was hostile to the empirical, experimental and realistic tenets of their positivist creed. The criminologists of today on the whole show indifference rather than hostility and largely for similar reasons. Also their hands are full and they cannot (even if some of them had the proper mental equipment and temperament) be expected actively to follow this philosophical orientation. But they should, as far as possible, take cognizance of it simply because it broadens and stimulates our understanding of some of the basic concepts of criminology and applied criminal science. It is precisely because modern

---

33 The annotated *Bibliography of Comparative Criminology* by Piers Bierne and Joan Hill (1991) is another illustration of this expanding interest.
34 The most recent example of the latter scenario is Richard J. Evans, *Rituals of Retribution – Capital Punishment in Germany 1600–1987* (1996) – a book easy to admire but difficult to imitate.

criminologists tend to be specialists, not to say sometimes narrow technicians, that no effort should be spared to build bridges of communication with philosophy and jurisprudence, however fragile these bridges may turn out to be. The same applies to some other major intellectual pursuits, especially in the fields of sociology and political science.

The criminology of Lombroso was much too wild. The criminology of Ferri was more subdued, nevertheless it was still much too one-sided and often guilty of propagandist simplification. Modern criminology has at last received academic recognition, but in order to maintain an honourable status amongst academic disciplines it must display an understanding of the way in which broader cultural, social and political forces shape attitudes to both crime and punishment. This means that it must guard against restrictive definitions of the scope and contents of the subject. Just as 'white collar criminality', 'victimology', 'feminist criminology' and 'political criminology' have become an integral and lively part of modern criminology, further accretions are bound to develop in response to the changing nature and dimensions of crime and systems of social control in contemporary societies.

One should not hesitate to reject the all-embracing claims of the two extreme schools of criminological thought: the classical and the positivist. Their battles belong to the past. As a matter of fact the concepts of 'school', or of 'theory', are much too often used in contemporary criminological literature. I am still inclined to stick to the definition given by one of my professors in Rome, R.A. Frosali, to whom a scientific school meant 'a vast current of ideas, all of which have a common direction and, being part of an organic system, differ from other currents of ideas in presenting a characteristic and distinctive originality of content'.[35]

The only current of thought in the criminological sphere which came close to the real meaning of the term 'school' was the Marxist interpretation of criminology and criminal policy. It emerged in the mid-nineteenth century and at first concerned itself primarily with the impact of economic conditions on crime within the context of societies which were the product of a capitalistic regime.[36] It soon expanded and covered many other vital aspects of criminal science and criminal law enforcement. It received a rigid and exclusive reaffirmation by the Soviet criminologists, but also a much more subtle and plausible redefinition in the gifted hands of a group of radical American criminologists. Often, deprived of its traditional trappings, and because of its

---

35 R.A. Frosali, *Sistema Penale Italiano* (1958), vol. 1, p. 17.
36 Leon Radzinowicz, 'Economic Pressures', in Leon Radzinowicz and Marvin Wolfgang (eds) *Crime and Justice*, vol. 1, *The Criminal in Society* (2nd edn, 1977), pp. 542–65. See also Leon Radzinowicz and Roger Hood, *op. cit.*, vol. 5, pp. 64–9.

tenuous linkage with the so-called conflict and labelling theories, the Marxist criminological doctrine is in danger of losing its bite and smoothly merging with other widely accepted sociological interpretations of crime and its control.[37]

I notice with satisfaction a marked decline in the belief that there can ever be a single criminological school, raising and answering all the essential questions in such a satisfactory way as to become the repository of a body of theory and a programme of penal action which would command general approval. And I welcome the eclectic, pragmatic approach, which concentrates upon identifying urgent current problems and dealing with them as they emerge. In general, the search for solutions in terms of wider principles, or as part of some grand strategy, has fewer supporters. Where attempts are still made to achieve some more comprehensive solution this is because of a priori adherence to a particular ideology, most frequently a political ideology. Today, more than ever, it is the imposition of political ideology on criminological premises and conclusions which should be regarded as the deadly threat to a balanced and fertile development of the discipline.

The famous epigram by Van Hamel, 'formerly lawyers bade man study justice but Lombroso bids justice study man', is being reappraised in the spirit of the eminent Professor of Criminal Law at Cambridge, Courtney S. Kenny, who commented: 'Each precept is good. But better still is the combination of the two.' Connected with this is a changing attitude towards criminal law proper. Positivist criminology, fighting a long and bitter war for scientific and academic recognition, regarded the criminal law as its enemy. The positivists would have liked to raze the whole structure to the ground and to have erected instead a loosely framed machinery of social defence, with the concepts of legal responsibility and punishment expunged for ever. The exponents of the traditional classical doctrine, firmly entrenched in seats of influence and power, responded with an invective intended to be both corrective and painful: *Gli Simplicisti di Diritto Penale* (*The Simplifiers of the Penal Law*). Today the prevalent criminological trend is neither to reject the criminal law, nor to attempt to alter it radically, but rather to enrich it. Hardly any voices advocate doing away with the concept of individual responsibility

---

37 See my piece, 'Kristian Georgevich Rakovsky: A Criminological Interlude', in Freda Adler and William Laufer (eds) *Advances in Criminological Theory* (1995), vol. 6, pp. 287–302, at pp. 294–5, and the three important references quoted there: Richard F. Sparks, 'A Critique of Marxist Criminology', in Norval Morris and Michael Tonry (eds) *Crime and Justice* (1980), vol. 2, pp. 159–210; David F. Greenberg, *Crime and Capitalism* (1981); and George B. Vold and Thomas J. Bernard, *Theoretical Criminology* (3rd edn, 1986), pp. 299–316. For a more recent orthodox and categorical reaffirmation of the Marxist doctrine see Michael Welch, 'Critical Criminology etc.', *Critical Criminology*, vol. 7, no. 2 (1996), pp. 43–58.

under criminal law, or leaving open the issue of insanity, or basing sentences exclusively on the presumed state of danger of the offender as determined by a sentencing tribunal.[38]

Under the best of circumstances the resources which criminology can marshal, in skill and in financial and technical means, are limited. It is therefore particularly important to ensure an economical and wise direction of efforts. Theorizing about the nature of crime and criminal behaviour and its connections with changing social structures, institutions and cultures should aways be regarded as fundamental to the development of our subject. On the other hand, theorizing detached from the realities of crime and societal responses to it tends to be sterile. Indeed I deeply regret the present-day paucity of thorough investigation into particular groups of criminals, their social background, mental make-up, criminal history and anti-social *modus operandi*. One of the reasons for this neglect may well have been that the concentration of research on the causation of crime tended to lead to the rejection of the approach to which I am referring as purely descriptive. A prominent place should also be given to analytical and critical accounts of trends in crime; of the status of victims of crime; of patterns in criminal conduct with special reference to processes of chronic involvement as well as desistance; of the effectiveness of existing types of sanction and of new alternatives or substitutes; of the prison system and of institutions connected with it; of the prosecuting organs including the institution of the police, of the courts, of sentencing processes and the nexus of problems to which they give rise; of the directing centres of law enforcement including ministries and departments; of the acts or omissions which should be brought within the orbit of the criminal justice system as well as of those which should cease to be penal or put at another level of the criminal scale; of the attitudes of public opinion in response to crime, properly differentiated; and of the significant developments – positive or negative – happening elsewhere.

In making a distribution of tasks along these lines, we should not allow ourselves to be intimidated by those who contrast, with a supercilious air, so-

---

38 Probably the only leading criminologist in the period between the two wars who favoured some of these solutions was Sheldon Glueck. In Germany I can quote only Fritz Bauer, *Das Verbrechen und die Gesellschaft* (1957); in Italy F. Gramatica, *Principes de défense sociale* (French translation 1964); in Britain at one time Barbara Wootton seemed to favour them but subsequently rejected them. They were adopted by the Greenland Criminal Code of 1954. Professor David Downes has given us a particularly felicitous reformulation of this dilemma, which will always remain disturbing: 'Ultimately, the individual *is* responsible, but choice and responsibility are not exercised in a vacuum. Certain circumstances encourage people to make choices rather than to resist them. Also, people do not simply leap from conformity to crime overnight. It is the job of governments to foster social arrangements that make the drift into delinquency less rather than more likely.' 'Why Inequality is still a Factor', *Times Literary Supplement* (1 September 1996), pp. 11–12.

called basic or pure research with applied research. The latter, if well conducted, will not only increase the social utility of criminology, but also bring with it a refinement in method and a more exact perception of the things which matter. In consequence, on closer examination attempts to distinguish between 'criminology proper' and 'administrative criminology' fail to reveal any difference in substance. Rather they convey an unattractive air of condescension.

The allocation and control of 'outside' research funds also causes me considerable concern. The prevailing mode is for the Home Office, the Department of Justice, or the Ministry of Justice, as the case may be, to propose or approve of a subject to be investigated and, when agreement is reached, to support it financially. This official involvement has marked a major advance in the recognition of the importance of criminology, theoretical and practical, for the administration of criminal justice. Yet it has its drawbacks. 'In fact,' stated the late Professor Hans Mattick,

> I have viewed the entire LEAA [Law Enforcement Assistance Administration] development as being rather unhealthy for criminal justice or research precisely because it constitutes a monopoly on research money and it gives the private foundations an easy way out; [the fact that] the Government, in effect, has a monopoly on research in an area as sensitive as criminal justice seems to me to be less wise and less healthy than to have some competition from private sources that could afford to be more critical.

This may have been expressed too severely but undoubtedly it contains a large kernel of truth.[39] For example, President Clinton has committed himself so unequivocally and so firmly to a considerable extension of capital punishment that it would be unrealistic to expect the Department of Justice to approve, and financially support, a piece of research which might prove the undesirability of capital legislation and of drastic changes in procedures to facilitate its more expeditious enforcement.

With the very great number of powerful, rich and independent foundations in the United States, the danger of stifling criminological inquiries which may go against the dominant official bent of criminal policy is very considerably reduced. But this is not the case in Britain, where between 80

---

39 For remarks actuated by similar considerations which, although uttered in the mid-1970s, are still topical, see Terence Morris, 'Some Thoughts on the Politics of Criminology', *Times Literary Supplement* (26 September 1975). This article was part of a symposium on 'Crime and Criminology' (fourteen pages long) launched by the then editor of the *TLS*, the distinguished literary critic John Gross. It was much superior to the edition on 'Crime' (1 September 1995).

and 90 per cent of current 'outside' criminological research depends exclusively upon the official backing of the Home Office and the Economic and Social Research Council (ESRC). Because of this substantial government involvement, support from philanthropic foundations with scientific preoccupations has become more and more difficult to obtain.

The officials directly responsible for decisions affecting the allocation of funds in support of outside, largely academic, research, however conscientious they may be, must nowadays obtain the approval of the minister, a political animal, who may wish to leave a distinctive mark on the selection of the topics, the way in which they are investigated, and determine the manner in which the findings should be made public. I believe that a stage has now been reached when the relationship between academic criminology and official backing should be looked into very carefully, and with a lot of understanding and goodwill on both sides. Researchers cannot always be given an unfettered rein. Those who carry out the heavy, and often ungrateful, task of administering criminal justice deserve all kinds of reassurances, many of which can be given without jeopardizing the basic integrity of a piece of research. But researchers, in order to be vital and innovative, also need to be able to work in a climate of trust in which their independence is respected. Perhaps the setting up a small committee of high standing to act as a go-between for the academic proposers and the official approvers might be a constructive forward step.[40]

Criminology is a relative newcomer and its subject-matter is intricate and fluid. The way in which its material and findings are presented is of cardinal importance. It is essential to avoid jargon, padding, over-elaborated statistical data, and hunting for far-fetched hypotheses. Pretentiousness and repetitiveness are deadly sins. It is no less essential to be highly selective in deciding what to publish. The danger is that what is ephemeral often submerges what is of more permanent value.

Connected with this point is the question of publication of criminological texts. In my early days it was extremely difficult to find a respectable publisher ready to take on and promote a criminological book. I may perhaps be

---

40 This should recommend itself even when criminological inquiries relate to the working of the judiciary. Two episodes seem to corroborate it. I refer to the Lord Chief Justice Lord Lane's abrupt decision in the early 1980s to end the inquiry led by the distinguished criminal lawyer, Professor Andrew Ashworth, and to the support Lord Lane received from Lord Hailsham, the Lord Chancellor of the day. More recently Professor Roger Hood was told that Crown Court judges had been instructed not to agree to be interviewed by him with respect to his innovative inquiry into *Race and Sentencing* (1992), pp. vi–vii.

allowed to mention that, when we in Cambridge envisaged the launching of a criminological series, Cecil Turner and I had to subsidize the publication of the first volume. Much later, when the series was doing quite well, we had to look for another publisher because the one we had felt that the income yielded by the volumes did not justify the investment required and expressed his intention to abandon the enterprise altogether. Today the situation has changed dramatically. Though criminological texts do not breed best-sellers, they now present, on the whole, a sound financial proposition which might lead to other attractive ventures. As I put it in another place, a new animal has emerged in our field and is galloping fast and far: I refer to the tempting publication of students' texts and collected articles. Of course there must be some books of this kind. But all of us must have the courage and determination to stick to real scholarship and research. Ultimately, prestige in the academic and political world depends upon it. I must confess that sometimes I am truly bewildered by the sheer volume of stuff that sees the light of day. I suspect that often it is the inevitable result of the principle adhered to in many academic institutions of 'publish or perish'. If so, it is a most regrettable pressure. Superficiality and repetitiveness are some of its inevitable dire consequences.

Crime is not the only social problem which confronts society. There are many others, some of which are as perplexing and disturbing as criminality. Modern criminology cannot ignore alcoholism, drugs, AIDS, mental inadequacies and retardation, neglect in education, abuse of women and children, chronic unemployment, acute poverty, ghettos of cities, indeed the hard-core of the sizeable under-class in quasi-permanent alienation and potential rage – all of which continue to crowd the agenda. Nor can criminology ignore the impact of international conflicts and tensions. But, as I stated in my report to the Bar Association of New York and the Ford Foundation,[41] measures for increasing the social welfare of the under-privileged in our societies are justifiable on grounds of ethics, of natural justice, of economics and of political expediency. Yet it must be borne in mind that improvement in social welfare may not necessarily lead to a reduction in crime. They cannot be identified as some sort of super-prophylaxis against delinquency. The fact is that crime takes different forms in different societies. In one it may be the fruit of poverty and lack of opportunities, in another of satiation, boredom or cupidity. But it can never be guaranteed that the amelioration of material conditions, or even the expansion of upward social mobility, will necessarily reduce it. To put it in a sentence and at the risk of indulging in an undesirable oversimplification, criminology and criminal policy, though they often

---

41 Leon Radzinowicz, *The Need for Criminology* (1965), pp. 28–32.

impinge upon social policy and social reform, must be kept distinct from them.[42]

Criminologists should avoid crusading zeal, dogmatic beliefs and narrow expertise. They cannot solve the problem of crime and should accept that crime is to a large extent inevitable; that it is an integral part of our society. It eludes the coercive or reformatory hand, at one time recoiling, but only for a fresh surge forward, at another assuming subtle changes of shape and proportion; sometimes because society itself postulates new offences, or breeds new possibilities for violating its laws, or simply because the art of crime is ever evolving new *modi operandi*. But it still abides, a constant symptom in all societies, whatever their racial, national, social, moral and economic conditions may happen to be. Criminologists cannot reduce criminality or influence its shape and trends. What they can do is to help us better to understand it, to avoid making mistakes in dealing with it, and to instil a little more humanity and reality in our attitudes towards the phenomenon of crime and its control.

Though it may at first sound paradoxical, the need for criminology is greater the more critical the condition of crime appears to be. One of the lessons which penal history teaches us is that it is almost always during such periods of tension, frustration or fear that solutions in the penological sphere are adopted primarily on emotional grounds or on opportunistic political calculations. More often than not they prove to be regressive temporary short cuts of hardly any value. It is in times like these that criminology is particularly qualified to prove its uses. But penal history also reveals that at these very times the voice of criminology is too often silenced or ignored even in countries in an advanced state of civilization.

The time has gone when criminology or penology were influenced, not to say directed, by persuasive, eloquent, passionate and vital personalities who, by their scientific work and public activity, transcended national frontiers and exercised profound and durable leadership. I am thinking of Dr Wines, Brockway, Lucas, Ducpétiaux, Dr Julius, Lombroso, Ferri, Von Liszt, Tarde, Prins, Ruggles-Brise, Paterson and many others. Criminology is becoming a

---

42 The theme of an intimate, inevitable causative connection between social policy and criminal policy appeared even amongst leading figures in the field of criminal law proper. 'The same great spiritual current', stated Franz von Liszt, 'which has given us social policy has also given us the concept of criminal policy. Our modern School of Criminal Law emerged as a transference of economic and political thought and exigencies into our specialised field of work ... This is what explains the rapid victory of our views.' See his speech at the meeting of the German Section of the IKV at Munich in 1912, in *Bulletin of the I.K.V.*, vo;. 19 (1912), pp. 376–400, at pp. 378 and 379.

product of teamwork, of collective endeavours patiently carried out, of laborious and steady exchanges of information. It has lost much of its intellectual lustre. It has become more imitative, more occupied with checking and cross-checking, more subordinated to methodological refinements. There are few bold crusaders proclaiming thrilling scientific discoveries, few architects offering blue-prints for broadly based penal betterment. Some may welcome this, as a sign that criminology is at last coming of age. To others it may signify the coming of old age, crippled by restraints and hesitations.

Not being a pessimist by nature and inclination, or an exuberant optimist beyond control, I would be deeply concerned if I were to convey the image that criminology is widely accepted, firmly established, amply funded to carry independent significant research, and well positioned to impart thorough knowledge in appropriate and professional settings.

To take an obvious example. No one can seriously question that the 'A' letter in any criminological alphabet of knowledge stands for criminal statistics. They constituted the primary ingredient in the nascent development and vision of criminological thought at the beginning of the nineteenth century. Yet the very sad fact stands out that in 1998, one hundred and seventy-three years after the publication in France in 1825 of the first criminal statistics in the world, the number of countries which collect and regularly publish reasonably satisfactory criminal statistics can be counted perhaps on the fingers of two hands.

In Europe they primarily emanate from the smaller countries: the four Nordic states plus the Netherlands and, though to a lesser degree, Switzerland and Belgium. Amongst the major European countries it is disappointing to register that criminal statistics in France and Italy, where they played so vital and illuminating a role in the formation of criminology and criminal policy, have suffered a steady and severe eclipse from which they do not seem able to recover. Germany is regaining the ground lost since the Nazi regime launched its deadly onslaught on the officially sponsored criminal statistics and the excellent special studies pursued during the Weimar Republic. Advances made in Britain in the field of criminal statistics since the 1950s cannot be otherwise described than as spectacular in the diversity, wealth and interpretation of raw material. Canada, several states in Australia and New Zealand continue to show care in developing this source of indispensable information.

I well remember the state of criminal statistics in the United States and the so frequently advanced criticisms of its leading criminologists. This also has changed beyond recognition and the progress made cannot fail to be admired. The Soviet bloc, from the very moment of seizing power, regarded the suppression of reliable criminal statistics, made available to the public, as the cornerstone of their unscrupulous manipulation of the apparatus of criminal justice to serve their immediate political ends. And to be realistic it will take a very long time before this reactionary trend can be reversed in the politically liberated countries. Virtually the entire South American continent is in this respect a perfect *terra incognita*. And so are the huge demographic giants – China, India and Pakistan. I am regrettably not sufficiently knowledgeable to express an opinion about the condition of criminal statistics in Japan.

To sum up, and taking a global view, it is not an exaggeration to affirm that at least three-quarters of the world is deprived of this vital penal, social and moral index. In some ways even more disappointing is the fact that the countries whose criminal statistics are poor or non-existent are making virtually no effort to remedy the situation.

Broadly speaking, criminology, on closer and more critical scrutiny, has a configuration very much akin to the status of its statistical ingredient. In South America the term 'criminology' is widely known far beyond the restricted circles connected with the governance of criminal justice. But the discipline – in its directions, substance and end-products – is still in an early stage of infancy. And again, the same observation is applicable to very many countries, big and small, across the world. Official China regards the subject with utmost suspicion and shows no restraint in readjusting criminology's image and findings to the needs of its arbitrary and cruel regime. The whole of the Middle East can be similarly disregarded. There was a time, I clearly remember, when Egypt entertained some criminological ambitions and an institute was even set up in Cairo. But the grandiose plans announced with great flourish produced very little. In contrast, in Israel a criminology in the Western European sense took root and has proved valuable and innovative.[43]

In spite of some promising beginnings criminology has yet to make much headway in Spain or Greece, while in Italy, with the exception of the Universities of Bologna and Macerata, little meaningful criminological research is being pursued. In contrast, in Germany, where the dogmatic and classical influences have always been very persistent, criminological research, and a more widely and eclectically perceived criminal policy, have made substantial advances.[44] No similar trend seems to have developed in Austria. The criminological enterprise in the Nordic countries and in the Netherlands continues to be distinctive and inspiring.

In Britain the growth of criminology was rather slow to start with.

---

43 My visit to Israel in 1969 as the Lionel Cohen Lecturer in the Hebrew University of Jerusalem and other Centres gave me ample opportunities to have my view confirmed.
44 The latest edition of Günther Kaiser's massive and rich *Kriminologie: Ein Lehrbuch* (1996), which appeared as I was revising this chapter of my book, and bears eloquent and convincing testimony to this development. The briefest of comparisons with the criminological texts of the past such as those by Sauer, or Mezger, or even Exner, show how far German scholarship in this field has advanced since Hans-Heinrich Jescheck promoted criminological departures at the Max Planck Institute in Freiburg over thirty years ago.

Despite the interesting and often important work which has been carried out by scholars up and down the country, criminology was not rewarded by full academic and public recognition until the first tenured and permanent chair was created in 1959, followed a year later by the first firmly established Institute in Cambridge. Thirty-four years later, in my address to the British Criminology Conference held in Cardiff in 1993, I noted the rapid and most encouraging expansion which had taken place since those early days. By 1993 there were, in the universities and other institutions of higher education in Britain, at least twenty-four Professors of Criminology, either with established chairs or promoted *ad hominem* and several criminological research centres. There were also many readers and an active cohort of lecturers. In the succeeding four years (up to 1997) more appointments have been made. The amount of research being carried out is considerable, with no diminution in scope or quality. A no less encouraging fact is the development of criminology as part of the academic curriculum. The subject is taught in most of the law schools, in virtually all Departments of Social Science, and it attracts a substantial crop of bright students, both undergraduate and postgraduate. Judged by international comparative standards I do not hesitate to repeat my view again: Britain's level of activity in this field is amongst the very best.[45]

And then, of course, there is the United States. During the first fifteen years of my studies I concentrated on the condition and evolution of criminology in Europe, paying hardly any attention to the subject within the North American context. This was largely justified because, in this respect, the United States was then still in what I was inclined to describe as its 'imitative phase'. It largely echoed what was going on at that time in Western Europe and, in approach and method, was often clumsy, oversimplified and superficial. Even the early and very rudimentary assumptions of Lombroso were still fashionable, and the initial reception extended to the theories of H.H. Goddard showed the popularity of attempts to connect, in a crude manner, criminal behaviour generally with some kind of inborn mental defect. And the spreading influence of the eugenic movement certainly proved an embarrassing ally.

In the years between the two world wars, the significance of criminological studies in the United States increased out of all recognition. The European influence was transcended and what I described as the 'imitative' phase came definitely to a close. Indeed, a strong reaction developed against the broad hypotheses unsupported by factual material, the rather crude methods of pseudo-scientific investigation, and the largely futile ideological strife which were so severely paralysing criminological thought in Western Europe at that

---

45 The second edition of *The Oxford Handbook of Criminology* (1997) edited by Mike Maguire, Rod Morgan and Robert Reiner is a vivid and invigorating example of this achievement.

time. In 1935 Professor Franz Exner of Munich, the distinguished scholar of criminal law and criminal policy, paid a visit to the United States to make a comparative assessment of what was being done in German penal administration and research. His conclusion was unequivocal. Some of 'the extensive researches of the Americans' could be criticized as well as admired, but he acknowledged that 'in one respect they are miles ahead of us in their clear perception of the meaning and practical necessity of criminological work'. He insisted that Germany should not fail to 'follow America's example'.[46] This comparison was true at that time not only of Germany but also of most of the rest of the world. I called it the 'germinal stage' of American criminology and tried rapidly to recapture the dynamic happenings of this 'vast laboratory'.[47] Vast indeed, but also inevitably uneven in quality. I would greatly reproach myself if I were to fail to pay a tribute to Professor Norval Morris (the initiator), and Professor Michael Tonry and their distinguished advisory board for giving us the ongoing series *Crime and Justice* – an informative and critical record of criminological developments unique of its kind and still going strong. I have just received Volume 22.

Nevertheless, when one takes stock of the condition of criminology on a world-scale, the picture has to be painted in much darker colours. A rigorous but fair count reveals that there are at present no more than fifteen countries where criminology has, so to speak, acclimatized itself and follows the course of a scientific discipline in the full meaning that this expression should convey. It is somewhat perplexing to note that the trajectory pursued by 'criminal statistics' is so closely akin to the one followed by 'criminology'. A hasty but tempting hypothesis would seem to suggest that the one is influenced by the other in a reciprocal causative relationship. It would, however, be wrong to make such an assumption. Rather, the affinity in their trajectories points to the influence of other factors which have determined the condition of both.

Good teaching is as important in the development of a discipline as good research. The recognition of this vital need has certainly not been overlooked, although in the early stages it sometimes assumed fanciful shapes. Thus as early as in 1875 the indefatigable Dr Wines drew up a 'Plan for Giving Breadth, Stability, and Permanence to the Work of Crime Prevention and Crime Repression' and enlisted influential support for it. It was to be 'some sort of Academy or Institute' to consist of

> the establishment of a great journal to be published in the four most widely spoken languages of the earth – in English, in French, in German, and Spanish – to be conducted by a staff of five editors, the

---

46 Franz Exner, *Kriminalistischer Bericht über eine Reise nach America* (1935), p. 84.
47 See Leon Radzinowicz, *In Search of Criminology* (1961), pp. 114–66.

editor-in-chief to have his office in London, and to be master of all four languages; the four assistant editors to reside severally in North America, South America or Mexico, France, and Germany; and all five to serve in the capacity of lecturers in the countries where they have their several residences – 'travelling luminaries' as Dr Woolsey has expressed it – giving courses here and there, now in one part of the country, now in another, lecturing perhaps to legislatures or to law schools and I will add also to students of the larger colleges, and even to popular assemblies.[48]

With the passing of time this conviction was gaining increasing recognition in many countries, especially in Europe, and the suggested solutions were, of course, becoming incomparably more realistic and coherent than the above quoted flight into colourful fantasy might suggest. The teaching of criminology, of criminal policy, of penitentiary sciences and the best ways of securing a proper professional specialization on the part of the judges, penal administrators, criminal lawyers and future academics, started to figure on the agenda of the leading international organizations leading to lively discussions, well-thought-out reports, and encouraging recommendations. In one of the appendices of my book *In Search of Criminology* I made a selection of all such material relating to the nineteenth and the beginning of the twentieth century.[49] A few years later, when invited by the international congress convened in Mendoza (Argentina) to act as a rapporteur on this very topic, I surveyed the development of criminological teaching in a forty-page report. In it I reviewed the place accorded to criminology (or to some of its aspects) within the legal, social, medical and psychological academic centres. I noticed some progress, but also much stagnation, one-sidedness and superficiality. My own, already noted, involvement in the planning and conduct of teaching at the Cambridge Institute and in the United States further enriched my experience. And I have continued to follow changes in the status of criminological teaching in several parts of the world.

Looking at this absorbing subject again at a point of time when I am about to send the manuscript of this book to the publishers (December 1997), I cannot fail to notice several substantial advances which have been secured in recent years, but also alas I must conclude that the overall picture remains far from satisfactory.

---

48 See E.C. Wines, *The State of Prisons and Child-Saving Institutions in the Civilised World* (1880; reprinted 1968). The Appendix (pp. 703–708) also contained some very interesting responses from distinguished contemporaries.
49 See 'Appendix I. Major International and National Congresses: Deliberations Concerning the Teaching of Criminology', in Radzinowicz, *In Search of Criminology* (1961), pp. 210–14.

In very many leading Departments of Sociology all over the world the trend is away from the study of crime and punishment as an independent subject, simply leaving some aspects of it to be dealt with under other headings (such as 'deviant behaviour' or 'social control') and even then not in a systematic manner but often no more than in the form of illustrations (although the American Sociological Association has an important 'Criminological Section'). This trend has gone too far to be reversed. I regret it. In the Departments of Social Studies (wherever they happen to exist) criminology fares much better. Their curricula often include a course closely akin to criminology, given by trained criminologists. Often there is a strong emphasis on practical matters, when criminology slides into criminal policy and penal administration. But these departments are not as frequently represented within universities as the Departments of Sociology and, if one may generalize, they do not, everywhere, carry the same prestige. The advances secured in Faculties of Law or Law Schools since the 1950s have been remarkable, especially in Europe. Very often, however, the course will not be given by a trained criminologist but by the professor of criminal law with wider interests. Criminological institutes or centres have by and large maintained their positions. Financial restrictions in so many universities across the world, and the increasing influence of regressive approaches to crime and punishment, have inevitably had an adverse effect on the expansion of advanced and graduate studies in criminology. The existing centres count themselves fortunate if they can maintain the very modest staff, libraries and research funds at the level of the early 1980s or even late 1970s.

In the United States the general picture is somewhat confusing and frequently not very encouraging, especially when compared with the rich achievements in research. First, the already noticed absence of criminology as an independent subject in the leading Departments of Sociology is faithfully reproduced in America today. Second, one cannot fail to register how scanty is the adoption of criminology in the curricula of the law schools, even amongst the major ones. In contrast, criminal law proper is taught in all of them. And although the quality of some of these outposts is outstanding when measured by the standing of their teachers and range of published work – the gospel does not seem to have made many proselytes. When I look at my notes extending over the past fifty years there seems to be always the same very modest nucleus of forlorn pioneers. Yet compensatory progress can be registered in the undeniable fact that criminology, or more precisely criminal policy and criminal justice, has had (and continues to have) a far-reaching influence on the teaching of criminal law proper. Many of the leading textbooks eloquently reflect this fruitful infiltration which in 1940 was so conspicuously initiated by Michael and Wechsler's textbook on *Criminal Law and its Administration*. A rapid comparison with the older textbooks shows how truly dramatic this change has been. This is all to the good, but much more is needed. Yet no more can be expected in the prevailing political climate. It should also be recognized that the interest evinced by American law students in these matters has never been very great and has certainly sharply declined since the mid-1970s. There are a few Schools of Criminal Justice up and down the country which are leaving a mark. And there is the extraordinary expansion of Criminal Justice Programs in colleges of one kind or another – at present some 150 such courses. They are primarily, but by no means exclusively, professionally oriented, and as such they discharge an essential role. But inevitably they vary in quality and scope, and consequently some of them must be viewed with ambivalence. In general, all over the world the task of adopting criminology as a worthy subject of teaching in higher education still remains daunting.[50]

I was privileged to start on my criminological journey at a point in time and in places when the discipline seemed to be securing signal achievements and unfolding exciting perspectives in so many of its sectors. Today, after nearly seven decades have passed by, if I were to be asked to assess the difference in the condition of criminology between the two periods which mark the beginning and the end of my scholarly life, I would find it difficult to resist plunging into a rather crude comparison and say it is like the difference between a veteran Ford car of nearly a century ago and a zippy Jaguar of the present. Indeed, it is fair to say that, in probing into the reality of crime and punishment, criminology has attained considerable successes in spite of the weaknesses of many of its hypotheses, of the limitation of many of its methods and techniques, of some excessively controversial contentions, and of the still very modest financial support afforded to it in so many parts of the world. Many old questions, of course, remain unanswered, and many new questions have arisen. But much solid and critical knowledge has been accumulated and it continues to grow. In some ways, the many doubts which criminology has fermented to challenge the status quo are as important as the explanations which it has succeeded in providing.

What I find profoundly disturbing is the gap between 'criminology' and 'criminal policy', between the study of crime and punishment and the actual modes of controlling crime. This gap, to put it in more general terms, between theory and practice had always existed and it will continue to persist, but it has become increasingly entrenched as the years have passed by, and there are no indications that it will be narrowed in the foreseeable future. This, however, has happened, not because of some fatal flaws in criminological thought and research findings but simply because standards in the administration of criminal justice in very many parts of the world are desperately low and lately have gone even further downhill.

---

50 It would be useful to update the survey of criminological teaching in Europe carried out by the Council of Europe in the 1970s and indeed to extend it to other parts of the world.

The stark fact stands out that, in the field of criminal justice, in spite of the output of criminological knowledge, a populist political approach holds sway. Indeed, it has become predominant. And perhaps I should end as I did when responding to the toasts of the Chairman of the Law Faculty and the Director of the Institute of Criminology at the dinner to mark my ninetieth birthday (Cambridge, 24 September 1996):

> Friends, I wish you well in all your endeavours. Face with courage the inevitable disappointments, and continue, through your teaching and research, to dispel the heavy clouds of opportunism, prejudice and oversimplification.

INDEX

Note: the alphabetisation of names with prefixes is in accordance with the conventions of the nationality of the name in question.

Aa, Simon van der 367
Abse, Leo 304, 306, 321n36
Acton, Lord 160
Adam, A.T. 396
Adler, Freda 46, 449n27, 456n38
Adler, Mortimer J. 61, 196
Adonis, Andrew 144n21
Adrian, Lady 234, 241, 341, 342, 347, 350n15
Adrian, Lord 179, 180, 187, 202, 211, 234, 239, 241
Agüeroy Bethancourt, de 377, 377n40
Ahmed, Humaira Erfan xv
Allen, Sir Carleton 82, 82n4, 117
Allen, Lady, of Hurtwood 325
Allen, Sir Philip (Lord Allen) 217, 228, 242, 306, 309, 352n23
Alper, B.S. 92, 403n65
Altavilla, E. 398
Amory, Viscount 335, 337, 341, 350n17
Ancel, Marc Plate 12, 130, 131, 131n25, 152, 195n5, 197, 197n6, 217, 227, 262n21, 291, 291n16, 329, 329n12, 359, 359n8, 374, 374n34 and n35, 375, 375n38 and n39, 395–6, 398
Andenaes, Johannes 131n25, 262n21, 340, 395, 398
Angell, Sir Norman 133
Annan, Kofi 394
Annan, Noel (Lord Annan) 178
Anttila, Inkeri 399, 400n61, 401, 403, 403n64
Ardigò, Roberto 4, 22

Armitage, Sir Arthur 212, 241, 272n38, 390
Arvold, Judge Carl 205
Ashworth, Andrew 424n13, 459n40
Astor, Viscount 270
Atkinson, Hon. Mr Justice Fenton 214
Attlee, Clement (Earl Attlee) 109, 126, 245, 250, 250n6, 322
Auerbach, Carl 420
Avison, N. Howard 240, 276n48
Ayer, A.J. 338n7

Bacon, Alice 334
Bacon, Francis 123
Baets, L'Abbé Maurice de 51
Bagot, J.H. 162
Balvig, Flemming 46
Banhofer, Stefan von 44, 44n9
Banton, Michael 276n48
Barker, Sir Ernest 202, 202n13
Barker, Dame Lillian 325
Barr, Revd James 246n2
Barry, Sir John 406
Barry, Sir Patrick 325, 326n8
Barry, Redmond 325
Barzun, Jacques 290n13
Bassett, David 350n17
Bassiouni, M. Cherif 403n65
Batson, Edward 408, 409
Bauer, Fritz 457n38
Bean, P.H. 398
Bebbington, N. 214
Beccaria, Cesare 8–9, 10, 19, 21, 116, 280, 281, 287, 291, 293, 374, 420, 453
Bedau, Hugo 289

470

INDEX

Behar, George *see* Blake, George
Bellot, H. Hale 154–5, 155n29
Beloff, Max (Lord Beloff) 253n10
Bemmelen, I.M. van 262n21
Bennett, William J. 430n3, 437n16
Benson, Sir George 133, 145, 152, 176, 180, 325, 327n2
Bentham, Jeremy 82, 83, 282n2, 421
Bentley, Derek 272, 272n40
Beria di Argentine, Adolfo 374n36
Bernard, Thomas J. 456n37
Berns, Walter 290n13
Bertrand, Ernest 64
Bichard, Hannah xv
Bierne, Piers 454n33
Binding, Karl 18, 73, 292n19
Bingham, Lord Chief Justice xii, 272n40
Birbeck, W.L. 117
Birkett, Sir Norman (Lord Birkett) 121–2, 144, 181, 181n28, 184, 324, 325n6
Birkmeyer, Karl von 36
Birley, Sir Robert 408
Bishop, Norman 398, 402n63
Black, Charles Jr 289, 289n12
Blackstone, Sir William 139
Blair, Tony 439, 439n20
Blake, George 294–5, 296n3, 297, 297n4 and n5, 301, 303n15, 313, 313n25, 314, 315–16
Blom-Cooper, Sir Louis 115n6, 254n12, 266, 310n19, 321n36, 327, 332n18
Bodson, Victor 150
Bonger, William Adrian 441, 441n4, 443n12
Borens, J.F. 403n65
Bottomley, A. Keith 207n15
Bottoms, Anthony E. 203, 240, 276n48, 321n36, 432n8
Boutros-Ghali, Boutros 394
Bowen, Elizabeth 258
Bowers, William K. 276, 277n50
Box, Stephen 276n48
Brandreth, Jeremiah 278
Breitel, Charles 410, 412–13
Brennan, A.J.E. 345n10
Brentford, Lord 344, 344n9
Bristol, Bishop of 325
Brockway, A.F. 115, 368n20
Brockway, Zebulon 63, 461
Brooke, Baroness 343
Brooke, Henry (Lord Brooke) 297, 315, 334–5, 343, 448, 448n24

Brougham, Lord 32
Brown, George 335
Brown, George K. 434n11
Brownell, Hon. Herbert 410, 411, 412
Buchwald, Art 295n2
Buckland, William 134
Buffelain, Jean 69n13
Bumke, Dr 368, 382n46
Burt, Sir Cyril 152, 203, 444, 444n15, 446
Butler, Josephine 165
Butler, Lady Molly 243
Butler, R.A. (Lord Butler) Plate 9, 126–7, 164–72, 176, 177, 180, 184, 186, 187, 189, 192, 193, 194, 209, 211, 219n17, 226, 238, 239, 239n37 and n38, 242–4, 255–6, 442, 447
Butterfield, Fox 430n3

Cadbury, Paul S. 215, 215n16
Cahn, E. 254n12
Caldecotte, Lord Chief Justice 143
Callaghan, James (Lord Callaghan) 303, 310, 325
Calvert, E.R. 254n12, 267n29
Calvin, John 26
Cameron, J.M. 425n14
Cameron, Mrs Elizabeth *see* Bowen, Elizabeth
Camps, Francis 424, 425, 425n13 and n14
Carlisle, Mark (Lord Carlisle) 311, 312, 321n36, 327
Carlyle, Thomas 160
Carnarvon, Lord 360, 360n10
Carpzow, Benedict 7
Carr, Sir Cecil 32
Carr, E.H. 73n1
Carr, Robert (Lord Carr) 312, 327
Carr-Saunders, Sir Alexander 446
Carrara, Francesco 4, 6–10, 7n1, 17, 19, 21, 23
Carroll, Denis 373
Carson, W.G. 276n48
Carter, President Jimmy 416
Carton de Wiart, Comte Henri Plate 5, 49, 65, 68, 69, 371
Cassin, René 150
Castan, Nicole 453n31
Castell, F.G. 308
Catherine the Great 282n2
Chamberlain, Neville 104, 125, 246

471

INDEX

Chapman, Dennis 276n48
Chapman, Richard A. 352
Chappell, Duncan 207n15, 407
Chester, Lewis 274n46, 329n13
Chorley, Lord 181, 185, 269, 329
Christiansen, Karl Otto 131n25, 384
Christie, John 166, 272
Christie, Nils 399
Christopher, James B. 254n12, 256, 256n15, 266, 266n28
Churchill, Sir Winston 95, 103, 127, 164, 248, 250, 432
Cilento, Diane 381
Cilento, Sir Ralph 381
Clark, Roger S. 403n65
Clarke, Ronald V. 173, 173n18
Clayton, Tom 302n13
Clemenceau, Georges 3
Clerc, François 30, 389, 389n55
Clifford, William 392, 407
Clinard, Marshall 46
Clinton, President Bill 289, 416, 458
Clokie, Hugh McDowall 252n9, 352
Cohen, Albert K. 196n5, 220
Cohen, Stanley 223n19, 276n48, 451n30
Coldham, Simon 292n17
Collins, Victor (Lord Stonham) 342, 344, 445, 446, 446n20
Colvin, Eric 207n15
Comte, Auguste 4, 5, 22, 440
Constant, Jean 390n56
Cooke, Terence Cardinal 414
Corben, A.E. 321n36
Cornil, Paul 262n21, 389n55, 395, 396, 398
Cowling, M.J. 188, 189
Cox, Revd Charles 278–9, 279n53
Craig, Christopher 272
Craven, Cicely 133
Cressey, D.R. 220
Critchley, T.A. 171
Croce, Benedetto 20
Croft, John 173, 173n19
Crofton, Sir Walter 360
Cross, J.H. 127n19, 129
Cross, Sir Rupert 131, 338n7
Crossman, Richard 314, 314n29
Crowther, Geoffrey 325
Crusen, Georg 370n24
Cubbon, Sir Brian 200, 242, 422
Cuche, Paul 64, 99
Cudahy, Patrick, Judge xiv, 416

Cunningham, Sir Charles 171, 177, 180, 183, 187, 242, 337, 339, 390, 391
Cutler, Lloyd xiv, 414, 416

Dallemagne, Jules 51
Darwin, Charles 4, 5
David, Pedro R. 219n18
Davies, Mr Justice Edmund (Lord Edmund-Davies) 350n17
Davies, Norman 73, 73n1
De Moor, Jean 51
de Vleeschouwer, Robert 150
Dean (hanged boy) 278
Deedes, William (Lord Deedes) 188
Delacourt-Smith, Lord 321n36
Delaquis, Ernst 43, 367, 386
Delierneux, Adolphe 63, 382, 383, 386
Denis, Hector 50
Dession, George 262n21
Devlin, Lord 325n6, 339
Dicey, A.V. 96, 139
Didcott, Peter 276n48
Digneffe, Françoise 51n2
Dilulio, John J. Jr 430n3
Disraeli, Benjamin 80
Dodd, David 240
Dohgna, Graf zu 98
Donnedieu de Vabres, Henri Plate 6, 24, 130, 262n21, 385
Donnem, Roland W. 411n2
Douglas-Home, Sir Alec (Lord Home) 335
Dove-Wilson, Sir John G. 96
Dowler, D.E.J. 297, 314, 315
Downes, David M. 229, 332n18, 457n38
Drogheda, Earl of 177, 325, 326, 326n8
Du Cane, Sir Edmund 336
Du Parcq, H. 96
Ducpétiaux, Edouard 53–4, 357, 461
Duff, Patrick 241
Dulaerts, Maurice 66
Dupont-Bouchat, M.-S. 53n4
Durkheim, Émile 440
Dybwad, Gunnar 98n16

East, Sir W. Norwood 96–7, 104, 446
Eaton, Gertrude 133n2, 376
Ede, James Chuter 109, 110, 122, 125–8, 129, 131, 152, 247, 248
Eden, Sir Anthony 269, 270, 271
Edwards, J.Ll.J. 131, 272n38
Ehrlich, Isaac 276, 276n49

INDEX

Eisenhower, Milton S. 414
Eliot, George 293
Elliot, Mrs Walter (Baroness Elliot) 325
Elliott-Binns, E.U. 262
Ellis, Ruth 272
Elwyn Jones, Lord 334n2
Endowes, M. 272n40
Engels, Friedrich 5, 45, 437n15
Ericson, Richard 207n15
Erikson, Thorsten 398
Evans, Harold 274
Evans, Richard J. 454n34
Evans, Timothy 166, 272
Ewing, A.C. 152
Exeter, Bishop of *see* Mortimer, Rt Revd R.C.
Exner, Franz 36, 92, 463n45, 465, 465n47

Fairbanks, Russell 420
Fairn, R. Duncan 215, 338n7
Faizant (cartoonist) 295n2
Farrer-Brown, Leslie 183
Farrington, David 240, 430n4
Fattah, Ezzat 442n10
Faulkner, David 200, 431n5
Felish, Dr 372n27
Ferracuti, Franco 195n5, 398
Ferri, Enrico Plate 1, 1–25, 32, 42, 45, 49, 51, 52, 73, 94, 149, 153, 195, 197n7, 203, 354, 374, 377, 383, 440, 440n2, 461
Fink, Arthur E. 449, 449n27
Fisch, Hamilton 360
Fisher, Geoffrey (Archbishop of Canterbury) 249
Fletcher, Joseph 122n17
Fletcher-Moulton, Hon. Silva 350n16
Fortas, Abe 276
Fortes, Meyer 242, 408
Fortescue, Sir John 82
Forth, Mrs Ruby 165
Foucault, Michel 45, 89
Fox, J.A. 277n50
Fox, Lady 219
Fox, Sir Lionel 109, 131, 171, 180, 212, 219, 219n17, 242, 340, 386, 388, 390, 391, 395, 398, 453
Fox-Andrews, Norman 258
Francis, F. 272n40
Francotte, Xavier 51
Frank, Hans 371
Frankfurter, Felix 262n21, 420

Frankowski, S. 79n4
Freisler, Roland 99, 382n46
Frencken, M. Eugène xv
Freud, Sigmund 3
Freund, Paul 420
Friedlander, Walter 42
Friedman, Milton 437n16
Frosali, R.A. 455, 455n35
Fry, Elizabeth 104
Fry, Lord Justice 140
Fry, Margery 132, 176, 177, 180, 325, 326, 376, 379, 444
Fry, Roger 132
Fyfe, Sir David Maxwell (Viscount Kilmuir) 184, 271

Gallie, W.B. 270n34
Garçon, Emile 64, 72, 99
Gardiner, Gerald (Lord Gardiner) 267n29, 334n2, 335
Garland, David 180n24, 198n9
Garofalo, Baron Raffaele 5, 12, 16, 354, 354n2, 440, 440n3, 441, 453
Garraud, Pierre 99
Gautier, Alfred 31, 39–40, 41
Gelhorn, Walter 420
Genn, Hazel 240
Gentile, Giovanni 19
German, O.A. 42, 44
Gibbens, T.C.N. 229, 276n48, 347, 350n15
Gibson, Violet 21, 21n6
Giddens, Anthony 440n1
Ginsberg, Morris 154, 162
Gladstone, Herbert (Viscount Gladstone) 95
Gladstone, William Ewart 138, 268
Gladstone-Smith, Peter 189n33
Glover, Edward 254n12, 267, 267n29
Gluckman, Max 338n7
Glueck, Sheldon 185
Goddard, H.H. 464
Goddard, Lord Chief Justice 117, 127, 249, 250, 272n40
Godin, Robert E. 116n7
Goebbels, Joseph 368, 382n46
Goldberg, W. Abraham 42
Goldschmid, Harvey 420
Goldstein, Abraham S. 220, 420
Goldstein, Joseph 420
Golsong, H. 398
Goode, W.M. 325
Goodhart, A.L. 86, 138, 139, 150, 184

473

INDEX

Goring, Charles 56
Gottfredson, Don M. 173, 173n18
Gould, Stephen Jay 197–8n8
Gowers, Sir Ernest 254, 254n12, 255, 255n13, 259–60, 260n18
Gowers, Sir William 254
Graham, Fred 226
Graham-Harrison, Carol 268
Graham-Harrison, Francis L.T. 177, 180, 183, 184, 242, 255–6, 257, 257n16, 260, 268, 325
Graham-Harrison, Sir William Montagu 255, 255n14
Gramatica, Filippo 374, 457n39
Grant, President Ulysses S. 360
Graser, Roland 409n1
Graven, Jean 30, 262n21, 395
Greef, Guillaume de 51
Greenberg, David F. 456n37
Greenwood, Anthony 170, 334n2
Griffith, Mr Justice 327
Griswold, Erwin 420
Gross, Hans 195
Gross, John 458n39
Grünhut, Max 94
Guillaume, Dr 44, 45n11, 367
Guizot, F. 285
Gurney, W.B. 279n53
Gürtner, Dr 382n46
Gutteridge, H.C. 43, 141

Hadden, T.B. 207n15
Hafter, Ernest 36
Hailsham, Lord 296, 304, 459n40
Haines, Herbert H. 290n14
Hale, Sir Matthew 82, 147, 148, 148n25
Halévy, Elie 86
Halifax, Lord 126
Hall, Livingstone 185
Hall Williams, Eryl 272n38, 276n48, 338n7, 340
Hamel, Gerard Anton van 19, 52, 370, 448, 448n24, 456
Hames, Tim 144n21
Hammond, Walter 423
Hancock, Dame Florence 257, 264n24
Hancock, R. 272n40
Hand, Judge Learned 420
Harcourt, Sir William 136
Hare, R. 338n7
Harris, José 114–15n5
Harris, Sir Sydney 113n3, 119, 119n12
Hart, A.W. 189

Hart, H.L.A. 119n11, 214, 265–6, 266n27, 338n7, 339
Hart, Philip 277, 414
Harty, Russell xv
Haseltine, H.D. 138
Hatchard, John 292n17
Haus, J. 50
Havard, John 424
Hawkins, Gordon 434n12
Hawkins, Keith O. 207n15
Hay, Will 432n9
Hayes, Paul 420
Hayes, President Rutherford B. 360
Heald, Henry T. 410
Healy, William 92
Heath, Sir Edward 296, 351–2
Héger, Paul 51
Héger-Gilbert, F. 55
Heidensohn, Frances 276n48
Helm, Bronhilda 408
Henkin, Louis 420
Hentig, Hans von 95, 95n13, 141n18, 288, 288n8
Hepple, Bob 408
Herbert, A.P. 252–3
Herrnstein, Richard J. 450n28
Herschel, Lord 422
Heyworth, Lord 241
Hill, Alan xiv, 231–2, 231n25, 232n26
Hill, Alfred 420
Hill, David xiv, 231
Hill, Joan 454n34
Hill, Martin 382, 386
Hitler, Adolf 73n1, 382n46
Hoare, Sir Samuel (Viscount Templewood) 96, 96n14, 104–6, 108, 109, 110, 125, 128–30, 131, 152, 165–6, 167, 171, 246, 254n12, 269
Hobhouse, Stephen 115, 368n20
Hodgkinson, Peter 292n17
Hoenigswald, Frances xv
Hogarth, John 207n15
Hogg, Quintin *see* Hailsham, Lord
Hollis, Christopher 272n40
Hollond, H.A. (Harry) Plate 8, 141, 158–9, 161
Holmes, Mr Justice 135
Holtzendorff, F. von 288, 288n8
Hood, Roger Plate 11, xi, xiv, 56n7, 83n5, 92, 93, 173n16, 207n15, 225, 238n36, 240–1, 273n42, 274n45, 276n48, 277n50, 291, 291n16,

474

INDEX

400n61, 434n11, n12, 435n14, 443n11, 444n14, 455n36, 459n40
Hopkins, Admiral Frank 302n11
Horder, Lord 152
Horne, Alistair 167, 167n6, 168, 168n10
Houzé, Emile 51
Howard, Anthony 166, 166n4, 168n8, 239
Howard, John 52, 404
Howard, Michael 439
Hruska, Roman 414
Huber, Barbara xiv
Huber, Eugene 31
Hughes, Emrys 251n8
Hulsman, Louk 398, 402
Humphrey, Hubert 357
Hurd, Douglas (Lord Hurd) 167
Hurtado Pozo, J. 31, 33, 43, 43n5
Hurwitz, Stephan 262n21, 384
Hyde, W.N. 304, 306

Inskip, Lady 177–8, 325, 330n15
Iremonger, F.A. 122n17
Iremonger, T.L. 350n15, 350n17

Jackson, R.M. 141, 141n18, 241
Jacqart, C. 50
Janson, Paul-Émile Plate 4, 48, 49, 68, 69
Jasinsky, Jerzy 79n4
Jaspar, Henri 49, 52, 65, 68
Jaurès, Jean 3, 285
Jelf, General R.W. 188
Jenkins, Lady 314
Jenkins, Roy (Lord Jenkins) 166, 295n2, 296, 297, 301, 303, 303n15, 311, 313–17 (314n26) 342–3, 350, 350n15, 447, 447n22
Jennings, Sir Robert 241
Jescheck, Professor Hans-Heinrich xiv, 79n4, 463n44
Johnson, Elmer H. 79n4, 373n29
Johnson, President Lyndon B. 413, 414
Joly, H. 50, 64
Jones, Caradog 152
Jones, Howard 276n48
Joseph II of Austria 282n2
Jowitt, Lord 249, 326
Julius, Nicholaus H. 461

Kadish, Sanford H. 220
Kaiser, Günther xiv, 44, 44n9, 79n4, 463n44

Kan, Joseph van 443n12, 453n32
Kant, Immanuel 123
Kelly, Elizabeth xv
Kemper, Kenneth D. 207n15
Kennedy, Ludovic 272n40
Kenny, Sir Anthony 90n11
Kenny, Courtney Stanhope 83, 135, 137–41, 142, 145, 146, 147, 155, 155n31, 278n52, 456
Kent, John 122n17
Kerenski, Alexander Feodorovich 342
Keynes, Sir Geoffrey 233
Keynes, J.M. (Lord Keynes) 73n1, 233, 254
Keynes, Mrs 233–4
Kilbrandon, Lord 214
Kilmuir, Viscount *see* Fyfe, Sir David Maxwell
King, Joan 226, 240, 276n48, 329, 430n2
King, Roy D. 276n48, 320, 321n36
Klare, Hugh 176, 178, 238, 238n36, 254n12, 267, 267n29, 302, 303, 335, 396
Knight, Jill 303n15
Knightley, Philip 313n25
Koestler, Arthur 254n12, 265n26
Kohlrausch, E. 76, 371n26
Komarowsky, Mirva 416n5
Krarup, Helen xv
Kriegsmann, Herman 92
Kürzinger, Joseph xv

Laboulaye, Edouard René de 359
Labriola, Antonio 5
Lacassagne, Alexandre 288, 288n8
Lane, Lord Chief Justice 459n40
Langan, Patrick A. 430n4
Lantsheere, Léon de 57
Larcier, Ferdinand 69
Laski, Harold 325
Lasky, Melvin 78
Laufer, William 449n26, 456n37
Laugier, Henri 381, 382n45
Lauterpacht, Sir Hersch 150
Lawton, Lord Justice 205, 340
Le Jeune, Jules 49, 52
Le Peletier de Saint-Fargeau, M. 435
Lejeune, Anthony 186n31
Lenz, Adolf 195
Lévy-Ullmann, Henri 82, 82n2
Lewis, Sir Aubrey 186, 237, 338n7, 340
Ley, A. 55

INDEX

Liepmann, M. 288, 288n8
Light, Roy 321n36
Lindesmith, Alfred 196n5
Lipstein, Kurt 43
Lipton, D. 431n6
Liszt, Franz von 15, 18, 52, 55, 73, 76, 81, 99, 117, 354, 355n3, 357, 370, 370n24, 371, 372, 461, 461n42
Livingstone, Edward 282n2
Lloyd George, David 73n1, 254–5
Lloyd George, Gwilym (Viscount Tenby) 168, 269, 269n33
Lodge, T.S. 131, 173, 173n17, 214, 306, 444, 444n14
Logan, Sir Jack 179
Logoz, Paul Plate 2, 24, 25, 26, 29–30, 31, 36
Lombard, Elliot H. 414
Lombroso, Cesare 1, 18, 19, 33, 38, 51, 75, 198n8, 203, 455, 461, 464
London, Jack 80
Longford, Lord 173, 173n17, 183, 184, 334, 334n2, 444, 445, 445n19
López-Rey, Manuel 219, 340, 391, 442
Low, Peter 220, 420
Lowry, Richard 329n9
Lucas, J.M.C. 288, 288n8, 461
Luccini, O. 18, 73
Ludlam, Isaac 278
Lygon, Lady Maud 125
Lynch, Gerald 420
Lyttleton, Alfred 125

Macaulay, Lord 81
McClemens, J.H. 406
McClintock, F.H. Derick 162, 225, 240, 276n48
McConville, Seán 90n10, 207n15, 352n23, 360n10
Macdonald, Horace 264n24
MacDonald, Ramsay 6, 246
Mack, John 276n48
Mack Smith, Denis 20, 21n5
Macmillan, Daniel 231
Macmillan, Dorothy 167
Macmillan, Harold (Earl of Stockton) 164, 167, 168, 168n9, 231, 271
Macmillan, Lord 160, 161
McNair, Sir Arnold D. (Lord McNair) 150, 160
MacRae, Donald Gunn 195n5
Maddison, Hon. J.C. 405

Maguire, Mike 180n24, 332n18, 464n45
Maier-Katkin, Daniel 420
Maitland, Frederick 138
Maliniak, Wladyslaw 74
Mandela, Nelson 407, 409
Mann, John 257
Mannheim, Hermann 24n9, 178, 179, 181, 181n26, 182, 182n29, 197, 267, 267n29, 373, 392, 406, 444, 444n16
Manningham-Buller, Sir Reginald (Lord Dilhorne) 271
Mark, Sir Robert 300, 312
Marks, L. 272n40
Mars, Colin 186n31
Mars-Jones, W.L. 321n36
Marshall, T.H. 229
Martin, Henri 53
Martin, John 205, 206, 240, 276n48
Martin, Kingsley 270
Martinson, R.M. 431n6
Marx, Karl 3, 4, 5, 6, 45, 84, 89, 330, 436, 437n16
Matteotti, Giacomo 20
Mattick, Hans 458
Maugham, Viscount 160
Maurois, André 259, 268
Maxwell, Sir Alexander 81, 97, 105, 112, 120–1, 130, 152, 258, 325, 444
Mayr, Georg von 452n30
Mays, John B. 276n48
Melbourne, W.L. 164
Meltsner, Michael 289, 289n12
Melup, Irène xv
Merton, Robert 416n5, 449n26
Mezger, E. 463n44
Michael, Jerome 42, 61, 196, 467
Midgley, James 408, 409, 409n1
Mill, John Stuart 273, 285, 440
Millard, R.E. 321n36, 350n17
Mitchell, Frank 296, 300
Mitchell, Priscilla xiv
Mittermaier, C.J.A. 288, 288n8, 357
Mohl, Robert von 155n33
Molotov, V.M. 73n1
Montesquieu, Charles de Secondat 44
Montgomery Hyde, H. 180, 186n31, 237n31, 325n6
Moodie, Peter 207n15
More, Sir Thomas 444
Morgan, Kenneth O. 269, 269n33
Morgan, Rod 180n24, 318, 318n32, 319–20, 332n18, 464n45

476

INDEX

Morris, J.N. 339, 340, 350n17
Morris, Norval 291, 291n16, 406, 456n37, 465
Morris, Pauline 276n48, 302
Morris, Terence P. 214, 254n12, 257n16, 266, 275, 276n48, 334, 458n40
Morrison, A.C.L. 118
Morrison, Herbert (Lord Morrison) 250n6, 322, 324, 325
Morrison, Robert L. 240
Mortara, Ludovico 19
Mortimer, Right Revd R.C. 304, 306, 321n36, 331, 339, 347, 347n14, 350n15
Moser, Sir Claus 204
Mott-Hadclyffe, Charles 125
Mountbatten, Lord 292n2, 297, 299–305, 307, 308, 309, 311–15, 317, 318
Mucchielli, Laurent 441n8
Muirhead, Judge 406
Murray, Charles 450n28
Mussolini, Benito 20, 21, 22, 287

Namier, Louis 73n1
Napoléon Bonaparte 81
Nathan, Lord 184, 232, 237, 237n31, 241
Neustatter, Lindsay 423
Newsam, Sir Frank 388
Noble, Sir Thomas 321n36, 327
Nursaw, Sir James 162
Nuttall, Christopher 174n20
Nuvolone, Pietro 374n36

Oaksey, Lord 329n10
Olivercrona, L.R. d' 288, 288n8
Olmo, Rosa del 195n5
Oppenheim, A.N. 204
Overbeck, Alfred von 281n1
Overholser, Wilfred 262n21

Page, Sir Leo 325, 329n10
Pakenham, Lord *see* Longford, Lord
Paley, William 82, 83
Pannell, N.H. 189
Pansegrouw, Klaas 385
Parker, Lord Chief Justice 166, 204, 225, 226, 294, 421, 423
Parker, Roy 276n48
Passell, P. 277n50
Paterson, Sir Alexander 63, 86, 92, 94, 102, 102n20, 105, 109, 368, 376, 461
Paulsen, Monrad 214, 420
Pears, David 360n11
Peel, Sir Robert 84, 130, 164, 286
Perroux, François 289n10
Perry, Rosina 235, 235n29, 241
Peterson, Sir Arthur 122n16, 129, 129n23, 171, 242, 398
Petrzilka, Werner 69n13
Pettit, Philip 116n7
Pfander, Helen 43
Pfeiffer, Timothy N. 411n2
Pfenninger, Heinrich 41
Philipson, C.M. 276n48
Pierce, G.L. 277n50
Pierrepoint, Albert 257, 257–8n17
Pike, L.O. 155
Pilsudski, Józef 72, 73
Pinatel, Jean 373n29, 395, 398
Pincher, Chapman 292n2
Poll, Maurice 48
Pollock, Sir Frederick 135
Polwarth, Lord 376
Pompe, W.P.J. 262n21, 395
Porter, J.R. 347m14
Posner, Richard, Chief Judge 438n18
Potter, Harry 284n7
Pötz, P.G. 402n63
Pound, Roscoe 388n53
Powell, Enoch 144
Power, Sir John 246n2
Pownall, General Sir Henry 299
Price, Revd E. Shirvell 330n15
Prins, Adolphe 52, 54, 65, 67, 99, 369, 370, 380, 383, 461
Proust, Marcel 382n45

Quentin, Leopold 92
Quetelet, Adolphe 50, 153, 452

Radelet, M.L. 277n50
Radzinowicz, Sir Leon Plates 15 and 16, xi–xiii, 56n7, 83n5, 85n6, 86, 99n17, 113n4, 117n8, 118n10, 130n24, 139n14, 143n19, 144n20, 179n22, 182n29, 185, 186n31, 189, 195n4, 198n8, 200n12, 210, 226n23, 230n24, 231, 238, 239, 264n24, 273n42, 274n46 (275n47, 276n48), 279n53, 288n9, 310n19, 321n36, 329n11 and n13, 330n15, 336n5, 346, 346n13, 350n15, 354n1,

INDEX

375n38, 394, 400n61, 413, 420n8, 426n1, 430n2, 434n11, 435n14, n15, 441n6, 442n9, 443n11, 451n29, 455n36, 456n37, 460, 460n41, 465n47, 466n49
Ram, Sir Granville 325, 326, 326n8
Randall, C.D. 360n9
Ranieri, Silvio 195n5
Rappard, William 45
Rattenbury, Robert 179
Redlich, J. 155n33
Redman, General Sir Harold 184, 187
Rees, Merlyn (Lord Merlyn Rees) 312
Reid, Jacques 187
Reiner, Robert 180n24, 332n18, 464n45
Remarque, Eric Maria 122
Renkin, J. 57
Renton, David (Lord Renton) 165, 184
Reynolds, Mr 134
Richardson, Sir Ralph xv
Rivière, Marcel 28, 29n1
Roberts, Andrew 299, 299n6, 311n22
Robespierre, Maximilien 162
Robinson, J. William 252n9, 352
Rocco, Arturo 20, 149, 287
Rock, Paul 229, 276n48, 442n10
Rockefeller, David Jr 420
Roeder, Karl 8, 8n2
Roger, John 404
Röling, B.V.A. 434n11
Rolph, C.H. 170n13
Romilly, Sir Samuel 286, 404, 404n66, 421
Roosevelt, President 412
Rose, A. Gordon 132, 378n41
Rose, G.N.G. 225, 240, 276n48
Roseman, Hon. Samuel J. 312
Rosenfeld, Ernst 370n23
Rosenthal, Abe 420
Rostow, Eugene 412, 420
Rothschild, Lady 214, 321n36, 327
Rousseau, Jean-Jacques 26
Roux, Jean-André 163, 371, 372
Rozès, Simone 374n36
Rubens, E. 53n3
Ruck, S.K. 102n19, 109
Ruggles-Brise, Sir Evelyn 85, 92, 360n9, 364n15, 461
Runcie, Robert (Archbishop of Canterbury) 134
Rusca, Michèle 33, 38
Russell, Bertrand 450

Russell, Whitworth 357, 358
Rutherford, Andrew 99n18, 292n17
Ryall, R.A. 207n15
Ryan, Alan 116
Ryckere, Raymond de 50, 52, 65

Saleilles, Raymond 388, 388n53
Salisbury, Marquis of 249, 309
Samuel, Sir Herbert (Viscount Samuel) 119, 120, 122, 249, 285
Sandford, Revd the Rt Hon. Lionel 321n36
Sankey, Lord 122
Santoro, Arturo 24n9, 440n2
Sauer, L. 463n44
Savonarola, Girolamo 64, 136
Savey-Cassard, Paul 284n7, 289n10
Savill, Nancy 162
Schabas, William A. 283n5
Schichor, David 434n12
Schlyter, Karl 131n25
Schuessler, Karl 196n5
Schultz, Hans xv, 42, 44n10
Schuster, Ernst 81, 81n1
Schwartz, Louis 262n21
Scott, Sir Harold 152
Scott, Peter 304, 306, 307, 321n36, 327
Seabourne Davis, D. 131
Sechrest, D.K. 434n12
Sellin, Thorsten 24n9, 69, 131n25, 152, 161, 234, 262n21, 289, 420, 441
Semal, F. 51
Serota, Beatrice (Baroness Serota) 321n36, 325, 347, 350n15
Servais, Jean 67
Shaw, George Bernard 261
Shawcross, Sir Hartley (Lord Shawcross) 250, 250n6, 325
Shelley, P.B. 279n53
Shinwell, Emmanuel (Lord Shinwell) 296
Short, James F. Jr 414
Shute, Stephen 434n11
Sieverts, Rudolf 92, 364n15, 368n21, 398
Silken, S.C. 350n17
Silverman, Sydney 166, 251, 251n8, 254n12, 265, 265n26, 270, 271, 272n40
Simon, J.E.S. (Lord Simon) 104, 125, 180, 249, 250–1, 251n7, 269
Simonds, Lord 160
Simpson, Sir Joseph 187

478

INDEX

Skelhorn, Sir Norman 327
Slater, Eliot 258
Smith, Sir John 147
Smithers, Sir Peter 398
Snare, Anika 131n25
Snowden, Major L. 304, 306, 319n33
Sokalski, W. 92
Sollohub, Count Vladimir Alexandrowitsch 359
Soskice, Sir Frank (Lord Stow Hill) 317, 342–3
Sovern, Michael 420
Sparks, Richard 432n9
Sparks, Richard F. 207n15, 225, 226, 240, 276n48, 306, 319, 320, 456n37
Spearing, Nigel 312
Spencer, Herbert 4, 5, 6, 22
Spencer, John 141
Sprott, W.J.H. 276n48, 338n7, 340
St John Stevas, Norman (Lord St John) 304
Stalin, Joseph 73n1, 78
Stallybrass, W.T.S. 148
Stead, John 188, 188n32, 420
Steinberg, Harris B. 411n2
Stephen, Sir James Fitzjames 81, 82, 83, 135–7, 138, 140, 141, 155, 421
Stephen, Sir Leslie 136n4
Stephens, Lilian Mary 125
Stevens, Hilary 160
Stevens, J. 53
Steyn, Hon. J.H. 408, 409, 409n1
Stonham, Lord *see* Collins, Victor
Stooss, Carl 31, 32–3, 35–9, 41, 42, 44, 45, 46
Stow Hill, Lord *see* Soskice, Sir Frank
Strahl, Ivan 131n25, 262n21
Sutherland, Edwin H. 71, 89, 152, 154, 196n5, 448, 448n26
Swinnerton-Dyer, Sir Peter 276

Taget, R.T. 272n40
Tarde, Gabriel 203, 288, 288n8, 388n53, 461
Tarnawsky, Marta xv
Taylor, Harold 179, 241
Taylor, H.J. 304, 306
Taylor, Ian 442n10
Taylor, Laurie 229, 276n48
Taylor, Telford 420
Teeters, Negley K. 358, 358n7, 360n9, 364n15
Temple, William (Archbishop of Canterbury) 115n5, 122, 123, 125n18, 249, 284n7, 340, 444, 444n13
Templewood, Viscount *see* Hoare, Sir Samuel
Thatcher, Margaret (Baroness Thatcher) 165, 165n3, 332n18
Thiry, Fernand 50
Thomas, David 240, 424
Thomas, Trevor 179, 241
Thompson, Margaret xv
Thonissen, J. J. 50
Thorneycroft, Peter (Lord Thorneycroft) 238
Thorpe, Jeremy 301
Titmuss, Richard 408
Todd, Alphaeus 352, 352n21
Tomlinson, Penelope 276n48
Tönnies, Ferdinand 115n5
Tonry, Michael 456n37, 465
Topinard, P. 441, 441n5
Trasler, Gordon 276n48, 327
Travers, Maurice 355, 355n4
Treitel, Sir Guenter 131
Trevelyan, George Plate 14, 81, 161, 162, 199
Tsitsoura, Aglaia xv, 398, 402n63
Tuck, Mary 200
Tulkens, Françoise xv, 54
Tullio, Benigno di 373n29
Turati, Filippo 5, 20
Turner, J.W.C. (Cecil) Plate 7, 43, 113n4, 118n10, 130n24, 133–4, 139n14, 141, 143n19, 144, 144n20, 145, 146, 147, 150, 151–2, 157, 158, 159, 160, 162, 202, 230, 231, 354n1, 441n6, 460
Turner, William 278
Tuttle, Elizabeth Orman 254n12, 270n35, 272n38
Tutu, Archbishop Desmond 408
Twist, George 321n36, 329n9
Tyler, Judge R. 220

van Caenegan, Raoul 82, 82n3
van den Bergh, T. 272n40
van den Haag, Ernest 276, 290n13, 292n19
Vandervelde, Émile 49, 54, 56, 57, 65, 68
Vassalli, Giuliano xiv
Venn, J.A. 149
Verdier, Raymond 292n19

INDEX

Vernon, Wilfred, Major 445, 446n20
Vervaeck, Louis Plate 3, 54–6, 56n6, 57, 59, 59n8, 61, 64, 67, 68
Vetere, Eduardo xv, 393
Vold, George B. 456n37
von Hirsch, Andrew 131n25

Waaben, Knut 131n25, 398
Wade, Professor C.C.W. 141
Walker, Monica 162, 240
Walker, Nigel 214, 219n18, 327, 330n14, 338n7, 340, 352n23, 410, 423
Waller, Irvin 207n15
Waller, Mr Justice 327, 329n9
Waller, Sir Maurice 376
Walters, John P. 430n4
Walton, Paul 442n10
Warburton, Mrs Eliot 350n16
Warnotte, D. 51
Warren, William 420
Wasik, A. 79, 79n4
Webb, Sidney and Beatrice 103, 155, 226n20, 309–10, 310n19
Webster, Bethuel M. 411n2
Wechsler, Doris 420
Wechsler, Herbert Plate 10, 42, 227, 262n21, 411n2, 420, 420n8, 467
Welch, Michael 456n37
West, Donald 14, 225, 240, 276n48, 306, 319, 423
Wheare, Sir Kenneth 253, 253n10, 263, 263n23, 269n30, 322, 322n3, 352
Wheatley, Lord 350n17
Whitelaw, William (Viscount Whitelaw) 167
Widgery, Lord Chief Justice 321n36, 327
Wiersman, D. 398
Wigmore, Professor John H. 135
Wilberforce, Samuel 140
Wiles, Paul 240, 276n48
Wilke, Dr 99
Wilkins, Leslie 173, 444, 444n17
Wilks, J. 431n6
Willett, Terence 276n48
Williams, Sir David 241
Williams, Glanville 131, 147, 241
Wilson, Anthony 215

Wilson, Charles Frederick 295–6
Wilson, Harold (Lord Wilson) 314, 332n18, 334, 334n2, 342, 351
Wilson, James Q. 430n4, 450n28, 506n3
Windlesham, Lord 273, 273n42, 332n18, 346, 346n11, 434n11
Wines, Enoch Cobb 359, 360, 360n9, 365, 366, 367, 369, 380, 461, 465, 466n48
Winfield, Sir Percy 139, 141, 146, 150, 157–8, 159, 160
Witlock, J. 278n52
Wittgenstein, Ludwig 339
Wold, Terge 150
Wolfgang, Marvin E. 220, 226, 291, 291n15, 414, 420, 455n36
Wolfson, Sir Isaac 187
Wolfson, Leonard (Lord Wolfson) 187
Woodfield, Sir Philip 300, 305, 306, 312
Woolf, Lord Justice xi–xiii, xiv, 438, 439n20
Woolf, Virginia 136n4
Woolsey, Dr 466
Wootton, Barbara (Baroness Wootton) 153, 183, 232, 272n38, 283n4, 321n36, 327, 330, 330n14, 339, 346, 347, 350n15, 444, 444n18, 457n38
Worgan, David S. 411n2
Wright, Cecil A. 150–1
Wright, Lord 160
Wright, Martin 235, 241

Yallop, D.A. 272n40
Yardley, Sir David 340
Young, Colonel Sir Arthur 327
Young, Jock 442n10
Younger, Sir Kenneth 303, 306, 307, 319, 319n34, 321n36, 325, 326, 326n8, 327, 328

Zangwill, Oliver 241
Ziegler, Philip 301, 301n10, 302, 302n12, 305, 308, 309, 309n18, 311n21
Zimmern, Alfred 114–15n5
Zimmern, Helen 2
Zimring, Franklin E. 434n12
Zuckerman, Lord 311